VENICE

the Collected traveler

Also in the series by Barrie Kerper

CENTRAL ITALY
The Collected Traveler

PARIS
The Collected Traveler

PROVENCE
The Collected Traveler

MOROCCO
The Collected Traveler

VENICE

the collected traveler

FRIULI–VENEZIA GIULIA

INCLUDING THE VENETO AND

AN INSPIRED
ANTHOLOGY & TRAVEL
RESOURCE

Collected by Barrie Kerper

Three Rivers Press / NEW YORK

Although all prices, opening times, and other details in this book are based on information supplied to us at press time, changes occur all the time in the travel world, and Three Rivers Press cannot accept responsibility for facts that become outdated or for inadvertent errors or omissions. So **always confirm information when it matters**, especially if you're making a detour to visit a specific place.

Published by Three Rivers Press, New York, New York.
Member of the Crown Publishing Group, a division of Random House, Inc.
www.randomhouse.com

THREE RIVERS PRESS and the Tugboat design are registered trademarks of Random House, Inc.

Printed in the United States of America

DESIGN BY LYNNE AMFT

Library of Congress Cataloging-in-Publication Data
Venice : the collected traveler, an inspired anthology and travel resource / collected by Barrie Kerper.
1. Venice (Italy)—Guidebooks. 2. Travelers' writings. 3. Venice (Italy)—Description and travel—Sources. I. Kerper, Barrie. II. Series.
DG672.V458 2002
914.5′310493—dc21   2001054838

ISBN 0-609-80858-3

10 9 8 7 6 5 4 3 2 1

First Edition

For my great and dear friend Lorraine Paillard,
whose love of Venice began many years ago
when her father wore the hats of both public
affairs and cultural affairs officer in Trieste.
Mille grazie, Lorraine, for sharing the volumes
in your vast Venetian library with me, for
enthusiastically encouraging me, and for
traveling with me when six months pregnant
in the world's most beautiful city
and
For Sarah Schulte, whose passion for
La Serenissima is infectious, and whose
assistance and kindness extended to me has
been inestimable
and
For my mother, Phyllis, once again, who has
always believed my boxes of files held something
of value, and who has reserved a special corner
of her heart for Venice

acknowledgments

As I have noted in previous editions, publishing a book requires a staggering amount of work by a dedicated team of people. The number of people who work with a book, from its days as a manuscript to its finished stage on bookstore shelves, and who care passionately about its success, is enough to make one's head spin. Just a few of the folks at the Crown Publishing Group—with which I am so proud to be associated—who have been so dedicated, creative, and supportive include Al Adams, Alan Mirken, Alison Gross, Amy Boorstein, Amy Myer, Andrea Rosen, Becky Cabaza, Cara Brozenich, Doug Jones, Florence Porrino, Holly Clarfield, James Perry, Jill Flaxman, Joan DeMayo, Kathy Burke, Linda Loewenthal, Maha Khalil, Melanie Greco, Patty Flynn, Philip Patrick, Rachel Kahan, Rich Romano, Ronni Berger, Stephanie Fennell, Teresa Nicholas, Teryn Johnson, Tim Mooney, and Tim Roethgen. As always, special thanks are due to the art and production team of Derek McNally, Lynne Amft, and Whitney Cookman, with extra-special thanks to Mark McCauslin, who managed to take a nightmare and turn it into a book. Adam Korn, my wonderful intern from New York University, deserves particular thanks: he not only is equally concerned with ensuring every detail is correct, but routinely ponders the next step, the next link in the chain, and approaches every task I assign him with enthusiasm and determination. I extend my heartfelt thanks to Tia Furman, Executive Director of Save Venice, Armida Tarquinio and Dario Chiarini of the Italian Trade Commission in New York, and Marzia Bortolin and everyone—especially Anna Maria and Diana—at the Italian Government Tourist Board in New York. Thanks are also due to each of the individual writers, agents, and permissions representatives for various publishers and periodicals—especially Leigh Montville of The Condé Nast Publications and David Seitz of *The New York Times*—without whose cooperation and understanding there would be nothing to publish. I remain deeply grateful to Shaye Areheart, my editor *eccellente* and Venice enthusiast; to Chip Gibson, my boss, mentor, and friend for his support, wisdom, and guidance; and to my husband, Jeffrey, for being there always. Lastly, to my daughter, Alyssa, who may not remember in years to come how much she loved Piazza San Marco, the *vaporetto,* the gardens at Miramare, or the fountain in Piazza dell'Unita in Trieste, but will without doubt rediscover them again one day.

A very warm thank you to all the writers who generously donated to Save Venice!

contents

Il Veneto

A Tavola!—La Cucina Veneziana

Il Friuli–Venezia Giulia

A Tavola!—La Cucina Friulana

I Personaggi

Musei e Monumenti

La Bella Vita

Contents   *ix*

"The way to enjoy Venice is to follow the example of these people and make the most of simple pleasures. Almost all the pleasures of the place are simple; this may be maintained even under the imputation of ingenious paradox. There is no simpler pleasure than looking at a fine Titian, unless it be looking at a fine Tintoret or strolling into St. Mark's— abominable the way one falls into the habit—and resting one's light-wearied eyes upon the windowless gloom; or than floating in a gondola or than hanging over a balcony or than taking one's coffee at Florian's. It is of such superficial pastimes that a Venetian day is composed, and the pleasure of the matter is in the emotions to which they minister. These are fortunately of the finest—otherwise Venice would be insufferably dull. Reading Ruskin is good; reading the old records is perhaps better; but the best thing of all is simply staying on. The only way to care for Venice as she deserves it is to give her a chance to touch you often—to linger and remain and return. The danger is that you will not linger enough—a danger of which the author of these lines had known something . . . When you have called for the bill to go, pay it and remain, and you will find on the morrow that you are deeply attached to Venice."

—Henry James, *On Italy*

Introduction

"A traveller without knowledge is a bird without wings."
—Sa'di, *Gulistan* (1258)

Some years ago my husband and I fulfilled a dream we'd had since we first met: we put all our belongings in storage and traveled around the countries bordering the Mediterranean Sea for a year. In preparation for this journey, I did what I always do in advance of a trip, which is to consult my home archives, a library of books and periodicals. I have been an obsessive clipper since I was very young, and by the time I was preparing for this extended journey, I had amassed an enormous number of articles from periodicals on various countries of the world. After a year of reading and organizing all this material, I then created a package of articles and notes for each destination and mailed them ahead to friends we'd be staying with as well as appropriate American Express offices—although we had no schedule to speak of, we knew we would spend no less than six weeks in each place.

My husband wasted no time informing me that my research efforts were perhaps a bit over the top. He shares my passion for travel (my mother-in-law told me that when he was little, he would announce to the family exactly how many months, weeks, days, hours, minutes, and seconds it was before the annual summer vacation) but not necessarily for clipping. (He has accused me of being too much like the anal-retentive fisherman from an old *Saturday Night Live* skit, the one where the guy neatly puts his bait, extra line, snacks, hand towels, etc., into individual sandwich bags. In my defense, I'm not *quite* that bad, although I *am* guilty of trying to improve upon pocket organizers, and I do have a wooden rack for drying rinsed plastic bags in my kitchen.)

While we were traveling that year, we would occasionally meet other Americans, and I was continually amazed at how ill prepared some of them were. Information, in so many different forms, is in such abundance in the twenty-first century that it was nearly inconceivable to me that people had not taken advantage of the resources available to them. Some people we met didn't even seem to be having a very good time; they appeared to be ignorant of various customs and observances and were generally unimpressed with their experience because they had missed the significance of what they were seeing and doing. Therefore, I was surprised again when some of these same people—and they were of varying ages with varying wallet sizes—were genuinely interested in my little packages of notes and articles. Some people even offered to *pay* me for them, and I began to think that my collected research would perhaps appeal to other travelers. I also began to realize that even the most well-intentioned people were overwhelmed by trip planning or didn't have the time to put it all together. Later, friends and colleagues told me they really appreciated the packages I prepared for them, and somewhere along the line I was being referred to as a "modern-day hunter-gatherer," a sort of "one-stop information source." Each book in the *Collected Traveler* series provides resources and information to travelers—people I define as inquisitive, individualistic, and indefatigable in their eagerness to explore—or informs them of where they may look further to find it.

While there is much to be said for a freewheeling approach to travel—I am not an advocate of sticking to rigid schedules—I do believe that, as with most things in life, what you get out of a trip is equal only to what you put into it. James Pope-Hennessy, in his wonderful book *Aspects of Provence,* notes that "if one is to get best value out of places visited, some skeletal knowledge of their history is necessary. . . . Sight-seeing is by no means the only object of a journey, but it is as unintelligent as it is lazy not to equip ourselves to understand the sights we see." I feel that learning about a place is part of the excitement of travel, and I wouldn't dream of venturing anywhere without first poring over a mountain of maps, books, and periodicals. I include cookbooks in my reading (some cookbooks reveal much historical detail as well as prepare you for the food and drink you will most likely encounter), and I also like to watch movies before I leave that have something to do with where I'm going. Additionally, I buy a blank journal and begin filling it with all sorts of notes, reminders, and entire passages from books I'm not bringing along. In other words, I completely immerse myself in my destination before I leave. It's the most enjoyable homework assignment I could ever give myself.

Every destination, new or familiar, merits some attention. I don't endorse the extreme—you don't want to spend all your time in the hotel room reading books—but it most definitely pays to know before you go. Even if you've been to Venice before and you just want to do nothing but sit in caffès and *bacari,* you still have to do some planning to get there. So, the way I see it, you might as well read a little more; after all, as Sarah Quill notes in *Venice: The Stones Revisited,* "the Venetians are fond of saying that it takes more than a lifetime to know their own city." The reward for your efforts is that you'll acquire a deeper understanding and appreciation of the place and the people who live there, and not surprisingly, you'll have more fun.

"Every land has its own special rhythm, and unless the traveler takes the time to learn the rhythm, he or she will remain an outsider there always."

—Juliette de Baircli Levy,
English writer

Occasionally I meet people who are more interested in how many countries I've been to than in those I might know well or particularly like. If *well-traveled* is defined only by the number of places I've been, then I suppose I'm not. But I feel I *really know* and have *really seen* the places I've visited, which is how *I* define *well-traveled*. I travel to see how people live in other parts of the world—not to check countries off a list—and doing that requires immediately adapting to the local pace and rhythm and (hopefully) sticking around for more than a few days. Certainly any place you decide is worthy of your time and effort is worthy of more than a day, but you don't always need an indefinite period of time to immerse yourself in the local culture or establish a routine that allows you to get to know the merchants and residents of your adopted neighborhood. One of the fastest ways to adjust to daily life in Italy, wherever you are, is to abandon whatever schedule you observe at home and eat when the Italians eat. Mealtimes in Italy are generally well established, and if you have not bought provisions for an alfresco lunch or found a place to eat before two P.M., restaurants will be full and many shops closed. Likewise, dinner is not typically served at six, an hour that is entirely too early for anyone in a Mediterranean country to even contemplate eating a meal. Whether you're in the Veneto, the Dolomites, or some corner of Friuli–Venezia Giulia, the earliest the locals sit down to dinner is about eight o'clock, after the evening *passegiata* (stroll). Adjust your schedule, and you'll be on Italian time, doing things when the Italians do them, eliminating possible disappointment and frustration. I would add that it's also rewarding to rise early in Italy, even in the north. It may be difficult to convince holiday travelers who like to sleep late to get out of bed a few hours earlier, but if you sleep in every day, you will most definitely miss much of the local rhythm. By nine A.M. in Italy—and in any Mediterranean country—much has already happened, and besides, you can always look forward to a delicious afternoon nap.

About fifteen years ago, the former Paris bureau chief for *The New York Times,* John Vinocur, wrote a piece for the travel section entitled "Discovering the Hidden Paris." In it he noted that the French have a word, *d'épaysement,* which he translated into English as meaning "the feeling of not being assaulted by the familiarity of things, a change in surroundings where there is no immediate point of reference." He went on to quote a French journalist who once said that "Americans don't travel to be *dépaysés,* but to find a home away from home." This is unfortunate but too often true. These tourists can travel all around the world if they desire, but their unwillingness to adapt ensures they will never really leave home. I am of like mind with Paul Bowles, who noted in *Their Heads Are Green, Their Hands Are Blue,* "Each time I go to a place I have not seen before, I hope it will be as different as possible from the places I already know. I assume it is natural for a traveler to seek diversity, and that it is the human element which makes him most aware of difference. If people and their manner of living were alike everywhere, there would not be much point in moving from one place to another."

Similar to the *dépaysé*-phobic are those who endorse "adventure travel," words that make me cringe as they seem to imply that unless one partakes in kayaking, mountain climbing, biking, rock climbing, or some other physical endeavor, a travel experience is somehow invalid or unadventurous. *All* travel is an adventure, and unless "adventure travel" allows for plenty of time to adapt to the local rhythm, the so-called adventure is really a physically strenuous—if memorable—outdoor achievement. Occasionally I hear descriptions of a biking excursion, for example, where the participants spend the majority of each day in the same way: making biking the priority instead of working biking into the local cadence of daily life. When I ask if they joined the locals at the *caffè* for a morning cappuccino or an evening *aperitivo,* shopped at the outdoor *mercato,* went to a local *festa,* or people-watched in the *piazza,* the answer is invariably no. They may have had an amazing bike trip, but they do not know Italy—one has to get off the bike a bit more often for that sort of knowledge. And if a biking experience alone is what they were seeking, they certainly didn't need to fly to Italy: there are plenty of challenging and beautiful places to bike in the United States.

I believe that every place in the world offers *something* of interest. In her magnificent book *Black Lamb, Grey Falcon,* Rebecca West recounts how in the 1930s she passed through Skopje, Yugoslavia (formerly the Yugoslav Republic of Macedonia) by train twice, without stopping, because friends had told her the town wasn't worth visiting. A third time through she did stop, and she met two wonderful people who became lasting friends. She wrote, "Now, when I go through a town of which I know nothing, a town which appears to be a waste land of uniform streets wholly without quality, I look on it in wonder and hope, since it may hold a Mehmed, a Militsa." I, too, have been richly rewarded by pausing in places (Skopje included) that first appeared quite limiting.

"Travel is fatal to prejudice, bigotry, and narrow-mindedness."
—Mark Twain

"The world is a book, and those who do not travel read only a page."
—St. Augustine

I am assuming if you've read this far that something compelled you to pick up this book and that you feel travel is an essential part of life. I would add to Mark Twain's quote above one by Benjamin Disraeli (1804–81): "Travel teaches toleration." I believe travel is indisputably significant in fostering understanding among the diverse cultures of our world, and people who travel with an open mind and are receptive to the ways of others cannot help but return with more tolerance for people and situations at home, at work, and in their cities and communities. James Ferguson, a nineteenth-century Scottish architect, observed this perfectly when he wrote, "Travel is more than a visitor seeing sights; it is the profound changing—the deep and permanent changing—of that visitor's perspective of the world, and of his own place in it." I find that travel also ensures I will not be quite the same person I was before I left. After a trip, I typically have a lot of renewed energy and bring new perspectives to my job. At home, I ask myself how I can incorporate attributes or traits I observed into my own life and share them with my husband and daughter. I also find that I am eager to explore my own hometown more fully (when was the last time you visited your local historical society, or the best-known tourist site in your part of the country?), and in appreciation of the great kindnesses shown to me by people from other nations, I always go out of my way to help tourists who are visiting New York City—Americans or foreigners—by giving directions, explaining the subway, or sharing a favorite museum or place to eat.

The anthologies in the *Collected Traveler* series offer a record of people's achievements and shortcomings. It may be a lofty goal to expect that they might also offer us an opportunity to measure our own deeds and flaws as Americans so that we may realize that, despite cultural differences between us and our hosts in *any* country, we have much more in common than not. It is a sincere goal, however, and one that I hope readers and travelers will embrace.

About This Series

The *Collected Traveler* editions are not guidebooks in the traditional sense. In another sense, however, they *may* be considered guidebooks, in that they are books that guide readers to other sources. Each book is really the first book you should turn to when planning a trip. If you think of the individual volumes as a sort of planning package, you've got the right idea. To borrow a phrase from a reviewer who was writing about the Lonely Planet Travel Survival Kit series years ago, *The Collected Traveler* is for people who know how to get their luggage off the carousel. If you enjoy acquiring knowledge about where you're going—whether you're planning a trip independently or with a like-minded tour organization—this series is for you. If you're looking for a guide that simply informs you of exact prices, hours, and highlights, you probably won't be interested in the depth this book offers. (That is not meant to offend, merely to say you've got the wrong book.)

A few words about me may also help you determine if this series is for you. I travel somewhat frugally, less out of necessity than because I choose to. I respect money and its value, and I'm not convinced that if I spent $600 a night on a hotel room, for example, that it would represent a good value or that I would have a better trip. I've been to some of the world's finest hotels, mostly to visit friends who were staying there or to have a drink in the hotel bar. With a few notable exceptions, it seems to me that the majority of these places are all alike, meant to conform to a code of sameness and predictability. There's nothing about them that is particularly Italian or French or Turkish—you could be *anywhere*. The cheapest of the cheap accommodations don't represent good value either. I look for places to stay that are usually old, possibly historic, with lots of charm and character. I do not mind if my room is small; I do not need a television, telephone, or hair dryer; and I most definitely do not care for an American-style buffet breakfast, which is hardly what the locals eat. I also prefer to make my own plans, send my own letters and faxes, place telephone calls, and arrange transportation. Not because I think I can do it better than a professional agent (whose expertise I admire) but because I enjoy it and learn a lot in the process. Finally, lest readers think I do not appreciate elegance, allow me to state that I think you'll quickly ascertain that I do indeed enjoy many of life's little luxuries, when I perceive them to be of good value to me.

This series promotes staying longer within a smaller area. Susan Allen Toth refers to this approach in her book *England as You Like It,* in which she subscribes to the "thumbprint theory of travel": spending at least a week in one spot no larger than her thumbprint covers on a large-scale map of England. She goes on to explain that excursions are encouraged, as long as they're no more than an hour's drive away. As I have discovered in my own travels, a week in one place, even in a spot no bigger than my thumbprint, is rarely long enough to see and enjoy it all. *The Collected Traveler* focuses on one corner of the world, the countries bordering the Mediterranean Sea. I find the Mediterranean endlessly fascinating: the sea itself is the world's largest, the region is one of the world's ancient crossroads, and as it stretches from Asia to the Atlantic, it is home to the most diverse humanity. As Paul Theroux has noted in his excellent book *The Pillars of Hercules*, "The Mediterranean, this simple almost tideless sea, the size of thirty Lake Superiors, had everything: prosperity, poverty, tourism, terrorism, several wars in progress, ethnic strife, fascists, pollution, drift nets, private islands owned by billionaires, Gypsies, seventeen countries, fifty languages, oil drilling platforms, sponge fishermen, religious fanatics, drug smuggling, fine art, and warfare. It had Christians, Muslims, Jews; it had the Druzes, who are a strange farrago of all three religions; it had heathens, Zoroastrians and Copts and Baha'is." Diversity aside, the great explorers in the service of Spain and Portugal departed from

Mediterranean ports to discover so much of the rest of the world. "This sea," writes Lisa Lovatt-Smith in her beautiful book *Mediterranean Living*, "whose shores have hosted the main currents in civilization, creates its own homogeneous culture, endlessly absorbing newcomers and their ideas . . . and is the one I consider my own." I, too, consider the sea my own, even though I live thousands of miles away from it.

With the exception of my Morocco book, this series focuses on individual cities and regions rather than entire countries, as readers who are not new to *The Collected Traveler* already know. While I do not plan to compile a book on all of Italy, for example, I am mindful that Italy is a member of two communities, European and Mediterranean; one could even say that northeastern Italy feels part of yet more communities, Balkan, Central European, and Asian included. I have tried to reflect this wider world sense of community throughout the book, especially in the *La Cronaca Mondana biblioteca*. I have enough material on Venice alone to publish a volume as thick as a dictionary or encyclopedia. It was tempting to limit this edition to Venice; it surely would have been easier (I probably would have met my deadlines, making my production manager very happy), and I love the city incredibly much. But when I was first discussing this edition with my editor, I happened upon a 1925 travel guide, *Le Tre Venezie*, published by the Touring Club Italiano. The book included not only Venice but all the towns of the Veneto out to the far reaches of Lago di Garda, up to the Brenner Pass, south through Friuli–Venezia Giulia, and (this being 1925) down the entire length of the Istrian peninsula. A short while later I read the following passage in Waverly Root's *The Food of Italy:* "The protohistoric people called the Veneti have bequeathed their name to the three northeasternmost regions of Italy. . . . Around the proud city of Venice, three Venezias have gathered, by a process of accretion. Veneto, or Venezia Euganea, of which Venice itself is the capital, joins to the province of Venice those of Rovigo, Padua, Verona, Vicenza, Treviso, and, reaching all the way to the Alps, Belluno. To the west is Venezia Tridentina, also called Trentino–Alto Adige. This is made up of two provinces, Trento and Bolzano, the latter being the Alto Adige, before World War I the South Tyrol of Austria. Venezia Giulia, also called Friuli–Venezia Giulia in recognition of the importance of the Ladin-speaking population of Friuli, is the farthest east. It is made up of the provinces of Udine, Gorizia and Trieste." Still later, I learned that the Italians themselves do not think of Venice in isolation from the lands around it, and it seemed that for me to think otherwise would be to deny an established fact and would indeed be inconsistent with geography. As much as I love Venice, I was actually happy about this discovery, because the landscapes and towns of the surrounding Veneto, Trentino–Alto Adige, and Friuli–Venezia Giulia are more than worthy of a detour and are deserving of a good deal of attention on their own. I also knew that, due to the limited materials on Friuli–Venezia Giulia and Trentino–Alto Adige, I would never publish individual editions on these two areas and that they would therefore never be included in any of the volumes I hope to do on Italy. Finally, to understand Venice fully, it is essential to know and see the extent of its reach. The *tre Venezie* may initially seem to represent too big a thumbprint; but rest assured that they can manageably be seen together (ideally in three or four weeks).

Of the *tre Venezie,* Friuli–Venezia Giulia is probably the least known; foreigners may not always recognize the name, Trentino–Alto Adige, but they do recognize the Alpi Dolomiti—or at least their English name, the Alps—even if they've never been there. In describing Friuli–Venezia Giulia, I turn to no better source than Fred Plotkin, author of *La Terra Fortunata:* "First, look at the name of the region. It is a joint name. Friuli refers to 80 percent of the land and 70 percent of the population. It covers the provinces of

Udine and Pordenone and part of the province of Gorizia. Venezia Giulia, as a name, was coined in the late nineteenth century in Gorizia, but represents an ancient concept. Trieste, Grado, part of the zone of Aquileia, plus the eastern side of the Isonzo River, the Carso, and Gorizia constitute an area of a native population that fell under the sway of the Romans and many other peoples up to the Austrians in the nineteenth century and the Slavs in the twentieth so it is a mistake to refer to the whole region as Friuli, as is often done, because this denies the presence of everything that Venezia Giulia represents. Friuli is separated from Venezia Giulia by a narrow stream called the Judrio River. You barely notice it as you drive over, but it is historically important. While all of this land was Roman, at various points in history the zones were divided. The word 'Friuli' is a corruption of *Forum Iulii*, which means Julius' Forum, named for Julius Caesar. Ptolemy referred to Aquileia this way, and later the town of Cividale had the same name. Venezia Giulia roughly means 'the Venice of Julius,' but this is not accurate because this area was a flourishing civilization centuries before the birth of Venice."

With the history of its name established, Plotkin also describes the very essence—a true distillation, if you will—of the region: "It is impossible to think of Friuli–Venezia Giulia without acknowledging nearby Istria. Politics, not culture or tradition, created the new border. This notion of borders is a key issue in the region. A man named Gabriele Massarutto, who lives in Tarvisio in northern Friuli, created an initiative in the 1990s that had important international significance. Friuli–Venezia Giulia is distinct because it is the point in Europe where three principal cultures converge. Just outside Massarutto's city of Tarvisio is the place where Latin Europe (Italy) meets Nordic/Germanic Europe (Austria) and Slavic Europe (Slovenia). The term 'crossroads of Europe' is very overworked by chambers of commerce across the continent, but Tarvisio is, if not the crossroads, the point where Europe meets. Massarutto under-stood the importance of this and created an initiative called *Senza Confini* (Without Borders) to ask people with warring ideologies and ancient hatreds to put them aside. To do this, he persuaded Austria and Slovenia to join Friuli–Venezia Giulia to make a joint bid for the 2006 winter Olympics. This would be the first time the games would be hosted by more than one country. Part of the underlying thought was to embrace the newly emerging nations of eastern Europe and to beat back extremist ideologies, including that of Jörg Haider, governor of the next-door Austrian province of Carinthia. This bid was a finalist for the games and, while it did not win, the *Senza Confini* concept took hold and now is expanding to commerce, culture, and other areas. As Massarutto told me, if God created land without borders, there is no good reason for man to create them. What Massarutto raises is something fundamental and essential in the story of Friuli–Venezia Giulia. This is a place that has an ancient native people, but has known outside invasion and domination for all of its history. What became important here was identity, not ideology, which was a luxury the people could not afford. Identity came through language, land, common suffering, shared food and wine, and the realization that it was pointless to engage in civil conflict when, all around them, wars raged that were based on ancient ethnic and religious hatreds. That the mixed soci-ety of the region of Friuli–Venezia Giulia never had serious internal battles is remarkable."

Venice, of course, quite unlike Friuli–Venezia Giulia, is known to everyone, even if only in the pages of books and magazines and on film. As the incomparable H. V. Morton wrote in *A Traveller in Italy*, "Venice and Rome are alike in offering not the sharp stab of discovery but the gentler nudge of recognition: it is almost as though one were living a second time and visiting scenes familiar in a former life." To its detriment, Venice is perhaps *too* well known, almost too well trodden, almost cliché. "No stones are so trite as those of Venice, that is, precisely, so well worn. It has been part museum, part amusement park, living off the entrance fees of tourists, ever since the early eighteenth century, when its former sources of revenue ran dry," noted Mary McCarthy in *Venice Observed*. But as trite as Venice was and is, it remains a stunningly beautiful, endlessly fascinating, and decidedly different sort of place—claustrophobic to some perhaps, not lively or hip enough to others; but for the vast majority of us, Venice is irresistible and intoxicating. I have a photo I took in Campo San Stefano on my first visit to Venice. It's a shot of a contemporary sculpture, a life-size human figure that is tilted a bit to one side with arms extended in a soaring motion. When I saw it, I felt it was the perfect image for the happiness I felt at being in Venice. I was reminded of H. V. Morton again, when he wrote, ". . . and I felt how good it was to be alive and how fortunate I was to be in Venice." I bought a piece of handmade marbleized paper from a Venetian shop and had the photo mounted on it and framed. Every time I look at it in my bedroom, I am reminded of how I was bursting with happiness—and how I still am—whenever I am fortunate enough to stand on the stones and bridges of *La Serenissima*. In a special issue of *Wine Spectator* (April 30, 1994) devoted to Venice, Thomas Hoving, former director of the Metropolitan Museum of Art in New York, wrote, "No one ever forgets the first trip to Venice. Mine came in 1956. We arrived from the Byzantine magnificence of Ravenna, through the Padua of the artists Giotto and Donatello, past the country estates designed by Palladio and thought we'd seen some pretty high and mighty works of art. But, on arrival, we were struck dumb by Venice, realizing instantly that this watery kingdom of heaven is the greatest art masterpiece Western civilization has ever produced." First visits to many cities are memorable, but perhaps none are as overwhelming as Venice.

Each section of this book features a selection of articles from various periodicals and an annotated bibliography relevant to the theme of that section. (The *Informazioni Pratiche* section is a bit different—the books listed there are part of the A–Z listings.) The articles and books were chosen from my own files and home library, which I've maintained for over two decades. The selected writings reflect the culture, politics, history, current social issues, religion, cuisine, and arts of the people you'll be visiting. They also represent the observations and opinions of a wide variety of novelists, travel writers, and journalists. These writers are authorities on Venice, the Dolomites, the towns of the Veneto, or Friuli–Venezia Giulia, or Italy, or all three; they either live there (as permanent or part-time residents) or visit there often for business or pleasure. I'm very discriminating in seeking opinions and recommendations, and I am not interested in the remarks of unobservant wanderers. Likewise, I don't ask someone who doesn't read much what he or she thinks of a particular book, and I don't ask someone who neither cooks nor travels for a restaurant recommendation. I am not implying that first-time visitors to Italy have nothing noteworthy or interesting to share—they very often do and are often very keen observers; conversely, frequent travelers are very often jaded and apt to miss the finer details that make Venice and northeastern Italy the exceptional places they are. I am interested in the opinions of people who want to *know* this corner of Italy, not just *see* it. I've included numerous older articles (even though some of the specific information regarding prices, hours, and the like is no longer accurate) because they are either particularly well written, thought provoking, or unique in some way and because the author's view stands as a valuable record of a certain time in history. Often, even with the passage of many years, you may share the same emotions and opinions of the writer, and equally as often, *plus ça change, plus c'est la même chose*. I have many, many more articles in my files than I was able to reprint here. Though there are a few pieces whose absence I very much regret, I believe the anthology you're holding is very good.

A word about the food and restaurant sections, *A Tavola: La Cucina Veneziana* and *A Tavola: La Cucina Friuliana:* I have great respect for restaurant reviewers, and though their work may seem glamorous—it sometimes is—it is also very hard. It's an all-consuming, full-time job, and that is why I urge you to consult the very good food and restaurant guides I recommend in each section's *biblioteca,* among them *Eating and Drinking in Italy* by Andy Herbach and Michael Dillon, *Eating in Italy* by Faith Heller Willinger, *Italy for the Gourmet Traveler* by Fred Plotkin, *La Terra Fortunata* also by Fred Plotkin, *Osterie d'Italia 2001,* by Slow Food reviewers, *Ristoranti d'Italia* by *Gambero Rosso* reviewers, and *Trattorias of Rome, Florence & Venice* by Maureen B. Fant. Restaurant (and hotel) reviewers are, for the most part, professionals who have dined in hundreds of eating establishments (and spent hundreds of nights in hotels). They are far more capable of assessing the qualities and flaws of a place than I, who have eaten in only about three dozen places in northeastern Italy and stayed at fewer hotels and can therefore tell you only about my limited experience, or than your in-laws, who perhaps went to Venice once for three days and spent their entire time on the well-beaten path between the Gritti Palace, the Zattere, and Harry's Bar. I don't always agree with every opinion of a reviewer, but I am far more inclined to defer to their opinion over that of someone who is unfamiliar with Venetian food, for example, or who doesn't dine out frequently enough to recognize what good restaurants have in common. My files are bulging with restaurant reviews, and I could have included many, many more articles about *ristoranti* and *trattorie,* but it would have been too repetitive and ultimately beside the point. I have selected a few articles that give you a feel for eating out in this part of Italy, alert you to some things to look for in selecting a truly worthwhile place versus a mediocre one, and highlight some dishes that are not commonplace in America. My files are equally bulging with hotel recommendations, but as with restaurants, I urge you to consult one or more of the great books I recommend in *Informazioni Pratiche*.

The annotated bibliographies (one for each section) are one of the most important features of this book, and together they represent my own favorite aspect of this series. Reading about travel in the days before transatlantic flights, I always marvel at the number of steamer trunks and bags people were accustomed to taking. If it were me traveling then, however, my bags would be filled with books, not clothes. Although I travel light and seldom check bags, I have been known to fill an entire suitcase with books, secure in the knowledge that I could have them all with me for the duration of my trip. Each *biblioteca* features the titles I feel are the best available and most worth your time. I realize that *best* is subjective; readers will simply have to trust that I have been extremely thorough in deciding which books to recommend. (I have read them all, by the way, and I own them all, with the exception of a few I borrowed.) If the lists seem long, they are, but the more I read, the more I realize there is to know, and there are an awful lot of really good books out there! I'm not suggesting you read them *all*, but I do hope you won't be content with just one. I have identified some books as *"essenziale,"* meaning that I consider them required reading; but I sincerely believe that *all* the books I've mentioned are important, helpful, well written, or all three. I keep up with book publishing and don't miss much, but there are surely some books I've not seen, so if some of your favorites aren't included here, please write and tell me about them.

I have not hesitated to list out-of-print titles because some very excellent books are declared out of print (and deserve to be returned to print!) and because many, many out-of-print books can be found through individuals who specialize in out-of-print books, booksellers, libraries, and online searches. I should also mention that I believe the companion reading you bring along should be related in some way to where you're going. Therefore the books listed in *La Bella Vita* are mostly novels that feature characters or settings in Venice, the Veneto, or Friuli–Venezia Giulia or that feature aspects of Italy and the Italians (such as *Dead Lagoon, Romeo and Juliet, Italian Neighbors,* and *Across the River and Into the Trees*). Biographies make up most of the books in the *I Personaggi* section. The selection isn't meant to be comprehensive—there are many more I could have included—but it represents a variety of books about a variety of interesting people, one or more of whom may also interest you. The *Musei e Monumenti* section, therefore, doesn't include biographies of artists, as I thought it better to separate art history books and museum catalogs—with their many reproductions of artworks—from memoirs and biographies.

Together the articles and books will lead you onto and off the beaten path and present a "reality check" of sorts. Will you learn of some nontouristy things to see and do? Yes. Will you learn more about the better-known aspects of Venice and Trieste? Yes. The Piazza San Marco, Castello di Miramare, the Alpi Dolomiti, the Roman arena in Verona, a perfect cup of cappuccino in Padua, and a quiet *campiello* in Venice are all equally representative of the region. Seeing them *all* is what makes for a memorable visit, and no one, by the way, should make you feel guilty for wanting to see some famous sites. They have become famous for a reason: they are really something to see, the Piazza San Marco included. Readers will have no trouble finding a multitude of other travel titles offering plenty of noncontroversial viewpoints. This book is my attempt at presenting a more balanced picture. Ultimately, it is also the compendium of information that I wish I'd had between two covers years ago. I admit it isn't the "perfect" book; for that, I envision a soft Italian-leather volume encased in a waterproof jacket and pockets inside the front and back covers, pages and pages of accompanying maps, lots of blank pages for notes, a bookmark, mileage and size conversion charts—in other words, something so encyclopedic in both weight and size that positively no one, my editor assures me, would want to read it. That said, I am exceedingly happy with *The Collected Traveler,* and I believe it will prove helpful in the anticipation of your upcoming journey; in the enjoyment of your trip while it's happening; and in the remembrance of it when you're back home.

As I reread and edit this introduction, it is in the aftermath of the horrific and senseless terrorist attack on New York's World Trade Center and the Pentagon in Washington, D.C. It has struck me profoundly that not only do I refuse to be made to feel like a prisoner in my own city and my nation, but places in the world like Venice—and towns like Padua, Verona, Vicenza, Treviso, Udine, and Cividale del Friuli and the truly international and multicultural city of Trieste— have in a matter of days become ever more precious and exceptional, more important than ever to see at least once. I will exercise caution and plan carefully, but I will continue to fly overseas, and I hope my fellow American citizens and Canadian neighbors will reach the same conclusion: that we must not allow terrorists to win. I believe that, contrary to one's initial reaction, staying home does not make us safe. The first goal of all terrorists is to intimidate and inspire fear in people. Staying home is equal to a victory, a major one, for terrorists. It is at this point, when people are scared and start canceling their travel plans, that terrorists strike again, defeating us twice, making the world an even more dangerous place and guaranteeing that they win the war they are waging. In an enlightening article in Condé Nast Traveler *entitled "Terrorism: Weighing the True Risks" (July 1996), the reporters prepared a "Targets of Terror" timeline from 1972 through April 1996. Some of the attacks on the timeline included the following: Palestinian terrorists kidnap and murder eleven Israeli athletes at the Munich Olympic Games (September 5, 1972); eight Palestinian terrorists open fire on a Tel Aviv beach (March 5, 1975); two IRA bombs explode in London's Hyde Park and Regent's Park (July 20, 1982); IRA bomb explodes outside Harrods department store in London (December 17, 1983); Palestinian gunmen hijack the Italian cruise line ship* Achille Lauro *in the Mediterranean (October 7, 1985); explosion at the World Trade Center in New York (February 26, 1993); Hamas suicide bomber blows up a bus in downtown Tel Aviv (October 19, 1994); Palestinian terrorists bomb La Belle nightclub in West Berlin (April 5, 1986); Arab terrorists throw a bomb from a passing car into a crowd at the Paris department store Tati (September 17, 1986); Shining Path guerrillas detonate a car bomb in front of a Lima, Peru, hotel (May 24, 1995); and Algerian Armed Islamic Group bombs the St.-Michel Metro station in Paris (July 25, 1995). The conclusion I draw from this list is that terrorist attacks happen not only on airplanes but on cruise ships, in department stores, at beaches, in parks, in nightclubs, and on public transportation—in short,* anywhere, *to* anyone, *for reasons as random—it seems to me—as wearing purple socks. (Perhaps the attack that most exemplifies this randomness was the one on April 18, 1996, when Islamic Group terrorists killed eighteen and wounded another fifteen Greek tourists in Cairo, mistaking them for Israelis.) If terrorist attacks are always within the realm of possibility, then so are the mundane activities of our daily existence, such as walking out the front door and picking up the morning newspaper, standing on a ladder and cleaning the leaves out of the gutter, or carrying clothes a few blocks away to the dry cleaner—each of which carries the risk of falling down and hitting our head on the sidewalk or the stone steps or the fire hydrant—not to mention drunk driving accidents, street crimes, hate crimes, heart attacks, rape, or murder. If we never leave our homes, we are effectively living in fear; if we travel with fear, we are victims of that fear, real or imagined, even if not a single incident happens while we're away. As an aside, I have just learned from a colleague at Visit Italy Tours that Italian hoteliers have been quietly allowing stranded Americans who cannot fly home to remain in their hotels, free of charge. So far this generosity has not been publicly acknowledged but deserves to be; you may repay the hoteliers' generosity by making a trip and thanking them in person.*

There are very good reasons why Giuseppe Verdi is known to have said, "You may have the universe if I may have Italy," and why Robert Browning, who spent much of his life in Venice, passionately wrote, "Open my heart and you will see / Graved inside of it, 'Italy.'" I hope you will discover them. *Buon viaggio!* on all your journeys to this vastly interesting corner of Italy in the new millennium.

Informazioni Pratiche
(Practical Information)

"The great thing to remember when using the ACTV services is that you are not the first non-Italian-speaking tourist to do so: all you have to do is smile and make enquiring gestures and the officials will put you on the right boat—and, what is more important, going in the right direction. It is less humiliating to do this than to find yourself in the wrong boat and having to pretend that your destination was a different one."
— J. G. Links, VENICE FOR PLEASURE

A–Z Informazioni Pratiche

Accommodations

If you arrive in Venice without a room, booking services are available at the Venetian Hoteliers Association (AVA) booths located at the Stazione Ferrovia Santa Lucia (train station), the Marco Polo Airport, the parking garage at Piazzale Roma, Tronchetto (described as Europe's largest parking garage), and the Venice exit on the *autostrada*. You must show up in person (as opposed to calling on the phone) and are required to leave a deposit, which is then refunded by the hotel. You may contact the main AVA office for both last-minute and advance reservations (041.522.22.64 or 800.843.006 toll-free within Italy; fax: 041.522.12.42).

Accommodation services are less likely to be available outside of Venice and Trieste, although it has been my experience that the staff at even the smallest tourist office in the smallest town in Italy will be able to assist you in finding a place to stay. They may not place telephone calls for you or make reservations, but they will tell you what choices there are, give directions, and help in any way they can. Unless you are traveling for an extended period of time throughout the region or throughout Italy, I don't recommend showing up without a room, especially in July or August, during *Carnevale,* and during the Christmas and New Year holidays. (This means the days leading up to Christmas as well.) Many of the most wonderful lodgings are quite small, with only a few rooms, and they can fill up fast even during the off-season. We all have a limited number of precious vacation days, and searching for a place to stay can be a most time-consuming and frustrating experience and certainly not what you came to Italy to do. Unless you're traveling around by train and a backpack—and therefore are probably going from youth hostel to youth hostel—you will probably want to carefully select the places you'll call home for a few days or longer. Some might argue that the choice of lodgings isn't important, since you won't be spending much time in your room anyway; but I disagree with this notion. Meeting the owners of a family-run hotel or *agriturismo* property, getting to know the front desk clerk at a posh *palazzo,* or simply returning to a nicely kept room for an afternoon siesta are all part of a memorable and enjoyable trip. I can find no reason *not* to devote some time to researching where you will stay—the only problem will be narrowing your choices, because there are so many great places to stay. Note that lodgings almost never close in Venice proper and the Veneto but that places on the Lido and Lake Garda often close during the winter. It's the reverse, of course, in Trentino–Alto Adige, where winter is a big season. Summer is popular in the mountains as well, so typically hotels and inns will close for some period in the spring or fall. Friuli–Venezia Giulia follows a pattern similar to Venice and the Veneto, but don't be surprised to find that some of the more remote establishments are not open year-round. Also, keep in mind that the Italian government's star rating system for lodging establishments awards stars based on the quality of rooms and the amenities provided, paying special attention to the number of bathrooms and toilets compared with the number of rooms. The stars have almost nothing at all to do with charm or quality of hospitality. For example, two hotels where I stayed recently were both given a rating of two stars. The first, the Al Teatro, is a once-grand building in Trieste, located steps away from the Piazza Unità d'Italia. The building served as British headquarters during the Second World War and is recommended in every guidebook as a good (as opposed to fancy) place to stay in Trieste. The thing of it is, it should be a *great* place to stay in Trieste—the rooms are larger than most, with high ceilings and nice moldings, and the location can't be beat; but unfortunately there is a stale, frayed-around-the-edges air to the place, and the rooms facing out toward the piazza are noisy at night. In the hands of a new owner, the building could be spruced up without too much of an investment and be returned to its former glory, or at least to something less depressing. Conversely, at the Due Mori in Vicenza, also rated two stars, everything is light, airy, very clean, and neat; it is also located on a pedestrian-only street. The rooms have ceiling fans, enabling you to close the window in the summer to keep out mosquitoes and noise, and the furniture in the rooms is tasteful and a cut above what you might expect from a two-star. Compared with the Al Teatro, the Due Mori is a much better value and should not be in the same category.

All of this is to say that you cannot depend on Italy's star rating system alone. Generally speaking, a one-star establishment is equated with simple accommodations and usually shared bathroom facilities. Two- and three-star establishments can be bed-and-breakfast or regular hotel accommodations, with a private bath. Four- and five-star hotels represent the highest standards of service and can be either quite luxurious or less so. All classified hotels, of whatever type, are required to display their rating on their facades, and the Italian State Tourist Board features all its rated hotels on its website (www.enit.it). You may, in your research and travels, discover places that have no rating; this is not because the tourist office has rejected them but rather because these establishments have not requested to be reviewed. I have stayed in a number of places with no rating, and they were all perfectly fine and clean, some even quite deserving of two or three stars; it's much better to read a thorough description of a place so you know exactly what you're paying for, and ignore the stars. Following are the types of accommodations you'll find in this corner of Italy:

Agriturismo (translated as "agricultural tourism") was not widely known—inside Italy or abroad—as recently as fifteen years ago. Though most visitors to Italy recognize the name now as representing accommodations offered on farms or agricultural estates, *agriturismo* as an organized concept is much more than that. Officially the program began in 1965 and was introduced by the Italian government's agricultural department. The idea was a good one: to help struggling farmers supplement their income by allowing them to offer simple accommodations to tourists (Italians included) and sell their homegrown produce directly to anyone who came to the farm to purchase it. Hoped-for added benefits would be a reduction in rural flight (after World War II, Italians left the countryside in huge numbers seeking opportunities in the nation's cities) and the preservation of local traditions, crafts, cuisine, and customs that seemed to be on the brink of extinction. Now, more than thirty-five years later, it can be said that *agriturismo* has been a great success, but for many years even most Italians didn't know about *agriturismo*, and those who did had an erroneous conception of it: that visitors received extremely basic accommodations (interpreted as uncomfortable and dreary) and peasant food in exchange for laboring in some manner on the farm. The truth is that accommodations range from basic to luxurious, on small working farms and larger estates. Readers should know in advance, however, that the primary purpose of an *agriturismo* property is the daily operation of the farm. You should not expect the same services that you would receive at a hotel or an inn—your room(s) may not be cleaned daily, so you should be prepared to tidy up yourself. Also, as *agriturismo* properties are in the countryside, a car is essential. Confusion still seems to exist as to the exact definition of *agriturismo* and its interpretation by each member property (for example, in some parts of the country a certain percentage of the land apparently must be given over to the cultivation of produce or wine). There are *agriturismo* member participants from all of Italy's regions, but the highest concentration of properties is in Tuscany and, happily for readers of this book, Trentino–Alto Adige. (The fewest exist in Calabria, Basilicata, and Campania.) The best sources for *agriturismo* accommodations throughout Italy are the directories published by three national organizations: Associazione Nazionale per l'Agriturismo (Corso Vittorio Emanuele 101, Rome 00168; 06.6852342; fax: 06.6852424; e-mail: agritur@confagricoltura.it); Turismo Verde (Via E. Franceschini 89, Rome 00155; 06.3220113; fax: 06.36000294; e-mail: info@turismoverde.it); and Terranostra (Via 14 Maggio 43, Rome 00187; 06.4682370; fax: 06.4682204; e-mail: terranostra@coldiretti.it). The directories, for which a fee is charged, are in Italian; but the lack of English text is really not a problem. I have a directory from the Associazione Nazionale entitled *Guida dell'ospitalità rurale: Agriturismo e vacanze verdi*, and it's not difficult to figure out the basic information for each listing, and each one has a photograph. An excellent website to browse for *agriturismo* properties is www.agriturismo.net. Viewers select a region and/or a province to review all the available places, and each entry includes a photo with a good description, driving directions to the property (some entries include a map), and contact information. Icons to click on for more information include "Pets," "Heating," "Pool," "Air Conditioning," "Daily Cleaning," "Handicap," "Open All Year Long," "Jacuzzi," "Satellite Television," "Golf," "Playground,"

"Washing Machine," "Biological Products," "Biking," "Credit Cards," "Tennis," and more. It's really incredibly comprehensive, and viewers can also browse by selecting "Farm Holiday," "City Apartments," or "Deluxe Country Houses." If you prefer that someone else do the legwork, one U.S. company that arranges *agriturismo* is Italy Farm Holidays (547 Martling Avenue, Tarrytown, New York 10591; 914-631-7880; fax: -8831; www.italyfarmholidays.com). When I last browsed its website, I found three farms in the Veneto: one in Bovolenta near Padua (a traditional house on a vineyard and horse farm), one in Selvazzana, west of Padua (a castle and tower in a majestic nine-hundred-year-old estate), and one in Barbarano, near Vicenza (a fifteenth-century castle with lemon orchard and garden). Two good articles worth tracking down that I did not include in this book are "Farmhouse Hospitality: Tucked Away Among Vineyards and Olive Groves, Italy's *Agriturismi* Offer All the Comforts of Home" (Faith Heller Willinger, *Gourmet,* May 1999, which highlights special places to stay in Friuli–Venezia Giulia, Piedmont, Tuscany, Campania, and Sicily; the recommended property in Friuli–Venezia Giulia is La Subida, in the Collio wine-growing district, owned by Josko and Loredana Sirk, proprietors of the highly regarded *trattoria* Al Cacciatore; Willinger also shares some good tips, such as, if you're fond of sleeping late, avoid farms with animals), and *"Agriturismo:* My House Is Your House" (Raffaella Prandi, *Gambero Rosso* no. 22, 2000, which is the most detailed article on *agriturismo* I've yet seen; the writer profiles three properties, one near Liguria, one in Umbria, and one in Campania, and the in-depth descriptions of each really prepare travelers for the experience). Another unique *agriturismo* property in Friuli's Collio wine district is located on the grounds of the well-regarded Venica & Venica winery. *"Casa vino e vacanze"* (house of wine and vacation) is this beautiful property's motto, and in addition to lovely rooms complete with a kitchen, there is a pool and a tennis court. Guests can also walk among the vines, bike ride, visit the parks of Plessiva and Bosco Romagno, tour nearby Cividale del Friuli . . . and savor the wines! (Venica & Venica, a family operation since 1930, produces a range of twelve whites and five reds and cultivates both native and imported grapes.) The winery is about 25 kilometers from Udine, 100 kilometers from Venice, and 20 kilometers from Ronchi dei Legionari Airport. Contact the Venica family for more details and to make reservations at Località Cero–Via Mernico 42, 34070 Dolegna del Collio (GO); 0481.61264; fax: 0481.639906; e-mail: venica@venica.it; www.venica.it.

Albergo is the Italian word for "hotel" but is generally a smaller operation. It is not always cheaper, however.

Bed and breakfast accommodation, like *agriturismo,* is relatively new to Italy. Some people make the mistake of using these terms interchangeably, but they are different: an *agriturismo* property may also be classified as a bed and breakfast, but a bed and breakfast is very often *not* an *agriturismo* property. The best guide, in my opinion, for seeking out B&B accommodations is *Caffèlletto: High Quality Bed*

& Breakfast in Italy (Edition Le Lettere, Emmebi 3 s.r.l., Via di Marciola 23, 50020 S. Vincenzo a Torri, Florence; www.caffelletto.it). This great paperback book is printed in both English and Italian and, to my knowledge, is no longer distributed in the United States. The *Caffèlletto* is the first guide to high-class bed and breakfast hospitality to be published in Italy, and the organization requires all its members to meet certain criteria of hospitality: "The hosts should be people whom it would be interesting to meet in any circumstances, who enjoy receiving guests and who take pride in their home and the corner of Italy in which they live, often for generations. Their homes should also have historic associations, beautiful gardens and views, and be furnished with taste, as well as offering every comfort to guests, starting with breakfast which must be of a very high standard." There are two accommodation listings for Friuli–Venezia Giulia, two for Trentino–Alto Adige, and thirty-three for the Veneto, including three for Venice. Listings are ranked in three categories. (A symbol of three candles means there is a private bathroom; four candles means that your room is part of a highly prestigious property; and the Caffèlletto logo means that the particularly discerning traveler will find luxurious accommodation in a beautiful mansion of historical significance or situated in a beautiful location.) Color photos and a good description accompany each very appealing place, and each region of Italy is outlined in a paragraph or two and includes a small map and a recipe unique to the region. (Barley Soup has been chosen for Trentino–Alto Adige, Red Radicchio Salad for the Veneto, and Custard Pudding for Friuli–Venezia Giulia.) Prices for Caffèlletto properties range from about $30 to $90 per person, and reservations can be made either directly with the hosts or through the Caffèlletto offices. (There is no charge for this service, and it includes the confirmation of your reservation, a map, and instructions for reaching the property, as well as the staff's assistance with any queries.)

Another book to consult—one perhaps easier to find—is *Karen Brown's Italy: Charming Bed & Breakfasts* (Nicole Franchini, Fodor's Travel Publications). The subtitle of this guide is *Italy's Finest Bed & Breakfasts at Reasonable Prices,* and though these lodgings are less expensive than those listed in *Karen Brown's Inns & Itineraries,* they are no less charming or special. Rates for the properties recommended in this guide range from $65 to $200. (Note that the title of this guide is a little misleading because all the listings in this guide are actually *agriturismo* properties. I've listed it here instead of above because I felt it would be too confusing.) I find the organization of Karen Brown's guides to be maddeningly cumbersome— the lodgings are listed alphabetically by individual city, town, or village, but the maps are at the back of the book, so you end up constantly flipping pages back and forth to evaluate all the available choices in any given region; but the description of each property is thorough and candid, and I trust the author that a stay at any of these places would be memorable. There are fifteen listings for the Veneto and ninety-two (!) for Trentino–Alto Adige, but none, unfortunately, for Friuli–Venezia

Giulia. The listings aside, some of the features I like best about Karen Brown guides in general are the sample Reservation Request letter (in Italian and English so readers can construct a letter, fax, or e-mail of their own) and the tips that appear in the introduction, such as that credit cards are rarely accepted at bed-and-breakfast establishments. Also included in this guide is a helpful list of regional farm names, such as *borgo, fattoria, locanda, podere, tenuta,* and so on.

Ca' or *casa* is Venetian dialect for "house" or "palazzo." You won't run across many establishments with this name, but you can equate a *ca'* with hotel-like service.

Campeggio (camping) can be a viable option for those who have a car and a lot of time. The thing to understand about the European conception of camping is that it is about as opposite from the American conception as possible. Europeans do not go camping to seek a wilderness experience, and European campgrounds are designed without much privacy in mind, offering amenities ranging from hot-water showers, facilities for washing clothes and dishes, electrical outlets, croissants and coffee for breakfast, and flush toilets to tiled bathrooms with heat, swimming pools, cafés, bars, restaurants, telephones, televisions, and general stores. If you find yourself at a campground during the summer months, you may notice that entire families have literally moved in (having reserved their spaces many months in advance) and that they return every year to spend time with their friends, the way we might return every year to a ski cabin or a house at the beach. It's quite an entertaining and lively spectacle, and camping like this is not really roughing it! The only campground I've stayed at in this part of Italy is Camping Fusina Tourist Village near Venice (Via Moranzani 79, Fusina 30030; 041.547.0055; www.camping-fusina.com). It is quite a nice campground, open all year and complete with a restaurant/bar/trattoria, supermarket, breakfast bar, Internet access, and—best of all—hourly shuttle boat service to Venice and the beach. (The boat drops you off at Zattere.) There are, however, more camping spots along the Litorale del Cavallino, that narrow strip of land beyond Burano. (You can see this well on one of the Baedeker's map inserts.) But some of these campsites are actually quite luxurious, as reported in the Rough Guide, and it's worth noting that "price can be a problem here—when you've added on the fare for the forty-minute boat trip into the city you're not left with a particularly economical proposition." For details on these specific camping sites, contact Assocampings, Via Fausta, Ponte Cavallino, Cavallino 30013; 041.658813; or Consorzio Lido Ca' di Valle, Corso Italia 10, Cavallino 30013; 041.968148. For more complete information about the region's campgrounds, the tourist offices here and in Italy have specific information. Ask for the campground directory, *Campeggiare in Italia,* or contact the Federazione Italiana del Campeggio e del Caravanning directly for a copy (Federcampeggio, Casella Postale 23, 50041 Calenzano, Florence; fax: 55.882.5918). It's been my experience at municipal *campeggiare* that during the off-season no one ever comes around to collect fees. The campgrounds are still open and there is running water, but the thinking seems to be that it just isn't worth it to collect money from so few campers. (This will not hold true at privately run campgrounds.) If you plan to camp for even a few nights, I recommend joining Family Campers and RVers. Annual membership (valid for one year from the time you join) is $25. FCRV is a member of the Fédération Internationale de Camping et de Caravanning (FICC) and is the only organization in America authorized to issue the International Camping Carnet for camping in Europe. Only FCRV members are eligible to purchase the carnet—it cannot be purchased separately—and the membership fee is $10. The carnet is like a camping passport, and since many FICC member campgrounds in Europe are privately owned, the carnet provides entry into these member-only campsites. A carnet offers campers priority status and occasionally discounts. An additional benefit is that instead of keeping your passport overnight—which hotels and campgrounds are often required to do—the campground staff simply keeps your carnet, allowing you to hold on to your passport. One FICC membership is good for the entire family: parents and all children under the age of eighteen. To receive an application and information, contact the organization at 4804 Transit Road, Building 2, Depew, New York 14043; 800-245-9755; phone and fax: 716-668-6242.

Home exchange might be an appealing option: I've read wildly enthusiastic reports from people who've swapped apartments or houses, and it's usually always an economical alternative. Some services to contact include Trading Homes International (P.O. Box 787, Hermosa Beach, California 90254; 800-877-TRADE; fax: 310-798-3865; www.trading-homes.com); Worldwide Home Exchange Club (806 Branford Avenue, Silver Spring, Maryland 20904; 866-898-9660; www.homeexchange.com); and Intervac International (Box 12066, S-291, 12 Kristianstad, Sweden; 800-756-4663; www.intervac.com).

~Consumer Reports Travel Letter presented a special report on home exchange in its November 2001 issue (to request a copy, send $5 to *CRTL*, 101 Truman Avenue, Yonkers, New York 10703-1057), and the report noted that the number-one complaint filed by exchangers is cleanliness. Obviously, different people interpret "clean" in different ways (males and females do too), so this is something to keep in mind when making arrangements.

Hotels are, of course, where most of us stay when we travel, and I feel that books exclusively about hotels are better than recommendations from general guidebooks. As with guidebooks, the right hotel book for you is the one whose author shares a certain sensibility or philosophy with you. It's important to select the right book(s) so you can make choices that best suit you and your style. I believe that in the same way you put your trust in the author of a guidebook, you put that same faith in the author of a hotel guide. Once you've selected the book you like, trust the author's recommendations, make your decisions, and move on to the next stage of your planning. I have never understood those people who, after they've made a reservation, seek some sort of validation for their choice—by searching the Internet, for example, for other travelers' comments and opinions. I find this serves no good purpose and is a poor use of one's time, and it makes me wonder why those people consulted the hotel books in the first place. Remember: *You don't know the people writing reviews on the Internet, and you have no idea whether the things that are important to you are also important to them.* And remember that authors of hotel guides carefully share their standards with you and explain the criteria they use in rating accommodations. I believe—because I read a lot of travel guidebooks and hotel guides—that most of the time authors are clear about what they look for and expect in hotel establishments, and though you may not always agree, you may at least understand how they arrived at their conclusions.

Following are some books I like to use when searching for a hotel in northeastern Italy. I have found that it is never difficult to learn of places to stay in either the luxury or the budget category; harder is finding beautiful and unique places that fall in between, which is why the following titles are my favorites:

Charming Small Hotel Guides: Venice & North-East Italy (Fiona Duncan and Leonie Glass, Duncan Petersen Publishing, London / Hunter Publishing, Edison, New Jersey). This series features the kind of places where I most like to stay. The authors explain that some of the qualities they look for include "a calm, attractive setting in an interesting and picturesque position; a building that is either handsome or interesting or historic, or at least with a distinct character; bedrooms which are well proportioned with as much character as the public rooms below; ideally, we look for adequate space, but on a human scale: we don't go for places that rely on grandeur, or that have pretensions that could intimidate; decorations must be harmonious and in good taste, and the furnishings and facilities comfortable and well maintained. We like to see interesting antique furniture that is there because it can be used, not simply revered; the proprietors and staff need to be dedicated and thoughtful, offering a personal welcome, without being intrusive. The guest needs to feel like an individual." Two types of entries are found in this guide: full page (which detail places that have nearly all the qualities listed above) and half page (which recommend hotels that are still charming but don't have as many of the qualities the authors look for; after all, as they note, you can't have stars on every page). Featured are forty full-page listings for Venice, five for the lagoon, twenty-seven for the Veneto (plus five from the Lombard side of Lake Garda), five for Friuli–Venezia Giulia, and nineteen for Trentino–Alto Adige, plus thirty pages of half-page listings, any one of which would make a memorable night's stay. The authors also provide an inside peek at riding the Venice-Simplon Orient Express, at the back of the book.

Cheap Sleeps in Italy: Florence, Rome, Venice (Sandra Gustafson, Chronicle Books). A companion volume to Gustafson's *Cheap Eats in Italy,* this is a great resource for best-value places to lay your head. Lest you get the wrong idea about

Gustafson's aim, she states, "It is important that you know *Cheap Sleeps in Italy* is not for those travelers who are looking for a list of the cheapest beds in Florence, Rome, and Venice. It is for those who are concerned with having a better trip by saving money and not sacrificing comfort, convenience, and well-being in the bargain. Life is too short not to treat it as a grand adventure." She also wisely reminds us that value is not always equated with price. The Venice section, which is organized by neighborhood, contains fifty-eight pages of hotel and apartment listings (which include hotels with apartments or kitchen suites), two pages for camping, six pages for student accommodations, and ten pages dedicated to listings for shopping (antiques, art, bookbinding, ceramics and porcelain, department stores, dolls, glass, glass beads and jewelry, lace and vintage clothing, markets, masks, photography, silk, stationery, and shopping destinations). With some splurges included, this is a book for *everyone*.

Hello Italy! An Insider's Guide to Italian Hotels $50–99 a Night for Two (2nd edition, Margo Classé, Wilson Publishing, Los Angeles, California, 1999). The author traveled alone to twenty-six of Italy's most popular cities and discovered this selection of clean, safe, centrally located, and inexpensive places to spend the night. Listings include rooms for single, double, and triple occupancies, and Classé notes that showing her book to the proprietor may result in a discount! Classé also provides directions to each hotel, tips on making reservations, and what to pack. I really like this book and have stayed at a few places Classé recommends; but recently I had a hard time finding it, though it is in print. I do encourage you to seek it out—even placing a special order for it—if you are looking for moderately priced accommodations, because this book is one of a kind.

Hotel Gems of Italy (compiled by Luc Quisenaerts, written by Anne and Owen Davis, D–Publications, Belgium). This is a beautiful book in the Hotel Gems of the World series. Most of these places are to die for, with prices to match, but still I'd rather spend my money on one of these places than on an international chain hotel. Each hotel is described in four to six pages with photos that make you want to pack your bags *immediatamente,* and practical information—prices, contact information, etc.—appears at the back of the book. Of the thirty-six hotels featured, seven are in northeastern Italy.

Karen Brown's Italy: Charming Inns & Itineraries (Fodor's Travel Publications). My husband and I have found some of the most wonderful places to stay with the help of Karen Brown's guides. In addition to the thorough descriptions of lodgings (some of which are in palazzi, old mills, and buildings of historic significance), this guide to inns includes tips for travelers, such as to be aware that some hotels will accept a credit card to hold a reservation but won't allow you to pay the final bill with a credit card. The itineraries presented in the book are useful for planning your route in advance and deciding whether you want to travel by car, but the descriptions of individual towns and sites are not detailed enough to warrant bringing the book along—this is really a before-you-go book. As I noted previously, I find the organization of these guides maddeningly cumbersome. But this frustration is really a small price to pay for the opportunity to stay in memorable *alberghi* and *pensioni*. This edition features more than twenty places to stay in the Veneto and Trentino–Alto Adige but only one for Friuli–Venezia Giulia. It's a good guide to consult even if you don't plan on going to other parts of Italy.

Rivages Hotels and Country Inns of Character and Charm in Italy (4th edition, Hunter Publishing). The French Rivages guides have been popular in Europe for years, and I think they are a welcome addition to lodgings literature here in the States. All the guides feature color photographs of the properties, with one-page descriptions and good road maps. There are twenty-two pages of listings for Trentino–Alto Adige, sixty-seven for the Veneto, and no listings, unfortunately, for Friuli–Venezia Giulia. At the back of the book is a section featuring restaurant recommendations, with three pages of listings for Trentino–Alto Adige and eleven for the Veneto. Some of the listings will be familiar to readers of other guidebooks, but many do not appear in any other books. "Character and charm" are not exclusively equated with four-star luxury, but there are lots of three- and four-star listings in this guide; and even though this book will never be of interest to the serious budget traveler, there are a number of two-, one-, and no-star choices. As I mentioned earlier, stars often have nothing to do with charm or quality of hospitality, and the reason some of the listings in this guide have no stars is simply that the owners never asked the government to rate them.

Alistair Sawday's Special Places to Stay: Italy (edited by Susan Pennington, Alistair Sawday Publishing, Bristol, England; distributed in the United States by Globe Pequot Press, Old Saybrook, Connecticut) is another guide I very much like. I'm a big fan of this series (I've used the Paris, Spain, and France editions with great success), and it seems to me that the majority of these places do not appear in other accommodation guides. Each entry is described, with a color photograph, on one page, and entries include palazzi, monasteries, vineyard estates, farmhouses, villas, and even a cistern in Emilia Romagna. The Sawday authors like places that are "interesting, highly individual, owned by delightful people and often in stunning areas." There is only one entry for Trentino–Alto Adige and two for the Veneto (none for Friuli–Venezia Giulia), but if you enjoy traveling to Italy, this is a good book to have. Included is also a two-page glossary, travel tips, twelve pages of color road maps, and an Italian-English reservation form.

~Often, newspaper and magazine articles are very good sources for hotels. The writers have more space to describe lodgings more thoroughly and can go into greater detail about service, amenities, and flaws. Accompanying photographs are also of better quality than those on websites. Three good articles about Venetian hotels that I've used are "Venice by the Numbers" (Christine Ryan, *Travel Holiday*, April 2000), which profiles three small hotels on the Grand Canal);

"Thirty Affordable Hotels". (Henry Shukman, *Condé Nast Traveler,* February 2001, which singles out wonderful hotels in fifteen cities—Venice included—that represent good value; in other words, they are less than $200 a night; Shukman recommends five hotels in Venice); and "As Good as It Gets (Trust Us)" (Christopher Petkanas, *Travel & Leisure,* September 2000, which highlights the Cipriani, Gritti Palace, Danieli, Hotel Monaco & Grand Canal, Grand Hotel dei Dogi, Il Palazzo at the Bauer, and Pensione Accademia).

A very special hotel experience I have read about is to stay at the Villa Emo, a Veneto country house that Palladio designed for the Emo family in 1556. The grounds of the villa were once a farm, but the villa itself has been transformed into a twelve-room hotel. I have not yet stayed there, but I think it would be a once-in-a-lifetime experience. To inquire, contact the Villa Emo at Via Stazione 5, Fanzolo; 423.476.414; fax: 423.487.043. Another special place is Al Leon d'Oro, a nineteenth-century farmhouse on a canal just fifteen miles from Venice and very near the villas of the Brenta. I read of it in an article entitled "Small Hotels, Part 2" (*Gambero Rosso* no. 28, 2001), and it was the only hotel featured in northeastern Italy. The Leon d'Oro is also home to Gianni Forzutti (who cooks at the Ristorante San Giorgio in Venice) and his wife Margherita Kaufman and their daughter. The hotel is surrounded by a garden (many rooms have their own private outdoor spaces), and there are two swimming pools and a sauna. Plus, eleven of the twenty-three rooms are designated nonsmoking. Breakfast is included, and the rates for a double room are from about $100 to $130 (Via Canonici 3, Mirano; 041.432.777).

Hotel groups often represent properties that aren't featured in other publications. My favorite organization, which I first learned about while researching my *Central Italy* book, is Abitare la Storia (Hospitality in Historical Houses), founded in 1995. The association combines independent accommodation facilities for tourists situated in historical dwellings both in towns and in the country, all over Italy. Abitare la Storia "extends a unique welcome to those receptive to the traces of history and art that the passing of the centuries has imprinted on these sites." Travelers who have visited the Iberian Peninsula may be familiar with the *paradores* of Spain and the *pousadas* of Portugal; these are government-run, however. A closer equivalent is the *estancias* hotel group of Spain, which, like Abitare la Storia properties, are privately owned. To quote from its brochure, Abitare la Storia "wishes to promote facilities situated all over the country and suggests connecting itineraries between the various associate facilities; it recommends secondary routes still unknown to most tourists and aims to enhance the value of all those marvelous artistic, scenic, gastronomical and oenological riches which abound in Italy, but are often not shown off with the sense of pride they deserve." In 2001 there were forty-one Abitare members, but only two in northeastern Italy: one in the Veneto (Villa Odino) and the other in Friuli–Venezia Giulia (Villa Lupis, where I had the great fortune to stay on my last visit—see *La Bella Vita* for a description). For a brochure and information, contact the association at Via Veneto 183, 00187 Rome; 064.201.2138; fax: 064.202.7980; e-mail: mailbox@abitarelastoria.it; www.abitarelastoria.it.

Relais & Châteaux is a well-known hotel group that is almost fifty years old. R&C has more than 450 member properties, hotels, and restaurants in forty-seven countries and has remained loyal to its five "C's": courtesy, charm, character, calm, and cuisine. R&C has only one hotel property in northeastern Italy, the Villa del Quar in the Veneto, and only one restaurant, the Ristorante Le Calandre in Padua. Recently the L'École des Chefs program (profiled in my *Paris* book) became affiliated with R&C, so visitors to Italy now have the opportunity to participate in this unique restaurant experience (see Cooking Schools for more details). The hefty (680 pages) R&C guide is a good resource for discerning travelers. For a copy and more information, contact Relais & Châteaux at its North American office, 11 East 44th Street, Suite 707, New York, New York 10017; 800-735-2478 or 212-856-0115, fax: -0193; rc-usa@relaischateaux.com; www.relaischateaux.com.

Locanda is the Italian word for "inn," and they are often family-run, but you'll also see this word in names of restaurants.

Monastic lodgings are sometimes overlooked, but they are a unique—and quiet—alternative. Two good books to consult are *Bed and Blessings—Italy: A Guide to Convents and Monasteries Available for Overnight Lodging* (June Walsh and Anne Walsh, Paulist Press, 1999) and *The Guide to Lodging in Italy's Monasteries: Inexpensive Accommodations, Remarkable Historic Buildings, Unforgettable Settings* (Eileen Barish, Anacapa Press, Scottsdale, Arizona, 1999). Average prices for a room range from $20 to $80 per night, and the rooms themselves range from simple to luxurious. Note that credit cards are not uniformly accepted, there is sometimes a curfew, and foreign languages are rarely spoken (a good incentive to brush up on your Italian!). There are twenty-one listings for Venice and the Veneto in the first book, and twenty-nine listings for the Veneto, Venice, Trentino, and Friuli–Venezia Giulia in the second book.

Ostelli della gioventù (youth hostels) are another choice for those seeking budget accommodations (and keep in mind that hostels are not just for the under-thirty crowd). I would take back in a minute my summer of vagabonding around Europe, meeting young people from all over the world, and feeling that my life was one endless possibility. I now prefer to share a room with my husband rather than five twentysomethings, but hosteling remains a fun and exciting experience. Younger budget travelers need no convincing that hosteling is the way to go; but older budget travelers should bear in mind that although some hostels offer individual rooms (mostly for couples), comparing costs reveals that they are often the same price as a room in a real (albeit inexpensive) hotel, where you can reserve a room in advance and comfortably keep your luggage (when hosteling, you must pack up your luggage every day, and you can't make a reservation); additionally, most hostels have an eleven

P.M. curfew. Petty theft—of the T-shirts-stolen-off-the-clothesline variety—seems to be more prevalent than it once was, and it would be wise to sleep and shower with your money belt close at hand. There are several youth hostels in northeastern Italy (in Venice, Trieste, Verona, Vicenza, Trento, Padua, and others), each of which is detailed in the excellent *guida* (guide) that the Associazione Italiana Alberghi per la Gioventù (AIG) publishes annually. This guide—in Italian and English—is also available at tourist offices in North America, and interested travelers should definitely make sure they peruse a copy. Granted, it doesn't include ratings or opinions about each hostel (like the *Hostels France & Italy* guide, below), but it does list the hostels' facilities and includes e-mail addresses, opening and closing times, phone and fax numbers, public transportation routes, and the like. For complete hostel listings for all of Italy, contact the AIG headquarters (Via Cavour 44, 00184 Rome; 06.487.1152; fax: 06.488.0492). Hostels do not have age limits or advance bookings but many require membership in Hostelling International. The HI national headquarters are located at 733 Fifteenth Street, N.W., Suite 840, Washington, D.C. 20005; 202-783-6161; fax: -6171; www.hiahy.org. Hours are 8:00 A.M.–5:00 P.M. Eastern Standard Time, with customer service staff available until 7:00 P.M. An HI membership card is free for anyone up to his or her eighteenth birthdate. Annual fees are $25 for anyone over eighteen and $15 for anyone fifty-five or over. HI also publishes several guidebooks, one of which is *Europe and the Mediterranean*. The price is either $10.95 or $13.95, depending on whether you purchase it from the main office or from one of its council affiliates around the country. (HI staff have addresses and phone numbers for affiliates nearest you.) I think a better book to get is *Hostels France & Italy: The Only Comprehensive, Unofficial, Opinionated Guide* (2nd edition, Paul Karr and Martha Coombs, Globe Pequot Press, Old Saybrook, Connecticut). This is one book that lives up to its no-nonsense title. It's a funny yet very practical guide. In "How to Use This Book," the authors state that "what you're holding in your hands is the first-ever attempt of its kind: a fairly complete listing and rating of all the hostels we could find in France and Italy." They invite you to take a quiz ("What is a Hostel?"), and they don't hesitate to tell it like it is, using such adjectives as sedate, educational, hoppin', quiet, plain, dirty, chaotic, strict, okay, small. There are little party hat icons for some entries (indicating that these are places where sleep is not a priority) as well as thumbs up and down (indicating the authors' likes and dislikes). Twelve listings are included for Venice and the Veneto, one for Trento, and none, unfortunately, for Friuli–Venezia Giulia. In addition to the usual contact information, the authors also note which hostels accept credit cards, how many beds each hostel offers, and if private or family rooms are available.

Pensioni are, like hotels, a very common option for travelers in Italy. *Pensioni* (singular is *pensione*) are generally simple but nice accommodations that are less expensive than hotels. Sometimes a *pensione* is a family-run guest house, and sometimes it is a much larger establishment, more like a hotel, and can be rather fancy. You can expect service to be similar to that of a hotel. So far I have not come across a book, in English or Italian, devoted to *pensioni,* but you will find recommendations for them in guidebooks and some of the hotel guides listed above.

Renting an apartment or villa might be a suitable choice depending on how long you'll be in the area and the number of people traveling together. While I very much like staying in inns and hotels, I also like the idea of renting because it can be a quick way to feel a part of the local routine—you have daily chores to accomplish just like everyone else (except that I would hardly call going to pick up provisions at the local *mercato* a chore). Though your tasks are mixed in with lots of little pleasures, sightseeing, and trips, you often avoid the too-much-to-do rut. What to eat suddenly looms as the most important question of the day, the same question that all the local families are trying to answer. Renting, therefore, forces you to take an active part in the culture rather than catch a glimpse of it. A comprehensive listing of organizations that arrange short- and long-term rentals would fill a small book, and it is not my intent here to provide one. Rather, following are some sources that have either come highly recommended or with which I have had a positive experience:

Barclay International Group (3 School Street, Glen Cove, New York 11542; 516-759-5100; 800-845-6636; fax: 516-609-0000; www.barclayweb.com) offers one of the world's largest and most reputable collections of apartments and villas in Europe, focusing especially on the Mediterranean destinations of Italy, France, Greece, Spain, and Portugal; when I last checked, it had nearly forty listings for apartments in Venice (there were none for Friuli–Venezia Guilia, the Veneto, or Trentino–Alto Adige), and they accommodated a minimum of one to three people and a maximum of five to eight in a variety of price ranges. An innovative offering from Barclay is its "Apartment Within a Villa" option, which is for small groups that can't fill up an enormous villa but want a villa experience; Barclay selected villas that were divided up into smaller apartments, each with kitchen and bath, and now offers this alternative at a fraction of the price of an entire villa. Guests have access to amenities such as a pool or a private garden, but of course they must share them with others who may be staying there in another apartment. Barclay is also a good resource for reserving extras like car rentals, sight-seeing tours, theater tickets, rail passes, cell phones, and laptop computers.

The Best in Italy (in Italy only: 055.223.064; fax: 055.229.8912; www.thebestinitaly.com) is a company founded in 1982 by Count and Countess Brandolini d'Adda. The countess is American-born, and when they began renting their own property near Siena to acquaintances in the United States, their friends asked them to rent *their* villas in Tuscany, Umbria, Amalfi, Rome, and the Veneto as well. These properties, which total over eighty, are located in the most prestigious locations in Italy. This is an outstanding resource if you're looking for truly exquisite places: all the properties—whether it's a villa, castle, palazzo, or country home—

come with a staff and swimming pool, and many have tennis courts and riding stables. Two properties in the Veneto that I browsed were quite exceptional, and one was designed by Palladio. The Best in Italy also organizes private tours for small groups to venues not usually open to the public; wine tastings with renowned experts; private boats; business conferences; film locations; and cooking classes.

Homebase Abroad Ltd. (29 Mary's Lane, Scituate, Massachusetts 02066; 781-545-5112; fax: -1808; www.homebase-abroad.com) has assembled its portfolio of private homes personally, working with individual owners, and is proud to state that the staff adds homes by referral from those who are already member properties. Most of the homes featured are privately owned, occupied occasionally by the owners during the year. Homebase's directors travel to Italy many times a year to meet with the owners, review listings, and add new ones, resulting in their being very familiar with all aspects of a home as well as the staff, neighboring towns, and local points of interest. Of all the rental companies that have a Web presence, I have found this one to be the most thorough in describing its properties and defining what is and isn't included in the fee.

The Parker Company (152 Lynnway, Lynn, Massachusetts 01902; 781-596-8282 or 800-280-2811; www.theparkercompany.com) has as its motto "Italy is all we do and we do it very well," and the staff arranges rentals of cottages, castles, villas, farmhouses, and apartments. Parker is the cherry-picker of the industry, selecting less than 10 percent of what it sees. A plus to my mind is that an agent in Italy is assigned to renters, just to make sure everything goes as planned. Parker also arranges rentals of cars and cell phones and organizes wine tours, cooking schools, and painting and creative writing classes. It also offers real estate.

Rentvillas.com (Internet company based in the United States: 700 East Main Street, Ventura, California 93001; 800-726-6702 or 805-641-1650; fax: 805-641-1630), after sixteen years in the villa business, "is dedicated to being the most experienced, the most innovative, and the most customer-focused company in the industry," according to its promotional material. All the staff members of Rentvillas.com love to travel and make clients feel as though they're receiving the staff's undivided attention. When I last checked, there were twenty-eight properties available for rent in Venice itself, eighteen in northern Veneto, thirty-one in southern Veneto, six in Friuli–Venezia Giulia, and none in Trentino–Alto Adige. Rentvillas.com also produces a newsletter, in which travelers who've rented from Rentvillas write about their experiences and the staff offer tips for renters; you can subscribe online.

VeniceRentals (in the United States: 252 Farrington Street, Quincy, Massachusetts 02169; 617-472-5392; www.venicerentals.com; or in Italy: Via Lepanto 10, Lido, Venice 30126; 041.276.9798) is a favorite company of mine to contact for rentals in Venice and the Lido, not only for its selection of properties but because the company is owned and operated by a charming American woman and her Italian husband who live in Venice. VeniceRentals is their main business, and they are 100 percent available to clients twenty-four hours a day. They offer studio, one-, two-, and three-bedroom self-service apartments as well as luxury flats in all six *sestieri* of Venice. At the time of this writing, they have no palazzi on the Grand Canal, but by the time this book is published, there will probably be one or a few. A very great feature—included in the fee—is that clients are met at the nearest *vaporetto* stop and accompanied to the property. In addition to securing apartments, VeniceRentals arranges baby-sitting and can provide translations, tour guides, shopper's service, and theater and restaurant reservations. The "Last-Minute Deals" section on its website is also worth a look if you are making plans in a hurry. A fan letter about VeniceRentals is perhaps the best endorsement I can share with you about this company: "Denise and Maurizio made this the perfect vacation. They really went out of their way to make the apartment comfortable for us. They are more than honest and trustworthy. They are super people too! With VeniceRentals, you get more than just a wonderful apartment—you get Denise and Maurizio. We plan to rent from them again and again!"

General accommodation notes to keep in mind: ~Ask for reservation confirmation in writing. Though I may place an initial call to an inn or hotel, I prefer that communication be by fax. This allows for any language errors to be corrected in case my Italian was faulty, and it serves as an official document. While fax alone does not guarantee something won't go wrong, it certainly helps if you can produce one at check-in. If you arrive at your lodging and the staff cannot honor your reservation, be polite but firm in asking for a better room elsewhere in the hotel (at the same price) or a comparable room at another lodging. (You could also push the envelope here and ask that they pay for your first night, this being their mistake and an inconvenience to you.) The hotel is obligated to find you comparable alternative lodgings—not to pay for your night someplace else—but I figure this is part of a bargaining process in arriving at a solution. You should also ask them to pay for your transportation to the other location (should this be the result), which the staff should not hesitate to do.

~When you first arrive at your hotel, ask to see your room first. This is a common practice in Europe, and it is understood that if a room is not to your liking, you may request a different one. This is also your opportunity to ask for a room upgrade; if the hotel is not fully booked (and it rarely will be during low season), you may end up with a much nicer room at the same rate. It never hurts to ask.

~Speaking of fully booked: if you've been told that you can't get a room, call again between four and six P.M. and double-check. This is the time of day when many establishments cancel the reservations of guests who haven't shown up.

~If a hotel you choose also has a reservations office in the United States, call both numbers. It is entirely possible that you will be quoted different rates. Also, some of the more expensive hotels offer a rate that must be prepaid in full, in advance of your trip, in U.S. dollars, but that is lower than the local rack rate.

~No matter what type of lodging you choose, *always* inquire if there is a lower rate. Reservationists—and even the owners of small inns—always hope the rate they quote will be accepted, and if you don't ask about other possibilities, they will not volunteer any. In addition, ask if there are corporate rates; special rates for seniors, students, government and military employees; weekend rates (this usually only applies to city hotels, as business travelers will have checked out by Friday); and even special prices for newlyweds. Hotels and inns large and small all want to fill their rooms, and if you'll be staying four nights (sometimes three) or longer, you may also be able to negotiate a better rate. Most important, ask for how long the rate you're quoted is available and how many rooms at that price are left. In smaller places especially, a day can mean the difference between securing a reservation or losing it.

~Breakfast taken at a hotel is rarely a good value, especially in Italy, where an Italian breakfast typically consists of a coffee drink and a roll. Save some money—and get the same thing, often better—and join the locals at the corner *caffè*.

~When renting a property, don't forget to ask thorough questions and read the fine print. Some questions to ask include: "Is there air conditioning?" (air conditioning is rare, not only in Italy but throughout the Mediterranean; so inquire if there is cross-ventilation or a ceiling fan), "How is the water pressure?" "Is hot water available at all times?" "Are children or pets welcome?" "Is there a crib for a young child?" "What is the charge for use of the telephone?" "How close is the nearest canal, and how badly does it smell?" (if it's summer in Venice), "Are toilet paper, sheets, and blankets provided?" "Are there coffee filters?" (if there is a coffee maker), "Is there a corkscrew in the kitchen?" "Is there a mosquito coil?" (screens are rare in windows in Mediterranean countries, and if you spy a mosquito coil—either the kind you light with a match or the kind that plugs into the wall—that is your clue that pesky bugs will be about after the sun goes down, and you'll be happy to have the protection), "Is there construction going on nearby?" and "How close (or far) is the food market?" (Some of the most appealing houses in the country are in rather rural areas, so keep in mind that you may be some distance from a main road.) In addition to these questions, and a few of your own unique to your situation, keep in mind the following good advice from Homebase Abroad: "Renting abroad is an adventure, no matter the level of house you're considering. If the myriad differences between an Italian home and your home, between the Italian lifestyle and your lifestyle are unwelcome, you might have to conclude this is not the right trip for you and your group." ~Useful vocabulary: *il cuscino* (pillow); *la chiave* (key); *biancheria da letto la coperta* (blanket); *il asciugamano* (towel); *acquà caldà* (hot water); *incluso* (included, as in "is breakfast"—*la prima colazione*—"included in the price?"); *il singolo* (one bed); *il doppio* (two beds); *il matrimoniale* (double bed); *avete una camera più silenziosa?* ("Do you have a quieter room?"); *avete una camera meno cara?* ("Do you have a less expensive room?").

Acqua Alta

Literally translated as "high water," *acqua alta* occurs at the peak of high tide, when the Adriatic has been flowing into the Venetian Lagoon for six consecutive hours. All visitors really need to know about these flood tides is that they usually occur between November and April (though this certainly does not preclude them appearing in the summer or early fall), and if the waters have reached a serious level, you'll need nothing less than a pair of Wellington boots to get around. If you don't feel like packing your Wellies, you won't have any trouble finding a pair (or something similar) around town; lots of shops sell boots and galoshes for the occasion. And while it is a good idea to bring a small umbrella to Venice at *any* time of year, I would definitely make sure to pack one in winter.

Airfares and Airlines

We all know that not everyone pays the same price for seats on an airplane. One reason is that seats do not hold the same value at all times of the year, month, or even day of the week. Recently I was researching some fares to Paris for a long weekend. One of my calls produced a particularly helpful representative who proceeded to detail all available fares for the entire month of September. There were approximately fifteen different prices—based on a seemingly endless number of variables—within that month alone. The best way, therefore, to get the best deal that accommodates your needs is to check a variety of sources. Flexibility is, and has always been, the key to low-cost travel, and you should be prepared to slightly alter the dates of your proposed trip to take advantage of those airline seats that hold less value. If you think all the best deals are to be found on the Internet, you're mistaken: airlines, consolidators, and other discounters offer plenty of good fares over the telephone and through advertisements. In order to know with certainty that you've got a good deal, you need to comparison-shop, which requires checking more than one source. I believe that on any day of the week, the lowest fares can be found equally among websites, wholesalers, airlines, charters, tour operators, travel agents, and sky auctions; no website, not even newcomer Orbitz, can claim to offer all choices for all travelers, and you don't know who's offering what until you inquire.

I like flying a country's own airline whenever possible, and Italy's official airline is Alitalia, one of the pioneers in commercial air travel when it was founded in 1947. Alitalia has grown to become the leading carrier to Italy, and it ranks fifth among European airlines, serving 133 destinations across Europe, Africa, Australia, the Near East, and Asia. Alitalia's two major hubs are Milan's Malpensa International Airport and Rome's Leonardo da Vinci International Airport. The airline's North American gateways include New York (JFK and Newark Airports), Miami, Boston, Chicago, Los Angeles, San Francisco, and Toronto. Alitalia offers some of the best rates and packages for travelers in the off-season. (Note, however, that months designated "off season" in Italy—especially in Venice—are few in number, mostly limited to January and part of February, as the country is so popular with foreigners.) As of this writing, Alitalia does not offer direct service to Venice from North America. (Travelers must first fly to either Milan or to Rome and then transfer for a flight to Venice.) Alitalia offers its own tours to Venice and other Mediterranean destinations, and I encourage you to consider what the airline is offering at the time when you are making your plans. For information, contact Alitalia at its office (666 Fifth Avenue, New York, New York 10022) or view its website at www.alitaliausa.com; for reservations, call 800-223-5730.

As I think is obvious, researching airfares and airlines is essential but fairly time-consuming. If you are really determined to turn over every stone, you'll find a lot of avenues to explore in Peter Greenberg's excellent book *The Travel Detective: How to Get the Best Service and the Best Deals from Airlines, Hotels, Cruise Ships, and Car Rental Agencies* (Villard, 2001; see General Travel for more details). Some airline "tricks" include split ticket fares, back-to-back ticketing, add-on legs for no additional cost, and buying a full-fare ticket and then returning it if you find a better deal at the last minute—these are all detailed in Greenberg's book. I admit I find some of these tactics to be more time-consuming than they are worth, and I don't usually have the time to conduct an exhaustive search, but some sources I typically consult before I buy anything include 800-AIRFARE; 800-FLYCHEAP; 800-FLY4LESS; 800-6LOWAIR (just to clarify, this is the toll-free number for a firm called Air 4 Less); 800-CHEAPAIR (this is the number for American Travel Associates, a company dealing mostly with domestic flights, though some international discounts are available); www.orbitz.com; www.travelocity.com; www.expedia.com; www.cheaptickets.com; OneTravel.com; www.trip.com; www.flights.com; www.lowestfare.com; www.qixo.com (pronounced KICK-so); STA Travel (STA means "Student Travel Association," but it plans trips for "generations X, Y and Z"; 800-777-0112 or www.statravel.com); Council Travel (known as "America's Student Travel Leader," this fifty-four-year-old company also offers good fares for adults and a host of useful stuff for students and teachers; 800-2COUNCIL or www.counciltravel.com); and the travel section of *The New York Times* (my local daily newspaper), which I scan for ads of all the area agencies offering low prices. Many of these ads typically reveal the same low fares by one or two particular airlines. The airlines are almost always smaller foreign lines currently trying to expand their business in the United States. So, for example, while researching fares for my last trip to Venice, all the agencies I called were featuring cheap flights on Sabena and KLM (with connections in Brussels and Amsterdam). At the time, Delta was the only airline offering nonstop service from New York to Venice, and it obviously really had the advantage on this route, so prices were over $1,200 per person. Note that the Internet sites listed here began their life as search engines for airfares only but now offer a wider range of services, including rental cars and hotel accommodations. Also, remember to consider alternative airports in your area, not just the obvious major hubs. Where I live in New York, for example, there are always different fares when I compare flights departing from Newark, New Jersey, or JFK Airport on Long Island. And if you're already in Italy and want to fly somewhere else within Europe, check with Europe by Air (888-387-2479; www.europebyair.com).

Internet booking. Booking travel on the Web works best for people with simple requirements and lots of flexibility. In fact, if you can leave on really short notice, some great deals may be in store for you: a website specializing in just such spur-of-the-moment travel is www.lastminutetravel.com, which offers last-minute fares from a number of airlines, and the carriers then have the opportunity to reduce fares if seats aren't selling. Another site is www.11thhourvacations.com. With both, make sure to check their fares against the airlines' to ensure you're really getting a last-minute bargain. Participating in sky auctions (via www.priceline.com or www.skyauction.com, for example) is not appealing to me personally. If you have a lot of questions, as I always do, you can't get them answered and are setting yourself up for potential headaches. I never seem to be able to find a flight scenario that works with my schedule, and I don't like that I can't more finely narrow the criteria when submitting my initial bid—what *time* of day I fly is just as important as the date. The time it takes to continue submitting bids (my initial bid is never accepted) seems wasteful to me, time I could be spending getting concrete information from other sources. Additionally, I have read that the idea of submitting your own price for a ticket is illusory; in fact, the Internet firms buy discounted seats from the airlines but sell those seats at fares only above an established threshold. Bids below that level are rejected. Also, travelers seldom have control over which airlines they'll fly or, if it's a connecting flight, which cities they'll stop in. And most don't allow you to earn mileage points.

In the controversy over paper tickets versus e-tickets, I'm for old-fashioned paper. Currently, if an airline has to route passengers on another flight or another carrier, holders of paper tickets are ahead of the game because computers between airlines can't communicate with each other, so e-tickets are impossible to verify. Airline representatives will serve holders of paper tickets first, while e-ticket holders have to wait in line to have their e-tickets converted into paper, then wait in another line to be confirmed on another flight. As travel guru Peter Greenberg notes, "The e-ticket is NOT your friend."

A word about travel agencies: Though it was perhaps inevitable that a great number of travel agencies would close due to the arrival of the Internet, do not underestimate what a quality agent can do for you. Readers who have one already know this: good travel agents are indispensable, worth their weight in gold. Resourceful travelers will often be able to put a detailed trip together on their own equally as well as an average agent, but even the most resourceful and determined traveler will not be able to match the savvy of a top-notch agent. I believe that at the end of the day, the Internet is a great resource tool, but it's not a human being watching over every last detail for you. The more specialized or complicated your trip is, the more reason you should employ the services of an experienced agent. To read more about exactly what a good agent is capable of, see "Miracles Are Us" (Wendy Perrin, *Condé Nast Traveler,* June 2000). Perrin identified seventy travel consultants described as "better connected than the Internet, faster than a T3 line, able to book the unbookable." Of the seventy, sixty-three of them are members of the Virtuoso network, which specializes in leisure travel for discerning clients. Fewer than 1 percent of consultants in the Americas are accepted for membership in Virtuoso, which utilizes a worldwide network of four hundred cruise, tour, adventure, property, and ground operator partners in sixty countries. Contact Virtuoso at 800-401-4274 or www.virtuoso.com.

Consolidators. Don't be afraid of reputable consolidators, but recognize that their lower fares come with restrictions. If your flight is canceled or delayed, you have no resource with the airline since it didn't sell you the ticket directly. (This holds true with tickets purchased through discount Internet companies too.) If you want to make any changes, you have to pay a penalty. The question to ask of a consolidator is "Do you accept credit cards?" The rule of thumb is, if it doesn't, go elsewhere; but I will tell you that on two occasions I purchased tickets with cash and had absolutely no problems.

Charter flights. Reputable charter flights too should not be feared. I've had three good experiences on charter flights and encourage you to investigate them. The limitations are that most charters offer only coach class and tend to be completely full—in fact, a charter operator is legally allowed to cancel a flight up to ten days before departure if it doesn't fill enough seats. I wouldn't, therefore, travel with children or plan a honeymoon around a charter flight. Although I did not experience any problems on my charter flights, I understand that delays do happen, and—as with consolidators—passengers don't have any recourse. But operators who organize charter flights are required to place passengers' flight payments in an escrow account, so if the flight is canceled or if the operator doesn't abide by its agreement, you receive a refund. A publication call *Jax Fax Travel Marketing Magazine* lists more than five thousand scheduled charter flights to more than one hundred destinations worldwide. Previously available only to industry folks, the general public can now subscribe. Contact *Jax Fax* at 48 Wellington

Road, Milford, Connecticut 06460; 800-9JAXFAX or 203-301-0255; fax: -0250; www.jaxfax.com.) A single issue can be purchased for about $5 as well as a one- or two-year subscription.

Couriers. Flying as a courier is no longer the amazing deal it once was, but it can still be a good deal if you're a light packer. (Luggage is usually limited to one carry-on bag.) Couriers also can't usually reserve a seat for more than one person, although your traveling companion could purchase a ticket on the same flight. Air couriers are cogs in international commerce; they are completely legal and legitimate, and the demand for them exceeds the supply. They are a necessity simply because companies doing international business send a large number of documents overseas, and those documents can get held up in customs unless accompanied by a person. Couriers are responsible for chaperoning documents through customs and then hand-delivering them to a person waiting outside the customs area. Several companies in the United States arrange courier flights, but the one I'm most familiar with is Now Voyager (74 Varick Street, New York, New York 10013; 212-431-1616). To review more options, consider joining the International Association of Air Travel Couriers (P.O. Box 980, Keystone Heights, Florida 32656; 352-475-1584; fax: -5326; www.courier.org). Members receive a regular bulletin with a variety of international routes being offered by air courier companies departing from several U.S. cities. Reservation phone numbers are included so you can make inquiries and schedule your trip yourself. I have seen some *incredible* bargains, and some fares were valid for several months. The website also features courier stories and back issues of *The Shoestring Traveler.*

Code-sharing. If you're making arrangements directly with an airline, ask if your flight is a code-share. Code-sharing is complicated, to say the least. (Betsy Wade, former travel columnist for *The New York Times,* once wrote that "the general theory of relativity is not too much more complex" than the code-sharing network.) In a very small nutshell, code-sharing is an agreement between airline partners that allows them to share routes, but what it means for the consumer is that each airline sharing a code may offer a different price for the same trip or the same leg of a multistop journey. Find out which other airline(s) is in on the code, and compare prices.

General guidelines and reminders about traveling in the friendly skies: ~*Overbooking.* Airlines are not required to offer much to passengers who experience flight delays or cancellations, and they can cancel flights or change schedules seemingly at whim, with very few penalties to themselves. If you have visions of free meals, hotel rooms, and flights, you may be in for a disappointment. According to the U.S. Department of Transportation's Aviation Consumer Protection Division, "Contrary to popular belief, airlines are not required to compensate passengers whose flights are delayed or canceled. . . . compensation is required by law only when you are 'bumped' from a flight that is oversold. Airlines almost always refuse to pay passengers for financial losses resulting from a delayed flight. If the purpose of your trip is to close a potentially lucrative business deal, to give a speech or lecture, to attend a family function, or to be present at any time-sensitive event, you might want to allow a little extra leeway and take an earlier flight. In other words, airline delays and cancellations aren't unusual, and defensive counterplanning is a good idea when time is your most important consideration." You can read this, and more, for yourself in the DOT's fifty-eight-page, pocket-size brochure "Fly Rights: A Consumer Guide to Air Travel," which you can obtain by writing to the Consumer Information Center, Pueblo, Colorado 81009 (fee is $1.75, which includes postage), or view it online at www.dot.gov/. (Click first on "Airline Complaint?," then on the "Booklets and Fact Sheets" prompt at the bottom of the page entitled "Air Travel Service Problems," and then finally select "Fly Rights" on the "Aviation Consumer Protection Division Publications" page.) I found this website to provide quite an interesting bounty of information. For those who might not know, overbooking is not illegal, "and most airlines overbook their scheduled flights to a certain extent in order to compensate for 'no-shows.'" Curious readers can select "Baggage," "Airfares," "Reservations and Tickets," "Smoking," "Passengers with Disabilities," "Frequent Flier Programs," "Contract Terms," "Health," "Airline Safety," and "Complaining" from the website too, and if you *do* have a complaint you'd like to file (keeping, of course, all of the above in mind), write to the Aviation Consumer Protection Division, U.S. Department of Transportation, Room 4107, C-75, Washington, D.C. 20590. Each airline has its own Conditions of Carriage, which you can request from an airline's ticket office or public relations department, but the legalese is not identical from airline to airline. From what I can tell, the airline employees who stand at the gates are the ones who have the authority to grant passengers amenities, so if you *don't* ask them for something (a seat on the next flight, a long-distance phone call, a meal, whatever), you *definitely* won't get it. It seems to me that passengers who patronize an airline frequently, or those who *politely* complain, may be first in line for any amenities.

~*Standby*. Technically, airlines no longer allow passengers to fly standby at a discount; but I've been told that for flights that aren't full, seats are occasionally sold at reduced prices. An official standby service is offered by Whole Earth Travel Airhitch (two U.S. offices: 2641 Broadway, 3rd floor, New York, New York 10025; 800-326-2009 or 212-864-2000; fax: -5489; and 13470 Washington Boulevard, Suite 205, Marina del Rey, California 90292; 800-834-9192; fax: 310-574-0054; www.4cheapair.com). Very affordable flights are available for worldwide destinations, but you must be flexible, seeing that Airhitch selects the date you travel based on a five-day range that you provide. Like a consolidator, Airhitch offers seats on commercial airlines that are about to be left empty, and the company's philosophy is one akin to *The Collected Traveler:* "The experience of travel is a benefit that should be available to everyone. It is through travel that we each learn to accept the differences in others while realizing the similarity in our common goals. We believe travel is the best road to peace and understanding, and it's a whole lotta fun!" Airhitch also offers an option called Target Flights: you supply the dates of travel and desired destination, plus the best quote you've obtained, and Airhitch will respond in twenty-four hours if it can buy a similar ticket at a cheaper price. (When I checked, this feature wasn't yet available on its website, but travelers can call the New York office—number above—for details.) I've been told that one of the best days of the year to show up at the airport without a ticket is Christmas Day. I can't personally confirm this, and it's doubtful that an airline employee can either. Perhaps this is either a very well kept secret or a myth, but if you're able to be that flexible, it would be worth trying.

Airports and Getting Around

Venice and the Veneto are served overwhelmingly by Marco Polo Airport (thirteen kilometers north of Venice, about a twenty-minute to a half-hour ride). There are also airports in Treviso (Aeroporto di Treviso) and Verona (Aeroporto Valerio Catullo), but these are served only by flights from limited European cities and would be good choices only if you were beginning your trip in the Dolomites or other far reaches of the Veneto. Passengers flying in or out of Marco Polo Airport can call 041.260.9266 for flight information, twenty-four hours a day, or view the airport's website (www.veniceairport.it/vce/ita/default.htm). Getting around and about the Veneto, Friuli–Venezia Giulia, and even into the Dolomites from the region's airports is not problematic—there is a good network of public transportation and taxi service. Getting into Venice proper, however, is a bit more complicated. Part of the reason Venice has remained as untouched as it has is because one can't get to it by automobile. From Marco Polo, travelers have several choices: a regular taxi (about $35 to Piazzale Roma, where you then transfer to a *vaporetto* or water taxi); the Alilaguna water bus (about $12, which departs from right outside the airport arrivals entry you don't need a porter unless you have a *lot* of luggage, as it's a short, two-minute walk to the dock; Alilaguna stops at Piazza San Marco, Arsenale, the Lido, and Murano, so you must then make your way from these stops to your final destination); a water taxi (about $77 for door-to-door service; note that this fare is the same for one passenger or up to eight); an ATVO bus (about $3.50 to Piazzale Roma, with departures timed with arrivals; tickets can be purchased at the ATVO counter in the arrivals hall or on board, and the trip is about twenty-five minutes; note that this is the blue bus, not the orange one, which is ACTV); an ACTV bus (about $1.50 to Piazzale Roma, with service every thirty minutes). If you're driving from Marco Polo to Venice, there are parking garages at Piazzale Roma (on the Grand Canal) and Tronchetto (south of Venice proper, which also allows for camping vehicles).

Trieste and Friuli–Venezia Guilia are served by Ronchi dei Legionari Airport, 32 kilometers west of Trieste. There is taxi service to Trieste (about $56, 30 to 35 minutes); Udine (about $63, 40 to 50 minutes); Gorizia (about $35, 20 to 25 minutes); and Pordenone (about $112, 60 minutes or a little longer). Airport shuttle service is offered to the Trieste bus station (about $10.50, 40 minutes, from 5:30 A.M. to 11:30 P.M.) and the bus stations in Udine and Gorizia (again about $10.50, 50 minutes, twice daily). SAITA public bus service is offered hourly from 5:00 A.M. to 11:00 P.M. to the Trieste station (about $3.50, 40 minutes) and to the Udine station (about $4.20, 60 minutes). Service to the Gorizia station is offered twice daily (about $2, 30 to 40 minutes). For airport information, call 0481.77.3224.

Alpi Dolomiti

The alpine mountain range known in English as the Dolomites, or the South Tyrol, is the major range in northeastern Italy. It's said that on exceptionally clear days, one can see the foothills of this range from the top of the Campanile in Venice. (I have apparently never been in Venice on an exceptionally clear day, because while I could see quite a distance from the lookout of the Campanile, and while the view is truly quite spectacular, I have never been able to see *that* far.) The Dolomiti may not be as renowned as the Alps in the far northwestern corner of Italy (where Mont Blanc—or in Italian, Monte Bianco—is nestled), but they are stunningly beautiful (I'll never forget the first time I saw the range, twenty-two years ago, by train, and according to the authors of the Cadogan guide, "the air and light in autumn are so sharp and fine they can break your heart") and quite formidable (not for nothing did the creators of a B movie spin-off of *Shaft* name the main character—a large, tough African American man—Dolomite, also the name of the film). Again according to the Cadogan guide, the mountain range was named after a French mineralogist, Dieudonné Sylvain Guy Tancrede de Gratet de Dolomieu, "who in 1789 was the first to describe their mineral content." As in other alpine regions of the world, opportunities for skiing and hiking abound in the Dolomiti—see the Hiking entry below for more details. Though the range falls almost entirely in Trentino–Alto Adige, I decided not to devote a separate section to either the mountain range or the region in this book. This omission is not meant to slight the region—it is quite interesting historically and culturally—but the vast majority of articles written about Trentino–Alto Adige focus on its physical beauty and the skiing and hiking activities associated with it. (There are no less than three national parks within the boundaries of the range.) Though the Dolomiti range extends to the western edge of Friuli–Venezia Guilia (where it is known as the Dolomiti Orientali), more of it falls in the Veneto, so I've included articles about it in this section. (More than half of Friuli–Venezia Giulia, by the way, is covered by mountain ranges: in addition to the Dolomiti Orientali, the region is defined by the Alpi Carniche—which provide the border between it and Austria—and the Alpi Giulie, which provide another border between it and Slovenia.) Marmolada is the highest peak (10,961 feet) in the Dolomiti, while seventeen other peaks top 10,000 feet. Though there are glaciers even in the summertime, there are also "massive bouquets" of wildflowers, to quote again from the Cadogan guide. The Brenner Pass is in the Dolomiti and has long been the easiest and chief highway across the Alps. Readers may recall, however, that after a collision and fire in a neighboring alpine tunnel—St. Gotthard—in November 2001, the Brenner became clogged with traffic and may remain so for quite some time. There are eight crossings over the Alps between France, Switzerland, Austria, and Italy: the Frejus Tunnel, the Mont Blanc Tunnel, the Great St. Bernard Tunnel, the Simplon Tunnel (which is the route used by the Venice-Simplon Orient Express), the St. Gotthard Tunnel, the San Bernardino Tunnel, the Reschen Pass, and the Brenner Pass, and according to an article in *The New York Times,* more than 110 million tons of freight traveled through these tunnels and passes in 2000, representing a 97 percent increase since 1980. An Alptransit rail tunnel is currently under construction in Switzerland, under the St. Gotthard Pass, which should help to ease the congestion; but it will not be completed for at least another decade. Austria also has plans for a tunnel project under the Brenner Pass, and France is considering a plan for its side of the Alps. So as transalpine trade continues to expand, the Alpi—no matter which country they fall in—will definitely be a part of Europe to watch in the years ahead.

~Lake Garda is the easternmost lake of the Italian lake district (in fact, most Italians think of the east side of the lake as being part of the Veneto and the western side as being in Lombardy), and it is almost completely surrounded by the foothills and peaks of the Dolomiti. Lago di Garda has been referred to as the most Mediterranean of the alpine Italian lakes, and there are indeed some spots along its shores where you would swear you were much farther south. In addition to swimming and sunbathing, Garda offers hiking and horseback riding trails, natural and aquatic parks, spa treatments, windsurfing, sailing, canoeing, fishing, yachting, mountain biking, and at resorts, tennis and golf. Besides outdoor activities, Garda boasts Roman settlements, noble villas, Romanesque and Baroque churches, opera and dance performances. The best introductory information I've found on the lake is the "Lago di Garda" brochure published by the Italian Tourist Office in its series Laghi d'Italia. This hefty booklet, published in four languages, includes some background historical information as well as exhaustive listings for hotels, campsites, and rental properties complete with addresses, telephone numbers, and websites for each area around the lake. Another good source is the www.dolomiti.it/eng/zone/howto-get.htm website, which is among the better sites I've seen anywhere. An overview of how to reach the Dolomites by car, bus, taxi, and train is provided, and viewers can click on particulars such as "Seasons," "Weather," "Services," "Nature," "Hotels," "Farm Holidays," "Events," "Maps," and "Sports"; an excellent selection of books and guides is available from the Libreria Campedel in Belluno. (Books can be purchased online; the selection includes titles on geology, history, flora and fauna, mountaineering, cycling, photography, and so on.)

~Val Gardena—also known as the Holiday Valley of the Dolomites—offers year-round activities for adults and children. Inquire at the Italian Tourist Office in North America for the Val Gardena brochure, which details accommodations, history, and programs for summer and winter. (Val Gardena's other moniker is "An Enormous Outdoor Fitness Center," and indeed the list of outdoor activities is staggering—ski runs for every level, cross-country trails, ice climbing, tobogganing runs, ice skating, astronomy excursions, track and field, skateboarding, alpine golf, riding, mountain biking, paragliding, guided mountain tours—the list is practically endless, and it's quite extensive for kids too, with ski specials in the winter and a Children's Club in the summer). Interested readers may also browse the www.val-gardena.com website for further information.

~When you need a break from outdoor activities, be sure to pick up a copy of *Guide to Religious Art,* first published by the Azienda per la Promozione Turistica del Trentino (APT) in 1997 but still available. (I found my copy at the Italian Tourist Office in New York; other offices in North America should still have copies.) This excellent eighty-page guide traces the history of the region from the pagan age and the early Middle Ages up to and including the nineteenth and twentieth centuries. Trentino, as noted in the introduction, "which draws great numbers of visitors for its skiing, its excursions, its spa baths, its cooking and many other attractions, is also of great interest to tourists for its array of religious art . . . the artwork to be seen in Trentino today is the result of a whole series of different factors. Venetians and Lombards from the south and Bavarians, Danubians and Tyroleans from the north. Thus in art, as in history, Trentino stands between two worlds: Italy and Germany." The guide also features a four-page glossary on how to identify attributes of saints, as well as fourteen itineraries complete with accompanying maps. There is also an extensive bibliography on the province of Trentino (though all the works listed are in Italian), and perhaps even more helpful, contact information is provided for the main APT office (Azienda per la Promozione Turistica del Trentino, Via Romagnosi 11, Trento 38100; 0461.497353; fax: 0461.260277; www.provincia.tn.it/apt) as well as for fifteen local APT offices and eleven syndicates of local tourist offices.

Associazione Buona Accoglienza (Good Welcome Association)

This relatively new organization was founded by a group of Venetian restaurants whose management decided to charge everyone, tourists and locals alike, the same prices. Restaurants often have a different price scale for tourists, which I have never felt is entirely a bad thing. Financial breaks have long been offered to "regulars" everywhere around the globe, and occasionally I have been on the receiving end of them. While I don't think it's fair to be taken to the cleaners, I also do not mind paying for the privilege to be in Venice in the first place. Inquire at the tourist office in Venice for a list of these restaurants or for contact information for the association.

Azienda del Consorzio Trasporti Veneziano (ACTV)

ACTV operates the lagoon transport network, which consists of buses and water buses in Venice proper. Most visitors—and residents too—probably know it more for its water-bus service. Types of ACTV water-bus traffic include the *vaporetto* ("little steamer," a name that dates from the time when *vaporetti* were introduced, in the late 1800s, and ran on steam; now a *vaporetto* runs on diesel fuel); the *diretto motoscafo* (a *diretto* is not as slow, cumbersome, or boxy as a *vaporetto,* the workhorse of Venetian waterways; a *diretto* makes fewer stops along the Grand Canal and is meant to provide a faster way of getting between San Marco and the Santa Lucia train station); the water taxi (which may provide personal service or transport you with other passengers; either way, the price is the same—expensive—but is worth every euro if you are having difficulty navigating a *vaporetto* with a lot of luggage; plus, if your hotel is on the Grand Canal, a taxi will drop you right in front, whereas a *vaporetto* stop may not be very convenient); and the *traghetto* (as there are only three bridges across the Grand Canal—Scalzi, Rialto, and Accademia—*traghetti* were offered as another means of getting back and forth; a *traghetto* is essentially a public gondola that ferries a number of passengers at a time across the Canal, and passengers typically stand up during the crossing. There are eight points along the Canal where *traghetto* service is offered: Ferrovia, San Marcuola, Santa Sofia, Riva del Carbon, San Tomà, San Samuele, Santa Maria del Giglio, and Dogana.) The various types of ACTV transport have different schedules, and they are not the same from summer to winter. Even the *traghetti,* for example, operate in summer only between certain hours, and in winter service is sometimes suspended altogether. It would be foolish of me to try to offer an outline of ACTV's water-bus schedules here, not only because this book isn't about such details but also because the various lines are often renumbered and routes change frequently. As the author of the Rough Guide to Venice notes, the water-bus routes operated by ACTV "can seem bewilderingly complicated, and the company sometimes seems bent on maximizing confusion by altering the routes and numbers for no readily apparent reason—indeed, ACTV have been known to produce a new full-colour map of the latest network immediately prior to introducing yet more changes." He adds, however, that as a general rule, the routes displayed at *vaporetto* stops are accurate, though at stops in outlying areas of the lagoon they can't always be relied upon to be up to date. The ACTV map available at the tourist office is useful, if incomplete. For the most thorough picture of the system, see the ACTV's website (www.actv.it) or get a copy of a publication entitled "Servizio accelerato con vaporetti Lido–Canal Grande–Piazzale Roma." J. G. Links, in his unsurpassed book *Venice for Pleasure,* says that "to retire to an island in the Lagoon with this matchless publication would be bliss indeed." In fact, I refer every reader to Links for the most appreciative—and fascinating—overview of the water-bus network ever written. He devotes nine pages of *Venice for Pleasure* to "The Services Provided by ACTV" and writes, "It may seem presumptuous to write in prose about the ACTV timetable. What is there to add to the pellucid yet dramatic words of the timetable itself?" Actually, Links has plenty to add, tips for visitors included: "I have used the name 82 for this service to fix in the reader's mind but no one in Venice calls it anything but the *diretto,* just as No. 1 is always called the *vaporetto* (though even Venetians may be confused by the proliferation of numbers). The official names for the two services are, respectively, *servizio diretto con motoscafi* and *servizio accelerato con vaporetti* and it is not for us to criticize the names although we may wonder what No. 1 did before it was accelerated and why the distinction is drawn between the two modes of propulsion since, in fact, they both use the same method, i.e., diesel. What is important for us to remember is that when asking for our ticket we specify *diretto* when we want to travel by it; if we have the wrong ticket we may not be allowed to board it when it comes. The difference in the type of boat used is easily recognizable, the *motoscafo* almost entirely covered in whereas the *vaporetto* has an 'inside' and an 'outside, the 'outside' having only a metal roof."

The *vaporetto* network seems to confound a great many visitors to Venice; I think it is a sensible and straightforward transportation system, but on my last visit I tried to ascertain exactly what was vexing tourists so. Here are some observations: ~None of the guidebooks explain that most *vaporetto* stops, whether they are served by one line or many, have two passenger platforms, one for each direction up or down the Canal. This may seem obvious, but I lost count of the number of passengers who seemed always to be standing on the wrong platform. Perhaps they were not paying attention and genuinely believed they were standing in the right place; but it really is a simple matter to check the route map that is displayed at each platform, showing all the stops along the way either up or down the Canal. If you discover you're standing at the wrong one, simply walk over to the other platform, which is usually just a few steps away (except notably in the case of the Santa Lucia train station, Rialto, San Marco, and San Zaccaria, where you will have to walk a bit farther). ~Note that if you want to go to Piazza San Marco, you should get off at San Zaccaria or Vallaresso (which apparently used to be called San Marco). ~Something I noticed that I haven't been able to explain—or have explained to me—is that occasionally you will board a boat, going in the right direction, and the attendant will announce that it is not making all the local stops you thought but rather is going straight on to the next "major" stop, such as Rialto or Ferrovia. Something similar happens with New York city subway trains, when they are running behind schedule; in an effort to catch up, trains will not stop at a few local stations in order to quickly move along until additional cars are added to the line. Whatever the reason, it does happen, most often in the summer months, and you just have to make the best of it and backtrack if you need to. ~Though Venetians receive a better discount for their use of the water boats (they have a Carta Venezia, which is available only to residents), tourists are eligible for a number of discounted options too. These are clearly displayed at ticket windows, so read them all and decide which is best for you: one-day, three-day, and seven-day, as well as twenty-four-hour tickets for groups of three, four, and five people (good for families). If you're unsure of your schedule, a good option would be to at least purchase the twenty-four-hour pass, which is dated from the exact time you purchase the ticket. ~Most of the tickets you purchase will be stamped (validated) by the vendor, but if you have a ticket that has not been stamped, you must validate it by inserting it into one of the orange machines on the platforms. I have rarely seen boat attendants checking tickets, but if you are caught without a valid ticket, you can be fined quite a considerable amount of money.

B

Biennale

The Venice Biennale (pronounced bee-eh-NAHL-ay) is arguably one of the most—if not *the* most—important venues for contemporary art in the world. Held biannually, the Biennale is 107 years old this year (2002), and though the art is typically loved as much as it is criticized, few collectors and serious connoisseurs of modern art would miss the installation. Though other cities and countries have biennial art shows, Venice's is the oldest and most prestigious. At the very first show, in 1895, the American James Abbott McNeill Whistler won the painting prize. For many years the Biennale was small enough to be contained in the Giardini di Castello, not very far from Piazza San Marco. Nowadays the art exhibits spill over to the Arsenale and to various museums, churches, and piazzas around the city. Tickets may be purchased on site, but to inquire about the next Biennale, in whatever year, contact the Italian Tourist Office in North America or in Venice for details.

Biking

Biking opportunities abound in northeastern Italy, though not in Venice proper, unless you enjoy carrying your bike up and down *a lot* of steps and ramps. The countryside of the Veneto and Friuli–Venezia Giulia, however, offer great terrain both for relatively easy routes and for more challenging ones. For recommendations on local biking routes, I suggest contacting the local tourist offices in the region. The majority of "biking in Italy" books I've seen tend to focus on longer, multiday bike trips as opposed to shorter circuits that take riders through the countryside for a day, for example. ~A few tour operators that offer biking trips I'm particularly fond of include Bike Riders Tours (P.O. Box 130254, Boston, Massachusetts 02113; 800-473-7040; www.bikeriderstours.com), which offers tours to other places besides Italy—Canada, New England, France, Ireland, Spain, and Portugal—as well. Its tours stand apart from others because each group is small in size (sixteen), accommodations are located in places that give a sense of a region's architecture and history, there are no preset meals at restaurants, it has the best bikes in the business, and the routes are carefully designed to showcase the best of a region and allow riders to enjoy the day. Most routes average no more than thirty-five miles per day, though if energetic riders want to cover more ground, the staff can accommodate. The company's tour in this part of Italy is "Dolce Vita in the Veneto: Blissful Biking Through Renaissance Towns and by Palladian Villas," which winds along the Brenta Canal to Asolo, Bassano del Grappa, Follina, and the Strada del Prosecco. The trip is six days in length, and the terrain is flat to gently rolling hills.

Butterfield & Robinson (70 Bond Street, Toronto, Ontario, Canada M5B 1X3; 800-678-1147 or 416-864-1354; fax: 416-864-0541; www.butterfield.com), founded over thirty-five years ago, is the leader in luxury active travel around the world, specializing in biking and walking (though it offers kayaking and multisport expeditions too) and offering about a hundred trips on six continents. It is probably the most recognized name in the business, and a few words from one of its beautiful catalogs sums up its philosophy: "We love exploring new places. We think biking and walking are the best way to see a region's people, history and culture. And at the end of each day, we like to treat ourselves well with a great meal and a great hotel. So that's what B&R does." In northeastern Italy, B&R offers one trip in particular that includes biking: "Venice & the Veneto: Biking and Walking from Villas to the Grand Canal" begins in Verona and ends in Venice, with stops in Vicenza, Asolo, and Follina and including visits to the Villa Rotonda, the Villa Emo, and the Villa Barbaro. The biking is on a good mix of flat and rolling terrain, while the walks are on well-maintained trails and paths through farmland and vineyards. "We've always focused on immersing ourselves in a region's culture, on seeing things from a totally new perspective," writes founder George Butterfield in a recent B&R Expeditions catalog. He adds that "these one-of-a-kind experiences bring into relief what every B&R trip comes down to: the incomparable sensation of living a moment that's never been lived before." Besides the quality of B&R trips, I like that the company established the B&R Fund, a charitable initiative with a mandate to support grassroots community projects, particularly in the developing world. The fund allows B&R to show its appreciation and respect by supporting community development projects in B&R destinations around the globe.

Ciclismo Classico (30 Marathon Street, Arlington, Massachusetts 02474; 800-866-7314 or 781-646-3377; www.ciclismoclassico) has been a specialist in Italian active vacations for almost fifteen years, concentrating on cycling and walking tours. Staff members are self-proclaimed world travelers at heart, but "the piece of the planet that we love and know best is *La Bella Italia!* Our staff's love and dedication to all things Italian is more than a hobby, it is a way of life and we crave sharing this world, this incurable passion, with each and every guest." All the company's guides are native Italians and have worked for Ciclismo for over five years. Impressive to me is that Ciclismo clients have remarked over the years that the guides are rather extraordinary, often going above and beyond the call of duty. "Villas & Gardens of Veneto" is the seven-day trip Ciclismo offers in this corner of Italy. The itinerary takes riders through Treviso, Asolo, Possagno, Monte Grappa, Follina, and Vittorio Veneto, and it includes rides along the foothills of the Dolomites, architectural visits to Renaissance villas, grappa tasting in Bassano, wine tasting along the Strada del Vino, a hiking tour with a local guide in Asolo, and an exclusive two-wheel tour of Palladian villas with a local guide. The trip averages twenty-four miles a day and the terrain is flat to rolling hills.

Randonnée Tours (249 Bell Avenue, Winnipeg R3L 0J2; 800-465-6488 or 204-475-6939; 204-474-1888; www.randonneetours.com), founded ten years ago by ecologist Ruth Marr, offers "distinctive self-guided vacations" for travelers interested in walking or cycling (and skiing too). Randonnee offers two cycling tours in the Veneto: the easier follows the Po delta, where the terrain is very flat, and follows a route beginning and ending in Padua (with stops in Este, Porto Viro, Chioggia, Venice, and the Brenta Canal). The more difficult route also begins in Padua, and for four days riders cycle to Este, Porto Viro, and Chioggia. On the fifth day, riders are picked up and transferred to Asolo for another two days of riding in the area.

~Note that if you have your own bike and are traveling with it on Italy's trains, you are allowed to take it on every train except those labeled *Pendolino* (intercity, first class only). You'll notice on the timetable a little bicycle icon next to the lines that allow bikes. But in almost all cases, your bike must be broken down and put in a bag or case. The proper thing to do to avoid any possible problems is to notify a train official that you have a bike, and he or she will tell you where you should install it on the train. Sometimes, especially if a train is not full, or if it is a *regionale, interregionale,* or *diretto* (short-to-medium-distance trains), you will be allowed to carry the bike on without dismantling it. If you are with a group of riders, be aware in advance that some trains cannot accommodate more than six bikes at once, and plan accordingly so everyone ends up in the same place. Riders carrying a bike on a train have to purchase a special ticket, *in addition to* a ticket for themselves. It isn't expensive, but it's something to know. If you'll be studying or working in Italy for an extended period of time, you can get a yearly ticket that allows you to transport a bicycle free on all *local* trains (that is, not long-distance trains headed for other parts of the country or other countries entirely). Inquire at the tourist offices in Italy for information on purchasing this pass, or if you're a student, the institution you're affiliated with will surely have details on its price and where to buy it. Though this is covered below under Trains (Ferrovie dello Stato), remember that you must validate your ticket by inserting it in the machine at the head of each platform.

Bookstores

Like Italians (and most Europeans in general), I prefer to buy whatever goods and services I need from specialists. One-stop shopping is a nice idea in theory, but it has not been very appealing to me, as convenience seems its only virtue. Therefore I buy fish from a fishmonger, flowers from a florist, cheese from a real cheese shop, and so on. And when I'm looking for travel books, I shop at a travel bookstore or an independent bookstore with a strong travel section. The staff in such stores are nearly always well traveled, well read, very helpful, and knowledgeable. An aspect of nationwide chain stores I don't like is that travel guides tend to be shelved separately from travel writing and related history books, implying that guidebooks are all a traveler may need or want. Stores that specialize in travel take a wider view, understanding that travel incorporates many different dimensions. Following is a list of stores in the United States that offer exceptional travel book departments. (I've also included a few stores specializing in art books and cookbooks, as some of these titles are mentioned throughout this book.) Note that all of them accept mail orders, and some publish catalogs and/or newsletters:

CALIFORNIA

Black Oak Books
1491 Shattuck Avenue, Berkeley
510-486-0698

Bon Voyage! Travel Books, Maps, & More
2069 West Bullard Avenue, Fresno
800-995-9716
www.bon-voyage-travel.com

Book Passage
51 Tamal Vista Boulevard, Corte Madera
415-927-0960 (locally); 800-999-7909
www.bookpassage.com

The Cook's Library
8373 West Third Street, Los Angeles
323-655-3141

Distant Lands
56 South Raymond Avenue, Old Pasadena
626-449-3220; 800-310-3220
www.distantlands.com

The Literate Traveller
8306 Wilshire Boulevard, Suite 591, Beverly Hills
310-398-8781; fax: -5151
800-850-2665
www.literatetraveller.com
~In addition to its regular catalog, The Literate Traveller publishes "Around the World in 80+ Mysteries."

Pacific Travellers Supply
12 West Anapamu Street, Santa Barbara
888-PAC-TRAV
www.pactrav.com

Rizzoli
117 Post Street, San Francisco
415-984-0225

The Travellers Bookcase
8375 West Third Street, Los Angeles
323-655-0575; 800-655-0053
www.travelbooks.com

COLORADO

Tattered Cover
2955 East First Avenue, Denver
303-322-7727; 800-833-9327
www.tatteredcover.com

WASHINGTON, D.C.

Travel Books and Language Center
4437 Wisconsin Avenue, N.W.
202-237-1322; fax: -6022
800-220-2665
www.bookweb.org/bookstore/travelbks

ILLINOIS

The Savvy Traveller
310 South Michigan Avenue, Chicago
312-913-9800 (in Chicago); fax: -9866
888-666-6200
www.thesavvytraveller.com

MASSACHUSETTS

Brattle Book Shop
9 West Street, Boston
617-542-0210; fax: 338-1467
800-447-9595
www.brattlebookshop.com
~Brattle's specialty is art books, but it also stocks more than 250,000 used, rare, and out-of-print books.

Globe Corner Bookstore
500 Boylston Street, Boston
617-859-8008; 800-358-6013
www.globecorner.com

Jeffery Amherst Bookshop
55 South Pleasant Street, Amherst
413-253-3381; fax: -7852
www.jeffbooks.com

MINNESOTA

Books for Travel, Etc.
857 Grand Avenue, St. Paul
651-225-8007; 888-668-8006
www.booksfortravel.com

NEW YORK

Archivia: The Decorative Arts Book Shop
1063 Madison Avenue, New York
212-439-9194; fax: 744-1626
www.abebooks.com/home/archiviabooks
~A beautiful store with a beautiful selection of decorating, garden, style, history, and art titles, some in Italian.

Bonnie Slotnick Cookbooks
163 West Tenth Street, New York
212-989-8962
~Bonnie deals almost exclusively with out-of-print cookbooks.

The Complete Traveller
199 Madison Avenue (at 35th Street), New York
212-685-9007
~In addition to having a great selection of current books, this store reserves a separate room for rare and out-of-print

travel books. Owners Harriet and Arnold Greenberg and their superb staff will do their very best to track down your most obscure request.

Hacker Art Books
45 West 57th Street, New York
212-688-7600; fax: 754-2554
www.hackerartbooks.com
~John Russell, former art critic of *The New York Times,* has written of Hacker that "for an all-round art book-store, this one is something near to ideal." On a recent visit to Hacker, three students were sitting on the floor surrounded by books and papers and discussing Cézanne, a customer was conversing in French with one of the staff, another customer began talking to me about the work of Albert Marquet, yet another customer came in rather breathless saying she just wanted to stop by to say hello, and another staffer was on the phone assisting a customer, exactly the atmosphere a good bookstore should exude. "Know art, know life," I read somewhere recently . . . to walk into Hacker (even though one has to take the elevator to the fifth floor) is to be reminded of this intensely.

Kitchen Arts & Letters
1435 Lexington Avenue, New York
212-876-5550; fax: -3584

The Metropolitan Museum of Art Bookstore
Fifth Avenue, New York
212-535-7710
www.metmuseum.org
~The Met has other outposts in New York—including one on the prome-nade at Rockefeller Center—and around the country, but the bookstore at the museum itself is outstanding. The museum's collection of Italian drawings, paintings, and decorative works is impressive (and may be unsurpassed in North America), and the bookshop reflects the museum's strong Italian collections and the traveling exhibits it has hosted as well as an extensive selection of titles for serious Italian-art enthusiasts and new admirers. Additionally, the bookstore staff is very knowledgeable and helpful, and on the rare occasion when the shop didn't have a book I was looking for, staff members were quick to recommend other art specialty stores, not just in New York but nationwide.

Joseph Patelson Music House
160 West 56th Street (behind Carnegie Hall), New York
212-582-5840; fax: 246-5633
e-mail: info@patelson.com
www.patelson.com

Rizzoli
31 West 57th Street, New York
212-759-2424; 800-52-BOOKS

Strand Book Store
828 Broadway (at 12th Street),
New York
212-473-1452; fax: -2591
800-366-3664 (mail orders)
www.strandbooks.com

Strand Book Annex
95 Fulton Street, New York
212-732-6070; fax: 406-1654

NORTH CAROLINA

Omni Resources
1004 South Mebane Street, Burlington
336-227-8300; 800-742-2677
www.omnimap.com

OKLAHOMA

Traveler's Pack, Ltd.
9427 North May Avenue,
Oklahoma City
405-755-2924
www.travelerspack.com

OREGON

Powell's City of Books
1005 West Burnside, Portland
503-228-4651; 800-878-7323
www.powells.com

Powell's Travel Store
701 Southwest Sixth Avenue, Portland
503-228-1108; 800-546-5025
www.powells.com

PENNSYLVANIA

Franklin Maps
333 South Henderson Road,
King of Prussia
610-265-6277; fax: 337-1575
800-356-8676
www.franklinmaps.com
~This store has an extraordinary selection of foreign and domestic maps as well as books. One journalist wrote, "What travelers will find at the 15,000-square-feet Franklin Map store are maps, charts, and books covering almost every square inch of earth and universe."

VERMONT

Adventurous Traveler Bookstore
P. O. Box 64769 (mail orders)
245 South Champlain Street,
Burlington
802-860-6776; 800-282-3963
www.adventuroustraveler.com

WASHINGTON

Wide World Books & Maps
4411A Wallingford Avenue North,
Seattle
206-634-3453; 888-534-3453
www.travelbooksandmaps.com

And because some books I recommend are British publications, I include three excellent stores in London, all of which also fill mail orders: The Travel Bookshop (13–15 Blenheim Crescent, W11 2EE, 44.020.7229.5260; fax: 7243. 1552; www.the travelbookshop.co.uk); Books for Cooks (a few doors down from The Travel Bookshop at 4 Blenheim Crescent, 44.020.7221.1992; fax: 020.7221.1517; www.booksforcooks. com); and Stanfords Maps, Charts, Books (12–14 Long Acre, Covent Garden, WCZE 9LP, 44.020.7207.730. 1354, plus three other locations in and around London. Stanfords has its own dedicated phone and fax for international mail-order service: 44.020.7836.1321; fax: 44.020.7836. 0189; www.stanfords.co.uk).

Additionally, I must mention two favorite mail-order book catalogs: *A Common Reader* and *Bas Bleu*. Both are issued monthly and offer an excellent selection of travel writing, biographies, history, cookbooks, and general fiction and nonfiction books for adults, as well as selected books for children. *ACR*'s selection is more extensive, but this does not make *Bas Bleu*'s offerings any less appealing. James Mustich Jr. is the man behind the *ACR* venture, and his reviews are of the sort that wander here and there and make you want to read every single book in the catalog. (His writing has been an inspiration to me for the annotated bibliographies in *The Collected Traveler*.) Not content simply to offer new books, Mustich even arranges to bring out-of-print books back into print by publishing them under his own Common Reader Editions imprint. To add your name to these catalog mailing lists, contact *A Common Reader* (141 Tompkins Avenue, Pleasantville, New York 10570; 800-832-7323; fax: 914-747-0778; www.commonreader.com) and *Bas Bleu* (515 Means Street N.W., Atlanta, Georgia 30318; 404-577-9463; fax: -6626; www.basbleu.com).

~If your favorite bookseller can't find an out-of-print title you're looking for, try contacting members of Book Sense, a network of more than eleven hundred independent booksellers around the country (888-BOOKSENSE or BookSense.com), or search one of the following websites: www.longitudebooks.com (a wonderful source for travel books—which they define as comprehensively as I do, including travel narratives, art, archaeology, novels, essays, guidebooks, etc.—and maps; when you select a destination,

you can view an "Essential Reading" list plus an accompanying map); www.abebooks.com (American Book Exchange, which I like because you purchase books directly from an independent bookseller); www.elephant-books.com (which specializes in rare and collectible books); or www.alibris.com (if a regular search doesn't prove fruitful, alibris also offers its "Book Hound" service, which keeps "sniffing" around for another thirty days).

SPECIALTY BOOKSTORE IN VENICE

Libreria Filippi & Filippi L.
calle del Paradiso
Castello 5763
041.523.5635

Venice has no shortage of bookstores, English-language included, but this shop stands out from every bookstore anywhere in northeast Italy. Filippi & Filippi is also a prestigious Venetian publishing house known for its works on Venetian history, literature, food, and local traditions. The shop is worth visiting for its collection of old photographs alone, but there are also works on aspects of the Veneto and Friuli–Venezia Giulia. The store has been described as "inestimable," an opinion with which I fully agree. There is another branch in San Marco (calle de la Bissa, 041.523.6916) though I've not visited it.

Buon Viaggio: A Bouquet of Reminders

This is actually the title of the final chapter of Kate Simon's wonderful book *Italy: The Places in Between,* about which more is said below under Guidebooks. (The book is out of print.) The chapter is nothing more than a list of reminders, but it is so good, and so appropriate to the spirit of *The Collected Traveler,* that I feel it is indispensable to this volume:

Remember that a little learning can be a pleasant thing. Italy gives much, in beauty, gaiety, diversity of arts and landscapes, good humor and energy—willingly, without having to be coaxed or courted. Paradoxically, she requires (as do other countries, probably more so) and deserves some preparation as background to enhance her pleasures. It is almost impossible to read a total history of Italy. There was no united country until a hundred years ago, no single line of power, no concerted developments. It is useful, however, to know something about what made Siena run and stop, to become acquainted with the Estes and the Gonzagas, the Medicis and the Borgias, the names that *were* the local history. It helps to know something about the conflicts of the medieval church with the Holy Roman Empire, of the French, Spanish and early German kings who marked out large chunks of Italy for themselves or were invited by a nervous Italian power. Above all, it helps to turn the pages of a few art and architecture books to become reacquainted with names other than those of the luminous giants. The informed visitor will not allow himself to be cowed by the deluge of art. See what interests you. There is no Italian Secret Service that reports on whether you have seen *everything.* If you try to see it all except as a possible professional task, you may come to resist it all. Relax, know what you like and don't like, and let the rest go. By moving ruminatively, all antennae out and receptive, you may learn—in the gesture of an old woman's finger stroking the arm of a baby as if he were the Infant Jesus, in the warmth and pleasure of friends meeting on a street, in the loud rumble of angry café voices when a father boxes his young son's ears, in the infinite bounty of concern among the members of a family, in the working-class coins that drop into the cap of a beggar—more about living, and Italy, than in miles of magniloquent buildings and seas of paint.

Everything about this excerpt remains true, to a degree, all over Italy.

Buses

The only occasions I've ridden a bus in northeastern Italy were when I was getting to and from the Piazzale Roma and Marco Polo Airport. Venice and Trieste excepted, it is seldom necessary to ride the bus in the city centers of Vicenza, Padua, Treviso, Verona, Udine, and Cividale dei Friuli, for example; they are small enough for visitors to walk from end to end without public tranport. Also, I have found the train network to be terrific, and to go from city to city, I typically choose the train over the bus. But as thorough as Italy's train network is, it doesn't go everywhere, and if you are traveling without a car, you'll need to take the bus to get to some of the towns in the Dolomites, to Asolo and the Palladian villas in the Veneto, and to some of the smaller villages throughout the region. Additionally, a train journey sometimes includes a bus connection—this is not as complicated as it might seem, as almost always in Italy the train station is very close to the *autostazione* (bus station), so you won't have to go very far to make your connection. A potentially confusing aspect of bus travel in Italy is that in addition to SITA, the state-owned company, there are a great number of privately owned services. Lazzi is the company that offers long-distance service within Italy and beyond, and it therefore serves the Veneto and the rest of the Northeast; but so do a handful of other lines. The prices among the lines are all about the same, by the way, with only minor differences in service. Tickets—whether you're riding a city bus in Trieste or a long-distance line—need to be purchased in advance of boarding and can be bought at bus stations, bus stop offices, newsstands, bookshops, bars, automatic machines, or *tabacchi* (tobacco shops; as in other European countries, nearly anything can be purchased at the corner tobacco shop). You need to validate your ticket by having it stamped in the machine at the front of the bus, and don't let Italy's honor system fool you: inspectors do check for tickets, and they are not forgiving. Within cities several different types of tickets are usually available, in addition to a monthly pass. Think about what you want to do in town, and inquire about your options, which usually include a *biglietto 60 minuti* (valid for one hour of travel), *biglietto 3 ore* (valid for three hours), and *biglietto 24 ore* (valid for 24 hours).

~Note that bus (and train) schedules do not always accommodate tourists, making it necessary, for example, to choose between seeing a small village in an hour or two, or spending the night there in order to catch the bus out the next morning. The schedules in more remote areas favor local school hours, which also means that there may be no service at all during school holidays. Plan accordingly. ~If you're making a round-trip journey, it's always a good idea to purchase tickets for both legs; smaller villages may have only one ticket outlet, which may very well be closed at the time of your departure. ~The tourist office in Trieste offers a great bus trip for visitors called "Trieste by Bus: Giro della Città in 13 Tappe," which is a good opportunity to get to know the city by making thirteen stops, at Piazza

Libertà, Caffè Tommaseo, Borsa Vecchia, San Giusto, Piazza Oberdan, Teatro Verdi, Stazione Marittima, Pescheria, Museo Ferroviario, Museo Revoltella, Piazza Unità d'Italia, and Piazza della Repubblica. It is offered only during the summer months, however, and children under ten years of age ride free. For details and a brochure, inquire at the Azienda di Promozione Turistica di Trieste (APT) office (see Tourist Office entry).

C

Canalazzo

Canalazzo is the word Venetians use to refer to the Canal Grande (Grand Canal).

Carnevale

Venice's Carnevale is probably the most famous pre-Lenten celebration in the world. The word is derived from "taking meat away" (*carne* means flesh and *levare* is the verb for to raise or lift up; the reflexive form means to get up or arise) and is celebrated twelve days before Ash Wednesday. Carnevale actually has its roots in spring fertility rites, and by the Middle Ages it had become legendary in Venice, and was celebrated for months at a time. Napoleon put a stop to all the merry-making in 1797, and it really was not fully revived as a major event on Venice's social calendar until 1979. Costumes are, of course, a big part of the festivities, allowing residents and visitors to become someone else for a while and perhaps realize a (temporary) fantasy.

Many of the Carnevale costumes have been inspired by the commedia dell'arte, an improvisational comic form of theater that thrived in sixteenth-century Italy (Arlecchino, Pantalone, and Pulcinella are the best-known characters; Puncinella became Mr. Punch in England—of Punch and Judy fame—and Arlecchino became Pierrot in France). The commedia dell'arte paved the way for puppet shows throughout Europe, as well as mime in France and pantomime in England and Denmark.

Readers interested in visiting Venice during Carnevale should reserve accommodations and flights well in advance and know that rates will not be a bargain. Most Carnevale festivities are staged out of doors, such as the best costume competition and the Flight of the Colombina, both of which take place in Piazza San Marco (the Flight of the Columbina may be one of the most impressive events ever: a mechanical dove soars down from the belltower and deposits massive amounts of confetti on the cheering crowd). The final weekend of the festival is typically the most jam-packed, and the two big public events are the flotilla of decorated boats along the Grand Canal and the closing ball. For more detailed information, readers may consult the official website of the APT office in Venice, www.turismovenezia.it (click on events, then festivities and fairs, and type in Carnevale). But I have repeatedly read that schedules of events—both public and private—are always subject to change, even on extremely short notice. The best approach is simply to make your plans and partake in the events that are happening while you're in town. When you arrive in Venice, you should immediately head for the nearest APT office and pick up a detailed schedule, which will be more accurate than anything you find on a website. For an advance preview of this "expression of popular joy and theater," you may want to watch the videotape *Venetian Carnevale* offered by the Discovery Channel (to order by phone, call 800-207-5775; about $19.99).

Car Rental

You can't rent a car in Venice, of course, and it is not essential—or even desirable—to have a rental car in Trieste, Verona, Vicenza, Padua, Treviso, or any of the smaller towns of the northeast. Train and bus service, direct or with connections, is available to just about everywhere. But for anyone wanting to visit the Palladian villas in the Veneto, the wine routes, or the countryside of Friuli–Venezia Giulia, I highly recommend renting a car. Perhaps best of all is a trip that combines train travel with a car rental. Here are some tips and reminders:

~*Car rental problems.* My favorite feature of travel publications is the section featuring readers' letters. I have probably learned more from these letters than from any other source, and the largest number of complaints seem to be about problems encountered when renting a car. But no matter what you read, hear, or assume, the only word that counts is the one from your policy administrator, be it a credit card or insurance company. If you have any questions about renting a car overseas and what is and isn't covered on your existing policy (including collision damage waiver), contact your provider in advance. Request documentation in writing, if necessary. It is your responsibility to learn about your coverage before you rent a car. I have never encountered any rental car problems, but then again I make it a habit to first inspect the car for any damages that could become problematic later before I drive it off the lot, and I always state to the company representative, "When I return the car to you, I will not pay anything more than this amount" while pointing to the total on my receipt; this gives the representative the opportunity to say, "Oh, well now that you mention it, there is one other possible charge . . . ," which opens the door to a final discussion about what I am expected to pay. I follow the "no surprises" rule: I bring up everything I can think of and ask any questions I may have at the outset of renting the car. The majority of the complaints I read about are due to false assumptions that were never clarified or questioned at the time the car was rented, and it is nearly always impossible—or best, very difficult—to resolve a dispute with a rental car agency once you've signed the bill, returned the car, and returned home.

~*Vouchers.* Hertz offers a competitive rate with its prepaid car rental voucher. The conditions are that you prepay in U.S. dollars in advance of your trip, and the vouchers are typically faxed to a U.S. fax number or mailed to a U.S. address. The prepaid rate does not include such things as drop charges, car seats, a collision damage waiver, or gas: these must be paid for in local currency at the time you pick up the car.

~*Maggiore,* a Budget Car Rental partner, is the largest car rental company in Italy. By making arrangements with Central Holidays in the United States in advance of your trip, rates are discounted as much as 50 percent (800-935-5000).

~*International driver's license.* You don't need an international driver's license in Italy. Save the ten-dollar fee for driving in less developed countries, where the absence of the license could open the door for bribery to cross a border.

~*Leasing.* For information on leasing a car (as well as renting), contact Europe by Car (62 William Street, New York, New York 10005; 800-223-1516; in New York: 212-581-3040; www.europebycar.com). Europe by Car has been offering low-priced rentals and tax-free leases since 1954, and in a recent Reader's Choice Awards roundup in *Condé Nast Traveler,* it was rated first among the top-ten car rental companies for best service and rates. It truly offers one of the best values around: in addition to offering good overall rates (with special rates available for students, teachers, and faculty members), clients can select the tax-free, factory-direct new car vacation plan. This is a good deal because technically the program operates more like a short-term lease, which makes the rental car exempt from European taxes. The cars are from Peugeot, Citroën, and Renault, and prices include unlimited mileage; insurance with liability, fire, collision damage waiver, and theft; and emergency assistance twenty-four hours a day via a free phone. The only catch is that you have to pay for the car for a minimum of seventeen days— you don't have to *keep* the car for seventeen days but the price is the same if you drop it off earlier. All clients receive special discounts at selected hotels and motels (and budget hotels costing about $26 a night) as well as free parking. ~Kemwell Holiday Autos (106 Calvert Street, Harrison, New York 10528; 800-678-0678; fax: 914-835-5449; www.kemwel.com) also offers a Peugeot short-term leasing program (which they refer to as the best-kept "secret" in the business) as well as regular car rentals, chauffeur-driven cars, carpass vouchers, and motorhome rentals, all at competitive rates. The carpass voucher program allows a traveler to purchase a rental voucher in three-day segments; you buy as many segments as you think you'll need, and any unused vouchers are fully refundable upon your return. (This is particularly helpful if you're not sure you need to rent a car at all or don't know how long you might need one.) I have used Kemwel on two occasions and have been very pleased. The materials one receives include charts for mileage, miles-to-kilometers, and international road signs; a handy little fold-out guide called "Travel Talk," with basic phrases in English, Italian, French, German, and

Spanish; and charts for clothing sizes, kilos-to-pounds, centimeters-to-inches, gallons-to-liters, temperatures, and time differences.

~*Kilometers*. It's helpful to begin thinking in kilometers instead of miles. I jot down sample distances to use as a ready reference as I'm motoring along the *strade principali* or *strade statale* or trying to keep up on the *autostrade:* 1 mile = 1.6 kilometers, so 12 km = 7 miles; 16 km = 10 miles; 40 km = 25 miles; 80 km = 50 miles; 160 km = 100 miles; 320 km = 200 miles, and so on.

~*Routes*. Road maps and atlases obviously employ route numbers for large and small roads; but most of the highway and road signs you'll see in Italy (and in Europe in general) typically indicate cities or towns quite far away rather than road numbers. (Initially, this threw me off and reminded me of a sign I used to see years ago just outside Philadelphia for a restaurant at the New Jersey shore; the sign advertised that the restaurant was "minutes away" but was in fact two *hours* away.) Begin thinking in terms of *direction* rather than road number, and consult your map(s) often—you'll find that it's quite a sensible way of getting around, and it forces the visitor to be better versed in geography.

~*Auto clubs*. The two automobile clubs in Italy are Touring Club Italiano (TCI) and the Automobile Club d'Italia (ACI). The ACI has a twenty-four-hour hotline in English (06.44.77), and although its services aren't free, rates are reasonable. (Note, however, that ACI does not provide roadside assistance; your car will be towed to the nearest ACI affiliate garage.) Most of the *autostrade* have emergency push-button call boxes every two kilometers; travelers in distress can also dial 116 at any time from any phone—an emergency number for car accidents or breakdowns. If you'll be living in Italy for any length of time, you might want to become a member of ACI.

~*Gasoline*. Gas prices in Italy are the highest in Europe. Years ago visitors crossing into Italy by car were eligible for discount gas coupons by the Touring Club Italiano. Unfortunately, these are no longer available; so budget accordingly, and think about some of the services that are paid for with the money generated from gas prices, and the next time a senator or congressman suggests raising the price of gas in the United States, let it be known that he or she has your support!

~*Tolls*. Tolls in Italy, as elsewhere in Europe, are extremely expensive. It's a good idea to purchase a Via Card if you'll be driving a fair amount on the *autostrade*. The Via Card is like a debit card: you purchase it in units of either 20,000 or 50,000 lire, and amounts are then deducted from the card. It can be purchased at tollgates (look for the Punto Blu service centers at the larger toll stations) or at ACI offices.

~*Speed limit*. The speed limit on the *autostrade* is 130 kilometers per hour (80 mph), while on regular main roads it's 110 kph (68 mph). Driving through towns, the limit is 50 kph (about 30 mph), and on smaller roads outside of town centers it's 110 kph (about 65 mph).

~Lanes. Driving in the fast lane on a European road can be a bit disconcerting, as any car suddenly looming up behind you is closing in at a *much* faster speed than we're accustomed to in the United States. These drivers usually have no patience for your slowness and will tailgate you and flash their lights until you get out of the way. So if you're going to pass, step on the gas and go, then return quickly to the right lane.

~Tickets. I've read conflicting advice on parking tickets, so I would not recommend taking a chance if you're in doubt. Rental agencies do have your credit card number, and it seems to me they can eventually bill you for any tickets you've received and add a service charge if they're so inclined.

~Gas stations. Gas stations offer full service on weekdays, but many keep the same hours as other businesses and close during the lunchtime siesta. Stations on the *autostrade,* however, remain open continuously. At night and on weekends, there may very well not be anyone about, or you may find someone around who is not employed by the station but who will service your car for a tip, anywhere from L500 to L1,000. (Ordinarily, gas station attendants do not receive tips.) Most stations have automatic self-serve pumps that accept 10,000 and 50,000 paper lire.

~An important word of advice for anyone returning a car to the parking garage at Piazzale Roma in Venice: If you are returning the car on a Sunday, ask the rental agency *what time the office closes* and *if it is open at all* on Sunday. The last time I was in Venice, I drove my rental car from Vicenza on Sunday morning, intending to arrive at Piazzale Roma by late morning with enough time to drop my bags off at the hotel and be seated at a particular *ristorante* I'd wanted to try by one o'clock. Readers should know that first of all, there is only one huge parking garage at Piazzale Roma, and all cars are directed into it. Even though the rental car offices are in plain view at the street level of this enormous structure, you cannot drive up in front of them and park your car. You must drive into the garage, take a ticket, and park your car. The instructions are that you leave the keys in the car with the doors unlocked. You then empty the car of your belongings and trudge down to street level to the appropriate office. The catch is that if it's Sunday and twelve noon, all the rental offices that line this level of the garage are closed and don't open again until Monday morning. I was standing on the sidewalk in front of these closed offices on my last trip while my friend Lorraine went to find out where the Maggiore office was located. (Through the good folks at Visit Italy Tours—see the Tours entry for more details—I had rented a car from Maggiore, which, it turns out, is the *only* office open on Sunday afternoon.) While I was waiting, no fewer than four Americans came by to return their cars, only to learn that their respective office was closed and that, according to the fine print in their agreements, *they would be charged an additional day* if they did not return the car before noon on Sunday. It was quite obvious that not a single one of these travelers had been informed of either the fine print or the restrictions on this particular day of the week. I heard some language I cannot repeat here, but suffice it to say that those rental agencies were going to get an earful on Monday. Now, returning to my own situation: Lorraine returned, informing me that the Maggiore office was in fact behind this giant parking garage, so we wheeled and carried our bags (and my daughter) all the way around to the back. Once there the Maggiore representative told me I had to retrieve my car from the parking garage, where I had parked it— on the top level, of course, as every other level was full—because the attendant told me I had to do so. So I walked back alone to retrieve the car, parked at the exit, and walked over to the pay counter, where a kind cashier saw that I had parked only for twenty minutes and ripped up the ticket. I returned to the Maggiore office and finalized everything, and we waddled a short distance to board a water taxi, which dropped us at our hotel—at two o'clock, when all the restaurants were finished serving lunch. A mediocre pizzeria near the hotel had room for us, but I couldn't help thinking that if only the attendant hadn't misinformed me about parking in the garage, or if only I had taken the train instead . . . My advice: remember Maggiore, and remember that the office is behind the *parcheggio* (parking), allowing you to bypass the garage entirely!

~*Driving tours*. A great book to get if you'll be driving at all in northeastern Italy is *Italy's Best-Loved Driving Tours: 25 Unforgettable Itineraries* (Paul Duncan, Frommer's). Of particular interest are tours 5 ("The Gentle Veneto," which makes a loop from Feltre down to Asolo and Vicenza, over to Mestre, up to Treviso and Conegliano, and back across to Possagno via the Strade del Vino Bianco), and 6 ("Beyond Venice—Inland Veneto," which loops from Verona down to Nogara, east to Monselice, up to Bassano del Grappa, down to Vicenza and back over to Verona). Unfortunately, there are no routes in Friuli–Venezia Giulia or in Trentino–Alto Adige.

~Useful vocabulary: *autonoleggio* (car rental agency); *gasolio* (diesel gas); *super* or *benzina* (regular gas, petrol); *senza piombo* (unleaded gas); *senso unico* (one way); *senso vietato* (no entry); *polizia stradale* (highway police); *divieto di sosta/sosta vietata* (no parking); *uscita* (exit); *accostare a destra* (merge to the right) or *accostare a sinistra* (left); *sottopassaggio* (underpass); *rallentare* (slow down); *pedaggio* (toll); *pericolo* (danger); *guasto* (breakdown); *sempre diritto* (straight ahead); *vicino* (near); and *lontano* (far).

Children

Most everybody, even if you are not a parent, has heard that Italy is a great country to travel in with kids. As the authors of *Italy with Kids* (below) state, "All of Italy is family-friendly. Children are national shrines. Even the maître d' in the most posh of restaurants has a special smile for the youngest of diners." Until you have done it, you have no idea how true this is. While working on this book, I realized I needed to make a return trip to update some material and better familiarize myself with this corner of Italy. My husband was positively unable to join me at the time I needed to go, and he was also unable to assume full-time baby-sitting duties, so I had no choice but to bring my two-and-a-half-year-old daughter with me. Nothing I had read prepared me for the experience of traveling with her; in no way could I have predicted the surprises that awaited us, the opportunities that were afforded me, the different ways of looking at things, and the different ways of being received. I could fill several pages of this book recounting all the ways the Italians I encountered were extraordinarily kind to me, but I will not bore you and will share only a few with you: I was in Venice, walking in one of the narrow streets off the Piazza San Marco with my daughter in the stroller, when a man called after me, "Signora, Signora!" I turned to find an elderly gentleman handing me a soft, cloth-covered book that, upon closer inspection, was for a child. I concluded that he thought we had dropped it, so I gestured that the book was not ours. He seemed confused and kept handing it back to me. Finally, he handed it to Alyssa, patting her on the head and saying, *"Che bella!"* He turned and walked into a bookshop, and I realized the book was brand-new and was a gift. Another time in Venice, I was in a rather expensive shop selling ceramics and other items for the table, and Alyssa kept exclaiming at all the ceramic animals she saw, like chickens, ducks, and rabbits. I did make a significant purchase, but I was still unprepared for the kind owner's offer of a gift to Alyssa: a salt and pepper shaker set in the shape of two swans. Additionally, the restaurant and *enoteca* proprietors all over this part of Italy never once offered less than a welcoming smile when I entered with my daughter, even on occasion refusing money for the nibbles of food she ate or the Fanta she drank. Nearly every *pasticceria* and *alimentare* we entered resulted in a free sample for Alyssa, and every time I approached a difficult set of stairs or a door that wouldn't stay open, an Italian appeared to lift the stroller, take Alyssa's hand, or hold the door.

When I first began working on this series, I could not find a single book devoted to traveling with children in Italy. Happily, this situation is changing, and publishers have rightly recognized this as a publishing niche to be filled. Some guidebooks (including many of those mentioned below under Guidebooks) offer excellent suggestions for things to see and do with kids; but a book that parents might be glad to have is *Italy with Kids* (Barbara Pape and Michael Calabrese, Open Road Publishing, Cold Spring Harbor, New York, 2001). Open Road's motto is "Be a Traveler, Not a Tourist!" and the authors do share a few tips for getting somewhat off the beaten path, or as off it as is possible with kids. (Usually, it's the really famous and big things that kids love.) The cover photo features two children feeding the pigeons in Piazza San Marco, your first clue that you may be asked/forced to do this more than once. (My daughter went four times, and it was easily the highlight of the trip for her.) Feeding the pigeons isn't as trite as it sounds; if there is more than one adult, one of you can sit down at Florian's and have a coffee or a Prosecco while the other is making sure the kids aren't scared when an aggressive pigeon lands on someone's shoulder. The book covers Rome, Venice, Verona,

Florence and Tuscany, Naples and the Amalfi Coast, Milan and the Lake District. Within each section the authors offer itineraries (which I didn't find that useful), fun facts, parent tips, restaurant and hotel suggestions (the selections for Venice were, unfortunately, nearly all categorized as "very expensive" or "expensive," with only three "inexpensive" options), and kid's corner suggestions of fun things to do. I think the book could be a tad more detailed, but it's really very good, and I think parents (and grandparents, older siblings who may be called upon for baby-sitting duties, and other relatives and friends) will find it useful. Books about traveling with kids in general that I've enjoyed include *Have Kid, Will Travel: 101 Survival Strategies for Vacationing with Babies and Young Children* (Claire Tristram with Lucille Tristram, Andrews McMeel Publishing, Kansas City, Missouri, 1997). Claire Tristram has visited all fifty states and thirty countries, and Lucille, her daughter, has been named "the best baby in the world" by several strangers sitting next to her on long-distance flights. Among her best words of advice: "Above all, don't let a bad moment become a bad day, and don't let a bad day become a bad week." Another is *Travel with Your Baby: Experts Share Their Secrets for Tips with Your Under-4-Year Old* (Fodor's Travel Publications, 2001). Readers around the country contributed their real-life travel stories and tips to this small, pocket-size edition. It has good checklists and packing lists, and I think the best overall suggestion is KTWF—Keep Them Well Fed. I have culled a lot of good ideas from this book and am now awaiting the *over*-age-four edition! None of the tips in either of these books, however, prepares parents for a situation like the one my friend Katie found herself in. She, her husband, and their one-year-old son, Jack, were on an airline terminal van at the Nice airport when Jack suddenly and inexplicably projectile-vomited all over everyone in the vicinity, on both sides of the van. After Katie and Gary hastily apologized and tried their best to clean everyone off with pieces of their own clothing, Jack repeated the performance. They did their best once again to wipe everyone off—searching desperately in their bags for *any* piece of clothing that hadn't been previously used—but by now they were also concerned that something was really wrong with Jack, as he had never done that in his short life and had not shown any signs of sickness. (As it turned out, the airport's resident doctor did detect a little sickness coming on, but everything ended up fine, except that their flight was delayed three hours.) There are just some things you can't prepare for, and some situations when you really need a sense of humor.

An observation that parents will be sure to notice: In Italy—as in most other Mediterranean countries—young children stay up late at night, even at restaurants and *trattorie*. Do not be surprised if it's midnight and there are lots of kids running around. I've never seen the children looking unhappy or tired, and it seems to make sense in a country with a tradition of an afternoon siesta.

Following are some tips that worked for me that you may want to try: ~Build excitement about the trip by reading some appropriate books in advance, or save one or two for the airplane. A few we liked are *Getting to Know Italy and Italian* (written by Emma Sansone, illustrated by Kim Woolley, Barron's Educational Series, 1992); *Strega Nona* (Tomie dePaola, Aladdin Paperbacks, 1975); *Strega Nona Meets Her Match* (Tomie dePaola, Paperstar/Putnam & Grosset, 1996); *Tom* (Tomie dePaola, Paperstar/Putnam & Grosset, 1997); *Daughter of Venice* (Donna Jo Napoli, Wendy Lamb Books, 2002) and *The Voice of the Wood* (Claude Clement, paintings by Frederic Clement, Dial Books, 1989; originally published in Belgium in 1988 as *Le Luthier de Venise* by Pastel, an imprint of L'École des Loisirs). ~Take the kids to your favorite food store—I chose our local natural foods store—and let them select snacks for the trip. These are good not only for the airplane but for all those times when you might need a distraction (waiting on line, riding on a *vaporetto,* frolicking on the beach at the Lido, sitting in the stroller, and so on), and if they pick out the snacks themselves, there is a much greater chance they will eat them. ~Select an overnight flight, if possible. Kids are used to going to sleep at night, so you don't upset their schedule as drastically. ~Bring along some "surprises" for the flight over. About a month before our departure, I started a pile of new books, games, and activities and kept them hidden from my daughter so that she would see them for the first time on the plane. ~My mother-in-law, Sheila, bought my daughter a tracing set of cardboard animals and colored string as an airplane activity. (The animals had holes all around tracing their shape, and you thread the string up and down through the holes until they're all filled in.) This turned out to be a great idea, even if Alyssa couldn't always follow the shape in a recognizable pattern. ~For older kids, buy an inexpensive disposable camera and let them take their own pictures. ~For kids of all ages, buy a blank journal and help them create a record of the trip. (The photos they take will go nicely in here.) ~When you arrive in Venice, find a souvenir stand (the majority of these are clustered at Piazzale Roma and along the Zattere) and buy one of those floaty pens—you know, the kind where a gondola floats back and forth—so kids can use it to write in their journals. ~When you arrive at an art museum, first buy some postcards. (This is not an original idea but I've expanded upon it.) If you have more than one child, tell the kids that whoever finds the most paintings or works of art first wins a special prize. (You must decide this in advance; it could be three scoops of *gelato* or a gondola ride—whatever your budget allows—but make sure it's something they will want to compete for.) If you have one child, tell him or her to find all the artworks—there is no race—to receive a special prize. I asked Alyssa to select five postcards from the racks in front of the Accademia, which she did with enthusiasm. Then, once we were inside, we came upon a mini version of the bookstore about a quarter of the way through the galleries, and I saw a wooden box of colored pencils. I bought the pencils (which she loved), and she then colored on the reverse sides of the postcards. This activity enabled me to walk slowly around every room in the museum. I saw everything in a leisurely fashion, and she never once asked if we could leave. ~Strollers are both a blessing and a curse in Venice proper (I found it *much* easier to get around with a stroller in any other city—Trieste, Vicenza, Padua—than in Venice): on the one hand, when your child needs to take a nap, he or she will fall asleep quite easily in the stroller; on the other, sometimes naptime is precisely when you've reached the steps of the Rialto Bridge. After a few days of leaving the hotel early in the morning and not returning until late in the evening, I decided to change course—the stroller was just becoming too difficult for me to handle alone, even with the help of friendly Venetians and fellow tourists. So I planned our days differently, making sure we left early in the morning with not too great a distance to go—so Alyssa could walk—and returning to the hotel in time for lunch and a siesta. In midafternoon we would set out again, occasionally with but mostly without the stroller, making the days less physically exhausting for me.

~The Lido is often overlooked by visitors to Venice, but it shouldn't be: it's pretty, pleasant, far less frenetic than Venice proper, and only a short boat ride away from San Marco. But especially for parents, the Lido should not be ignored. And here's the thing of it: you don't even have to stay in one of the grand—and expensive—hotels to enjoy the beach, because nearly all the hotels offer their beach services to day guests. I had read about this in a few of the guidebooks, but most of the writers were not parents, so the idea of paying a rather high fee to use the beach and facilities was, to them, simply abhorrent. But I was determined to give it a try, because I was determined *not* to go to the free beach, where there would be no place to change diapers, sit under an umbrella, wash up, or leave my valuables unattended. I inquired at the beautiful Hotel des Bains what the rates were and was pleased to discover that, first of all, there are varying rates for a variety of amenities. I was not interested in a private cabana, which costs more; but for the equivalent of $38, I was given two comfortable deck chairs with umbrellas and a table on a manicured lawn; I changed in a dressing room and my clothes and valuables were locked up; the stroller was handed over for storage; when it was time for a shower, we were shown to the outdoor warm-water showers and were given two big, fluffy white towels; the bathrooms had changing-table facilities; and we had access to all the dining facilities (two modest cafés and a more expensive restaurant) and, of course, to the beach, on which we frolicked about for four hours. I met a mother of three from Australia whose husband had business in Venice, and she told me they had made the decision to stay on the Lido because it was much more accommodating to the children. Granted, the Hotel des Bains is quite an expensive hotel, but this particular mom thought it was worth the expense. She told me that she and the kids divided up their days about fifty-fifty, spending about half the day on the beach or around the hotel, and half in Venice itself. But families could just as easily do the reverse, staying in Venice (at a more affordable hotel) and making several trips over to the Lido as frequently as desired. It's only a ten-to-fifteen-minute walk from the dock to the Hotel des Bains (the first grand hotel one reaches upon turning to the right at the end of the main street, Gran Viale Santa

Maria Elisabetta), there are plenty of casual places to eat along the way, and the kids won't get so tired of being dragged here and there in Venice. I offer my thanks to the Hotel des Bains, and others like it that allow beach guests for the day, and I would gladly pay for the privilege again. The *spiaggia comunale* (free beach) on the Lido is fine if your kids are past the diaper stage and you don't mind carrying provisions with you; but I think the fancy hotels' beach services represent one of the world's better values, and I highly recommend them to parents.

~Fruit juices are not widely available in restaurants, at least in this part of Italy, but orange soda is. We do not keep soda in our home, so orange soda was not exactly what I considered a welcome addition to Alyssa's diet. But when traveling, a child who eats what he or she wants is a happy child, and I do not think it is productive to argue about food or drink in a restaurant. Parents all choose what battles they will wage with their children, and my own advice is that this shouldn't be one to add to the list. Alyssa ate plenty of pasta, bread, and bottled water, she tasted nearly everything on my plate, and she ate cereal, fruit, and cheese for breakfast; but when she wanted potato chips, pizza, gelato, or chocolate pudding, I did not deny her request, and as a result she felt that eating out in Italy was great fun. *And* she understood perfectly when we were back home that we had returned to the ways of our household, and I explained that we ate differently in Italy because there is different food in Italy. (You could always try telling very young children that orange soda and chocolate hazelnut spread aren't available in America, but watch out if you're caught in your white lie at the grocery store!)

~Two final resources that I deem indispensable are *Venice for Pleasure* by J. G. Links (see the entry for Walking Guides under Guidebooks for details) for the chapter entitled "Venice for Children's Pleasure and The Delights of the Brenta"; and *The Riddles of Venice: A Book of Six Treasure Hunts in Venice* by Douglas M. Sardo with an introduction by John Julius Norwich (see description under the Save Venice entry). The J. G. Links book is available at most good bookstores and through the *Common Reader* mail-order catalog (see Bookstores entry for contact information); but *The Riddles of Venice* is available only through Save Venice (again, see the Save Venice entry for contact information).

A few handy vocabulary words are *una tazza* (a small cup, usually referring to a cup used for an espresso; this is useful in restaurants because it seems there are no child-size cups in Italy, and drinks for children are always brought in large cups and glasses); *un bicchiere piccolo* (*bicchiere* is the word for "glass," usually referring to a wine glass, but by adding *piccolo*—"small"—you can get across that you'd like a small glass *per la bambina*—"for the little girl"—or *per le bambino*— "for the little boy"); *un cucchiaino* (a teaspoon, pronounced kook-yah-EE-no; again, this is useful because if you don't ask, silverware brought for children will often be adult-size; for a fork, you could say *una forchetta piccola*, meaning "small fork"); *la paglia* or *la cannuccia* (straw, or drinking straw—even though the second word may be more correct, I used both words and was not misunderstood; again, a helpful word to know for small children who can't quite grasp a glass or who find it more festive to drink from a straw).

Chiuso (closed)

Hopefully, this is a sign you won't often see, as you will have quickly adjusted to the daily rhythm of life in Italy. But occasionally the interior of a church you had hoped to see will be closed for renovation, or the proprietor of a shop was just too hungry and went home a little early for lunch, or the museum you wanted to visit changed its hours . . . or, the family-run trattoria is *chiuso per ferie* (closed for vacation). Welcome to Italy. It's no use having a cow about what you cannot control; what you *can* control, and what will limit the occasions you encounter *chiuso* during your visit, is your itinerary, so plan for the Italian day accordingly.

Clothing

The way I see it, you can hardly talk about clothing without talking about packing, but I have included a separate Packing entry to address luggage issues and share packing tips. I pack light, and unless I have plans to be at fancy places, I pack double-duty items (stuff that can go from daytime to evening) in low-key colors that also mix and match so I can wear garments more than once. Remember that Italians tend to dress up a bit more than Americans, so reserve your jeans for casual daytime wear and the most casual of places at night, and leave the color-coordinated jogging suits at home. (The athletic look is considered athletic, and is not stylish for any other purpose.) Italians also remain conservative when it comes to visiting their religious houses of worship. Visitors will earn respect and goodwill by refraining from wearing sleeveless shirts, and short skirts and shorts, no matter how hot it is. You may find this odd in a country where topless sunbathing is permitted on the beaches, but make no mistake about it: it is still frowned upon, especially in smaller villages, to dress inappropriately around town and in churches. Suits and ties are necessary only at the finest restaurants, and polo shirts and khakis will always serve men well. Although comfortable shoes are of the utmost importance, I never, ever bring sneakers—my husband is positively forbidden to bring them—and you might not either once you realize that they scream "American." I prefer Arche, a line of French walking shoes and sandals for men and women, but several other lines are available that are also stylish *and* comfortable.

The following mail-order catalogs offer some practical clothes, shoes, packing accessories, and gadgets for travelers. ~L. L. Bean Traveler (800-221-4221; www.llbean.com) offers some noteworthy items that include no-iron oxford cloth shirts for men; universal packers—zippered cubes with mesh tops to keep clothes folded and separated, in three sizes and six colors; and personal organizers, which are sized for from one to five days, come in eight cool colors, and have hooks so you can hang them up on a shower or closet rod. ~At Magellan's (800-962-4943; www.magellans.com), I like the Splash Caddy, a waterproof pouch with a waistband you wear when at the beach or in the water; the wine companion, complete with corkscrew, foil cutter, knife, fork, can/bottle opener, and cocktail stir; and toothettes, for brushing your teeth without water. Plus, the catalog includes a country-by-country chart indicating the world's electrical and telephone connections, *and* it offers adaptor plugs for each. Also good is TravelSmith (800-950-1600; www.travelsmith.com), which offers a great reversible coat for women, a travel blazer for men that defies wrinkles and pickpockets, and stretch canvas sneakers. I know readers may be surprised by this last since I just grumbled about sneakers, but these are terrific! I like them because they're stylish in a European way, weigh only twenty-two ounces, are incredibly comfy, and make locals think twice before summing the wearer up as American. The Territory Ahead (888-233-9959; www.territoryahead.com) offers the most stylish clothing of the bunch, especially shorts and footwear.

Coins

If you have leftover euros in the form of coins, you can always save them for a future trip; but perhaps a better idea is to give them to a great cause: UNICEF's Change for Good program, a partnership between UNICEF and the International Airline Industry. The program is designed to redeem normally unused foreign currency and create value by converting passengers' foreign change into life-saving materials and services for the world's neediest children. Since 1991 more than $31 million has been raised through Change for Good. Thirteen airlines currently participate in the program: Aer Lingus, Air Mauritius, Alitalia, All Nippon Airways, American Airlines, Asiana Airlines, British Airways, Cathay Pacific, Crossair, Finnair, JAL, Qantas, and TWA. On flights back to the United States, flight attendants pass out small envelopes to passengers. When you consider that approximately $72 million in inconvertible foreign coins and low-denomination bills are forfeited each year by international travelers, Change for Good is a remarkably wonderful idea. UNICEF notes that the average passenger carrying two dollars in foreign change, for example, could buy thirty oral rehydration packets (a life-saving mixture of salt and sugar that prevents death from dehydration), or twenty-five immunization needles, or enough high-dose vitamin A to protect thirty toddlers from blindness caused by vitamin A deficiency for one year. If you've never received an envelope on a flight and want to contribute, you may send your coins (and low-denomination bills) directly to Travelex America, Attention: Jessica Lynch, Change for Good for UNICEF, JFK Airport, Terminal 4 IAT, Jamaica, New York 11430. For more information, view the UNICEF website at www.unicefusa.org or contact UNICEF at 333 East 38th Street, New York, New York 10016, 800-FOR-KIDS.

Cooking Schools

The best single source for cooking schools in Italy—and the entire world—is the *Shaw Guide to Cooking Schools: Cooking Schools, Courses, Vacations, Apprenticeships, and Wine Instruction Throughout the World* (ShawGuides, New York). Established programs that may be familiar to cooking enthusiasts are listed, as well as lesser-known classes, and interested food lovers can also view updates to the guide at its website: www.shawguides.com. ~Another good source for classes is The International Kitchen (1209 North Astor, no. 11-N, Chicago, Illinois 60610; 800-945-8606; fax: 847-295-0945; www.intl-kitchen.com). Founded by Karen Herbst in 1994, The International Kitchen specializes in more than forty unique cooking trips to Italy and France. Herbst personally handpicks the chefs, locations, and excursions and works to ensure that every experience is professional and rewarding. Three great trips to northeastern Italy include "Dining in the Secret Gardens of Venice" (a five-day trip, based at the Hotel Cipriani, that includes visits to private gardens in Venice, cooking lessons and demonstrations, wine, cheese, and olive oil tastings, tours of the Veneto and its vineyards, a private tour of the Peggy Guggenheim Museum, and a gala "Arrivederci" banquet at the Cipriani); "Spa and Cooking in the Veneto" (a luxurious six-night trip, based at Abano Terme—the leading spa resort in Europe, twenty-five miles from Venice—that includes spa treatments, cooking lessons, gourmet meals, and excursions to Verona, Lake Garda, Bassano, and Venice); "Veneto Cusine at Villa Luppis" (a five-day trip, based at one of my most favorite places in the world—the wonderful Villa Luppis in Fruili–Venezia Guilia—that is mostly a series of cooking lessons with the chef at Villa Luppis, with wine tastings and excursions to Villa Giustinian, Treviso or Asolo, Venice, and the Palladian and Venetian villas along the Brenta River). ~Epiculinary (321 East Washington Avenue, Lake Bluff, Illinois 60044; 888-380-9010 or 847-295-5363; fax: 847-295-5371; www.Epiculinary.com) offers twenty "distinctive cooking journeys" in Italy, France, and Spain and was founded by Catherine Merrill, a former travel agent specializing in European and culinary vacations. Its two northeastern Italy trips include "Vero Veneto" (a five-night trip with accommodations at the Villa Luppis—my favorite, as noted above—and including cooking lessons with chef Antonino Sanna and visits to a Palladian villa, Asolo, Sacile, a prosciutto factory, and the Collio wine-growing district of Friuli–Venezia Giulia) and "Venice by Sailboat" (a four-day trip around the Venetian Lagoon via the *Eolo*—the last boat still in navigation belonging to the category called *bragosso*—with visits to Chioggia, Sant' Erasmo island, and Torcello; and a cooking lesson with Fulvia Sesani). ~L'École des Chefs Relais Gourmands (11 East 44th Street, Suite 707, New York, New York 10017; e-mail for brochure requests: info@ecoledeschefs.com; 800-877-6464; www.ecoledeschefs.com) is perhaps the most appealing program I've ever heard about. I first profiled L'École des

Chefs in my *Paris* book; readers may recall that this unique program—which is not a traditional cooking school but an opportunity to work in restaurant kitchens—was founded by Annie Jacquet-Bentley, a Parisian now living in the United States. She created the program after she spent time studying with some French chefs and wanted to make the experience available to others. In the spring of 2001, however, the prestigious Relais & Châteaux hotel group acquired L'École des Chefs, broadening the program to include nearly one hundred Relais Gourmand restaurants in seventeen countries. Classes are mostly in two- and three-star Michelin restaurants, and although they're for nonprofessionals, applications receive an extremely thorough review. A *stage* (stage, or length) is either for two days or for five days, and apprentices may be asked to work for up to twelve hours at a time. As I write this, there are no L'École des Chefs restaurants in northeastern Italy; but this is sure to change, and in the meantime, I encourage interested would-be chefs to consider applying for a position at two participating restaurants near Mantua, just over the Veneto border in Lombardy: Ristoranti Ambasciata (a Michelin two-star in Quistello, just outside Mantua) and Restaurant dal Pescatore (a Michelin three-star, also just outside of Mantua). To read about some first-hand L'École experiences, see "The College of Hard Cheese: Blood, Sweat and Tuna" (Andy Birsh, *Forbes FYI*, November 2001), "How Great Paris Restaurants Do It" (*Saveur* no. 35, 1999), and "Gourmet Adventurism" (*Paris Notes*, March 1999). Additionally, L'École was recommended first on a list of holiday gift ideas in the December 2001 issue of *Bon Appétit*. Personally, I think it is a gift idea *per eccellenza*, and I wish some thoughtful person would give it to me! L'École des Chefs courses are priced from about $1,100 to $1,400 for two days and about $1,900 to $2,600 for five days. ~Finally, an unusual class I found by browsing www.initaly.com is "Painting and Cooking in Venice," which is a full-day program of watercolor painting and cooking with an American woman named Celia, who has lived in Venice for over twenty-five years. A typical day begins at nine o'clock at the Rialto market, where participants select items for the evening meal; but first Celia takes the group (of no more than six people) to a quiet corner where you paint a still life of your culinary purchases. In the evening, guests gather at Celia's apartment for a hands-on cooking lesson and meal. Celia also offers a morning hands-on cooking lesson followed by lunch. Contact her at www.initaly.com/ads/celia/celia2.htm.

Customs

There seems to be a lot of confusion over which items can and positively cannot be brought into the United States—on the part not only of travelers but of customs agents too. The rules, apparently, are not as confusing as they might seem, but sometimes neither customs staff nor travelers are up to date on what they are. Some examples of what's legal and what's not: olive oil yes, but olives no (unless they're vacuum-packed); fruit jams and preserves yes, but fresh fruit no; hard cheeses yes, but soft, runny cheeses no; commercially canned meat yes (if the inspector can determine that the meat was cooked in the can after it was sealed), but fresh and dried meats and meat products no; nuts yes, but chestnuts and acorns no; coffee yes, but roasted beans only; dried spices yes, but not curry leaves; fresh and dried flowers yes, but not eucalyptus or any variety with roots. If you think all this is unnecessary bother, remember that it was quite likely a tourist who carried in the wormy fruit that brought the Mediterranean fruit fly to California in 1979. Fighting this pest cost more than $100 million. For more details, call the U.S. Department of Agriculture's Animal and Plant Health Inspection Service at 301-734-8645 or view its website: www.aphis.usda.gov (click on "Travelers' Tips").

D

Doge

Doge is pronounced DOE-jay. H. V. Morton, in *A Traveller in Italy,* noted that when Napoleon ended the Venetian Republic in 1797, "there had been a hundred and twenty Doges in direct and unbroken succession from Polo Lucio Anafesto, who was elected in 697. The Popes and the Doges were the two most ancient dignitaries in the world." Perhaps, unlike me, you are one of those incredibly gifted people who has memorized the British royal line of succession. I like to think I have a good memory, but I don't think it crucial to memorize all the Venetian doges. I do think, like J. G. Links, that it is important to know a few, namely the first doge (Paoluccio Anafesto, 697–717); the most wicked doge (Enrico Dandolo, 1192–1205); the unluckiest doge (Marin Faliero, 1354–55, who "failed to understand what was expected of him. He tried to exercise some power, was charged with conspiracy against the state and lost his head. . . . In place of his portrait in the great Council Chamber, where all the Doges may be seen, there was put a black square. It is still there."); and the last doge (Ludovico Manin, 1789–97).

Dov'è

Dov'è is a good "D" word to know, meaning "Where is?" and pronounced DOE-vay. Even if you don't know how to pronounce what follows it, you'll at least establish that you are looking for something, and someone will be able to point you in the right direction.

E

Eating In, Eating Out, and Taking Away

"The Subject Is Eating" is the title of an essay in Kate Simon's *Italy: The Places In Between.* The essay is an excellent summation of eating Italian-style, and I think it's also an excellent beginning to this entry:

In the portfolio of misconceptions carried on a first voyage there is often a vision of Italian food that is a simplified reduction to pasta and veal drowned in tomato sauce which would taste of iron filings, if it weren't heavily laced with garlic. Garlic in tomato sauce is, however, not the national elixir; north of Naples you will find it in comparatively few dishes or unobtrusively wafted through a more complex sauce. Unlike the bread you are served at Luigi's or Joe's around the corner, Italian bread—from a crusty, huge country loaf through half-empty rolls, to wheels and deformed little planes that have the brittle consistency of pretzels—frequently lacks salt. It is taken for granted that the drippings one wipes up will supply the missing flavor.

An Italian's concept of hot and cold differs considerably from yours; his palate abhors intense heat and cold. If you want your soup hot, ask for it *caldo, caldo,* and if you want your coffee cold (*caffè freddo,* black and sweet), have the barman give you a piece of *ghiaccio,* ice. Outside the major cities, it is a struggle without rewards; near-warm and near-cold are the best you will be able to achieve. Accommodating as he would like to be, it is difficult for an Italian to understand the masochism of searing or freezing one's tongue and taste buds, or exchanging temperature for flavor. Thus fruit, bred for intensification of flavor, not looks, is allowed to perfume your table at room temperature. It may, in the country, still be wrapped in spider webs, still inhabited by a patron spider (all taken care of by a bowl of water served with the fruit), but it never arrives as pretty little corpses done in by white chill.

An Italian bar, in our sense of alcoholic succor, is not. Although it often adorns itself with salable bottles of whisky and liqueurs, its purpose is to nourish sagging spirits bored with the day's work, aching to know the latest soccer news, incapable of lasting the long hours before the midday meal. The bar is first-aid station for these and other ills, dispatching visiting nurses in the guise of solemn, long-aproned boys with trays to those mired in one of life's unspeakable tricks, like jobs and weather. The black, condensed coffee it serves is taken in the twinkling of an eye, the speed of an injection. For slower ingestion—but always fast the barmen steam out of their glistening machines the white-foamed cappuccino (named for the garb of Capuchin monks) and caffe-latte, coffee and nonagitated milk. Bars heap, depending on location and degree of style, open sandwiches, thin sandwiches on white bread, pizza dough and rolls in fetching, unusual combinations—cold fried egg and tomato, flattened artichoke hearts and bits of chicken, most of it bordered in baroque curlicues of mayonnaise. Less sturdy early-morning tastes are fed sweet rolls closely related to the French classics, brioche and croissant. The method of paying for these goodies may seem complex but in actuality makes for speed and efficiency. In large bars on main streets, price markers appear with each category of sandwich or cake. You make your tentative choice, tell the cashier the price, and how much with coffee? She gives you a slip, after payment is made, to be presented to the men at the counters. In smaller places, habitués pick up their selections with tongs, place them daintily in small paper napkins (it is very crude to eat out of the naked hand) and then approach the cashier.

The late-afternoon transfusion for men is an apéritif, usually bitter, herbal and undoubtedly salubrious. The ladies content themselves with coffee and cakes in the wintertime, awaiting patiently the bounty of warmer seasons: *frullato di frutta,* a nectar derived of fruits mingled and mashed in a blender; *granita di limone,* lemon ice; *granita di caffè,* coarse coffee ice heaped with whipped cream unless one is quick to say, *"senza panna."* Or *la signora* may decide to refresh herself with ice cream *(gelato),* never more than a few feet away and portable in a cone with no loss of dignity.

The *tavola calda* (hot table, literally) is an amorphous institution of variations on the cafeteria theme. One selects from a repertoire of basics, then takes the dish to a counter and stool and eats it quickly; a *tavola calda* is designed for inexpensive, fast turnover rather than conviviality. Solitaries often eat in *tavole calde* because of their impersonality and the speed of order, ingestion and departure that takes the sting off eating alone, a sad thing anywhere and tragic in Italy. A *tavola calda* can be its own entity or part of a large café that sets aside one corner for the chairs and table, to which waiters bring one's selection, or they can be attached to delicatessens. These latter provide a wide range of cold meats, stuffed tomatoes and peppers, a few fried items for reheating and, always, pasta out of a ceaselessly boiling caldron. It would be unjust to expect too much of these places; a split personality rarely functions well. However, there is often the pleasant surprise and, always, the undemanding price.

For cheap, voracious feeding look out for signs on rural roads that hail a *sagra*—a country food fair of nuts, fruits, pork, pasta, sausage, bread; anything in season and abundance. The supply will necessarily be monotonous but ringed with country jollity and, besides, you may find regional specialties that rarely appear on menus.

Should you begin to feel immoral and hear your seams groaning, it will be comforting to know that most pasta can be ordered in half portions *(una mezza porzione di . . .)*. Soups are generally full-bodied, or you can substitute for soup or pasta, particularly in rural restaurants and trattorie in big cities, a delicacy called *bruschetta,* thick-sliced country bread toasted on an open fire, rubbed with garlic and doused with oil. Other possibilities are *porcini,* enormous, rich mushrooms that appear in late summer and fall or, in the spring and early summer, an artichoke omelet. A variation on pizza is calzone, pizza dough folded over melted cheese and ham.

One menu per table, whether that table is set for one or four, seems to be a strict rule. It is not impossible, though difficult, to get another. Insist. Be an ugly American.

Many of the lovely words that purl out of Italian mouths, you will notice, deal with eating: *"Ha mangiato bene?"* *"Sì mangia bene."* *"Che mangiamo oggi?"* *"Dové mangiamo?"* All are invitations to long, animated discussions. Should you be on an Italian excursion bus that takes off at, let us say, 8:00 A.M., the exchange of greetings and autobiography will last until about 9:00, to be followed—first from one quarter, then another and soon burbling through the bus—by requests for a coffee stop, which will include a nibble of cake or a small sandwich. At 10:30 paper parcels will unfold and chunks of bread, slices of prosciutto and medicine bottles full of wine come into action. From that time on, until the lunch stop at 1:30, lascivious fantasies are exchanged about delicious possibilities: pasta, chicken or veal, salad, fruit and wine, always familiar, always a promise of pleasure.

The lack of interest in diversity, in new dishes (cookbooks are for foreigners to take home), the deep contentment with the accustomed, bespeaks an attitude toward a meal that makes of it a daily *festa*—like other *feste,* eagerly anticipated and tradition bound—whose opening ceremony is placing the slithering heap of gleaming pasta on the alta-table. Italian *joie* and conversation, the gurgle of wine out of carafes, the waiters who swoop, dance and murmur under their offerings are seductive ornaments that deny monotony, as paper hoops and garlands of electric bulbs deny the poverty of a *festa* street. As soon as a restaurant menu becomes "international," no matter how good, the ebullient life seeps away, a hush settles. Unpretentious, friendly wines are discussed too lengthily, the ingredients of a dish described too respectfully, the waiters are no longer brothers or fathers; one is dining in an imitation of the French manner, cut off from the ruddy, noisy zest of eating in Italian.

The pace of an authentically Italian meal is distinctly musical. The first movement, the pasta or soup, is a *presto agitato,* fast and eager. The meat is cut, lifted and chewed in a calmer *allegro,* while the fruit introduces a stately *adagio* of slow, careful selection, aristocratic discarding, exquisite peeling with knife and fork, the deliberate, slow jaws returned to serenity. We have now reached the interminable *lento.* Although your bread, wine and first course were brought with the speed that accompanies emergencies—a hungry man is a man in serious trouble—the waiter, having fed you, turns to more urgent matters, rather like the physician who no longer finds you interesting after the acute ailment disappears. It may be that, like other Schweitzers, he scorns thanks and money. Whatever, getting your check will take time and more time. And no one but your wife and the Americans at the next table will understand your impatience. Why should you be annoyed when you've been so quickly and fully fed while others, *poveretti,* are tearing their bread in agony?

One learns, in time, to sit out the waiter's evaluation of the state of his patients and begins to realize that the passion for Italian food is less a need for veal in six styles or chicken in three than a yearning for Italianness. So, even if your diet forbids you *penne, agnellotti,* fettuccine and spaghetti with a hundred names, you will eat pasta because you see it eaten with a total joy, a concentration of pleasure, as if it were a rare Lucullan dish rather than the habitual staple served at least once a day. You will plunge and wallow in the manipulating, slurping, moistly shining, sexy happiness, not so much to eat as to share the buoyant Italian greed for experiencing deeply, everything, from roaring in a winner at the races to the wash of peach juice in the mouth.

Like other European countries, Italy offers a variety of eating and drinking establishments to residents and visitors. Though there is sometimes a fine line between what distinguishes a restaurant from a *trattoria,* for example, it's important to recognize the differences and know what you should—or should not—expect from each place. What follows is a list of all the kinds of establishments you may encounter, a few of which are unique to Venice or to Friuli–Venezia Guilia:

bacaro: unique to Venice, a *bacaro* (pronounced BA-car-oh, plural: *bacari*) is, to me, not much different from an *enoteca* (see below), and in fact I'm not at all certain I could point to one and definitively say it was a *bacaro* and not an *enoteca.* Saying a *bacaro* is a neighborhood wine bar is not incorrect, it's just that it isn't always only that. (But perhaps it is enough to know that if you want a glass of wine—or bottled water or a choice of other libations—you'll find it at a *bacaro.*) This entry introduces readers to two other distinctly Venetian words: a glass of wine is referred to as an *ombra* (meaning "shade," derived from the days when wine vendors set up their carts in Piazza San Marco; as the day went by, the vendors moved their carts to keep the wine out of the sun by following the shadow of the Campanile), and the snacks and little nibbles one eats at a *bacaro* are known as *cicheti* or *cicchetti* (pronounced chee-KET-ee). Venetians go *bacaro* hopping the way Americans go bar hopping.

bar: as in other European countries, a bar serves coffee, tea, and soft drinks as well as alcoholic drinks and some food, such as *panini* (sandwiches) or *cornetti* (breakfast rolls in the shape of a croissant, plain or with filling). Bars are neighborhood places where patrons typically consume their food and drink standing at the bar; they do not always have tables.

bottiglieria: before wine bars became fashionable, a *bottiglieria* (pronounced bow-TEEL-ee-yeh-REE-ah) was where one went to drink wine and eat a light meal. The word translates as "bottle shop," which is why nowadays you see so many bottles of wine, which is drunk by the carafe or glass. Don't count on finding much to eat at a *bottiglieria,* which is also known as a *fiaschetteria* or *cantina.*

caffè: similar to a bar in terms of its offerings, but a *caffè* always has both counter and table service.

enoteca: a wine bar, found in urban settings in Italy, that serves wine both by the glass and by the bottle, along with a small selection of bite-size things to eat—like olives, nuts, and sliced ham and cheese—or small plates of food, like *insalata caprese,* roasted fennel, or omelets. An *enoteca* is also defined as a "wine library or collection" and can therefore be used to describe a wine store or a wine bar—where one would go to look at a range of bottles—or even a *trattoria* that has a strong emphasis on the wine list. As with a *bacaro,* the distinction is blurred, as some wine shops offer wine tastings and some wine bars sell bottles of wine.

frasca: unique to Friuli–Venezia Giulia, a *frasca* (plural *frasche*) actually translates as "branch," from an old tradition of hanging or displaying a branch in the front of a property or over a doorway to indicate that new wine was available to sell. *Frasca* also referred to a small farm or wine property that served a copious meal with the new wine to paying guests, outdoors. "Dining al *frasca*" thus became a phrase in Friuli–Venezia Giulia, and there are a number of *frasche* that visitors can frequent today. Some have evolved into *agriturismo* properties, and all serve food local to the region, much of it grown on the property. A great article, and one of the very few, on the *fraschi* of Friuli is "Italian Farmhouse Feasts" by Eugenia Bone with photographs by Paolo Destefanis (*Saveur,* no. 35).

gelateria: shop or street-side cart selling *gelato* (ice cream).

locanda: an inn in the countryside with a casual restaurant serving regional food and wine. The dining room is often set with long communal tables where eating is family style.

osteria: according to Italian food writer Maureen Fant, the words *osteria* and *hostaria* are both "virtually meaningless" in Italian, as nowadays they are simply another way to say restaurant. She notes that "etymologically, this is any place with an *oste,* host, meaning landlord, innkeeper, publican, or the like. Traditionally, this was the place where the neighborhood men would gather for conversation, card games, and wine poured into carafes from a barrel. Food was of secondary importance; often the customers brought their own (this is the origin of the 'bread and cover' charge still in use today)."

paninoteca: panino is the word for "sandwich," *panini* is its plural form, and so a *paninoteca* serves . . . sandwiches.

pasticceria: a pastry and cookie shop.

pizzeria: while it may seem unnecessary to translate this word, readers may not know that a *pizzeria* is a restaurant, serving made-to-order pizza, and is open only in the evening. A *pizza al taglio* is a more casual storefront operation where pizza is sold in slices (or squares, usually) by weight and is open from midmorning to midafternoon.

ristorante: a restaurant, which can be quite casual or top-of-the-line formal and can specialize in local food or Italian food from any region of the country.

rosticceria: specializing in roasted chicken and meat, a *rosticceria* (pronounced roast-ee-chair-EE-ah) is essentially a deli, but many of them have tables and chairs.

tavola calda: the words mean "steam table," and in these establishments, just as in the States, one can take the food away or eat it at a table cafeteria-style.

trattoria: pronounced tra-tor-EE-ah, this is almost always an informal restaurant, often family run, offering what we in America might refer to as comfort food, the kind of food that is fairly time-consuming to prepare and therefore not many people make it at home anymore. Beware, however, that a *trattoria* can also be a rather expensive, trendy place and may or may not have a kitchen staff with an adequate foundation in classic Italian cooking. Note that a *trattoria-pizzeria* indicates that the establishment is a *trattoria* that also serves pizza.

~As in other European countries, the price you pay for food and drink is different depending on where you sit. You'll notice that Italians mostly stand at the bar, especially in the morning when they down little cups of espresso. If you sit at a table, you can expect to pay up to twice as much (although you can also expect to remain in your seat for as long as you like). In many bars and *caffès*, it's customary to pay the cashier first and then take your *scontrino* (receipt) to the counter, where you usually repeat your order. It is also customary to give a tip of 100 or 200 lire to the person who hands you your food or drink.

~Don't let the words *menu turistico* necessarily turn you away from a potentially great meal. Just like the *menu del dia* in Spain or the *prix fixe* meal in France, the *menu turistico* in Italy is often a good value and nearly always includes a carafe or half bottle of wine.

~Mealtimes in this corner of Italy follow a northern Italian rhythm, not a southern one. Breakfast, such as it is (usually a quick cup of espresso and a *cornetto,* the Italian version of a croissant, with or without a filling), is served early, from about 6:30 or 7:00, and though you can obviously order coffee and tea drinks all morning, the pastries usually don't last past 9:00. Lunch is served beginning at 12:00 or 12:30 but is positively over by 2:00. You may, on occasion, be able to talk your way into a place after 2:00, but don't count on everything on the menu being available, especially the day's specials. Dinner is served beginning at around 7:30, although this is generally a bit early for locals.

~Some good words of advice from *Cheap Eats in Italy* by Sandra Gustafson: "Italians believe that God keeps an Italian kitchen, and so everyone should enjoy *la cucina italiana.* . . . Dealing with Italian waiters is similar to crossing Italian streets: you can do it if you are brazen enough, showing skill and courage and looking all the time as though you own the place. A good waiter should explain the dishes on the menu and help you select the wine. But if you order coffee or tea during the meal, ask for the ketchup bottle, or request a doggie bag . . . watch out, you will be in big trouble."

~As Kate Simon has noted, meals in Italy are a procession of dishes. Keep in mind that unlike in America, where many of us are used to the "meat and two veg" concept (you know, where you receive a meat selection with two vegetables on the side, all on the same plate), individual courses are served separately in Italy. It is expected that you will order an antipasto, followed by a pasta, a choice of meat, chicken, or fish, and a *contorno* (vegetables). The *contorno* may arrive at the same time as your meat, or it may arrive before or after, but either way it will be served on a separate plate. It is acceptable, however, to simply order an antipasto and a pasta, or perhaps pasta, a *contorno*, and a glass of wine, or pasta and a meat dish; but salad is most often served at the end of the meal, so if you try to order pasta and a salad *at the same time*, for example, do not be surprised to receive a quizzical look from the waiter.

~Useful vocabulary: *Vorrei un tavolo, per favore/piacere* ("I want to reserve a table, please"); *vorrei un tavolo, per favore, dentro* ("I'd like a table, please, inside"; as opposed to "outside," which is *fuori*, or "on the patio," which is *sulla veranda*); *potrei vedere il menu?* ("may I see the menu?"); *primo/i* ("first course," singular and plural); *secondo/i* ("main course," singular and plural); *contorno/i* ("vegetable or salad side dish," singular and plural); *dolce/i* (dessert); *vorrei un bicchiere di vino rosso/bianco/rosato, per favore* ("please bring me a glass of wine, red/white/rosé"); *quali sono gli ingredienti in questo piatto?* ("what's in this dish?"; this question is useful if you are allergic to certain things, but obviously, if you won't be able to understand the reply, you might want to select something more straightforward); *cosa mi consiglia?* ("what do you recommend?", the waiter's favorite question, which you could ask if you eat everything); *il conto, per favore* ("the check, please"); *e incluso il servizio?* ("is service included?"); *errore* (a mistake); *una mancia* (tip); *zona per non fumatori* ("no smoking area," although don't expect there to be one, or for it to be enforced); *mi porta un portacenere, per favore* ("please bring me an ashtray," something smokers will probably never have to ask for, as they are always around; *portacenere* is pronounced porta-chay-NARE-ay); *freddo/a* ("cold"); *caldo/a* (hot); *troppo cotto* (overcooked); *non e fresco* ("this is not fresh"); *acqua minerale* ("mineral water," which will sometimes automatically be brought to your table; note that it isn't free, so if you don't want it, ask for *acqua di rubinetto*—tap water); *non ho ordinato questo* ("this is not what I ordered"); *il rapporto qualita/prezzo* (good value, what the French call *qualité-prix*); and *da porta via* means you'll be taking food away, as when you're ordering a *panino* (sandwich) from an *alimentare* (combination store/deli, also known as a *salsamentario* or *salumeria*). Often an *alimentare* is located next door to a *fornaio* (bakery), so you can count on the bread being good and fresh. Order the filling for your sandwich in two ways: either by the *fette* (number of slices) or by the *etto* (weight, an *etto* being about four ounces). Finally, to show your appreciation for a fine meal, you can say *grazie, era delizioso/eccellente/squisito* ("thank you, it was delicious/excellent/exquisite"), or if you have had the great good fortune to be a guest in someone's home, you could say *molte grazie per il pasto* ("many thanks for the meal").

Elderly Travel

The two best-known organizations for elderly travelers are Elderhostel (11 Avenue de LaFayette, Boston, Massachusetts 02111; 877-426-8056; fax: -2166; www. Elderhostel.com) and Interhostel (University of New Hampshire, 6 Garrison Avenue, Durham, New Hampshire 03824; 800-733-9753; fax: 603-862-1113; www.learn.unh.edu/interhostel). I've listed them here instead of under Tours because I wanted them to stand apart from the more general travel companies.

Euro

See Money entry.

F

Film

I'm aware that the FAA maintains that sending film less than 1000-speed through an X-ray scanner won't harm picture developing; but my friend Peggy, a freelance photographer, maintains that multiple trips through the scanner will indeed harm the film. Avoid packing your film in checked bags—the scanners that inspect them are stronger than those for carry-on bags.

~I always keep rolls of film—no matter what speed—accessible and hand them to the security inspectors before I walk through the scanner. (Remember to retrieve them after you pass, however!) ~If you take a lot of photos, you might want to buy some lead-lined pouches from a camera store. They're inexpensive and will even protect film in checked bags. ~Professional film (which is very sensitive and must be kept refrigerated until used and developed a day later) aside, a general guideline for us amateurs is that the higher the film speed, the faster the film—and fast film requires less light. So think about the situations in which you anticipate taking pictures and select film accordingly. ~I happen to be very fond of black and white photos, so I always include a roll or two in my bag.

Fogolar

Fogolar is a word unique to Friuli–Venezia Giulia, referring to a raised hearth, typically in the center of a room called the *chase* (CA-say), which means "home." Note its similarity to the word *focolare,* meaning "fireplace" or "hearth."

Fondaco

A *fondaco* (plural: *fondachi* or *fondaci*) is another typically Venetian word that refers to a building whose ground floor is devoted to a warehouse. The concept originated with the numerous communities of foreigners *(foresti)* who have lived in Venice, mostly for trade and commerce. *Fondachi* were typically located on a canal, and the two most famous were on the Grand Canal: Fondaco dei Turchi (representing the Turkish community and now a museum) and the Fondaco dei Tedeschi (representing the German community and now a major post office).

Frequent Flier Miles

From what I've read, it seems the airlines wish they'd never created mileage-award programs. The year 2001 marked the twentieth anniversary of the frequent flier program, which was initially introduced by American Airlines. Fewer and fewer seats are now reserved for frequent fliers, and you need even more miles to earn these seats. You can also earn more miles—by *not* flying—than ever before. (According to an annual feature report in *Consumer Reports Travel Letter* in September 2001, at least 40 percent of frequent flier miles are earned by means other than flying.) Call me a *pessimista,* but I believe that there is no free lunch, and while it may seem appealing to sign up for a new credit card, buy a cell phone, buy quantities of a particular product, or shop at certain retail establishments to earn extra miles, I think that at the end of the day you are spending more money than it would cost you to purchase a discounted ticket through other means. Unless you are a true frequent flier—and let's face it, the frequent business or pleasure traveler is exactly who the mileage-award programs originally targeted—you can almost never spend enough money to make your efforts worthwhile. Even if you are spending money on goods or services that you would buy anyway, it is more than likely that just when you accrue the number of eligible miles to fly to Venice, the airline will increase its qualifying points, ensuring that a trip to Venice remains slightly out of your reach. To my mind, the miles aren't really worth having unless you accrue upward of 500,000 or 1,000,000, which entitles you not only to lots of destinations worldwide but also to business and first-class upgrades and VIP treatment. Should you happen to have enough miles and want to fly to Venice, plan to redeem those miles about six months ahead or plan to fly in the off-season. (It's also possible that airlines will reduce the miles needed for the off-season flight.) Don't immediately give up if your initial request can't be confirmed: apparently the airlines tinker with frequent flier seats every day as they monitor the demand for paying customers. If the number of paying travelers is low as the departure date approaches, more frequent flier awards may be honored. Apparently, seats for both paying passengers and frequent fliers become available 331 days in advance of a flight; but not every airline will allow you to reserve a seat that far in advance for especially popular routes. Venice is not as popular as Rome, for example, so technically you should be able to redeem your miles a year in advance without a snafu. ~Check to see if your accrued miles have expired before you try to redeem them. All airlines have expiration dates on frequent flier miles, but they don't all adhere to strict enforcement of those deadlines. ~If you're desperate for miles, you can always buy some through Miles4sale.com (8235 Douglas Avenue, Dallas, Texas 75225; 866-630-8717). In addition to purchasing airline miles and upgrades for yourself, you can also buy some as a gift. The last time I checked the website, the participating airline partners were American, Continental, Delta, and Northwest. I think this is probably a more expensive way of earning miles than buying goods or services, but that's why they call it desperation. ~Finally, try to reserve your valid mileage for expensive flights rather than for those that you can get for a good price anytime.

G

General Travel

Here are some good books to consult about trip planning in general: *The Travel Detective: How to Get the Best Service and the Best Deals from Airlines, Hotels, Cruise Ships, and Car Rental Agencies* (Peter Greenberg, Villard, 2001). As long as the title is, it could be even longer, as Greenberg covers—and uncovers—so much indispensable information on all aspects of travel. If I could have, I would have excerpted nearly every entry in Greenberg's book in my own. You want to read this book. It's remarkably interesting, and *essenziale*. *The New York Times Practical Traveler Handbook: An A–Z Guide to Getting There and Back* (Betsy Wade, Times Books, 1994) and *Wendy Perrin's Secrets Every Smart Traveler Should Know: Condé Nast Traveler's Consumer Travel Expert Tells All* (Fodor's Travel Publications, 1997). It may seem that these two books cover the same ground, but in fact there is very little overlap, and I refer to both of them all the time. Wade's book really is an A–Z guide, organized alphabetically, covering such topics as airline code sharing, customs, hotel tipping, closing up the house, and the wonderful WPA guides. Perrin's book is divided into eight sections plus an appendix; the anecdotes featured were all previously published in the "Ombudsman" column of *Condé Nast Traveler*. She covers the fine art of complaining; what to do if your luggage is damaged or pilfered; travel agents and tour operators; car rentals; shopping; cruises; and so on, as well as the ten commandments of trouble-free travel, which I think should be given to every traveler before he or she boards the plane.

~In a similar but different vein, I highly recommend *Traveler's Tool Kit: How to Travel Absolutely Anywhere!* (Rob Sangster, Menasha Ridge Press, Birmingham, Alabama, 1996). "Tool kit" really is the best description of this travel bible, which addresses *everything* having to do with planning, packing, and departing. Who is this book for? Everyone, really, or at least people who are curious about the rest of the world; people who are thinking about their very first foreign trip; budget travelers; business travelers; people who want to travel more independently; and people who know "that life offers more than a two-week vacation once a year." It's a *great* book, with lots of great ideas, tips, and advice. I've found Sangster's checklists at the back of the book particularly helpful, and his bibliography is the most extensive I've seen aside from my own.

Carlo Goldoni
World-famous playwright Carlo Goldoni (1707–93) was a native Venetian, and his plays are today still performed in the Venetian dialect. He was especially noted for satirizing the rich, and in the eighteenth century, when the commedia dell'arte was in decline, he borrowed its characters to create his comedies of manners.

Guidebooks
Choosing which guidebooks to use can be bewildering and frustrating. I have yet to find the perfect book that offers all the features I need and want, so I consult a variety of books, gleaning tips and advice from each. Then I buy a blank journal and fill it with notes from all these books (leaving some pages blank) and end up with the "perfect package" for me: the journal plus two or three guidebooks I determine to be indispensable. (I don't carry them around at the same time.) In the end, the right guidebook is the one that speaks to you. Place yourself in front of the Italy section of a bookstore, and take some time to read through the various guides. If you feel the author shares a certain sensibility with you, and you think his or her credentials are respectable, then you're probably holding the right book. Recommendations from friends and colleagues are fine only if they travel in the same way you do and seek the same qualities as you in a guidebook. Also, if you discover an older guide that appeals to you, don't immediately dismiss it. Background information doesn't change—use it in combination with an updated guide to create your own "perfect package." Keep in mind, too, that guidebooks within the same series are not always consistent, as they aren't always written by the same authors. What follows is a "Guide to the Guidebooks":

Baedeker's Venice (Baedeker Stuttgart; distributed in the United States by Fodor's Travel Publications). No book sums up the excitement and romance of travel to me like an old hardcover Baedeker guide. (If you're a nut for them like me, The Complete Traveller in New York always seems to have a good assortment— see Bookstores for address and phone.) The first Baedeker guide appeared in 1844, and the series has been the authoritative leader ever since. Current guides are still red, paperback, and less textbookish, with color photos and an easy-to-read format. The best feature of a Baedeker is the fold-out map. (In the old editions, it was glued to the back cover; in the updated guides, the map is completely separate from the book itself and is housed in a plastic sleeve at the back of the package.) The book is divided into three, color-coded sections: "Nature, Culture, History" (blue); "Sights from A to Z" (pink); and "Practical Information from A to Z" (yellow). In keeping with Baedeker tradition, sites are described in alphabetical order and are rated with one star (especially worth attention) or two (outstanding). A new feature of contemporary guides are "Baedeker Specials," essays on subjects such as "Festival of the Masks," "The Gondola—a Quaint Conveyance," "Cristallo, Aventurin and Millefiori," and "Venetian *bacari*—an *ombra* with a *cicheti.*" (In this last, the writers explain that the Venetians trace their name back to the Veneti, "a derivative of Eneti [from the Greek 'enos,' meaning wine], and therefore regard themselves as wine people par excellence. 'Bacari,' reminiscent of Bacchus, the god of wine, is the name given to the typical Venetian wine-bars serving vins ordinaires and simple 'cicheti,' tasty morsels made from local ingredients.") Filled with color photos, Baedeker's is, in my opinion, the easiest guidebook to use and the least cluttered, although still quite basic. *Essenziale* for the map, this is a better before-you-go read than a bring-along.

Blue Guide: Venice by Alta Macadam and *Blue Guide: Northern Italy—From the Alps to Bologna* by Paul Blanchard (A & C Black Publishers, London; distributed in the United States by W. W. Norton). Perhaps because it is so authoritative, like Baedeker, I always feel like I *have* to check in with the Blue Guide. In fact, the Blue Guide series has been around since 1918, and the original founders were the editors of Baedeker's English-language editions. Blue Guides are very straightforward and practical, with a no-nonsense approach that sets the series apart from so many others. Blue Guide editions are known for their comprehensive historical, architectural, and artistic material, and they do not disappoint. The *Venice* edition, which is very good, includes an atlas of fifteen maps at the back of the book. If one is not planning on leaving *La Serenissima,* this edition alone would be fine; but for those going a bit farther afield, I strongly recommend the *Northern Italy* guide in addition, even though it also includes northwestern Italy and Emilia-Romagna. There are separate sections on Trentino–Alto Adige, the Veneto, Lake Garda, and Friuli–Venezia Giulia. The author of this edition notes in his introduction, "Though the sinking of Venice is certainly the most dramatic environmental issue that Italy has faced in recent years, it is not the only one. As the country gradually takes stock of its California-like disposition towards earthquakes, landslides, drought and flooding, and of the aggravating factors brought by prosperity and development, Italians are beginning to realize that the proper attitude towards the land is one of care, not heedless exploitation. In a word, they are rediscovering nature. Especially in the northern regions, the proliferation of small, profitable industries that, in the not-so-distant past, had turned demographic patterns topsy-turvy (causing the country folk to move to the cities) and created an urgent demand for infrastructures (more roads!) has slowed, thanks largely to the information revolution. . . . This is good news for travellers like us. It translates as more good restaurants, charming hotels, tastefully renovated bed-and-breakfasts, music festivals, theatre festivals, film series, galleries, museums and exhibitions even in out-of-the-way places. And more hiking trails, cycling trails, back-country ski trails, parks and nature reserves. Today a new and more adventurous northern Italy awaits you." In both books there is an index of artists and a glossary of special terms. Highly recommended, but not necessarily as bring-alongs.

Cadogan: Northeast Italy (Dana Facaros and Michael Pauls, Cadogan Books, London; distributed in the United States by Globe Pequot Press, Old Saybrook, Connecticut). Cadogan (rhymes with *toboggan*) guides are almost all written by the Facaros-Pauls team (they've written more than twenty now), and I consider them to be of the bring-along variety. They're discriminating without being snooty, honest, witty, and interesting. The authors are not very easily impressed, so when they enthuse about something, I pay attention. I'm most especially fond of the "History" and "Topics" sections in the front of each book, which reveal how perceptive the authors are and introduce the reader to their style. There are lodging and dining recommendations for all budgets, and good commentary on sights both famous and little-known. The walking tours are good, and there are the usual maps, menu vocabulary, glossary, bibliography, and list of architectural, artistic and historical terms. This edition represents the new format for the Cadogan series, and the authors have credited a colleague, Mike Usiskin, with assisting in the task of updating. A twenty-eight-page color photo essay—in this edition by John Ferro Sims—is a new feature of Cadogan guides, and I find it a welcome addition. Definitely my favorite all-around guidebook, and most definitely *essenziale*.

Exploring Venice (Fodor's Travel Publications). The Exploring imprint is a line in the Fodor's family that complements the Gold Guides. Unlike the Gold Guides, each Exploring book is filled with color photographs (I could not find even five pages without a photo or illustration) and is printed on thick glossy paper. Maps are featured on the inside front and back covers, and there is a multipage atlas section at the very back of each book. One of my favorite features in Exploring guides is the suggestions for walks and drives; for this Venice edition, four walks are outlined: the Accademia to Piazza San Marco; a circular walk from the Rialto; San Marco to the Arsenale; and the Accademia to the Frari. I also like the "Venice Is" and "Venice Was" pages in the very front of the book, as well as some of the sidebars that appear throughout. An eighteen-page section on excursions outside Venice—to Padua, Verona, and Vicenza—is included. I wouldn't recommend this guide as a bring-along, but it's worth browsing before you go.

Eyewitness Travel Guide: Venice & The Veneto (DK [Dorling Kindersley] Publishing). Like the Knopf Guides, the Eyewitness series features bold graphics, cutaways and floor plans, full color photos, maps, and illustrations. Unlike Knopf Guides, Eyewitness Travel Guides feature lots of bird's-eye views of historic buildings and street-by-street maps, as well as a running timeline from prehistoric times to the present. I am crazy for the bird's-eye views and timelines, and I like the introductory section, "A Portrait of the Veneto," as well as the following one on historical themes, such as "Roman Veneto," "The Birth of Venice," "The Queen of the Adriatic," "Glorious Decadence," and so on. The Venice section is divided into sections for each neighborhood plus one for the Grand Canal and another for the lagoon islands. The "Venice Street Finder"—composed of eight pages of maps and a four-page street name index—is pretty helpful, but I wish it were separate from the book so you wouldn't have to also hold the somewhat heavy book while using it. The "Veneto" section has individual chapters on the Veneto plain (which includes Vicenza, Padua, Asolo, Treviso, Montagnana, and Portogruaro), Verona and Lake Garda, and the Dolomites. As with all Eyewitness Guides, the practical-information pages are found at the back of the book. Overall, I feel that Eyewitness guides are more visually appealing than substantive, and I do not think they are bring-alongs; but they are very much worth reading before you go, especially the introductory section of each book, and the practical-information pages at the back always seem to include some tip or another that is not in other guides.

Florence, Venice & the Towns of Italy (Robert Kahn, series editor, The Little Bookroom, 2001). This little (approximately 4 by 6 inches) volume is positively a must-have. I loved the first edition in the series—featuring Rome—so much, I could barely breathe until this one was published. Subtitled *Artists, Writers, Architects, Curators, Historians and Gourmets Reveal Their Favorite Discoveries in the Ultimate Insider's Guide,* it is truly one of a kind. The contributors are all members of the American Academy in Rome and/or Save Venice, and in addition to all their recommendations, the book contains an index of recommended reading, an index of contributors, and some lined pages for notes. A complaint I have is that only four pages are devoted to Friuli–Venezia Giulia, and for the entry on Udine, the contributor writes, "There's not much to see in Udine." Udine is an extremely interesting and pleasant town, and I suspect the contributor didn't stay long enough. I love what one contributor wrote about Piazza San Marco: "Pick up any guide to Venice and you are directed straight to the Piazza San Marco. The façade of the Basilica is described in hallowed terms, praise is heaped on the palazzo of the Doges, the campanile, the clock tower. Every author repeats Napoleon's description of the Piazza as the most elegant drawing room in Europe. *Feh!* How long since you had a really good time in a drawing room, the 18th century? It's the new millennium, and if you want a great experience, turn on your heels and head for the Campo Santa Margherita in the Dorsoduro district." *Essenziale.*

Fodor's Venice and the Veneto (Fodor's Travel Publications). I typically crave more information than Fodor's guides seek to provide, but I think the entire line of Fodor's guides just keeps getting better and better every year. I've noticed that whenever Fodor's introduces a new feature—such as color photos, a pull-out map, whatever—all the other guidebooks follow suit. I *always* read the appropriate Fodor's guide before I go, and I *always* discover a handful of useful tips. This Venice guide also includes Friuli–Venezia Giulia as well as the Dolomites, though the Friuli section is only twenty-three pages and Trentino–Alto Adige is covered in six and a half. I used this Gold Guide for the initial "Smart Travel Tips" section and the section immediately following it—"Destination: Venice and the Veneto"— with the essay entitled "The Most Glorious and Heavenly Show Upon the Water" and "What's Where," "Pleasures and Pastimes," and "Fodor's Choice," a roundup of choice restaurants, little-known corners of Venice, best Madonnas, hotels, and special memories.

Fodor's upCLOSE Italy (Fodor's Travel Publications). The upCLOSE series is aimed at travelers on limited budgets, but not necessarily the Let's Go crowd. The book offers lots of money-saving tips throughout, as well as information on rail passes, youth hostels, and studying in Italy, but it also provides a wealth of practical information for *all* types of travelers, not just students. The range of options for transportation, lodging, and dining is wide, there are numerous maps, and—my favorite feature—there are interesting "trivia boxes" all through the book, like "Radical Filibuster" (about the Council of Trent), "Courtly Gestures" (about the human chess game in Marostica in the Veneto), "Come Hell or High Water," and "Wine-Snob Etiquette." The historical background is too thin for my taste, but this series is particularly welcome because I believe this audience—intelligent travelers who want an authentic experience on a modest budget—accurately reflects the majority of people traveling today. There are individual chapters devoted to Venice and the Veneto, and the Dolomites and the Northeast (which includes Friuli–Venezia Giulia). Not recommended as a bring-along, but it's worth reading the introductory "Basics" section and the northeastern Italy chapters before you go.

The Heritage Guide: Venice (Touring Club of Italy). It was good news a few years ago when Abbeville Press began distributing these TCI guides in English. TCI maps are the equivalent of IGN maps in France and Ordnance Survey in England, so it's no surprise that this edition includes a twenty-five-page city atlas and nineteen walking tours indicated on individual neighborhood maps. In addition to Venice proper, the islands of Murano, Burano, Torcello, and the Lido are included, as well as the Riviera dell Brenta. Although I prefer even more historical information and more detailed practical information, the Heritage Guides provide better, more thorough details on noteworthy things to see and do than nearly any other guidebook. The opening chapters, "A City in the Sea of History" and "Instructions for Use," are particularly good. The gray pages at the back of the book make up a section of selected listings for hotels, restaurants, *bacari,* and places of interest, including shops, crafts, and fine art. Highly recommended as a bring-along.

Insight Guide: Venice (APA Publications, Singapore; distributed by Houghton Mifflin). I have been an enormous fan of the Insight Guides for years. When they first appeared, about twenty years ago, they were the only books to provide outstanding color photographs matched with perceptive text. The guiding philosophy of the series has been to provide genuine insight into the history, culture, institutions, and people of a particular place. The editors search for writers with a firm knowledge of each city or region who are also experts in their fields. I do not think that recent editions are quite as good as the older ones. The introduction (the best section, in my opinion, in *all* the books) is a series of magazine-style essays on architecture, food, markets, the people, history, the arts, and politics: "The Venetians," "Supreme Statesmen," "Heydey of the Venetian Republic," "Sunset on the Serene Society," "Artists of Color and Light," "The Casini," "Regattas and Water Festivals," and "La Fenice: The Fire and the Passion." Not necessary to bring along, but I make sure I copy some essays and passages by hand into my journal for reading when I'm there.

Italy: The Places In Between (Kate Simon, Harper & Row, 1970). Sadly, this wonderful, wonderful book is out of print, but it does occasionally turn up. If you ever run across a copy, buy it without hesitation. There are no more travel writers quite like Kate Simon, except perhaps Jan Morris and Barbara Grizzuti Harrison. A quote from the jacket reads, "How splendid is Kate Simon, the incomparable Kate Simon, whom no one has ever rivaled in the long, long history of guidebooks." Like her books on Paris, Mexico, and New York, this is an uncommon guidebook and indeed is like no other guidebook ever published. At the end of each chapter (there is, unfortunately, no separate one for Venice or anywhere else in northeastern Italy) is an essay, such as "The Subject Is Eating" (excerpted on pages 79–82), "Knowing the People and the Language," and so on. These essays are brilliant observations that make this book unique. Simon does not approach things to see and do in a predictable fashion, which I think encourages travelers to approach Italy in an unpredictable manner. This is a very special, inspiring book. *Essenziale.*

Italy's Finest (Bona dei Frescobaldi, Edizioni del Titano). Not exactly a guidebook, but something better: personal recommendations for everything from antiques, bread, ceramics, museums, hardware stores, caterers, flowers, cultural associations, fabrics, galleries, glassware, medical tests, household linens, laundries, shoes, veterinarians, toys, wine—nearly *everything,* and it's not just for tourists as the list attests (though special places of interest are listed for each region of Italy). This clothbound, eight-hundred-page-plus book is very special and is not available outside Italy. I first learned of it in an article about the Frescobaldi family in *Wine Spectator* a few years ago, and since then I have made sure to get a copy every year. Bona dei Frescobaldi is passionate about sharing "the best of one of the next millennium's great civilizations" (quoted from the 2000 guide), and she has a great many friends who are just as eager to compile "Italy's finest" in a single volume. It has individual sections on Trentino–Alto Adige, Friuli–Venezia Giulia, Venice and the Veneto. Each section begins with a map of the highlighted region followed by ABC listings, recommended hotels, restaurants, and wines, and a recipe unique to the city or region. It seems not enough copies are printed each year, because I have asked around, only to be told "finished" by bookstore staff in early summer. But if you visit Italy often, or simply want to be kept up to date on its *da non perdere* (not to be missed) attributes, this is a must-have. A number of bookstores in Venice carry the book regularly, as do a few in Trieste—I'm not certain about its availability elsewhere in the Northeast, but as the Frescobaldi family is Tuscan, the guide is perhaps most widely available in Florence bookshops. Make looking for it a priority once you land—this is a true insider's book, of interest to anyone spending more than a few days in Italy.

John Kent's Venice: A Color Guide to the City (text and drawings by John Kent, Chronicle Books, 1992; originally published in the U.K. in 1988). Though this slender, attractive paperback contains information about the history, cuisine, architecture, music, and monuments of Venice, its real value is for the thirty-nine-page chapter on the Grand Canal. Kent had the brilliant idea of illustrating the major palazzi and other buildings exactly in the order they appear along the Canal, from Ferrovia to Piazza San Marco, with one side of the Canal running along the top of the pages and the other running along the bottom. This allows the visitor to hold the book open while navigating the Canal—it doesn't matter at which end you begin, or even if you begin in the middle—and identify the buildings and learn a little about their significance. I personally recommend starting at one end of the route and finding an appropriate seat in front of a Number 1 *vaporetto*—by "appropriate," I mean if you're traversing the Canal from Ferrovia, choose a seat on the left side of the boat so that nothing will obstruct your view; vice versa if you're beginning at San Zaccaria or thereabouts. Truly it is one of the most enjoyable, and educational, means of traveling the length of the Canal imaginable, and for that reason this book is *essenziale*. In addition to this wonderful feature, there are atlases for both the left and right banks of the Canal—not for buildings directly on the Canal but those farther in each *sestiere*. Highly recommended.

Knopf CityMap Guide: Venice (Alfred A. Knopf, originally published in France by Nouveaux-Loisirs, a subsidiary of Gallimard, Paris). This series of map guides, whose motto is "Open, Unfold, Discover," debuted in the States just as I was planning a trip to Venice. So I wear-tested the Venice edition, so to speak, and I'm happy to report that it's not only great but indispensable. After my first day, I left all the other maps I'd brought back at the hotel. I got into the habit of spreading out the big maps that fold into a bewildering number of panels on my bed, so I could see everything and get the big picture when I needed to; but I didn't carry those behemoths around with me, and I sure wasn't going to open one up, say, on the Number 1 *vaporetto*. The concept behind CityMap Guides is that cities are broken down into neighborhoods. A fold-out map of each neighborhood is accompanied by a list of landmarks and cultural sites and some recommendations for places to eat, drink, and shop. As visitors to Venice quickly learn, getting lost is a concern. On the bigger maps, some of the street names are so small, you can't even decipher them. Thank God for this CityMap Guide. When you have to consult it, you'll look not like a helpless tourist but like a savvy visitor, perhaps even a resident. I can also confirm that a parent can hold the guide, while opened to a particular *sestiere,* in the same hand that grips the stroller.

Knopf Guide: Venice (Alfred A. Knopf, originally published in France by Nouveaux-Loisirs, a subsidiary of Gallimard, Paris). I'm fond of the Knopf Guides in general, and the Venice edition is no exception. I like the bold design, and I love the various sections in the front of the book ("Natural History," "The Battle of Lepanto," "The Bucintoro," "Mosaics," "Steering and Propelling a Gondola," "Sarde in Saor," "Venice as Seen by Painters," etc.). I also like the fold-out page for Piazza San Marco. The practical-information pages (the gray-colored section at the back of the book) are actually quite extensive and include two pages devoted to Venice for children and others for where to find works by Titian and music in Venice. Surprisingly, for such a *luxe* book, there are a number of listings for one-star hotels, plus youth hostels and student dormitories. The islands of the lagoon and Chioggia are included, but there is no section on travel farther inland in the Veneto. As visually appealing and chunky as Knopf Guides are, they are actually surprisingly short on in-depth information. I wouldn't use this Venice edition exclusively, but it's a great companion to a more substantial guidebook.

Let's Go: Italy (Let's Go, Inc., distributed by St. Martin's Press). "The World's Bestselling Budget Travel Series" is the Let's Go slogan, which is hardly debatable. Let's Go is still the bible, and if you haven't looked at a copy since your salad days, you might be surprised: now each edition contains color maps, advertisements, and an appendix that features a wealth of great practical information. A team of Harvard student interns still offers the same thorough coverage of places to eat and sleep and things to see and do, and true to Let's Go tradition, rock-bottom budget travelers can find suggestions for places to sleep under ten dollars a night (sometimes it's the roof), and travelers with more means can find clean, cozy, and sometimes downright fancy accommodations. The inside back cover of this Italy guide features important phrases, phone numbers, Italian symbols, a Celsius/Fahrenheit chart, and a ruler with inches and centimeters, providing a quick reference that's easy to read. This Italy edition is divided into different geographic sections, and the "Northeast Italy" section devotes a rather large portion to Venice. It also features four useful street maps with bus routes and plotted night spots, restaurants, and hotel accommodations. Areas of the Veneto, Friuli–Venezia Giulia, and Trentino–Alto Adige are also highlighted. Along with several detailed maps of Rome, there is a color map of Venice at the front of the book. Within each city in a given region, there is typically one detailed street map highlighting recommended accommodations, but these maps are quite small and are in black and white, so supplemental maps are likely necessary. I think the presentation of facts and history is quite substantive in Let's Go, and I would eagerly press a copy into the hands of anyone under a certain age (thirty-five?) bound for Italy.

Living, Studying, and Working in Italy: Everything You Need to Know to Fulfill Your Dreams of Living Abroad (Travis Neighbor and Monica Larner, Henry Holt, 1998). Just as the title indicates, here's the book you need to inspire and prepare you to go. The authors lived in Italy, separately and in different cities, for a combined total of more than ten years, and they wrote this book because they couldn't find one that addressed the practical side of living in Italy. Readers will find great information on looking for a job, including more than nine hundred addresses and Internet sites; freelance, seasonal, part- and full-time employment options, language schools, American colleges and Italian universities; tips on money and banking; and a great appendix with telephone and mail, times, measurements, and the like. It's obviously most useful for long-term visitors, but short-term visitors with a serious interest in Italy will be glad to have it as well.

Lonely Planet: Italy (Helen Gillman, Damien Simonis, and Stefano Cavedon, Lonely Planet, Sydney, Australia). Lonely Planet guides have been among my most favorite for many years. Tony and Maureen Wheeler founded the series in Australia in 1973 and originally focused solely on Asia; but about a dozen years ago they realized that the Lonely Planet approach to travel was not exclusive to any particular geographic area of the world. The series is aimed at independent travelers, and each book is organized into chapters such as "Facts for the Visitor" (covering everything from health issues and gay and lesbian travel to pickpockets and legal matters), "Getting Around," "Things to See & Do," "Places to Stay," "Places to Eat," and so on. I am fondest of the opening chapters, covering history, politics, ecology, religion, economy, and practical facts; the information on sites to see is not nearly detailed enough. I like that hotels and restaurants are presented from least expensive to most expensive, and I like the candid opinions of the contributing authors. As I have mentioned so often, I do not prefer books devoted to an entire country, but Lonely Planet does not yet have an edition for northeastern Italy. I like the series so very much that I didn't want to omit it from these listings, and I do think readers would benefit from taking a look at this all-Italy edition. The book features a section on Italian art and architecture with color photographs. A percentage of each book's income is donated to various causes such as Greenpeace's efforts to stop French nuclear testing in the Pacific, Amnesty International, and agricultural projects in Central America.

Michelin Green Guide: Venice. A Michelin guide might be more trustworthy than your best friend. Its famous star-rating system and "worth a detour" slogan may have become a bit too formulaic, but it's a formula that works. The series was created in 1900 by André Michelin, who compiled a little red book of hotels and restaurants. Today the Michelin Red Guide is renowned for the stars it awards to restaurants. The Green Guides, for tourists, first made their appearance in 1926; each is jam-packed with information and easy to pack. It will come as no surprise to readers that I prefer even more detail than Michelin offers, but I find it an excellent series, and each guide I've used has proven to be exceptionally helpful. This edition covers not only Venice proper but also the outlying islands of the lagoon and the villas of the Brenta (it goes no farther into the Veneto, however). I often sit on the fence when considering whether to take a Michelin guide along, and ultimately I pack it about half the time. I cannot conceive of not consulting the guide at all, but it is of most value to me in seeing how the various historical sites and museums are rated. On my most recent trip to Venice, I decided at the last minute to pack this edition, but I think what prompted me was that I have a slim, exterior zippered pouch on my Dakota bag that doesn't accommodate much else, so I figured, *perché no?* (why not?). But I admit I did not carry the book around with me most days, though I consulted it often in my hotel room. The decision is yours, and this edition is so lightweight it hardly matters if you bring it and never open it. Each Michelin guide is complemented by a Michelin map, of course. A new route-planner service—which I happen to think takes much of the joy out of trip planning—is available by visiting www.michelin-travel.com. Viewers type in start and finish points and are provided with a suggested route, travel time, distances, road numbers, and any tolls.

The Rough Guide to Venice and the Veneto (Jonathan Buckley, distributed in the United States by Penguin Books). When the Rough Guides first appeared, in the early 1980s, they had limited distribution in the United States. Then the guides were sort-of-but-not-quite the British equivalent of Let's Go. I sought them out because I found the British viewpoint refreshing and felt the writers imparted more knowledge about a place than was currently available in U.S. guidebooks. Series editor Mark Ellingham was inspired to create the Rough Guides series because at the time current guidebooks were all lacking in some way. They were strong on ruins and museums but short on bars, clubs, and inexpensive eating places, or they were so conscious of the need to save money that they lost sight of things of cultural and historical significance. None of the books mentioned anything about contemporary life, politics, culture, or the people and how they lived. Now, since the Rough Guides opened a New York office in the late 1990s, the series has evolved into one that is broader-based but still appealing to independent-minded travelers who appreciate the Rough Guides' honest assessments, and historical and political backgrounds. (These last are found in the "Contexts" section of each guide, and my only complaint is that this section should appear at the beginning of each book instead of at the end.) Like their cousin Let's Go, Rough Guides offer specifics on working and studying in Italy, gay and lesbian life, and hotels that are frequented both by the backpacking crowd and by those who carry luggage with their hands. Some of the features I particularly like about this Venice edition include the entire initial section, "The Basics" (which is incredibly thorough—the text boxes feature such subjects as "The Government of Venice," "Venetian Glass," and "Aldus Manutius"); and the more practical ones covering "Main Veneto Train Services," "Padua's Combined Tickets," and "Vicenza's Museum Passes"; and the numerous listings for accommodations and restaurants for each *sestiere*. Seven color maps are found at the back of the book—including one for the main water-bus services—and the "Contexts" section is, as always, excellent. Overall, each edition in the Rough Guides series is dependable and informative, and I highly recommend that this Venice edition be considered as a bring-along. Online updates to Rough Guides can be found at www.roughguides.com for those who feel this is essential.

Time Out City Guide: Venice (Penguin Books). Published by the same hip folks who brought London's *Time Out* magazine to New York, Time Out City Guides are compact (each book measures about 5" × 7"), well written, and jammed with information. The style and tone are similar to the Rough Guides and Lonely Planet, but the *Time Out* City Guides are "written and updated by resident experts who have striven to provide you with all the most up-to-date information you'll need to explore the city or read up on its background, whether you're a local or a first-time visitor." *Time Out*'s specialty, for those who've never seen the magazine, is listings, an exhaustive plethora of them, so this Venice edition is particularly good on contemporary art, film, the Biennale, gay and lesbian life, music and nightlife, late-opening bars, discos and clubs, performing arts, festivals, and sports and fitness. Some of the features I particularly like this guide for include the six-page feature on the Grand Canal; lists for top-five Tintorettos, don't-miss Titians, Ruskin recommends, and best beaches; the essays entitled "Venetian Green" and "A Galley in Just a Few Hours"; suggestions for lagoon picnics; and the initial "In Context" section, with nine feature boxes on a variety of themes. The guide also includes a few pages of good suggestions for entertaining children in Venice, twelve pages of color maps, and a section on the Veneto (plus a page on Aquileia but not Trieste or anywhere else in Friuli–Venezia Giulia). The Italian vocabulary section is particularly good, as in other *Time Out* City Guides: in addition to the usual useful stuff, you can learn words for a come-on—"what's your name?" *(come ti chiami?)*, "would you like a drink?" *(vuoi bere qualcosa?)*; a brush-off—"I'm married" *(sono sposato/a)*, "I'm going home" *(vado a casa)*; and an offensive brush-off—"idiot" *(stronzo)*, "what the hell are you doing?" *(che cazzo stai facendo?)*, and *merda* and *vaffanculo* (both of which I think you can figure out). Also, for those who need weekly updated information, *Time Out* guides can be accessed via the Internet: www.timeout.co.uk.

Louis Vuitton City Guide: European Cities VI: Rome, Florence, Milan, Venice (Louis Vuitton Malletier, Paris). As I noted in my *Provence* book, when I first learned of this Vuitton series, my initial reaction was *"non, grazie"* as I envisioned page after page of ritz and glitz, with the sort of snooty drivel that makes my skin crawl. But I think this series—now in its fourth year—is excellent and is not at all just for the Vuitton-toting crowd. The series is sold as a boxed set of slender paperbacks (volumes cannot be purchased separately) and is positively addictive. Each guide features a remarkably concise and accurate profile of each city, a page of practical information, and listings for hotels, restaurants, bars, cafés, tearooms, shopping (Louis Vuitton stores are, naturally, highlighted in a box), galleries, museums, nightlife, outings, and excursions). This edition, which devotes about forty pages to Venice and the lagoon islands, includes a boxed list of historical and must-see sights and, like the rest of the entries in the book, includes both predictable and off-the-beaten-path selections. (The shopping recommendations are particularly enlightening.) Even though it includes three other cities, this book is lightweight enough to bring along. If you know Venice and its history well, it might be the only book you'll need to bring along. If it's your first trip, it's a good companion to, say, *Venice for Pleasure* or *Strolling Through Venice*. The Vuitton books are available only at Louis Vuitton stores and boutiques nationwide and via the www.eluxury.com website. *Essenziale* or highly recommended, depending on what type of traveler you are and how well you know Venice.

Guides for Walking

Though books outlining walks are often lumped in with guidebooks, I wanted the books below to stand apart because they're *not* standard guidebooks, and they are so outstanding and excellent, I wanted the opportunity to extol their virtues in such a way that readers would be inspired to seek them out. *Strolling Through Venice: Walks Taking in the History, Monuments and Beauty of Venice* (John Freely, Penguin Books, 1994) and *Venice for Pleasure* (J. G. Links, Pallas Athene, London, 1998, sixth revised edition; first edition published in 1966) are two books that are *essenziale*. More than any book mentioned above, I recommend these two; I would positively not get off the plane, upon landing at Marco Polo Airport, if I discovered I had forgotten these. No, I take that back, because they are both sold in bookshops throughout Venice! I was unaware that Freely had written the first book until about five years ago, but I was already very familiar with his *Strolling Through Istanbul*—also indispensable—and so I already knew him to be a worthy companion, the kind one really cannot be without. As Freely writes in the introduction, this book is a "guide to the city and its lagoon, both as they were in times past and as they are today." In addition to individual chapters on the Piazza and Basilica of San Marco, there are chapters on each *sestiere* plus one on the islands of the lagoon. Within these Freely takes walkers to "every one of the 115 churches of Venice and its thirty-three museums, as well as identifying some three hundred of the city's *palazzi*." Freely is simply a guide *per eccelente*, so find this book at all costs.

You must also, of course, find J. G. Links's *Venice for Pleasure*, which I found in the *Common Reader* mail-order book catalog (see Bookstores entry for contact information). The first distinctive thing about this book is its shape: it's about five inches by seven, horizontally, and therefore really stands out if you're looking for a copy on a bookstore shelf. (Not enough bookstores stock this title, sadly, so you may not be searching *any* shelves for it.) I happily used two editions of this book before this final revised edition appeared, and it was in this final edition that I learned that Links had passed away in 1997, just shy of his ninety-third birthday. Tears rolled down my cheeks as I read some of the printed snippets from his obituary. Of these, what affected me most were the words of Sir Michael Levey, who defined Links as "someone infinitely kind, perceptive, generous and life-enhancing." It greatly saddens me that Links will no longer be able to add footnotes to his great work, but it does not need updating in the way that annual guidebooks do. This is decidedly not a guidebook in the usual sense; rather, as Links noted in his introduction, "it is a guide to the pleasures of Venice without its pains. Its simple object is to guide the reader to places he might otherwise miss and, having reached them, to tell him what he might wish to know and then leave him there to admire, to enjoy or, perhaps, to be disappointed." He is quick to add, however, that readers of his book "will probably not be disappointed in Venice. It is, on the whole, not a disappointing city, even to those with enviable powers of imagination." Links presents four walks in Venice, a city made for walking as "there is not a building in the city proper that cannot be reached on foot." In describing his readers, Links confidently asserts that they are "prepared to sacrifice the famous and illustrious for the little known and charming if there is not time for both." He is also describing himself, as can be seen in the following passage: "We must seriously consider going back to the Scuola S. Rocco when we are refreshed and examining its Tintorettos, which made it, in Ruskin's opinion, one of the three most precious buildings in the world—bracketed with the Sistine Chapel and the Campo Santo of Pisa. We may well be asked on our return what we thought of these Tintorettos and it would be unthinkable to visit Venice without seeing them. Never let it be said that I suggested such a thing. I only point out that the stairs are steep, the pictures, though wonderful, profuse and that they will still be there tomorrow, and, indeed, on our next visit to Venice." (In fairness, he does let us know that he is not an especial fan of the three Ts, Tiepolo, Tintoretto, and Titian, preferring Carpaccio and Bellini.) Links is also humorous and informative in the same paragraph: "On our left is 'the frightful façade of S. Moise,' as Ruskin described it, 'one of the basest examples of the basest school of the Renaissance,' and, while baseness is being considered, the façade of the Bauer Grunwald Hotel across the way may be worth a glance. We may wonder how Moses came to be canonized but my book of saints is silent on the subject. He is by no means the only Jewish saint with a church in Venice, though; he has Jeremiah, Job, Zaccariah and Samuel to keep him company." Parents should take special note that the "Venice for Children's Pleasure and the Delights of the Brenta" chapter is wonderful, with some good ideas (count well-heads and winged lions, hunt the bell-tower) and even use the illustrations in this book as part of a counting game. Links also shares some important advice, if you are setting out on a walk or to do anything: "Timing is important. Most churches close at midday, the big ones to open again at two-thirty or three, some not until four. Ask the concierge of your hotel who may well have to telephone the church for advice. If you start at nine in the morning, a good time to start, the walks will sort themselves out as far as timing is concerned." You must positively find this book, and Freely's, before you go to Venice, even if you have been there a hundred times before.

H

Health

Staying healthy while traveling in Italy should not be a challenge, but things do happen. I was once very sick with diarrhea in Florence after drinking water from the tap, so for years I never drank anything but bottled water—even to brush my teeth—in Italy (except in Rome, which has excellent and delicious water from wells). But on my last trip to northeastern Italy, I drank plenty of water from the tap with no ill effects. I do think, however, that water in the North is generally better than in the South. A good general reference book to consult is *The Rough Guide to Travel Health* (Dr. Nick Jones, Rough Guides, distributed by the Penguin Group, 2001). In addition to an A–Z listing of diseases and health risks, it provides good coverage on being prepared (including homeopathic suggestions) as well as summaries of potential health concerns region by region around the world. Travelers with special needs—asthma, diabetes, epilepsy, HIV, disability, pregnancy, and so on—are also addressed, and a very thorough directory with a wide range of resources is found at the back of the book. Another good overall book is *Travelers' Health: How to Stay Healthy All Over the World* (Richard Dawood, M.D. [former medical editor for *Condé Nast Traveler*], foreword by Paul Theroux, Random House, 1994). This thick, six-hundred-plus-page book isn't for bringing along, it's for consulting before you go. In addition to Dr. Dawood, sixty-seven other medical experts contributed to this volume, which covers everything from insect bites, water filters, and sun effects on the skin to gynecological problems, altitude sickness, children abroad, immunizations, and the diabetic traveler. It also features essays on topics like "The Economy-Class Syndrome" and "Being an Expatriate."

Not related to travel to Italy specifically but related to flying to and from is deep vein thrombosis (DVT), sometimes called coach-class thrombosis or economy-class syndrome. Visitors flying from the East Coast of the United States or Canada to Italy are probably not at great risk for DVT, as even if there is a connecting flight, total flying time is only about eight or nine hours; but travelers flying from other parts of North America are prime candidates for this condition, in which prolonged periods of sitting in one position cause blood clots in the leg veins that can travel to the lungs and get stuck there, causing death. Though long plane flights are not the only cause of DVT—sitting for long periods at an office desk, on a train or bus, or in a car are equally bad—it's important to remember to get up and walk up and down the plane's aisles while en route. My chiropractor tells me I should never sit for more than twenty minutes at a stretch because I have lower-back problems. Now I have another reason to get up and move about. Concerned travelers should contact the Aerospace Medical Association, 320 South Henry Street, Alexandria, Virginia 22314; 703-739-2240; www.asma.org. Two recently introduced items may provide some relief while on a long flight and may aid in preventing DVT: Hyland's makes homeopathic tablets for leg cramps, and one of the active ingredients is quinine. The tablets are 100 percent natural and do not interact with other medications. Call 800-624-9659 for details. Two companies—Wolford America and Mediven—have introduced travel compression stockings for men and women. (It offers tights for women and knee socks for men, but women have the choice of both.) Long Distance is the name Wolford is using for its stockings, but no matter the name, they are tightest at the ankles and knees to prompt blood flow away from the feet and toward the heart. Ask for them at department stores, travel shops, or pharmacies and expect to pay from about $21 to $45, depending on whether they're tights or knee socks.

~Travelers with diabetes might want to refer to *The Diabetes Travel Guide* (American Diabetes Association, 2000), which is filled with good tips and info. ~Disabled travelers may not already know about the Society for Accessible Travel and Hospitality (347 Fifth Avenue, Suite 610, New York, New York 10016; 212-447-7284; fax: 725-8253), a nonprofit organization that celebrated its twenty-fifth anniversary in 2001. Its website, at www.sath.org, is a seemingly inexhaustible resource for related information and other Internet links. Two other useful websites are www.access-able.com (representing Access-Able Travel Source) and www.disabilitytravel.com (representing the travel agency Accessible Journeys, 35 West Sellers Avenue, Ridley Park, Pennsylvania 19078; 800-846-4537 or 610-521-0339; fax: 610-521-6959). ~Some travel health websites to consult include www.cdc.gov/travel, which is the online site for the federal Centers for Disease Control in Atlanta. The content on the website is from the CDC's *Yellow Book: Health Information for International Travel*. Travel Medicine Inc.'s site is www.travelmed.com, which complements *The International Travel Health Guide* by Dr. Stuart Rose (Chronimed Publishing). The very best site, in my opinion, is www.tripprep.com. This site's "Travel Health Online" section is prepared by Shoreland, a trusted resource of travel medicine practitioners around the world. When I clicked on "Italy," I found good—though fortunately not lengthy—information on vaccinations (as well as excellent overall information on other aspects of the country). The report noted that some doctors may recommend vaccinations against hepatitis B, tick-borne encephalitis, or influenza, depending on one's itinerary in Italy. It also suggested reviewing routine immunizations for tetanus, diphtheria, and childhood diseases. Another site, www.medicinePlanet.com, is good for names of local health care providers and general recommendations. ~To find English-speaking doctors, you can contact the International Association of Medical Assistance to Travelers (417 Center Street, Lewiston, New York 14092; 716-754-4883), which provides a directory of English-speaking doctors around the world. IAMAT is a nonprofit organization, and while membership is free, donations are greatly appreciated. In addition to the directory, IAMAT mails members other material on malaria, immunizations, and so on, as well as a membership card, which entitles them to member rates should they have to pay for medical help. ~Travelers can also always contact the closest American embassy or local U.S. military installation for a list of local physicians and their areas of expertise. Additionally, some credit cards offer assistance: American Express's Global Assist program, available to all cardholders at no extra fee, is a full-service program offering everything from doctor and hospital referrals to emergency cash wires, translation assistance, lost item searches, legal assistance, and daily monitoring of your health condition. When abroad, travelers can call cardmember services at 800-528-4800; international collect at 1.336.393.1111; or the local American Express office.

Hiking

There are lots of opportunities for hiking in northeastern Italy. Though Tuscany and Umbria may have more "gentle" routes, the presence of the Italian Alps presents more challenging routes for experienced hikers and for those who simply prefer trails that are less traveled. Walking in Italy is generally not a wilderness experience, but there are very few places in Europe—now or ever—where you can backpack into completely isolated areas and not encounter roads, people, or towns. Conversely, there are few—if any—places in the United States where you can backpack and be assured of finding a place to sleep in a bed, plus a meal with wine or beer at the end of the day. As I noted in my *Provence* book, Friedrich Nietzsche once opined that "only those thoughts that come by walking have any value." I believe that whether one walks leisurely or hikes with a goal in mind, spending some time getting around via your own two feet makes you feel a part of a place in a special way. Ramblers and serious hikers will both be rewarded in this corner of Italy, whether for a day hike or a longer trek with stays in alpine huts. Some good resources to consult if you plan on doing some hiking include *The Independent Walker's Guide to Italy* (Frank Booth, Interlink Books, Northampton, Massachusetts, 1996). I took an immediate liking to Booth because he explains that although he has written a guide about walking in Italy, his book is also about escaping and avoiding DROPS (Dreaded Other People). "Even with this book in hand," he writes, "you will not always be able to completely avoid the DROPS, but you will have a strategy to retain your independence and sanity." This is your clue that he has lots of surprises in store for the visitor who wants to escape from the beaten path from time to time. Featured walks in northeastern Italy include "Bolzano: Oberbozen to Bolzano," "Merano: Algund to Merano," "Dolomites: Sortisei to St. Christina," "A Valley Walk: St. Christina to Selva/Wolkenstein," and "Lago di Garda: Marniga to Castelletto." In addition to these, there are ten thematic itineraries: "Ancient Ruins," "Great Castles and Walls," "Famous Cathedrals, Churches, and Abbeys," "Fabulous Feasts, High Hills and Massive Mountains," "Captivating Coasts and Beaches," "Inland Waterways," "Great Art Centers," the "Must-See Itinerary: All the Greatest Sights," and "Author's Favorite Walks." (One of the ten is in northeastern Italy: Lago di Garda.) For those inspired to embark on a more serious hike, Booth recommends the Grand Tour, which is simply all the walks in the book in order, which he calls "peerless as a vehicle for an in-depth discovery of Italy." A map and trail notes accompany each walk, and the book is a small paperback meant to be a bring-along. ~The *Lonely Planet Walking in Italy* guide is another good book (Helen Gillman, Sandra Bardwell, Stefano Cavedoni, and Nick Tapp, 1998). Four walks in the Dolomites are featured. A helpful chart in the front of the book gives a description of each walk, the duration, the best season to do it, and the level of difficulty, and there are a few color photos. ~A third book, with more color photographs, is *Wild Italy: A Traveller's Guide* (Tim Jepson, Interlink Books, Northampton, Massachusetts, 1994). This is one edition in the Wild Guides series (others include France and Spain), and in this edition Jepson—who has contributed to several guidebooks on Italy—identifies all the most beautiful landscapes in Italy that are still unspoiled by the modern world, the Dolomites included. The maps are very good, and the practical information is very detailed.

~The Cicerone Press publishes an enormous variety of books for outdoor enthusiasts, including *Alta Via: High Level Walks in the Dolomites, Classic Dolomite Climbs, Walking in the Dolomites,* and *Walks in the Julian Alps.* (The Adventurous Traveler in Vermont—see Bookstores entry for details—stocks the full array of Cicerone Press titles.) ~The three major areas of Friuli–Venezia Giulia for hiking are Piancavallo, Carnia, and Tarvisiano; interested readers should contact the appropriate APT office for detailed information: Azienda di Promozione Turistica di Piancavallo Cellina—Livenza, Piazza Duomo, Aviano 33081 (PN); 0434.651888; fax: 0434.660348; Azienda di Promozione Turistica della Carnia, Via Umberto 1, 15 Arta Terme 33022 (UD); 0433.88767; fax: 0433.886686; Azienda di Promozione Turistica del Tarvisiano e Sella Nevea, Via Roma 10, Tarvisio 33018 (UD); 0428.2135; fax: 0428.2972. (Additionally, the APT office in Trieste will have general information: Azienda Regionale per la Promozione Turistica, Via G.

Rossini 6, Trieste 34132; 0403.63952; fax: 0403.65496. ~Two good books to read about walking in general that I highly recommend include *The Walker Within* (editors of *Walking Magazine,* Lyons Press, 2001) and *Wanderlust: A History of Walking* (Rebecca Solnit, Viking, 2000). ~Some tour operators that offer walking and hiking trips include Alternative Travel Group (69–71 Banbury Road, Oxford OX2 6PJ England; 011.44.1865.315678 / www.atg-oxford.co.uk). ATG is a long-established company that offers a variety of trips in northeastern Italy: "Flowers of the Dolomites," "Venice," and "The Brenta Dolomites." Several friends and colleagues who've attended ATG trips have raved about the quality and sincerity with which the company approaches walking. I personally was especially impressed with its winter 2001 brochure, in which the staff, addressing the September 11 tragedy, stated, "If we allow our lives to be disrupted and do not travel, the economic damage will be decisive. Terrorism will win, and we will have only ourselves to blame." I also admire that ATG has established the ATG Trust for the Environment, which aims to raises funds for conservation projects in the areas they visit. The trust is young and has so far completed only two projects, in Umbria: the restoration of a two-thousand-year-old path once used by pilgrims visiting the notable abbey of San Eutizio, and the restoration of two medieval wooden sculptures in Bevagna.

~Butterfield & Robinson (see contact information under Biking entry), as noted, is one of the world's leading biking and hiking tour operators. In northeastern Italy it offers "Italian Alps: Walking to Mountain Villages in the Dolomites" (starts in Bolzano and finishes in Venice, with about seven to eight miles of hiking daily on varied terrain); "Venice and the Veneto: Walking the Foothills to Palladian Villas" (starts in Conegliano and finishes in Venice, with walks through woods and fields, on an ancient Roman road, in vineyards, and in the foothills; highlights include visits to the Villa Maser, Asolo, the Villa Emo, the Villas Pisani, and the Villa Malcontenta, a boat cruise and picnic on the Brenta River, and a walk to the quaint fishing village of San Pietro); and "Family Walking Adventure in the Italian Alps," a trip for kids from age eight and their extended family members—aunts, uncles, and grandparents included. This last is just one in B&R's Family Trips program, and it offers plenty for the kids to do with good supervision, as well as lots of free time for relaxation for the adults.

~Country Walkers (P.O. Box 180, Waterbury, Vermont 05676-0180; 800-464-9255; www.countrywalkers.com), a tour operator nearly twenty-five years old, has as its motto "Explore the World One Step at a Time." It offers one trip in northeastern Italy, "Alpine Serenity in the Dolomites," a seven-day journey beginning and ending in Bressanone. Walks average four to ten miles a day, and the terrain is moderate, with challenging options. Accommodations are all in deluxe Tyrolean hotels, including one Relais & Châteaux property.

Internet Access

I'm including this here only for business travelers. If you're traveling for pleasure and feel you need to surf the Web, perhaps you should save your money and stay home. (I take the view that vacations are for removing yourself from your daily grind; visiting another country is about doing *different* things and putting yourself in unfamiliar situations.) Overseas telephone services are not as reliable as in the United States, ensuring that connecting to the Internet is neither as easy nor as inexpensive. Business travelers who need to check in with the office via e-mail should consider what it will cost for a laptop, power adapter, disk, and/or CD-ROM drives, plus any other related accessories, as well as how heavy it all will be to carry. You may conclude that cybercafés (or Internet cafés) are more economical (and easier on your back). Fees for access to the Internet vary, but when you compare a hotel's charges for the same access—often at slower speeds—cybercafés represent good value. I found more than sixteen cybercafés in Padua, Trieste, Treviso, Castelfranco, Venice, Vicenza, and Verona, by searching www.cybercaptive.com and www.netcafes.com. Additionally, I've noticed that some public telephone booths at airports are equipped for Internet access, and more and more hotels these days are installing hookups in guest rooms.

Istituto Italiano di Cultura (Italian Cultural Institute)

The Italian Cultural Institute is a great organization to help keep you immersed in all things Italian, both before you leave and when you return. I have attended some truly memorable events at the Institute here in New York, and the center has a great library and offers Italian-language classes. In addition to the New York Istituto (686 Park Avenue, New York, New York 10021; 212-879-4242), there are other locations in North America: Chicago (312-822-9545); Los Angeles (213-207-4737); Quebec (514-849-8351); San Francisco (415-788-7142); Toronto (416-977-1566); and Vancouver (604-688-0809). The website for the New York Istituto (www.ital-cultny.org) is a useful resource, as it offers a forum for Italian teachers, a bulletin board for a wide variety of inquiries, Italian government grants for translations, and a calendar of events.

Italian Trade Commission

Readers who are in a retail, restaurant, or service profession that has some link to Italy will already be familiar with the Italian Trade Commission. Others may never have heard of the ITC, which celebrated its seventy-fifth anniversary last year. But the ITC is a worthwhile group for the general public to know about and can be a tremendous resource for those embarking on any sort of an Italian-related business or research project. The ITC is the official trade development and promotional agency of the Italian government and is headquartered in Rome, with sixteen offices in Italy and eighty-one abroad. (In the United States it has five offices, in Atlanta, Chicago, Los Angeles, and Seattle, with headquarters in New York.) Its general mandate has been to promote, assist, and develop Italy's international trade, with particular regard to small and medium-size enterprises. The ITC also works very hard to establish the difference between premium quality "Made in Italy" products versus those that are imitation "Made in the Italian Style." The Food and Wine Center of the ITC may be of most interest to readers. A few of its excellent publications include *A Journey Through the Flavors of Italy: The Art of Eating Well* (part of the ITC's "Naturalmente Italiano" promotion, with some great recipes, including a few from northeastern Italy: Prosciutto di San Daniele and Castelmagno Cheese Spread, and Risotto with Radicchio Rosso di Treviso and Grana Padano Cheese, plus a delicious recipe for Peach Pudding). *From Italy with Flavor,* another Naturalmente Italiano booklet, outlines premium Italian wines and food products that—in 2001—were seeking a U.S. importer. Readers who like to cook Italian food but live in isolated areas of North America may be interested in the list of U.S. importers—if so, they may contact the ITC directly about locating retailers that carry the particular Italian products they are looking for. *A Guide to Italian Regional Specialties* is an outstanding, region-by-region reference to the cheeses, fruit, vegetables, grains, fresh and cured meats, extra virgin olive oils, wines, and organic products of Italy, including the qualities of DOP and IGP products and DOC and DOCG wines. *VINO—Italian Wines: The Quality of Life* (see the *La Cucina Veneziana biblioteca* for details) is a great little booklet by Burton Anderson. Finally, *Foods of Italy,* the most recent publication to date, is also written by Burton Anderson. To receive complimentary copies of any of these publications, contact the ITC's main office at 33 East 67th Street, Food and Wine Center, New York, New York 10021; 212-980-1500; fax: 758-1050. The website for the trade is www.italtrade.com, while www.italianmade.com is for consumers.

J

Jewish History in Italy

"Set apart, much hated, the Venetian traders shared a strand of the Jewish destiny, which was interwoven with their own in a fabric commonly thought of as 'eastern.' The Jews were the last representatives of the Eastern bazaars to remain in Venice; when the Star of David set in the eighteenth-century ghetto, Venice herself was extinguished." Mary McCarthy's quote (from *Venice Observed*) is an apt reminder that Jews, though a minority community in Venice, played a vital role in the history of *La Serenissima*. To visit the Ghetto today in Cannaregio is to explore *Venetian* history, not just Italian Jewish history. *Not* to visit is the equivalent of going to Florence without setting foot in the Boboli Gardens, or to Paris without seeing the Place des Vosges. (Besides, the Ghetto is quite a lovely and quiet spot, and the synagogue interiors are stunningly beautiful.) McCarthy also reminds us that "Shylock, of course, was not the Merchant of Venice. The Merchant was the hero, Antonio. Shylock was only a moneylender. But popular belief declines to make the distinction and persists in thinking that Shylock was the merchant, i.e., that Venetian merchants were all Shylocks. Anti-Semitism is often traced to a medieval hatred of capitalism. To the medieval mind, the Jew was the capitalist par excellence. But this could also be said of the Venetian, whose palace was his emporium and his warehouse." It is easy to see that we have the Venetians to thank for a number of inventions, including the income tax, statistical science, the floating of government stock, state censorship of books, anonymous denunciations (in the form of the *bocca del Leone*), the gambling casino, and the Ghetto.

Jewish roots are widespread in Italy: Rome is home to the second-oldest continuous Jewish community in the world (after Jerusalem). Italian Jewry is unique in Judaism. Within the northeastern corner of Italy—in the Veneto especially—there are a great number of things of Jewish interest, including the sites of the only two concentration camps established in Italy by the Nazis: Trieste and Vo' Vecchio, southwest of Padua. (Vo' may perhaps represent the greater tragedy, as it served as a camp only from December 3, 1943, to mid-July 1944; forty-seven people were deported to Auschwitz, though the camp had held sixty to seventy people at a time.)

~The best book to consult for travel in the Veneto is *Venice and Environs Jewish Itineraries: Places, History and Art* (edited by Francesca Brandes, Marsilio Publishers, New York, 1997), a volume in the paperback Jewish Itineraries series. (Others cover Emilia-Romagna, Piedmont, Tuscany, and Lombardy; I'm not sure if there are editions for Friuli–Venezia Giulia or Trentino–Alto Adige.) Slender enough to pack, it highlights Jewish cultural heritage throughout the entire region and presents three itineraries with accompanying maps. According to the author, the Ghetto was established on March 29, 1516. Initially seven hundred or so Jews of both Italian and German origin were enclosed in what was then an isolated area of the city, formerly the site of a foundry. It was considered unhealthy, and "thus the first ghetto in history came into being. The etymology of the name that was to become sadly synonymous with segregation continues to be a matter of debate among scholars: some say it derives from the German word *gitter* (iron grill), from the Hebrew word *get* (divorce) or again from the German *gasse* (alleyway). However, the most widely accepted theory is that the word comes from the Venetian verb *getar*, to smelt." The origins of the island of Giudecca—directly across from Piazza San Marco—are equally unresolved. It is said that the city's Jewish community lived on Giudecca from the eleventh to the thirteenth centuries, but "there is no certain proof that the name derives from a Jewish connection, and a more plausible theory explains Giudecca as deriving from the Venetian word *zudega* (tried or judged) . . . the question is far from being settled, despite the vast amount of documents on the history of the Jewish community in Venice (particularly for the ghetto period)." The book is filled with color photos, good descriptive text, and a glossary but no specifics on visiting hours for museums, synagogues, and such.

~An illustrated hardcover book with color photos of the interiors of the five Ghetto synagogues is *The Venetian Ghetto* (Roberta Curiel, Bernard Dov Cooperman, Rizzoli, 1990). Selected treasures from the Museum of Jewish Art in Venice are also featured. ~*Italy: Jewish Travel Guide* (Annie Sacerdoti and Luca Fiorentino, Israelowitz Publishing, Brooklyn, New York, 1993) is another good book—though much less attractive—but covers all of Italy. It has a thirteen-page section covering Friuli–Venezia Giulia, and a five-page chapter for Trentino–Alto Adige. (The Veneto is represented in over twenty pages.) ~*Gardens and Ghettos: The Art of Jewish Life in Italy* (edited by Vivian Mann, University of California Press, 1989) is a beautiful catalog that accompanied an exhibit of the same name at the Jewish Museum in New York (September 17, 1989 to February 1, 1990). As Mann notes in the foreword, "The Jews of Italy would not have developed their distinctive character had they not shared common traits with fellow Italians, who were and are comparatively tolerant and humane, generally curious and respectful of the mores of the person next door, and endowed with the virtue of disobedience when afflicted by unjust rulers. Our communities seldom found themselves in a situation of isolation or estrangement from their surroundings. Even our ghettos were never airtight shtetls. In their houses of worship, ritual objects, and life-styles, Jews and Gentiles in Italy over the centuries have revealed a shared love for beauty and harmony, formal order, pride in good craftsmanship, intellectual curiosity, and humor." She adds that this is not just a "Jewish" story: it's the history of a community and a country that is both European and Mediterranean, at a crossroads of both east and west, north and south; and it points to "a new dimension of the Jewish presence at the very roots of European civilization." ~A bigger book is *A Travel Guide to Jewish Europe* (Ben Frank, Pelican Publishing Company, Gretna, Louisiana, 1996), which includes only Venice from northeastern Italy. A wonderful book of related interest is *Benevolence and Betrayal: Five Italian Jewish Families Under Fascism* (Alexander Stille, Summit Books, 1991), which is unfortunately out of print but can still be found.

L

Language

I do not speak Italian, of which I am not proud; but I do know some key words and phrases that rarely fail to bring a big smile to the faces of my hosts. The natives of *any* country love it when visitors try to speak their language. Italian may not be as widely spoken around the world as French, for example, but that doesn't mean you shouldn't attempt to learn some Italian vocabulary—it's a beautiful language, and if you've studied Latin, you'll learn it in a snap. *Me* expressing what an invaluable ability it is to speak a second (or third or fourth) language will not likely be persuasive; but recently I read an essay in *The Washington Post Book World* by John Keegan, who has been referred to as our greatest living military historian. (He's the author of a good many excellent books, including *The First World War*—see the *La Cronaca Mondana biblioteca* for details.) The essay's broad title was "The Writing Life"; *Book World* periodically invites writers to contribute a piece about the life of a writer, and at the end of Keegan's piece, he addresses what factors help him in the art of writing. He shares that he feels he has long had an ear for the rhythm of prose, which is essential to readability. "The other great help was foreign languages. I had been taught Latin and Greek until I was sixteen and had learned French very well. Knowledge of foreign languages is the best of guides to the structure and subtleties of one's own. It is, alas, dying out in the English-speaking world, which all foreigners now want to join. The result is that English-speaking writers don't write as well as those even of the last generation did, while strange varieties of English are taking form outside its historic heartland. The absolute certainty of touch that came so naturally to Rudyard Kipling and Evelyn Waugh is probably gone forever. I deeply regret its disappearance." Though I realize Keegan is writing about literature, mostly, I think his statement may be applied to North American travelers as well. It is never too late to begin learning another language, and if you are a lover of the arts, Italian is a useful one to learn.

The Tuscan dialect is considered "standard" Italian, and if that is the dialect you know, you'll find that almost everyone will recognize it and will most likely be happy to converse in it as well. You should be aware, however, that the Venetian dialect is unique in Italy, and if you travel all around this corner of Italy, you will discover a great number of dialects spoken in Friuli–Venezia Guilia and Trentino–Alto Adige. About the Venetian dialect Jan Morris has noted that it "is very fond of Xs and Zs and as far as possible ignores the letter L altogether, so that the Italian *bello,* for example, comes out *beo.* There are at least four Italian-Venetian dictionaries, and from these you can see that sometimes the Venetian word bears no resemblance to the Italian." Dialects aside, a few Italian pronunciation guidelines apply no matter where you are in Italy: *ch* before *i* or *e* is pronounced as *k,* such as in *radicchio, chiesa, zucchini, bruschetta.* The letter *c* preceding *e* or *i* is pronounced as *ch,* such as in *ciao, piacere.* The letters *gl* together are somewhat swallowed, so that each letter is not sounded separately, as in *bullion.* (The painter Modigliani, for example, is NOT pronounced mo-dig-lee-AH-nee but rather mo-deal-ee-AH-nee.) The letters *gn* together are pronounced as in *onion.* When you see the word *pesce* (fish), it is pronounced PESH-ay, as *sce* is equivalent to *sh;* similarly, *sci* is pronounced as *she* in English.

~The best language course I've used is Living Language. There are others—Berlitz, Barron's, Language/30, and more—but Living Language has been around longer (since 1946), the courses are continually updated and revised, and in terms of variety, practicality, and originality, I prefer it. Italian courses are available for beginner, intermediate, and advanced levels, in both audiocassette and CD editions. The "Fast & Easy" course (referred to as "virtually foolproof" by the New York *Daily News*), for beginner business or leisure travelers, is a sixty-minute survival program with a cassette and pocket-size pronunciation guide. The "Ultimate Course" is for serious language learners and is the equivalent of two years of college-level study. In a co-publishing venture with Fodor's, Living Language also offers the pocket-size *Italian for Travelers,* which is a handy book/cassette reference—designed for business and leisure travelers—with words and phrases for dozens of situations, including exchanging money, using ATMs, and finding a hotel room, and it also includes a two-way dictionary. To help build excitement for young children coming along, there's the *Learn in the Kitchen* and *Learn Together for the Car* series. These book/cassette kits are for children ages four to eight, and include a sixty-minute bilingual tape; sixteen songs, games, and activities; a forty-eight-page illustrated activity book with color stickers; and tips for parents on how to vary the activities for repeated use. The *All-Audio Course in Italian* (also published by Living Language) may be better suited to readers who want to learn on the go, so to speak, as it's popular in the car, with a Walkman or Discman. Both the cassette and CD programs come with six, sixty-minute recordings and a sixty-four-page listener's guide. The All-Audio course is available only at the beginner and intermediate levels. The Living Language *In-Flight: Italian* course is yet another way to get some words and phrases under your belt. "Learn Before You Land" is the program's motto, and it's meant for beginner business and leisure travelers. It's a sixty-minute course, with a CD, featuring just enough to get by in every travel situation, including greeting and polite expressions, asking for directions, getting around, checking into a hotel, or going out on the town. Fodor's has created a nifty credit card–size, fold-out magnet called *Fodor's to Go: Italian for Travelers.* You can conveniently keep it in your pocket and unobtrusively retrieve it when you need to look up a word or phrase. It is also great for pretrip quizzing: you can keep it in your kitchen on the refrigerator at eye level and, while holding a glass of Soave, for example, in one hand, unfold the magnet with the other and test your memory. Note, however, that as it is a magnet, you have to make sure it doesn't touch your credit cards or any other data-storage items.

~If you prefer learning by videotape, try the four-hour, two-video course by the Standard Deviants (available through the Discovery Channel, 800-207-5775). For newborns to age two, there is also *Baby's First Steps in Italian,* a book and CD set. This program is an easy introduction to understanding and nurturing a child's natural talent for learning languages and covers sounds, rhymes, and songs. The seventy-three-page booklet is excellent and includes resources and references for parents. I have to add that though my daughter is three—supposedly beyond the scope of this package—we have found the French edition to be entertaining and educational. As an aside, I would like to stress that it is never too early to begin teaching young children another language. Even my husband was pooh-poohing me when I would read to Alyssa in French, or teach her Italian words. But she knows over a dozen words and phrases in French and said *buon giorno, ciao, grazie,* and *Piazza San Marco* constantly when we were in Venice—simply because I repeated them over and over.

~For help with translating a fax, e-mail, letter, or text of any kind, try logging on to www.world.altavista.com. Users input the (Italian or other language) text they want translated and click on "Translate." It works the other way too. I have found this particularly helpful when viewing websites that are exclusively in Italian.

~An essential book to have is *501 Italian Verbs* (Barron's). In addition to giving really good descriptions of the various tenses, a full page is allotted to each verb, showing all the tenses fully conjugated, plus the definition and a useful selection of "Words and Expressions Related to This Verb" at the bottom of each page. As if this weren't enough, there are also chapters on "Verbs Used in Idiomatic Expressions," "Verbs with Prepositions," "Verbs Used in Weather Expressions," "Thirty Practical Situations for Tourists and Popular Phrases," and "Words and Expressions for Tourists." If you're serious about learning or brushing up on Italian, I really can't see doing it without this book.

~Some related books for Italian-language lovers are *Latina pro Populo (Latin for People)* (Alexander and Nicholas Humez, Little, Brown and Company, 1978) and *Le Mot Juste: A Dictionary of Classical and Foreign Words and Phrases* (Vintage Books, 1991), which includes classical languages, French, German, Italian, Spanish, and a smattering of other languages around the world. It's a great reference book, and what I'm reminded of each time I consult the Italian pages is the great number of words we use for music and art that derive from Italian.

The League of Cambrai

The League of Cambrai could have been the undoing of Venice, but it wasn't, and as it is referenced so often in historical overviews of Venice, it is worth knowing a bit about. The league dates from 1508–10 and was an alliance formed in the majority by Emperor Maximilian I, Louis XII of France, Ferdinand V of Aragon, and Pope Julius II; the emperor and the king of Hungary also joined the bandwagon. What prompted them to join together was that Venice had decided that she needed to expand a bit, and the logical place for that expansion was Emilia-Romagna, known then simply as Romagna. This expansion was viewed as an attempt to usurp the lands of Christian powers. (The region had been under the control of the pope but was now in utter disarray, a fact that was not lost on the Venetian powers that were.) As Jan Morris explains it, "Venice's prices were high, her terms were unyielding, and her political motives were so distrusted that in the League of Cambrai most of the sixteenth-century Great Powers united to suppress 'the insatiable cupidity of the Venetians and their thirst for domination.'" So the group was formed, and each member put in a bid for a portion of Venice's empire: the pope wanted Romagna back, Spain wanted the Apulian ports, France wanted Cremona, the emperor wanted Friuli and the Veneto, and the king of Hungary wanted Dalmatia. The big offensive was launched from France on May 14, 1509, and the league defeated Venice at Agnadello in the Ghiara d'Adda. French and imperial troops occupied the Veneto, and the situation looked grim for *La Serenissima*. But once again Venice extricated herself by her efforts and political skill. The Apulian ports were ceded in order to reach an accord with Spain, and the pope was placated when he wisely perceived how much more dangerous Venice would be destroyed than intact. Andrea Gritti recaptured Padua in July 1509. Spain and the pope broke off their alliance with France, and Venice regained Brescia and Verona from France. After seven years of war, Venice regained her domains on the mainland up to the Adda (a river that is closer to Milan than to Brescia), all of which she held on to until the end of the republic. Though Venice was victorious, Morris reminds us that "even when, in the seventeenth and eighteenth centuries, she stood almost alone for Christendom against the triumphant Turks, Venice was never embraced by the nations. She was like a griffin or a phoenix, on the outside of a rookery."

Lion of Saint Mark

As you will see the lion of San Marco not only in Venice but throughout the Veneto and in parts of Friuli–Venezia Giulia, it might be useful to know the story of how it became the symbol of Venice. A winged lion is one of four beastly beings that the Apostle John described in Revelation (". . . and in the midst of the throne, and round about the throne, were four beasts full of eyes before and behind. And the first beast was like a lion, and the second beast like a calf, and the third beast had a face like a man, and the fourth beast was like a flying eagle. And the four beasts had each of them six wings about him; and they were full of eyes within; and they rest not day and night, saying, Holy, holy, holy, Lord God Almighty, which was, and is, and is to come. And when those beasts give glory and honour and thanks to him that sat on the throne who liveth for ever and ever"). In the fourth century, Saint Jerome interpreted the images of these beings and attributed them to the four Evangelists. The lion became Mark's attribute because his gospel emphasizes Christ's regality and the lion was, of course, a symbol of royalty. Saint Mark apparently came to the lagoon to preach, and there he established the Patriarchate of Aquileia (on the Adriatic in Friuli–Venezia Giulia, about an hour's drive from Venice). The legend goes, according to John Julius Norwich in *A History of Venice*, that when Saint Mark was traveling from Aquileia to Rome, his ship happened to stop at the islands of Rialto en route. "There an angel appeared to him and blessed him with the words *'Pax tibi, Marce, evangelista meus. Hic requiescet corpus tuum.'* ['Peace be unto you, Mark, my evangelist. On this spot shall your body rest.' The first of these sentences must be familiar to all visitors to Venice, since it is inscribed upon the open book that the ubiquitous winged lion of the city holds in his paw. One of the few exceptions is the stone lion outside the Arsenal; the message being thought too conciliatory for so warlike an institution, his book is held defiantly closed.] The historical evidence for this story is, to say the least, uncertain; the prophecy—since Saint Mark later became Bishop of Alexandria and remained there till he died—would have seemed improbable; but the legend certainly came in very handy when, in 828 or thereabouts, two Venetian merchants returned from Egypt with a corpse which they claimed to be that of the Evangelist, stolen from his Alexandrian tomb." Norwich points out that the details of this theft are, unsurprisingly, all over the map; but the generally accepted details are that the Christian guardians of the shrine were effectively persuaded to step aside and allow the robbery to go forward. The body of Saint Mark was put into a large basket and carried down to the harbor, where, conveniently, a Venetian ship was waiting. An obvious question that the astute reader might ask is "What about the smell of the decayed body?" Norwich tells us that one chronicler wrote of the stench that "if all the spices of the world had been gathered together in Alexandria, they could not have so perfumed the city." The worldly-wise Venetians covered the body with quantities of pork, the first sight of which horrified the Muslim inspectors. The body was wrapped in canvas and hoisted up to the yardarm, where it remained safe until the ship reached Venice. This story, according to Norwich, "is something more than just another of those legends in which early Venetian history is so rich." It is generally believed, as historical fact, that a body thought to be that of Saint Mark was brought to Venice. Giustiniano Participazio, the current doge, ordered that a special chapel be built for the relic. A doge didn't have to be a rocket scientist to figure out that if the Venetian Republic were to command proper respect in Europe, the city needed prestige above and beyond maritime supremacy and obvious wealth. Politics and religion were still one and the same in the Middle Ages, and "the presence of an important sacred relic endowed a city with a mystique all its own." The relic was also that of an Evangelist, which set Venice apart one spiritual—and political—step more. "History records no more shameless example of body-snatching; nor any—unless we include the events associated with the Resurrection—of greater long-term significance. But once the Venetians had the Evangelist safely among them, they adopted him as their own, more wholeheartedly than any other tutelary saint in any other city. As their guardian, over the centuries, they were to work him hard and to try him sorely; but as their patron they were never to fail him in their love and veneration. And he, for his part, was to serve them well." What may not be obvious in this explanation is that before

Saint Mark, Theodore was the city's patron saint. (That's him standing on top of the crocodile on one of the two pillars in the Piazzetta beside St. Mark's; as Jan Morris tells us in *The World of Venice,* no guidebook will explain the significance of Theodore and that crocodile, "for the good reason that nobody is quite certain what their significance is: most writers hazard a brief conjectural biography of the saint, but evade the crocodile altogether.") Additionally, an open book held by the lion of Saint Mark is meant to indicate a time of peace, while a closed version is equivalent to war.

Luggage

I've read of a syndrome—really—called BSA (baggage separation anxiety), which you may at first be inclined to laugh at; but as reports of lost luggage have escalated in the last few years, I'm not at all surprised that fear of losing luggage is now a syndrome. (All the more reason, I say, not to check bags, and *definitely* the reason to pack at least some essentials in a carry-on bag.) Essentials, by the way, don't add up to much: it's remarkable how little one truly "needs." Recently one of my bags did not turn up when I reached my destination, and the airline representative was honest enough to tell me that when flights are full, sometimes not all the bags are loaded onto the plane—intentionally (#&!). As distressing as this is, at least it explains part of the problem, and it is one more reason to keep essentials with you. Nearly every luggage manufacturer, including leaders in the field such as Tumi and Samsonite, have created a variety of bags at varying prices that are meant to hold enough stuff for about three days of traveling—about the time it takes for a misrouted bag to show up, assuming it isn't lost altogether! Even if you are the sort of traveler who cannot lighten your load, you will still probably bring a carry-on. As I write this, the standard limit for carry-on luggage is 9 by 14 by 22 inches, otherwise known as 45 linear inches to the airlines. Before the September 11 tragedy, the biggest misunderstanding about carry-on luggage was the 22-inch bag. Some airlines would (and still will) accept these as legitimate carry-on luggage, while others did not (and still won't). I still recommend the 20-inch bag, even if you have to check it, simply because it is, in the end, more practical. In the aftermath of September 11, much of what we knew and understood about carry-on luggage applies no longer. As I edit this, the FAA has issued new directives on what constitutes a carry-on item; but as I found out when placing calls to several airlines, interpreting these directives is really up to each individual airline. Essentially, there is no universal standard among North American carriers as to what constitutes a carry-on *personal item* or even a carry-on bag. Representatives I spoke with told me the list of carry-on items was subject to change daily, at the discretion of the airline. Airlines reserve the right—and I'm glad they do—to spot-check passengers as they are passing through the gate, and decisions about the items you're carrying are made on a case-by-case basis. It may seem obvious that razor blades and pocket knives are not allowed in carry-on bags, but aerosol cans are sometimes confiscated too, as well as safety pins and cigarette lighters, and photography equipment is often examined very carefully. What a woman defines as her tote bag or purse is open to scrutiny (a tote bag filled with clothes is usually considered not personal and therefore must be checked), though a large cosmetic case is typically considered small enough to be personal. A backpack is a carry-on personal item, but put it on wheels and it becomes checked luggage. Computer laptop cases may also be singled out for inspection: if anything is stashed in the bag besides papers, the computer, and writing utensils, it could be seen as a candidate for checked baggage. The only way to confirm what is and isn't allowed is to call the airline you're flying with directly. Don't wait until you're at the airport to discover that you should have left an item at home. And be sure to ask about medical prescriptions, syringes, and metal items that might sound the security alarm. I have actually welcomed the limits on carry-on bags, as I have always been annoyed with people who try to sneak on more baggage than they should be carrying in the first place. Storage space on planes is limited, and less baggage means more on-time schedules and better passenger safety. I endorse the words of Antoine de Saint-Exupéry: "He who would travel happily must travel light."

The ubiquitous—and always black—suitcase on wheels has taken a beating of late. Some travelers complain that it's too heavy to lift in and out of an overhead bin without hitting someone on the head, and that trying to find one at a baggage claim is like Harry the dog trying to find his family's umbrella at the beach in the children's book *Harry by the Sea*. Plus, they've become decidedly unhip: a writer for *The Wall Street Journal* claims that "the wheelie has become a fashion faux pas—the suitcase equivalent of a pin-striped suit on a casual Friday." I may be the lone voice in the wilderness, but the wheelie is essential for those of us with back problems. (I am extremely happy with my Dakota 20-inch wheelie, and it's forest green, by the way. The entire Dakota line is one of the better-kept secrets in the luggage world: "the hardest working bags in the business" are a division of Tumi and are equally as well made, for about half the price.) Also, I like the freedom of not having to depend on only one type of ground transportation. With a wheelie, I don't need a porter or a luggage cart, and I can choose from all forms of public (and private) transportation. Travelers in a hurry, and those who really worry about someone else walking off with their bag, should make their bags distinctive so they'll stand out on the luggage carousel. Short of buying a lemon yellow suitcase, you could use unique luggage tags, or really go out on a limb with something called the Lock It Spot It set, which includes two locks, a large identification tag, and a thick nylon strap that you wrap all the way around your bag—in either shocking pink or bright green. It seems like a good compromise to me, rather than buying that lemon yellow bag. (For more information, contact Christine Columbus, P.O. Box 2168, Lake Oswego, Oregon 97035; 800-280-4775; www.christinecolumbus.com—this is a very cool company, by the way, offering products "uniquely well-suited for the woman traveler.")

M

Maps

Getting lost is usually a part of everyone's travels, but it isn't always a bonus—except when you're in Venice proper, where getting lost is not only inevitable but desirable. As Frederic Vitoux notes in *Living in Venice,* "With its passageways, windings, and squares, Venice presents itself less as a city to be methodically explored, than as a city always full of surprises." It's true that the surprises one discovers when lost in Venice are almost always greater than those discovered when following the beaten path. But occasionally we don't *want* to be lost—we are, for whatever reason, in somewhat of a hurry to reach our destination. Not that a map always helps in Venice, as H. V. Morton explains in *A Traveller in Italy:* "I thought it should be easy, with the help of a map, to walk across Venice from the statue of Colleoni to the Friary Church on the opposite side of the Grand Canal, and I started off with success, crossing to the other bank by the Rialto Bridge; but I found myself hopelessly lost. I regained the Grand Canal and took a vaporetto, which landed me near a large Franciscan church."

I wish I could refer you to an amazing, foolproof map of Venice—one that the locals swear by—but I'm afraid I haven't yet discovered one. I very much recommend *Knopf CityMap Guide: Venice* (see Guidebooks for more details) for carrying around every day. In an ideal world, I think everyone should have *Knopf CityMap Guide: Venice* and a large, overall map of Venice (both *Baedeker's Venice* and *Fodor's CityPack: Venice* have good ones that are separate from the books themselves) for looking at in your hotel room. For driving in the Veneto, Friuli–Venezia Giulia, and Trentino–Alto Adige, the best choices are the large, bound edition of *Atlante stradale d'Italia* (published by Touring Club Italiano) and the fold-out *Carta turistica stradale* (also published by TCI), for *Italia centrale,* foglio 2, at a scale of 1:4000,000. This volume, at a scale of 1:200,000, is available in three editions: Nord, Centro, and Sud (Nord obviously being the edition you want for northeastern Italy).

Mercate (markets)

Outdoor markets are one of the unrivaled pleasures of Italy. Even if you have no intention of purchasing anything, you should not miss walking around an outdoor (or indoor) market. The Rialto in Venice, for example, is world famous and is positively *da non perdere* (not to be missed). Prices for food seem to be displayed and fixed at markets in Italy, but for other things bargaining is the accepted method of doing business. (The merchant will tell you if it's not.) Therefore, a visit to the market should not be an activity you try to do in a hurry: take your time, remember to stop for something to eat or drink so your stomach (or companion) doesn't grumble, and enjoy searching for a unique *ricordo* (souvenir) or soaking up the atmosphere. While most of my own bargaining efforts have been practiced in Turkey, Morocco, and Egypt, here are some tips that work well for me in Italy:

~Walk around first and survey the scene. Identify the vendors you want to come back to, and if prices are not marked, try to ascertain what they are for the items you're interested in. If you don't have any idea what the general price range is, you won't have any idea if you're paying a fair price or too much. Even better is to learn the prices that leather gloves, handbags, or jewelry sell for here in the States before you leave home—then you'll also know how much (or how little) savings are being offered. ~If you do spy an item you're interested in, try not to reveal your interest; act as nonchalant as you possibly can, and remember to be ready to start walking away. ~It's considered rude to begin serious bargaining if you're not interested in making a purchase. This doesn't mean you should refrain from asking the price of an item, but to then begin naming numbers is an indication to the vendor that you're a serious customer and that a sale will likely be made. ~You'll get the best price if you pay with cash, and Italy isn't in the vanguard of credit card acceptance anyway. I prepare an assortment of paper lire and coins in advance so I can always pull it out and indicate that it's all I have. It doesn't seem right to bargain hard for something and pay for it with a big note. ~Occasionally I feign interest in one particular item when it's a different item I *really* want. The tactic here is to begin the bargaining process and let the vendor think I'm about to make a deal. Then I pretend to get cold feet and indicate that the price is just too much for me. The vendor thinks all is lost, and at that moment I point to the item I've wanted all along, sigh, and say I'll take that one, naming the lowest price from my previous negotiation. Usually the vendor will immediately agree to it, as it means a done deal. ~Other times I will plead poverty and say to the vendor that I had *so* wanted to bring back a gift for my mother from "your beautiful country—won't you please reconsider?" This, too, usually works. ~Finally, remember that a deal is supposed to end with both parties satisfied. If, after much back-and-forth, you encounter a vendor who won't budge below a certain price, it's likely that it's not posturing but a way of letting you know that anything lower will no longer be advantageous. See my *Morocco* edition for a much more extensive section on bargaining.

Money
The best way to travel is with a combination of local cash, American Express traveler's checks (other types are not universally accepted), and credit cards. If you have all three, you will *never* have a problem. (Note that you should not rely on wide acceptance of credit cards, especially in the countryside.) How you divide this up

depends on how long you'll be traveling and on what day of the week you arrive: banks, which offer the best exchange rate, aren't generally open on weekends and, in Italy, aren't open continuously on weekdays. (Usually banks close for lunch, then may reopen for only an hour or two.) If you rely solely on your ATM card and you encounter a problem, you can't fix it until Monday when the banks reopen.

Overseas ATMs. Overseas ATMs may limit the number of daily transactions you can make, as well as place a ceiling on the total amount you can withdraw. ~Make sure your password is compatible with Italian ATMs (if you have too many digits, you'll have to change it), and if, like me, you have memorized your password as a series of letters rather than numbers, write down the numerical equivalent before you leave. Most European cash machines do not display letters, and even when they do, they do not always appear in the same sequence as in the United States. ~Call your bank to inquire about fees for withdrawals, and ask if there is a fee for overseas transactions. (There shouldn't be, but ask anyway.) Find out if you can withdraw money from both your checking and your savings accounts or from only one; and ask if you can transfer money between accounts. ~Though I think this is a bit anal-retentive even for me, it's possible to view in advance the exact street locations of ATM machines in Italy online. To see where Plus systems are, go to www.visa.com; for the Cirrus network, go to www.mastercard.com/atm. Once at the website, select "ATM Locator," and you'll be given an opportunity to select a country, city, street address, and postal code. (It's not essential to provide the postal code, but for best results, enter the cross streets and the city.)

~*Local currency.* Savvy travelers always arrive with some local currency in their possession. (I feel most comfortable with about a hundred dollars' worth.) While the rates of exchange and fees charged obviously vary, it is far more important not to arrive empty-handed than to spend an inordinate amount of time finding out how much money you'll save—we are, after all, talking about a very small sum of money, and when you get off the plane with the ability to quickly make your way to wherever you're going, you'll feel it's money well spent. After a long flight, who wants to exchange money, especially while looking after luggage and/or children? There are very often long lines at the exchange counters and cash machines, and cash machines are sometimes out of order, or out of cash. (Once I even had the admittedly unusual experience of going directly to a large bank in a capital city, only to find a posted sign stating that the bank was closed because it had *run out of money!?*) Smart travelers arrive prepared to pay for transportation, tips, snacks, personal items, or unanticipated expenses. If you're too busy to get the cash yourself, call International Currency Express and request its Currency Rush mail-order service. With two offices, in Los Angeles and Washington, D.C., the company offers excellent rates. Call 888-278-6628 and request either UPS second-day or overnight service.

~Traveler's checks. Traveler's checks should be cashed at banks, as vendors prefer not to deal with them. The reason is not that Italy has a dim view of traveler's checks but that Italy remains very much a cash economy.

Credit cards. Credit card *(carta di credito)* acceptance is vastly wider than it was even five or ten years ago, but be aware that—especially outside large cities and towns—many small inns, country restaurants and wine bars, street vendors, and shopkeepers accept only cash. *Posso pogare con la carta di credito?* ("Am I able to pay with a credit card?") is a good question to ask if you're not sure.

~The euro. Significant not only economically but symbolically, the new single currency is expected to keep the Continent from finding reasons to go to war. In this respect, the European Union is viewed as a model of higher authority which respects regional and ethnic identities. Euro paper notes and coins have now replaced local currencies in Austria, Belgium, Finland, France, Germany, Greece, Ireland, Italy, Luxembourg, the Netherlands, Portugal, and Spain. At the time of this writing, the U.S. dollar and the euro were very close in value (with one U.S. dollar being about equal to 1.10 euros). Readers interested in learning more about the euro can view an informative website, www.eurolandia.tin.it.

~Refrain from wearing one of those ubiquitous waist bags, or as my friend Carl says, "Make our country proud, and don't wear one of those fanny packs!" Tourist plus fanny pack equals magnet for pickpockets. I know of more people who've had valuables stolen from these ridiculous pouches than I can count. Keep large bills, credit cards, and passports hidden from view: in a money belt worn under your clothes, in a pouch that hangs from your neck, or in an interior coat or blazer pocket. My husband had great success while we were traveling in Morocco with a money belt worn around his leg, underneath his pants. This obviously won't work with shorts, but it's quite a good solution for long pants. Also, the Socaroo tube sock is another good alternative: it's a cotton sock meant for joggers that also happens to be great for travelers, as it holds cash and credit cards in a small, two-by-three-inch pocket. A pair of socks is about five dollars, and readers may view the website (www.socaroo.com) or call 310-559-4011 for more information. ~If possible, don't keep everything in the same place, and keep a separate piece of paper with telephone numbers of companies to contact in case of emergency.

~Useful vocabulary: *monete* or *spiccioli* (coins); *denaro* (money); *assegni di viaggio/per viaggiatori* (traveler's checks).

La Mostra del Cinema

La Mostra—officially known as La Mostra Internazionale di Venezia—is Venice's annual film festival, founded in 1932. The festival, while not nearly so famous as the one in Cannes, takes place each year in September on the Lido. I have never yet attended, but I have read that, though still star-studded, La Mostra is a little less frenzied than the springtime gathering in Cannes. Most of the festival's screenings are held at Palazzo del Cinema and the Astra Theater, and a number of shows are open to the public at regular movie prices. For more information, call 041.521.87.11 or send a fax to 041.523.63.74.

Movies

Plan a meal from one or more of the cookbooks mentioned in the *La Cucina Veneziana biblioteca,* and invite some friends and family over for dinner and a movie. Some suggestions: *Breaking Away, Pane e Tulipani* (Bread and Tulips), *Summertime, Top Hat, From Russia with Love, Morte a Venezia* (Death in Venice), *Casanova, Don Giovanni* (adaptation of the opera), *A Little Romance, Marco Polo, Indiana Jones and the Temple of Doom, Carrington, Everyone Says I Love You, The Talented Mr. Ripley,* and *Dangerous Beauty.* (On a related note, a great film that has for fifty years lured people of all ages into the world of opera is *The Great Caruso,* which admittedly romanticizes the life of the great tenor Enrico Caruso and stars the tenor idol of the 1940s and 1950s Mario Lanza, as well as Ann Blyth and soprano Dorothy Kirsten.) While you're cooking, get in the mood by listening to some appropriate music: *Viva Italia!: Festive Italian Classics* (RCA) and *Italy by Night* (EMI), *Mob Hits I,* and *Mob Hits II,* are all great, toe-tapping choices that will have you ready to say *cin-cin* (pronounced cheen-cheen, the Italian equivalent of "cheers!") when your guests arrive. (For some less kitschy music selections—opera and works by classical musicians who lived and/or worked in Venice—see the Music entry.)

Museums and Monuments

Italy's art treasures face an unfair number of obstacles to their survival: pollution, earthquakes, fires, floods, terrorist bombs, theft (more than half a million works have been stolen since 1970, and only about a third have been recovered), enormous numbers of tourists, lack of money, and even apathy. Museum hours used to be somewhat of a joke in Italy, but in the last five or so years, a number of Italy's major museums standardized their hours and are now open all day long, without a three-hour break for lunch (and some have bookstores and cafés). Some museums remain open until ten P.M., later even than museums in France, which has a long tradition of caring for its *patrimoine.* Additionally, *The New York Times* reported in December 2001 that a law was about to pass that would partially privatize Italy's museums. The Italian government planned to take bids for the management of Italy's some three thousand museums. But it will retain legal ownership of the museums and remain responsible for the preservation of Italy's "extravagant share of the world's art treasures." According to Giuliano Urbani, Italy's minister of culture, about 30 percent of Italy's artistic heritage is in storage, and "because we have so much of it, we can't afford to get it out of the basement."

~Remember that many museums in Italy are closed on Mondays. Some of the smaller museums and monuments are open, however, as well as churches. Be sure to check in advance. ~With the exception of the San Marco basilica and the campanile in Venice, long lines are relatively rare. This is not to say there won't be a crowd at the Accademia or the Palazzo Ducale, or at Miramare in Trieste, but even in high season you shouldn't have to wait more than ten minutes.

Music

Novelist Michael Dibdin, in the foreword to a great book called *Venice: A Cultural and Literary Companion*, offers some practical advice to visitors interested in Venetian music: "Before you go, explore the recorded repertoire and make a few compilation tapes. Unless you have an invitation to stay in a palazzo, I would suggest that you concentrate on the vocal and notionally religious music. (Most secular music—sonatas, concerti, and solo cantatas—was performed in private spaces.)" Dibdin then advises us to become creatures of the night by leaving our hotel after dark, turning on our music selections (presumably in some sort of headphone apparatus), and getting lost. "Venice is one of the safest cities in the world, and you will eventually spot one of the nocturnal *vaporetti* which keep circulating all night long. Hop on, see the city from the water, then try and find your way back on foot. You will have the place virtually to yourself—the greatest luxury it has to offer—and if the sounds pouring into your ears do not put you into a very intense personal and private communion with the ghosts of Browning's 'dear, dead women' and men, then for you I feel nothing but pity." For readers even remotely interested in the subject, a very good survey is *Five Centuries of Music in Venice* (H. C. Robbins Landon and John Julius Norwich, Thames & Hudson, London, 1991; first American edition published by Schirmer Books, an imprint of Simon & Schuster Macmillan, New York, 1991). Norwich notes in the introduction, "One of the most astonishing—and occasionally, it must be said, the most irritating—aspects of the people of Venice down the ages has been their ability to turn their hand to virtually anything, and then to do it quite superbly well." In addition to the Venetians' skills as seamen, merchants, imperialists, political theorists, international statesmen, and visual artists, they were musicians: "And here again Venice's record is enough to leave us gasping. Not quite all the heroes of the pages that follow were natives of the city; but in almost every case Venice gave them shelter, or inspiration, or encouragement, or patronage, or a combination of the four; every one of them, I suspect, would have been proud to call himself at least an honorary Venetian, and a good many of them did. . . . For in Venice—far more, surely, than in any other city in Italy—music mattered; indeed, it still matters today, just as it has for the past five hundred years." Chapters of this lavishly illustrated book cover the sixteenth through twentieth centuries, and—best of all—there is a two-page discography with recording recommendations for Palestrina, Lassus, Gabrieli (both Andrea and Giovanni), Schütz, Monteverdi, Cavalli, Strozzi, Vivaldi, Bach, Handel, Rossini, Verdi, Wagner, Stravinsky (who loved Venice above all other cities and whose grave is on San Michele), Britten, Maderna, and Nono.

Some readers may have noticed, with regret, the absence of entries on opera in my previous books *Central Italy* and *Paris*. (I did, I think, have the good sense to include a wonderful piece in the *Central Italy* book entitled "A Musician's Florence" by writer Harvey Sachs, but it was not exclusively about opera.) I regret the opera omission and admit that it's due to my limited knowledge of this beautiful art form. My limited knowledge is expanding, however, due to three people. My cousin, Abbie F., sings soprano and currently lives in Berlin. (Until a few years ago, the only opera recordings I owned were *Carmen* and *La Bohème;* Abbie kindly gave me a list of her top ten recommendations for beginners.) Ann Patchett wrote a great piece for *Gourmet* (June 2001) entitled "An Affair to Remember," in which she relates how she came to opera in midlife—like me—and aptly notes, "One way to find great music in Italy is to blindfold yourself and throw a dart at a map of the country. Wherever it pierces the boot, there is sure to be extraordinary music." She adds, "No city seems more suited to opera than Venice," though Florence is generally credited with being the city where opera was born. Finally, Fred Plotkin, whom you may know for his excellent Italian cookbooks. In fact, Plotkin has taught about opera all over the world, written much about opera, and was performance manager of the Metropolitan Opera in New York. The result is his *Opera 101: A Complete Guide to Learning and Loving Opera* (published in 1994 by Hyperion). Ann Patchett, in her *Gourmet* article, nicely praises *Opera 101* as "something of a bible even for sophisticated opera buffs. What Mr. Plotkin offers is basically a college course in opera." I would have to agree: Plotkin presents a history of four hundred years of opera and informs how one can become an opera cognoscente, including going to the opera; he provides a discography; he deals with eleven operas in individual chapters; and he includes four appendices, the last one being a complete list of opera houses around the world for travelers. As inspiring and authoritative as Plotkin's book is, opera mavens and almost-mavens will naturally crave more.

~General books for those who seek to further their knowledge about opera include *The Story of Opera* (Richard Somerset-Ward, Harry N. Abrams, 1998). Do not be misled by the bland title: this elaborate history book includes beautiful color photographs, historic documents, and individual stories that will enlighten younger and/or newer opera fans as well as jog the memories of older opera fans. *Opera as Drama: New Edition* (Joseph Kerman, University of California Press, 1988) is a controversial opera criticism book that explores opera history and can be appreciated by a wide audience. *Ticket to the Opera: Discovering and Exploring 100 Famous Works, History, Lore and Singers with Recommended Recordings* (Phil G. Goulding, Fawcett Books, 1999): Goulding, though not musically trained himself, brings opera to a wider audience with lucid explanation and offers suggested recordings. *History Through the Opera Glass* (George Jellinek, Pro Am Music Resources, 1993): an opera aficionado of the "old school" offers historical analyses of different operas and the events on which they are based.

~The greatness of specific operas is not just about the wonderful music and the intriguing drama, however. The interpreters of various roles have made operas such as Puccini's *Tosca* and Verdi's *Aïda* staples at opera houses and festivals all over Italy, including the world-renowned outdoor festival at Arena di Verona. Among the books about singers is *Singers of the Century*, vol. 3 (John B. Steane, Amadeus Press, 2000): esteemed opera writer and *Gramophone* columnist Steane offers a splendid account of singers, their voices, and their respective interpretations of their best roles. *Callas at Julliard: The Master Classes* (John Ardoin, Amadeus Press, 1998) is an exact account of the famed 1971–72 master classes given by Maria Callas, one of the most celebrated, if not *the* most celebrated, interpreter of Italian opera's heroines and who is remembered for her great performances with tenor Giuseppe di Stefano, among others, at La Scala in Milan. A good biography of her is *Callas: Portrait of a Prima Donna* (George Jellinek, Dover, 1986). *Leonard Warren: American Baritone,* Opera Biography Series, no. 13 (Mary Jane Phillips-Matz and Tony Randall, Amadeus Press, 2000) is a biography of one of the greatest Verdi baritones of the twentieth century; he performed little in Italy but continues to be a standard of greatness all over the world.

~A great source for both opera and film enthusiasts is *Opera on Film* (Richard Fawkes, Duckworth, 2000). Among the films is Cecil B. DeMille's 1915 *Carmen,* which made the early-twentieth-century soprano Geraldine Farrar a film star. The rest of the book similarly discusses famous film directors' interest in putting excerpts from or entire operas on film, and how opera stars like Enrico Caruso, Giovanni Martinelli, and Rise Stevens became stars of the big screen.

National Italian American Foundation

The National Italian American Foundation (1860 Nineteenth Street, N.W., Washington, D.C. 20009; 202-387-0600; fax: -0800; www.niaf.org) was founded in 1975 as a nonprofit, nonpartisan organization and is the major advocate for nearly 25 million Italian Americans, the nation's fifth-largest ethnic group. NIAF's mission is to preserve and protect Italian American heritage and culture, and it offers a wide range of programs that provide grants, legislative internships in Congress, conferences, cultural seminars, and travel programs for students. (In 2001 NIAF introduced "The Gift of Discovery," a ten-day trip for Italian American students between the ages of eighteen and twenty-three; the expenses-paid program includes round-trip airfare between New York and Italy and features cultural lectures, meetings with government officials and leaders, and visits to government offices and museums.) Travelers may be most interested in the illustrated guide to

Italian language and culture courses that NIAF publishes. The guide highlights courses at academic and commercial institutions all over Italy, as well as nonacademic studies in art restoration, architecture, fashion, interior design, tourism, and hotel management. Additionally, U.S. universities with study-abroad programs in Italy are also featured. The 252-page guide costs $19.95 including postage and handling and is available only though NIAF. Readers interested in joining NIAF may do so online (there are eight membership categories) or by mail. ~A notable bit of trivia I learned from the website: Connecticut is the state with the highest percentage of Italian Americans, with 16.4 percent. Rhode Island is second, with 15.9 percent, and New Jersey is a very close third, with 15.4 percent.

Orario continuato (continuous hours)
In other words, "open all day," as more and more businesses in Italy are these days.

P

Packing
Most people, whether they travel for business or pleasure, view packing as a stressful chore. It doesn't have to be, and a great book filled with excellent suggestions and tips is *Fodor's How to Pack: Experts Share Their Secrets* (Laurel Cardone, Fodor's Travel Publications, 1997). You might think it silly to consult a book on how to pack a suitcase, but it is eminently practical and worthwhile. Cardone is a travel journalist who's on the road a lot, and she meets a lot of fellow travelers with plenty of packing wisdom to share. Buying luggage, filling almost any suitcase, nearly crease-free folding, finding the right wardrobe for the right trip, and packing for the way back home are all thoroughly covered. ~Some pointers that work for me include selecting clothing that isn't prone to wrinkling, like cotton and wool knits; when I *am* concerned about limiting wrinkles, I lay out a large plastic dry cleaning bag, place the garment on top of it, place *another* bag on top of that, and fold the item up between the two bags. The key here is that the plastic must be layered in with the clothing; otherwise it doesn't really work. ~If I'm packing items with buttons, I button them up before I fold them. The same with zippers and snaps. ~If I'm carrying a bag with more than one separate compartment, I use one for shoes; otherwise I put shoes at the bottom (or back) of the bag opposite the handle so they'll remain there while I'm carrying the bag. ~Transfer shampoo and lotions to travel-size plastic bottles, which can be purchased at pharmacies—and put them inside a Ziploc bag to prevent against leaks. ~Don't skimp on underwear—it's lightweight, it takes up next to no room in your bag, and it's never a mistake to have more than you think you need. ~Belts can be either rolled up and stuffed into shoes or fastened together along the inside edge of your suitcase. ~Ties should be rolled, not folded, and stuffed into shoes or pockets. ~Some

handy things to bring along that are often overlooked: a pocket flashlight, for looking into ill-lit corners of old buildings, reading in bed at night (the lights are often not bright enough), or, if you're staying at a hotel where the bathroom is down the hall, for navigating the dark hallways (the light is usually on a timer and always runs out before you've made it to either end of the hallway); binoculars; a small travel umbrella; a penknife/corkscrew; if I'm camping, plastic shoes—referred to in the United States as jellies—that the Italians have been wearing on some of their rocky *spiaggi* (beaches) for years and years—for campground showers; an empty lightweight duffel bag, which I fold up, pack, and use as a carry-on bag for gifts and breakable items on the way home; copies of any current prescriptions, in case I need to have a medicine refilled; photocopies of my passport and airline tickets (which should also be left with someone at home).

Pane e coperto

About six years ago there was a movement to try to stop Italian *ristoranti* and *trattorie* from charging a *pane e coperto* fee (supposedly for the bread and rent of the silverware), which ranged from two to six dollars. (The authors of *Eating and Drinking in Italy* refer to it as "a small charge just for placing your butt at the table.") Although *pane e coperto* is no longer ubiquitous (it was even an institution at campground restaurants), I have it on good authority from the Italian Tourist Office that, regrettably, some establishments still charge it. It's not really a big deal and certainly not worth arguing over, but if you're just stopping for a plate of pasta and a glass of wine, the *coperto* could cost half as much as your meal.

Parla inglese?

"Do you speak English?", a phrase you might be asking quite often. While many Italians are not *fluent* in English, nearly everyone knows a few words, or sometimes they will run and fetch someone who does.

Passeggiata

Known in Italy as the *passeggiata,* the evening stroll is an ages-old Mediterranean custom (it's called the *paseo* in Spain and Morocco, for example, and goes by other names in Croatia, Egypt, and Greece). I am convinced the evening *passeggiata* is one reason why Italians and Mediterranean people in general are healthier than Americans. The combination of regular exercise, smaller food portions, a bigger meal at lunch, and wine and alcohol in moderation is not a secret code to be deciphered. What could be more pleasant than taking an evening stroll around town (or village) before dinner? The *passeggiata* provides a relaxing and rejuvenating experience for residents and visitors alike, and has also historically served as a venue for young men and women to meet each other. *Everyone* turns out for the *passeggiata*—grandparents, babies, teenagers, and toddlers. The stroll flows a bit better on straight stretches of cobblestones, macadam, or marble, but even in a curving city like Venice the *passeggiata* is a ritual not to be missed. Even elderly people who may not feel up to walking will meet their friends at a particular bench in the closest *piazza* to find out the news of the *sestiere*. An essay in the wonderful *The Walker Within* notes about the *passeggiata* that "were Americans to take up this custom, the rate of criminal violence would surely drop, for it's easier to gun down strangers than people with whom you've passed the time."

Passports

For last-minute crises, it *is* possible to obtain a new passport or get a necessary visa. Two companies that can meet the challenge: Travisa (2122 P Street, N.W., Washington, D.C. 20037; 800-222-2589) and Express Visa Service (353 Lexington Avenue, Suite 1200, New York, New York 10016; 212-679-5650; fax: -4691).

~As in most other countries, hotel and inn proprietors are required to ask to see your passport. Details from your passport are recorded in the inn's ledger and are also shared with local authorities, which is why passports are often not returned to guests until the following day. This is not cause for alarm or mistrust; proprietors are merely following the letter of the law. If you have an imperative reason for hanging on to your passport during the first twelve to twenty-four hours of your stay, let the staff know and they may be able to return it within an hour or so. If you are only staying one night at a particular lodging, make sure your passport is returned to you when you check out. This may seem obvious, but it does happen that both reception staff and guests forget. An extreme example of this happened to my friend John, who was traveling in northern Italy on his honeymoon. He and his new bride were on a train en route to their next destination when they realized their passports had not been returned to them upon checkout at the previous inn. When they telephoned, the reception staff reported it did not have the passports, and that they had been returned. (It has never actually been fully investigated if the passports were stolen.) Rather than return to the inn, the newlyweds chose to report to the U.S. embassy and apply for new passports, a fairly time-consuming and frustrating experience. Have you ever tried to convince someone that you are who you say you are? Or tried to prove you are an American citizen? (The bride, who had lived previously in Boston, was asked a series of questions about local professional sports stars, which she positively could not answer, causing the embassy official to doubt she knew Boston at all. It was only after it was revealed that she was familiar with local politics that a breakthrough occurred, as she knew every state and national politician in eastern Massachusetts.) I, too, had my own passport experience upon checking out of a very fine hotel in Friuli–Venezia Giulia. I was simply preoccupied while paying the bill, mad at myself for getting a later start than I had wanted, and just not paying close attention. It was not until two hours later that I realized what had happened. When I called the inn, the staff was unable to send someone to deliver the passport until the next day. I was concerned about checking in to my hotel in Trieste that night, but the staff said it would not be a problem—they called the Trieste hotel and gave them my passport information. I then selected a spot for a rendezvous the following day for the passport return, at 1:00, and the bigger problem then turned out to be lunch. If I haven't hit you over the head about mealtimes yet, it's worth repeating once more: plan your days carefully and don't find yourself in a town at 1:30 with all the shops closed and restaurants full. As it happened with me, the hotel representative was a little late, and after he returned the passport, I asked him for a nearby recommendation for lunch. He checked his watch, and a look rather like panic registered on his face. He told me we would have to hurry and that I was to follow him. I could barely keep up with his driving, as he sped around the country roads, and sure enough, the place he most wanted me to eat at was full, and the second place was closed on that particular day of the week. Resigned and defeated, the rep said, with embarrassment, that he would drive me to the only place left: a shopping mall on the highway that kept an *horario continuato* schedule. (Though I shared his disappointment, even fast food in Italy is better than in America: for the equivalent of five dollars, I had a fresh tomato, mozzarella and basil sandwich—which was quite good, as the tomatoes were real and ripe, not those plastic, mealy things American produce distributors have the audacity to call tomatoes, and the mozzarella was creamy—and a generous glass of white wine, which would of course *never* be allowed at a fast food outlet in a U.S. shopping mall). Okay. I think I've now exhausted two important topics: your American (or Canadian) passport is a valuable commodity, and mealtimes are taken seriously in Italy.

Pazienza (patience)

Kate Simon, in her book *Italy: The Places In Between,* defines *pazienza* as "the capacity to endure with serenity," a quality very much worth remembering when traveling in Italy.

Periodicals

Following are some newsletters and periodicals, a few of which are not available at newsstands, that you may want to consider subscribing to in advance of your trip—or upon your return, if you want to keep up with goings-on in Italy:

~*The Art of Eating:* Named "Most Nourishing Food Quarterly" by *Saveur* in 1999 and described as "one of the most respected publications in the food world" by *Chef's Edition* on National Public Radio, this is, in my opinion, one of the very best publications ever, of any kind. Some readers may already know of this absolutely excellent, critical, and superbly written quarterly newsletter by Edward

Behr. Although not exclusively about Italy, Behr has devoted several issues to various aspects of Italian food and restaurants over the years, and each of them is worth the effort to special-order. Of particular interest is the Spring 1999 issue, devoted to Venice. Of this issue, I would say: don't go without it! *The Art of Eating* is really *essenziale* reading, so don't wait until the last minute to order back issues ($9 each, $7.50 for four or more). If you want to learn about the food traditions of Italy and other countries and care about the food you eat and its future, you'll want to subscribe to this stellar periodical. Some cookbook and cookware stores sell individual issues of *The Art of Eating* (Kitchen Arts & Letters in New York stocks it regularly), but to receive it in your mailbox you should subscribe: Box 242, Peacham, Vermont 05862; 800-495-3944; www.artofeating.com.

~*Dove Dossier:* This monthly magazine is in Italian and is devoted to *"vacanze e tempo libero"* (vacation and free time). Although I do not speak or read Italian, I find the magazine useful for the names and addresses of restaurants, places to stay, and things to do, and the maps and color photos are great.

~*Events in Italy:* This bimonthly magazine is published in Florence but is in English, and features art, music, and museum events going on all over Italy as well as sections on places to stay, news and culture, travel, fashion, food and restaurants, and classified ads. It's available on some of the bigger American newsstands, or you can subscribe by contacting the magazine directly: Lungarno Corsini 6, Florence 50123; 055.215613; www.events-italy.it.

~*Gambero Rosso:* This quarterly magazine devoted to wine, travel, and food in Italy is among my favorite publications. I can't describe it better than its own promotional motto: "A magazine for intelligent travelers, gourmets on a budget, value-conscious buyers of nothing but the best." I anxiously wait for each issue to appear in my mailbox, but *Gambero Rosso* can also be found at better newsstands; to subscribe, contact the magazine's U.S. distributor: Speedimpex USA, 35-02 48th Avenue, Long Island City, New York 11101; 800-969-1258; fax: 718-361-0815; to subscribe to the Italian version of the magazine, contact the main office in Rome: Via Arenula 53, Rome 00186; 39.06.68300742; fax: 39.05.6877217; e-mail: gambero@gamberorosso.it; www.gamberorosso.it.

~*Italian Cooking & Living:* This magazine debuted in the spring of 2001 and is available on newsstands. It isn't so very different from other food magazines—such as *La Cucina Italiana*—but I like it because it represents just one medium of The Italian Table, founded by Paolo Villoresi in Italy. Villoresi's mission is to familiarize everyone with authentic Italian cuisine. "After all," as he notes, "cooking is about far more than food: it is about people, about tradition, about culture. *Italian Cooking & Living* is for everyone: it is for food lovers who wish to become food experts, for people who have little time to devote to cooking but want to enjoy honest Italian food, and for those who want to create exciting menus to have fun dining with friends." The *Italian Cooking & Living* website—www.italiancookingandliving.com—features food, recipes, information on wine, travel tips, cooking techniques, discounts, and a calendar of food and wine activities across North America.

~*Italy Italy:* "A Guide to All Its Best" is this bimonthly magazine's motto, and each issue offers a variety of articles pertaining to history, contemporary events, travel, personalities, and the arts. What's harder to convey here is how beautifully printed the magazine is, and how in-depth the articles are. This is absolutely one of my most favorite magazines about Italy, and thankfully it's available at some of the larger newsstands in the United States. To subscribe, contact IAM Italian American Multimedia Corporation, P.O. Box 1255, New York, New York 10116; 800-98-ITALY; fax: 212-982-3852; www.italyitalymagazine.com.

~*Meridiani:* This beautiful monthly magazine is published in Italian but is worth a look even for visitors who don't know the language. It focuses on the history and culture of Italy, and each issue is devoted to a single city or region. The issue from the summer of 2001 (no. 75) is devoted to Venice, and it's filled with color photos and features about *acqua alta,* La Fenice, the Ghetto, San Lazzaro, the artwork of Gabriel Bella, and more, as well as book, music, and restaurant reviews, a calendar of events, art itineraries, and a pull-out map. Other issues I've seen are as comprehensive, and all are worth the cover price (about $6). *Meridiana* can be found at almost every newsstand in Italy; I'm not sure if international subscriptions are honored, but readers can inquire by contacting the magazine at Editoriale Domus, Servizio Abbonati, Casella postale 13080, Milan 20130.

Per piacere, per favore, permesso, più lentamente, and prego

Some good Italian *P* words to know. *Per piacere* and *per favore* mean "please"; *permesso* means "permission" (a polite way to ask if you may enter, sit down, take something, ask a question, etc.); *più lentamente* is useful when you want to say "please speak more slowly"; and *prego* is an all-purpose word used to mean "please," "you're welcome," "okay," "of course," "go ahead."

Photography

I would rather have one great photo of a place than a dozen mediocre shots, so I like to page through photography books for ideas and suggestions on maximizing my picture-taking efforts. Here are some books I've particularly enjoyed.

The Traveler's Eye: A Guide to Still and Video Travel Photography (Lisl Dennis, Clarkson Potter, 1996). Dennis, who began her career in photography at *The Boston Globe,* writes the "Traveler's Eye" column for *Outdoor Photographer.* I like her sensitive approach to travel photography and find her images and suggestions in this book inspiring. After chapters covering such topics as travel photojournalism, shooting special events, and landscape photography, she provides an especially useful chapter on technical considerations, with advice on equipment, film, packing, the ethics of tipping, and outsmarting airport X-ray machines.

Focus on Travel: Photographing Memorable Pictures of Journeys to New Places (text by Anne Millman and Allen Rokach, photographs by Allen Rokach, Abbeville Press, 1992). This book is more of a tome than *The Traveler's Eye,* although it doesn't cover video cameras. The authors offer much more information on lenses, filters, films, and accessories and offer separate chapters on photographing architecture, shooting subjects in action, and taking pictures in a variety of weather conditions. The appendix covers selecting and preparing your photos after the trip, fill-in flash guidelines, a color correction chart, and a page-by-page reference to all the photos in the book.

Kodak Guide to Shooting Great Travel Pictures (Jeff Wignall, Fodor's Travel Publications, 2000). Unlike the books above, which should be consulted before you go, this very handy, small paperback is good for bringing along as a reference. Six chapters present specific photographic challenges—such as city vistas, stained-glass windows, close-ups of faces, mountain scenery, motion, lights at night, and taking pictures through frames—and each is dealt with in one page. This guide is meant for experienced *and* point-and-shoot photographers; many of the images featured in the book are from the Eastman Kodak archives, a great number of which were taken by amateurs. The final chapter is devoted to creating a travel journal.

Piazza

In other towns and villages of Italy, the piazza is, of course, the central square where much of the life of those towns and villages takes place. In Venice there are dozens and dozens of *campi* (fields) and even a *campiello* here and there, but to Venetians there is only one piazza: Piazza San Marco. Equally as pleasant, though not as grand, is the Piazza Unità d'Italia in Trieste, which faces the sea.

Ponti

Ponti is Italian for "bridges," of which there are quite a lot in Venice. I regret I was unable to include in this book a wonderful piece entitled "A City Defined by Its Bridges" (Louis Inturrisi, *New York Times,* December 22, 1996), in which Inturrisi informs us that Venice is "stretched over 116 islands and crisscrossed by more than 150 canals." The four hundred or so bridges in Venice are more than a means of crossing canals; they are reliable points of reference. As Darlene Marwitz notes in *Italy Fever,* "Venetians live ninety-nine bridges from the train station, twenty-six bridges from the closest shoe repair shop, or six bridges from their favorite bar." When you are asking directions, you may notice that Venetians will often say that the site you are seeking is *do ponti da qui* (two bridges from here) or *al di là del ponte* (on the other side of the bridge). Inturrisi also tells us that a Venetian will suggest an after-dinner stroll by using the phrase *andar' per ponti,* "to walk the bridges." I don't know if anyone has ever published a book on the *ponti* of Venice—surely someone must have; I just haven't found it yet—but as the bridges are all different, I think it would make a remarkably interesting book, similar to a volume I have on the fountains of Rome. In truth the bridges of Venice are very much alike, as they are all made of stone. (Long ago they were all made of wood and were flat, so that carts and cattle could pass over them easily into the fields, or *campi,* as all the piazzas in Venice—with the exception of San Marco—were once called.) But the bridges do range in length, from the long, two-mile causeway that connects Venice to the mainland to little private walkways leading to a residence. ~A tip: the stone bridges can be treacherous when wet, so roam with caution.

La Posta

If you'll be traveling on to Rome, mail all your postcards, letters, or packages from an *ufficio postale* (post office) in the Città del Vaticano (Vatican City) as it's the only place in Italy with reliable mail service. Your postcards *(cartolini)* will actually arrive at their destinations if you mail them from there. Postcards mailed from Venice *may* arrive; just don't be surprised if they don't. Actually, I have never had a problem on the occasions I was mailing items home to myself, but the utter disarray inside a typical Italian post office—especially in smaller towns—has led me to think many times that I would never see the items I mailed again. If you're mailing anything of value or if it's very large, you might want to consider a packing and shipping service. I don't recommend trying to pack and mail something yourself, unless you have an *abbondanza* of patience, because Italian postal requirements are so complex, your head will hurt. Much better to inquire at the tourist office about a service, one that is familiar with the proper way to wrap and the proper stamps, seals, and paperwork. ~I learned of a wonderful new worldwide delivery service while I was at the Accademia: FlyBooks. Visitors can buy all the books they want without worrying about the weight. I don't know exactly how this works because I didn't try it—though believe me, there were a great number of books I wanted to buy in the museum's bookstore—but FlyBooks is a home delivery service offered by the Accademia in collaboration with Verona 83—Stagehand and the Italian publisher Electa. Interested readers should inquire at the ticket office for the necessary forms and information. ~As in other European countries, *francobolli* (stamps) are also sold at *tabacchi* (tobacco shops) in Italy.

Può aiutarmi, per favore?

"Can you help me, please?" (pronounced pooh-O i-u-TAR-mee). It is a very useful phrase, as everyone always wants to be helpful.

Real Estate

If you find northeastern Italy *bella* and decide you want to stay for the rest of your life—or if you're a student or have been temporarily transferred overseas—two good books to consult are *Living in Italy: The Essential Guide for Property Purchasers and Residents* (Yve Menzies, Robert Hale Limited, London, 1999) and *Buying a Home in Italy* (David Hampshire, 1999). Both books address identity cards, banking, insurance, taxes, and so on, and if you can't find them in your favorite bookstore, you can order them direct from Seven Hills Book Distributors (1531 Tremont Street, Cincinnati, Ohio 45214; 800-545-2005; fax: 888-777-7799; www.sevenhillsbooks.com).

Riposo settimanale

Riposo settimanale is a good Italian phrase to know as it refers to a regular day of the week that an establishment is closed. You'll often see it posted on a sign, and the day is often Monday.

Rolling Venice

Through Rolling Venice, travelers between the ages of fourteen and twenty-nine can obtain valuable information, including a guidebook to direct them to Venetian hot spots and to make their trip more economically accessible. They are eligible for inexpensive rates for accommodations and food, and special rates for museums and theater. Brochures for this program are available at Italian tourist locations.

S

Saints' Days

Nearly every day of the year is a saint day somewhere in Italy, at both the national and local levels. National saints' days fall on November 1 (*Tutti Santi,* All Saints' Day) and December 26 (*Santo Stefano,* Saint Stephen). Offices and stores are typically closed on national saints' days, as well as on feast days that honor local patron saints. ~Public holidays are known as *giorni festivi,* and *chiuso per ferie* (closed for the holidays) is a phrase you'll hear often in August, when Italians (and most Europeans) are on vacation. A *ponte* (bridge) is the equivalent of our long weekend, when a holiday falls on Thursday, Friday, Monday, or Tuesday.

Save Venice

Save Venice is a wonderful organization that was born after the city's most infamous flood, on November 4, 1966. That terrible flood, ironically, proved to be the best tragedy to ever befall Venice, as it attracted the attention of concerned citizens around the world. In response to the flood, more than thirty international private committees—organized under the administrative umbrella of UNESCO—were formed to restore and protect Venice's masterpieces. (twenty-five of them are still active), as the Venice Committee of the International Fund for Monuments. In 1971 the late John and Betty McAndrew (John was professor of art history at Wellesley College) and Sydney J. Freedberg (then chairman of the department of fine arts at Harvard University) founded Save Venice from the Venice Committee of the International Fund for Monuments. Today the International Fund for Monuments is known as the World Monuments Fund, and it funds projects all over the world, while Save Venice, a purely American organization, confines its activities to Venice.

Can Venice be saved? Should it be saved? I passionately believe that it can and should, and I hope that both first-time and repeat visitors to *La Serenissima* will believe so too. Were it not for the efforts of organizations like Save Venice, some or most of Venice would exist solely in art history books today; its supporters recognize that to allow such a treasure to disappear would be a tragedy for all humanity. "Yet again I must rejoice in the miracle that has enabled Venice to survive for thirteen hundred years," wrote the incomparable J. G. Links in *Venice for Pleasure*. "It cannot be long," he continued, "in terms of a city of Venice's age before the water returns, and we are enjoying a privilege which, the experts tell us, may well be denied to our grandchildren and certainly to theirs." Writer Evelyn Waugh noted, "If every museum in the New World were emptied, if every famous building in the Old World were destroyed and only Venice saved, there would be enough there to fill a full lifetime with delight. Venice, with all its complexity and variety, is in itself the greatest surviving work of art in the world." Who can save Venice? Only her own citizens and local politicians, in combination with groups and individuals around the globe, and certainly Save Venice can help enormously.

The mission of Save Venice, Inc., a nonprofit U.S. organization, is to protect the cultural patrimony of the city by raising funds to restore its monuments and works of art. It does not work in isolation; the Superintendencies of Monuments and of Fine Arts in Venice direct all restoration work carried out by Save Venice. Once the superintendents have identified projects in urgent need of care, the board of Save Venice chooses projects from this wish list and raises money to fund the work. No project is completed without the efforts of Venetians *and* others. But since its formation, Save Venice has been the most active of the private committees in the international effort to conserve the treasures of this beleaguered city. The works that it has preserved are truly extraordinary, many of them glories of Western civilization. Here are just a few: preservation of the facade of the Ca' d'Oro, the most famous and elegant private fifteenth-century palace in Venice (1968); restoration of Tintoretto canvases and installation of a climate control system in the Scuola Grande di San Rocco (1970); repair and cleaning of Donatello's *Saint John the Baptist* sculpture in the Church of Santa

Maria Gloriosa dei Frari—this painted wooden sculpture is the only example of the sculptor's work in Venice, and when cleaned, Donatello's signature and the signed date of 1438 were revealed, ending many years of scholarly debate (1973); structural reinforcement, roof repair, installation of a heating system, and much else in the Scuola Levantina, the baroque synagogue in the Ghetto dating from 1678 (1974); cleaning and repair of *Paradise* by Tintoretto, the largest painting on canvas in the world, in the Sala del Maggior Consiglio of the Doges' Palace (1983); cleaning of Titian's altar painting *Annunciation,* for many decades nearly invisible under heavy layers of dirt, in the Church of San Salvador (1989); restoration of three historic Venetian boats in the collection of the Naval Museum at the Arsenale (1995); clearing, cataloging, and restoration of the old Jewish cemetery, Lido (1998); and the fresco cycle in the presbytery and apse of the Church of San Samuele, dedicated to the Old Testament seer Samuel (Venice being the only city in Italy where Old Testament prophets were venerated as saints). Since 1998 Save Venice has been working on the restoration of the facade of the Scuola Grande di San Marco. Save Venice also has an educational mission to teach people about the city's culture and history. One way in which it does this—and this is perhaps what impresses me most about Save Venice and what I think separates it from other charitable organizations—is to sponsor fellowships for extremely qualified scholars specializing in conservation and art history. In addition to four fellowships in Venice, the organization also sponsors a stone-conservation course in Venice for thirty students from around the world.

Besides the central office in New York, Save Venice has two chapters in the United States, both of which are extremely active. Save Venice supporters have the opportunity to participate in numerous events sponsored by the organization throughout the year. In addition to lectures and concerts, the annual Masked Ball in celebration of Venetian *Carnevale* has become one of the most popular fundraising events in New York, and since 1987 Save Venice has organized a biennial Regatta Week Gala, a five-day cultural celebration in Venice that includes dinners in private homes and a ball in a Venetian palazzo. (The theme for the 2001 gala was "Music in Venice.") Save Venice also publishes a number of excellent publications, including "Venetian Treasures Restored & Preserved" (detailing its projects from 1968 to 1998), a quarterly newsletter, and a biannual scholarly journal published on the occasion of Gala Week. Additionally, an absolutely essential and fun book entitled *The Riddles of Venice: A Book of Six Treasure Hunts in Venice* is available through the organization, and it is among the very best books I've ever seen, for both adults and children. (See the entry for Children for more details.) My personal plea to you is to contact the Save Venice office in New York, even if you live far from the city, and get involved. (A good way to begin might be to view its website, www.savevenice.org.) There is no better way to ensure the continued existence of the world's most compelling and radiantly beautiful city. I will be the first to admit that there are hundreds of enjoyable ways to part with one's money in Venice, but none is as significant, satisfying, or long lasting as making a donation, however small or large, to Save Venice (15 East 74th Street, New York, New York 10021; 212-737-3141; fax: 249-0510; newyork@savevenice.org). Though I am surely teetering on the brink of being annoying, I encourage you to join in the effort to preserve Venice's unique and very fragile heritage. Please support Save Venice!

Scusi (excuse me)
Another good Italian word you'll hear often is *scusi*. It's used to make your way through a crowd, on public transportation, or to get someone's attention.

Sempre Dritto
Translating as "straight ahead" (the equivalent of *tout droit* in French), *sempre dritto* is a Venetian phrase with a history, and no one can explain it better than J. G. Links: "Accost the first passer-by without a camera, smile and say, for example, 'Zattere?' His answer will be *'sempre dritto'* (straight on), which will not help much as nothing is straight on in Venice. He will, however, add gestures to his answer which will, at any rate, set us off in the right direction. In all probability, he will insist on personally escorting us, whether he happened to be going in our direction or not. If he does not answer *'sempre dritto,'* he is not a Venetian and his directions must be treated with caution; he may be just another Englishman showing off by walking about Venice without a camera. Venetians *always* answer *'sempre dritto.'* James Morris, by far the city's best twentieth-century chronicler, tells us (in *Venice* [Faber, 1983]) how Pepin attempted to take Venice in 809 and reached Malamocco, which the Venetians had abandoned in favour of the group of islands called Rivo Alto–Rialto. 'Only one old woman had stayed behind in Malamocco, determined to do or die, and this patriotic crone was summoned to the royal presence. "Which is the way to Rivo Alto?" demanded Pepin, and the old woman knew her moment had come. Quavering was her finger as she pointed across the treacherous flats . . . tremulous was her voice as she answered the prince. *"Sempre dritto,"* she said: and Pepin's fleet, instantly running aground, was ambushed by the Venetians and utterly humiliated.' So it has been ever since."

Single Travelers
Those traveling alone (not necessarily looking for romance) might be interested in a great book: *Traveling Solo: Advice and Ideas for More Than 250 Great Vacations* (Eleanor Berman, Globe Pequot Press, Old Saybrook, Connecticut, 1997). Berman offers the names of tour operators for different age groups and different types of trips and asks all the right questions in helping you determine if a proposed vacation is right for you. ~Female *and* male solo travelers should beware of revealing

too many personal details about their travels. If you admit that you're traveling for an indefinite period of time, for example, the perception will be that you are probably carrying a lot of money. I met an Australian man who had the bulk of his money stolen from a youth hostel safe, and he was certain it was taken by a fellow hosteler whom he had befriended (but who had since disappeared).

Slow Food

Though Slow Food is an international movement, it's based in Italy (in the Piemonte region), so I felt it would not be out of place to mention it here. To my mind, it seems that only the Italians or the French could create such a wonderful response to American fast food. The Slow Food movement was founded in 1989, and is active in forty countries with sixty thousand members and five hundred convivia (chapters). Slow Food U.S.A. has over five thousand members and fifty convivia. Slow Food is for food and wine enthusiasts who care about and promote traditional foodstuffs from around the world and who "share the snail's wise slow-itude" (the snail, appropriately, is the organization's symbol). As Carlo Petrini, president of Slow Food, has stated, "Food history is as important as a baroque church. Governments should recognize cultural heritage and protect traditional foods. A cheese is as worthy of preserving as a sixteenth-century building."

A highlight from the organization's manifesto is "in the name of productivity, Fast Life has changed our way of being and threatens our environment and our landscapes. So Slow Food is now the only truly progressive answer." There are several programs and divisions that encompass Slow Food: The Ark (a project aimed at documenting and promoting foods and beverages in danger of becoming extinct); Events (the biennial *Salone del Gusto* in Turino is the largest food and wine event in the world, and its biennial Cheese in Bra (Italy) is the largest cheese show in the world; in addition to these, there are wine conventions and tasting sessions across the United States, various food festivals around the world, and each convivium organizes educational tastings, cooking courses, trips, visits to restaurants, and lectures for its members); Publications (in addition to the excellent *Vini d'Italia*—published in conjunction with *Gambero Rosso* and detailed in the *La Cucina Veneziana biblioteca*—Slow Food publishes *Italian Cheese*, the first guide to traditional Italian cheeses, with 205 artisanal specialties described and documented; *Slowine*, a seventy-page magazine reporting on wine culture around the world; and an outstanding and insightful journal entitled *Slow: The International Herald of Tastes*, which is published in English, German, Italian, and French; Fraternal Tables (Slow Food funds projects in Nicaragua, Hekura (Brazil), Zlata (Bosnia) and Colfiorito in Umbria; and Slow Cities (a group of towns and cities in Italy committed to improving the quality of life of their citizens, especially with regard to food issues; the best known Slow City in northeastern Italy is San Daniele del Friuli, and readers can view the entire list online).

Personally, I think Slow Food may save the planet, and is one of the more worthwhile groups to support. Interested readers may join Slow Food U.S.A. by contacting the group by snail mail (P.O. Box 1737, New York, New York 10021), telephone 212-965-5640, e-mail (pmartins@slowfood.com), or by viewing its website (www.slowfood.com). A $60 membership entitles you to four issues of *Slow*, four newsletters of *The Snail*, two issues of *Slowine*, invitations to all Slow Food events, and discounts on Slow Food publications and merchandise (I have to admit I'm hooked on the snail pins and aprons).

Squisitezza
This beautiful Italian word means "exquisiteness," "daintiness," or "delicacy." You will in all likelihood never use it, but it's such a great word, I couldn't leave it out of this compendium.

Stendhal Syndrome
Named for the sick, physical feeling that afflicted French novelist Stendhal after he visited Santa Croce in Florence, Stendhal Syndrome is synonymous with being completely overwhelmed by your surroundings. (My translation: "seeing and doing way too much.") Though it happened to Stendhal in Florence, it could just as easily have happened in Venice, and visitors who arrive with too long a list of must-sees are prime candidates. As Truman Capote said in 1961, visiting Venice is "like eating an entire box of chocolate liqueurs at one go." There is simply too much to see; accept it, and come back. My advice: organize your days, factor in how long it takes to get from place to place, and see what you want. There will be no quiz.

Storage
If you plan on traveling around Italy or beyond for extended periods of time (say, a month or longer) and want to store some baggage or other belongings, you should first investigate the left-luggage facilities at Santa Maria Novella train station in Florence or at the *stazione* in other towns of Italy. A locker at a station may prove to be ideal if you'll be traveling by train. Otherwise, check with the tourist office and ask for recommendations for storage companies.

Strade (streets)
Just as the Venetians have their own dialect, they even have their own curious names for different types of "streets," which I put in quotation marks because a Venetian *strada* is not like any other street in the world, except perhaps in Treviso or Amsterdam. For the following definitions, I have borrowed when necessary from J. G. Links: a *calle* (plural *calli*) is a long and narrow street, or a lane. A *campo* (plural *campi*) is an open space, usually always near a church *(chiesa)* and,

as noted earlier, is Italian for "field," since that is what these open spaces were originally. Therefore, a *campiello* is a small *campo,* but note that a *campazzo* is an abandoned place, used for rubbish. A *corte* is something akin to our enclosed courtyard, though usually small. A *fondamenta* (plural either *fondamenta* or *fondamente*) is a paved walkway on the banks of a canal. An important *fondamenta* may be referred to as a *riva*. A *molo* is a quay. A *punta* is a point, and so the extremities of Venice are sometimes referred to as Punta di ——. A *ramo* (plural *rami*) is a little offshoot from a larger street. Some *rami* are so narrow that only one person may pass at a time, reminding me of a narrow alley in a Moroccan *medina*. And by narrow, I mean you have only to stick out your elbows to touch the walls on both sides. A *rio* (plural *rii*) is a canal, any canal except the Grand Canal and the Canareggio Canal. A *rio terra* is a filled-in canal that has thus become a street. A *ruga* is a street with shops, or even houses, along both sides; a *rhugetta* is a little *ruga*. A *sacca* is a stretch of water into which two or more canals run. A *salizzada* or *salizada* is one of the principal streets of a parish; Jan Morris notes that a *salizzada* is a paved alley, "once so rare as to be worth distinguishing." A *sottoportico* or *sotoportego* (another of my favorite words) is a small street entered by an arch under a building, and it may be covered the entire way. And related to the Venetians' unusual street names is their unusual numbering system. Again according to Links, a Venetian's postal address is the name of the *sestiere* in which one lives followed by a number. The numbers are consecutive in the truest sense: one number follows another going all the way down a *calle,* around to a *corte,* and back up the other side of the *calle* so that two houses facing each other have numbers that are quite far apart. Often, you will see addresses given with only the *sestiere* and a number ("Dorsoduro, 1234," for example). This is not helpful, and even residents have trouble with such meaningless numbers. By all means, before you set out looking for a particular address, ascertain the nearest landmark, be it a *campo,* church, museum, restaurant, whatever, and get as many precise details as you can. A few times, in desperation, I have taken my vague addresses to the tourist office, and together we would trace out a route on my map. Of course, if you spy a postman, you're in the best hands possible.

Studying in Italy

Not surprisingly, Italy has dozens and dozens of study opportunities for North Americans, sponsored either by colleges and universities or by other educational institutions. The majority of these programs are available in central Italy and Rome, but there are some in the Veneto, Friuli–Venezia Giulia, and Trentino–Alto Adige as well. If you are a college-age student seeking a program, my advice is to select one that allows you to stay a year or even longer. And if you have to change your major to go, do it—you won't regret it! Spending a semester abroad is a great experience, but there is no replacement for staying a year. Alternatively, investigate attending an Italian college or university. Studying in Italy isn't limited to language (courses are also offered in the fine arts, photography, painting, business, literature, and so on) or age (plenty of programs welcome adults, and plenty of adults attend). *The* guide to begin your research is *Directory of Italian Schools and Universities* (Michael Giammarella, EMI International, P.O. Box 640713, Oakland Gardens, New York 11364-0713; 718-631-0096; fax: -0316; e-mail: mgiamma@prodigy.net). The guide, $19 plus $3 for first-class shipping, details a variety of the programs— not just language—offered throughout Italy. Giammarella also handles bookings for the programs. (He also publishes directories for Spain and France, among others.) A good school featured in Giammarella's guide is Istituto Venezia, located in the *sestiere* of Dorsoduro in Venice; it offers language courses and special programs on cuisine, among other things. Another good school is the Centro Culturale Italiano in Verona, which offers language classes year-round. ~Tourist offices here in the States, and the offices of the Istituto Italiano di Cultura in the United States and Canada have numerous brochures on language and cultural programs in Italy. Additionally, a group called WorldWide Classroom (Box 1166, Milwaukee, Wisconsin 53201; fax: 414-224-3466; www.worldwide.edu), which I learned about by browsing the excellent www.initaly.com website, offers a number of programs in northeastern Italy, including Accademia di Belle Arti in Venice; British Institutes Vicenza; Centro Studi Alberti and Istituto Trentino di Cultura in Trento; Italo American Association of the Region Friuli–Venezia Giulia and The British School in Trieste; The English International School and Istituto Linguistico in Padua; and the Giulietta e Romeo Centre of Italian Studies in Verona. WorldWide is among the largest international consortium of schools, providing information about 10,000 schools in 109 countries.

T

Telephones

Remember that Italy is six hours ahead of Eastern Standard Time, seven ahead of Central time, eight ahead of Mountain time, and nine ahead of Pacific time. To call Italy from the United States, dial 011 + 39 + local number (011 = the overseas line, 39 = country code for Italy, and the local number includes the appropriate city code). The city code for Venice is 041. Verona is 045, and Trieste is 0431. Note that when calling any city or town in Italy from the United States, you must include the initial 0, and all phone numbers in this book include it. To call the United States from Italy, dial 00 + 1 + area code + number. Within Italy, to reach an Italian operator for local assistance, dial 12. To reach an operator for assistance outside the local area, dial 175. To reach an English-speaking operator, dial 176. For tourist information, dial 110. In an emergency (the equivalent of 911 in the United States), dial 113. ~Do not be alarmed that some Italian phone numbers have more digits than others. I can't explain it—it's just Italy. ~Almost all public phones in Italy no longer accept *gettoni* (tokens). A *carta telefonica* (phone card) is now the way and can be purchased at Telecom Italia offices and at *tabacchi* (tobacco shops). You can also place calls at Telecom Italia offices, where there are individual cabins and you pay after you make the call. Inquire at the tourist office about the least expensive times of day to call—it's usually after 6:30 P.M. during the week, from 10:00 P.M. to 8:00 A.M. on weekends and holidays, and after 1:30 P.M. on Saturdays.

~*Telefonini* are cellular phones, and you'll quickly notice that Italians use them constantly. I won't elaborate on my feelings about cell phones here, but at least the Italians have the excuse that their public telephone system is at best unreliable and at worst horrendous. If you feel you really must have your own cell phone, check with your service provider first to ensure the phone is programmed to be compatible with European communication systems. Renting a compatible cell phone may be a better option: a few companies that offer them are Cellhire (offices in New York, Los Angeles, Dallas, and Washington, D.C.; 866-CH-ONLINE; www.cellhire.com); WorldCell (International Mobile Communications, 801 Roeder Road, Suite 800, Silver Spring, Maryland 20910; 888-967-5323; fax: 301-562-1379; www.worldcell.com); and Roberts Rent-a-Phone (150 East 69th Street, New York, New York 10021; 800-964-2468 or 212-734-6344; fax: -3780; www.roberts-rent-a-phone.com). You can expect the basic rental fee to be about $40 a week, plus the cost of shipping the cell phone to you before you depart. Additionally, there are charges for both outgoing and incoming calls, from about $1 to $3 a minute. Points to keep in mind are that renting a cell phone is not an inexpensive option (though it may be less expensive than making calls from your hotel), and not all companies are the same when it comes to what's in the fine print. Find out in advance exactly what you're going to be charged, and ask about service fees and taxes.

~Useful vocabulary: *elenco telefonico* (telephone directory); *un colpo di telefono* (a telephone call); *scatti* (units used on the telephone card).

Terrorism

This is the first time I have had to include this entry, and unfortunately it will now be a permanent entry in all my books. It is easy to refer to the days before September 11 as "normal," especially regarding international travel. But I don't believe we should pine for those days, which really were "abnormal," as events have shown us. American travelers—and Canadians, too—must accept the fact that we are no longer immune to terrorist acts, on our own soil or on that of other nations, and that we will probably have to pay more to travel and to help pay for the new (and expensive) security systems and programs we must now install in our airports and other public transportation centers. Additionally, I think we can count on travel taking longer than it once did (at every time during the year, not just during holidays) and some of us will need to practice the arts of courtesy and patience while we are all trying to figure out how to foil terrorists. At one time a trip to Italy did not mean that a call to the U.S. State Department was a necessity; but I urge readers planning a trip to northeastern Italy to first read the State Department's profile of Italy. When I recently browsed its website (http://travel.state.gov/travel_warnings), I found a surprising amount of information about where the embassies are located, crime, previous episodes of violence in Italy, medical facilities and insurance, traffic safety, road conditions, and more. As recently as mid-2001 to January 2002, Italy was included on the State Department's list of public announcements to Americans traveling abroad (public announcements are "a means to disseminate information about terrorist threats and other relatively short-term and/or trans-national conditions posing significant risks to the security of American travelers. They are made any time there is a perceived threat and usually have Americans as a particular target group. In the past, public announcements have been issued to deal with short-term coups, bomb threats to airlines, violence by terrorists, and anniversary dates of specific terrorist events."). Note that a public announcement is not the same as a travel warning, which is issued when the State Department decides, "based on all relevant information, to recommend that Americans avoid travel to a certain country." I mention all of this not to create reasons for travelers to be afraid of traveling to Italy; I've read that the State Department is extremely liberal in issuing travel warnings and public announcements; they cannot leave any stone unturned in its efforts to inform the public, so I think smart travelers should embrace a policy of "know before you go": read up on everything, but do not allow yourself to be unnecessarily alarmed at insignificant incidents. I have found the State Department's consular information sheets particularly helpful—they're very detailed and less alarming. Readers may also call 202-647-6575 for information on travel warnings and public announcements. ~Though some of the following tips may seem obvious, I think they are worth repeating for further reflection as you prepare for your trip: register with the nearest embassy if it would make you feel better upon arrival; select either very expensive hotels or budget hotels (the logic here is that moderately priced hotels tend to attract package tourists, a more obvious target); and pack clothes that don't make you immediately stand out from the locals (this includes not bringing that really comfortable sweatshirt with the American flag emblazoned on the front, or your favorite college T-shirt). I do want to add here, however, that I personally am not going to stay in expensive hotels just to feel more secure. If I choose to stay at a high-end place, it will be because I want to, not because I'm afraid to stay at a more modest place. I believe that aware travelers are always on their toes, regardless of the threat of a terrorist attack. ~A book you might want to take a look at is *The Worst-Case Scenario Survival Handbook: Travel* (Joshua Piven and David Borgenicht, Chronicle Books, 2001). Though there is some humor here, this is meant to be a helpful volume, perhaps saving your life or someone else's. Some of the more threatening entries include "How to Escape When Tied Up," "How to Survive a Hostage

Situation," and "How to Survive a Riot." Other entries that may apply to travel in Italy include "How to Survive a Riptide," "How to Foil a Scam Artist," and "How to Pass a Bribe." The appendix also includes tips on general travel strategies, packing, flying, hotels, travel in dangerous places, and a glossary of foreign emergency phrases.

Theft

Whether of the pickpocket variety or something more serious, theft can happen anywhere: in the finest neighborhood, on the bus, in a park, on a street corner. It bears repeating not to wear a fanny pack, which is nothing but a neon magnet for thieves. I read about a lot of incidents that could easily have been avoided. In 1998 a lengthy piece in the travel section of *The Philadelphia Inquirer* told about a husband and wife traveling in France whose pouch with all their valuables in it was stolen. What made this story remarkable was that they were shocked. *I* was shocked reading their tale because they seemed to think it was a good idea to *strap their pouch under the driver's seat of their rental car*. This couple had apparently traveled all over Europe and North America every year for twelve years, so they weren't exactly novices. I think it's a miracle, however, that they hadn't been robbed earlier. Rental cars are easily identified by their license plates and other markings, which may not be so obvious to you and me but signify pay dirt to thieves. Do not leave anything, *anything at all*, in the car, even if you're parking it in a secure garage. My husband and I strictly follow one rule when we rent a car: Never put items in the trunk unless we're immediately getting in the car and driving away, as anyone watching us will then know there's something of value there.

Some pointers: ~Hatchback-type cars are good to rent because you can back into spots against walls or trees, making it impossible to open the trunk. ~Do not leave your passport, money, credit cards, documents, or camera equipment in your room. The hotel safe? If the letters I read are any indication, leaving your belongings in a hotel safe—whether in your room or in the main office—is only slightly more reliable than leaving them in plain view. Sometimes I hear that valuable jewelry was taken from a hotel safe, which I find baffling as there really is only one safe place for valuable jewelry: your home. No occasion, meeting, or celebration, no matter how important or festive, requires that you bring valuable jewelry. *Leave it at home*. I also happen to find it ostentatious to display such wealth.

~While reading the State Department's consular sheet on Italy, I learned that a scam reported primarily in northern Italy is that one or more persons will befriend a traveler and offer drugged food or drink. Also, thieves have been known to impersonate police officers in order to gain the confidence of tourists. The thief shows the prospective victim a circular plastic sign bearing the words "police" or "international police." If you find yourself in this situation, ask to see an identification card *(documento)* as thieves tend not to carry forged documents.

~Pickpockets employ a number of tactics to prey on unaware travelers. Even if you travel often, live in a big city, and think you're savvy, professional thieves can usually pick you out immediately. (They'll quickly identify you as American if you're wearing the trademark sneakers and fanny pack.) Beware the breastfeeding mother who begs you for money (while her other children surround you looking for a way into your pockets), the arguing couple who make a scene (while their accomplices work the crowd of onlookers), the tap on your shoulder at the baggage security checkpoint (when you turn around, someone's made off with your bags after they've passed through the X-ray machine)—anything at all that looks or feels like a setup. For a look at some common tricks, you might want to see *Traveler Beware!*, a video directed by a seventeen-year undercover cop, Kevin Coffey. This eye-opening program shows all the scams that thieves use to target business and holiday travelers. Coffey was founder of the Airport Crimes Detail and investigated literally thousands of crimes against tourists. He's been a guest on *Oprah* and *20/20* and has been featured in *The Wall Street Journal* and *USA Today*. The seventy-minute cassette is available from Penton Overseas (800-748-5804; e-mail: info@pentonoverseas.com) and costs $14.95. ~If, despite your best efforts, your valuables are stolen, go to the local police. You'll have to fill out an official police report, which will help later when you need to prove you were robbed. Call your credit card companies (which is why you have written down those numbers in a separate place), make a trip to the American Express office if you've purchased traveler's checks, and go to the U.S. embassy to replace your passport.

Tipping

Tipping in Italy is not the mystery some people perceive it to be. Service is included in nearly every bill; it will appear on a receipt as *servizio compreso*. Otherwise, tipping is always at the discretion of the client, and as a general guideline a tip is usually 10 percent of the bill. But tipping is expected, in small denominations, for small services: water-taxi drivers usually expect about a 5 percent tip; local tour guides should be tipped the equivalent of two to four dollars per person, depending on his or her ability and the length of the tour; a porter carrying your bags expects some coins, and perhaps more if the bags are numerous and/or heavy (I happen to very much appreciate someone carrying my bags, so I am probably considered a generous tipper to porters; I think nothing of giving the equivalent of a dollar a bag); and custodians who open locked doors for you also expect something in return, usually the equivalent of a dollar or two, plus the obligatory *grazie*, of course.

Toilet Paper

Never set out each day without stuffing some in your pockets or your bag. Public toilets—even in some of the nicest places—can be abominable and often do not have toilet paper, which is *carta igienica* in Italian. I have always found good American-style toilet paper in the bathrooms at American Express offices.

Tourist (as in, being one)

Whether you travel often for business or are making a trip for the first time, let's face it: We're all tourists, and there's nothing shameful about that fact. Yes, it's true that you feel a real part of *la vita quotidiana* when you blend in and are mistaken for a native; but since that's not likely to happen unless you live there, it's far better to just get on with it and have a good time.

Tourist Office

I cannot stress enough how helpful it is to contact the Italian Government Tourist Board as soon as you learn you're going to Italy. Think of it as the ultimate resource: all the information you need is there, or the staff will know how to direct you elsewhere. At the New York office, I have never stumped anyone with my questions and requests, and I think readers have observed that I ask a lot of questions about a lot of little details. A word of advice for dealing with tourist offices in general: it is not very helpful to say you're going to Venice and would like "some information." Allow the staff to help you by providing them with as many details about your visit as you can: Is it your first trip? Do you only need information about hotels? The offices are stocked with mountains of material, but unless you ask for something specific, it will not automatically be given to you.

A good guide to request from North American tourist offices is *Planning Your Trip to Italia,* which is published annually. Additionally, some really excellent and helpful brochures and booklets are available at the tourist offices in Venice that I urge you to pick up. Though new ones will undoubtedly appear after this book goes to press, a few are regularly published on a weekly and monthly basis, and the offices usually always have a surplus of materials that aren't always displayed. The weekly *Un Ospite a Venezia* is indispensable, and *Leo: The Venice Magazine* features articles and color photos about topics of interest and also includes the insert "Bussola," a complete guide to the city. Others that I think are particularly worth obtaining include *Venezia Beyond St. Mark's* (published by the Touring Club Italiano), and *Venezia a Tavola: The Official Guide to Restaurants, Typical Venues, Bars and Nightspots* (which also features historical and cultural neighborhood highlights). From the various offices in the Veneto, I think the following are excellent: "Tiepolo in Vicenza and Its Environs," "Vicenza: Città del Palladio," "Discover Bassano: Free Guided Tours," and "Discover Vicenza: Guided Tours." (This list is most valuable as it details the dates and times of guided tours and gives specifics about the four types of special visitor cards to Vicenza, which include museums, palazzi, and monuments and is valid for one month from the day of issue.) And from APT offices in Friuli–Venezia Giulia, I particularly enjoyed "Diocesan Museum and Tiepolo Galleries," "Trieste Awaits You" (with a city map), and the Udine fold-out map of sites and historic center. There are four tourist offices in North America: at 630 Fifth Avenue, Suite 1565, New York, New York 10111; 212-245-5618; fax: 586-9249; brochure hotline: 212-245-4822; at 500 North Michigan Avenue, Suite 2240, Chicago, Illinois 60611; 312-644-0996; fax: -3019; brochure hotline: 312-644-0990; at 12400 Wilshire Boulevard, Los Angeles, California 90025; 310-820-1898; fax: -6357; brochure hotline: 310-820-0098; and at 175 Bloor Street East, Suite 907, South Tower, Toronto, Ontario M4W 3R8; 416-925-4882; fax: -4799; brochure hotline: 416-925-3870. Travelers can also visit the website www.italiantourism.com.

~*Azienda de Promozione Turistica (APT) and Ente Nazionale Italiano per Il Turismo (ENIT)*: An APT is a local tourist office, and ENIT is the national tourist network of Italy. Just to make things more Italian, there is also the Ufficio Informazione Turistiche, the municipally run office, and the Azienda Turistica office for each region of Italy. No matter what the offices are called, look for the little *i* sign. The main tourist office in Venice is at San Marco 71F, Piazza San Marco (041.529.8711; fax: .8734; www.turismovenezia.it). Other branch offices are located at the Marco Polo Airport arrivals hall, the Santa Lucia train station, San Marco 2, Palazzetto Selva, Giardinetti Reali; and Piazzale Roma. There is also an office on the Lido.

Tours

A list of full-service tour companies would fill a separate book, and it is not my intent to promote only one company or one type of trip. Following are some companies that have appealed to me and offer an authentic experience:

Alternative Travel Group (69-71 Banbury Road, Oxford, OX2 6PE, England; 011.44.1865.315678; fax: 011.44.1865.315697; info@alternative-travel.co.uk). "The best way to see a country is on foot" is the ATG motto. I have been very impressed with this group's philosophy and lengthy catalogs.

Archetours (260 West Broadway, Suite 2, New York, New York 10013; 800-770-3051; fax: 646-613-1897; www.archetours.com). I admit that I first discovered Archetours—whose motto is "World Leader in Architectural Travel"—at the Spanish Tourist Office here in New York. I was preparing for my next book, on northern Spain, and amid all the other tour operator brochures on the shelves, the Archetours brochure really stood out, so I picked it up and read it and knew I had found a like-minded company. While I admit that I have not traveled with Archetours to Italy, I did experience the company's services in Bilbao, and I can report that they were top notch. Expert guides are Archetours' specialty, and they are typically designers, architects, and art and architectural historians who accompany the small group for all or part of each trip. Daniel, our guide to the Guggenheim Museum in Bilbao, made the building and its collection come alive in a way I have never experienced before. "Palladian Villas of the Veneto: Life on a Grand Scale" is the trip Archetours offers to northeastern Italy, and it includes visits to Villa Barbaro, La Rotonda, and Villa Foscari, and private visits to Villa Pisani Ferri, Villa Cornaro, and some others (fifteen in all), and two Renaissance gardens. Visitors are put up in a beautiful restored villa twenty minutes outside Venice.

Cross-Culture: Foreign Travel Programs Designed for Travelers Rather Than Tourists (52 High Point Drive, Amherst, Massachusetts 01002; 800-491-1148 or 413-256-6303; fax: 253-2303; www.crosscultureinc.com). Cross-Culture describes its trips as "group travel for people who think they don't like group travel, designed for travelers rather than tourists." For seventeen years, the company has offered cultural special-interest tours and hiking programs in Europe, the Caribbean, Australia, and New Zealand. Its many trips to Italy include one called "Art of the Veneto: Venice, Vicenza and Verona," which includes visits to Lake Garda and Padua.

Esperienze Italiane: Unparalleled Experiences of Italian Food, Wine and Culture (c/o Felidia Ristorante, 243 E. 58th Street, New York, New York 10022; 800-480-2426 or 212-758-1488; www.lidiasitaly.com). Founded by cookbook author, restaurateur, and PBS host Lidia Bastianich, this unique travel company specializes in food and wine holidays in Italy. When the company began, it focused on prearranged itineraries; but today its specialty is customized itineraries for travelers who are interested in going behind the scenes to visit wine and food producers. Lidia, as readers may know who are already familiar with her PBS show or will definitely know by the time they finish this book, grew up in Istria and Friuli–Venezia Giulia. Her son, Joseph, is a partner in Italian Wine Merchants here in New York, and there is a family winery in Friuli. Between the two of them, you can only imagine how many purveyors they know personally and work with, so this is really a one-of-a-kind experience for foodies.

The Italy Italy Experience (Via Trebbia 5, Rome 00198; 06.8424.2655; fax: 06.8530.4276; e-mail: italy.italy@flashnet.it; www.italyitalymagazine.com). The same people who publish the wonderful *Italy Italy* magazine offer "made-to-measure" travel arrangements in Italy. What makes the Italy Italy Experience unique is that as the travel division of *Italy Italy* magazine, it is able to draw on the resources of a publication that has been dedicated for over twenty years to promoting the best of Italy. The staff has truly discovered and rediscovered Italy's great sights and hidden places, and the best of Italy offers exclusive experiences, such as after-hours visits to museums, accommodations in castles, monasteries, and aristocratic palaces, private fashion shows, private operatic concerts, personalized shopping, and visits to cloistered convents. The Italy Italy Experience also organizes special interest tours and personalized itineraries. A trip it recently developed is a Jewish heritage tour in Trieste and Gorizia. The tour includes visits to: the two synagogues in both cities; Umberto Saba Bookshop (named after the famous Italian-Jewish poet), with a lecture on Italian-Jewish literature; famous cafés in Trieste that were meeting places of Saba, Svevo, and other contemporary intellectuals; the Wagner Museum; the Morpurgo Museum; and an excursion to Gorizia. A second itinerary begins in a seventeenth-century villa. A count, who is also an art historian, guides visitors through the castles and villas of the area. Both itineraries include wine tastings. Other tours in Friuli–Venezia Giulia include the Grado Lagoon and World War II sites.

R. Crusoe & Son (566 West Adams Street no. 505, Chicago, Illinois 60661; 888-490-8047; fax: 312-980-8100; www.rcrusoe.com). The price tags on R. Crusoe trips are among the highest in this business, but these folks are definitely doing things the right way. To quote from a brochure: "Our definition of a traveler (vs. a tourist) is someone who *likes* getting away from the familiar. There is no more engaging way of finding out who you are, who you might be. Travelers, by nature, want to see *inside stuff*, go *behind the scenes,* come home with good stories that are *actually true* (and that their friends haven't already heard)." The nine-day "Venice & the Ravishing Italian Lakes" includes Venice, Vicenza, Verona, and the lakes north of Milan. The thirteen-day "Investigating Italy" includes Venice, Asolo, Florence, Siena, the Amalfi coast, Pompeii, Capri, and Rome.

Smithsonian Study Tours (1100 Jefferson Drive, S.W., Washington, D.C. 20560-0702; 877-EDU-TOUR; www.SmithsonianStudyTours.org). Smithsonian's tours are among my favorite; they are also among the most expensive, but they tend to be longer than most other trips, and travelers also have the added benefit of an excellent study leader. Its trip to northeastern Italy is "Palladian Palaces and Venetian Masters: Lombardy and the Veneto." (Okay, they do sneak into Lombardy a bit, but this is very much of a Veneto trip.) The eleven-day itinerary includes visits to Padua, Vicenza, Castelfranco, Venice, Verona, Lake Garda, and Mantua, and some highlights are the Scrovegni Chapel in Padua, La Rotonda and Villa Valmarana, a wine tasting in Valpollicella, and Mantegna's frescoes of the Gonzaga court in Mantua. The study leader holds a master's degree in art history and teaches in Florence, but her knowledge extends to all aspects of Italy's culture.

Travel France with Carol (29 McGettigan Road, Milford, New Hampshire 03055; 603-673-6715; fax: -5741; www.TravelFrancewithCarol.com). I'm sure you must be wondering why I am recommending a company that so obviously specializes in France. Well, the reason is that a person can love Venice and Italy just as much as France, and if that person is the exuberant Carol Bonow, travelers are in for an unrivaled experience. After years of organizing unique trips to various regions of France, Carol has ventured into Italy. She has led trips to Tuscany and Umbria, but she recently decided that it's the *coastlines* of Italy that most intrigue her. (She's currently trying to put together a bicoastal "Cinque Terre–Venezia" trip.) Carol's Venice trip focuses on Venice proper and the islands of the lagoon, and it is from ten to fourteen days in length. Two particular highlights are a sailing trip with chef Mauro Stoppa (who was profiled in *Saveur* magazine) and a night on Torcello. "Venice: A Shimmering Dream" was created for "those who are drawn not only to the wonders of art and architecture, but who also want to experience a particular culture—its people, laughter, neighborhoods, pride, and deep sense of place." Carol is an extraordinary human being who embodies much of what *The Collected Traveler* is all about. Note that in addition to the trips she plans herself, Carol has custom-designed countless trips for people with wide-ranging interests, such as antique doll hunting, castle hopping and dressage, and anniversary and birthday celebrations.

Visit Italy Tours (9841 Airport Boulevard, Suite 1424, Los Angeles, California 90045; 800-255-3537 or 310-649-9080; www.visititalytours.com). This tour operator—known as "the finest Italian tour operator"—works mostly with other operators, but it also arranges customized itineraries for travelers. In addition to my own personal experience with Visit Italy, what I particularly like about the organization is that its promotional material asks the very good question "What do you look for in a tour company to Italy?" and the replies it offers are: "They should know the country from north to south, east to west" [we do], "Their service should be friendly and efficient, no problems" [we agree], "Myself, I like really good prices" [and so do we]. Visit Italy also has an office in Rome, so that if anything should go wrong while you're in Italy, the homebase office can help you out. Among its organized trips are several to northeastern Italy, and it also offers fly and drive trips, Italy by train, and the lowest car rental rates in Italy.

~If you do select a tour operator, ask a lot of questions so you know what to expect. For starters, ask if the operator employs its own staff or if it contracts with another company to run its trips. Remember, however, that standards differ around the world, and operators don't have control over every detail. For example, many beautiful old villas and inns do not have screens in the windows, and many first-class hotels don't have air-conditioning. The price you pay for accommodations may not be the same as the posted rates, but you have to accept that you're paying for the convenience of someone else booking your trip. Tour operators also reserve the right to change itineraries. If you have special needs, talk about them with the operator in advance.

Trains (Ferrovie dello Stato)

The Italian train network offers some reduced fares to riders in addition to rail passes, but the choices are not quite as bewildering as in France, for example. The *carta d'argento* (silver card) is for seniors (men over sixty-five, women over sixty); the *carta verde* (green card) is for those twenty-six and under. Families traveling together are eligible for a discount, and the *biglietto chilometrico,* which is valid for three thousand kilometers, can be used by up to five adults. The Flexi Card Pass is available three ways: four days of unlimited travel within a nine-day period, eight days of travel within twenty-one days, and twelve days of travel within thirty days. The best rail pass for those planning on lots of train travel is the *biglietto chilometrico libera circolazione,* which allows for unlimited travel in either first or second class and is available only to nonresidents, so you must show your passport when purchasing it. A *carta blu* is a reduced-price ticket for the disabled. Depending on what type of ticket you have, you may be required to purchase supplements for the super rapido, rapido, and intercity trains. Remember to buy the supplement when you purchase your ticket, or you'll be charged extra for it once you're on the train. Also, remember to stamp your ticket in the yellow machine at the head of each platform. It isn't always so noticeable, so allow some extra time for finding it. Unstamped tickets usually result in a fine. No one wants to waste money, but I do not find train fares in Italy prohibitively expensive. One or two short trips may cost less at the regular fare—make sure you will get the most out of a special discount, and make sure the option you're considering isn't simply a discount for first-class travel, which you may not have wanted in the first place. You can purchase some rail passes in advance from CIT Tours (800-CIT-RAIL; fax: 888-2-FAX-CIT; www.cit-tours.com). Both the Italy Rail Card and Italy Flexi Rail Card are available for a variety of time periods, as well as the Eurailpass and Europass, which are valid in Italy and most of Europe.

In addition to different types of tickets, there are also different types of trains. The *pendolino* is for intercity, first-class-only service. The *eurocity* is international express service. The intercity is the national express train. *Espressi* are long-distance express trains within Italy that do not travel as fast as the intercity. *Diretti* and *interregionali* are slower than *espressi* and making most of the stops. *Locali* or *regionali* provide local service, making all stops, no matter how small. Individual cars are labeled with a number one or two, indicating first or second class, and there are also symbols indicating where smokers can sit. Some trains have bar and dining cars. The Ferrovie dello Stalo (FS) publishes two timetables twice a year: the pocket-sized *Pozzorario* is for all of Italy; a smaller version called *Pozzarario: Nord e Centro* is for everything above Rome. The *Orario delle FS* is in two volumes, *Nord Centro Italia* and *Sud Centro Italia.* These are indispensable bibles.

~After having reviewed all these types of trains and tickets, my best advice to anyone riding the rails in Italy is to never assume anything and check every piece of information you're given two, three, or more times. I say this not because I don't like riding trains—I am an enormous fan of train travel, in any country—but because the word *unbelievable* in its truest sense best applies to train travel in Italy. Schedules really mean nothing: do not be surprised if the track you thought your train was departing from changes at the last minute; if you have to connect to another train, sometimes you are kept waiting for *hours* at a tiny station in the middle of nowhere; simply determining the track number your train is departing from is itself a challenge as it isn't printed on your ticket and lines are listed by final destination, and when a number of trains are departing for the same final destination within a few minutes of each other, it can be *quite* confusing; track numbers typically disappear from the schedule a few minutes before a train departs, meaning that if you are running late, you will probably miss the train as the absence of the track number indicates that the train is in fact leaving; you may find that suddenly, everyone around you is moving to the other side of a platform, or to a different one entirely, so pay attention, as it's likely that a change was announced and you missed it; you may also find that suddenly, everyone on your train is gathering up their belongings and moving to another car—this is probably because the train is going to split at some point up ahead, with half the cars going one way and the other cars heading in the opposite direction; and you may also find that your train trip is blessedly free of any mishaps or confusion. In short, though you may receive a variety of answers to your questions about platforms, tracks, seat assignments, discounts, arrivals, and departures, bear in mind that this is in part due to the language barrier (unless you speak Italian), as many agents and staff do not speak English. Accept all the answers you receive, repeatedly confirm them, don't fret, and before the train you're on starts moving, be sure it's the right one. For more information about trains, contact the tourist office nearest you or view the Ferrovie dello Stato website, www.fs-on-line.com.

~Useful vocabulary: *un biglietto andata* (one-way ticket); *andata e ritorno* (round trip); *binario* (platform); *deposito bagaglio* (left-luggage locker); *biglietteria* (ticket office or window); *orario* (timetable); *prima classe* (first class); *seconda classe* (second class); *una prenotazione* (a reservation); *fumatore* (smoking); *non fumatore* (no smoking); *la porta* (door); *la finestra* (window).

Travel Insurance

I have never purchased travel insurance because I have never determined that I need it, but it's worth considering if you think the risks to you are greater without it. Ask yourself what it would cost if you needed to cancel or interrupt your trip, and how expensive it would be to replace any stolen possessions. If you have a medical condition or if a relative is ill, insurance might be a wise investment. First check to see if your existing health or homeowner's policy offers some protection. If you decide you need to purchase additional insurance, read all the fine print and make sure you understand it; compare deductibles; ask how your provider defines *preexisting condition* and inquire if there are situations in which it would be waived; and check to see if the ceiling on medical expenses is adequate for your needs. ~Emergency medical insurance may be something to consider if you have a medical condition that could quickly put you at serious risk. Elderly travelers may want to consider it in any event, and they should be aware that Medicare does not cover expenses incurred outside the United States. Travel insurance generally consists of five parts: trip cancellation or interruption coverage; trip delay coverage; emergency medical expenses during travel; emergency medical evacuation; and full-time medical and travel assistance. With a typical cancellation policy, you will be compensated for the nonrefundable deposit if the cancellation is due to a medical problem involving either yourself or a family member—essentially, for that which is uncontrollable. I have read repeatedly that it is not wise to use the insurance policies offered by a tour operator or cruise line, simply because the policies serve more to protect the enterprise than to benefit you or me. ~Predictably, there is new concern over coverage in the event of a terrorist attack. Travel Guard International (1145 Clark Street, Stevens Point, Wisconsin 54481; 800-826-4919; www.travelguard.com) is one particular insurance company that has been in the spotlight since the tragedy because it has expanded its policy to cover acts of terrorism for people traveling to places where an incident has occurred within the previous twelve months.

V

Value-Added Tax (VAT)

Imposta valore aggiunto (IVA) or value-added tax (VAT) is the tax amount that visitors to Italy (except those from EEC member countries) are entitled to receive as a reimbursement. I have an entire file on conflicting information about the VAT, so even if you meet the eligibility requirements, be prepared for a potentially confusing procedure. Frankly, the procedure seems to be a lot of bother unless you are making a significant purchase, and I think it would be worth asking the retailer simply not to charge any tax. (Retailers are not required to participate in the program nor to match the dollar amount, so ask first.) But for those who are determined, here's what you must do: produce your passport at the time of the purchase; spend at least 150 euros at one store; and produce receipts *and* merchandise for inspection at customs. The paperwork must be stamped by customs officials *before* you enter the United States. Problems seem to arise when the customs desk is closed, although if you'll be in any other country before you return to the States, a customs stamp from that country is also valid (if the officials are willing to validate your forms). Also, it seems customs officials are rather lax at some borders, vigilant at others. ~For a 20 percent fee, Global Refund will handle your refund through the Europe Tax-Free Shopping (ETS) network, and many stores in Italy are now affiliates; the ETS refund form is known as a Shopping Cheque. Once your forms are stamped you're able to receive a refund—in the form of cash, check (in euros), or charge card credit—right away at an ETS counter. (Or you can mail the forms from home.) ~If you have attempted to have your forms validated in Italy and were thwarted in your efforts, or if it has been more than three months since you applied for a refund, contact Global Refund (707 Summer Street, Stamford, Connecticut 06901; 800-566-9828; fax: 203-674-8709; www.taxfree.se).

Verona

I've included this entry for readers who may want to inquire about tickets to performances at the Estate Teatrale Veronese. Verona's Roman Theater is the venue, from June to September, for an annual Shakespeare Festival (one of the oldest in Europe, dating from 1948), classical and modern ballet and folklore dance performances, and an international jazz festival featuring new musicians from around the world. For information about schedules and tickets, contact Comune di Verona—Estate Teatrale Veronese, Piazza Bra 1, Verona 37100; 045.807.7500; e-mail: spettacolo@comune.verona.it; www.comune.verona.it.

W

Weather

Northeastern Italy is perhaps most beautiful in the fall, but each season offers its own delights. Picking the "perfect" time of year is subjective; when it's rainy and cold—and it does get quite cold in the winter months—you don't have the pleasure of picnicking and hiking outdoors, but prices drop and you'll have little trouble securing reservations at hotels and restaurants. Go when you have the opportunity, and that will be your experience, your Italy. It's true that peak season means higher prices and more people, but if you've determined you want to be in the Veneto in July, then the cost and the crowds don't matter. I've visited Venice in the middle of summer twice, and I never once wished it were another season. If you're a weather maven, you'll love *Fodor's World Weather Guide* (E. A. Pierce and C. G. Smith, 1998; published in 1998 in Great Britain as *The Hutchinson World Weather Guide, New Edition* by Helicon Publishing, Oxford). As frequent business or pleasure travelers know, average daily temperatures are only a small part of what you need to know about the weather. This guide features weather specifics for more than two hundred countries and territories and includes a map of the world's climate regions; humidity and wind-chill charts; a centigrade and Fahrenheit conversion table; a rainfall conversion table; and a bibliography. ~Some good weather sites are: www.weather.com, which allows you to explore historical data for 7,462 locations, ten-day forecasts for 77,000 locations worldwide, record lows and highs, and other useful information; www.weatherbase.com, which provides monthly data with just as useful information, for perhaps fewer cities; and www.initaly.com/travel/weather, which gives you the mean range of temperatures for various Italian cities for each season and provides you with a link to *USA Today*'s website weather resource, where you can access current five-day weather forecasts and month-to-month climates of several Italian cities. ~Finally, just something to keep in mind about the weather in Venice: according to Tami Calliope, translator of Paolo Barbaro's magnificent work *Venice Revealed,* Venetians have many different words to describe varieties and nuances of fog, including *nebbia, nebbietta, foschia,* and *caligo.*

Websites

Personally, I don't find a single one of the following websites better than the tourist office or the appropriate book, but a few offer some good features:

www.travel.it: This site provides information and reservations for hotels, spas, ground transportation, trekking, youth hostels, archaeology, art and culture, and more. Selecting some of the icons, I found three tour operators (Italplan Travel Express, Siesta, and Contribus) and two organizations that arrange rentals of apartments, villas, cottages, farmhouses, and offices.

www.initaly.com: This is one of the best sites I've ever seen. It is incredibly useful for visitors to Italy, with more links than you can even dream about.

www.malox.com/arcigay/link.htm: This is a site for gay travelers to Italy, with a link to Venice.

www.tin.it/fenice: This is the La Fenice opera house site, where visitors can find out about tickets to performances at PalaFenice, the huge white tent that was erected on a neighboring island after La Fenice burned to the ground (again) in 1996. A special *vaporetto* marked "La Fenice" leaves from the Vallaresso stop forty-five minutes before each performance.

Women Travelers

Whether a woman is traveling solo or not, lots of great advice is offered in *Travelers' Tales: Gutsy Women, Travel Tips, and Wisdom for the Road* (Marybeth Bond, Travelers' Tales, San Francisco; distributed by O'Reilly & Associates, 1996). This packable little book is filled with dozens and dozens of useful tips for women of all ages who want to travel or who already travel a lot. Bond has traveled all over the world, much of it alone, and she shares a wealth of advice from her own journeys as well as those of other female travelers. Chapters address safety and security; health and hygiene; romance and unwelcome advances; money, bargaining, and tipping; traveling solo; mother-daughter travel; travel with children; and more. ~The Women's Travel Club may be of interest. Founded by Phyllis Stoller, this organization plans numerous domestic and international trips a year and guarantees everyone a roommate. Its great list of travel safety tips was featured on NBC's *Today* as well as in *Travel & Leisure* (August 1999). Membership is $35 a year, and members receive a newsletter. Contact them at 800-480-4448; e-mail: Womantrip@aol.com; www.womenstravelclub.com.

World Heritage Sites

The list of World Heritage Sites, founded by UNESCO—the United Nations' cultural branch—encompasses 630 natural and cultural sites "of outstanding value to humanity" in 118 countries. UNESCO reports that two-thirds of the world's historical artistic heritage sites are in Italy. Italy's northeastern World Heritage Sites are: Venice and its lagoon, the city of Vicenza and the Palladian villas of the Veneto, the Botanical Garden (Orto Botanico) of Padua, the archaeological area and the patriarchal basilica of Aquileia, and the city of Verona.

The World Monuments Fund

The World Monuments Fund (WMF), founded in 1965, advocates the preservation of important works of art and architecture from around the world and, through contributions, supports special conservation projects. The World Monuments Watch (WMW) program was initiated in 1996 by WMF and by its founding sponsor, American Express. Every two years, WMF produces the *List of 100 Most Endangered Sites* to bring to the public's awareness the need to support special projects for these monuments. Since 1996, the sites listed for northeastern Italy include the Botanical Garden of Padua University (Padua), Santa Maria in Stelle (Verona), and the Bartolomeo Colleoni Monument (Venice).

Venice: The Grand Arrival

BY BILL MARSANO

᠊ᢙᢙ᠊

editor's note

....

Writer H. V. Morton *(A Traveller in Italy)* thinks that the best way to arrive in Venice is by train. He may be alone in expressing this opinion; nearly everyone else, including the writer of this piece, feels the only proper way to arrive is by boat, which was once the only way one *could* arrive. I for one would have to agree. Writer Marsano also believes that it would not be outside the realm of possibility to consider taking a bus to Piazzale Roma, but if arriving by car, forget it: as he says, "A person who would drive to Venice cannot be saved."

BILL MARSANO is a freelance writer specializing in a wide variety of Italian topics. His work was featured in the *Central Italy: Tuscany and Umbria* edition of *The Collected Traveler,* and he has been honored six times with the Lowell Thomas Award, an award given for distinctive travel writing sponsored by the Society of American Travel Writers.

Some cities are best seen in special ways—in a certain season or slant of light—and Venice is among them. By *seen* I mean not "toured" but "beheld." For the first time, at least, Venice should be beheld as the old tart/empress herself would prefer, which is to say from her good side and with some little ceremony to mark the occasion.

Therefore whether you are going to Venice for the first time or for the hundredth but with some virginal niece in tow, give your eyes or hers the pleasure of a grand arrival. Here is how to do it.

If you're arriving at Aeroporto Marco Polo, skip this paragraph and the next. If traveling by train, book your ticket for, and be certain to get off at, Mestre, the hideous industrial warren on the mainland. It is the one and only stop before Venice. If you foolishly continue, your arrival will have all the glory of "Venice, last stop. Everybody off," be encumbered by several hundred other luggage-bearing passengers, and occur in a grimly functional public facility. To wit: a train station.

Exiting at Mestre, you descend to a less crowded platform with only a half-dozen other passengers, none of them tourists, and seek bus transport to Aeroporto Marco Polo, a few minutes away. "Use the regular bus service of ACTV—Azienda del Consorzio Trasporti Veneziano—at the front of the station," counsels my old colleague Cesare Battisti, sage of the Veneto tourism office. "The number fifteen bus leaves for the airport every thirty minutes." Buy tickets in the station at one of the *tabacchi,* the bar, or the newspaper kiosk. Of course you could take a cab, but—"not economic," says Cesare.

At the airport, air and train passengers alike will seek boats and be ferried across the lagoon. Here everything absolutely depends on choosing the right boat. There are several small, sleek, dashing, privately owned speedboats and one slow, scuffed, dowdy thing that is that maritime equivalent of a crosstown bus.

Take the bus.

The speedboats, sad to say, speed not, neither do they dash. They must crawl lest they create destructive wakes, and to crawl in craft meant to travel at fifty miles per hour is agonizing. And because time is money and so is gasoline, they take the shortest route to your hotel—always through a dreary and sometimes smelly warren of unattractive back canals.

The "bus" is plain old public transportation—even slower but only a fifth of the price. It potters along the edge of the lagoon making one or two stops out in nowhere, but then things begin to get interesting. After stopping at the Lido, one of the barrier islands that enclose the lagoon, the bus makes a hard turn to starboard. At about that time you'll want to move up to the bow for the best possible forward view. For now Venice in all her faded grandeur arises from the mists or from golden bathing sunshine; all of the legendary sights rise from their thousand thrones before you. This is the Pearl of the Adriatic, the Venice that for centuries has left visitors goggle-eyed and dumbstruck. Straight up the Grand Canal you go, your tubby little bus seeming decidedly less dowdy as you faintly hear trumpet fanfares in your head.

For me, disembarking is the best part: I get off at Piazza San Marco, feeling like Marco Polo every time.

La Cronaca Mondana
(The Daily News—
Points of View)

"In Italy, Communism and Catholicism, urban chic and peasant simplicity, an almost shocking self-regard and great personal generosity, are part of a uniquely satisfying whole."
—Denis Judd, from the Preface to
A TRAVELLER'S HISTORY OF ITALY

"Italy is still a country of limitless opportunities. It offers stage settings for all kinds of adventures, licit or illicit loves, the study of art, the experience of pathos, the weaving of intrigues. It can be gay, tragic, mad, pastoral, archaic, modern, or simply dolce.*"*
—Luigi Barzini, *THE ITALIANS*

Berlusconi, The Rerun

BY ALESSANDRA STANLEY

~

editor's note

....

This piece about Italy's prime minister, Silvio Berlusconi, appeared before he was elected on May 13, 2001. I have included it because I think the piece reveals more about Berlusconi than others that appeared after the election. In the final days of his campaign, Berlusconi signed a five-point contract with Italians that effectively commits him to relinquish his office if he fails to deliver on at least four. The five points were tax cuts, the creation of a million and a half new jobs, an increase in pensions, vast public works projects, and new anticrime measures. By the time this book is published, Berlusconi may no longer be in office—his first government, in 1993, collapsed after seven months, and Italy has, after all, had fifty-eight governments since World War II; but even if he is no longer prime minister when you read this, Berlusconi is a name we will likely continue to hear about in future Italian politics.

ALESSANDRA STANLEY is the Rome bureau chief for *The New York Times*.

The richest man in Italy did two small things on his way to an international political conference on the French Riviera. Before boarding his Gulfstream jet, Silvio Berlusconi stopped in at a Milan courthouse where he had been called to testify in a trial of two of his employees charged in 1994 with committing perjury. (He didn't answer any questions, however, pleading an Italian version of the Fifth Amendment, as was his legal right since he is a defendant in a related bribery case.)

As he left, surrounded by a jostling horde of aides, bodyguards, and reporters, he paused long enough to help a distraught woman. She grabbed his sleeve and begged for help, tearfully explaining that she had left her abusive husband, had no job or house, and risked having her five-year-old taken away by welfare authorities. Berlusconi instantly invited her to Arcore, his eighteenth-century estate outside Milan. "Today," he told her with the beaming magnanimity of a television game show host, "is your lucky day."

It was a classic Berlusconi moment, blending the beneficence of an Old World *padrone* with a more modern sense of media spin. His day in court, part of an endless legal saga that bores most Italians, received perfunctory news coverage. But the media homed in on Filomena Esposito, thirty-three, who with her young son and other relatives in tow did in fact receive advice and, ultimately, $2,500 in cash, a watch, and an AC Milan soccer ball from the busiest man in Italian politics.

Silvio Berlusconi, sixty-four, is a self-made billionaire whose private holding company, Fininvest, controls, among other things, the AC Milan soccer team and the country's three largest private television networks. As the head of Forza Italia, the insurgent conservative party he built from scratch, he is confidently preparing to become Italy's next prime minister in parliamentary elections next month. Should he succeed, as is widely expected, it would mark a revanchist return to power after his first conservative government collapsed in 1994 after only seven turbulent months in office.

Then, Italy's bloated, debt-ridden economy was the laughing-stock of Europe. Few believed the country would ever straighten its finances enough to qualify for membership in the Euro. It did, just barely, in 1998. When Berlusconi left office, the country was in the throes of *Tangentopoli* ("bribesville"), a vast criminal investigation into political and financial corruption that traumatized the nation and eventually toppled an entire political class that had ruled Italy without interruption since the end of World War II.

Italy has changed over the past seven years, and so has Berlusconi: both are a little calmer, better organized, and more in tune with the rest of Europe. But Italian politics remains bafflingly baroque. And so does Berlusconi.

He is easily caricatured, but he cannot be dismissed or narrowly defined. His economic platform is familiar—a blend of tax cuts and free-market capitalism borrowed from Margaret Thatcher and Ronald Reagan. His regal-populist style, however, is more startling, even by American standards: on the stump, he comes off like a wired Steve Forbes with a touch of Eva Perón.

For the last seven years, as leader of the opposition, he has held center stage as the beleaguered leftist government's most assiduous adversary. Promising to shake off what he calls a straitjacket of taxes, bureaucracy, and state regulations, Berlusconi says he wants to strip down the inefficient Italian state and make it a model for the rest of Europe. Italians are less optimistic, but they do yearn for change, as long as it is not too tumultuous. Berlusconi describes his candidacy as a "sacrifice," his "gift" to the Italian people. He says he genuinely believes that he—and he alone—can transform the nation. Italy needs an entrepreneur, he tells voters, not a smooth talker.

Berlusconi, as it happens, is both. His charm is legendary, a sudden high beam of warmth and enveloping attention. "America? I love America," he gushes to an American reporter in a gold-and-cream reception room in the seventeenth-century Baroque palace that is his Roman *pied à terre*. "I am on whatever side America is on, even before I know what it is."

He laughs self-mockingly as he speaks, the kind of engaging good humor shared by the best Italians—the art of laughing gently at others' foibles while including themselves in the joke. But Berlusconi also speaks with braggadocio, an unfettered self-aggrandizing streak that alienates many ordinary Italians.

Berlusconi recently lamented to reporters that he had never mastered English and knows only French, Latin, and Greek. "I am a

Greek scholar," he said. "I used to compose Greek verses off the top of my head." That brashness, along with his Reaganesque, flag-waving patriotism—taboo in Italy since the days of Mussolini—makes the Italian intelligentsia cringe.

Berlusconi even invented a word to describe himself—*entusias-matore*—an adjective that conveys the high-energy salesmanship that helped him rise from real estate developer in Milan to Italy's richest tycoon. His fortune, estimated at $12.8 billion, won him fourteenth place on *Forbes* magazine's list of the world's richest people. He made his mark—and much of his wealth—by creating Italy's first commercial television networks, introducing striptease quiz shows and American soap operas to Italian viewers.

His opponent in the election, Francesco Rutelli, forty-six, the former mayor of Rome, offers a liberal platform that is a gentler version of Berlusconi's: more cautious tax cuts and a steady liberalization of the economy. But Italy's leftist coalition is so internally divided and unstable (four governments and three prime ministers in the last five years) that only Rutelli's own pollsters—who include Stanley Greenberg, a campaign adviser to Al Gore, Tony Blair, and Ehud Barak—express much confidence.

Berlusconi, on the other hand, says he is so sure of victory that he is already meeting with European prime ministers, seeking the international legitimacy that eluded him in his first term. Indeed, Europe is edgy about several aspects of a Berlusconi government. His center-right coalition includes former Fascists led by Gianfranco Fini, as well as Umberto Bossi, the volatile leader of the Northern League. So far in the campaign, Bossi has been on his best behavior, but his platform and own past statements are veined with anti-immigrant, antihomosexual sentiments that are too close to those of Austria's Jörg Haider for comfort.

And then there is Berlusconi's money. Except to shrug it off as a political attack, Berlusconi has never acknowledged the conflict of interest presented by his three networks, a film company, Italy's leading publishing group, and a financial network that spans insurance, real estate, and banks. He has said he would resurrect a 1994 proposal in Parliament to resolve the matter, but it is hard to see how. State television has been privatized a little, but top network executives are still political appointees, and Berlusconi could well go into office with all of Italy's major networks—public and private—in his pocket.

He has talked about putting his assets in a blind trust, but what he really seems to want Italians to do is elect him on blind faith. "Italians think two things, and this shows up in the focus groups," he says. "One, it is better to send someone into office who doesn't need to steal because he is already rich. And they think that anyone who is under the spotlight can never get away with going against the general interest to favor his own interests." Growing exasperated, he adds: "I don't see how anyone can think that it is possible to do something against the interests of others and in favor of myself. It's impossible! Impossible! I would instantly lose my consensus. It is a nonproblem and a false problem."

His supporters, however, put it differently, arguing that what's good for Fininvest could be good for the country. "He knows his business well," says Carolo Corassa, a prosperous farmer from Emilia-Romagna who attended an agriculture conference on mad cow disease in Rome. Corassa stood and applauded vigorously as Berlusconi swept in, two shades tanner than any farmer in the room. "If he can do well by Italians while doing well for his own business," the farmer said, "that is fine with me."

Berlusconi is a great performer, whether the audience is a room full of Forza Italia "seniors," his party's senior citizen group, or a news conference with less doting reporters. Unveiling his campaign pledge to increase the minimum retirement pension, he sat at a table behind a giant campaign poster and confidently fielded questions about his conflict-of-interest problems, tax cut proposals, and dubious political allies.

In the course of the news conference, a man stood up, introduced himself as a reporter for an obscure monthly, *L'Attualità,* and delivered a lengthy diatribe about the Italian phone company's decision to lay off thousands of workers. (In point of fact, the workers were not fired but merely furloughed at almost full pay. Firing workers in Italy is extremely difficult, one of the inflexibilities of the labor market that Berlusconi promises to fix.)

Berlusconi ignored these complications, instead expressing his admiration for the antifascist writer Gaetano Salvemini, whose followers founded *L'Attualità.* He then cited a Salvemini bon mot, mocking the mentality of Italian industrialists: "Profits are for us alone, but losses are shared by all." Berlusconi paused and then uttered grandly, "When we are in power, these things will not happen."

Even in style-conscious Italy, Berlusconi's attention to image stands out. Standing only five feet six inches, he is self-conscious about his height. When he sits down at a conference table, his aides slip a cushion onto his seat to ensure that his height aligns with the others. When they stand for a group photo, Berlusconi rises on tiptoe just before the camera lights flash.

There is an electoral strategy beneath the strutting, however. Berlusconi was treated for prostate cancer in 1997, a fact he revealed only last year, explaining that he has fully recovered. Running against Rutelli, a telegenic opponent who is almost twenty years younger, Berlusconi sometimes jokes about the contrast, but mostly he tries to dismiss it. "My doctors tell me I have the physique of a forty-year-old," he proudly assured a television interviewer.

Berlusconi knows how important a *bella figura* is to Italians.

"He understands the weaknesses of Italians because he shares them," says Indro Montanelli, ninety-one, Italy's most respected conservative columnist. Montanelli edited *Il Giornale,* Berlusconi's newspaper, but was forced out for failing to lend sufficient support to the political ambitions of his boss. "I had a lot of fun with Berlusconi," Montanelli recalls, almost wistfully. "You cannot imagine his ability to lie. Not necessarily to cheat you, just for the sheer gusto of it. He persuades himself at the same time he persuades you. But he is a brilliant salesman—he can persuade Italians that he will deliver on promises that are unkeepable."

He persuaded enough voters in 1994 to get elected, but his not-ready-for-prime-time government quickly collapsed under the weight of criminal investigations that followed him into public office. He still faces trials on corruption charges but blames a broad left-wing conspiracy for his legal troubles. Most Italians really don't care, either because they agree that the prosecutors have a political motive, or because they assume that Berlusconi was only taking the same illegal shortcuts that most entrepreneurs used in the 1980s and 1990s to succeed in business, Italian-style.

In the most humiliating moment of his public life, Berlusconi received an *aviso di garanzia,* an official notification that he was under criminal investigation, while he was presiding over an international conference on organized crime in Naples. Berlusconi still broodingly refers to that incident as a "coup" and talks so passionately about the red menace that one has to pinch oneself to remember that the Italian Communist Party lost in 1948 and never did get a chance to erect gulags on the Lago di Garda. "He doesn't see the attacks against him as just political," his spokesman, Paolo Bonaiuti, explains. "For him, it is very personal."

But when he resigned in December 1994, it was because of an in-house insurrection. Bossi, his current coalition partner, pulled his support in Parliament, calling Berlusconi a "dictator" and

"Berluskaiser." Berlusconi ran again in 1996 but lost to Romano Prodi, who, like Berlusconi in 1994, campaigned as an outsider but carried far less ideological and personal baggage.

Prodi and his successors managed to straighten out Italy's finances. But major efforts to fix the pension system, reform the electoral laws, or streamline the judiciary were thwarted both by the center-right opposition and by the government's own querulous coalition partners, who spanned the ideological range from Catholic centrists to Communists.

The Italian economy, powered for the most part by small family-owned companies, is remarkably vigorous given the hurdles of regulations, red tape, and high taxes, like a one-legged skier who learns to shift his torso to slalom. But its productivity lags in the new Europe. The Italian political system, rigged to prevent any one party from accruing too much power, makes it almost impossible for any government to see through needed long-term reform. Instability is the one constant for Italian governments, of which there have been fifty-eight since the end of World War II.

Some critics predict that for all his ambitious plans for economic growth, public-works projects, and modernization, Berlusconi will face the same endemic political obstacles as his predecessors, namely having to rely on allies who could bolt and bring him down.

Umberto Bossi says he has given up his dream of having Northern Italy secede in exchange for Berlusconi's promise to introduce a federalist system. So far, Bossi is acting like a more reliable partner than he has been in the past, telling his supporters that he was wrong about Berlusconi in 1994—though he tends to do so with a roguish twinkle.

He remains a politically incorrect ally and a volatile one. Berlusconi says he has tied Bossi down with so many incentives, pacts, and joint programs that he would never pull out. But the ropes and chains crisscrossing their alliance only underline Bossi's

Houdini side. Berlusconi's strategists admit that they need Bossi's strength in the North to win a definitive mandate. But they also insist they will have so many of their own parliamentary seats that they won't need Bossi's to govern.

Bossi says the opposite. "If at the last minute he wants to drop us, he can win the election," he says. "But he wouldn't be able to govern. He would have to strike accords with the old Christian Democrats, and he would never be able to bring about real change. Without us, he will fail."

Berlusconi is far better positioned to govern than he was in 1994. Back then, Forza Italia was at best a loosely organized marketing vehicle for his candidacy. Now he has built it into a real political party, with grassroots organization and credible candidates. Unlike in 1994, Berlusconi's coalition has hashed out a program of cutting income tax, eliminating the inheritance tax, and enacting other measures meant to stimulate growth.

But Italy doesn't have the same freedom to reroute economic policy that Reagan and Thatcher wielded. Last year Italy's ratio of public debt to gross domestic product was 110 percent, nearly twice as high as Germany's. Any tax cuts would need to be offset by spending cuts to avert a collision with Brussels. "This government has already cut taxes significantly," warns Francesco Giavazzi, an economist at the Bocconi University school of economics in Milan. "The only realistic way to cut spending is to reform the pension system. Until I know what Berlusconi intends to do, I remain worried."

Berlusconi has promised to increase the minimum monthly pension check to $500 a month (from about $350 now), under the slogan of "more dignified pensions." But he has not unveiled what he will do about a pension system that eats up 30 percent of government spending and threatens to collapse under the weight of the country's aging population and low birthrate.

Off the podium, he can be quite frank about why he won't discuss his programs. "Look, Europe is going to make the decisions for us," he says. "When that happens, we'll do what we have to do. But in an election campaign, we do not discuss the program because it doesn't bring us votes."

He also grows flinty on the subject of his fortune and what he could gain in public office. Instead, he muses about what he has already had to give up. "Let me list some of the things that politics took away from me." He proceeds to tick off a long list of companies that he was discouraged from acquiring or forced to divest—Omnitel, one of Italy's largest cell phone companies, three pay-TV stations, another TV network, radio stations, and the newspaper and magazine division of Mondadori, a publishing group that he bought in 1990 and that then owned fourteen newspapers, including *La Repubblica*. "I am the businessman who was most punished by politics in the history of the republic, no doubt about it," he says.

Asked whether he shouldn't take Fininvest public, a move that would earn him money and bring some transparency into the dealings of the family business, Berlusconi lets loose. "No, look, excuse me, but I have worked my entire life," he says. "I am doing my country a favor. I don't need to go into office for the power. I have houses all over the world, stupendous boats, including Murdoch's yacht, which I just bought. I have beautiful airplanes, a beautiful wife, a beautiful family."

He adds: "I am making a sacrifice for my country, and then I also have to take away the fruits of my labor from my children? I pay two million in taxes a day. I am the Italian who pays the most, and they still want to punish me? Let them all go to the devil."

Venice: The Art, Mass Tourism, and High Water

BY RANDOLPH H. GUTHRIE

editor's note

Acqua alta is a serious threat to Venice's existence, but uncontrolled tourism may prove more difficult to check. As John Julius Norwich wrote in his foreword to *Venice: The City and Its Architecture*, "We have no wish to see some of the most dazzlingly beautiful buildings in the world becoming part of a waterlogged museum, the thinking-man's Disneyland. Surely, if Venice is to survive at all, it must be as a living, working city, in which ordinary Venetians will still be proud and happy to make their homes."

RANDOLPH H. GUTHRIE is chairman of Save Venice. This piece is an expanded version of a lecture he gave on January 22, 2001, as part of a Save Venice seminar program in New York.

Venice is the most improbable and fragile city in the world. Improbable because people do not dwell on tidal mud flats unless driven there by desperation and because a lagoon village is not expected to become the richest society in history and produce much of the greatest art and architecture the world has ever known. Fragile because the city is old with weakened structures, because she is still half above and half below water and hostage to the god of storms, because she is being overrun with hordes of people who pick at her day by day.

The Art

On November 4, 1966, Venice flooded. It was not the ordinary flood that arrives to a depth of a few inches many times a year. This was a tempest. For fifteen hours the water surged four feet deep through the Piazza San Marco with driving wind, rain, and waves. Many feared that Venice's thousand years had come to an end. One could think of Oliver Wendell Holmes's great poem on the Constitution: "Leave her to the god of storms, the lightning and the gale." Then, when all seemed lost, the storm passed, the winds fell, and the water gently receded. Most of Venice had been inundated. The world was shocked.

The storm had also flooded Florence. The threat to not one but two of the principal repositories of Renaissance art stirred the world to action. Private rescue committees were formed in many countries. UNESCO assumed leadership and established a framework within which the private committees could operate. Along with twenty-five other committees, Save Venice was born, first as the Venice Committee of the International Fund for Monuments and shortly afterward in its own name.

It was immediately recognized that the problems in Florence and Venice were quite different. In Florence the keepers of the Arno dam above the city had released too much water in response to the rainfall, and this had spilled over the banks of the Arno into the city. Heating oil tanks had been filled in October. The high water flowed into these tanks through their vent pipes, and oil, being lighter than water, had floated up the vent pipes and spread throughout the city. In Florence many treasures are kept on the ground floors, and these were covered with oil. Restoration in Florence consisted of removing oil.

In Venice the water had done relatively little damage. Had there been no other problems, preservation efforts would have consisted simply of drying the ground floors. Venetians had long since learned not to keep anything valuable on the ground floor, so this would have been no great task. What the flood did for Venice was to reveal centuries of neglect. Everything was filthy—the buildings, the statuary, the paintings, everything. The art could hardly be seen. Many works, which are today seen in the same places in all their incomparable glory, were thought lost because they had not been visible in centuries. The stones and canvases were buried under thick layers of soot and wax from four hundred years of heating by soft coal and lighting by candle fire. Mixed into the dirt were the acid chemicals from modern industrial pollution. Inside the stones was a high concentration of weakening salt from centuries of sea-water inundation. The literal "icing on the cake" was the layer of acid pigeon guano covering the buildings and statuary throughout the city.

There was a day, of course, when the *Serenissima* (the Most Serene City) was the "Queen of the Adriatic," the richest, most populated, and most powerful city in the West. At its height in the fifteenth and sixteenth centuries, Venice was new and pristine. Great wealth was producing new and glorious buildings. Their facades were painted in fresco, and a trip through the city was a burst of color and beauty. Titian and Giorgione painted the vast facade of the present post office on the Grand Canal. The greatest century of artists the world has known were at work—the Lombardi, Palladio, Sansovino, Longhena, the Bellinis, Carpaccio, Vivarini, Cima, Giorgione, Titian, Lotto, Bassano, Veronese, Tintoretto, Piombo, Palma. Their works of art were still bright. The land was higher, and flooding was a rarity. The stones were new and not full of salt. There was no industrial pollution. The smoke from fires and candles had not yet obscured the surfaces of the city. The pigeons were systematically destroyed.

The fall of Venice from Queen of the Adriatic to a backwater came slowly. The sea route around Africa was discovered in the late fourteenth century. Within a few decades, the thousand-year-old silk route across Asia, with its sea connection across the Mediter-ranean and through Venice, was abandoned for the superior speed, safety, and cost of the new all-sea route. Venice, for five hundred years, had "held the West in fee" through her control of the Eastern trade, and this was gone. From the wealthiest society the world had ever known, she declined into one of the poorest. Napoleon conquered and looted the city in 1797. The Congress of Vienna refused to restore Venice's independence and gave her to Austria. By now, a third of the city's population were beggars, a third prostitutes, and a third impoverished noblemen. 1830 and 1848 saw ill-fated revolts. 1867 saw the city absorbed into the new Italian state, which was itself impoverished by two world wars. By the time of the Great Flood of 1966, Venice was not even a pale shadow of its days of glory.

The Superintendencies of Fine Arts, UNESCO, and the twenty-five private committees surveyed the city's treasures and set to work. The task was daunting. Hundreds of buildings and thousands of artworks awaited identification, cataloguing, and evaluation, after which they had to be restored and preserved one by one. In the beginning, because no restoration had been done, there were few restorers. Those few gradually trained more. Progress was slow.

Money was hard to come by. The outside world did not understand why it should help restore art in Italy. Didn't we have enough needs to fill at home? In America it took a while for us to understand that we are children of the Renaissance, that our emigration from the Old World was economic, not cultural. We had not abandoned our heritage. It belongs to us as much as to anyone. Italy cannot maintain this heritage alone. Half to 60 percent of the Renaissance is in Italy. The Italians spend ten times as much as we per capita on the arts, but they are not rich enough to take care of all that is under their care. It is not they who need help. It is the art that needs help, and without help, the art will be lost forever.

For twenty years UNESCO maintained an office and a staff in Venice to oversee the restoration efforts. With no overhead, the private committees were able to apply one hundred percent of the money they raised to restoration projects. When the twenty-year "campaign" was over, the private committees formed their own organization (Association of Private Committees) to take the place of UNESCO as an administrative umbrella, and the work continued. Between twenty-five and thirty committees have been active at one time or another. Not all of them have done a project every year. Some have disappeared, and new ones have taken their places. The American Committee, Save Venice, the English Committee, and Venice in Peril became the leaders, accounting for some three-quarters of all the money spent. Save Venice, over the years, has contributed more money than all the other committees combined.

Venice is unique in that most of its art is still to be found in its original sites. Art in a museum is rarely at the eye level for which it was created, and its perspective is wrong. It is also out of context. A painting has a rounded top because it was made to fit in a specific altar and to be framed by stone carved to match the work. Side-by-side matching paintings may have been covers for organ doors and meant to open to show another set of matched paintings inside. These and many other distinctions cannot be appreciated when works are separated from their original sites.

The dispersal of Venice's art throughout the city makes restoration more costly and difficult. Personnel and materials cannot be concentrated in one place. Transportation and travel are required. Electricity has to be brought in. Sites have to be walled off from the public during restoration. The height and architectural projections of church walls often require elaborate scaffolding to reach and restore a work. Churches are dark, cold, and dank, and sometimes their sacristans are cranky. It would be easier to work in a well-lit, warm museum laboratory with a nearby library and ready-at-hand colleagues for consultations.

The neglect of centuries has not been all bad. The art of Venice escaped the restorations of the nineteenth century, which, in retrospect, were poorly performed. It was not understood that the inner layers of shellac were mixed with the outer layers of paint and that removing all of the black (oxidized) shellac would cause paint to be lost forever. Knowing this, you will now recognize many of these mistreated works in major museums. They are "skimmed." They appear too light, almost white. Their definition is a bit vague. This is especially true of Tintoretto, who used very thin, watery paint and displayed his subtle genius in the last few layers. When these are gone, a Tintoretto looks like it is seen through a white screen. Today's restorers never remove the deeper shellac. One day in the future we will find a method that will leach out all of the shellac without removing any paint. In the meanwhile nothing is lost. The paintings in Venice escaped the nineteenth century and still have all their paint. Poverty is a protector of art.

A number of steps have been taken to prevent the restored art from renewed pollution. The government has prohibited the burning of anything but natural gas to reduce the smoke and carbon dioxide in the air. Smoke makes the city filthy, and carbon dioxide combines with water to form carbonic acid that dissolves stone. The churches have been strongly discouraged from burning candles in front of the altars. As for the pigeons, the private committees have lobbied hard for their control. Unfortunately, they are encouraged by seed sellers and by tourists who have themselves photographed covered with the birds. If any of these adventurous souls were to pick up a pigeon wing and see the infestation of lice, they would not be so enamored of such close contact. Twenty years ago the private committees, with great difficulty, convinced the city to allow the committees to feed the pigeons treated seed that would render them sterile. This treated seed was, by all tests and appearance, identical to normal seed, with which it was mixed prior to feeding. As fate would have it, the pigeons were able to recognize the treated seeds, and they snapped up every last untreated kernel and left behind every treated one. The committees had to pay to clean up the piazzas. The pigeons have, so far, had the last laugh.

Mass Tourism

As the artworks have been restored, Venice has revived as a center of tourism. When all was black, invisible, and covered with pigeon dung, people came to Venice to swim and play on the Lido. Today people spend their days exploring the historic center of the city, searching out the rediscovered and refurbished treasures of times past. As the fame of the city has increased, so has the number of visitors. This number has reached the point where it is a serious problem.

Venice is lilliputian. Everything is small—the thoroughfares, the buildings, the entranceways, the hotels, the restaurants. There are few sanitary facilities, and those that exist are hard to find. Venice can handle only so many people, and the numbers that come exceed that capacity. The merchants are hungry for customers and resist controls. The European Parliament, which now runs roughshod over everyone and is accountable to no one, has forbidden cities to limit their visitors. Entrance fees are prohibited. The worst is that the majority of tourists, who arrive in buses, trains, and cruise ships, are not interested in or knowledgeable about the art of Venice. They have simply heard that it is something to see, and here they are, courtesy of whatever travel agency has arranged their holiday.

With seemingly no way to stem the tide, the tourists are overwhelming Venice. They arrive by the thousands every morning, having slept overnight in long-distance buses or trains. The buses and trains cost next to nothing, thanks to packaged tours and Eurorail passes. The horde wears the same clothes for a two-week trip through Europe, traveling each night and stopping each day in another city. They alight in Venice carrying a bottle of water and a sandwich. They spend no money. They move through the city like locusts, scavenging anything not firmly attached and leaving behind their plastic bottles, their sandwich wrappings, and their bodily functions. Like the goat herders of the Dark Ages gazing on Roman ruins, they have no knowledge of the civilization that produced Venetian art and architecture or any appreciation of its glory. At five o'clock the horde returns to the bus and train stations. Tomorrow is Florence.

As if the buses were not enough, consider the usual cruise ships. They hold three to five thousand or more people. They dwarf the city with ten to fifteen decks. They occupy a thousand feet or more along the Ducal Palace waterfront. They are both a source of over-crowding and a visual abomination. Often there are five or more at a time. They affront the scale and beauty of Venice. Their crews and passengers are no different from those from the buses and trains. They crowd and use the helpless city, leaving nothing behind. They may buy a few trinkets and beads, but they eat and sleep on board. At five o'clock the horde returns to the boat. Tomorrow is Dalmatia.

Some solution must be found soon. Another five years of increase at the present rate, and no one who is of value to the city will want to return. The emigration of citizens will accelerate; the streets will be impassable; the public transportation will be swamped; all facilities will be overwhelmed; and good order will simply break down. It is all well and good for the politicians to pander to the crowds with talk of democracy and open access, but what will be the use of their platitudes when the city is no longer habitable?

High Water

The sixty-odd islands of Venice are individual mudflats in the Brenta River delta, whose main channel is the Grand Canal. They have always been half above and half below water, depending on wind and tide. The early Venetians raised the islands by surrounding them with pilings and shoveling mud inside.

Italy is part of the African geologic plate and is moving north, diving under the European plate. This is why the Alps are rising. It is also why Venice is sinking—about an inch and a half a century. In the early years after the war, the problem was exacerbated by Veneto industries pumping water from the deep aquifers under Venice. The city subsided a foot into the emptied spaces.

High water results from natural and man-made causes.

Natural
    Low local atmospheric pressure
    High tide
    South winds pushing water north
    Heavy rain on the mainland
    The Sessa (a rocking of water in the Adriatic like that in a bathtub)
Man-made
    Deepening the lagoon entrance channels, enabling water to rush in faster
    Reducing the size of the lagoon by
        Putting up walls around it, blocking expansion into the flood plain
        Filling in the lagoon for land reclamation
        Enclosing parts of it with impermeable walls to make fish farms
        Allowing the bottom, including the canals, to shallow up with silt

The result today is that Venice is often flooded. Mean high tide, coming twice a day, is twenty-six inches above mean water (average sea level). The Piazza San Marco is at twenty-eight inches. Tides reach thirty-two inches, flooding the piazza to a depth of four inches a hundred times a year. You cannot walk in four inches of water without taking off your shoes and socks and rolling up your pants. You also cannot see what your bare feet are walking on. There is broken glass. There are dog and pigeon contributions. It is unpleasant. Tides reach forty-four inches, flooding the piazza to sixteen inches eleven days a year. Tides reached fifty-two inches, flooding the piazza to two feet, twice last year. On November 4, 1966, the piazza flooded to four feet with waves rolling on top.

The high water in Florence was fresh (albeit mixed with oil). In Venice it was salt. To understand the damage done by salt water, you must know how the buildings are constructed. First, wooden pilings are sunk into the ground. Heavy structures cannot be built on the mud. The pilings reach down to the solid clay, twenty to thirty-five feet below. On top of the pilings is laid Istrian stone, which is very water-resistant. On top of the stone are built walls of brick. For important buildings, the brick walls are faced with marble. The Istrian stone is meant to cover the whole rise and fall of the lagoon water. If the water falls below the stone and exposes the wooden pilings to air, they quickly rot. If the water rises above the stone, the brick absorbs it like a sponge. The water rises in the brick and evaporates, leaving behind its salt. The salt disrupts the integrity of the chemical bonds in the brick. Marble in contact with the brick is similarly affected. After enough soakings in salt water, brick and marble become so soft ("sugarized") that they can be scraped with a fingernail.

High water is also very demoralizing to the inhabitants, driving 2,500 out of the city every year. Postwar population was 200,000 and is now 60,000 and falling. Venice cannot be only a collection of museums, hotels, and restaurants. It needs a population pursuing a normal life to maintain a vibrant community. Without daily maintenance of properties by the thousands of private owners, most of the buildings would rapidly disintegrate.

The Center for Global Warming in Geneva estimates that water levels in the world will rise twenty inches in the next century. Left unattended, this means the end of Venice within just a few decades. Clearly, something must be done. There are four solutions frequently mentioned.

1. Reduce the depth of the three openings into the lagoon between the Lido islands and zigzag them to slow tidal and storm water.
2. Control the lagoon openings with movable gates.
3. Re-expand the lagoon volume by
    Breaking down the walls around the lagoon
    Breaking down the walls around the fish farms
    Removing the landfills
    Dredging the lagoon bottom.
4. Raise the level of the perimeters of the city islands.

Numbers one and two would eliminate the higher tides by slowing the entry of water into the lagoon. If slowed enough, a high tide would fall before all of its water was able to penetrate. Number three would accomplish the same effect by enlarging the volume to be filled. (You can fill a tub faster than a swimming pool.) Number one raises the level at which high water is a problem, allowing one and three to be more effective and two to be used less often.

In 1984 Rome passed the "Special Law for Venice." It created the Consorzio Venezia Nuova (CVN), comprising the fifty largest engineering and construction companies in Italy, and charged it with finding a solution to the water problem. It also established the Commitatone, composed of heads of major government departments and chaired by the prime minister, to supervise the effort.

In 1989 the CVN submitted its recommendations:

Raise the island perimeters to forty inches above mean water.
Build movable gates to block the entrances to the lagoon.
Dredge the lagoon canals.

It concluded that removing the walls around the lagoon would do little because the surrounding land has been built up and the floodplain is gone. Computer models showed that removing the landfill and fish farms would not make a significant difference.

Today every island in Venice, except San Marco, has had its perimeter walls raised to forty inches. Dredging of canals is well along. We now await the gates. They are not new in design. They have already been used in the Thames below London and outside Maastricht. The gates are sixty feet wide, sixty feet high, and ten feet thick. The twelve-hundred-foot-wide south and central lagoon openings require twenty gates each, and the northern opening requires thirty. Each gate is hollow. It is connected to a cement base on the sea floor by hinges. When filled with water, the gate lies on the bottom. When the water is pushed out by compressed air, the gate swings up to float. A line of raised gates across an opening can sustain a nine-foot difference in water level from outside to inside. Water rushes between the gates and through the hinges but too slowly to fill the lagoon before the tide turns.

Opposition to the gates appeared immediately and has increased as the environmental movement has grown. The environmentalists fear that any restriction of tidal action will stagnate the lagoon. They want to raise the city islands another twelve inches. The CVN says that the gates, with present occurrences of high water, would be elevated for only four hours, ten times a year. The Greens reply that, if the CVN accepts that the water will rise twenty inches this century, the gates will be elevated much more often. The

CVN replies that such a rise in water makes the gates all the more necessary. Those on the side of the CVN say that the Greens would rather have a sunken city in distilled water than a live city in a less-than-perfect lagoon. And on it goes. Neither side will give in, and the politicians find it easier to take no stand than to alienate anyone.

The government in Rome, unable to reach a decision in the face of the controversy, established an independent commission composed of experts from MIT, the University of Padua, and A. D. Little & Company (based in Cambridge, Massachusetts). In 1997 the commission reported that raising the lagoon perimeters another foot would create enough pressure to cause water to burrow under the walls and bubble up in the center of the islands. It would also require raising the height of many of the entrance doorways in Venice. The commission unequivocally supported the construction of the gates and stated that, even with the expected water rise in the next century, the gates would require elevation only forty times a year for four hours at a time.

In December 1998 the environmental minister, naturally under the influence of the environmentalists, rejected without explanation the commission's report. The Veneto Region sued, and the highest court in Italy ruled in favor of the Veneto (and the gates) in June 1999. One assumes that the gates will now be built. The environmentalists will likely appeal to the European Parliament and European Court, which will delay matters awhile longer, but in the end Venice will probably get its gates. Whether or not they will work remains to be seen. We can only hope.

This piece grew out of a lecture originally entitled "History of Venice on the Water," Copyright © 2002 by Randolph Guthrie. Reprinted with permission of the author.

Biblioteca

The Civilization of Europe in the Renaissance, John Hale, Atheneum, 1994; first American edition, 1993. I first picked up this book because the title was so similar to Jacob Burckhardt's *The Civilization of the Renaissance in Italy.* In the reviews on the back cover, the book was indeed compared not only to Burckhardt's classic but also to Fernand Braudel's *The Mediterranean in the Time of Philip II.* I needed no further justification to purchase the book. Featuring more than one hundred black-and-white illustrations, this volume covers the period from about 1450 to 1620. Some of Hale's other works, which are ideal companion volumes to this one, include *Renaissance Europe, 1480–1520* (1971); *Renaissance War Studies* (1982); *War and Society in Renaissance Europe* (1985); and *Artists and Warfare in the Renaissance* (1990).

Europe: A History, Norman Davies, Oxford University Press, 1996. In the opening line to his preface, Davies states that "this book contains little that is original," but I would disagree. From the chapter titles ("Hellas," "Roma," "Origo," "Pestis," "Renatio," "Dynamo," and so on) to the manner in which ideas and material are presented, plus the useful appendixes and notes at the end of the book, this *is* an original work, highly recommended.

Fifty Years of Europe: An Album, Jan Morris, Villard, 1997. At last count, I discovered I'd read all of Jan Morris's books except three. Hers are among the very first books I distinctly remember as being responsible for my developing wanderlust. When I saw this volume, I thought, Who better to be a reader's companion on a tour of Europe on the brink of the twenty-first century? She's traveled to all of Europe's corners more than, I believe, any other contemporary writer, and one of the most appealing aspects of this book is that she often includes multiple perspectives, relating her observations to the first time she visited a place as well as to more recent visits. The five chapters are sandwiched between ruminations on Trieste, which Morris refers to as "the cusp of Europe . . . where I can look one way toward Rome and Paris and London, the other toward Belgrade and Bucharest and Athens." The final chapter, "Spasms of Unity: Six Attempts to Make a Whole of Europe, from The Holy Roman Empire to The European Union," is perhaps the best.

The First World War, John Keegan, Alfred A. Knopf, 1999. A definitive account of the Great War, which created the modern world. As Keegan notes, there were in the end *twelve* battles of the Isonzo (in Friuli–Venezia Giulia) in that war. In the first, nearly 2,000 Italians were killed and 12,000 wounded. "There were to be three more battles of the Isonzo in 1915, in July, October and

November, each incurring a heavier toll of killed and wounded, 6,287, 10,733, and 7,498 dead respectively, for almost no gain of ground at all."

History of the Present: Essays, Sketches, and Dispatches from Europe in the 1990s, Timothy Garton Ash, Random House, 1999. The bulk of this insightful book is made up of "analytical reportages" that were originally published in *The New York Review of Books.* Ash admits that the phrase "history of the present" is not his but was coined by American diplomat and historian George Kennan in a review of Ash's book *The Uses of Adversity,* in the 1980s. The phrase is the best description for what Ash has been trying to write for twenty years, combining the crafts of historian and journalist. I really like the way he has written this book, with a chronology for each piece and diarylike sketches inserted throughout that are drawn from his own notebooks and recollections. It's an unusual way of reporting history, but an effective one, I think. Italy is mentioned often in the course of events.

Holy War: The Crusades and Their Impact on Today's World, Karen Armstrong, with a new preface, Anchor Books, 2002; originally published in hardcover in Great Britain by Macmillan, 1988, and subsequently published in revised editions in the United States by Doubleday, 1991 (hardcover) and Anchor Books, 1992 (paperback). It is of course impossible to understand Venice without simultaneously understanding the Crusades, and this newly reissued book is an excellent source. Venice's role in the Crusades was somewhere between non-confrontational and duplicitous, which is to say entirely secular and capitalistic: the Venetians had no desire to fight the Muslims, anywhere, because their very (profitable) existence depended on the trading markets they had established in the Levant. An infamous example revealing the Venetians' true colors occurred in 1202, when the Crusaders made a treaty with the Venetians. Doge Enrico Dandolo (the one who was blinded during a brawl in Constantinople) agreed that for the sum of 85,000 marks he would provide transport and food for 4,500 knights, 9,000 squires, and 20,000 infantry. But at the same time Dandolo was negotiating this treaty (though it does not seem that there was any negotiating at all, rather a single offer), his staff was promising Sultan al-Adil that he would not endorse an attack on Cairo. "By June 1202 the Crusaders had assembled in Venice, but unfortunately only half the number they had expected had taken the Cross and only two thirds of the money they owed Dandolo had been collected. When Dandolo found that they could not pay him in full, he took control. He crammed the Crusaders onto the tiny island of St. Nicolo di Lido and threatened to cut off their food supplies unless they paid up or else helped him in a project of his own before they went to the East. Venice had recently been in conflict with Hungary for control of the Dalmatian trade routes, and the Hungarians had just seized the key port of Zara in modern Yugoslavia. Dandolo wanted the Crusaders to capture Zara for him with their huge army. To their credit, some of the Crusaders were disgusted by the idea of attacking a perfectly innocent Christian city and they left the Crusade, but those who stayed on to cooperate with Dandolo were probably more confused than wicked. Like many modern Crusaders, they would have felt, when they turned their Crusade into a Crusade against Christians, that the end justified the means." It is clear from reading about the Crusades—which took place in the eleventh, twelfth, and thirteenth centuries—that Venice's motive in each offensive was always profit. I am not condoning the actions of the Venetians when I say that, in contrast to other Christian nations, they stood a bit apart from the fray: they were savvy operators but were not despicable.

The Crusades Through Arab Eyes, Amin Maalouf, Schocken, 1989. This very good book differs from Armstrong's work in that Maalouf presents eyewitness accounts and medieval Arab scripts, and so the entire book is revealed through the lens of Arab eyes. Interestingly, while the Arab view sees the Crusades as unprovoked and brutal to the point of disbelief, it also proudly honors Saladin, who was sultan of Egypt in 1175 and precipitated the Third Crusade by his recovery of Jerusalem in 1187. Saladin was renowned for his knightly courtesy and made peace with Richard I of England in 1192. He is a hero among the Arabs for delivering the greatest defeat ever to a non-European society. To say that this book and Armstrong's are important is a simplified understatement. In attempting to understand the Crusades, I am reminded of Bernard Lewis's *A Middle East Mosaic,* in which he states that "in medieval Europe no Muslim presence was tolerated," perhaps the single best quote to keep in mind. The Crusades' legacy of religious violence is still with us, and as Armstrong notes, "it is important for Western people to consider these contemporary holy wars in connection with the Crusades, because they remind us of our own input, involvement and responsibilities." At the end of her preface, she adds that the Crusades showed religion at its very worst: "I was so saddened by the conflict between the three Abraham traditions that I decided to embark on the research for my book *A History of God.* [See my *Morocco* edition for details of this excellent work.] I wanted to demonstrate the strong and positive ideals and visions that Jews, Christians and Muslims share in common. It is now over a millennium since Pope Urban II called the First Crusade in 1095, but the hatred and suspicion that this expedition unleashed still reverberates, never more so than on September 11, 2001, and during the terrible days that followed. It is tragic that our holy wars continue, but for that very reason we must strive for mutual understanding and for what in these pages I have called 'triple vision.'"

The Penguin Atlas of Ancient History (1967; reprinted 1986), *Medieval History* (1968; reprinted 1992), *Modern History—to 1815* (1973; reprinted 1986), and *Recent History—Europe Since 1815* (1982), Colin McEvedy, Penguin Books. This is a brilliant idea: a chronological sequence of maps that illustrate political and military developments, which in turn illustrate history via geography. Each individual volume is remarkably fascinating, and the four volumes as a whole present an enlightening read. Maps appear on the right-hand pages while one page of explanatory text accompanies them on the left-hand pages. *Essenziale* for history novices and mavens alike.

Travel Guide to Europe—1492: Ten Itineraries in the Old World, Lorenzo Camusso, Henry Holt & Co., 1992; originally published in Italy in 1990 under the title *Guida ai viaggi nell'Europa del 1492* by Mondadori. This unique book, published to coincide with the five hundredth anniversary of the discovery of the Americas, deserves more than short-lived appreciation. Italian historian Camusso presents ten real (or probable) journeys, in chronological order, so that readers may imagine the passing of time and events. The first section of the book gives an overview of Europe in the fifteenth century and includes descriptions of what travel was like by horse, river, and seaworthy boats; the condition of roads; inns; money; royal families; artists and artwork; food and drink. Of the ten itineraries, Venice—whose population at the time was 100,000—is featured in one.

The Mediterranean: History, Natural History, and Personal Narratives

The First Eden: The Mediterranean World and Man, Sir David Attenborough, William Collins Sons & Co., London, 1987. The four parts of this book deal with natural history, archaeology, history, and ecology, and there is very good coverage of Mediterranean plants and animals.

The Inner Sea: The Mediterranean and Its People, Robert Fox, Knopf, 1993.

The Mediterranean, Fernand Braudel, first published in France, 1949. English translation of second revised edition, HarperCollins, 1972. Abridged edition, HarperCollins, 1992. Still the definitive classic. *Essenziale.*

Mediterranean: A Cultural Landscape, Predrag Matvejevic, translated by Michael Henry Heim, University of California Press, Berkeley, 1999; previously published as *Mediteranski brevijar,* Zagreb, 1987; *Breviaire méditerranéen,* Paris, 1992; and *Mediterraneo: Un nuovo breviario,* Milan, 1993. A beautiful, unusual book combining personal observations with history, maps, maritime details, people, and language.

Mediterranean: From Homer to Picasso, Xavier Girard, translated by Simon Pleasance and Fronza Woods, Assouline, 2001. This recent book is perhaps in a category by itself. Divided into five chapters—representations, narratives, figures, places, and arts—I've been waiting for a volume just like this, which is filled with color and black-and-white illustrations and photos. As quoted in the prologue, "The Mediterranean," wrote Bernard Pingaud in the pages of

L'Arc in 1959, "is nothing other than the image we make of it for ourselves. The unusual thing is that we all make an image of it for ourselves, and that it is still a magnet for all those who are lucky enough to discover it one day. Herein lies a secret. It is perhaps not the secret conjured up by the 'land where the orange tree blooms.' It is the secret of this image itself, the secret of a dream which paradoxically contrasts abundance and drought, merriness and poverty, moderation and excess, joy and tragedy. Who can say why we need the Midi? If the Mediterranean didn't exist, we would have to invent it."

Memory and the Mediterranean, Fernand Braudel, Alfred A. Knopf, 2001.

On the Shores of the Mediterranean, Eric Newby, first published by Harvill Press, London, 1984; Picador, 1985, paperback. You have to travel with Eric and Wanda Newby to other places around the Mediterranean besides Venice—the former Yugoslavia, Greece, Turkey, Israel, North Africa, the Côte d'Azur, and Spain—but it's a pleasure every step of the way.

The Pillars of Hercules: A Grand Tour of the Mediterranean, Paul Theroux, G. P. Putnam's Sons, 1995.

Playing Away: Roman Holidays and Other Mediterranean Encounters, Michael Mewshaw, Atheneum, 1988.

The Spirit of Mediterranean Places, Michel Butor, Marlboro Press, 1986.

World War II in the Mediterranean, 1942–1945, Carlo d'Este, with an introduction by John S. D. Eisenhower, Major Battles and Campaigns Series, Algonguin Books of Chapel Hill, 1990. One of the few single volumes devoted to this arena of the Second World War, and though it's a bit dry at times, it's an interesting, informative read with black-and-white photographs and good maps. Though greatly overshadowed by the D-day landings, the Mediterranean theater of war was hardly insignificant; Eisenhower, in his introduction, reminds us that during just one Mediterranean campaign, battle deaths among Americans, British, and French totaled 32,000 men. "That staggering figure almost equals that of the 33,000 American troops killed during the entire Korean War (1950–53). It even compares to the number (47,300) killed in the ten-year Vietnam conflict (1963–72). . . . By no means do these figures denigrate the traumas undergone by our soldiers in other conflicts; they merely explain our wonder at how such a large campaign as the Mediterranean could be treated as 'secondary.'" Events in Italy—on Sicily and at Anzio, Rome, and Monte Cassino—are all well documented.

Mediterranean Architecture and Style

Mediterranean Color: Italy, France, Spain, Portugal, Morocco, Greece, photographs and text by Jeffrey Becom, foreword by Paul Goldberger, Abbeville Press, 1990.

Mediterranean Lifestyle, photography by Pere Planells, text by Paco Assensio, Loft Publications; distributed in the United States by Watson-Guptill, 2000.

Mediterranean Living, Lisa Lovatt-Smith, Whitney Library of Design, Watson-Guptill, 1998.

Mediterranean Style, Catherine Haig, Abbeville Press, 1998; first published in Great Britain in 1997 by Conran Octopus, London.

Mediterranean Vernacular: A Vanishing Architectural Tradition, V. I. Atroshenko, Milton Grundy, Rizzoli International Publications, 1991.

Villages in the Sun: Mediterranean Community Architecture, Myron Goldfinger, Rizzoli, 1993.

Playing Away: Roman Holidays and Other Mediterranean Encounters, Michael Mewshaw, Atheneum, 1988.

Italy

Bazaar to Piazza: Islamic Trade and Italian Art, 1300–1600, Rosamond Mack, University of California Press, 2002. In chapters that focus on silks, carpets, ceramics, glass, bookbinding, lacquer, and inlaid brass, Mack presents a history of the Mediterranean trade in luxury goods and how this trade made such a strong and lasting impression on Italian taste and production during the early Renaissance. This excellent book is quite timely, and with the recent release of Deborah Howard's *Venice & the East* (see *Venezia biblioteca*), it represents what I hope is a new wave of scholarly books about this important link. While Howard's book deals exclusively with Venice, this title covers all of Italy—though Venice was obviously the "frontline city" when it came to East-West artistic exchange. (Readers may be familiar, by the way, with the painting reproduced on the cover of this beautiful book: *Saint Mark Preaching in Alexandria* by Gentile Bellini, which hangs in the Pinacoteca di Brera in Milan.) Mack concludes that consumers, whether Eastern or Western, acquired a range of tastes that craftsmen on either side learned to satisfy. "Furthermore, such competition and exchange clearly neither hindered the development of a strong Ottoman artistic culture nor threatened the Italian one. Sixteenth-century East-West trade and artistic exchange softened a clash of civilizations, establishing a historical precedent for cultural coexistence and mutual enrichment." During the early years of the Renaissance, Italian craftsmen were inspired by the dazzling wares that arrived in Europe via Italian merchant ships. But even after their own versions of some of the luxury goods surpassed the quality of the originals, Italians continued to collect, imitate, and adapt objects from the Ottoman Empire and China. "The Ottomans permitted the Venetians to establish consulates in Cairo and Aleppo, the first, the principal market for spices, the second, for cotton and silk arriving by caravan." This subject has not been exhausted, but this book is extremely thorough, vastly interesting, and comprehensive. *Essenziale.*

Cento Città: A Guide to the "Hundred Cities & Towns" of Italy, Paul Hofmann, Henry Holt, 1988, hardcover; Owl, 1990, paperback. "Whenever Italians want to stress the cultural variety of their nation, or nostalgically mention places where they really would like to live, they speak of the Cento Città (CHEN-toh Chee-TAH). The alliterative phrase must be translated as the 'hundred cities and towns,' because the word *città* means either. The townspeople of Todi (population 16,000) and the 7,000 residents of Asolo, referring to their habitat, say *'città'* the same way as the three million Romans." This is one of the most treasured books in my Italy library, and Hofmann, for many years the *New York Times* bureau chief in Rome, is one of my favorite writers. The hundred *città* (a word that is both singular and plural—one of the exceptions in Italian grammar—for city or town) featured in this book are his personal favorites, and it would be ridiculous to disagree with his selections; they are, individually and collectively, singularly sensational. The first section of the book is devoted to "The Serene Venetias" and the *città* included are Padua, Adria, Chioggia, Trieste, Udine, Cividale del Friuli, Asolo, Bassano del Grappa, Treviso, Vicenza, Cortina d'Ampezzo, Ortisei/St. Ulrich/Urtijei, Bressanone/Brixen, Bolzano/Bozen, Merano/Meran, Trent, Rovereto, and Verona. The bigger cities—Rome, Florence, Venice, Milan—are not included; this is a book for those who want to get off the predictable circuit and better understand *regions* of Italy. The appendix contains practical information, such as postal and telephone codes, recommended hotels and restaurants, museums, and the like, much of which may obviously be outdated, but the mileage distances and traveling times by car or train are still applicable. With seventy-four black-and-white photographs. *Essenziale.*

The Civilization of the Renaissance in Italy, Jacob Burckhardt, introduction by Hajo Holborn, Modern Library, 1954. In his introduction, Holborn refers to this definitive and much-quoted work as "the greatest single book ever on the history of Italy between 1350 and 1550." If the title sounds dry, it's misleading. This is an endlessly fascinating and brilliant book, *assolutamente essenziale* for *all* visitors to Italy.

Henry James on Italy, Barrie & Jenkins, London, 1988; published in the United States by Weidenfeld & Nicolson, New York. A handsome hardcover package with color reproductions of period paintings matched with text from James's *Italian Hours.* Most of the time, I am not fond of book excerpts, and certainly *Italian Hours* deserves to be read in its entirety; but this is such an appealing collection and I have enjoyed it so much that I am happy to include it here. Though James travels all about Italy, the first two chapters are "Venice" and "The Grand Canal." Within them are some of the oft-quoted—but worth quoting again—words about the city: "Venice has been painted and described many thousands of times, and of all the cities of the world is the easiest to visit without going there. Open the first book and you will find a rhapsody about it; step into the first picture-dealer's and you will find three or four high-coloured 'views' of it. There is notoriously nothing more to be said on the subject. Every one has been there, and every one has brought back a collection of photographs. There is as little mystery about the Grand Canal as about our local thoroughfare, and the name of St. Mark is as familiar as the postman's ring. It is not forbidden, however, to speak of familiar things, and I hold that for the true Venice-lover Venice is always in order." Great to keep or give as a gift.

Image of Italy, special issue of *The Texas Quarterly,* vol. 4, no. 2, Summer 1961, edited by William Arrowsmith, photographs by Russell Lee. Although it's an edition of *The Texas Quarterly,* this is actually a hardcover book, with unforgettable photos and superb text. The fact that it was published in 1961 is irrelevant; today's "image" of Italy is just as various and complex as it was then. As stated in the foreword, our image of Italy is occasionally distorted in part because of Italy's "staggering diversity" of people and landscape. "Her politics have been polarized by the Cold War, her Communist party is proportionally the largest in Europe, while her economic policies vacillate between state socialism and uncontrolled laissez-faire capitalism. Add to this war (and the civil war which was its consequence), overpopulation, underemployment, a growing gap between rich and poor and South and North, the flight of the peasantry from unproductive farms to cities, continual emigration, the desuetude of old ways and old customs, and the violent alterations in landscape and living, and the impression is utter variety and change. In a half hour's drive out of almost any city in Italy you can pass through three or four successive centuries, all of them simultaneously alive and even competitive, each one with its distinctive way of being Italian, and its Italian hunger for change." This is not a record of contemporary Italian culture, nor a venue for representative Italian writing. Rather, it suggests how the ideas of Italy and of being Italian are formed and how they are shaped by the work of Italian writers and thinkers. Some contributors are Carlo Cassola, Cesare Pavese, Carlo Levi, Paolo Volponi, Gabriella Parca, and Elena Croce. A wonderful, outstanding collection.

Italian Days, Barbara Grizzuti Harrison, Ticknor & Fields, 1989. My enthusiasm for this beautifully written and superb book, no matter how many times I reread it, is endless. I am incapable of praising it sufficiently. In an endorsement from *The Washington Post Book World,* a reviewer wrote that it "will be the companion of visitors for years to come." It was published over a decade ago, and I hope that it remains true. I cannot imagine going to Italy without reading it, can't imagine anyone with a serious interest in Italy not reading it, can't imagine my life without having read it. *Essenziale.*

Italian Dreams, photographs by Steven Rothfeld, introduction by Franco Zeffirelli, Collins, 1995. With writings by Gertrude Stein and others to accompany the dreamy photographs by Rothfeld, this is a special treat to buy for yourself. (It also makes a nice gift for your favorite Italophile.) The images—handmade Polaroid transfers—are not the Predictable Pictures of Italy one sees in so many other books. It's a beautiful package for those who appreciate beautiful things.

Italian Hilltowns, Norman F. Carver Jr., Documan Press, Kalamazoo, Michigan, hardcover and paperback, 1979, 1995. This is one of my most treasured books. Carver, an architect, has also spent a considerable number of years photographing folk architecture in the Mediterranean region as well as Japan and Mexico. It's not only that these color and black-and-white photographs are exquisite, but that Carver is passionately concerned with preserving Italy's hilltowns and sharing what we can learn from them. He highlights many towns, throughout all of Italy, which are hardly mentioned in guidebooks: Pierele, Grisolia, Sorano, Caprancia, Archidosso, Postignano (which is featured on the cover), Castelvecchio Calviso, and the Val di Fafora, a valley west of Florence where there are seven tiny villages perched on hilltops, none of which overwhelm the environment. None of the featured villages are in the Northeast, but this is still a rewarding book to read.

Italian Hours, Henry James, Ecco Press; originally published by Houghton Mifflin, 1909. There are twenty-two essays in this wonderful book, which James wrote during the 1870s. *Essenziale.*

The Italian Way: Aspects of Behavior, Attitudes, and Customs of the Italians, Mario Costantino, Lawrence Gambella, Passport Books, an imprint of NTC/Contemporary Publishing Co., 1996. One of my favorite books, this is a slim, handy A-to-Z guide to a multitude of key traits of the Italians. Costantino and Gambella have compiled an interesting and useful list including abbreviations and acronyms that tourists will need to recognize; the numerous ways the Italians have of attracting attention; the finer points of compliments, appreciation, criticism, and gallantry; a brief history of *Carnevale;* Italian films; *Il Malocchio, Il Palio,* and *La Vendemmia; Lo Sciopero,* pro loco; sports; ways of conveying information; and women. *Assolutamente essenziale.*

The Italians: A Full-Length Portrait Featuring Their Manners and Morals, Luigi Barzini, Atheneum, 1964. *Still* the classic, *still* the best book of its kind. If I were to recommend only one book, this would be it. Don't bother trying to understand Italy or grasp the Italian character without reading this, or rereading it if it's been a while since you first picked it up. Each chapter is well written and thought provoking but a few that really stand apart are "The Problema del Mezzogiorno," "Illusion and Cagliostro," and "Sicily and the Mafia," which might be the best essay I've ever read on the history and influence of both the *mafia* (defined by Barzini as a state of mind, a philosophy of life, a conception of society, and a moral code, prevalent among *all* Sicilians) and the Mafia (the illegal organization that makes headlines). *Essenziale.*

Italians First!: An A-to-Z of Everything First Achieved by Italians, Arturo Barone, third edition, Renaissance Books (an imprint of Global Books), Folkestone, Kent, England, 1999. The only book of its kind I've ever seen, this is a handy and truly amazing cross-indexed listing of Italians and the areas in which they achieved "firsts," such as: In 1350 gold wire was first made in Italy; Giorgio Vasari became the first art historian in 1550; the first newspaper was published in Venice in 1563; Venice established the first coffee house in the Western world in 1645; in 1871 Antonio Meucci applied for a telephone patent (Alexander Graham Bell's application came in 1876); in 1889 Giuseppe Pirelli made the first motorcar tire; Giovanni Battista Amici discovered the sexual process in flowering plants—the list is endless (more than eight hundred entries). Barone also provides commentaries for some topics, which provide an interesting diversion from the entries.

The Italians: History, Art, and the Genius of a People, edited by John Julius Norwich, Thames and Hudson, London, 1983; 1989 edition published by Portland House, a division of Dilithium Press, Ltd. A wonderful, wonderful book that I would include in the *essenziale* category. Norwich is an engaging historian and is also the distinguished author of *A History of Venice, Byzantium,* and others. He has gathered an impressive bunch of authors to answer the question How did the qualities of "Italianness" that make Italy unique arise in history? Individual chapters cover ancient history, humanism, the Renaissance, romanticism, and modern Italy from 1800 to the present. With an equally impressive collection of color and black-and-white illustrations, this is really an essential read.

Italy Fever: 14 Ways to Satisfy Your Love Affair with Italy, Darlene Marwitz, Portico Press, Fredericksburg, Texas, 2000. Darlene Marwitz is one of my soul mates. She doesn't know this, and we've never met, but we both have what others might refer to as an insane, irrational obsession with Italy. Unfortunately, I did not discover Marwitz's joyful book until my *Central Italy* manuscript had been completed; otherwise I would have shared it with readers then. I bought it and read it the same day. I knew we were of like mind when I read this passage from the preface: "Obsessing on Italy is relentless. Each day I uncover new writers, old writers, great writers who share my passion. Each week I meet others who have traveled to, lived in, or desire to go to Italy. Each fellow Italy lover fuels me forward into something bigger than was first imagined." And at the preface's close, she writes, "In no way am I able to capture even a fraction of what is grand and intimate about Italy. I make no attempt to do so except in terms of my personal aspirations and private love affair with this country. I've never lived in Italy, nor do I have longtime acquaintances who live there. Instead, my expertise lies in my passion, the knowledge I seek about all things Italian—stemming from my first glimpse of a Renaissance villa in Vicenza, Palladio's Villa Rotonda. It was love at first sight, not only for what the villa displayed architecturally, but for what it represented in spirit to me." Like me, Marwitz does nutty things like talking to a map of Italy hanging on her wall, collecting old postcards of Venice and Rome, sampling *gelato* combinations and calling it "research," and overdosing on Verdi and Puccini. If you too are smitten—or think you might be one day—you will love this book. Marwitz helps readers discover, interpret, and incorporate pieces of Italy into their own lives, and for this it is invaluable.

Modern Italy: A Political History, Denis Mack Smith, University of Michigan Press, 1997; first published in the United States as *Italy: A Modern History* by University of Michigan Press in 1959, revised 1969. This is *the* volume to read on Italy from just before 1861 to 1996. Smith is a fellow of the British Academy, has been awarded a dozen literary prizes in Italy, and is a *commendatore* of the Italian Order of Merit. He is also the author of *Italy and Its Monarchy* (Yale University Press, 1989), among other works. "The best starting point for a political history of modern Italy," he notes, "is March 1861 when, at long last, Count Cavour was able to proclaim that a united Italian kingdom was in existence." From this point, Smith takes readers up to the confusing political mess of recent years, and his final chapter is the best summation I've read on this transitional period. The book is very well organized and clearly written and also provides an appendix of prime ministers, heads of state, and popes and their terms. Impressively, more than a dozen editions of the book have been used as texts in schools and universities in Italy.

Letters from Italy, J. W. von Goethe; many editions; mine is a rare volume translated by Rev. A.J.W. Morrison, M.A., Anna Swanwick, and Sir Walter Scott, published by Robertson, Ashford and Bentley, 1902. Even more than Henry James and D. H. Lawrence, Goethe and his writings on Italy are *essenziale* in any library of Italian books. Readers will notice that Goethe's letters are referenced in a great number of sources, and with good reason: they are a delight to read, filled with the sort of observations and insights that make such good quotations.

Out of Italy: 1450–1650, Fernand Braudel, translated by Sian Reynolds, Editions Arthaud, 1989; English translation Flammarion, 1991. I had known Braudel only as the author of *The Identity of France* and *The Mediterranean* before I ran across this beautiful and fascinating book, illustrated with color reproductions by Michelangelo, Raphael, Titian, Ghirlandaio, Van Eyck, Rubens, Poussin, and others. Braudel examines Italy's dominant position in Europe and around the Mediterranean during the two centuries of the Renaissance, Mannerism, and the Baroque period, and analyzes the interaction among art, science, politics, and commerce in terms of how they contributed to Italy's influence abroad. This is Braudel's specialty—looking at history simultaneously with other social studies—and readers will find this book *essenziale*.

Sprezzatura: 50 Ways Italian Genius Shaped the World, Peter D'Epiro and Mary Desmond Pinkowish, Anchor Books, 2001. What a great word: *sprezzatura,* which means "the art of effortless mastery." As the authors note in the preface, "functionality and beauty are the very essence of Italian civilization. From the beginning, Italian genius has tended to be practical, down-to-earth, and concerned with getting things done, but it has also emphasized form, harmony, and radiance." They present here fifty outstanding Italian contributions to world civilization out of a possible fifty thousand. Apart from the authors' personal preferences, their selection has been guided by "the wish to focus on significant achievements that have been realized by Italians first, best, or most influentially over the past twenty-five centuries or so." They also clarify that for the purposes of the book, they have defined Italians as people who were born in Italy and spent at least the formative part of their lives there. Among the fifty people and concepts are the Roman calendar; Ovid's *Metamorphoses;* Saint Francis of Assisi; banks, bookkeeping, and the rise of commercial capitalism; Brunelleschi, Donatello, and Masaccio; Cosimo and Lorenzo de'Medici; the violin and the piano; Venice; the art of apparel; and Andrea Palladio. This is a brilliant idea for a book, and each essay is addictive.

La Storia: Five Centuries of the Italian American Experience, Jerre Mangione and Ben Morreale, HarperCollins, 1992. I've included this book here because of the significant number of Italians who have emigrated to the United States and because of this line from *The New York Times Book Review:* "And it is a book that should be read by all Americans interested in what binds us together, despite our different backgrounds and histories." The size and scope of this book is amazing, and each chapter is fascinating. The authors focus on three historical periods, including the years 1880–1920, when the largest number of Italians arrived, the overwhelming majority from the *mezzogiorno.* There is and has been for a long, long time a unique Italy-America (or "La Merica" as many Italians called it) bond, which may, depending on where you travel, become overwhelmingly apparent to you in Italy.

That Fine Italian Hand—What Makes the Italians Italian: A Wry Close-up of a Resourceful People, Paul Hofmann, Henry Holt & Co., 1990. Another wonderful book by Hofmann, this one covers such topics as pasta, pizza, and espresso; red tape and anarchy; the Mafia, the two Italys, the *carabinieri,* the family, and more—all of which are referred to as having "that fine Italian hand," which "has long meant the particular way Italians like to do things, preferring adroitness to sheer force." *Essenziale*.

A *Traveller in Italy,* H. V. Morton, Dodd, Mead & Co., 1964. Morton has been described as "a fine traveling companion," and it would be difficult to find a better one. His books on Rome, Spain, and southern Italy are among the best ever published, despite the fact that they're all, including this one, out of print. Chapters 8, 9, and 10 are devoted to the Veneto and Venice. (Unfortunately, Morton did not travel to Friuli–Venezia Giulia.) Of the many memorable passages in this book, three in particular stand out. The first is about the Council of Ten, a body that once held the real power in Venice, controlling the police, the judiciary, and the secret service funds. They were, Morton tells us, as feared as the Gestapo. "That the rule of the Ten," Morton writes, "founded on suspicion and a depressingly cynical view of human nature, should have worked for more than a thousand years, is one of the many amazing things about Venice. For centuries the rest of Europe looked at the Republic with awe and envy as an example of a miraculously stable state, one that went on its glorious golden course age after age, untouched by internal strife or dynastic or religious wars." About the Palazzo Ducale, Morton notes, "One has to be a tremendous enthusiast to be genuinely interested in the enormous river of Venetian history which flows round the walls and overflows on the ceilings: Venice triumphant; Venice resurgent; Venice conquering the Turk; Venice capturing Crete; Venice always successful. It was an unwritten law that one had to be successful. No matter what a man's past triumphs, should he fail, it was assumed that there was treachery somewhere and he was probably impeached. In contrast to the modern cult of personality, Venice cultivated impersonality. The individual was nothing: Venice was everything." And finally, sadly: "History has few sadder footnotes to greatness than the decline of Venice in the eighteenth century. As trade grew less, life became more costly and spectacular, and Venice became the gayest city in Europe. The last Doge, Ludovico Manin, surrendered Venice to a young man of twenty-eight, a Corsican with untidy hair and a general's sash across a yet slim waistline. The Doge left the Council Chamber under the gaze of his mighty predecessors, and entered his apartments to be disrobed by his valet. Removing the *corno* from his head, the symbol of Venetian greatness, he handed it to the man with the remark that he would not be needing it again. Napoleon saved his last insult until the end. He sold Venice to Austria." A helpful appendix features the famous families of Italy. Wonderful, and *essenziale*.

A *Traveller's History of Italy,* Denis Judd, Interlink Books, New York, 1994. This edition is one in a great series for which I have much enthusiasm. I'm not sure what the series editor's vision is, but *my* idea of it is to give readers a compact, historical overview of each place, highlighting the significant events and people with which every visitor should be familiar. Each edition is a mini "what you should know" guide, with a minimum of milestones to help you really appreciate what you're seeing. Judd reminds us that "the history of Italy is central to the European experience, but also curiously detached from it. It was, of course, through the supremacy of Rome that Italy enjoyed its greatest influence. Roma power stretched from the Atlantic to the borders of Mesopotamia, and from the Scottish Lowlands to the Sahara Desert. It is understandable that the Mediterranean was believed to lie at the centre of the civilized world, or that early-twentieth-century Russian and German emperors assumed a local variation of the title Caesar. Nor did Italian influence vanish with the collapse of Rome: a new, spiritual Caesar exercised a global sway from the Vatican; Italian banking techniques and artistic genius shaped European and world attitudes; a Genovese discovered the Americas in 1492; and Machiavelli was to statecraft what Marconi became to radio communications. Yet modern Italy has often been on the sidelines of world events. Despite its nineteenth- and twentieth-century pretensions, Italy was of little account in the European balance of power, and its empire consisted largely of the scraps left over by the major imperial predators. To travel down the length of Italy is a reminder that though the country's northern regions are thoroughly European, its southern extremities are almost North African in character and climate." The eight chapters in this volume cover the major periods in Italian history, from the stone age, the Etruscan civilization, and the *Rinascimento,* to fascism and postwar and contemporary Italy. Additionally, there are charts of emperors, popes, Venetian doges, Italian artists, and prime ministers; a twelve-and-a-half-page chronology of major events; a chart showing election results to the Chamber of Deputies, 1946–1992 and 1994–1996; a bibliography; and an A–Z historical gazetteer that can be used to cross-reference towns, sites, and buildings of historical importance.

Towns of the Renaissance: Travellers in Northern Italy, David D. Hume, J. N. Townsend Publishing, Exeter, New Hampshire, 1995. I am very fond of this book although it is not written by a noted historian or scholar in Italian studies. Hume has one quality, however, that is equally important: a sincere love and enjoyment of Italy, as well as an insatiable curiosity about things Italian. He writes about Italy and travel very much in the spirit of *The Collected Traveler,* and when I read in his "Author's Note" that "my wife Cathy and I learned a lot about that wonderful country while we were there and perhaps twice as much by reading about it both before and after we went on these visits," I immediately liked him. He presents a good bibliography and offers lots of practical tips for traveling and interesting observations and thoughts. The book features Renaissance towns from Venice to Rome. The chapters entitled

"Crime in Italy," "Cars and Their Pilots," and "The Boys of the Renaissance" are good, and "Understanding Italian and Italians" is worth reproducing in full, as it is an excellent encouragement for *anyone*, of any age, to learn a foreign language. Parchment endpapers featuring a map of Italy as far south as Perugia and nice drawings by the author are included. Highly recommended.

Were You Always an Italian?: Ancestors and Other Icons of Italian America, Maria Laurino, W. W. Norton, 2000. A great companion read to *La Storia*, this is an engaging, touching, funny, and thoughtful memoir. And you don't have to be Italian to appreciate its window onto ethnic and cultural identity in America.

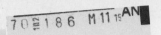

CONVALIDA ↑ ↑ ↑

AEROPORTO
MARCO POLO-VENEZIA
BIGLIETTO - TICKET
C.S.- AEROPORTO-23

L. 5000   €2,58
DA VENEZIA - P.ROMA
A AEROPORTO M.POLO
COMPRESO BAGAGLIO
P.I. 00764110276
11:02 86 G1 186 10043
VEDI AVVISO A TERGO

ISTITUTO VENETO
DI SCIENZE, LETTERE ED ARTI
PALAZZO FRANCHETTI

salviamo Venezia

ITALIA   L.20

Venezia—
"La Serenissima"
(The City of Venice—
"The Most Serene Republic")

"And there is no use pretending that the tourist Venice is not the real Venice, which is possible with other cities—Rome or Florence or Naples. The tourist Venice is Venice: the gondolas, the sunsets, the changing light, Florian's, Quadri's, Torcello, Harry's Bar, Murano, Burano, the pigeons, the glass beads, the vaporetto. Venice is a folding picture-postcard of itself."
—Mary McCarthy, VENICE OBSERVED

"Nothing in the world that you have heard of Venice is equal to the magnificent and stupendous reality. The wildest visions of the Arabian Nights are nothing to the piazza of St. Mark, and the first impression of the inside of the church. The gorgeous and wonderful reality of Venice is beyond the fancy of the wildest dreamer. Opium couldn't build such a place, and enchantment couldn't shadow it forth in a vision. . . . It has never been rated high enough. It is a thing you would shed tears to see."
—Charles Dickens, IN A LETTER, 1844

America's Venice

BY JOHN LUKACS

〜

editor's note

We are probably much more familiar with the British presence in
Venice, but as the writer reveals in this piece, Americans too have long had
a presence in *La Serenissima* (sometimes dubiously, as sometimes it seems
the city is positively America-on-the-lagoon).

JOHN LUKACS is the author of *Five Days in London: May 1940* (Yale
University Press, 1999), *Destinations Past: Traveling Through History with
John Lukacs* (University of Missouri Press, 1994), and *Confessions of an
Original Sinner* (St. Augustine Press, 2000). His work has also appeared in
the *Provence, Côte d'Azur and Monaco* edition of *The Collected Traveler*.

What could be more different than Venice and an American
city? One pretends to represent the continued existence of
the past. The other pretends to represent the ideal of progress, of
the future. In their separate ways both are illusions, but no matter.
The relationship of the Old and the New Worlds is not simple. It is
like that of the sexes: opposites may repel, but often they attract.
Thus there are towns named and emulating Venice across America.
And there exists a long record of American presence in Venice,
reaching well beyond what brings American tourists there today.
The history of Americans' attraction to Venice is more than two
hundred years old.

In 1789, when the United States was born, there were but two
other republics in the entire world. One was the Republic of Venice,
the other the city-state of Geneva. Many of the Founders were
aware of their existence but had no wish to emulate their examples.
They were aristocratic republics, with constitutions that had little

appeal even for the more conservative of the Founders. At least Geneva was Protestant, but the government and the society of Venice seemed to represent much that was corrupt in the Old World. Many Americans were acquainted with *Venice Preserved,* a popular, often-performed play by the English dramatist Thomas Otway: "Curs'd be your State, cursed your constitution / The curse of growing factions and divisions." No, the new American Republic had to incarnate something that was the very opposite of Venice.

Still, it was the task of that new republic, for reasons commercial even more than diplomatic, to establish consulates abroad, especially in the main ports of Europe. In 1796 Timothy Pickering, Washington's secretary of state, wrote William Willis, a proper Philadelphian, instructing him to take the post of the first American consul in Venice. Willis, who was involved in a business dispute with a dubious Italian middleman in Leghorn, was about ready to move across Italy and establish himself in Venice when Bonaparte marched into that city in May 1797, putting an end to the Venetian Republic after thirteen hundred years. Willis never got to Venice. He turned around and sailed first to the West Indies and then to New York, where he wrote a detailed letter to the secretary of state about Venice and the French. In November 1798 he was posted American consul at Barcelona. By then the Republic of Geneva had been eliminated too, annexed to France, and Bonaparte had traded Venice to the Austrian Empire.

William Willis had missed a great experience: the approach to Venice. Two hundred years ago the only way to get there was by water, from the lagoon or the sea. And that way was—and remains—incomparable. Allow me, then, to suggest something to American travelers two centuries after Willis—that is, if they will afford a small amount of extra time. The dazzling approach, the literal revelation, of Venice is that from the lagoon to the south. There is the fishing town of Chioggia, on a spit of land, not difficult to get to, a few miles from Vicenza, at the end of the Brenta Canal, which is dotted with Palladian villas. Chioggia is a little Venice, its canals lined with fishing boats even now. A small steamer wends its way north from there, calling at a few of the lagoon villages, and then makes straight for the pier at St. Mark's. An hour or so before the traveler's arrival, Venice rises from the sea, a coruscating beauty immediately recognizable, the fabulous vista immortalized by its own Canaletto and Guardi and by hundreds of other great painters, including Americans. If one elects to spend the night at Chioggia and take the morning boat, the eastern sun paints the grand theater of Venice with gold.

The approach by train is not bad either. Once you emerge from the crowded Santa Lucia station, there is the Grand Canal, with a plenitude of color and waterborne business. From the airport north of Venice you will arrive by water: again, not a great loss, since, as with a beautiful woman, every side of Venice, including her back, is admirable. (Don't take a *private* motorboat from the airport; it will cost you a small fortune.) One thing is to be avoided, if possible: the approach by car. The enormous parking garage at the western end of Venice is nowadays often so full that many motorists must leave their cars at a garage in the mainland industrial port of Mestre and, panting, lug their bags to its indifferent railroad station, there to wait for the next local across the lagoon.

In 1807 an American consulate was finally established in Venice. It functioned until the 1960s, when the number of U.S. consulates abroad was reduced. But for American travelers in the early nineteenth century, Venice was seldom on the itinerary. Emerson visited it in 1837. He did not like it. "It is a great oddity—a city for beavers—but to my thought a most disagreeable residence . . . any thing but comfort. I soon had enough of it." But much would change after 1847, when the Austrian administration built the long railway bridge connecting Venice with the mainland. That was around the beginning of popular tourism, including the spread of eclectic interest in architecture, especially in their Italianate forms. In 1848 the Venetians rose against the Austrians, proclaiming, for a short time, the independence of Venice. The American consul William A. Sparks sent his felicitations to the Venetian leader Daniele Manin. Manin answered instantly: "We have been impressed with the salutations of the Consul of your great Republic as he greeted our Rebirth; we have welcomed it as the happiest of auguries. . . . We are divided by the Ocean but united by Sympathy, and Liberty, like the electric Telegraph, traversing the seas, will bring us your examples."

Poor Sparks, poor Venice. The former was very ill and died a year later. Venice was reconquered by the Austrians without much trouble. Sparks's secretary Peter C. Ebenkofler reported to Washington on July 1, 1850: "I regret saying that since the Austrian government had thought it proper to deprive Venice of the *free* port, with a view, it is generally supposed, of favouring Trieste, this place is entirely fallen . . . in point of fact, commerce is *null.*" Yet his pessimism was not warranted. It was not only that sixteen years later the Austrians left Venice, which was then united with the kingdom of Italy; it was that notwithstanding the decline of maritime commerce, during those sixteen years the attraction of Venice rose to a previously unimagined extent, drawing masses of visitors and, for the first time, many Americans.

The U.S. consulate had its troubles. Of no fewer than seven consuls between 1849 and 1861, one declined the appointment "in consequence of the inadequacy of the emoluments," and two died at their posts. Then in 1861 Abraham Lincoln gave William Dean Howells the consulship, a serendipitous choice for at least two reasons. It was in Venice that Howells discovered his talent for writing novels; eventually, he turned out to be one of the best American novelists of the nineteenth century. And his *Venetian Life,* written between 1863 and 1865, is still one of the finest of the hundreds of books about Venice, recognized not only by his American critics but by many of the most erudite and sensitive English Venetophiles. At first Howells thought of writing letters from Italy for *The Atlantic,* but its editors rejected them. After that his "Letters from Venice" appeared seriatim in the Boston *Daily Advertiser.* They were the work not of a journalist but of a novelist. As he himself wrote later, "I was studying manners, in the elder sense of the word, wherever I could get them in the frank life of the people around me.

"I took lodgings, and I began dining drearily in restaurants." Not too much change there since. From a gastronomic tour of northern Italy, Venice might as well be omitted. There *is* good food to be found in Venice, but mostly in some of its luxury hotels. Here and there, in a dark *calle* or around a sudden turn, tucked away in the corner of a small stone-paved square, one may find a fine little trattoria, above and beyond all gastronomic criticism. But don't attempt to dine on St. Mark's Square or near La Fenice Opera; the food will be appallingly expensive and not very good. Those places are for coffee and ices—very good coffee and very good ices, worth the money, which will be considerable.

There are a few exceptions to such generalizations. Perhaps typical of the Venetians' customary thrift, one of the few traditional and very good Venetian dishes is *fegato alla veneziana,* a calves' liver that is nearly classic; the other one is both Venetian and Adriatic, the *fritto misto,* a lightly breaded and fried medley of calamari and scampi and whitebait and small fish—delicious, accompanied by a green salad. There is one bargain, the wines of the Veneto, of the Venetian mainland provinces, crisp, light white wines (among them, for instance, the relatively recent American importation of Pinot Grigio). However, there is no reason to worry. Where else in the world can you lunch or dine on an airy terrace of a hotel, under a softly flapping canvas, leaning your elbow on a fine stone balustrade, looking out on the great theatrical traffic of the Grand Canal?

Howells wrote, "I felt curiously happy in Venice from the first." It seems that Venetians had despised his predecessor, J.J. Sprenger, "whose unhappy knowledge of German threw him on his arrival among people of that race," even though he was a "vivid" Pennsylvania Republican. Howells met few Americans in his first year, but that would soon change. The Venetians called Americans *inglesi*, their name for the English; the *inglesi* were open-handed, while the *tedeschi*, the Germans and Austrians, were stingy. At the Armenian Convent in San Lazzaro, "a sharp, bustling, go-ahead Yankee rushed in one morning, rubbing his hands, and demanding 'Show me all you can in five minutes.'" Howells was wonderfully observant. His official duties were few "during a year of almost uninterrupted tranquillity." He met an old man who had known Byron and pretended to have swum with him. "Is it worth observing that there are no Venetian blinds in Venice?" Near the end of his first year in Venice, he married Elinor Mead; their first child was born in Venice and given the un-Venetian name of Winifred; they had their Saturday evenings, their *conversazioni*. They moved to the Casa Falier, with its entrance on a dark *calle* but with its windows on the Grand Canal. On the wall, a small plaque, affixed in 1961, marks the Venetophile Howells's residence. Like all other consuls, he rented not a house but an apartment. "Our dear little balcony at Casa Falier! Over our heads dwelt a Dalmatian family; below our feet a Frenchwoman; at our right, upon the same floor, an English gentleman; under him a French family; and over him the family of a marquis in exile from Modena." Another neighbor was a witch, yet another a duchess of Parma.

He was not the first, or the last, to remark that Venetians are "insensible to and ignorant of Art. . . . I would as soon think of asking a fish's opinion of water as of asking a Venetian's notion of architecture or painting, unless he were himself a professed artist or critic." And that was Howells's strength too: unlike so many other writers, he did not aspire to vault suddenly to the near-celestial spheres of high art criticism. "I could not, in any honesty, lumber my pages with descriptions or speculations which would be idle to most readers, even if I were a far wiser judge of art than I affect to be." A very wise judge of art he was not. When he looked at Titian's *Martyrdom of Saint Lawrence* on a bitter-cold day, he felt envious of the saint's being poked by a hot fork, toasting comfortably "amid all that frigidity." He brought with himself plenty of New England Protestant prejudices: "there is so little in St. Mark's of the paltry or revolting character of modern Romanism." He disliked the Baroque: "The sight of those theatrical angels, with their shameless, unfinished backs, flying off the top of the rococo facades of the church of the Jesuits, has always been a spectacle to fill me with despondency and foreboding." He called the Church of the Jesuits "a dreary sanctuary." The very fine English connoisseur James Lees-Milne took him to task for that. "How could this jolly American consul be so disapproving of a building calculated to bring beauty and pleasure to a congregation in a poor district who feasted their eyes and senses on the splendour and luxury which they regarded as theirs?" Still, James (later Jan) Morris, no mean critic of Venice, called Howells's *Venetian Life* "a charming book." Which it is.

During the last year of his consulship, Howells and his wife moved into the Palazzo Giustiniani. Was there "any house with modern improvements in America, which has also windows, with pointed arches of marble, opening upon balconies that overhang the Grand Canal?" Their apartment had six rooms, "furnished with every article necessary for Venetian housekeeping. We paid one dollar a day which, in the innocence of our hearts we thought rather dear." Well, more than nostalgia is in order here. Hotels in Venice are frightfully expensive. Crowded they are too. But then some of them are *very* beautiful. The Gritti and the Danieli are world-famous and traditional palaces on the water. A fine addition is the Cipriani, positioned at the end of the island of Giudecca, built about thirty-five years ago, and pricey all right but, if you can afford it, worth every cent or lira. Its private motorboat will ferry you across the lagoon, to St. Mark's, in a few minutes, across the grandest sea—and island—and cityscape—of the entire world.

It is not possible to ascertain how much of an effect *Venetian Life* had on American tourism after 1865. But it is ascertainable that soon after 1865 the high period of American Venetophilia began. The city began to attract American painters. In 1872 Henry James met "on the Piazza on the evening of my arrival a young American painter who told me that he had been spending the summer just where I found him. I could have assaulted him for very envy." Among the most famous American painters, John Singer Sargent, James McNeill Whistler, William Merritt Chase, William S. Horton, and Maurice Prendergast painted many, and very different, canvases of Venice. But the most celebrated and most industrious American painter of Venice was Thomas Moran, otherwise known as the pioneer landscape painter of the Rocky Mountains. In 1898 the publishers Brown & Bigelow printed an edition of 22 million of one of Moran's Venetian paintings, an extraordinary number considering that the population of the United States was then about 76 million.

John Ruskin wrote that Venice was "a golden clasp on the girdle of the earth," about as fine a phrase as one can imagine. Such a clasp had appeal in the Gilded Age. By about 1880, Venice was no longer just a somewhat exotic bauble in the garland collected by American tourists, an extraneous feature on their rapid tours of Europe. Now one or two rich Americans had rented entire palazzi on the Grand Canal, and in 1882 Mr. and Mrs. Daniel Curtis of Boston bought the two upper floors of the Palazzo Barbaro, perhaps one of the most historic and surely one of the most sumptuously decorated palaces of Venice. Sargent, who disliked Venice because it was "cold," painted the group portrait of the Curtis family in the ballroom of the Barbaro. Their guest list was stunning: Sargent, the aged Robert Browning, Mrs. Jack Gardner (who used the Barbaro as a kind of model for her Boston townhouse, now the Gardner Museum), Edith Wharton, and Claude Monet. Howells was, of course, gone, but there was Henry James. He had come to Venice first in 1869, in the same year as Mark Twain, who, Yankee skeptic as he was in *The Innocents Abroad,* was more impressed by Venice and wrote better about it than James, who wrote to his brother that Venice reminded him of Newport: "The same atmosphere, the same luminosity." Luminosity, perhaps, but atmosphere? Well, he learned fast. He came again in 1872 and then in 1881; he knew the Curtises, he stayed in the Palazzo Barbaro, and he came often thereafter, staying long, very long. He wrote at least three articles about Venice, and he wrote two of his novels, *The Aspern Papers* and *The Wings of the Dove,* there. In the latter, he described the ballroom of the Palazzo Barbaro in a sentence that runs to more than 130 words. Let us, instead, cite him on the gondola: "The little closed cabin of this perfect vehicle, the movement, the darkness, and the plash, the indistinguishable swerves and twists, all the things you don't see and all the things you do feel—each dim recognition and obscure arrest is a possible throb of your sense of being floated to your doom, even when the truth is simply and sociably that you are going out to tea. Nowhere else is anything as innocent so mysterious, nor anything so mysterious so pleasantly deterrent to protest."

～

A century later, don't let yourself be talked into a gondola or a private motorboat, as you issue, with eyes blinking, from the railroad station. Don't let yourself be talked into a gondola at high noon anywhere. Gondolas are for the twilight or the evening. Then the theatricality falls away, and velvet shadows appear not only on the water but under the small cast-iron bridges and the houses close to whose stone walls the gondola slides with a melancholy sigh, the silence punctuated only on occasion by the soft plash of the gondolier's oar. During the day the best way to get around, when not on foot (Venice can be crossed walking in an hour at the most), is on the *vaporetti*, the water buses, crowded with working people getting off and on at so many stations, as they stitch the line of their progress from one side of the canal to the other, back and forth.

Americans tended to like gondoliers—James Morris mentions a generous American lady who in her will left a house to each of her boatmen—and gondoliers liked Americans. "The prestige of the United States was very high in Venice," Morris writes. "When a team of gondoliers took their craft to the [1893] Chicago World Fair, they came home to Venice as heroes, and lived comfortably on the experience for the rest of their lives." Lagoons, gondoliers, Venice: they appealed to the imagination of many Americans. How many American towns are named Venice! In California, replete with canals, in Florida, but also in Illinois, Michigan, Louisiana, New York, and Ohio.

Ever since the sixteenth century, the finest observers and admirers of Venice have been Englishmen and Englishwomen. Another maritime power, but how different! Perhaps the sense of contrast—architectural, theatrical, historical—is also what had drawn so many Americans to Venice, the sense of being able to experience a city where an ever more ancient past is palpable and alive at every corner. For unlike other Old World attractions, Venice is not a museum; it is, rather, a magnificent and panoramic seaborne bazaar, where each turn of small street or canal is a living reminder of something in the past. Venice is not a city of fantasy. It is not fantasy but imagination that is vitalized by its thousands of sights.

The American consulate had a gondola and employed a full-time gondolier. In 1910 the consul, John Q. Wood, reported that the consulate's situation was "fairly convenient" but that there was "difficulty for tourists of finding Consulate without a gondola." By that time, the main business of the consulate involved not commerce or problems with tourists but the emigration of workers to the United States from the Veneto, a small but significant portion of the huge wave of Italian migration to America, many of them accomplished artisans and stonemasons, and their families.

In the 1920s the consulate estimated that about 29,000 Americans visited Venice every year. In the Depression year of 1931, the number fell to 18,000, but soon it rose again. There was now another attraction to Venice: after plein air painting, plein air bathing, on the Lido. Across from Venice proper, a few minutes' boat ride across the lagoon, on its narrow sandy strip the hotels and the casino of the Lido stretch out. The Lido of Venice was probably the most fashionable summer place in Europe during the 1920s and 1930s; indeed, many Americans stayed at the luxurious Excelsior or at the Hôtel des Bains, rather than in Venice, which they could visit easily by boat. Cabanas with their striped awnings; silk pajamas on the beach and on the hotel terraces; bands playing American tunes, so different from the melancholy nineteenth-century opera and operetta music that floated from the plangent strings of the small orchestras of the cafés on St. Mark's Square: the atmosphere of the Lido was suffused with the fevered social and sexual ambitions and appetites of the period. Henry James and Edith Wharton and Thomas Moran were gone; it was now the period of Ernest Hemingway and Cole Porter and the supermodern Biennale and Peggy Guggenheim's no less supermodern museum.

One emblem of this American imprint on Venice was the establishment of Harry's Bar in 1931 (not on the Lido), marking the rise of the talented Cipriani family; the name "Harry's Bar" soon to be repeated on thousands of American lips, eventually becoming an American rather than Italian cliché. (Cliché or not, many Americans claim that it is one of the few places in Europe, if not the only one, where you can get a first-class American martini.)

Twentieth-century American writers wrote about Venice, foremost among them Hemingway, Gore Vidal, and Mary McCarthy. Ezra Pound chose to be buried there. Hemingway wrote an entire novel, *Across the River and Into the Trees,* set in the winter in Venice and on the lagoons, not one of his better ones. Perhaps the finest twentieth-century American book about Venice is Mary McCarthy's *Venice Observed* (1956). About St. Mark's, for example: "And it can take you unawares, looking beautiful or horribly ugly, at a time you least expect. Venice, Henry James said, is as changeable as a nervous woman, and this is particularly true of St. Mark's facade." A gondolier talked to McCarthy, with exquisite taste, about colors. "There spoke Venice, the eternal connoisseur, the voice of her eternal gondolier."

Venice preserved! There was, and there is, more of the American presence than the tangible remnant works of American artists and the words of American writers, and more than the surely fleeting memories of the hundreds of thousands of American tourists who must now push their way through the enormous crowds that make passage so difficult as to be nearly impossible, at least around St. Mark's, and not only during the months of high season. The American love, and respect, for Venice endures in many ways. American-born historians have written precise and scholarly works about odd periods of Venetian history. Americans have contributed—and not only financially—to important works of Venetian restoration. In 1902 the great bell tower, the campanile on

St. Mark's square, collapsed. The Venetians swore that it would be rebuilt perfectly, the way it had been and where it had been: *com'era, dov'era*. By 1912 that was done. One of the principal contributors to its restoration was J. P. Morgan. In 1967, after a sudden tidal flood had damaged the beautiful Church of Santa Maria del Giglio, American art students came and worked hard to restore portions of the interior and floors. There is a small plaque commemorating their endeavors. The plaque is difficult to find, hidden in one of the recesses of the church, but then Venetians are not an expressive people, and fulsome gratitude is not among their habits. There was a time, shortly after the Second World War, when Italy, including Venice, attracted American writers and bohemians and all kinds of expatriates, worthy and unworthy ones, much as did Paris in the 1920s. Frank Lloyd Wright wanted to build a house next to the Palazzo Balbi, at the turn of the Grand Canal. Fortunately, he didn't.

To Plan a Trip

You can fly to Venice via a number of European gateways, but Delta, leaving three times a week from JFK Airport in New York City, offers the only nonstop flight from the United States.

Two classic meditations on Venice are still in print and well worth reading: Mary McCarthy's *Venice Observed* (Harcourt Brace) and James Morris's *The World of Venice* (Harvest). The best account of its past—and Venice has a past wholly different from that of any other city on earth—is John Julius Norwich's great *A History of Venice* (Vintage).

There are any number of guidebooks, but one of the most lively, helpful, and intelligently designed is Richard Saul Wurman's *Access Florence & Venice* (HarperPerennial); another valuable work, as readable as it is knowledgeable, is Hugh Honour's *The Companion Guide to Venice* (Boydell & Brewer). And do not set out for this miraculous place without first acquiring a copy of *Venice for*

Pleasure by J. G. Links (Bishop Museum Press), which the London *Times* called "not only the best guide-book to that city ever written, but the best guide-book to *any* city ever written." Although a deep—indeed, omniscient—student of Venetian history and culture, Links is a relaxed, affable, funny companion in his book, which is divided up into four walking tours of this most walkable of all cities. Something of the spirit of the guide is evident in the first paragraph of "Walk 2: The Riva degli Schiavoni, SS. Giovanni e Paolo, the Rialto Bridge": "The first object of our next walk is to reach a charming café on one of Venice's most attractive canals; the second is to enter another picture gallery. Fear not; it is a very special gallery and has but nine pictures."

Reprinted by permission of AMERICAN HERITAGE, INC.

More Than a Dream: Venice

BY ERLA ZWINGLE

editor's note

Here is a good piece presenting an overview of contemporary Venice. Despite Venice's daunting ills, I am reminded of an article I read years ago by A. L. Rowse, an emeritus fellow of All Souls College in Oxford, England, in which he wrote, "It has been said a thousand times before, but it must be said again: Venice is unique, the most wonderful creation among historic cities. I regard New York as the most splendid urban creation of our twentieth century, but it has taken many centuries to build up the fabulous creation that Venice is, on its islands and waterways. There is nothing to equal it."

ERLA ZWINGLE was an assistant editor at *National Geographic,* where this piece originally appeared in 1995. She is now a freelance writer and lives in Venice.

Enrico Mingardi spent a good part of the morning with me explaining his ideas on how to improve the water-bus service in Venice. Being the chairman of the ACTV, the public transportation company, he discovered that some of his ideas weren't very popular. But he did think it would be easy enough to change the timetable on one line.

Almost immediately, he told me, a petition was delivered from people who liked it better the old way. "They collected 750 signatures against the change," he recalled, "so I said okay, I'll put it back." He put it back. Another petition arrived. This one carried 1,500 names of outraged residents protesting the reversion; they had liked it better the new way.

"Were some of the names the same?" I asked, joking.

He shrugged. "Sure," he replied.

Venice. The mere name summons associations from its astonishing 1,500 years, an incomparable legacy of art, politics, and commerce. Ten million visitors a year arrive to marvel at the remains of its glory, the architecture and paintings, and to be seduced by the dreamlike allure of a place that seems to exist somehow apart from real life, a kind of Baroque elegy adrift in its lagoon, floating in mist and shadow, entranced by the ceaseless murmur of the water as it never tires of kissing the stones.

But Venice is not a dream. In these days it is facing more than its share of reality. In fact, as the episode of the bus petitions demonstrated yet again, Venice at heart is a classic small town, trapped in the body of a monument.

To begin with, Venice actually *is* small. The sweep of the vistas across the Venetian Lagoon, the immense, moody arc of the sky, the grandiose facades all give the illusion of amplitude; it comes as a shock to learn that Venice, dense as a diamond, covers a mere three square miles. You could walk from one end to the other in an hour. And you will walk, because the streets are usually the size of an average sidewalk, or less. Walking, as much as the surrounding water, dictates the shape of Venetian life: the reasonable pace, the sudden streetcorner encounters with friends, the pause to talk. Among the many things the Venetians love about their town—no cars, virtually no crime—this intimacy is the best. They like to say their city is like a living room.

Is Venice still sinking? This is the question everybody outside Venice seems to ask. In a word, yes, though the rate has slowed, mainly because the pumping of groundwater for industries on the mainland has been stopped. The catastrophic flood of November 4, 1966, inundated parts of the city with as much as four feet of water for twenty-four hours. Since then a tremendous international effort has been made to repair the palaces and churches, restore the works of art, and protect the surrounding lagoon from future tidal calamity.

But today a rising tide of troubles is more likely to swamp the city. A new sense of desperation seems to have taken hold. Businesses have moved out; the population has shrunk over the past thirty years from 138,000 to a mere 70,000; 1,500 people a year leave Venice, especially young families unwilling to cope with the cost of living and finding a good job and an affordable house or apartment. These are the unglamorous facts of life in any city, but in Venice they have been compounded by the political favoritism and corruption that have beset the rest of Italy.

Venetians can't get over the fact that while everyone seems to love their city, hardly anyone seems to care about them. Randolph Guthrie is president of an American committee called Save Venice, which raises some $500,000 a year to restore the buildings and works of art. But, he admits, "there's no point in preserving the artifacts if the city itself can't survive."

Venice's fate is also tied to a city just across the bridge that no one ever hears of: Mestre. Since 1926 the political entity called Venice has included Mestre, which with about 180,000 people is more than twice the size of island-Venice. As a city planner put it bluntly to me, "Venice is not a city, it's a small village. *Mestre* is a city." Thus the mayor of Venice is responsible for two virtually opposite towns, each inevitably convinced that he secretly favors the other.

As in any small town, Venetians can be conservative, self-absorbed, addicted to gossip, obsessed by minutiae, full of opinions, and amazingly quick to note the speck in their brother's eye. They are also kind, curious, and generous. Most of them have known one another from birth. They are also essentially island people, living offshore in their own self-contained universe. "I don't like going to the mainland," one elderly gondolier told me, with a flourish. "When I need mountain air, I go to the top of the Accademia Bridge." The Venetians even speak their own language, a sibilant tongue from which most of the consonants have long since been worn away. I suspect they may like the notion of being difficult to understand; in any case, it may be one of the few ways they can sustain at least the illusion of privacy in what must be one of the world's most public cities.

"The Venetian really closes himself in," said Ninalee Craig, once married to a Venetian count. "But there are eyes everywhere in Venice. If I left the palazzo to go to the Piazza San Marco, by the time I got there, two cousins and three nieces would know what color hat I was wearing."

Today the sadness and anxiety of the Venetians have become something more complex than you could account for by listing the problems. It is a sensation deeply involved with their own lost grandeur, the echo of the centuries when Venice was an independent city-state, ruler of the eastern Mediterranean, providing ships and funds to crusaders' armies, and deviser of a form of government so tolerant and stable for its day that the framers of the United States Constitution studied it. Venice fell to Napoleon in 1797; then came an Austrian army, then annexation to Italy. Some remnant of anguish remains, a synthesis of longing and fatalism. And there is that unfathomable beauty.

"Venice is a place that overwhelms you," Clarenza Catullo said frankly as we sat at dinner one winter evening. She is a senior assistant at a museum; her Venetian parents moved to the mainland, but she moved back. "Every time I leave Venice, I have not only psychological pain but physical pain too. Deep pain. It's stupid; I can't explain it. When you're away, you feel that something is lost. Because here people are different, relationships are different, houses are different, *everything* is different. When I see the lagoon from the airplane, I thank God that I'm back."

Dawn in Venice. The water awakens first. Along the smaller canals there is a tentative rippling. The air is chilly with three kinds of coolness: from the darkness, the stones, and the damp. Beneath a translucent violet sky the Grand Canal is empty, except for the faithful Number 1 water bus, the local, progressing along the litany of the stops (S. Silvestro, S. Angelo, S. Tomà, pray for us . . .) toward the more open water of the Basin of San Marco and beyond it to the slender barrier island called the Lido. Although the streets are still deserted as the water bus pulls up to the floating bus stop, I am surprised to see so many passengers, people already going to or from work. To the east a dull, orange sun, so huge and flat it seems cut from paper, begins to lift itself slowly above the pinnacles, domes, and towers. Above the tangled finials of the Basilica of San Marco, it pauses. The water makes little clapping sounds.

In the dawn light, joggers appear along the wider pavements at the water's edge. At a corner of the Campo San Vio, the rich smell of bread pours from the bakery into the street. At six o'clock, up in the farther reaches of the quarter called Cannaregio, Andrea Cerini, a former professional soccer player, is opening up his newsstand.

Men on their way to work will begin to buy copies of *Il Gazzettino*, one of two local papers dependably full of cranky letters to the editor, the latest in the operatic political wrangles over every aspect of city life, and a steady supply of obituaries in this aging town. (The average age is forty-six, the highest in Italy.) Later, students on their way to the nearby school of nursing will stop in for candy, cigarettes, ballpoint pens. Even later, housewives will come for stamps, lottery tickets, water-bus tickets.

By seven-thirty the canals have begun to rumble with the workaday barges. They move heavily, unfurling heavy waves, usually with a dog at the prow as self-appointed guard, lookout, and alarm system. The barges are loaded with anything: bags of cement powder, towering stacks of clean hotel laundry, mounds of luggage, crates of bottled mineral water. At the Rialto market, just beyond the famous bridge, Luigi Smerghetto has just finished loading his barge with the day's orders of produce and is about to begin his rounds. Paola Cristel, my interpreter, and I climb aboard.

The Grand Canal looks remarkably less grand viewed above piles of cauliflower, oranges, and broccoli. There are transport companies, but Luigi is independent. He lives on the nearby island of Sant' Erasmo and is up every morning at four, sometimes not getting home again till past eight at night. He's been doing this for twenty years.

We cross the wide Giudecca Canal toward the island cluster called La Giudecca and head for number 517, Amerigo Avezzu's shop. Here Luigi unloads the daily standing order of leeks, celery, oranges, tomatoes, bananas, eggplant, and a huge bag of California walnuts. We proceed to the canteen for the power company, leaving cartons of fennel and bags of potatoes destined to form part of the day's four hundred lunches. Then we tie up at the water entry to the Passageway of the Grapes, and Francesco Sambuco arrives with a helper to carry the produce to his stand in the nearby square.

The Venetians say that their city is expensive because everything has to arrive by boat. It sounds logical, but Amadeo Rumor, president of a small transportation company at the Rialto market, disputes this. It's not that boat transport is inherently more costly, he says, but that the price of goods and labor is high. Because there isn't enough space in the city for large warehouses, cargoes have to be smaller and are therefore more costly. And to move any item from the boat to its destination requires people, usually pushing some variety of wheelbarrow. The narrow streets and bridges dictate a boutique approach to commerce, and until there is no more water, this will undoubtedly be the case.

Venetians don't worry about the water the way outsiders do. They're used to high water; although it can occur as often as forty times a year, usually between November and May, it doesn't necessarily rise very high, and in any case it doesn't stay more than a few hours.

Slithering, sucking, sloshing through the silvery fog in winter, the aquamarine radiance of spring, the brilliance of noon in summer, when the tops of the waves seem to be scattered with blinding chips of glittering mica, the water is never silent. Venetians even call the mainland terra firma, as if their own city were somehow less than solid. The floating bus-stop platforms creak and sway, the pavements undulate. The entire city seems suspended in a liquid medium: you not only hear the water, you feel it. In the winter the damp, chill fog seeps into your skin; in the summer the air can be soggy and heavy.

To the inevitable question, Francesco Bandarin replies, "Venice will always sink." Bandarin has been working with a group called the Consorzio Venezia Nuova (New Venice Consortium) to restore the lagoon. "Venice wasn't built very high, and the city is built on sand, silt, and hard clay, which tend to compact. It's not much each year, but over history this natural sinking alone comes to thirty inches. Then when they pumped out the groundwater on the mainland, the entire area sank almost another five inches.

"I don't think there's much you can do," he concludes matter-of-factly. "You can't lower the sea or raise the city."

But memories linger of the disastrous flood of 1966. Because that flood was the result of an unprecedented combination of circumstances, the likelihood of another is small. Yet there was an irresistible urge to try to do something to control the tide. The result: a vast floodgate project informally called Operation Moses.

A series of empty metal caissons would be submerged at the three entrances to the lagoon; with the arrival of an unusually high tide, the caissons would be filled with air to float up and form a barrier against the incoming water. But ten years have passed since the project was begun. Now public enthusiasm has waned; money is short. The prototype is parked beside the Arsenal, waiting for more funds to be approved.

Happily, scores of more humble projects well under way in the lagoon are already benefiting Venice. The consortium is restoring tidal marshes, reclaiming shoreline, and building jetties on the string of barrier islands to prevent beach erosion. It also monitors polluting runoff from the 720-square-mile drainage basin that empties into the lagoon, especially the agricultural chemicals that for years have been feeding floating mats of voracious algae. It hopes, perhaps ten years from now, to have brought pollution under better control. For the moment it simply controls the algae, sending out a flotilla of machines to rip it out.

The worst offenders along the shoreline, primarily the petrochemical plants in Porto Marghera, have either adopted more stringent controls on effluents or closed. "In the late eighties we reduced the toxic pollution to one-fifth," Alberto Bernstein, the consortium's environmental planner, told me. But the public seems ever ready to believe the worst. "You may have clear water that is toxic and green, muddy water that is not," he says. "The mayor says he used to be able to swim in the lagoon when he was little, but it was much more dangerous then than it is now."

Actually low tide is as much of a problem as high tide. Because of political wrangling over how to spend certain allotments of money, the canals have not been dredged for thirty years. Consequently some canals have silted up to the point where they are dry at low tide, a serious problem for ambulances and fireboats. Finally, though, money and a reasonable plan for using it are both in hand, and dredging began last fall. The engineers thought it best to wait till then; they weren't sure the tourists could stand it.

Midday in Venice. On a springtime Saturday the flood of tourists is rising. I had heard Venetians complaining, but it wasn't until now that I could see what they meant. I was hurrying to an appointment not far from the Piazza San Marco, which is where every tourist eventually heads, and it was clear I wasn't going to make it. The streets were completely filled with sluggish streams of people shuffling along, looking in shop windows, peering around, stopping suddenly to grapple with their maps. It was maddening. I couldn't understand why they had to take up every inch of space, oblivious to everyone else. I asked them to excuse me, and I began to push.

Tourists are at the core of most debates about the future of life in Venice. The Venetians know they need tourists in order to survive but can't figure out how to reduce their impact, how to make coping with them every day somehow less of a struggle. Apart from the inconvenience, their constant presence represents a kind of silent battle for emotional ownership. And the commercial diversity of the city has shrunk drastically over the years; though the port and the glass furnaces are still active, beleaguered artisans and small shopkeepers struggle to prosper as taxes consume up to half of their gross. Everyone senses a danger for the city in depending almost completely on tourists for survival.

"We have 50,000 visitors between eight A.M. and eight P.M.," said Silvio Testa, a political reporter for *Il Gazzettino*. "I think the main point is that in Venice there should be a new class formed by businessmen working to revitalize Venice but not bound only to tourism. To give back to Venice the character of a complete city."

The irony is sharp. The power of Venice was once largely based on commerce; rice, coffee, sugar, spices found their way to Europe through Venetian hands. Even without considering Marco Polo, a random look at just a few street names reveals the city's former strength: the Street of the Spice Dealer, of the Almond Dealer, of Beans, Wine, Oil, Iron Pots, Oysters, the Gondola Yard; inevitably, the Street of Lawyers and, my own favorite as a sort of subcontractor, the Street of the Assassins. The stupendous palaces and churches were the outward and visible sign of the almost inconceivable wealth of these businessmen, yet it is the allure of these palaces and churches that now provides the city's only economic muscle. In a way, the Venetians have become victims of the very beauty that sustains them; no one asks or expects more of the city than just to be there. "The problem is that Venice is beautiful," Mara Vittori, a young Venetian, told me. "That's all."

Two critical events showed the pressure at its worst. On "black Sunday," May 3, 1987, some 150,000 tourists arrived in the city; it was one of several days that spring when the police had to be called out to deal with the crush. Then, on July 15, 1989, the rock band Pink Floyd gave a concert from a raft tied up near the Piazza San Marco. Hordes of fans—reportedly 200,000—overwhelmed the city, leaving mountains of trash. The breakdown seemed complete when one young man was videotaped urinating against the doors of the basilica. "I understand that tourism is a big resource and that we earn a lot of money without doing anything," said a retired

Venetian businessman. "But there will be a point at which it won't work anymore."

To be fair, it doesn't appear that many Venetians do much to resist or reduce the general sense of degradation. To stand on the crest of the Rialto Bridge, for instance, admiring the elegant sweep of the Grand Canal, is almost inevitably to hear the approaching gondola bearing an accordion player and a tenor bellowing "Santa Lucia" or "O Sole Mio!" which are songs from Naples. (One especially horrifying day the tenor switched to singing "My Way.") When you ask the gondoliers why you hear these songs so often, and not Venetian ones, the answer is a bland "People ask for them."

Gianfranco Mossetto is one of several people I met who are trying to come up with new ideas on how to improve the situation. Young, energetic, and a professor of economics, he is the new deputy mayor for culture, tourism, and museums. He has even published a book with the intriguing title *The Economics of Art Cities.*

"Economically speaking, there is a difference between a useful good and a beautiful one," he told me eagerly. His office is on the Piazza San Marco, and his windows look straight into the face of the basilica. As he spoke, I watched the sinking sun set the angels' wings on fire and strike sparks of gold from the mosaics. I wasn't sure why beauty could not also be useful. But this was exactly his point.

The crux of the problem is how to preserve the artistic heritage while accommodating the hordes who come to admire it. "If you have 120,000 people in a town like Venice, as we did last Saturday, you run the risk of having the good destroyed," Mossetto said. "You can't afford it." His solution: ration access to the city. This could mean either selling tickets to limit the total number of people allowed into the city or organizing itineraries so they don't all arrive at San Marco by the same route at the same time. The theory makes sense, but many Venetians aren't convinced.

"Mossetto's not Venetian, and he's very rational," said one

young professional woman. "My friends think his ideas are a bit too strict. It's not democratic. This isn't Russia."

I suppose every activity could eventually be traced to tourism, but there is a sturdy, workaday Venice devoted primarily to itself (in fact, 40,000 people commute into Venice to work every day). The street sweepers and trash collectors throwing piles of plastic bags of garbage into the hydraulic maw of a waiting barge; the neighborhood barber, through whose shop window I glimpsed a serious little boy perched high in the chair, watching his haircut as if it were happening on television; architects drawing plans for somebody's new kitchen or extra bathroom. Dry cleaners, bus drivers, grave diggers, bank tellers.

Meanwhile, somewhere in or around the Church of San Pantalon, Don Ferruccio Gavagnin is also hard at work. He is always working: he's the priest of what is technically the smallest parish in Venice, but his congregation won't stay small. "The other priests are a little bit jealous," he says. "But I can't refuse people. If they need help, they know they can find me."

Don Ferruccio has been at San Pantalon for the past twenty-six of his forty-one years as a priest. He's balding and compact, and his keen, kind eyes framed by steel-rimmed glasses miss nothing. He has a tendency to bustle, and a let's-get-on-with-it way of talking. He's up at five o'clock to pray, do paperwork, and look after his ninety-three-year-old mother, who lives with him in the small house attached to the church. At seven he opens the church, and eventually, being a shepherd, he heads out to check on his flock.

In and out of shops and cafés, a quick cup of coffee, a quick word, a smile, a wave—into the butcher shop, into the optician's shop, into the firemen's headquarters. (He's their parish priest.) We stride down the street past the Church of San Silvestro—"The ugliest church in Venice"; we pause in the Church of the Carmini, where he speaks with one of the friars about the bishop's impending visit. I notice that the friar smiles at him with particular coolness—the interparish rivalry continues.

There's always too much to do. Catechism classes, visiting the sick in four different hospitals, planning a funeral or a wedding. "Yesterday was a hard day, and at the end of the day I received two young people who asked me to marry them. They met at a hospital—they both had an eye disease. I told the boy, 'You probably didn't see her properly.'"

I can't lure Don Ferruccio into a long conversation; he has no time and less inclination. Favorite Bible story? He twinkles at me; not a chance. Besides, "I don't believe in words," he tells me briskly. "I believe in fact. Words are not important."

There is a long, slender crack in the austere, dark-brick facade of the Church of San Pantalon. Don Ferruccio says it's always been there; a surveyor recently reported that it might, or might not, get worse over time. As long as Don Ferruccio is there, I don't think it would dare get worse.

Evening in Venice. The twilight sky gleams with opal and silver, the mainland succumbs to the mist. The dancing water in the lagoon glows with the light it has been gathering all day. The Venetians begin to turn homeward. It is a domestic moment of the day in what at heart is a deeply domestic city. By nine the shutters will be closed, dinner will almost be finished, the televisions will begin to come on. They are at home.

But homes are one of the biggest problems in Venice. Any discussion of the city's prospects ends up with housing. The basic difficulty is an exotic tangle of laws that, in one way or the other, work against both the owners and the tenants.

The price of housing is just as problematic. With 23,000 students attending the two universities and several smaller institutions, rents keep rising. If an owner can charge six students the equivalent of $400 each every month, he's not likely to offer the space to a Venetian for less. There's something about Venetians cutting one another out of their own city in this way that especially stings.

But worst of all are the empty houses. Over the years many foreigners—Americans, Japanese, French, even wealthy Italians—have bought houses in Venice. They restore them, which is good, but they use them mainly for vacation.

"On the street where I live, there remain only three Venetian families," one Venetian man told me. "Most of the other houses have been bought by strangers. They just come to stay for fifteen days each year. The top floor of the palace facing my house has been bought by Fiat heiress Susanna Agnelli, and she comes to Venice maybe two or three days a year. It would have been better if it had been sold to people living in Venice—even if very wealthy people, but *living* here."

Venetians know the houses in the same intimate way they know one another.

"Do you see that little yellow house?" Sandro Gaggiato, an art dealer, asked me as he rowed me down the Grand Canal in his small boat toward the Rialto Bridge. I saw it, flanked by two impressive palaces that are undoubtedly in the guidebooks. "That's where my wife and I lived just after we were married. We had such a wonderful view."

"Do you see that red house?" I heard a man saying as I walked down a street near the Campo San Barnaba. "I was born there, behind the window with the balcony. I lived there till I was twenty-two. My mother used to put tomatoes on the windowsill to ripen, and I would throw them at the gondoliers."

"I love this corner," Paola, my interpreter, suddenly said as we turned near the Campo Sant' Angelo. "That was our first house in Venice. I was nine. We lived on the top floor. I remember there was a cat on the roof next to ours, and she had babies. We used to throw her little pieces of meat."

Claudio Orazio, the new deputy mayor for housing, is working hard to help Venetians move back. He recognizes—as do most Venetians—that the big challenge is to encourage middle-class people to stay in Venice, till now the very class least likely to qualify for municipal help.

"Housing is the main reason people move out," Orazio explained. "There are enough habitable houses in Venice, so the main problem is the money."

New programs are already under way: low-cost loans to help homeowners make repairs, and subsidies to young families trying to buy their first home. Orazio is also beginning to induce owners to be more willing to rent. "The point is to make them aware that solving the problem of housing is important for everybody," he said. "It's a problem of Venice."

The problems of Venice. On a golden spring afternoon, I wandered along the shore of Poveglia, a deserted island in the lagoon. To the northwest, on the hazy shoreline, were the metal towers and pinnacles of the industrial zone of Marghera, flaring with gas burn-off, a kind of infernal mirror image to the towers and pinnacles of Venice. It was difficult to judge which seemed more unreal. I wondered why Venice's problems had come to seem so overwhelming. I remembered an exchange between two young professional women.

"One good thing is that there are people willing to do things for Venice," Gilda had been saying. "They still believe in this town and Venetians, and they do everything they can to bring it alive again. But most of them aren't Venetians—they're foreigners."

"It's just because the Venetians are lazy," Giovanna retorted.

"Maybe they're used to belonging to a golden circle," Gilda mused. "They're used to having people do things for them."

"They just care for themselves, and that's it," Giovanna said firmly. "If you look at most Venetian houses, inside they're beautiful. They don't care about the facades, but everything is new inside. They don't care what people see outside. 'Why do I have to do it and not somebody else?' That's the question each Venetian is asking himself."

The Venetian outlook: my notes are littered with the things they say about themselves. "The Venetian will complain even if he doesn't need to," said Enrico Mingardi at the ACTV. "He has a lot of habits he doesn't want to change."

"These problems aren't so difficult to solve," said Giulio Zannier, an architect. "But everything you do in Venice, you find someone who says, 'No, we can't do it.'"

"They just live for the day, because they were merchants, living by chance with no way to plan," said a young woman who works as a tourist guide. "So they say, 'This is today—why worry about tomorrow?'"

The real problem, Deputy Mayor Mossetto believes, is that the town lacks a ruling class and has been at the mercy of a string of political opportunists. This is true. Yet some Venetians also acknowledge that there hasn't been any need, till now, to try to change. With the constant donations of money, the endless supply of tourists, and the years of political scavenging and manipulation, the Venetians have become passive, introverted. They recognize the problems but can't see how to get a grip on them. Yet their love for their city seems to grow at the same rate as their frustration. "The quality of life is very high here," Gilda said simply. "If you care about life."

～

Night in Venice. The streets are silent, except for the sound of my heels as I walk slowly toward the Grand Canal. I pass through a tiny street smelling of jasmine and cat urine and am just crossing the Bridge of the Tree when I hear music: a woman singing to a piano accompaniment. I pause. Looking up, I see the slightly open shutters of a Gothic window; golden light slips out with the sweet, unaffected melody. A young couple stops, then a middle-aged blond woman in a red dress. Nobody speaks. We simply stand there together in the empty street, unable to leave.

For the first time that day I wasn't thinking about the problems. I was remembering some of the people who weren't waiting for someone else to come up with an idea. I thought again of the elderly gondolier; he'd said, "There is a hand that sustains Venice, an army of angels with chains of gold that keep it up." It had seemed extravagant at the time.

Near the Campo Santo Stefano is Giuliano Nalesso's classical music shop. Every day recorded music ripples into the Street of the Spice Dealer as a kind of benediction. Often it is pieces by the great Venetians, especially Vivaldi, whose shimmering music seems to be the water itself transcribed for orchestra.

"Until eight years ago there wasn't a music shop in Venice," Nalesso told me as we sat in the courtyard among various pieces of Venetian sculpture. "I was a violin teacher in the conservatory, and the professors and students were forced to go outside. Venice, the center of the world of music in the sixteenth century! So I invented myself as a shopkeeper. It was an abandoned courtyard, and the shop used to be a potato warehouse."

Now he sells not only tapes and CDs but also books, instruments, and sheet music; he even prints music. But he is looking at more than business. "I want to speak about transformation," he said thoughtfully. "This very place where we're sitting could show what Venice could be in the future. Restore the buildings and create cultural activities too."

It is because of Nalesso that live music also pours from the quartets playing at two cafés in the Piazza San Marco. "This city was born for music," he said. "So every corner should resound with music. And the attitude of the citizens should change. A new type of Venetian citizen should be created with a grand cultural conscience. We should be aware that every step is on holy pavement."

And the lost Venetians have been comforted today. On the northern edge of the city there is a shelter called Betania, where for ten years a gentle deacon named Tiziano Scatto has tended the homeless. Anyone who needs a good dinner can come here any night of the week; they can also have a shower, wash their clothes, be seen by a doctor or dentist, talk with a psychologist or a lawyer.

"The idea was not only to create a shelter," Tiziano explained as we sat in the tranquil upstairs kitchen with its high white walls, "but to create a testimony of the church in Venice. You have to love the poorest people, because through the love of your brother you can reach God." This is not the only organized shelter in Venice, but it may be the most personal. As surprised as I was to discover derelicts in Venice—fifty to sixty people come to Betania every day, primarily men—it was even more remarkable to learn that as many as four hundred Venetians volunteer to help them.

"We don't only try to assist people," Tiziano said in his quiet way, "but also, when we can, to restore them. In this way six years ago we opened a place where people could go and talk about themselves, in order to find out what was really the problem, or to help them find work.

"And at the end we also provide the coffin when they die."

What kind of future could there be for a city like this? Rinio Bruttomesso is the director of the International Centre Cities on

Water and a professor of urban design. He thinks about this question in a large way.

"You can't always think about Venice; you must think about Mestre too," he told me one hot afternoon in late spring. We opened the windows over the canal, but *that tenor* kept drifting by and we finally had to close them again. "We should think of Venice as a metropolitan area. Then we'd have some sort of way to choose activities for Venice that are better for its particular urban fabric.

"I think in the future the waterfront area will be a crucial spot for linking Venice and Mestre." He pointed on a map to the shoreline. "We've been studying how we can replan this area where the oil refineries are. In my opinion in ten to fifteen years these refineries will close. So this could be a very important area for Venice."

He is especially keen on establishing ashore a scientific and technological park, which could naturally draw on the two universities in Venice and the nearby University of Padua. I had heard others, including the new mayor, mention this idea. The talent is already there, and the benefits to the city would be many.

"A lot of people are realizing that we are arriving at a crucial moment for the future of Venice," Bruttomesso said frankly. "Will it become just a museum? The strange thing is, we realize it's a crucial moment and we *should* make a choice. But there's no will and no ability to create a consensus.

"I foresee the risky thing is that in twenty years, no decision will have been made. And on your next visit you'll find a city with 40,000 people, merchants, Carnival mask sellers, and this would be the end of Venice. It would be Disneyland, not Venice, even if we're very close to Disneyland now."

Disneyland. It's a word that is often spoken with a kind of horror, because the Venetians know that, as Giuliano Nalesso puts it, "The real life of the city is in the normal things." They can't imagine living in a city in which, in fact, nothing is real anymore.

I walked to the top of the Accademia Bridge and gazed at the Grand Canal. The city was silent, except for the murmur of the water. It was as if, behind the veil of darkness, Venice were returning to her true self, a creature of the lagoon rising on the brimming water trying to join the stars. I often heard Venetians talk about the canals as the city's blood; they didn't see that they themselves were its blood. The city felt deserted, a suddenly terrible sensation. Venice without Venetians?

"We are still in time to save Venice," a friend had told me with conviction. "Anyone who loves Venice is a part of Venice. We can still save what we have."

Why should Venice be saved? I used to think the answer was obvious. But the answer has become more elusive, though no less compelling. I think the Venetians would simply say, because our children were born here and our parents are buried here. It's home.

One darkening winter afternoon I was out on the lagoon having a rowing lesson. The shallow water was clear as glass and perfectly smooth except for small patches scuffed by the breeze. The pale sun set, and the distant skyline blurred, woven into the soft fibers of the gathering fog. We paused to simply float, and invisible wavelets made gentle stroking sounds against the boat. Then out of the darkness came the heavy, tolling note of the bell in the campanile of San Marco. It is the voice of Venice. The city had completely disappeared, yet the bell was surprisingly strong. At that moment it all seemed very sad. So why do I remember it with so much happiness?

Erla Zwingle/National Geographic Society Image Sales. This piece originally appeared in the February 1995 issue of *National Geographic*.

The Stars of Venice

BY NAOMI BARRY

~

editor's note

Since 1979, when this piece was written, the Countess Vedremina has passed away, and the Dottoressa Maria Francesca Tiepolo is no longer "the vestal of the Archives of the State." But they may still rightly be referred to as "stars," and Venice has many more contemporary—and eccentric—lights that shine just as brightly.

NAOMI BARRY lives in Paris and was for more than twenty years a regular contributor to *Gourmet*. She was also a features writer for *The International Herald Tribune* and is the author of *Paris Personal* (E. P. Dutton, 1963) and *Food alla Florentine* (Doubleday, 1972). Barry's work also appeared in the *Paris* edition of *The Collected Traveler*.

Venezia, a name more magic than Camelot, confers a rare feeling of privilege, beginning at the airport. A waiting motorboat carries you across the lagoon, down highways marked upon the water by wooden pilings, toward the floating city. The driver drops to minimum speed as you enter a narrow canal, threading his way into the basin of San Marco. At the Gritti on the Grand Canal, he assists you out, and you are ready for your Venetian adventure.

The floating deck, the outdoor antechamber to the hotel, is the most elegant grandstand on the Grand Canal. While you have breakfast, lunch, dinner, or drinks, you are a first-row spectator at the passing show: goods-laden barges; sleek gondolas; police boats; motorboats; the *vaporetto,* that local streetcar beyond Desire; the flower-decked gondola of a bride; the gorgeous pageant of the Regatta Storica. At the table in the rear right-hand corner, Proust was supposed to have sat for hours staring at Santa Maria della Salute.

The Gritti was constructed at the end of the fifteenth century as a palazzo for a noble family. As a hotel, it has never quite forgotten its seigneurial start. One of the most beautiful hotels in the world, it is the flagship of the CIGA chain.

Rooms are important. On one occasion while staying there, I had been given sumptuous accommodations furnished with antiques and one of those tender personal bouquets the house-keeper does so well. However, the bed was narrow, and I wondered how a hotel could afford to let such spacious quarters to a single person. Later I discovered that the beds had been changed in case I might feel badly that I was alone.

The floor plan is split into three levels. The clerestory windows look out on the Grand Canal: the gold dome of the Dogana; the huge church of the Salute; the handsome Palazzo Dario; the low white house of Peggy Guggenheim, the last *dogaressa*.

Nico Passante, director of the Gritti, spent part of his childhood in Venice, which he recalls as a wondrous place for children. He remembers strolling through the Mercerie with his grandfather and stopping before a spout in a wall outside a shop. The grown-ups pressed a handkerchief to it and walked on. The spout gave off eau de cologne. Alas, it is not there any longer.

The Cipriani

In contrast to the palatial Gritti, the Cipriani is a rambling resort set in a garden surrounded by a lagoon at the tip of the Giudecca. It offers an Olympic-size swimming pool and the relaxed atmosphere of a jovial multinational houseparty where many of the guests already know each other.

Some people mistakenly assume that the two hotels are bitter rivals. Actually, they are more like two gentlemen jockeying for position. Director Natale Rusconi is a superb hotelier, as is Passante of the Gritti. Under their management, both hotels vie for the best teachers for the cooking-school programs and the most inspired lecturers for the cultural day programs.

A knowledgeable visitor to Venice (assuming he is well-loaded with ducats) operates on the triangle principle. He sleeps either at the Gritti or the Cipriani and takes a meal or two in the establishment where he is *not* bedded. The third point of this extraordinary triangle follows.

Harry's Bar

If there were not a soul in Venice, Harry's would still be full. It is the gossip mart that succeeded the Rialto. The combination is some sort of alchemy—a compound of comfortable crowding, hawk attention to detail, and a small repertory of perfectly prepared dishes. Small wonder that Hemingway patronized it so often.

Dining

Venice has its own language sparkling with words and expressions incomprehensible even to other Italians. The singsong inflection is recognizable even to a foreigner, and there is a soft whir to the omnipresent letter Z.

And the food is as distinctive as the dialect. The Adriatic provides a bounty of shrimp, crab, scampi, mussels, squid, and fish one doesn't seem to find elsewhere.

Risi e bisi is the Venetian ode to spring, a fluffy *risotto* made with rice and the first new peas of the season. *Sjogie in saor,* baby sole in a sweet-and-sour sauce, was one of the ritual dishes of the Doges when they entertained. It is a favorite at the Gritti. Meat, fowl, and game in a *peverada* sauce was a favorite with populace and patrician during the Renaissance. The Cipriani recently revived it with guinea hen.

Certain dishes created by Harry's Bar have become so famous

they are now trademarks of Venetian cuisine. *Carpaccio* consists of raw beef filet (the finest) sliced so thin as to be translucent and dribbled with a discreetly spiced mayonnaise. *Risotto primavera* is a lovely combination of creamy risotto and barely cooked, diced fresh vegetables. It too is a specialty that has traveled far.

For pure sin, deliver yourself to a *gianduiotto*—a rectangular block of chocolate ice cream set upright in a glass of whipped cream.

La Contessa

The Countess Vendramina Marcello, high-arched patrician nose, straight back, passionate about the well-being of her city and its people, has never forgiven the Austrians for their nineteenth-century occupation and takes a dim view of Rome for its administrational lording over the once proudly independent republic. The countess is about eighty, stylish without being modish, speaks fluent French and German, claims she could not breathe if she left her adored Venice and consequently has refused all invitations to travel.

Shouldering the responsibility of the traditional aristocrat, she has organized benevolent groups to bring food to house-bound invalids, to visit inmates of the prison. If she goes regularly to church, it is not because she is such a confirmed Catholic but because her position, she says, demands the setting of an example. She also agitates for improved housing conditions and jobs for the young.

Winter, when Venice folds in upon itself, the Countess reads voraciously and lately has been delving into the Koran, which she finds full of wisdom. Summer she can be seen, tall and alert, at art shows and cultural manifestations. Friends arrive from all over the world and her dinner parties, with the servants in livery and white gloves, are prized invitations.

Only someone so grand could allow a ground-floor section of the immense Palazzo Marcello to be turned into a popular wine bar to sell the family wine and others. It's the *bacaro* on the Rio Terà degli Assassini: wine is sold by the glass from eight A.M. to ten P.M., and the customers are workers, boatmen, lawyers, engineers— everybody.

The Two *Dottoresse*

"I am the vestal of the Archives of the State," says the Dottoressa Maria Francesca Tiepolo, with a shy, winning smile.

For the past twenty-seven years, this woman with the celebrated name has been the record-keeper of the story of Venice. The documents, which begin with the year 847, if laid out would stretch for sixty-seven kilometers. Proudly she walks her visitor through the tunnels of books and boxed papers. The Archives are lodged in two former convents by the Frari church—one S. Nicolo della Lattuga. "A miraculous lettuce grew in the garden," she comments, explaining the name. "It still grows there. We eat it sometimes."

The *dottoressa* says that when she came, the students using the files were all in the fine arts. Now they are interested in the social aspects of the republic: urbanization, sanitation, administration, class structure. The Archives cooperate with exhibitions held by the city, aiding with the bibliography and catalogs.

Has the family been long in Venice? she is asked. "Giacomo Tiepolo was doge from 1229 to 1249."

And the painter? The sweet-faced *dottoressa* shakes her head negatively and smiles. "You can't have everything."

The Dottoressa Chiappini is superintendent of the Correr Museum. Right now she is doing a study on the velvets and other fabrics produced in fifteenth-century Venice. Her theme is their importance in the economic development of the city and the wealth brought to it by foreign workers.

Wars and strife in Lucca once sent masses of the population into exile. The textile workers found asylum in Venice, whose generosity paid off rich rewards. The records of the fabrics can be seen in paintings around the city. You can trace the history of cut velvet, incised velvet, uncut velvet by the Madonna's robes.

The Working World of Venice

BY WILLIAM G. SCHELLER

editor's note

I was especially happy to read this piece because it is one of the very few that addresses everyday life as it's lived in Venice by ordinary Venetians.

WILLIAM G. SCHELLER is a freelance writer who contributes periodically to *Islands*, where this piece first appeared in 1995.

This afternoon Venice smells like laundry. Not like noisome summer canals or damp plaster in a tilting palazzo; not like fish sizzling in a trattoria or sea mist and doom. I am in a working-class neighborhood known as Santa Elena, and Venice smells like the garlands of laundry strung across the street.

Of all the world's cities, Venice most enjoys—or suffers—the cachet of being a place where fantasy looms larger than reality, where work runs a poor second to play. This is partly Venice's own fault. During the days of her eighteenth-century decline, she worked hard at cultivating the playground image. The image stuck, and the tourists kept coming.

Venice also answers for her sheer gorgeousness: in a world where aesthetics and economy are driven by the cold Calvinist north, any place this delightful to the eye must have been built to be a fey little theme park. Venice's great landmarks—St. Mark's basilica and its piazza, the Grand Canal with its palazzi and quayside cafés, the Palace of the Doges and the Bridge of Sighs—stand in the mind's eye as the stuff of romance and the backdrops to a holiday.

The truth is that no city ever worked so diligently to such serious purpose, ever strove so mightily after the almighty ducat—or did so much to set up shop for the rest of Western civilization in the bargain. If Venice is impossibly beautiful, it is because its builders saw no reason why beauty and work should be incompatible. The senators, artisans, and merchants of Venice had no trouble inventing commercial banking, while at the same time wringing a few extra decades of poetry from the vocabulary of late Gothic architecture.

But still the laundry had to be done, as it was being done this day in the secluded far eastern corner of the city, where I stood beneath this festoon of fresh linen. I had spent the past few days exploring outward from the Venetian epicenter of St. Mark's, making it my business to look beyond the Rialto Bridge, beyond the great paintings of the Accademia galleries, beyond the apricot-tinted sunsets behind the Church of Santa Maria della Salute.

Without ignoring gondola rides and Titian-filled churches, I wanted to see past the treasure gloss of Venice and to sense its everyday pulse. I wanted some glimpse of life in a city that dates back fifteen hundred years, to the days when the first mainland refugees fled the barbarians' sack of Rome's Adriatic cities and settled on the marshy, unpromising islands of the Venetian Lagoon.

I got my glimpse, and then some. I found what I was looking for on a narrow street, scant blocks from the fabulous Tintoretto ceilings of the Scuola di San Rocco, in the neighborhood of San Polo, where a metalsmith worked at his anvil in the back of a dusty shop while his wife tended a brazier of coals. I sensed workaday Venice as I looked through a shop window to watch an artisan with a single strong needle craft a mattress from yard goods and cotton batting.

I sensed it again on the soccer field at the naval academy, where the heirs of one of the world's greatest maritime traditions butted and booted their ball around. And I watched as two young civil engineers set up their transit to survey for a new footbridge across a canal on the island of Giudecca.

At another canal in another quarter, where workers had drained the water away so they could shore up a Gothic foundation, I saw brown mud where, on any other day, there would have been shimmering reflections.

"Do you ever find anything interesting when you drain a canal?" I asked one of the workmen.

The man shrugged and gestured with his cigarette toward the mud. There was his answer: bricks, last week's empty wine bottle, a couple of broken flowerpots.

I was disappointed. One of my favorite Venetian stories concerns the eighteenth-century magnifico who impressed his guests by having his golden tableware tossed out the window after each course of a banquet. Of course, he had servants down below, holding a net above the water. But it's fun to imagine that a fork or two might have missed the net.

I went to that most modern and prosaic of institutions, the supermarket. Two or three exist even in Venice. In one I discovered the just-home-from-work-gotta-throw-dinner-together versions of all the Venetian classics around which two-hour restaurant meals are built. Here was *pasta e fagioli,* the rich local soup of macaroni and beans, dried and bagged by Buitoni. A frozen, shrink-wrapped assemblage of squid and shellfish was called *"misto per risotto."*

There was also a display of cat food large enough to fill the shelves of a giant American supermarket, its presence a reminder that Venice is a city of independent cats fed by everyone as a sort of community project. They aren't strays; they know exactly where they are. They aren't homeless; Venice is their home. They are the heirs of the comfortable kitty beneath the banquet table in Veronese's *Feast in the House of Levi,* on exhibit in the Accademia, and none of them ever get run over by cars.

But streets that are safe for cats are losing their appeal for people who would dearly love to hop into their Alfa Romeos and drive to work. The maître d' at the rooftop restaurant of the Hotel Danieli lives in Padua, and it takes him two hours to get home. As I finished my grappa on a slow night, he had nothing but praise for proposals to ease travel in and out of the city.

"Someone wanted to build a new bridge into Venice, from the Lido di Iesolo in the north," he said, "and a metro line—a subway under the Grand Canal from the train station to the Rialto and St. Mark's. But the ecologists always say no. No one wants anything to be built in Venice."

The upshot, according to the maître d', is that not only do many Venetians move to the mainland and commute to jobs in Venice; some stay in the city and commute to the mainland to work.

So Venice makes it hard to live in Venice. Yet someone is buying the frozen risotto mix; someone ordered the handmade mattress; someone is hanging out the laundry. Someone employs the press-man wearing the traditional square cap made out of a newspaper page, whom I saw walking into a bar for lunch. And someone, other than a tourist, buys produce from the little fruit and vegetable barges that tie up along the sidewalks.

Someone, with a Mac or a PC tucked behind Renaissance walls, must have been happy to see the printout banner in the window of a computer store that heralded: "Finally Venice has a connection with the Internet." *La Serenissima,* the Most Serene Republic, is on the information supercanal.

Of course, there are Venetian yuppies. There are so many Venetians walking around with cellular phones nowadays that if one asked another, "What news on the Rialto?" the answer would undoubtedly be, "*Un momento*—just let me check."

Suits are everywhere in Venice—even the old pensioner, his dogelike profile turned toward the winter sun as he naps in the public gardens, is turned out better than an American banker. But you can always tell when there's mercantile purpose in a Venetian's stride.

What is in short supply, sadly, is a new generation of Venetians. Of Venice's population of some 75,000 souls—down from nearly 150,000 about fifty years ago—fewer than 4,000 are children.

One afternoon I turned off the Fondamenta della Croce, between Palladio's Church of the Redentore and the eastern tip of the island of Giudecca. Before continuing on to the *vaporetto* stop at Le Zitelle for the short ride to the island and Church of San Giorgio Maggiore, I ducked into the narrow lanes of the housing project that lies between two of Venice's most exclusive institutions—the "Garden of Eden," a walled private enclave planted by an Englishman with that paradisaical surname, and the plush Cipriani Hotel.

The pathway I followed led to a grassy courtyard, surrounded by two-story apartment blocks that could have stood anywhere between Minsk and Minneapolis. I felt like an intruder in someone's yard. There was no one around except for a woman on a second-floor balcony; I tossed her a clothespin she had dropped.

But not long after I turned my back on the courtyard, I felt something small and hard hit the back of my neck. I heard giggling and turned. Half a dozen urchins, like the funny little snot-nose kids in Fellini's *Amarcord,* were ducking under a portico.

The game began. Every time I turned my back, another pebble would hit me; when I spun around, they'd jabber and point at each other as if to say, "Not me, it was him." Only four thousand kids in Venice, and I had to run into this bunch.

They followed me out the alley before losing interest. Once I got inside the Church of San Giorgio Maggiore, though, I didn't feel so bad: there was Tintoretto's *Martyrdom of Saint Stephen,* showing the saint being pelted to death with stones.

Among the grown-up pursuits of Venice, perhaps none strike as familiar a chord with the outside world as those having to do with the lagoon city's signature craft, the gondola. By no means are the gondoliers themselves anything less than authentic—the redoubtable Mario, who took me from the Grand Canal quay called the Riva degli Schiavoni and back via a labyrinthine route I could never hope to retrace, told me that his pedigree as a Venetian was untraceably long and that his father and grandfather had been gondoliers.

But the men who guide the long black boats are, finally, in the front line of the tourism industry. The men who *build* gondolas are a step closer to the old pulse of Venice.

The small canalside yards where gondolas are constructed are called *squeri,* and there are four of them in operation in Venice today. Equipped with a map and some vague directions from the gondoliers who congregate in back of St. Mark's piazza, I finally found the *squero* of D. Manin on the Rio di San Trovaso.

The scene there was impossibly medieval. Wooden balconies, their railings crowded with geraniums, lined the two-story tile-roofed buildings around the little gondola yard. Two partly built gondolas lay half beneath a shed roof at the head of the sloping ways. One was overturned, its bottom being sanded and caulked with pitch. Even where I stood, across the canal, the pungent smell of pitch was in the air.

The *squero* I really wanted to visit was the one belonging to Tramontin and Sons, which Mario had told me made the best gondolas. He has a Tramontin, sixteen years old, and when it has run out its useful life in perhaps five years, he will replace it with another, at a cost of about $22,000.

Tramontin's establishment was in an even more remote part of the Dorsoduro neighborhood, at the intersection of two obscure canals. I was able to see the yard before I could figure out how to get to it; finally, I guessed that a gray steel door in a narrow alley was the only possible entrance. I rang a bell alongside the locked door, and in a moment I was buzzed in by Roberto Tramontin, whose great-grandfather Domenico had started the business.

A busy man, Roberto Tramontin, or else a man of few words. I asked if I could come in and look around; he said yes. When I thanked him, he responded with a brief *"Prego,"* the all-purpose Italian word that includes "you're welcome" among its meanings.

It was a privilege to be allowed so nonchalantly into one of the most rarefied manufacturing establishments on earth, and it was quite a surprise when Roberto soon disappeared and I was in the *squero* alone. It was like being left alone in an old small-town garage when the mechanic has gone out for a part, only this was a world of wood, not of metal.

There are eight different kinds of wood in a gondola—among them elm for the ribs, oak for the bottom, and walnut for the *forcola,* or oarlock. The seasoning stock was fragrant in racks beneath the rafters. A single gondola lay overturned, its bottom still only partly planked. Along one wall a long work table held an array of hand tools that might have been laid down by men who had gone off to join the Fourth Crusade.

I was standing there staring at the tools and at an old photo of Domenico Tramontin, framed beneath two mock wooden *ferri* (the crested and serrated steel ornaments that grace gondolas' prows) when an old man walked into the shed. He went over to the partly constructed boat and began hand-sawing planking very slowly and with methodical sureness.

"*Buon giorno,*" he said, and that was all. I let myself out by the steel door.

In a water city, the water is the place to look to see the day's work being done. Watching the traffic on the lagoon and on the larger canals is like watching the rest of the world with its wheels removed, sending up a wake. As I stood for a few minutes along the Fondamenta Nuove, the broad quay on the north side of Venice, I saw a speeding ambulance, a shipment of oranges, a veterinarian's boat (a cat emergency?), and a fire boat. A brown-and-white boat went by with UNITED PARCEL SERVICE emblazoned on its side. Another boat was carrying a new dishwasher, and on the prow was the single word WHIRLPOOL. And—startling yet perfectly logical— a hearse boat chugged past with a shiny mahogany coffin on deck. San Michele, the cemetery island of Venice, was only a few hundred yards away; behind me, along the Fondamenta Nuove and its little side streets, the marble workers were busy cutting and polishing headstones and tombs.

One afternoon I set out across the water, to a corner of the lagoon between Venice proper and the long barrier beach called the Lido, to visit a little-known religious and intellectual outpost. Here, in this city of churches and of the original Jewish ghetto—where Hasidim still keep a strict Sabbath in the streets where Shylock walked—one of the busiest retreats of the godly is on the little cypress-studded island of San Lazzaro degli Armeni, home of the mother house of the Armenian Catholic Mechitarist fathers.

The Mechitarists have been here since 1717. Within these walls Byron once studied classical Armenian, and today fifteen priests and as many seminarians edit and publish editions of old Armenian manuscripts (more than four thousand books and documents, some dating back to the seventh century, fill the community's library), along with modern works on Armenian culture.

A genial, dry-witted priest explained it all to me and to a small group of tourists I had come over with—that is, after he finished explaining where Armenia was.

"It's in Armenia," he answered drolly, after disabusing a geographical naif of the notion that it was in Israel. Fluent in Italian, English, German, and both the classical and vernacular versions of his native Armenian, he made it seem the most natural thing in the world for a tiny religious order with roots in the Caucasus to publish books in thirty-two languages on an island in the Venetian lagoon. The connection has a lot to do with the old saying that "the enemy of my enemy is my friend"; traditionally, Venetians and Armenians alike shared, along with a common Christianity, an antipathy toward the Turks.

To Turks and other enemies of the old Republic of Venice, one of the most feared sights on the high seas was a banner bearing the image of a lion holding a bound gospel—the lion of St. Mark, Venice's age-old symbol.

The lion is emblazoned all over the city, but as I rode the *vaporetto* back from the Mechitarists' island, I saw it at its most impressive: set in bronze on the superstructure of a giant freighter, the *Fenicia,* making its way down the Giudecca Canal. Painted on the stern was the ship's port of registry, VENEZIA. Here was a vivid link with the lagoon city's storied maritime past.

For centuries—almost since those first late-Roman refugees began to gather on this marshy little archipelago—Venice understood that its destiny lay upon the water and its wealth lay in moving goods, at a considerable profit, from where they were made to where they were wanted. The *Fenicia,* no doubt, was delivering something other than spices and silks, and Venice is no longer master-merchant to the world. But that ship carried tradition and pride, and in its figurative wake all the commerce of the West had arisen.

On my last day in Venice, I went out into the countryside without ever leaving the city limits. The island of Sant' Erasmo is less than a half hour's *vaporetto* ride from the busy quay of Fondamenta Nuove, but it might as well be a hundred miles away. The morning sounds I heard there were not the bells and bustle of St. Mark's but the trill of songbirds, the crowing of a rooster, and the chugging of a tractor in a distant field. Another surprise, after a week during which I had seen nothing mounted on wheels other than baby strollers and handcarts, was that the people of Sant' Erasmo had bicycles, motor scooters, and cars. Like a train station in an American suburb, the *vaporetto* landing was surrounded by vehicles left for the day by commuters.

Sant' Erasmo is not merely a bedroom island. Venice's vegetables have to be grown somewhere, and that somewhere may as well be nearby. Sant' Erasmo is all farms and vineyards with a small village attached.

I walked down the narrow lane from the landing, past fields of salad greens, past the straight rows of pruned vines waiting for the warm spring sun to bring them into leaf. The soil was dark and rich. Houses were few and far apart, and people scarcer still.

Here and there someone was hoeing weeds; several times I was passed by women on bicycles, all of whom wished me good morning after looking a bit surprised that any outsider other than the mailman (who had been on my boat) would bother setting foot on Sant' Erasmo. With their black bicycles and sturdy woolen coats, the women seemed like phantoms from Europe's early postwar days as they cycled along the flat, tilled fields.

My hike around the island took two hours, and it was only at the end of that time that I came to the town center that served these farmers and their commuting kin. There was little more than a nursery school named after Pope John XXIII (the onetime patriarch of Venice), a small food market, and a new church with a Romanesque font inside for holy water.

Almost a millennium ago, when that font was freshly carved, the landholders of Sant' Erasmo were no doubt busy at the same fields and vineyards through which I had just passed. And some of them, the young and more adventurous, probably crossed the lagoon, like today's *vaporetto* commuters, to pitch in at the task of making Venice work.

Author's Tips

Because Venice tops the "must" list of just about everyone who travels to Italy, it's become commonplace to hear the complaint that the lagoon city has become an overcrowded day-tripper's destination. This is only true, however, if your visit takes you no farther than the immediate environs of St. Mark's square and some of the more popular haunts along the Grand Canal.

Even in summer there are quarters of Venice that outsiders seldom see. While the throngs jostle along the Riva degli Schiavoni and near St. Mark's, the savvy visitor can be walking the brooding, empty streets of the Ghetto or exploring the back streets south and east of the Arsenal. All it takes is willingness to get lost and the knowledge that no two Venetian points are as far apart as they appear on the maps. Besides, signs nearly everywhere point back to St. Mark's, the Rialto, and the train station *(ferrovia).*

Transportation in and around Venice is relatively uncomplicated. Most travel within the central city is done on foot, using pedestrian streets and bridges. (There are, of course, no autos, buses, or streetcars.) *Vaporetti,* so named because they were once powered by steam, constantly run up and down the s-shaped Grand Canal; and several *vaporetto* stops serve the Venetian out islands. Taxis are sleek, sumptuously furnished runabouts and are quite expensive. Gondolas—except for the *traghetti* that cross the canals—are excursion vessels only; they're quite pricey but worth every penny.

Venetian restaurant food is frequently bad-mouthed, but you can eat quite well if you avoid the *menu turistico* joints near St. Mark's and stick with simpler seafood and pasta dishes. Be sure to try Venice's signature *fegato alla veneziana,* calves' liver and onions. And after dinner have a grappa, the favorite local spirit.

Suggested Reading

There is no shortage of books to get you in the right frame of mind, from classic novels like Mann's *Death in Venice* to great nonfiction book-length essays, including Mary McCarthy's *Venice Observed* and Jan Morris's *Venice.* Dorling Kindersley's beautifully illustrated Eyewitness guide, *Venice and the Veneto,* has wonderful maps, plus a handy street-finder index.

The Serene Spaces of Venice

BY TONY HISS

~

editor's note

It may be difficult to fathom for first-time visitors, but despite what you may think, it really is possible to be in Venice, even in high season, and be quite far from the madding crowd. There are very well-worn routes throughout Venice, but once you are off them—and it doesn't take much to deviate from the San Marco-Rialto-Accademia-Ferrovia path—it's remarkable how quiet it can become, and how few tourists you'll encounter.

TONY HISS is the author of *The View from Alger's Window: A Son's Memoir* (Alfred A. Knopf, 1999; Vintage, 2000). He is visiting scholar at New York University's Taub Urban Research Center, and he contributed this piece to *Gourmet* in November 1997.

As a kindness to modern travelers, cautionary signs should be posted at all the exits of Venice's central train station. "WARNING," these signs should say. "ALMOST COMPLETE ABSENCE OF DANGER OUTSIDE. *You have now reached an abrupt sensory transition point.* Slow down at once. Open wide your vision and hearing, and readjust your perceptions. *Ciao.* Welcome to Venice!"

Venice amazes, even overwhelms, twentieth-century sensibilities and preconceptions: the idea of a working-for-a-living, going-about-its-business city in the water makes about as much sense as a metropolis in the clouds. Especially when the place is uncompromisingly *all city*. Bricks, mortar, marble, streetlights, front doors, window boxes of cascading geraniums, and bustling crowds fill every inch of space, right up to the water's edge.

And then, in the next inch, the water of the canals, grand and small, is steadfastly oceanic, an untamed arm of a living sea. Yet it also buoyantly supports a teeming human presence: *vaporetti* (water buses), water taxis, and gondolas; long, modern delivery barges, often with a dog up front, ears streaming in the breeze; and tiny wooden *sandoli* (meaning "little sandals," and indeed these boats seem to walk on, or skip across, the Grand Canal).

This neighborliness between watery wilderness and intense human habitation is only one of the surprises Venice presents. The city was a self-governing republic for a thousand years, with a constitution infused by the concepts of checks and balances and live and let live. Physically it's fully intact, spared by both world wars; it's unmodernized by the car; and in its fifteen-hundred-year history, it was looted only by Napoleon (many of whose takings were later returned).

But Venice is not perfect. Detractors think of the city as a place of faded brilliance. And it quite desperately needs more permanent inhabitants—there are now only 70,000, down from 150,000 at the end of World War II—and new businesses to offset seven million tourists a year, and it won't get them until it lowers rents and prices. Still, many mid-twentieth-century problems have in fact been solved, or are on the mend: the air is no longer fouled by fuel oil stoves; less factory waste gets dumped into the lagoon waters; and because mainland industries have stopped pumping out the groundwater beneath, the city is no longer sinking.

For those of us who grew up elsewhere, sudden contact with the Venetian world is simultaneously thrilling and bewildering, as if we were coal miners who had suddenly been catapulted up to sunlight. However ridiculous it may sound, as soon as you step into Venice—whether for your first time or your fiftieth—you are flooded with delight, and something within you leaps to life.

You've just left the station and entered one of the sixty-five or so public squares—the *campi*—that punctuate the city and organize its life. Here is an unremarkable-looking, gray marble veranda and a series of shallow steps, equally undistinguished, leading down to the Grand Canal. But just beyond lies Venice, the dazzling city whose every detail has been thought through so that even the echoes sound fine-tuned, the city that fits itself to your mind the way a ring slides onto a finger.

We think of Venice as sustained by waterways, but it's also a city dedicated to walking—a place so compact that the longest walk of all, from one end of town to the other, takes only about an hour (assuming one doesn't get lost!). Moreover, it's entirely unmotorized. So you feel a surge of energy that, for once, is not being drained by the vigilance and wariness that must be switched on whenever you have to share a public space with people who have temporarily encased themselves in a few thousand pounds of steel, glass, and rubber. Your feet seem to have new power, and your body seems to expand and starts to respond to the volume of space in the streets and squares you're passing through.

The public spaces narrow and swell every few steps, as there's no need for them to be a uniform width—and you can, at any moment, dart around a corner and even use the ground floor of a building as a public passageway. A walk takes on the shape of a melody: you speed up to slip through a narrow stretch, vault over a tiny bridge, and then slow down to a saunter and stop when you hit an open square, wondering whether it might be time for an ice cream cone.

The lack of cars might also contribute to Venice's low crime rate. How can anyone hope to make a quick getaway? Certainly peacefulness cradles every nerve ending, and in the absence of the blare produced by thousands of cars, trucks, and buses, you can tune in to the sounds that mark the progress of a day: sea gulls; small waves lapping against a stone pier; laughter; bargaining; farewells; deep-toned chimes of church bells; the cry of a strawberry seller in the vegetable market; thirty grade-schoolers singing their anthem at a graduation ceremony on the far side of a high garden wall; two cats fighting to see which one gets to sleep under the shade of a ladder; homeward-heading children bouncing a ball against a *campo* wall; swifts twittering overhead at twilight; a solitary footfall at ten in the evening.

Campi are the least decorated parts of town because the city's houses were built to present their beautiful sides and front doors to the open water. But *campi* are marvelous in their own ways. In former centuries the squares collected pure drinking water; raindrops seeping down between the paving stones of each square filtered through underground sandboxes and trickled into cisterns beneath community wells. Now the *campi* collect Venetians, who gather there to shop and eat and resume conversations.

The city's fueling stations—wine bars, coffee bars, sandwich shops, restaurants, pizzerias, ice cream stands—are concentrated in the *campi* and *campielli*, literally meaning "fields" and "little fields." (There's only one actual piazza in Venice, the famous central cathedral square of San Marco.) Venetians, because their city is organized around walking and stopping (each *campo* is about a three-minute walk from the next), are high-octane nibblers and sippers.

Crowds of day-tripping tourists who are quick-marched through the city by vacation packagers go home with barely a taste of its treasures—as the Italians say, *mordi e fuggi* ("bite and flee") is their lot. It is possible, when caught up in one of these packs as it inches its way through the Piazza San Marco or shuffles into a glass-making foundry on the island of Murano, to be as dispirited in Venice as anyone ever is on a gridlocked freeway in Los Angeles or in a stalled subway car under New York City. But there's always a way out, a chance to *fuggire*. The day trippers stick to assigned routes and rarely disperse; with the aid of a good street map, you can escape, bobbing and weaving at will. (The best of these maps, sold in most local bookshops, is the good-looking one with the green cover published by the Touring Club Italiano.)

~

My wife and I spent ten days in Venice last year along with our young son. We went in May, when the tour groups are not yet in full gear and the weather's apt to be excellent—and it was. (April, June, September, and October are the other generally reliable months.) The *campi* are the wellsprings of Venetian life, and among them we began to recognize recurring features. Many have large churches; others, more purely residential, are organized around the small palace of an area's founding family; they're all laid with rectangular gray stones; the liveliest have ground-floor neighborhood shops—dry cleaners and drugstores—in addition to bakeries and cafés. Some *campi* are so intimately proportioned, you feel as if you're sitting in an open shoebox. A number are long and skinny, and some, bounded by canals, have rounded edges. As a paved urban form, they took shape more than five hundred years ago— just after Columbus set sail for the New World.

Almost all of them give you a privileged, behind-the-scenes feeling: in the Campo delle Beccarie, for instance, near the Rialto Bridge, I was amazed to see an elaborate, solid-looking fish stall disappear before my eyes. It had a saillike canvas awning, which the fishmonger rolled up like a window shade. That took one minute. Then the frame beneath came apart like a Lego set, and everything was stowed in a couple of small boxes, loaded onto an aluminum handcart, and wheeled away—three more minutes. Swiftly the space was claimed by a nearby café owner, and a waiter set out lunch tables, unfurling their umbrellalike shades. It was as orderly and as mutable as the life of a coral reef.

It took us several days to recognize that the true heart of the city was Campo di Santa Margherita ("Santa Margarita" in Venetian dialect), a welcoming, untouristy, modestly decorated open space in Dorsoduro, the university quarter. Santa Margherita does have permanent presences, such as a row of shops and cafés along one side (in fourteenth-century houses); a flagpole; an eighteenth-century guildhall; and half a dozen trees plunked down haphazardly by a 1960s greening-of-Venice movement (most greenery is hidden away in private gardens). In addition, though, it has wide, almost wild mood swings.

If you sit in Campo di Santa Margherita for a day, this is what you'll see. In the morning stalls appear, and there's a bustling fish and vegetable market. By two P.M. the stalls have dematerialized and all is quiet, save for the leisurely scrapings of the street sweeper's twig broom. At four the schools let out, and there's a new liveliness, and lots of ducking into ice cream shops, and whispered conferences in front of the toy store window. One afternoon we saw a nun organize and then lead a spirited soccer game. Venice is for the most part a go-to-bed-early town, but at night, and even well past midnight, Santa Margherita is a noisy undergraduate hangout and the late-night ice cream shop is so busy that lire notes pile up uncounted and unstacked on the back marble counter for hours on end. Night is also a time of apparitions. On an evening stroll with a Venetian couple we'd met, we saw a dozen giant black Newfoundland dogs (trained in Italy as aquatic rescue dogs) as they were coming around a corner. "There are bears in the square," said the man, drawing back. "No, there are holes in the night," said the woman.

Today, delicately, with respect and mutuality, young and old, rich and poor share the city. What makes that possible? It's a matter of give and take, like the former republic's constitution—an ebb and flow, like the tides that rise and then fall by three feet every six hours in the canals.

Discerning travelers spend two or three days in the city, savoring its past and its patrimony—the lavishly beautiful churches, palaces, guildhalls, and bell towers, and the breathtaking sculptures, paintings, and frescoes amassed in museums, spanning ceilings, or spreading behind altars. And yet there's another way of approaching Venice—by treating it as inspiration for a more graceful, peaceful way of living. The twenty-first century will be the first in humanity's history in which more than half the world's population lives in cities. So it's a balm to know that what city planners elliptically refer to as "quality of life" or "urban livability" already has an abundant, effervescing, and enduring source in a great city eager for friends and imitators.

We first got a feeling for what truly governs Venice when we were out on the water in a *traghetto,* a ferry gondola that goes back and forth across the Grand Canal. *Traghetti* passengers traditionally stand, perhaps so the gondoliers can squeeze in more customers, and as we bobbed across the water, the canal was suddenly an enormous river; the four-story palaces behind and ahead of us became vast, almost mountainous; and a staid old *vaporetto* looked the size of a destroyer. The tiny *traghetto,* moving at right angles to the rest of the traffic, softly nosed left, then right, slipping past the other craft while they, even the looming water bus, adjusted their own speeds and directions. Everyone watched everyone else, and no horns blew.

There's a café in Campo di Santa Margherita that has a few tables outside, then an empty space, and then a much larger bunch of tables beyond the break. This odd configuration puzzled me—until the day I noticed that the blank patch functioned as a pathway for pedestrians, allowing the restaurant to accommodate both still pool and moving stream.

Venice began in the fifth century as a series of fishing villages on some of the 118 low, whale-shaped islands in the lagoon, and over the centuries, it has retained the shape and life of these villages. Without fanfare and almost without interruption, the city has concentrated for some fifty generations on making urban life as relaxed and as socially comfortable as life in the countryside, and on giving working life many of the refreshing qualities of a vacation. As a result, Venice is one of the sanest cities in the world.

To a greater extent than any other city, it has learned not only how to coexist with a watery nature that swirls past its doors but how to deeply satisfy human nature as well—on the basic, enduring level of the senses. Continuously. Generously. Gloriously.

Venice: "Having a Lovely Time . . . Glad You're Not Here"

BY LEIGH NEWMAN

∽

editor's note

There are some cities that really can be visited only at one or perhaps two particular times of year, either because the climate is too severe (hot or freezing) or because events, natural or man-made, happen only then. Venice, however, is one of those cities that is perhaps equally as captivating in the dead of winter as in spring, summer, or fall. Winter may in fact be the preferred season, if the number of articles in my files is any indication. Writer David Plante wrote that in winter, "you feel that Venice itself, for its own spiritual well-being, is going through a period of withdrawal. The world, the whole world, is too much with it in the summer, and, too, in the spring and, recently, at the carnival that takes place every year before Lent."

Following are two pieces that present two different views of visiting the city on the lagoon in winter.

LEIGH NEWMAN lives in New York and is a contributing editor of *Travel Holiday*, where this piece first appeared in 2001.

If there's one place in the world where you might just wish for bad weather, it's Venice. Okay, not really bad weather. A little nip in the air, a little ice on the cobblestones, a little dusting of atmospheric snow on the cornices of the palazzi lining the Grand Canal. What else can create a little mystery the way a swirl of fog can—uncurling down a narrow street like the velvet cape of a masked reveler you're trailing behind?

Mood aside, however, winter in Venice creates another city, one without crowds and lines, one filled with people who actually live here—in the cold and in the warm. Want to go to mass in San Marco's? Tour the Palazzo Ducale? Have coffee at Caffè Florian—without a wait? Why not? That's what the Venetians are doing. Well, at least some of them. (They're not the most religious of people.) Others are obsessing over those new oxblood pumps in Prada's windows along Via San Moisè, sipping coffee on an outdoor terrace swaddled in the world's only version of a sexy down coat, or watching their children play soccer in the neighborhood square. In other words, they're simply living—which, in Venice, isn't simple at all.

In many ways, this city isn't designed for living. And that doesn't just refer to the floods that threaten to sink it or the high (often very high) prices. These things make life difficult, but they also separate the Venetians from the Italians—and from anyone else. What's more difficult is that this life must be lived under the eyes of the world, in the flash of cameras going off. As busloads of tourists fill its streets, its restaurants, its cafés, Venice becomes part museum. Everyone—locals and visitors alike—and everything is constantly on display.

But in many ways, that's exactly what the town was built for—to impress, from the moment Renaissance traders first approached its massive skyline from the sea. You still see it while walking past the houses, the palazzi, the churches, the facades decorated with swirls of inlay and cotton-candy-colored marble and winged cherubs. Majesty is the norm here. And so the ordinary events and people you stumble on in winter—say, a woman dragging her wheeled grocery basket—become slightly extraordinary. In fact, the contrast between these two sides of the city, between the city-in-the-clouds and the down-to-earth people living in it, is what creates the real mystery here, the one that lives and eats and walks and shops and argues and laughs in the city's streets.

Green Lagoon

"The glory of Venice is built on nothing," says Nicolas Dona as he rushes me from twisting street to twisting street. "On rats. On mud." I've just met Dona when asking for directions, this thin, nervous harpsichordist you might mistake for a nineteenth-century dandy, with his aubergine velvet topcoat and waxed mustache. "Just look at these canals," he says. "The water is petrifying in them. You can smell the centuries in them."

No, I think, you can't. And thank goodness. In the summers, the only thing you smell in the canal water is the sewage—a condition made more pungent by the heat. But now, in the winter, the water flows clean-smelling (or so it seems when I test it) and antifreeze green, as though it were dyed just to enliven the white, pinks, and grays of the city's stonework. "In the winter," Dona says, "Venice breathes. In the summer, it sweats." Out here, our breath turns bright white as it hits the cold, damp, wet air—the city's own natural trinity that ensures winter is left to the Venetians and the truly devoted. Unless, that is, you're lucky and it's sunny, the way it is the next day. A hard dazzling light shines over the city's curvaceous marble skyline, causing gondoliers of every stripe to break out hand mirrors and pieces of tinfoil. Up and down the quays, I find them with faces tilted into the glass's bright reflection, changing the position of their chairs as the sun moves across the sky like a bunch of sunflowers, only with five o'clock shadows.

Starting at the Accademia Bridge—that rough wooden anomaly in this city of stone and gilt—I head to San Marco's square where (predictably) the pigeons burst up in flapping indignation. You can never really say that Venice is devoid of tourists. It just isn't. Even now, when the temperature holds steady at forty degrees, the old men are there, selling their bags of bird feed. The young women dressed up in powdered wigs and seventeenth-century ballgowns are still stuffing Vivaldi concert brochures into people's hands. The difference is they've only got about fifty people to approach (which seems not more than a handful in this huge square). And they seem half-hearted about it all, lighting cigarettes between their lace-gloved fingers, while ignoring the crowds of Japanese girls who stand with their heads tilted back, mouths open as if to taste some rain of gold dust falling from the Byzantine mosaics of the cathedral.

As I move on, toward the Rialto and the less-visited districts of Santa Croce and the old Jewish quarter, things quiet down as they always do when you move away from the lagoon (or the train station). The lagoon, that brackish mixture of river and seawater, is where Venice began in the fifth century A.D., when mainlanders were forced onto the islands by encroaching Lombards. It was water that gave rise to the city's enormous prosperity, once the Venetians, with their legendary fleet, had learned to trade salt, harvested on the flats of the lagoon, for spices and spices for gold.

Water, of course, may also end up being the cause of Venice's well-publicized demise. Most of the *acqua alta,* or high tides, take place in November (when the tides of the Adriatic are the strongest), but even in February you find platforms strewn around the squares like the still-setup tables of some wedding party after the guests have gone. "Until December, you hear the sirens wailing," says Rosa Beauavier, whose family has lived for seven centuries on Murano, the Venetian island famous for its blown glass. "In San Marco's square there's an Hermès store that has a button. They push it, and all of the pieces of furniture rise up to protect them from the floods."

Open the Doors, Where Are All the People

So misty, cloak-and-dagger weather doesn't appear on command. There are other marvels, namely, going to do what everyone does in Italy—look at art. Just about anywhere in this country, you can wander into a corner church and find a museum-quality Madonna and Child. And the pleasure comes from seeing it where it was meant to be. But nowhere will you find that experience more concentrated than in Venice. You don't just find the masterpieces in the corner church, you find them in the corner palazzo and the corner *scuole* (the Renaissance-era charitable institutions that used to commission everything from paintings to frescoes). With the exception of the venerable Accademia, even the few museums here are casual, housed in palazzo galleries that make you feel as if you're dropping in at the home of an old nobleman friend.

And what makes it all more bizarrely normal in the winter is that there aren't any crowds to remind you that, by the way, I don't know any noblemen. I can saunter along, imagining I own the place, if I wish. Here's how my experience went. The Accademia's Titians and Bellinis? No line. Peggy Guggenheim's palazzo filled with Jackson Pollocks and Max Ernsts? No line. The Scuola di San Rocco's fifty-odd masterpieces by Tintoretto? No line. The Palazzo Ducale? Well. A line. Of three people.

After a day's hard looking, you end up leaving the world of some wonderful painting, where, say, Saint George slays a rainbow-winged dragon to save a village, only to enter a world equally otherworldly—Venice at dusk, where the light turns shadowy and pink, blending the edges of the buildings into fuzzy lines of stone and air, exactly the way that Venetians' Renaissance masters did on their canvases, calling it chiaroscuro.

Shadow Play

The temperature drops (vanity's not the only reason fur is so popular with Italian women), and as your footsteps echo on the cobblestones, you find yourself looking for a well-lit window to have the night's first *ombre,* or shadow, that glass tumbler of wine, drunk down in a neighborhood *bacaro,* or wine bar. The name comes from the days when wine was served from a cart in San Marco's square. The cart was moved every few hours, following the shadows on the ground that kept patrons cool as they drank.

Today, these small corner shops—often selling wine by the bottle and various *cicchetti,* little appetizers like creamy salt cod spread on polenta, meatballs, grilled sardines—are where most Venetians go after work, before dinner, after a fight with a friend (to make up)—and so on. They're your home downstairs from home. The one I find myself in, Schiavi, isn't fancy, just a sunken cement floor lined with wooden shelves and bottles. But there's a little dog who jumps on the bar for a taste of pork sandwich. The phone rings. It's someone's wife or someone's husband looking for that someone. And everyone else just keeps on jabbering on to everyone, glass held in the direction of the bar. (Grizzled artist to bartender: "You want to know how to sell more wine? Fill up the glass.")

As I leave the *bacaro,* the thin lines of golden light waver along on the brick walls—reflections of the canal's currents thrown up like liquid shadows, and perhaps the real inspiration for the name *ombre,* coined by some wine-fortified Venetian centuries ago as he wandered home in the dark.

When Pigs Cry

Many people claim Venice in winter is the real Venice. But what is the real Venice? In many ways, this city—for all its columns and arches and balconies, its cosmopolitan cocktails-at-Cipriani's crowds—is just a small town. Since the 1950s, when people fled to the mainland in search of jobs and houses with roofs that didn't leak, the population has dwindled to just over 60,000.

With this small of a community comes a slow, even sleepy pace, which is obliterated in the summer, in the press and pull of visitors. Interestingly enough, this small-town pace does coexist with some big-city attitudes. Venetians are very open people. They like to go out, to meet people from all over the world, mostly because of their seafaring history, when Venice served as the doorway between the East and the West, and Venetians became a people made up of the world's people. It's hard to see this openness in the summer, because the sheer number of visitors forces them to retreat to locals-only places. But try talking with a Venetian in a café or *bacaro* during the winter, and see if you can get him to shut up.

In a week or so, though, the chatter will be harder to come by, when Carnival arrives and marks the end of winter, and tourists again invade in force. The citywide festival seems to come out of nowhere. No one speaks of their costumes or parties. Then a few mask-shaped strings of lights appear near the Rialto. Bits and pieces of a stage take shape in front of San Marco.

Finally it's Sunday, a cold and blustery winter one, with dark clouds on the horizon, which makes the little boy in the happy black-and-white cow suit seem all the stranger. He's stuffed into his costume, enormous pink teats hanging from his belly (an accessory that might be omitted in America), asking his mother to buy him a magazine at the newsstand in front of the Accademia.

Later, near San Marco's, I run into a Big Bird, strapped in his stroller, his face smeared with chocolate. I walk a little faster and find the entire square filled with frogs and princesses, dragons and piglets, cats and parents. The kids throw confetti and birdseed in the air. The mothers sit at the tables, ordering elaborate ice cream confections and coffees. This carnival could be taking place on

Main Street, except for the hundreds of stone arches and the extravagant, rambling gold roofline of the basilica. There are no beautiful masked revelers drinking champagne here. There is no eerie fog. But that doesn't mean there isn't atmosphere, especially when a ridiculously chic woman asks if her sugar-high piglet can rest at my table while she runs off to find her neighbor's child, a witch. Watching the boy's face inside his pink fur hood, I think of Nicolas, the harpsichordist, when he explained, "Venice is just a theater set. Everyone comes here to act out a part in their own fantastic play." But now I understand his conclusion: "That's why everyone also feels so comfortable here."

Venice: On Ice

To get to Venice, you have to fly through Rome, Milan, or another city, depending on your airline. I took Alitalia, which offers steeply discounted tickets during the winter (mine was about $400), as long as you don't travel close to the holidays. The city is usually in the chilly forties, so bring warm clothes.

Some hotels have a special winter deal, which can bring the sky-high Venetian hotel rates down to earth. The **Locanda Montin** is private, romantic, and right on the canal (winter, $91, summer, $114; 1147 Fondamenta di Borgo; 011.39.041.52.27.151). Another choice with a similar feel is **Pensione La Calcina** ($118 for a double room on the canal, $91 off the canal; 780 Dorsoduro 78; 011.39.041.52.06.466). The most famous hotel in town, the **Danieli,** starts at about $452 year-round (4196 Riva degli Schiavoni; 011.39.041.522.6480).

Venice isn't known as one of the premier food regions of Italy, but the food is often wonderful. Begin in a *bacaro,* or wine bar, such as the classic **Cantina Do Mori.** In these dark, comforting bars, you'll choose from among the snack-size dishes, or *cicheti,* like marinated baby octopus (San Polo 429, Calle dei Do Mori;

011.39.041.52.25.401). For lunch, try **Al Mascaron**—it's packed at dinner. The locals start a meal with a plate of *cicheti* and slices of grilled polenta. For a main course, try the pasta topped with clams, prawns, and mussels (Castello 5225, Calle Lunga Santa Maria Formosa; 011.39.041.52.25.995).

And dinner? A nonseafood choice is **L'Incontro**. The steaks make you want to write an ode to their tenderness. Homemade pastas, like the orecchiette in gorgonzola sauce, are similiarly inspiring (3062 Dorsoduro; 011.39.041.52.22.404).

The **Peggy Guggenheim Collection** is located in the Palazzo Venier dei Leoni, the **Palazzo Ducale** is at Piazza San Marco, and the **Gallerie dell' Accademia** is at Campo della Carità.

Venice in Winter

BY FRED PLOTKIN

∾

FRED PLOTKIN is the author of *La Terra Fortunata: The Splendid Food and Wine of Friuli–Venezia Giulia, Italy's Great Undiscovered Region* (Broadway Books, 2001), *Italy for the Gourmet Traveler* (Little, Brown & Co., 1996), *Recipes from Paradise: Life and Food on the Italian Riviera* (Little, Brown & Co., 1997), and *Opera 101: A Complete Guide to Learning and Loving Opera* (Hyperion, 1994). He is at work on a book on the life and travels of Michelangelo.

Venice in winter exudes a timeless quality. Walking the narrow streets, I find myself thinking, can this really be the year 2000? For here—where the sound of water lapping against palazzi is as it always was, where mists shroud the canals and narrow streets as they always have—it could be 1700, or even 1500. The very stillness evokes agelessness: Richard Wagner spent some of his winters here because he believed that only in the city's silence could he hear music. Winter is the *only* time of year when *La Serenissima* is, indeed, serene. Aside from the week between Christmas and New Year's—and the week of the annual *Carnevale,* when mayhem erupts—life is tranquil, just as the citizens like it. And it is only now that you will find restaurants, cafés, and wine bars filled with Venetians. The rest of the year, they retreat into their homes, taking refuge from the tourist stampede, so the fair-weather visitor misses a crucial element of life in Venice. To be in Venice without Venetians is to know the city's stones but not its soul.

Venetians are heirs to the legacy of the fifteenth-century Republic of Venice: its musical language, its sense of fun, its fierce love of both self and the inimitable *cucina* of the region. In winter its classic dishes are prepared with the greatest of care, and more important, foods appear that are never seen on a *menu turistico*. You might even come across a gondolier, dining out with his family, singing not for money but for the pure love of singing.

True Venetians eat all day. A cappuccino and a sweet bun in the morning tide them over until just before noon, when they might take a glass of wine and *cicchetti* (snacks of fish, meat, or vegetables). By late afternoon, when the last of the winter light has waned, they're back to the wine bar for a glass of Prosecco and another little snack. Then there's supper at nine, and later, somewhere between eleven and midnight, a coffee or a grappa with friends. How do most Venetians stay so trim and fit despite all this? They walk everywhere.

I have been a regular visitor to Venice since 1973, and when I want to eat out, I go where the locals go. But my first stop is always at a personal favorite, Pasticceria Dal Mas. Although it's on a very touristy street, not far from the train station, it remains authentically Venetian. My order is invariably an espresso and an *Arlecchino* (as in Harlequin, the commedia dell'arte character), a wedge of cake with layers of chocolate, white pastry cream, golden cake, beige nut cream, more chocolate, and so on. It puts me in a Venetian mood.

Later on, *la dolce vita* continues at Pasticceria Didovich, where, standing, I have a light lunch of the house specialty: a palm-size vegetable quiche. To my mind, two or three of these with a glass of Prosecco make a perfect meal. (And if the quiche with red radicchio is on the menu when you visit, do not fail to order it!) Then I treat myself to strudel, Sacher torte, linzertorte, or little pastries filled with jam or sweet cheese—the sort of pastry that might seem more at home in Vienna or Budapest (not so surprising when you remember that in the nineteenth century Venice was under Hapsburg rule for almost seventy years).

Another holdover from the Austrian occupation is the Venetian love of *panna montata* (fresh whipped cream). You will find it all over town, but I go to Hostaria da Zorzi, near Piazza San Marco. To my mind, an incomparable seasonal sight is the short, stout, fur-swathed Venetian ladies standing at the bar with a platter of whipped cream in front of them. Each diminutive matron is given two ice cream cones with which to gather up as much cream as possible. I've yet to learn how they manage so efficiently—I always manage to get more cream on my nose than in my mouth.

At Ponte delle Paste, you can get a cup of hot chocolate topped with fresh whipped cream and, in winter only, *frittelle veneziane* (fritters filled with either pastry cream or zabaglione). You will see *frittelle* all over town, but few are this good. Nearby is Pasticceria Colussi, an austere little bakery offering classic Venetian dry cookies such as *bussolai, baicoli,* and *zaletti; frittelle,* of course; and also little cakes. Here the *focaccia* (or *fugassa,* as it's known locally) is not the usual Italian bread of flour, salt, and oil but a sweet, eggy, lemony cake, cousin to the Milanese *panettone,* without the candied fruit.

Finding wonderful food in Venice is more difficult than locating lovely pastries. The overwhelming onslaught of tourists over the past fifteen years has turned gastronomic Venice into a tired old courtesan who mindlessly dispenses her favors with barely the suggestion that pleasure could be part of the transaction. The absolute low end of this unfortunate phenomenon is, of course, the ubiquitous *menu turistico*—spaghetti with canned clams followed by a greasy fry-up of scraps of seafood. Avoid it at all costs.

The scandalous high end, on the other hand, is found at Harry's Bar. Here the downstairs room is convivial and full of regulars, but tourists are relegated to a drab upstairs room where the walls are covered with puckered fabric and the staff has only the most perfunctory regard for either the food or the diner. After my Bellini (where—the question still niggles—did they find fresh peach juice in winter?), I ordered spider crab, which came with too much shell carelessly left in, followed by an only so-so house risotto and parched sea bass fillets with greasy artichokes, then a piece of dull apple pie. With my meal I had a mineral water, a very ordinary white wine, and a cup of coffee. For this "classic" Venetian experience I paid an outrageous 352,400 Italian lire (about $200).

Sadly, many visitors to Venice think that they are in the know if they dine at Harry's Bar, Osteria da Fiore, Al Covo, Trattoria alla Madonna, or Fiaschetteria Toscana. Osteria da Fiore collapsed under the weight of an article in the *International Herald Tribune* in 1994 that called it the best restaurant in Italy. An attractive though noisy place with warm and careful service, da Fiore has always produced perfectly nice food, including its famous baked scallops with fresh thyme. But the kitchen has too many misses, owing to careless preparation. It makes a laudable effort to achieve delicate cooking, but dishes can wind up being flavorless.

Al Covo has acquired an almost entirely American following, many of whom are directed there by the concierges of the Cipriani, Danieli, and Gritti Palace hotels. You will certainly enjoy good seafood, prepared by Cesare Benelli, whose Texan wife, Diane, supplies not only a cheery welcome but American desserts too. The problem here, from my point of view, is that Al Covo has become such a safe bet for visitors that it is now really an American-style restaurant that happens to serve Venetian dishes.

About Trattoria alla Madonna, near the Rialto Bridge, people say, "I eat here because there is nowhere else good left in Venice." The food is certainly decent, but nothing special. Fiaschetteria Toscana, on the other hand, is a very good choice. The food is all Venetian, and among the classics are *pasta e fagioli* with a creamy base of cranberry beans; scallops with almonds served as an appetizer in a tiny ramekin; *seppioline con piselli* (tender cuttlefish with peas and yellow polenta); and *fegato alla veneziana* (thin slices of calves' liver deftly sautéed with onions to the perfect degree of doneness). Fiaschetteria is justifiably proud of its *frittura della Serenissima,* a large plate of delicately battered and fried seafood and vegetables. This is the one restaurant with a large tourist clientele that is also frequented by Venetians, and the service is welcoming to newcomers, never condescending.

At Fiaschetteria, as at other restaurants where Venetians dine, you want to look for the special repertoire of winter foods. Foremost are *schie* (pronounced *skee*-ay), tiny shrimp boiled or fried and served on a small cushion of soft polenta. In some months you will find *moleche* (soft-shelled crabs). Also in abundance now are artichoke bottoms, typically sautéed in a little olive oil. In the Rialto market you will see vendors carefully remove the bottoms from the artichokes and soak them in cold water with lemon juice to keep them from turning brown.

Fritters and carnival pastries are everywhere, and wines of the most recent vintage are just making an appearance in town. American visitors tend to order a carafe of house wine when dining out, but for just a little more money it's possible to get an excellent local bottle.

Ristorante Riviera threatens to become the next restaurant for those supposedly in the know. Near both the cruise-ship terminal and the city's only real supermarket, Riviera has a following among the movie stars who come for the September film festival. The food here may be delicious, but little else is right about the place. It is so cramped that the one overworked waiter has to bone the fish on top of a fax machine, and the thirty tables are set so close together that cigarette smoke from anywhere in the room can overwhelm the food you are eating. The owner does not bother to recite specials for visitors, so they must order off the menu whether or not they understand Italian. And the minuscule wine list offers nothing that really complements the (admittedly excellent) risottos, pasta, and seafood.

Other restaurants have given me much more pleasure and, better yet, genuine Venetian company. Hostaria da Franz, near the Giardini della Biennale, is a modest-looking establishment with great food. Here Franco Gasparini, a large man with whiskers, cooks; his son runs the restaurant, occasionally with the help of Franco's daughter-in-law; and at times two grandchildren play charmingly underfoot. I order my favorite, *sarde in saor* (sweet-and-sour sardines), a Venetian classic. And I urge you not to miss the *moscardini al Prosecco* (baby octopus cooked in sparkling wine—a masterpiece of flavor and texture) or the exquisite *baccalà mantecato* (salt cod whipped with olive oil to a creamy froth).

At Antiche Carampane the home-style Venetian cooking is not fancy, but it is good. And you have to love a place with a sign in the doorway stating, "No pizza, no lasagne, no *menu turistico.*" One of the dishes I love is *spaghetti con lo scorfano,* with a sauce made from local fish. Another specialty of the house is the homemade traditional Venetian desserts (for which the owner refuses to reveal the recipes; they have been handed down through generations). Antica Locanda Montin, near the Gallerie dell'Accademia, has long been favored by artistic types like Ezra Pound and painter Arbit Blatas and his wife, opera star Regina Resnik, who made Venice their home. Here the food is reliable and the setting cozy. Antica Locanda Montin is famous for its beautiful enclosed garden in the back—unusual for a Venetian restaurant. Try the *spaghetti con nero di seppia* (with cuttlefish ink) and *coda di rospo* (monkfish). At Trattoria da Ignazio—a typically friendly Venetian restaurant—the starring dishes are *scampi fritti* (like delicate "Cajun popcorn") and grilled fish such as sole (ask to have it without added salt). At all costs, skip the baby octopus with balsamic vinegar.

If I could have just one restaurant meal in Venice, it would be at

Ristorante da Ivo, where the room is romantic and the food is delicious, including the *schie* and great fish fillets cooked with vegetables. Here you will enjoy the best risottos in Venice. A friend who had just finished da Ivo's risotto with cuttlefish ink told me, "My teeth may turn black, but I wouldn't trade this for pearls in my mouth."

Truth be told, I do most of my eating as the locals do—in the many *osterie* and *bacari* all over the city. In most, the clientele is strictly Venetian and the food caters to their demanding taste. There are two such places that call themselves *osteria,* but they are, in reality, much more than the word suggests. At the tiny Osteria alle Testiere, the menu changes daily according to what the sea provides. Shellfish is always a good choice, particularly the *caparozzoli allo zenzero* (clams ennobled by gratings of fresh ginger). Look for a splendid grilled *soaso* (tiny Adriatic turbot taken from the lagoons near Venice). All this, and a superb wine list, too. Osteria La Zucca is a paradise for vegetarians, though meat is also plentiful. Here you can enjoy the gentle service and intelligent wine list in the attractive dining room with conversation-friendly acoustics and a no-smoking section. Two special dishes are the pumpkin flan and the carrots with yogurt and curry.

It is common in Venice to go from one wine bar to the next, ordering a dish or two at each place plus a glass of wine to match. The Veneto produces some very fine wines, and the neighboring province of Friuli–Venezia Giulia is one of Italy's top three wine producers, responsible for the nation's best whites. I would start at Osteria Bentigodi da Andrea, near the old Jewish quarter. Everything here (but the pasta) is delicious. On one visit I ordered a glass of Müller-Thurgau with my endive, pecorino, and walnut salad, and the medley of flavors was positively stereophonic. At Bentigodi I make an exception to my rule of having only fresh fruit for dessert. For it's impossible to resist the *salame di cioccolato* (chocolate "salami"—a slightly crumbly roll with pine nuts). And, unlike most Venetian *osterie,* which are cramped and rustic, this one is light and airy.

Nearby is the Trattoria Ca' d'Oro, also called Osteria dalla Vedova, one of the most reliable in Venice. Starring dishes include *baccalà mantecato* and *polpette* (cold veal meatballs served with a vibrant tomato sauce and perfect vegetables). The soups, pastas, and accompanying wines are all really good too. Then go to Osteria alla Bomba. You can tell you've found it by the peals of laughter from men engaged in hearty discussion while feasting on superb salami from Treviso, local cheeses, vegetables, and grilled and fried fish. The *pasta e fagioli* is one of the best.

At Osteria ai Assassini, near San Marco, the pasta is mediocre but the soups are delicious. Fish dishes are thoughtfully cooked and presented: *cappe sante al pomodoro,* when available, are made with crushed tomato and herbs and baked in the shell—the most perfectly cooked scallop dish I've had in Venice. And the welcome is warm and genuine. Nearby, in a little cul-de-sac off the Frezzeria, is Osteria da Carla. If you arrive around eleven in the morning, you can make the first selection from gorgeous fish and vegetable preparations. There is arguably no better lunch in town.

When darkness begins to envelop the city at around four P.M., I head for Cantinone già Schiavi, near Locanda Montin. Here the *mamma* makes wonderful *baccalà mantecato,* plus open-faced sandwiches of caviar, sardines, tuna, vegetables, cheeses, salamis, or ham, while the *papà* and the *figli* pour wine from one of the best selections in all of Venice. (You can buy bottles to take home.) A local woman told me that she loves to come here and eat the sandwiches and have a glass of wine with her neighbors. "At home," she said, "I would be all alone with a bowl of pasta." This is indeed the most cheerful place I know, and genuinely Venetian. Nowhere feels warmer on a wintry evening.

At the close of day, I often find my way to the Piazza San Marco, a spot I avoid in other seasons. From a seat at the Gran Caffè Ristorante Quadri or the Caffè Florian, over espresso or hot chocolate, I admire the piazza's grand form, its sense of being an outdoor drawing room. Sometimes I will walk to the center of the square and stand completely still to absorb the silence of the centuries, breathe in the mist, and draw in my memories of another uniquely Venetian day.

Eating in Venice

Venice is divided into *sestieri* ("districts"). The central six are Cannaregio, Castello, Dorsoduro, San Polo, Santa Croce, and San Marco. When trying to find a restaurant, first identify the district and then the street. Most restaurants accept credit cards; some *osterie* and bars do not.

Restaurants and Osterie

al Covo, *Campiello della Pescheria 3968, Castello (041.522.3812)*

Antica Locanda Montin, *Fondamenta Eremite 1147, Dorsoduro (041.522.7151; fax 041.520.0255)*

Antiche Carampane, *Rio Terà de le Colone 1911, San Polo (041.524.0165)*

Cantinone già Schiavi, *Fondamenta Nani 992, Dorsoduro (041.523.0034)*

Fiaschetteria Toscana, *San Giovanni Crisostomo 5719, Cannaregio (041.528.5281; fax 041.528.5521)*

Harry's Bar, *Calle Vallaressa 1323, San Marco (041.528.5777; fax 041.520.8822)*

Hostaria da Franz, *Fondamenta San Isepo 754, Castello (041.522.0861; fax 041.241.9278)*

Osteria ai Assassini, *Rio Terà ai Assassini 3695, San Marco* *(041.528.7986)*

Osteria alle Testiere, *Calle del Mondo Nuovo 5801, Castello* *(Tel./fax 041.522.7220)*

Osteria Bentigodi da Andrea, *Rio Terà Farsetti 1424, Cannaregio* *(041.716.269)*

Osteria alla Bomba, *Calle dell'Oca 4297, Cannaregio* *(041.520.1438)*

Osteria da Carla, *Corte Contarina 1535, San Marco* *(041.523.7855)*

Osteria da Fiore, *Calle del Scaletter 2202, San Polo (041.721.308; fax 041.721.343)*

Osteria La Zucca, *San Giacomo dell'Orio 1762, Santa Croce* *(041.524.1570)*

Ristorante da Ivo, *Ramo dei Fuseri 1809, San Marco* *(041.528.5004; fax 041.520.5889)*

Ristorante Riviera, *Zattere 1473, Dorsoduro (041.522.7621)*

Trattoria alla Madonna, *Calle della Madonna 594, San Polo* *(041.522.3824; fax 041.521.0167)*

Trattoria Ca' d'Oro/Osteria dalla Vedova, *Ramo Ca' d'Oro 3912, Cannaregio (041.528.5324)*

Trattoria da Ignazio, *Calle dei Saoneri 2749, San Polo (Tel./fax 041.523.4852)*

Sweet Shops and Caffè

Caffè Florian, *Piazza San Marco 56 (041.528.5338)*

Gran Caffè Ristorante Quadri, *Piazza San Marco 120*
(041.528.9299; fax 041.520.8041)

Hostaria da Zorzi, *Calle dei Fuseri 4359, San Marco*
(041.520.8816)

Pasticceria Colussi, *Calle Lunga San Barnaba 2867/a, Dorsoduro*
(041.523.1871)

Pasticceria Dal Mas, *Lista di Spagna 150/a, Cannaregio*
(041.715.101)

Pasticceria Didovich, *Campo di Santa Marina 5908, Castello*
(041.523.0017)

Ponte delle Paste, *Ponte delle Paste 5991, Castello (041.522.2889)*

Islands of the Venetian Lagoon

BY NADIA STANCIOFF

editor's note

I don't have any idea what the statistics are on visitors who never leave
Venice proper and therefore never get to the islands of the lagoon, but my
guess is it would be rather a large percentage, which is a shame. It is well
worth deciphering the ACTV schedule and devoting a day, or even a half
day, to the discovery of Venice's less famous cousins.

NADIA STANCIOFF wrote for many years for *Gourmet,* where this
piece first appeared in 1991.

Venice, like Venus, rose from the sea. When the Lombards ravaged northern Italy in the sixth and seventh centuries, the inhabitants of Altinum and other cities at the northwestern corner of the Adriatic fled into the blue-gray mirage of what is now called the Venetian Lagoon. Extending some two hundred square miles, the lagoon was shielded by sandbars from the lashings of the sea and dotted with islands on which to settle—yet it was sufficiently marshy and mud-clogged to make negotiating it treacherous for enemies unacquainted with its secrets. Here the refugees chose perforce to live.

But these refined Roman citizens quickly learned to adapt to their new watery world. They abandoned their islands' sketchy roads for the lagoon's waterways and dredged deep canals through the marshy shallows that are still in use today. In time they became masterful boatmen and fishermen, and their skills took them beyond the lagoon to the brave, wide sea, which opened new vocations: they became far-roving merchants and tradesmen, and flourished.

In 727 the island communities elected their first doge, or duke, "to be the sovereign of them all and to represent them in dealings with the rest of the world." Consolidated by this union, Venice grew ever stronger, and three centers of lagoon life evolved: the island of Grado, seat of religious power; Eraclea, seat of the government (an island that has since disappeared); and Torcello, seat of trade.

Taking advantage of their political independence and isolated location between the Holy Roman and Byzantine empires, Venetians shrewdly became middlemen, exploiting both powers but paying allegiance to neither. So successful were they at treading this tightrope that by the eleventh century they controlled the profitable trade routes in the Mediterranean.

Gradually the power and population center of Venice shifted to the islands where it remains today. From the city's shipyard, the Arsenale, came splendid merchant galleons that sailed every year in five fleets to Constantinople, the Black Sea, Egypt, North Africa, and western Europe. Silks, marble, ebony, spices, and precious stones were shipped to the lagoon and haggled over; the world's first banks sprang up. Venice prospered and grew sophisticated. It glittered with shining domes, marble palaces, and beautiful courtesans, earning it the name "the city of pleasure." In their pursuit of magnificence, Venetians spared no effort or expense to make their city the richest and most powerful in the world.

Although Venice's power has long since dwindled and faded away, the city remains the most narcissistic in the world, unabashedly mirroring itself in the shimmering waters of the lagoon. It has cause to be vain, of course, more so than some visitors realize, especially those who restrict their movements to the heart of the city. For out beyond it is greater Venice, consisting of about two hundred islands, many little more than mudbanks but some large enough to support several villages. Theirs is a wild, lonely, and sometimes desolate beauty, isolated as they are between sea and sky. To know Venice fully, however, one must visit these islands—one must travel the lagoon.

We began our explorations of it last September, the time of year when the autumn light lends fascinating changes of color to the water: it can appear an intense azure on a clear morning, mauve-gray beneath passing clouds, and a rich russet at sunset.

Early one sunny day we headed north across a bright blue lagoon to Murano. In 1291 Venice's glass furnaces were moved to this island to prevent fires in the city proper and to restrict espionage, for Venice created Europe's finest glass, and the techniques used to make it were jealously guarded. In the sixteenth century master glassblowers were given patrician status and endless privileges to keep them from migrating with their secrets; those who attempted to do so anyway had a hand cut off or were tracked down by emissaries of the republic and murdered. No small wonder, then, that these men were for ages the only ones in Europe who knew how to make mirrors.

Glass is still blown on Murano using the same instruments and techniques that were so assiduously protected in the past. From generation to generation the intricate art has been handed down, although only a small number of craftsmen still make the delicate objects their forefathers prided themselves on. Visitors to the island can watch these inventive and dexterous artisans as they create bowls and vases in their workshops.

Unfortunately, the glass for sale in many of Murano's shop windows is disappointing, aimed as it is at the tourist market. Several of Venice's finer glass companies, however, maintain their only stores in the city on Murano. Two that have particularly interesting selections are Foscarini, at Fondamenta Manin, 1, and Barovier & Toso, at Fondamenta dei Vetrai, 28; they both sell lamps and lighting fixtures, and the latter also carries vases and art objects.

Before buying, it's wise to learn about Venetian glass by paying a visit to the Museo Vetrario, or Glass Museum, on Murano's Canale di San Donato. There you will see what has been called the most important collection of blown glass dating from antiquity to modern times. One display illustrates how glass is made, and in other galleries the evolution of techniques and the use of color are traced. Some very early Roman glass exhibits a pure simplicity of design; with each passing century, however, the museum's exquisite objects become more colorful and ornate. I was particularly struck by the famous fifteenth-century blue Barovier Wedding Cup, one of the oldest pieces of Murano glass in the collection.

Not far from the museum is the Venetian-Byzantine brick and marble basilica of Santa Maria e Donato, founded in the seventh century and rebuilt in the twelfth. Regrettably, it was subjected to an insensitive restoration by the Austrians in the last century, but it still has its beautiful apse, with two tiers of arches, facing the canal; its onion-shaped dome; and a splendid twelfth-century mosaic floor. The church also contains the relics of Saint Donato—and a few of what are identified as bones from the dragon he reportedly killed.

Across the Canale degli Angeli stands San Pietro Martire, a Dominican Gothic church worth visiting for its paintings, particularly for Veronese's *Saint Jerome* and the *Madonna* and *Immaculate Conception* by Giovanni Bellini. Despite two imposing crystal chandeliers, however, the paintings were so dimly lit that all we could see were their handsome gilt frames until an Italian child, who had been noisily nagging his mother for coins, dropped a one-hundred-lire piece into a mysterious slot. Then, as if by a miracle, a flood of light brought to life the figures on the canvases.

Just east of Murano lies the island of Sant'Erasmo, where you will find neither tourists nor the smart Venetians who linger at Florian's in the Piazza San Marco. Since the time of the republic, this largest island of the lagoon has been the fruit and vegetable basket of Venice. Neat rows of lettuce, peas, artichokes, leeks, corn, and onions corrugate its flat expanse, interrupted here and there by clusters of farmers' houses. What few people we saw were mostly elderly or children; the young have found work on the mainland.

Coming upon an old man weeding his onion patch, I tried to strike up a conversation but had great trouble understanding his thick dialect, a mixture of Italian, French, Slavic, Greek, and Arabic. When I managed to piece things together, it became clear that he was bemoaning his soil's lost fertility; in 1966 the worst high-tide flood in Venice's history washed over the island, killing its crops and leaving behind a crust of blighting salt.

South of Sant'Erasmo shine the straits toward which the doge would journey in his gilded barge every year on Ascension Day. When he and his retinue reached them, he would stand, his robes fluttering in the breeze, and throw a gold ring far into the sea, saying, "In sign of eternal dominion, We, the Doge, espouse you, the Sea!" Venetians have always been fully aware of their intimacy with the sea.

To the north of Sant'Erasmo lies Burano, an island dominated by an idyllic village of fishermen and lace makers, above which leans a campanile at a perilous angle. A burst of life and color, Burano demands not to be passed by. Its miniature canals, narrow alleys, and bright, Gypsy-colored houses bustle with activity; groups of muscular men with tanned, lined faces repair their nets, and women—seated before their front doorways, their backs turned to the street—stitch the lace for which Burano has long been famous.

It was in the 1400s that lace making first became a profitable enterprise on Burano, and for centuries thereafter it was a chief source of income for the islanders. But in the nineteenth century the last of the women to whom this painstaking craft had been passed down began to die off; in 1872, in an effort to preserve their knowledge, the Scuolo dei Merletti (School of Lace) was founded. Located on the Piazza Galuppi, it can still be toured today, along with an adjoining museum of lace.

When we paid a call to the school, we spoke with sixty-five-year-old Maria Memo, whom we found bent over her *tombolo* (work cushion), sewing stitches so tiny that one couldn't help but wonder that she still had her sight. From all she told us, it was clear that the *punto Buranese* (Burano stitch) may yet fall from use and be forgotten. "On this island there are only ten master lace makers left," said Maria, who is herself one, "and about four hundred women who make lace following simple designs and using thick thread; the result is very different from authentic Burano lace. I can't blame them, when you consider that one of our tablecloths takes 720 hours and that we are paid a mere 3,050 lire [about $2.40] an hour." She shook her head, discouraged. "I've been making lace since I was six. Before I go, I want to pass our art on to the young." Her task is made all the more difficult by the presence in Burano's shop stalls of cheap factory-made lace from China and Korea.

Burano will no doubt stay in your mind's eye for quite some time, but your palate might not be as impressed with the cuisine. The best-known *trattorie*, however, are Da Romano and Da Galuppi, where I suggest you stick to pasta, fresh fish, and salads.

In the canal behind Burano's main square and the Church of San Martino, you may find elderly boatmen who will take you at high tide on the short journey to San Francesco del Deserto (Saint Francis of the Desert). An enchanting haven of tranquillity protected by a screen of dark green cypress trees, the island is said to be the one on which Saint Francis of Assisi ran aground in a storm in 1220. Making the best of adversity, the saint built a hut, and when he planted his walking staff into the ground, tradition has it that it formed roots and burst into leaf. Several decades later a Franciscan monastery was established on the island.

The handful of Franciscan monks who work and pray there now are distracted only by the changing seasons, the cries of their three docile peacocks, and the intrusion of occasional visitors (who are allowed access from 9 to 11 and 3 to 5:30 daily). On the tour the monks give, one is taken to stand beneath the venerable pine tree that sprang from the saint's staff, and in the little church with the brick beehive-shaped tower, one is shown the original floor of Saint Francis's oratory.

The red-brick campanile of Torcello's medieval cathedral can be seen from a long distance across the water, rising high above the green, nearly deserted island that many feel is the most unforgettably evocative in the lagoon. Settled by the people of Altinum in 639, Torcello grew into the richest colony in Venice. During its heyday, from the ninth to the twelfth centuries, it had twenty thousand inhabitants, grand houses and glorious churches, and enough power for one twelfth-century scribe to write of the *"Magnum Emporium Torcellanorum."* Then it all crumbled. The approaches to the island silted up, halting trade, and malaria scourged the population. Those who survived moved south to Venice's main islands, returning to Torcello only to quarry the stones from its buildings for their new homes.

After being deposited at Torcello's landing stage, visitors follow a tree-shaded brick path along a trickling waterway leading inland to "a piazza that contains two of the most remarkable churches in all Italy, and very little else," notes the Cadogan guide to Venice.

The Cathedral of Santa Maria dell'Assunta and the Church of Santa Fosca, which flanks it, are relics of a city formed by the meeting of Rome and Byzantium; their architecture is a spiritual marriage of East and West. Inside the cathedral in the dome of the central apse, you will find a magnificent thirteenth-century mosaic, executed by Greek craftsmen, of the Teotoca Madonna—the God-Bearer, the Christ child in her arms. In *The World of Venice,* James Morris calls this "the noblest memorial of the lagoon." Isolated on a gold ground, the Madonna seems to watch you with her sad, dark eyes, following you in a somewhat reproachful way as you study the patterned marble floor and the vast mosaic on the west wall depicting the Crucifixion, Resurrection, and Last Judgment.

I always get an eerie feeling when I visit Torcello's cathedral, one of having been part of the place long ago. That impression, however, is left behind with staggering speed as soon as I step out onto the green of the village piazza and see the tourists taking photographs of each other sitting in the so-called Attila's Throne or posing with set smiles next to the postcard and souvenir vendors.

When Ernest Hemingway and his wife, Mary, went to Torcello in the autumn of 1948, it was long before the day of the tourist, and they found the island to their liking. They spent a month there, an interlude Hemingway passed in writing, duck shooting, and chatting in pidgin Italian and Latin with the parish priest as they ambled around the island's two churches and four houses. At dusk he would return to the island's only hotel, the Locanda Cipriani, to share the evening meal beside a fire with Mary. Supper usually consisted of fish or wild fowl from the lagoon, accompanied by the ever-present carafe of wine. ("Man's best friend is the vine," insisted the writer.) Hemingway felt a great kinship with Torcello; in a chapter of *Across the River and Into the Trees* it appears as a kind of dream oasis seen from the mainland shore.

When we lunched on Torcello, it was not at the Locanda Cipriani but—for a change—at the more reasonably priced Osteria al Ponte del Diavolo, a fairly new restaurant with a garden shaded by pines and mimosa trees. Our very good meal began with three different starters: *tagliarini alla marinara,* thin, homemade noodles with shrimp and mussels; *tagliarini* with a flavorful medley of mushrooms, peas, tomatoes, and eggplant; and a tangy risotto prepared with scampi and arugula. For our main course we chose a warm vegetable salad of julienne zucchini, eggplant, and roasted bell peppers. Sweet, scented wild strawberries with fluffy zabaglione ended our pleasant luncheon.

On the trip back to the heart of Venice, your boat will most likely pass the white-walled San Michele, the cemetery island. This is the last stop for all Venetians, as it has been for numerous famous foreigners who asked to be buried there. Lord Byron, John Ruskin, and Ezra Pound lie on San Michele, as do Igor Stravinsky and Sergey Diaghilev. I am not surprised by their choice; it is probably the most cheerful cemetery I have ever visited. Massive cypresses line the paths that run between miles of mausoleums and graves, around which sprout a colorful tangle of buttercups, wood anemones, and weeds.

Owing to limited space, however, only the recently deceased are allowed a plot of land on San Michele. The remains of those gone to a better world twenty-five or more years ago are disinterred and placed in a common grave marked by marble plaques decked in a riot of fresh and plastic flowers.

Among the handful of hotels in the world worth splurging on are two of Venice's most luxurious: the Gritti Palace Hotel, on the Grand Canal in San Marco, and the Hotel Cipriani, on the island of La Giudecca, just south of Venice proper. Occupying the fifteenth-century palazzo of the flamboyant womanizer Doge Andrea Gritti, the hotel that bears his name is nothing less than a Venetian dream come true. Owned by the Aga Khan's CIGA hotel group, the Gritti may be best known for its terrace restaurant, from which diners can watch the comings and goings on the Grand Canal. (CIGA also owns the nearby Hotel Danieli, a splendid Gothic palace adorned with silken walls, gilt mirrors, and plush Oriental rugs.)

The Cipriani is located at the tip of La Giudecca near the island of San Giorgio Maggiore, but the separation from the heart of Venice poses no problem, as the hotel's motorboats obligingly whisk guests back and forth. After a day spent braving the city's crowds, I find the Cipriani a comforting place to return to. Set in a tranquil garden of azaleas and oleanders, it has a saltwater pool, a fine restaurant, and views of the lagoon. Some rooms even provide guests with the luxury of facing one of Venice's most spectacular churches: Andrea Palladio's splendid architectural feat, the Church of San Giorgio Maggiore.

Although its first stone was laid in 1566, the church wasn't completed during the architect's lifetime, which was a pity, for it represented his solution to the Renaissance problem of how to put a classical temple front onto a traditional church with a nave and chapels. Ruskin may have thought that nothing could have been "more childish in conception, more servile in plagiarism" than this building, but many others concur with James Morris, who writes: "Nothing is cooler, and whiter, and more austerely reverent than

Palladio's church of San Giorgio Maggiore. . . . The proportions are perfect, the setting is supreme, and from the top of the campanile you get the best view of Venice."

As we strolled through San Giorgio's gardens one evening, we saw a fisherman, framed by a screen of myrtle and holm oak, draw his catch and row slowly away toward the island of San Servolo. At that moment his existence seemed strikingly silent and bereft of companionship, but in fact the people of the lagoon are a vocal and communicative race. They can be seen hailing each other in sign language from boat to boat, exchanging gossip from one laundry-draped window to another, and talking business or just plain shouting at each other in the *calli*. As Henry James observed, Venetians "assist at an eternal *conversazione*."

That night we returned to La Giudecca for dinner at Harry's Dolci, which belongs to Arrigo Cipriani, owner of Harry's Bar, but is more reasonably priced and serves primarily Venetian food. Though its decor probably won't impress you, the restaurant is roomy and quiet, and the food is unusually well prepared.

To start, we ordered jellied consommé with a squeeze of lemon, followed by ricotta- and spinach-filled cannelloni covered with a béchamel sauce tinged with tomato. For our main course, we had chicken with lightly fried peppers and zucchini. As is apparent from the restaurant's name, desserts are its specialty, so save room for them. Having done so ourselves, we were happily able to eat every bit of our *meringata al caffè*, a fluffy spongecake flavored with coffee and topped with meringue.

Our next venture into the lagoon led us southeast toward San Lazzaro degli Armeni and the Lido, but on the way we took a detour to Poveglia. A fan-shaped island with a tall campanile topped by tiles conformed in a pine cone–like design, Poveglia was inhabited by the retired servants of the doge from the ninth century on. Today, however, it is reputed to be abandoned, though the fields and vineyards that we saw surrounding its empty buildings seemed well cared for. Despite our curiosity to discover who the farmers were, our stay on the island was cut short by the abrupt entry onto the scene of three fierce dogs that chased us, growling, back to our motor launch. Clearly, Poveglia should be viewed from a distance.

That's not the case with San Lazzaro degli Armeni, an island that has been home to a monastery of Mechitarist Fathers of the Armenian Catholic Church since 1715, when the republic granted the order both the island and protection from the tyrannical Ottoman Empire. A center for Armenian culture, the monastery harbors one of the world's most complete libraries of Armenian manuscripts and publications. Furthermore, the monastery runs a celebrated polyglot press that can print in thirty-two languages. The monks have also published a magazine continuously for two centuries—a record at which no modern media mogul would sneeze.

Welcoming visitors only on Thursdays and Sundays at 2:45, the monks give a tour of the island that includes their small museum and picture gallery, as well as the room in which Byron devoted many a winter afternoon to learning Armenian. Every day for four months the poet rowed back and forth from San Marco to the island in order to spend time with his teachers. Speaking proudly of Byron as "a devoted friend of Armenia," the monks show visitors his portrait and the pen with which he compiled an Armenian-English dictionary and grammar.

As the seagull flies, the Lido—*the* Lido that lent its name to innumerable bathing spots and cinemas the world over—is a flip-flap away from San Lazzaro. In Byron's time this littoral separating the lagoon from the Adriatic was a sandy wilderness where the poet walked with Shelley—or dallied with his teenage mistress. By 1900, however, the Lido was crowded with oversize grand hotels and the aristocrats and the rich portrayed in Thomas Mann's *Death in*

Venice. Those gloried Belle Epoque days are long past, and the hotels now owe their continued existence to the Venice Film Festival, the Municipal Casino, and business conferences.

To my mind, the Lido has little to do with the magic of Venice. While technically part of the city, it doesn't look like it, mostly because cars and buses are permitted there. For gamblers and beach lovers, however, the island may offer a nice change of pace.

South of the Lido is another long barrier island, little more than a thin sandbar, called Pellestrina. In the early 1700s, after the island was battered by several violent storms, it became apparent that it might well be swept away, endangering all of Venice. To prevent such a catastrophe, the city began to build the Murazzi, sea walls of white Istrian stone that took forty years to raise and ultimately ran the length of the island. *"Ausu Romano—Aere Veneto"* reads the plaque on the wall: "With Roman audacity and Venetian money." From 1782 until the disastrous high-tide flood of 1966, the Murazzi held firm before the sea.

On Pellestrina lie two fishing villages, San Pietro in Volta and (confusingly) Pellestrina, each of which has a very good restaurant. Ristorante da Nane can be found in San Pietro in Volta, and San Marco da Celeste—my favorite—stands beside the water in Pellestrina. We went to the latter on a Sunday, and as we watched, a procession of families of islanders decked out in their best clothes pulled up in fishing boats. The fathers and children would jump out, followed more cautiously by the *mamme* and *nonne* carrying infants in starched dresses and embroidered bibs. For Venetians, such outings are pleasurable competitions of showmanship and noise. The lively conversations in which the families were engrossed on arrival never subsided; they didn't even seem to draw breath while tucking into their four-course meals.

The variety of local fish served at San Marco da Celeste is a wonder in itself. Much of the shellfish is particular to the lagoon and goes by confusing Venetian names: *cicale, lumache, datteri, capelunghe,* and *caparozzoli.* It may perhaps, then, be a blessing that the restaurant doesn't provide a menu. Instead, one delicious course after another is automatically brought to your table. Our waiter left with us first a starter of a mixture of seafood: what he called sea snails, crab served in its shell, tiny octopuses, and *gamberetti di laguna,* which he mysteriously identified as sea crickets.

Next we enjoyed mussels and scallops that had been briefly sautéed in oil, garlic, and parsley, folded together with egg yolk and bread crumbs, and then baked. We hardly had time to comment on how delicious the dish was before the house special arrived: *pasticcio di pesce,* bowls of *tagliolini* in a béchamel sauce with shrimp and sole.

Before bringing us the mixed grill of scampi, crayfish, sole, mullet, monkfish, and eel, the waiter kindly suggested we might like to have a *"riposino"*—a little rest—before tackling the remainder of the meal. The digestive *riposino* proved to be a refreshing lemon and vodka *sorbetto.* During the trip back to our hotel, we all agreed that our lunch at San Marco da Celeste was the best meal we had eaten during our stay in the city.

Our tour of the lagoon's islands may not have been exhaustive, but it was illuminating. Torcello, Murano, the Lido, and the others are as integral a part of Venice and its history as the palazzi on the Grand Canal. Sadly, the clock is ticking for all of Venice's islands, for the level of the Adriatic continues to rise, making the full-moon tides even more threatening than they have been; someday the city that rose from the sea may well return to it. In his "Lines Written Among the Euganean Hills," Shelley wrote forebodingly:

> Sun-girt City, thou has been
> Ocean's child, and then his queen;
> Now is come a darker day,
> And thou soon must be his prey.

But perhaps the tenacious Venetians will yet discover a way to save their home. I, for one, comfort myself with the thought that Venice is much too vain to die.

Hotels

Gritti Palace Hotel, Santa Maria del Giglio, San Marco, 2467, 30124 Venezia (041.79.46.11)

Hotel Cipriani, La Giudecca, 10, 30133 Venezia (041.52.07.744)

Hotel Danieli, Riva degli Schiavoni, 4196, 30122 Venezia (041.52.26.480)

Restaurants

Harry's Dolci, Fondamento San Biagio, La Giudecca, 773 (041.52.24.844)

Locanda Cipriani, Piazza Santa Fosca, 29, Torcello (041.73.01.50)

Osteria al Ponte del Diavolo, Torcello, 10 (041.73.04.01)

Ristorante da Nane, San Pietro in Volta, 282, Pellestrina (041.68.81.00)

San Marco da Celeste, Pellestrina, Isola di Pellestrina (041.96.73.55)

This article originally appeared in the August 1991 issue of *Gourmet*. Copyright © 1991 by Nadia Stancioff. Reprinted with permission of the author.

Pleasures of a Tangled Life

BY JAN MORRIS

∾

editor's note

Like Jan Morris, I, too, have a special affection for the island of Torcello, though I have not (yet) had the pleasure of spending the night. Though this piece is actually from the book *Pleasures of a Tangled Life* (Random House, 1989), it first made its appearance in the November 1989 issue of *European Travel & Life*, and I like it so much that I had to include it.

JAN MORRIS is the author of a great number of wonderful books, most recently *Trieste and the Meaning of Nowhere* (Simon & Schuster, 2001). Among her other works that I particularly adore are *The World of Venice*, *Among the Cities*, *Places*, and *The Matter of Wales*.

Few pleasures I know are more perfectly proportioned than a single night upon the Venetian island of Torcello, the one whose stalwart campanile you see, beyond the leaning tower of Burano, farthest away of all in the northern reaches of the lagoon. It is one of life's rules that most pleasures are too much of a good thing. They go on too long (like opera), they fill you up too much (like plum pudding), they are too wide like America or too hungry like Saint Bernard dogs. Only the very best of them come and go lightly, leaving you satisfied but not sated, with the sweet aftertaste in the mind that follows your awakening from a happy dream.

For me, just such a pleasure is the pleasure of a night in Torcello, even in these times of touristic overkill. By definition it cannot last too long, and by geography it cannot be too overwhelming, for the island is only about a mile around, has a permanent population of less than a hundred, and contains at the most a couple of dozen buildings. There are no cars on it, and no paved roads. That campanile greets its visitors with an easygoing tolerance still, knowing that though they may be here today, they will almost certainly be gone before tomorrow.

What I like to do is to board the slinky excursion launch that, every summer day at noon, takes the international tourists out from Venice for lunch at the Locanda Cipriani, the island's long-celebrated hostelry. This gives me a flashy reentry to Torcello, all among the rich and famous (for if they're not really famous, for the Cipriani lunch they'd better be fairly rich).

The experience offers a piquant mixture of sensations. The launch sails cautiously up the long narrow creek that is the main street of Torcello, beneath a bridge without a parapet (alleged to have been designed by the devil) until it reaches the fulcrum of relative bustle—a moored boat or two, a few spectators hanging around—which marks the presence of the *locanda*. This looks like a modest country tavern. Outside it a few locals sit dozily over glasses of red wine beneath the quayside pergola. Inside there is a garden of flowers, vines, and vegetables, floated among by swallowtail butterflies and supervised by the noble cathedral tower just over the wall.

But in the dappled shade of the restaurant, everything is vigorous greed and gobble, confident accents Parisian, Japanese, or New Yorker, gin fizzes and scampi and shrill laughter between tables. It is like a morality play. When I watch the great pleasure-launch sailing away again after the meal, all sunglasses, designer pants, and now vinous badinage, it is as though the great hard world itself is departing the island, leaving me naive upon its shore.

Not that Torcello is deserted in the afternoon. Not at all. The rich and famous may have gone pulsating away, but the more modest holiday-makers, those who have come on the public water bus, now stroll everywhere around the place. On the green piazza beyond the restaurant, elderly women in straw hats and floral dresses sell lace from a parade of canopied stalls rather as though they are offering sacred souvenirs at a place of pilgrimage. Children burble about the green, playing ball beneath Romanesque arcades, dangling their legs from the rough-hewn stone seat once popularly supposed to have been the throne of Attila the Hun. The attendant at the public lavatories, behind the small museum, comfortably reads a paperback on a kitchen chair in the sunshine, while young people with backpacks sit cross-legged here and there, singing gently discordant folk songs.

They come and go in waves through the afternoon, as the boats from Venice come and go, strolling leisurely up the long path from the landing stage, running down it when they see the upper works of the *vaporetto* sliding up the waterway beyond the foliage. By the early evening thay are gone too. The lace ladies are tying canvas sheets over their stalls, Attila's throne is empty, and the lavatory attendant has disappeared, locking up behind her. A hush descends upon the island and the few score souls that remain upon it. It is time to go for an evening walk.

A man told me once that he found Torcello "dead as old bones." He was speaking, though, as a Londoner, to whom such a half-abandoned place, once a thriving municipality with heaps of money, may well offer funereal vibrations. Actually, by the standard of these generally sterile waters, Torcello is like an animated oasis.

Dusty lanes take me through its fields, past brackish back canals, through plantations of sunflowers sagging with the weight of their blossom, beside meadows of indeterminate vegetables and indefinable salad plants, where solitary men are still laboring away with hoes in the gloaming, or tinkering with mechanical cultivators. Here and there a homestead stands in its garden rich in the blues and yellows of homely cottage flowers. Up a reedy creek a fisherman rows his boat from the lagoon, standing cross-oared in the old Venetian way.

Dead as bones indeed! Tadpoles squirm in the little rivulets, beetles stalk the grasses, seabirds squawk, hens and pigeons scrabble in yards, ginger cats eye me, dogs bark out of sight, lizards flick on fenceposts, tall asphodels stir in the breeze from the Adriatic. A distant bell rings across the lagoon, from Burano perhaps, or from the cypress-shrouded monastery of San Francesco del Deserto, and with a laborious gasp the great bell of Torcello itself awakens to boom mellow and melancholy through the twilight.

So night falls, and I feel myself enfolded in velvet privacy among the waters. All alone I wander after dinner through the quiet shadowy monuments of Torcello's lost consequence, its domes and its arcades, its crumbled pillars and indecipherable plaques, its campanile half-hidden in the darkness above. There is nobody about but me, unless some of those backpackers have unrolled their sleeping bags beneath the cathedral cloister; only me, the mosquitoes, the frogs that leap around my feet, and the little bats that forage in and out of the lamplight.

In the morning the swallows have taken over, whirling dizzily around the bell tower and the chimney pots. Now, after breakfast in the *locanda* garden, I look once more at the monuments. I have known them for nearly forty-five years, but I feel it my duty. Besides, they are not only few but marvelous. It was to this sedgy island, fifteen centuries ago, that the first of all the Venetians came as fugitives; the little cluster of buildings that is Torcello now represents the true beginning of all that we mean, all the dazzle and the beauty, all the power and the fizz and the sadness, when we speak the name of Venice.

What a claim! And what monuments, concentrated as they are within the space of a couple of hundred yards! Cool and calm is the simple domed form of the Church of Santa Fosca, as though some lovely outhouse, a dairy, a princely stable, has been converted for holy use. Infinitely touching is the lonely figure of the Madonna, high in her mosaic apse, that greets you in the bleached stoniness of the cathedral. Peculiar stone objects of unimaginable age litter the sacred purlieus, and it is a fine thing to sit on Attila's throne, before the children arrive, looking across the tiled domes to the mighty tower above. From time to time the bell whirringly assembles its energies again to announce that another Torcello hour has passed.

Twelve noon, it strikes. Time for a last meal at the house beside that demonic bridge. I ate my way into Torcello with the jet set; I eat my way out with the Italians, for the people who order their seafood salad or spaghetti with clams at the Osteria al Ponte del Diavolo come mostly from Padua, Vicenza, Treviso, or Venice itself. This gives the restaurant an organic, family feel, very pleasant to take with a glass of wine and one of the rough rolls that, distributed from table to table out of big wicker baskets, constitute Torcello's very bread of life. Merrily flows the conversation. Happily flows the wine. Imperceptibly turns the cycle of the island's life. I am hardly through the cheese when, looking up across the patio, I catch sight of today's boatload of cosmopolitans, looking just like yesterday's, sailing well-fed back to Venice from the *locanda* up the way.

Heavens, my own *vaporetto* leaves at two-fifteen! I pay the bill, I tip them well, I grab my bags and sprint to the landing stage just in time to see the humped shape of the Number 12 foaming up from Burano. And if I'm not in time? Well, I can always catch the next one; or I can start all over again, stay another night after all, with the frogs, the swallows, the mosquitoes, and the great grunting bell of the cathedral, and see how far a rule of life can be stretched—for to tell you the truth, two nights in Torcello is a pleasure I have never tried.

Biblioteca

Art and Life in Renaissance Venice, Patricia Fortini Brown, Harry N. Abrams, 1997. This paperback volume is one in the excellent Perspectives series published by Abrams. (Other editions feature *Renaissance Florence, The Art of Renaissance Rome, Gothic Art, Islamic Art,* and so on.) Brown—also the author of *Venice & Antiquity,* below—has reconstructed the visual world experienced by Venetians during the Renaissance in this book, profusely illustrated with color photographs and reproductions of paintings, drawings, book illustrations, and other related artworks. Within approximately 160 pages, Brown succinctly presents a slice of Venetian life during the Renaissance, revealing how the citizens of Venice lived during this time period, how its art differed from that of mainland Italy, and how, in fact, Venice itself was a "world apart in the nature of her participation in the Renaissance in Italy." (The first chapter is entitled "Venezianita: The Otherness of the Venetians," which is essential reading on its own.) Obviously, travelers with a serious interest in the Venetian Renaissance will seek works that are more thorough than this, but I think this is an outstanding introductory volume for everyone else.

A History of Venice, John Julius Norwich, Alfred A. Knopf, 1982 (hardcover); Vintage Books, 1989 (paperback). "First experiences should be short and intense," Norwich writes in the introduction to this superb book. He continues, "When my parents took me to Venice in the summer of 1946, we stayed only a few hours; but I can still feel—not remember, *feel*—the impact it made on my sixteen-year-old brain. With his usual blend of firmness and commonsense, my father limited to two the buildings we actually entered: the Basilica of St. Mark and Harry's Bar. For the rest of the time, wandering on foot or drifting gently in a gondola, I subconsciously absorbed the first essential Venentian lesson—a lesson, incidentally, that poor Ruskin, beavering away at his crockets and cusps round the Doges' Palace, never learnt: that in Venice, more than anywhere else, the whole is greater than the sum of the parts." While the family walked, Norwich's father talked about Venetian history, about this extraordinary city that had been mistress of the Mediterranean. In fact, Norwich senior had intended to write a definitive history of Venice, an opportunity that was lost to him when he passed away in 1954. Norwich junior took up the task, and though he is sincere when he admits that his only regret in writing this book is that it fell to him instead of to his father, "who would have done it so much more brilliantly," I cannot see how it is possible that anyone could have written a better history. In a review of it, writer Jan Morris referred to it as "the standard Venetian history in English, indispensable." Readers simply must start with this book. It's not a light read at 639 pages, but as Norwich notes, it's not a work of profound scholarship, so the narrative moves along at a good clip. The book is divided into four sections: "The Barbarian Invasion to the Fourth Crusade," "The Imperial Expansion," "A Power in Europe," and "Decline and Fall." There are five accompanying maps, two inserts of black-and-white photos, and a list of doges. *Essenziale.*

Letters from the Palazzo Barbaro, Henry James, edited by Rosella Mamoli Zorzi, Pushkin Press, London, 1998. James's letters are well known by anyone who reads even the tiniest bit about Venice, and they are available in several editions; but I particularly like this one, a beautifully printed paperback edition—sporting a textured blue cover with a watercolor illustration of the Palazzo Ducale—small enough to fit in a handbag or other tote. On the Grand Canal and quite close to the Accademia Bridge, the Palazzo Barbaro was home, in the 1880s, to Daniel and Ariana Curtis, a distinguished Boston couple. The Curtises sometimes rented the palazzo to another Bostonian, Isabella Stewart Gardner (who, Boston area readers know, built her own Venetian palazzo and filled it with a magnificent art collection that is now a museum), and over the years and generations a great number of other remarkable guests—including James, Robert Browning, John Singer Sargent, and Claude Monet—were guests at the Barbaro. James's letters reveal much and are entertaining, but this collection also includes letters by Curtis family members, and I find them equally as engaging, especially the last one, written by the Curtis's son, Ralph, and dated 2 September 1915: "Venice is like a lovely prima donna in deep mourning. All the gilded angels wear sack-cloth painted dirty grey. Anything that shines is covered. At night all is as black as in the dark ages. . . . All the hotels but the Danieli's are hospitals. No antiquaire is open. The only foreigners are those who own places here. Nobody is allowed to paint or photograph. At night the waiters at Florian's give change with pocket electric lamps for a moment on the table. . . . We are so exhilarated by the good news from all the fronts. At last the beginning of the end seems in sight, but we expect still another winter of it, and possibly 18 months." A thoughtful touch is a final memoir by Patricia Curtis Vigano, granddaughter of Ralph. Her recollection, in the words of Zorzi, gives us a "glimpse of a palace that has survived Napoleonic plunders and spoliation, ruin and wars, to continue the tradition of art, history, and of civilization into the next century."

My Venice, Harold Brodkey, Metropolitan Books/Henry Holt & Co., 1998. Brodkey first visited Venice in 1960, and this book gathers passages from several of his best works with previously unpublished notes and essays, along with photographs by Italian photographer Giuseppe Bruno. I'm sorry to say I had never read any Brodkey before I picked up this beautifully printed little book, so I did not recognize the essays that were excerpted from his other works. I found some of them insightful, but cannot say I agree with the publisher that the book deserves a place beside the works of John Ruskin and Mary McCarthy. Brodkey fans, however, will, I think, enjoy it very much.

Preserving the World's Great Cities: The Destruction and Renewal of the Historic Metropolis, Anthony Tung, Clarkson Potter, 2001. Though this excellent book—a first-of-its-kind account—features twenty-two of the world's great cities, Venice is one of them, so I include it here for the excellent chapter "Tourism Versus the Habitable City." As Tung notes, "Saving Venice is one of the most complex urban conservation problems in the world. As in other great cities, historic architectural preservation in Venice is not separable from the larger and intertwined issues of the whole metropolis—economic, social, political, and environmental. Nor are the quandaries of any city divorced from the broader developmental dilemmas of its nation and region. Yet Venice is more complicated. Its singularity as a historic built environment and the way these special characteristics clash with the forces that determine the vitality of modern cities is the reason. Its problems are extraordinary because there really is no other place—and has never been any other place—quite like it." This chapter is required reading for any serious visitor to Venice. Other Mediterranean cities included in the book are Athens, Cairo, and Jerusalem.

The Stones of Venice, John Ruskin, edited by J. G. Links, Da Capo Press, 1985; originally published by Hill and Wang, 1960. *The Stones of Venice,* is, of course, *the* classic work above all others on Venice. "By any standards," notes author Sarah Quill (just below), *"The Stones of Venice* was a massive undertaking; unrivalled in the beauty of its prose, Ruskin's survey of the buildings of Venice laid the foundations for art and architectural historians of the future." It is rather difficult to come across the original work, published in 1853, which consisted of 450,000 words in three volumes. (I've never seen it, though I'm told that serious students of architecture should try every means to find a set.) But this abridged version, by the wonderful J. G. Links, is no less scholarly or significant than the original. As Links explains in his introduction, Ruskin himself admitted that the 450,000 words of the original was a lot, and he published his own "abstract" as the traveler's edition in 1877. This edition was actually reduced to a quarter of its original length, but Ruskin left out some very fine passages and essays. Links, for the Da Capo Press edition, included much that Ruskin omitted and "left out many of what were, no doubt, his favorite parts, especially on Decoration." This abridged edition will serve both Ruskin's newcomers and established fans well. As *essenziale* as it is, however—and I know this will be blasphemous to diehard Ruskin fans—I recently decided I do not feel every interested visitor to Venice needs to read this book. When I first read it, in college, I devoured every word and filled half a notebook with drawings of architectural elements. But when I picked it up again recently, I came to the conclusion that Ruskin is not only not essential for casual visitors but also potentially not essential for even the most well-meaning literate travelers. I recommend *The Stones of Venice* as *essenziale* to those with an academic interest in architecture and as optional to everyone else. What I recommend as *essenziale* to *everyone* is *Ruskin's Venice: The Stones Revisited* (Sarah Quill, Ashgate Publishing, Hants, England, and Brookfield, Vermont, 2000). This brilliant project pairs selected passages from *Stones* with contemporary color and black-and-white photographs as well as Ruskin's own drawings and watercolors. Not every single building Ruskin mentioned is featured; Quill identified and photographed those buildings and details about which Ruskin had something definite to say, and rearranged the material into broad chronological sequence to help provide a visual guide to his aesthetic argument. "This compilation does not include paintings or interiors; it concentrates on the exterior architecture and sculpture described in the *Stones,* all of which may be seen from the street, or from the water, without entering a building." I think that what Ruskin *really* wanted people to do was *really* look at buildings. I'm not sure his great work would encourage every reader to do so, but I do think that Quill's wonderful book (even though it's hardcover, it's not too heavy to bring along) will encourage many travelers to reread or discover the observations of the master. As Quill notes, "For the traveller in Venice, Ruskin is still an entertaining and persuasive guide to the architecture of the city, which has changed remarkably little in its outline since his day." In addition to the buildings featured, there are chapters on Byzantine, Gothic, and Renaissance architecture in Venice, plus excerpts from letters, key dates, and—my favorite—a photo of the plaque dedicated to Ruskin in the Calcina on the Zattere, complete with the English translation.

Venetian Colour: Marble, Mosaic, Painting and Glass, 1250–1550, Paul Hills, Yale University Press, 1999. Hills, an Italian Renaissance art historian, explores for the first time Venetian color in relation to social, cultural, and environmental forces. He argues that Venetian color—in buildings, table glass, and dress as well as paintings—was the product of a lagoon site and a mercantile culture. He notes that there is no perceived relation between the land and the materials of the city—the materials of Venetian buildings were and still are brought from a distance. "In its unique location Venice, cut off from the earth, invited celestial comparison: the reaction of the Irish visitor of 1323 anticipates many a later eulogy: 'it is completely set in the sea, yet by the name of its beauty and the merit of its elegance it could be set between the star Arcturus and the shining Pleiades.'" It's not just that this book is beautiful; it's one of the few books to feature the close-up details of paintings, mosaic floors, frames, glass, and marble. *Essenziale.*

Venetian Life, W. D. Howells, with illustrations by Joseph Pennell, The Marlboro Press/Northwestern University Press, Evanston, Illinois, 2001; first published in 1866. Howells, an American who wrote a campaign biography of Abraham Lincoln, was rewarded for his efforts with the job of consul in Venice in 1860. Though he also served as the editor of the *Atlantic Monthly* and *Harper's* and wrote novels and dramas, he may be best known for his travel books about Italy. (*Italian Journeys* is his other famous book, profiled in my *Central Italy* edition.) Howells stayed in Venice for four years and was there at a crucial time in the city's history: when the Austrians were still in power and Venice was on the brink of becoming part of Italy. He noted then that "the present situation has now endured five years, with only slight modifications by time, and only faint murmurs from some of the more impatient, that *bisogna, una volta o l'altra romper il chiodo* (sooner or later the nail must be broken). As the Venetians are a people of indomitable perseverance, long schooled to obstinacy by oppression, I suppose they will hold out till their union with the kingdom of Italy." This is a classic, and sincere thanks go to the Marlboro Press and Northwestern University Press for establishing the Marlboro Travel series and bringing works like these back into print.

Venice & Antiquity: The Venetian Sense of the Past, Patricia Fortini Brown, Yale University Press, 1996. You will often read that Venice, unlike other Italian cities such as Rome and Florence, had no "antique" past of its own, so during the city's Golden Age—the thirteenth through the sixteenth centuries— Venetian authorities determined to create an image of Venice for posterity that might not have been exactly "antique" but was nonetheless unique and worthy, and which only Venice was capable of carrying out with skill. This ground-breaking book includes various writings, travel accounts, and art to illustrate the ways in which Venice successfully endowed herself with a new, richer past. Brown details how the city was influenced by antiquity, its Byzantine heritage, and its own historical experience. With numerous black-and-white and color illustrations and photographs, this is excellent and *essenziale.*

Venice & the East, Deborah Howard, Yale University Press, 2000. John Pemble, in *Venice Rediscovered* (below), wrote that to the British and French, Venice was more Oriental than much of the Orient. "The idea that Venice was Oriental probably accounts for a lot of the uncertainty and ambivalence in early nineteenth-century evaluations of the city. Visitors had difficulty in making up their minds about Venice because they had not yet made up their minds about the Orient. During the eighteenth century European hostility to the Islamic Orient had softened. . . . Goethe said that we are all Muslims. . . . The East was certainly no longer everything it had been. However, it had not out-lived all its traditional associations. . . . Though Islam in the Holy Land was no longer offensive, Islam in Greece was. Goethe said we are all Muslims, but Shelley said we are all Greeks; and much of the opprobrium shed by the Arabs was inherited by the Turks. In the philhellenism of Byron, Shelley, and Hugo, the old hatred of the Saracen lingers and the old horror of things Oriental persists." Jan Morris, too, in *The World of Venice* (below), wrote, "As I lean bemused against my pillar in this place, and let my mind wander, I find that Venice fades around me, west turns to east, Christian to Muslim, Italian to Arabic, and I am back in some dust-ridden, fly-blown golden market of the Middle East, the tumble-down *suk* at Amman, or the bazaars beside the Great Mosque of the Ummayads, in the distant sunshine of Damascus. . . . In Venice, as any gilded cockatrice will tell you, the East begins." I remember the first time I was in Venice, I stood in Piazza San Marco looking at the basilica thinking to myself, "It looks so . . . *Eastern*," though at this time of my life I had not yet been anywhere east of, well, Venice. I have been fascinated ever since by the associations of both East and West that are a part of Venice's history, and I was so pleased, therefore, to learn of architectural historian Howard's shared interest in this subject. It doesn't take long to ascertain the near-obsession the Venetians had (presumably they don't still) with their Arab trading partners: earrings in the shape of Moors' heads; the figures of two Moors ringing the bell on top of the clock tower on Piazza San Marco; words that derived from Arabic—*arsenale* is from *dar as-sina*—and the Campo dei Mori are only a few of the more obvious examples. This book is beautiful, with marbelized endpapers and loads of color and black-and-white photos and reproductions. But more important, it is an extraordinary work of research that is immensely interesting and rewarding to read—even if you have not spent much time thinking about the effect of Islam on Venice. In her foreword, Howard explains that hers is a book not about Orientalism or the Orient but about "the response of medieval Venice to the experience of oriental travel and its effect on the architecture of the city." When she first set out to write the book, she intended to address the cliché that assumes an oriental impact on the townscape of Venice. She felt her main task would be to carefully compare the visual characteristics between the architecture of Venice and that of the Islamic world, to discover similarities, differences, and "borrowings." "But the further I explored, the more I had to face up to the problematic nature of 'influence,' especially when it crossed a religious boundary. Fundamental questions accumulated and the vastness of the arena became daunting." So Howard restricted the scope of her inquiry to concentrate on an area roughly equivalent to the biblical world, an area of primary interest to the Crusaders—who departed for the Holy Land from Venice—and to Venice herself as it was crucial for her continued trade with Alexandria and Syria. As Howard notes, "It will be evident to the reader that the subject of east-west cultural transfer cannot be neatly wrapped and sealed." Geographic areas she could not, therefore, include in this project were Byzantium ("contact with Constantinople before 1453 did not involve the negotiation of a major religious divide that underlies my topic") and Greece ("I have leapfrogged over this transit point in order not to lose sight of the primary focus of my topic"). Howard examines the experiences of Venetian merchants overseas, focusing on their links with Egypt, Syria, and Palestine, and she argues that many of these merchants gained insight into Islamic culture through personal contacts with their trading partners. In the event you momentarily forget the Eastern association as you wander around Venice, just take a step back into the ducal chapel of San Marco, where you will be standing beneath the twelfth-century mosaics of the Pentecost dome, "the expression of the power of the apostolic mission to spread the Gospels across cultural boundaries. At the summit of the dome floats the dove of the Holy Spirit, source of the universal meaning of the Word of God. Here, in a curious transformation of the *Etimasia,* or empty chair, of Byzantine art, instead of soaring through the heavens the dove rests on a bed of rich oriental cushions and rugs. The image seems to invoke the power of Venetian traders to transport the Holy Spirit with their cargoes of textiles and spices, just as they carried the body of Saint Mark to its Venetian resting place. Immediately the blurring of trade and religion becomes apparent. In his account of the *translatio* a century later, Martino da Canal was to remark that, when Saint Mark's tomb was opened, a sweet smell emerged 'as if all the spices of the world had been brought to Alexandria.' In the Venetian consciousness, the world of the early Christian martyrs was inextricably bound up with their own mercantile fortunes in the lands of the apostolic missions." *Essenziale.*

Venice: The Biography of a City, Christopher Hibbert, HarperCollins, 1988. A word from the author himself may be the best introduction to this book and may clarify for readers, as it did for me, why he wrote it in the first place: "To add yet another to the great number of books about Venice requires a few words of explanation, perhaps even of apology. This book makes no attempt to rival John Julius Norwich's splendid history of Venice from the earliest times to the fall of the Republic in 1797. Nor does it pretend to compete either with James Morris's marvelous evocation of the city, or with the excellent guides by Hugh Honour, J. G. Links, Alta Macadam and the indispensable Giulio Lorenzetti. . . . It is intended for the general reader, as a well illustrated introduction to the history of Venice and of the social life of its people from the days of the earliest settlements on the islands of the Lagoon to the floods of 1966 and the Venice of today." Hibbert, in my opinion, need not make apologies: this is one of the finest books ever penned about Venice and belongs on the *essenziale* shelf with those other works he mentions. He has divided the book into three parts, the first two taking readers from 500 to 1987, and the third—which makes the book even more valuable than a biography—features a glossary, list of doges, notes on buildings and works of art, museums and art galleries, an excellent one-page essay on the gondola, and sources for further reading. Italophile readers will recognize historian Hibbert as the author of *Florence: The Biography of a City* and *Rome: The Biography of a City,* as well as others on various aspects of Italy.

Venice: The City and Its Architecture, Richard Goy, Phaidon Press, 1997. True fans and students of Venetian architecture will want to borrow or buy this outstanding book. Certainly I can do no better than John Julius Norwich in the foreword in explaining its virtues: "Countless books are written about the Serenissima, and I seem to have contributed forewords to a good many of them; but it has seldom been my good fortune to introduce a work as remarkable as that which you now hold in your hands. The author is not content to describe the Stones of Venice; he roots them firmly in their historical context, discussing not just the buildings themselves but why and how they came to be built, the purposes for which they were intended and even the degree to which those purposes were fulfilled." Besides the exceptional quality of the photos and reproductions for which Phaidon is known, this book stands out because the author advances on all previous works in depth and scope, and he does not take a chronological approach to the city's architecture. Rather, he has chosen four nuclei of the city—the Piazza, the Arsenale, the Ghetto, and the Rialto—to focus on. As Norwich says, "Each of them is in its way a product of Venice's unique way of government and outlook on life; each casts its own revealing light on the city and its people." It's a lot to read (there are 303 pages, plus the notes, glossary, and biographical notes on the architects), but each chapter is very well written and interesting. A fold-out map is at the back with a key to buildings' locations. *Essenziale* for those who are genuinely interested in Venetian architecture and history.

Venice: The Golden Age, 697–1797, Alvise Zorzi, Abbeville Press, 1980. Zorzi, a native-born Venetian and author of several important books on the art, history, and politics of Venice, here presents an extremely complete compendium of Venice that includes art, history, politics, and much more. Chapters include "Venetiae Caput Mundi," "The Keys to Power," "The Venetian Empire," "The Love of the Subjects," "The Territories of St. Mark," "Mercantile Enterprise," "Wars, Armies, Victories, Defeats," and "Eleven Centuries of Independence—Why?". Some of the sections I like best are those on the Arsenale, the Palazzo Ducale, Venetian building methods in the lagoon, and Venetian palazzi, each with diagrams and cross-section drawings. Also, aside from the lavish color and black-and-white photos, reproductions, and illustrations (more than 340), an extremely handy fifteen-page political chronology is found at the back of the book, along with lists of the doges of Venice, the patrician families (those still in existence, those now extinct, and the main non-Venetian families admitted to the patriciate, the regiments at the fall of the republic, and a glossary of Venetian place names. If you're seeking a large illustrated book of high quality that focuses on Venice's most famous span of years, this is one you'll want to consider. *Essenziale.*

Venice: Its History, Art, Industries and Modern Life, Charles Yriarte, translated from the French by F. J. Sitwell, International Press, John C. Winston Co., Philadelphia, n.d. This is a rare volume that I don't expect you to find easily, but if you collect old books on Venice, or if you simply appreciate quality bookbinding and good—though dated—writing, you might want to search for this volume, which features more than twenty-five black-and-white illustrations protected by tissue paper. The text could be said to be old-fashioned, but it is old-fashioned in the best sense. In the first chapter, we are reminded that "while Europe was yet plunged in the darkness of the Middle Ages, the Venetians went to the only two civilized peoples of our hemisphere, the Arabs and the Greeks, to borrow from them the elements of their delicate and exquisite arts. The more familiar we grow with the history of Venice, the more we come to marvel at the practical common sense of this handful of human beings, who, by the fourteenth or fifteenth century, were making more noise in the world, and filling a greater place, than the populations of the largest empires."

Venice: A Cultural and Literary Companion, Martin Garrett, foreword by Michael Dibdin, Interlink Books, Northampton, Massachusetts, 2001. This is one volume in Interlink's Cities of the Imagination series. Though it features a great number of monuments, museums, palazzi, churches, synagogues, and *scuole,* it's not a guidebook per se. The series is meant to offer in-depth cultural and historical guides to some of the world's greatest cities, and each book introduces visitors to the city's present-day identity and its links with the past. This Venice edition is divided into ten chapters, with the themes of history, monuments, the doges, palaces, islands of the lagoon, theater, religion, and literature, and one on the Veneto towns of Padua, Vicenza, and Verona. It is marvelously interesting, and the first two chapters on historic Venice—"Rise of a City State" and "The Long Decline"—are well written and succinct; they are, in fact, one of the best short histories of the city I've read. Garrett, in his preface, reminds us, "There is no substitute for going to Venice. The experience can, however, be enhanced by reading about the place. You can profitably read the long history of the Venetian republic. More poetically you can, say, wander in Henry James' Venice until it becomes part of your own." No photographs, but with black-and-white drawings.

Venice, Lion City: The Religion of Empire, Garry Wills, Simon & Schuster, 2001. Much-published historian Garry Wills has, with this book, added an important work to the groaning shelves of books on Venice. He has chosen to focus on Venice in the fifteenth and sixteenth centuries, when it was a "ruthless imperial city," not when it was a decadent and declining city. Wills also relates the history of the city to its art, which in turn illuminates the art through the city's history; more than 130 black-and-white and color photographs and artwork reproductions are featured. Among the many memorable passages for thought in this wonderful book is the following: "Venice poses a special problem for Americans, since we sometimes criticize ourselves, or feel uneasy about, what has been called our 'exceptionalism'—the belief that we are better than other nations, specially blessed, with a right to do things forbidden to lesser peoples. If that strain ever did exist in our history, it is infinitesimal next to the Venetian sense of superiority to other human beings. The whole myth of Venice is simply exceptionalism writ large. According to it, Venetians were the favorites of Christ, Mary, and Saint Mark. Their city's birth was miraculous. Their doge was a spiritual leader better than the monarchs who ruled elsewhere. He stood above popes and emperors—though not above the republic he served. That myth would become harder and harder to sustain as the empire fell away— Cyprus lost in the sixteenth century, then Crete in the seventeenth. Bravado tried to cover this decline with Baroque swagger, but the trappings of power call themselves in question when the reality of power is going or gone. There was one tempering element to the Venetian exceptionalism: at least it did think of itself as the exception among nations, not as a model for them. It had no missionary sense that it should spread its values to other people. Americans believed that we should not be an exception but a pattern. Others should emulate us. Our man from the North, John Winthrop, said it in 1630: 'He [God] shall make us a praise and glory, that men shall say of succeeding plantations, "The Lord make it like that of New England." For we must consider that we shall be a city upon a hill . . .' Our man from the South, Thomas Jefferson, said it in 1801, calling America 'the world's best hope.' Our man from the then-West, Abraham Lincoln, said it in 1854: 'The succeeding millions of free happy people, the world over, shall rise up and call us blessed to the latest generation.' Though Venice praised republicanism in general, a sense of its unique birth and circumstances meant that it never seriously thought there could be other Venices. It had this virtue in its megalomania, that it was not a redeemer nation, not a savior of others, only of itself. It was not out to convert or crusade, only to trade. It joined Crusades for what was in it for Venice, but it could always strike a deal with the other side. Its very worldliness made it tolerant of anyone who could offer a market. Venice had no *libido dominandi,* only a *libido vendendi,* a vendor's compulsion. This freed it from a lot of pious bullying in the Kipling vein. If Venice dominated its imperial holdings, this was done only so far as domination could be made profitable. People's souls were left alone as the merchants of the Rialto went after their purses." *Essenziale.*

Venice Observed, Mary McCarthy, Harcourt Brace Jovanovich, San Diego, 1963; originally published in 1956 in an edition that included both text and illustrations. I have, unfortunately, never seen the 1956 edition of this wonderful book, but if it's anything like the original illustrated edition of McCarthy's *The Stones of Florence,* I am most unfortunate, indeed. When I picked up my little paperback copy to review for this book, I noticed I had highlighted entire pages with a yellow marker. McCarthy was that sort of writer, her every observation memorable and quotable, irresistible to the pen, colored sticky-note, or bookmark. Whether you read it before you go (for the first time), or bring it along (it's a 158-page paperback), or reread it (for the tenth time), it's *essenziale.*

Venice Rediscovered, John Pemble, Oxford University Press, 1996. In this engaging paperback, Pemble explores the origins of our (Americans and Europeans) modern passion for Venice. In the introduction, he makes the observation that were Canaletto to return to Venice a hundred years after his death in 1768, he would not find the city to be drastically altered from the days when he was recording the city in paint for foreigners. (This is essentially true today as well.) But "a rare example of conspicuous change was in the increasing dilapidation and shabbiness of Venice, especially in its outlying areas. The change in perception is registered by the fact that this evidence of deterioration made the city not less but more attractive. . . . In the early 1800s Venice had been generally regarded as an odd and rather depressing wreck which could qualify as beautiful only when seen at a distance or by moonlight. By the end of the century the most fastidious sensibility was not only able but eager to contemplate the detail of its ruin." The three chapters of the book are "Unwritten History," "History Rewritten," and "Beyond History," followed by an epilogue and including black-and-white photographs in a twelve-page insert, one of which is of the original Accademia Bridge.

Venice Revealed: An Intimate Portrait, Paolo Barbaro, translated by Tami Calliope, photographs by Ken Aiken, Steerforth Italia (an imprint of Steerforth Press), South Royalton, Vermont, 2001. The Steerforth Italia imprint was new at the time I was working on my *Central Italy* book, and I made special mention of it in its *"La Bella Vita"* section. Its mission is to introduce American readers to fine books by Italians and about Italy. "The Italians," as the editors note in the Steerforth catalog, "have created one of the great national literatures of the twentieth century. . . . Above all the Italians have created a great literature of witness to the central struggle of the [twentieth] century between democracy and Fascism. Ignazio Silone and Natalia Ginzburg described the onset of Fascist authoritarianism under Benito Mussolini before the Second World War. Giorgio Bassani related the terrible fate of the Italian Jews in the Holocaust. Elsa Morante chronicled the everyday hardships of life during the war, and Carlo Levi recreated the heartbreaking chaos of a shattered Italian society when the war was finally over." This Venice book is the only one the imprint has introduced so far dealing with northeastern Italy, but I encourage readers to seek out the other titles Steerforth Italia has published, notably *Open*

City: Seven Writers in Postwar Rome, edited and with an introduction by William Weaver; *The Time of Indifference* by Alberto Moravia; and *Women of the Shadows: Wives and Mothers of Southern Italy* by Ann Cornelisen. (You may contact Steerforth Press directly at P.O. Box 70, South Royalton, Vermont 05068; 802-763-2808; fax: -2818; www.steerforth.com/italia.htm for further information about all its excellent titles, or inquire at your favorite bookstore.) The Venice that Barbaro presents to us is a journey of rediscovery (he returns after having left years ago to live and work in a number of other cities around the world), and it is the most balanced contemporary work we have on the city. As such, as you can imagine, it is honest in ways some travelers may not want to know about. "All that's going on already is deeply disturbing: exodus, pollution, deteriorations of every kind, holes in the bank of the canals, oil tankers trafficking in the middle of the lagoon, chemical wastes whose dangers we can't even guess at spewing out into the water along the whole shore from Marghera to Venice, toxic fumes unfurling into the sky, newer and deeper excavations in the goddamned channel for the big oil tankers, environmental imbalances of all kinds, *acque alte* ever higher and more frequent year after year, *acque basse* ever lower—all within, or a hand's breadth away from, the most beautiful, delicate city in the world. As if it were the safest and most protected place on the planet; or as if it were the most ignoble, the basest, the most utterly superfluous. But it's *Venice*. And all this, and all that seems to be headed our way in the future, is perhaps the threat that frightens us most, to the depths of our souls, whether we're Venetians or not; perhaps nothing could break our hearts more completely than the possibility of part or all of it sinking, the thought of this fragile miracle drowning, submerged beneath the waters from which it was created." Everything has changed and nothing has changed. "Now you might say there's no place in the city untouched by the great touristic machine in one way or another; no way to get there. That strange fascination, those voices are lost. We don't have many others to substitute for them, in Venice or in the world." As if we needed to hear it again, a waitress named Manuela tells Barbaro that Venice is "a whole other thing, it's as far away as America. *Anyplace* is different from here—it's *terrafirma,* country, continent . . . Mestre or Milan, Italy or America . . . it's not *here."* Finally, Barbaro can tell us that "even at its most derelict and degraded, this city-that-is-entirely-a-work-of-art is still wholly lived in and livable." *Essenziale.*

Venice 360°, photographs by Attilio Boccazzi-Varotto, sketches by Marco Filaferro, Random House, 1987. This is a volume in the 360° series, which I very much admire, but I think this Venice edition may be of benefit most of all from the large format and pull-out panoramas. The image of Piazza San Marco and the four-panel fold-out of the view of the city looking toward Mestre are the best I've ever seen. Anyone who's ever tried to take pictures in Venice can truly appreciate how valuable these views are: Venice is a city that completely lends itself to the panoramic style. In addition to the photos, there is a very good picture-by-picture section of explanatory captions that identify the landmarks pictured and give some of their historical and artistic context. Great to look at before you go, but even better to save for when you get home. And a wonderful gift for your favorite fan of Venezia.

Venice and the Veneto, photographs by Sonja Bullaty and Angelo Lomeo, text by Sylvie Durastanti, Abbeville Press, 1998. This beautiful coffeetable book is by the same winning team that produced some other favorite books on Provence and Tuscany. The multitude of photos of *La Serenissima*, the islands of the lagoon, and the villas, villages, and landscapes of the Veneto is a reminder of how we should all be living.

The Venetian Empire: A Sea Voyage, Jan Morris, Harcourt Brace Jovanovich, 1980. After the success of *The World of Venice* (below) Morris, by 1980, was the perfect candidate to create this book, which I absolutely love. What she has done here is to map the Venetian empire, so instead of a book about the history of Venice's conquests, this is a book about those all those ports of call and what life was like under the Venetians. So we visit many coastal cities of the former Yugoslavia, Corfu, the Cyclades, much of the coast of Greece, Cyprus, and Constantinople. Morris writes, "These islands, capes and cities of the sea were distant reflections of a much greater image. It is only proper that we start our journey through them, as we shall end it, in the very eye of the sun, on the brilliant and bustling waterfront before the palace of the Doges." Profusely illustrated with color and black-and-white photographs and reproductions, and including map endpapers, a gazetteer, and a chronology. *Essenziale.*

The World of Venice, Jan Morris, Harvest (Harcourt Brace & Co.), 1960, 1974, 1993. The third revised edition of this wonderful book (1993) includes a new foreword, which I'm especially happy about because Morris had the opportunity to present her observations about Venice over a period of time, revisiting it so to speak, and it isn't often readers are given such a special perspective. She reveals that when she first knew Venice, at the very end of the Second World War, the city retained a "sense of strange isolation, of separateness, which had made it for so many centuries unique in Europe." She liked this mixture of sadness and flamboyance, but by the 1970s Venice was different: it had captured the concern of the world after the disastrous flood of 1966, and with all the attention came the world's desire to spiff it up, make Venice new and exciting. Morris missed the *tristesse,* however, and thought she had fallen out of love with the city. Eventually, though, she came to terms with Venice, which she notes has "for better or for worse, got over some kind of historical hump. . . . Contemporary Venice is what it is: a grand (and heavily overbooked) exhibition, which can also play useful, honourable, but hardly monumental roles in the life of the new Europe." She concludes that she cannot pretend she still feels the same way about Venice as she once did. "Though Venice no longer compels me back quite so bemused year after year to her presence, I hope this record of old ecstasies will still find its responses among my readers, and especially among those who, coming to the Serenissima fresh, young and exuberant as I did, will recognize their own pleasures in these pages, and see a little of themselves in me." Though this is decidedly not a guidebook, Chapter 21, "To the Prodigies," contains some Venetian sights Morris feels are most worth seeing. There are two sixteen-page inserts of black-and-white photos (some not very good, but that only makes them more charming) and a very thorough chronology. The final page includes the most wonderful parting shot of Venice I've read anywhere: "When at last you leave these waters, pack away your straw hat and swing out to sea, all the old dazzle of Venice will linger in your mind; and her smell of mud, incense, fish, age, filth and velvet will hang around your nostrils; and the soft lap of her back-canals will echo in your ears; and wherever you go in life you will feel somewhere over your shoulder, a pink, castellated, shimmering presence, the domes and riggings and crooked pinnacles of the Serenissima." *Essenziale.*

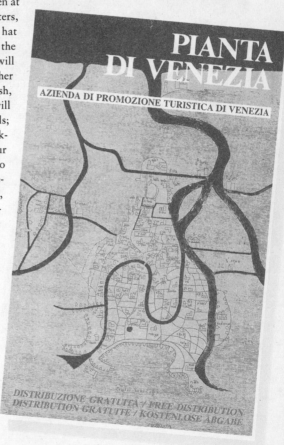

ITALIA L.300

Teatro Olimpico
Palazzo Chiericati
Museo Naturalistico-Archeologico

Prezzo 13000.
Price € 11.55.

Data
Date 08/07/2001

CUMULA12
00019713

Il Veneto
(The Region of the Veneto)

"Too many people fail to realize that behind the gorgeous mask of the city whose name it bears lie other wonderful cities, landscapes, Padua, Vicenza, Treviso, the valleys of the Adige and the Po, Lake Garda. An entire region offers the wealth of a diverse topography and innumerable important monuments and works of art."
　　　　　　　　　　—Gilles Plazy, THE TRAVELING GOURMET:
　　　　　　　　　　VENICE AND ITS REGIONS

La Dolce Vita

BY CATHARINE REYNOLDS

∿

editor's note

Here is a piece about renting a villa in Palladian country, and I enjoyed reading it so much, I very nearly picked the phone up and called the Best in Italy to make my own arrangements.

A warming footnote to this piece is that the author met her husband on this trip—he's the architect referred to in the text! A school friend of hers had a hunch that the architect and the writer might take to each other, and in fact Catharine told me it was "instant magic," which both credit to Palladio. Catharine also shared with me that this was not her only experience at a rental property in the Veneto. Another friend decided to celebrate her fiftieth birthday by inviting the ten women who had had the greatest impact on her life to spend a week with her at a palazzo in Venice. Rental companies are arranging ever more special occasions just like this one.

CATHARINE REYNOLDS, who wrote the wonderful "Paris Journal" column for Gourmet for more than twenty years (which was honored with a James Beard Foundation Award in 1998), is also a contributing editor of Gourmet, where this piece first appeared. She divides her time between Boston and Paris and is at work on a biography of Nicolas Fouquet, Louis XIV's first minister of finance.

We had decided to share this holiday with eight friends, all of them with wide-ranging curiosities and knowledge and differing backgrounds: here a lawyer, there a decorative arts historian; here a Californian, there an expatriate Englishman; here a Jamesian scholar, there a snap-happy chap. No two couples had met, though all were close friends of mine. That friendship and their interest in the architecture of Palladio were the unifying elements in this house party.

Simon met new arrivals with glass mugs of Prosecco, and we then showed them to their rooms. Our first dinner, at eight, set the mood of our stay. From squash risotto served in pretty pottery through a fruit tart with a symbolic birthday candle, we were launched in cele- bratory mode, awash in good talk and glee. This immediate aura of fellowship was sealed in the drawing room with a *razentino,* drops of grappa swirled through the dregs of espresso in our coffee cups.

Food at the villa is the pride of Clemy, the onetime family nanny whose kitchen talents have led her to open a restaurant at the foot of the drive. Her readings of the cooking of the Veneto—antipasti of ripe peeled figs and prosciutto; grilled vegetables; sliced chicken with arugula; spaghetti flecked with eggplant; grilled beef, veal, and bass; and luscious desserts that ranged from a sinful ice cream afloat in zabaglione to zesty lemon *sorbetto,* a drinkable dessert of lemon ice cream whizzed together with vodka and Prosecco—were so good that we were reluctant to dine out, in spite of the choice of tempting *trattorie* and restaurants within easy driving distance.

Occasionally we abandoned the house's dining room to convene down the hill at Clemy's *trattoria,* quickly discovering that we had to brake her generosity or else plan to march ourselves up the hill after supper to assuage our weighty consciences. The very drinkable wines of the region, from the omnipresent Prosecco to the subtle Villa Giustinian Riserva that we carried back after a visit to Roncade, fueled our merriment.

All the guests brought a wealth of information about the region to the table, whether from professional experience, wide reading, or hasty boning up. Talk ranged over architecture, Italian politics, and Renaissance history, through the nineteenth-century perception of the Venetian Republic and Ruskinian aesthetics that derided Palladio's classicism in favor of the Gothic. But there was nothing labored about the conversation, as the rippling laughter confirmed.

With this heady mix swirling through our brains, we the first morning set out for Vicenza, where the Padua-born Palladio had begun his career as a stonemason. His skills attracted the patronage of one of the town's great humanists, Gian Giorgio Trissino, who took him to Rome to expand his knowledge of the buildings of antiquity and the masters of the Roman Renaissance. We sought out Palladio's palazzi down the web of winding streets, pausing to marvel at the endearing examples of filigree Venetian Gothic and Roman remains spread among them.

And we sat captivated over a light lunch at the Gran Café Garibaldi on the Piazza dei Signori, riveted by the Basilica, the touchstone of Palladio's oeuvre. This arcaded masterwork is actually an elegant "slipcover" for an older council chamber. His Loggia del Capitaniato, opposite, came later; its pinky brick columns contrast with finely chiseled Corinthian capitals and bas-reliefs. We spent time at the Teatro Olimpico, Palladio's adaptation of an antique theater for Renaissance productions; his Palazzo Chiericati, which now houses the town's picture gallery; and Santa Corona, with the Valmarana chapel he designed in the crypt.

In planning the trip I had relied on *Historic Houses & Gardens Open to the Public: Italy* (Milan: Editoriale Giorgio Mondadori, 1996), which provides information on opening hours (brief and extremely idiosyncratic) and good directions to the villas. We wandered down lanes, enjoying the serendipity of our wrong turns, visiting the Villas Emo, Thiene, Saraceno, and Valmarana.

At Simonetta's suggestion, we organized one mad day for Contessa Maria Teresa Ceschia Santa Croce to lead us on a dizzying visit to five more villas: the Francesco Muttoni–designed Villa Loschi Zileri dal Verme at Monteviale, where we were dazzled by the Tiepolos; the Villa Cordellina Lombardi at Montecchio Maggiore, designed in 1735 by Giorgio Massari; La Rocca Pisana at Lonigo, Vincenzo Scamozzi's majestic solution for a hilltop site; Palladio's Villa Pisani ora Ferri, now impeccably restored; and another Muttoni work, the Villa Fracanzan Piovene at Orgiano, with its single majestic *barchessa* (farm building) where the owner displays his fascinating tractor collection. It took us days to absorb the kaleidoscope of images.

With each day we developed a clearer notion of the breadth of Palladio's work and of its felicities of volume. Working with a limited range of materials—brick, stucco, timber, and precious little stone—he distilled the classical idiom of Vitruvius with Renaissance developments, adding a measure of what architectural historian James Ackerman calls "Byzantine fantasy" and the "radiance of the provincial earlier Renaissance architecture of Venice" into the most human and compelling of styles.

We managed to visit more than half of Palladio's constructed villas as well as a goodly number of others designed by his disciples in succeeding centuries. Each offered a new insight into this multi-faceted man—from the Villa Cornaro ora Gamble, granddaddy of America's antebellum houses; to the Villa Almerico, known as La Rotonda, which inspired Monticello; to the Villa Badoer, which influenced Charles Cameron's Pavlovsk, outside Saint Petersburg.

We combined a visit to the Villa Foscari with a detour to Venice, bypassing San Marco for lunch on the Zattere with a view of Palladio's three largest churches: the Redentore; the Zitelle, or Santa Maria della Presentazione; and San Giorgio Maggiore.

Each couple had a car, so on occasion we paired off according to interests, one twosome gourmandising away to lunch at Da Gigetto in nearby Miane, another shopping for antiques and silks in Asolo, another crossing the Brenta at Bassano del Grappa on Palladio's covered bridge and sampling the eponymous *eau de vie* on its home ground.

Betweentimes we walked or sprawled on the banks above the valley, dreaming or chattering of cabbages and kings, of the past and imagined futures, nibbling the fat Concord-type grapes picked from the garden's vines.

Time flew and Sunday's farewells were deeply felt, with new friendships forged amid shared pleasures. We all had much to recall: Simon's wry smile as we called down to the kitchen each morning for still another pot of his excellent coffee; Elizabetta's shy acknowledgment as we admired her still life of fruits designed for snacking; our amazement at the polar bear in our party, who swam each crisp morning; the architect's quiet way of finding one sentence to sum up the group's diffuse commentary on a palazzo's cross-vaulting; the happy hours poring over the Touring Club Italiano map as we plotted the next day; and the ongoing debate between those who favored the frescoes of Palladio's contemporary Paolo Veronese and his school and those who preferred the Tiepolos, father and son.

Yes, we had missed visiting many of the villas—hardly through *dolce far niente*—but we would be back, seduced by Palladio, the Veneto, and the abiding notion of *villeggiatura*.

Renting a Villa of One's Own

The Best in Italy represents some ninety properties (accommodating from two to twenty-five) spread throughout the country. All are staffed and enjoy unique locations, ranging from palazzi in Venice and restored farmhouses in the Tuscan wine country to landmark historical estates. All have pools. For more information, contact:

Contessa Simonetta Brandolini d'Adda
The Best in Italy
Via Ugo Foscolo, 72
50124 Florence
Tel. 55.223.064; fax 55.229.8912
E-mail: bestinitaly@dinonet.it

Splendor in the Grass

BY DALBERT HALLENSTEIN

~⌇~

editor's note

....

I have several articles in my files about touring the Palladian villas, but this one, from the British edition of *Condé Nast Traveller,* is the best, complete with six different itineraries.

DALBERT HALLENSTEIN lives in the UK and writes frequently for *Condé Nast Traveller.*

L iving in Venice, arguably the world's most beautiful city, is and always has been notoriously claustrophobic. The houses and palaces face each other across the canals, and open views of the lagoon are rare. This near treeless city must have been especially suffocating in the hot summers of the Middle Ages, yet there was no escape for the Venetians, who were forbidden by law from owning property on the mainland. After the 1345 decree that permitted investments off the island, however, there was a rush to buy land and construct villas in the open countryside away from the sweltering city.

There were other reasons beyond the merely climatic for this massive land-acquisition and building boom. The aristocracy had accumulated huge fortunes by exploiting Venice's virtual monopoly on overland trade with the Orient. But this was broken when the Portuguese opened up the sea route to the East around Africa. Afterward the Venetians were quick to realize that investments in land were far less risky than the increasing uncertainties of overseas trade. Until the late eighteenth century, almost all the villas in the Veneto were also hard-working farms.

Equally significant was the fact that for the first time since the fall of the Roman Empire, a vast area of Europe was safe from foreign invaders and marauding bands of robbers. The Venetian mainland territories extended from what is now the Slovenian border down to the Po river and westward to Lake Garda and beyond. This enormous area was ruled with an iron hand by a Venice administration notorious for its ferocious justice and rigorous laws. While the rest of Europe was involved in warfare and civil strife, the Venetians could build elegant country houses in peaceful countryside—often without fences, let alone walls. "That ditch and iron fence down there in front of the villa," said Countess Caroline Emo (who lives in one of the most beautiful of the Venetian villas near Asolo, built in 1564 by the Venetian architect Andrea Palladio for the Emo family), "was only constructed in the late eighteenth century at the time of the French Revolution. Before then there was no barrier between the villa and the surrounding countryside. There was absolute peace."

It is their sense of peace, their perfect insertion into the natural environment, that makes these villas so enviable and, in a sense, so modern. Andrea Palladio (1508–1580) was one of the world's greatest architects, whose reinterpretation of classical Roman villas has had a huge influence on country houses and public buildings in Europe and the United States. For him, the link with nature was fundamental. He favored an elevated position for the views it afforded and for the fresh air. Palladio was convinced that a villa should "help conserve the health and strength of its inhabitants, and restore their spirits, worn out by the agitation of city life, to peace and tranquillity." Gardens also played a fundamental role. "The garden," he wrote, "is the soul of the villa." On a more practical level, he recommended building on a river or canal for easy access to Venice.

This harmony between architecture and nature fascinated travelers to northern Italy between the sixteenth and eighteenth centuries, especially the English. The hills south of Vicenza reminded them of their own rolling countryside. They longed to build similar country houses at home, but until the mid-seventeenth century this was impossible. An unfortified country villa was almost inconceivable in an England wracked by the upheaval of civil war.

Although Inigo Jones introduced Palladian ideas into English architecture in the seventeenth century, it was not until the civil peace of the eighteenth century that the Palladian concept of the country villa was able to take off. Palladianism quickly swept through Europe, reaching as far east as Russia. It also became a dominant influence in the United States, not only in domestic architecture—especially in the southern states—but also in the country's public buildings. The White House is a classic example of the Palladian influence on public buildings of the early nineteenth century.

There are an estimated 4,500 villas scattered throughout the Veneto. Palladio himself built fifteen and influenced many more. A lot are in an appalling state, ruined either by neglect or over-restoration; some are now next door to squalid suburban developments and lack their original park settings. Others have been taken over as town halls or have been converted into apartments. But hundreds still exist in excellent condition. Few of the classic Italian Renaissance and Baroque parks have survived intact, however, as many of them were converted in the nineteenth century into, somewhat ironically, English-style parks and gardens. Belying their grand facades, the villas' interiors are often intimate and full of light. Living areas, when furnished with family paraphernalia, are often distinctly cozy, despite the magnificent frescoes and solemn family portraits.

Not all the villas of the Veneto follow the Palladian model. Pre-Palladian villas are sometimes Gothic and are often based on the typical late-medieval Venetian palazzo. Others have ornamental turrets or decorative walls that flaunt the military glories of past ancestors. Some, built in the eighteenth century, emulate the vast palaces of the German and Austrian principalities while maintaining their essential Venetian style. Many of those along the Brenta canal were built as summer holiday residences, and it was in these that the sexual and social excesses of the final, decadent years of eighteenth-century Venetian high society, depicted in dramatist Carlo Goldoni's famous comedies, took place.

Itinerary One: Around Vicenza

Plan this for a Wednesday as it is the only day you can visit the interior of the Villa Almerico Capra Valmarana, known as La Rotonda.

Morning
Villa Badoer (1): This Palladian villa, 1556, at Cricoli was converted from a medieval structure by Giangiorgio Trissino, Palladio's first great patron. *Strada Marosticana 6, Cricoli; only viewable from the street, but worth the effort for its historical interest.*

Villa Negri Ceroni (2), also known as Ca' Latina, is a fine early-eighteenth-century country house in Palladian style. *Via Ospedaletto 148, Vicenza; only viewable from the outside.*

Villa Thiene (3): Now the town hall, this is the only wing that was built from plans by Palladio for an enormous villa. *Piazza IV Novembre 2, Quinto Vicentino (04.44.584211); open Mon–Fri 9.30 A.M.–12.45 P.M., Tues and Wed 5.30 P.M.–7.15 P.M.; other times by appointment.*

Villa Ghislanzoni Curti (4): A fascinating eighteenth-century villa set in open countryside and at present partly under restoration. *Via San Cristoforo 73, Bertesina (04.44.504674); visits by appointment only.*

Lunch

Da Remo: Excellently situated for La Rotonda and Villa Valmarana "Ai Nani," Da Remo is in an old farmhouse. It specializes in fish (try the calamari and sturgeon) although the most appetizing dish is probably the boiled meats. *Via Ca' Empenta 14, near eastern exit of the A4 motorway (04.44.911007; fax: .911856). From about £20 per head for three courses, with wine. Closed Sun. evening, Mon., end July–1 September and throughout the Christmas period.*

Or try **Locanda Grego,** which specializes in local dishes and excellent puddings. *Via Roma 24, Bolzano Vicentino (04.44.350588). From about £13.50 per head for three to four courses, without wine. Closed Sun. and Wed. evening, August, and the Christmas holidays.*

Afternoon

Villa Almerico Capra Valmarana (5), also known as La Rotonda (1566–1567) is the best known of Palladio's works. Its four classical facades face a lush landscape that is, miraculously, still pretty unspoiled despite its proximity to Vicenza. *Via della Rotonda 45, Vicenza (04.44.321793; fax: 98.791380); villa can be viewed from the grounds Tues.–Sun. 10 A.M.–12 noon and 3 P.M.–6 P.M.; the interior can be visited 15 March–15 October, Wed. between the same hours.*

Villa Valmarana "Ai Nani" (6): This seventeenth-century villa is a five-minute walk from La Rotonda. It exudes elegance and civilization. The cozy interior is embellished with frescoes by Giambattista Tiepolo; the inside walls of the *foresteria* (guesthouse) are almost covered with frescoes by Giambattista's son Giandomenico, and illustrate with astounding freshness scenes from peasant and aristocratic life. *Via dei Nani 2–8, Vicenza (04.44.543868). Open 15 March– 30 April, Wed.–Sun. 10 A.M.–12 noon and 2:30–5:30 P.M.; 1 May– 30 September, Wed.–Sun. 3 P.M.–6 P.M.; 1 October–5 November, Wed.–Sun. 2 P.M.–5 P.M.*

The Venetians constructed some of their most magnificent villas along the Brenta canal, a short boat trip from the city. The existing villas are now in settings of suburban squalor, so we suggest taking the Burchiello, a private water bus that leaves from Venice or Padua and visits the three major villas along the canal. From the water, at least, the shabby locality is less evident. The water bus visits **Villa Foscari,** otherwise known as **La Malcontenta (1),** in Mira, one of Palladio's greatest buildings (1559–1560); **Villa Pisani (2)** at Stra, a grandiose eighteenth-century palace with frescoes by Tiepolo, a vast park with maze, and curiously, Napoleon's wooden lavatory; and the frescoed one-wing remains of the **Villa Valmarana (3),** also at Stra, based on a design of 1541 by Palladio. *The day costs about £35 (children about £20), plus an optional £3.50 to visit Villa Pisani. The boat runs from 17 March to 28 October and departs from Venice on Tuesday, Thursday, and Saturday. It departs from Padua on Wednesday, Friday, and Sunday. Call 04.98.774712; fax: 763044; e-mail: burchiel@tin.it: website: www.ilburchiello.it*

Itinerary Three: Asolo area

The countryside around Asolo is full of fascinating villas, though most are viewable from the outside only.

Morning
Villa Contarini (1): Reasonably close to Asolo (44km) is Piazzola sul Brenta, where you will find this enormous, mainly seventeenth-century villa. More like a palace than a villa, it is said to have been an attempt by the Contarini family to outdo Versailles. *Via Camerini 1, Piazzola sul Brenta (04.95.590238). Open daily except Mon.: December–February, 9 A.M.–12 noon, 2 P.M.–5 P.M.; March–May, 9 A.M. to 12 noon, 2.30 P.M.–6.30 P.M.; rest of year, 9 A.M.–12 noon, 3 P.M.–7 P.M.*

The villas of Feltre and Belluno, with their stunning backdrop of the Dolomite mountains, are a short drive away. Asolo is about an hour's drive from Vicenza.

Lunch
Ca' Deton: One of the most original restaurants in the area. Try the *bigoli* (northern Italian spaghetti) with duck sauce, followed by tender lamb. *Piazza G. d'Annunzio 11, Asolo (04.23.529648); book ahead. From about £20 per head for three courses, without wine. Closed Sun. evening, Mon., the last two weeks of January, and all of August.*

Afternoon
Close to Asolo are two of Palladio's major works, both open in the afternoon only. **Villa Barbaro (2):** One of the great pieces of European architecture. Built in about 1560 by Palladio, the Villa Barbaro's sublime natural setting at Maser is unspoiled. The interior frescoes are among Paolo Veronese's finest. *Maser (04.23.923004); open April–September, Tues., Sat., and Sun. 3–6 P.M.; October–March, Tues., Sat., and Sun. 2–5 P.M.* **Villa Emo (3):** This surprisingly intimate villa by Palladio is decorated with vibrant frescoes by Giambattista Zelotti. The setting is superb. *Via Stazione 5, Fanzolo di Vedelago (04.23.476414); open November–March, Sat., Sun., and holidays 2 P.M.–6 P.M.; April–October, weekdays 3 P.M.–7 P.M. and Sun. 10 A.M.–12.30 P.M.; closed 18 December–13 January.*

Itinerary Four
──

Morning
To the southwest of Vicenza The best way to begin this tour is to drive down the A4 highway from Vicenza toward Verona and Milan. Leave it at the Montebello exit and head for Lonigo. On your left you will see the magnificent **Villa da Porto (1),** also known as La

Favorita, built in 1697. Restoration is likely to continue through the spring, but it is still well worth driving up the hill to look at it through the main gate. Next, drive to Lonigo and follow signs to the **Villa Pisani Ferri (2),** also known as La Rocca Pisana. This magnificent hilltop villa dominates the local countryside. It was built on the ruins of a medieval castle by the great architect Vincenzo Scamozzi, a pupil of Andrea Palladio who finished off some of his most important buildings, including Villa Almerico Capra Valmarana (known as La Rotonda—see Itinerary One) on the outskirts of Vicenza. Like La Rotonda, it has four main windows that face the four points of the compass, but there the similarity ends. This is one of the most original buildings ever built. It has a dome with an open *oculis* through which rain pours into the center of the house, following the style of the Pantheon, thus cooling it down in the hot summers for which it was built. The views of the Berici hills surrounding the villa are almost totally unspoiled, and the rolling countryside looks very much like England, which explains why English travelers between the sixteenth and eighteenth centuries felt so much at home here. *Villa Pisani Ferri, Via Rocca 1, Lonigo (04.44.831104). Open by appointment only, book at least two days in advance; gardens open 1 March–15 May, by appointment with the curator (04.44.831625). The Villa Pisani is available to rent (for more information see "Where to Stay").*

Before lunch it is worth visiting **Palazzo Pisani,** now the town hall. This sixteenth-century villa has an elaborate eighteenth-century staircase.

Lunch

La Peca: Elegant but relaxed, this is widely considered to be one of the best restaurants in northern Italy. Try the sweetbreads with truffles or the gnocchi with *baccala* (salt cod). The wine list is vast and excellent. *Via Principe Giovanelli 2, Lonigo (tel/fax: 04.44.830214); booking necessary. From about £35 per head for three courses,*

*without wine. Closed Sun. evening and Mon., and throughout
January and August.*

Afternoon
Villa Pisani di Bagnolo (3): One of Palladio's finest and most
exquisite creations (1542–45) set in unspoiled countryside.
*Via Risaie 1, Bagnolo di Lonigo (04.44.831104). Open 4 April–4
November, Wed. 10 A.M.–12 noon, 3 P.M.–6 P.M. The villa can be
viewed on other days between these dates, by appointment.*

Villa Pojana (4): One of Palladio's masterpieces, the villa has just
been carefully restored, together with its splendid sixteenth-century
frescoes. *Via Castello 41, Pojana Maggiore. For further information, call Pojana town hall (04.44.898033). Open all year,
Tues.–Sun. 10 A.M.–6 P.M.*

Villa Barbarigo-Rezzonico (5): This massive four-story country
villa, built at the end of the sixteenth century, is now in the center
of Noventa Vicentina and is used as the town hall. *Piazza IV
Novembre, Noventa Vicentina (04.44.788520). Open Mon.–Fri. 10
A.M.–1.30 P.M., Tues. and Thurs. 8 A.M.–1.30 P.M., 3 P.M.–6 P.M.*

Villa Saraceno (6): This small Palladian villa (c. 1545) has recently
been beautifully restored by the Landmark Trust, which owns it.
*Via Finale 8, Finale di Agugliaro (tel/fax: 04.44.891371). Open
1 April–31 October, Wed. 2 P.M.–4 P.M.; rest of the year by appointment. The villa can also be rented (for more information see "Where
to Stay").*

Itinerary Five: West of Vicenza

Morning
Villa Valmarana Morosini (1): Francesco Muttoni's masterpiece.
*Via Marconi 73, Altavilla Vicentina (04.44.333736; e-mail: centro-
congressi@cuor.it); visits by appointment.*

Villa Cordellina Lombardi (2): Worth a visit for Giambattista Tiepolo's frescoes. *Via Lovara 36, Montecchio Maggiore (04.44.696085); open Tues–Fri 9 A.M.–1 P.M., Sat., Sun., and holidays 9 A.M.–12 noon and 3 P.M.–6 P.M.*

Lunch
Ca' Masieri: This is one of the best restaurants near Vicenza. *Via Masieri, Trissino (04.45.962100); book ahead; closed Sun., Mon. lunch. From about £35 per head for a three-course meal, with wine.*

Afternoon
Villa Trissino Marzotto (3): Two villas (one now a romantic ruin), set in a fine private park. *Piazza Trissino 2, Trissino (04.45.962029); park open by appointment.*

Villa Piovene da Porto da Schio (4): A seventeenth-century villa containing works by Giambattista Tiepolo. *Via Villa 117, Castelgomberto (04.45.941084); park open 1 June–30 September.*

Itinerary Six: The Euganean Hills

Morning
From Vicenza, take highway 247 to Este, about 60km away. **Villa Contarini Maldura Emo (1):** An elegant Palladian-style, sixteenth-century villa. *Near Rivella, Monselice (04.29.781970); visits by appointment only.*

Villa Barbarigo Pizzoni Ardemani (2): From Battáglia Terme, head for Valsanzibio. This gardens of this mid-seventeenth-century villa contain a maze, fountains, and statuary. *Valsanzibio di Galzignano (04.99.130042); open March–November daily, 9 A.M.–12 noon and 1:30 P.M. to sunset.*

Lunch
Castelletto da Taparo: Honest home cooking and local wine. *Via Castelletto 43, Torreglia (04.95.211060); closed Mon., last week of January, and first week of February. From about £15 per head for a three-course meal with wine.*

Afternoon
Villa dei Vescovi (3): This sixteenth-century villa in late Renaissance style was a retreat of the bishops of Padua and contains a marvelous sixteenth-century bathroom. *Via dei Vescovi, Luvigliano di Torreglia (04.95.211118). Open Easter to 15 November (closed 15 July– 15 August), Mon., Wed., Fri., and the first Saturday of the month, 10:30 A.M.–12 noon and 3 P.M.–6 P.M.*

Villa Emo Capodilista (4): An atypical sixteenth-century villa and Renaissance arcade. *Via Montecchia 16, Selvazzano Dentro (04.9.637294); open Wed. and Sat. for group tours, 4 P.M. and 5:30 P.M.*

Design of the Times
Villas tend to open at times that make visiting several in one area in a day almost impossible. It is enough for a villa owner to have flu for the property to be closed on its only open day. It is therefore essential to call ahead to confirm opening times. Many villa owners prefer to open to groups only (who pay more than individuals), so it may be worth trying to attach yourself to an organized trip. The custodian of a closed villa will often allow you in if you slip him or her L10,000 (about £3.50) per person, the standard entry price.

Where to Stay
From near Vicenza, you have easy access to the main villas, plus those in the Euganean Hills southwest of Padua and around Verona. From around Treviso (try and stay in or near Asolo), you

can easily reach the important villas in the area as well as those around Belluno and Feltre. Some villas have been converted into luxurious hotels or unserviced apartments. These are recommended whenever possible.

Around Vicenza

Hotel Villa Michelangelo, via Sacco 19, Arcugnano (04.44.550300; fax: 550490). Ten kilometers from Vicenza, ten minutes from the A4 Milan–Venice highway, this four-star hotel, in a beautiful eighteenth-century villa with swimming pool, is perfect for exploring the Vicenza and Padua villas. Doubles from about £125 with breakfast.

Ca' Masieri, via Masieri 16, Trissino (04.45.490122; fax: .490455). About 20 km from Vicenza and 12 km from the A4 highway—ideal for the Vicenza and Padua villas—Ca' Masieri occupies a two-hundred-year-old aristocratic villa-farmhouse with a swimming pool. Doubles from £55; apartments from £75; breakfast about £5.

Locanda Grego, via Roma 24, Bolzano Vicentino (04.44.350588; fax: .350695). This comfortable hotel is at the heart of an area full of important villas, 10 km from Vicenza, close to the A4 highway. Doubles from about £40; breakfast £3–£3.50.

Villa Pisani Ferri, also known as La Roca Pisana, near Lonigo (04.98.759693; fax: .752499). Renting this celebrated villa is one of the greatest and most memorable experiences of European travel, although you will need three families or a group who are friendly enough to vacation together. Sleeps up to twelve. Villa costs from about £1,690 per week, plus expenses, mid-May to mid-September; minimum one-week stay.

Villa Saraceno, via Finale 8, Finale di Agugliaro. This perfectly pro-portioned Palladian villa, owned by the Landmark Trust, can be rented by groups of up to sixteen. Villa costs from £1,164 to £5,885 per week. From November to February the main villa can be rented for up to five people from £856 per week. Call 01628.825925 for a Landmark Handbook, £9.50 (refundable on booking); www.landmarktrust.co.uk.

Asolo and Surroundings

Villa Cipriani, via Canova 298 (04.23.952166; fax: .952095). One of Italy's finest hotels, in a villa once owned by the poet Robert Browning. Perfect for exploring Treviso and northeast Vicenza. Doubles from about £175 with breakfast.

Hotel al Sole, via Collegio 33, Asolo (04.23.528111; fax: .528399). An excellent four-star hotel in the town center. Doubles from about £120, including breakfast.

Hotel Duse, via Browning 190, Asolo (04.235541; fax: .950404). Comfortable if modest rooms and friendly staff. Doubles from about £60; breakfast about £4.

Near Padua

Villa Margherita, via Nazionale 416, Mira (04.14.265800; fax: .265838). This luxurious hotel stands by the Brenta Canal in an elegant seventeenth-century villa surrounded by fine parkland. Doubles from £95, including breakfast.

By Dalbert Hallenstein, © Traveller/The Condé Nast Publications Ltd.

Venezia in Campagna

BY NAOMI BARRY

The three main rivers that empty into the Venetian Lagoon are the Sile, the Piave, and the Brenta, this last the best known of the three because it's the one Venice chose for a canal, resulting in an attractive area for the Venetian aristocracy to build their summer villas. *Villeggiatura* (a season that lasts from about mid-June to mid-November, when wealthy Venetians would literally move to the country) was born, and it prospered from the sixteenth century to the eighteenth. The Venice tourist office publishes the very best information about touring the Brenta, better than anything you'll find in a guidebook. *Riviera del Brenta: The Guide* is a sixty-three-page guide covering all aspects of the area; the accompanying fold-out map of the *riviera* is very good and includes some history about the canal and the environment; and the *Il Burchiello* guide gives specifics of this wonderful boat trip along the canal. The *Burchiello* cruises every year from March to October and departs from Padua or Venice on alternate days. The trip includes visits to Villa Pisani, Barchessa Valmarana, and Villa della Malcontenta. (A great article to read, by the way, featuring gorgeous photos of the Villa della Malcontenta, is "The Most Beautiful House in the World" by Marella Caracciolo, photographed by Francois Halard, *House & Garden,* October 2001; according to this article, *La Malcontenta* means "the unhappy woman," and the name most likely has its origins in the term *mal contenuta,* meaning "badly contained," a reference to the river's former tendency to flood its banks at the site of the villa. "But the more interesting explanation behind the villa's name is the legend that the wife of one of the original owners was banished to the house for living too loosely in Venice.") If you travel farther inland, the Vicenza tourist office publishes a superb illustrated map of villas dating from 1400 to 1800 entitled *The Most Beautiful Villas in Vicenza and Surroundings*. If you're flying into Marco Polo Airport, you can pick up the Brenta brochures at the little counter the tourist office operates there. Otherwise, ask for them at one of the other Venice branches.

NAOMI BARRY, who was introduced on page 235, is at work on a biography of Natale Rusconi of the Hotel Cipriani.

Pazzo is a fine Italian word, full of *z-z-z-zing*. It means "crazy," nice crazy, like being *pazzo* about night-blooming flowers, pasta with pesto, brown-eyed blondes, or Byzantine icons.

Just prior to World War I a French guidebook writer who was *pazzo* about Venice (a city that generally inspires fanatic affection) boldly told his readers to leave the train at Padua and make their way to Fusina at the mouth of the River Brenta so they could approach *La Serenissima* by gondola across the lagoon—a little bit of ultimate. He spoke his mind even though he knew he was whistling up the creek because at the time most travelers wanted to go direct to Venice station and straight on to the Grand Canal. Furthermore, nobody went to the Brenta at that time. The noble sixteenth-through-eighteenth-century villas of the Venetians had sombered with neglect, decay that began with the fall of the republic in 1797; the once-animated stream meandered with all the melancholy of an untidy backwater. The currents of fashion had changed since Goethe's vivacious voyage downriver from Padua, punctuated by the joyous jumping ashore of passengers at each brief halt to gorge on fruits offered at the landings.

By the eighteenth century a villa on terra firma was considered a necessity by wealthy Venetians. The Brenta was but an extension of their Grand Canal. From their town houses in Venice they could be ferried without charge to the fields and vineyards of their country mansions, remaining always in direct communication with the lagoon. A good gondolier could make it from the Rialto in two hours, and the post and courier services were models of efficiency. Letters sent in the morning were oftentimes answered by night.

In its heyday the area along the river was a dreamlike hinterland of humanism where patricians patronized the arts in a bucolic playground. Each country house was a showplace for the talents of Venetian architects, fresco painters, stucco workers, and gardeners. A very young Tintoretto applied his brushes to frescoes of the Villa

Querini at Mira, Giovanni Battista Tiepolo painted the glories of the Pisani family on a ceiling of their villa at Stra, and Andrea Palladio designed the Villa della Malcontenta near Marghera for Nicolò and Alvise Foscari.

Abbot Marco Vincenzo Coronelli published a series of engravings in 1709 on the wonder of it all. Architect Gianfrancesco Costa recorded the scene even more precisely in two sets of engravings (1750 and 1762), entitled *About the delights of the River Brenta expressed in the villas and hunting lodges on its banks, from its mouth in the Venetian lagoon to the city of Padua*. Both collections, now in the Biblioteca Marciana on the Piazzetta of San Marco, are studied as the blueprints of the world that was.

Venezia in campagna in the eighteenth century was a round-the-clock *festa* in never-never land. Comedies were performed against the bosky backdrops of private gardens, and strains of Vivaldi sounded from the balconies of the ballrooms that were part of each great villa. Itinerant showmen set up their puppet stands for Arlecchino, Colombina, and Pantalone, and itinerant merchants erected their booths in the squares of the little villages that bordered the river like a string of country fairs. The playwright Carlo Goldoni, a frequent and popular houseguest at one villa or another, wrote poems about the jolly traffic on the river and plays about the hoopla of going to the Brenta countryside for the season.

In recent years there has been a creeping return of attention to the Brenta's exuberant domestic architecture. The Commission for Venetian Villas currently catalogs 294 villas in the province of Venezia alone. Most are in decay, but sixty-one have been restored as private residences or buildings for public use. Is there enough money to revive them all? Probably not, and even if there were, where would one find the servants to uphold the splendor?

Those *pazzo* about the past glories of Venice follow a pilgrim's route along the Brenta, bringing to the trip an archaeological eye that blocks out ugly modern encroachments and rebuilds imaginatively from the vestiges the gay and glorious environment that flourished there.

The most recommendable seasons are spring and autumn, when the Veneto goes luminous. As orientation, previous homework is necessary. Perusal of the much-reproduced Costa engravings is a good introduction. The most informative book we found was Clauco Benito Tiozzo's generously illustrated *Le Ville del Brenta* (Edizioni d'arte del Cavallino, Venice).

To capture the maximum of what has not vanished, it is advisable to go by car (although a bicycle would be even more suitable) and slowly drive along one bank of the river, returning via the other. The nonhighway side is more pastoral these days and as a result more evocative of the past.

From the beginning of May until the end of September, a small excursion steamer, *Il Burchiello,* floats between Venice and Padua, journeying up and back on alternate days. The trip takes a full day, with stops for lunch at a riverside restaurant plus two shore visits to the monumental villas Malcontenta and Pisani. Except for small boys in rubber dinghies and an occasional private motorboat, the passage of the *Burchiello* is today the only important navigation on this stretch of the Brenta. It is a nice pastime, but the eye level is too low, alas, for a good look at the villas as one passes by.

For eighteenth-century passengers the Brenta trip was a pleasure cruise.

> Muse, I sing of the Burchiello of Padua
> The delightful, comfortable vehicle,
> In which on the Brenta I traveled so beautifully.

Goldoni enumerated its charms: mirrors, paintings, inlay work, and even a little chamber for the unavoidable. Charles de Brosses, a distinguished visitor to Malcontenta, wrote back to France that the

Burchiello was like a beautiful little baby of the *Bucintore* (the ceremonial vessel of the doges). Literally, it was a floating apartment of two well-furnished, windowed rooms hung with Venetian brocades where, protected from cold and from heat, travelers could eat, drink, gossip, and gamble while boatmen poled the ornate craft across the lagoon. Once in the Brenta, the *Burchiello* was towed up and down by stout horses walking along the banks. Decks were awninged, and musicians often sat on the roof.

The estates produced wine, grain, dairy products, and the vegetables for which the lands around the lagoon have always been famous. They were gentlemen's farms around fun houses. In his high-spirited memoirs Antonio Longo, who lived in the Palazzo Bonfadini at Mira Porte, recounted entertaining fifty friends for whom he organized an orchestra of eighteen musicians.

We dined at the main hotel. When evening fell we reboarded our illuminated boats and, singing and laughing, we headed for Mira where we thought of passing the night at the Noblemen's Club to wait until the next day's gambling.

But passing in front of Senator Gianbattista Corner's villa we saw that it was blazing with light: wax torches at the windows, on the loggias, near the statues and pine torches scattered throughout the gardens.

Our orchestra began to play and immediately from the villa another orchestra replied, so we disembarked and the host came to greet us surrounded by a crowd of guests.

We started to dance, finishing at dawn, but the senator did not limit his hospitality to this but invited me and my fifty companions to stay on for a meal.

The reception lasted eight days, during which time Senator Corner and Senator Gradenigo gave six banquets each.

Stone steps still lead up the banks of the river at frequent intervals for laughing friends who no longer come. However, the disappearance of so many great houses on the river was due to more than the erosion of time. At the end of the last century, a tax was levied on conspicuous symbols of wealth, such as frescoes, doors more than a meter wide, and elaborately decorated chimneys. Some of the already-bankrupt heirs to the Brenta properties turned over their villas to the peasants, who whitewashed the interiors or sold them to speculators and antiques dealers, who stripped frescoes from the walls for resale. (That explains how one Tiepolo fresco turned up at the Musée Jacquemart-André in Paris and two at the Metropolitan Museum of Art in New York City.) Other owners ordered main houses to be blown up, sparing the outbuildings to which the crushing taxes did not apply. Fortunately, not all owners took such drastic measures.

The Villa della Malcontenta, the neoclassic temple Andrea Palladio finished building in 1560 for the brothers Nicolò and Alvise Foscari, is a perfect cube with its interior space daringly subdivided into a vast cruciform *sala* (hall) and a symmetry of large and small rooms filling the spaces around the arms of the cross like those puzzles whose components fit together into a single block.

The vaulted ceiling of that breathtaking central hall is twenty-four feet high, awe-inspiring for a private dwelling, but the proportions are so harmonious and the fusion of the frescoes with the architecture is so felicitous that even a quite normal-size person can settle down on one of the divans for coffee without feeling squelched by the emptiness overhead.

The architect, Andrea Palladio (1518–1580), was born in Vicenza but studied in Rome, where he was fascinated by the stateliness and proportions of the buildings that remained from ancient times. The antique inspiration is evident in much of Palladio's work: the Teatro Olimpico in Vicenza, the churches of the Redentore and San Giorgio Maggiore in Venice, and the private villas still standing in northern Italy. His treatise, *I Quattro Libri dell'Architettura,* was translated into every European language. The introduction to the English edition (1620) was written by Inigo Jones. The work so influenced seventeenth-century England and Ireland that the resulting style came to be known as Palladian. Its effects reached American shores, the most stunning example being Thomas Jefferson's house, Monticello. Palladio's only villa on the Brenta, however, is the Malcontenta.

A date inscribed on the outer front wall of the Malcontenta— July 27, 1574—records the passage of Henri III on his way to France from Poland, accompanied by a stupendous cortege. From then until now the villa has hosted distinguished visitors: Frederick IV of Denmark and Norway, Elizabeth II of England, Winston Churchill, Cole Porter, Sergey Diaghilev, Bernard Berenson, and Igor Stravinsky, to name but a few.

The Austrians quartered troops in the Malcontenta during their occupation of Venice in the mid-nineteenth century. When they pulled out, the house was taken over by peasants, who used it to store their grain, dry their grapes, and breed their silkworms. G. B. Zelotti's frescoes were covered by repeated coats of whitewash and forgotten.

By 1925, when Albert Landsberg, a Brazilian diplomat, felt the lightning of true *pazzo* strike, the Malcontenta was an abandoned ruin, dismissed by pessimists as "beyond hope." For the next forty years Landsberg repaired, restored, and exulted as each lost fragment came to light. With his death in 1965 uncertainty settled again upon the Malcontenta. In 1974 the most celebrated villa on the Brenta was acquired by Antonio Foscari-Widmann. Funds were granted by the Ente per le Ville Venete, and the Malcontenta resumed the aspect it displayed to the original Foscari.

The villa described by Palladio in his *Quattro Libri* is now open to the public several mornings a week, although it is wise to check schedules before setting out. The Malcontenta, nearest to Venice of all the villas, is mal-placed in a countryside now pockmarked by the factories and oil refineries of the industrial suburb of Marghera. But magic operates within the property: the house is so protected by a curtain of weeping willows that it might be as far from Marghera in distance as it seems to be in time.

When in 1736 the powerful Venetian family of Pisani finally saw one of its members elected doge, they commemorated the honor by demolishing their country house at Stra and constructing a villa more grandiose than anything ever attempted even by the Medicis in their prime. The stables at the end of a long perspective were as noble as a palace, and the labyrinth that figures in Gabriele D'Annunzio's novel *Il Fuoco* was designed by Girolamo Frigimelica, who worried even about making an icehouse as charming as a little belvedere. Costa's engraving shows an orangery to rival Versailles'.

Napoleon I bought the Pisani in 1807, possibly spent one night there, and installed Eugène de Beauharnais. Upon the unification of Italy, the Pisani became a royal palace, and it has been government property ever since, with its name changed to Villa Nazionale. As such, it is open to visitors. Despite the unkempt grounds, the grandeur of its ambition has not diminished. The palace has just undergone a face-lift.

If houses impose their own atmosphere, the Villa Foscarini at Mira Taglio must have had a quality that ignited passion. In 1622 Antonio Foscarini paid with his life for a compromising relationship with Anne, Countess of Arundel. The accusation subsequently was proved false, and the Venetian government rehabilitated Anne's and Foscarini's reputations, albeit a little tardily. A later Foscarini had the misfortune to lose his fascinating wife, Chiara, to a rival in a much-talked-of affair.

In 1817 George Gordon, Lord Byron moved into the villa, sharing it with Marianna Segati until he met Margarita Cognis, the beautiful wife of the baker in the neighboring town of Dolo, with whom he had a short and stormy relationship. In September 1818 Byron turned over the villa to Countess Guiccioli, requesting the privilege of being her houseguest. After the countess left, the poet forsook Mira.

Elia Fornaciari, head of the government commission for the villas of the Veneto, lists as his favorite along the Brenta the Villa Querini because "it is the most human." Its story is also the most human. Clauco Benito Tiozzo was born in Mira, a village of the Brenta, the son of a local tradesman. At six Benito knew he was going to be a painter. When he married his childhood sweetheart, Anna de Liberali, the couple decided they would bring back to life one of the crumbling villas, part of the patrimony of their region. Eventually in 1972 they acquired the Querini in their hometown.

Tiozzo by then was one of the foremost restorers of Italy, responsible for the frescoes at the Palazzo Labia in Venice, as well as a best-selling painter with his tenderly romantic landscapes of the Brenta. However, he did not have the kind of money required for a major restoration. Benito consequently taught the art of restoration to Anna and their two young sons. With courage, patience, sacrifice, and hard labor the family went about the massive task. The work is impeccable, and the house has rewarded them. It is a jewel, and it is alive.

The floor plan of the Querini repeats itself upstairs and downstairs. The long central drawing room on the ground floor is a masterpiece of grace and nobility. When upon mounting the frescoed staircase one comes upon a second drawing room of the same exquisite proportions, the mind boggles. Through a carefully calculated trick not noticeable to the unwarned eye, one wall measures eighteen meters whereas the other is only seventeen and a half. The

Brenta curves slightly in front of the Querini; by cleverly manipulating his measurements, the architect was still able to front his house squarely on the river.

Anna and Benito Tiozzo are a modest but proud pair. Benito has his studio in the right-hand *barchessa* (wing), as well as a *cantina* (cellar) for the wine from his grapes. The second *barchessa* is being altered now, in accordance with the Costa drawings. Under its arcades, Anna envisions a long table for feeding friends al fresco. Next year, perhaps, she will give a masked ball for Carnival as friends did this year in another villa a few miles up the Brenta. She adores her house, quite understandably. For serious students who ask permission in advance, it is her quiet pleasure to introduce them to this wonder of *Venezia in campagna*.

Life along the Brenta was Venice with an added dimension. Thus, the food of this part of the Veneto was the same as that served on the tables of Venice. Several features distinguish Venetian cuisine. The use of cinnamon, nutmeg, and clove reminds one that for centuries the republic dominated the flourishing spice trade with the East. An ancient recipe for turkey and pomegranate juice speaks of the link with Byzantium and the caravan routes of Persia.

The refinement of the Orient was revealed in the *salsa peverada*, a piquant sauce much in favor during the Renaissance and so popular that it appeared in both the silver sauceboats of the nobles and the terra-cotta bowls of the people. It accompanied chicken, boiled meats, game, and birds of all kinds. The ingredients included sausage, liver, and generous doses of pepper. The *peverada* was reputed to have aphrodisiac powers, which made it all the more popular.

The Adriatic was the fortune of *La Serenissima*, and the shellfish and fish of this long arm of the Mediterranean are the basis of *la cucina veneziana*. Delicate and full of flavor is *broèto*, the

Venetian equivalent of *bouillabaisse*. *Scampi* (shrimp), *gamberoni* (large crayfish), *gamberetti* (small crayfish), *calamaretti* (baby squid), *seppioline* (tiny inkfish), miniature eels, and giant crabs are the bounty of the lagoon. The noble fish are the *sogliola* (sole), *rombo* (turbot), *sgombro* (mackerel), *San Pietro* (John Dory), and *coda di rospo* (monkfish tail). In Venice the head of the *rospo* and the tail *(coda)* are sold separately, the former for fish soup and the latter to be baked or grilled.

At the popular *trattoria* La Colomba in Venice, the specialty is a savory mixture of fish, rich and poor, with tomatoes and olives baked *al cartoccio* (in a paper sack). A fish risotto is the Veneto on a plate. The great vegetable risottos incorporate zucchini or a mixture of spring vegetables, in which case the dish is called *primavera*. There is a beauty that calls for asparagus tips, but its season is short. The vegetables grown on the islands of the lagoon are noted for their special flavor, which is imparted by the salt air.

The Queen of the Adriatic receives her admirers by the hundreds of thousands each year. She feeds them, amuses them, bedazzles them. Herewith is a small selection of places for happy eating and sleeping in Venice.

The top trio are Harry's Bar, the Gritti Palace Hotel, and the Cipriani. Harry's Bar represents the most polished professionalism in Europe. No matter how crowded (during the season the walls must be elastic), the management copes. Actually the juxtaposition of the famous, not so famous, and infamous simply heightens the excitement. The vegetables come from the restaurant's own garden on the island of Torcello. The *tagliarini* is an example of pasta perfect. The fish are the finest daily selection to be found on the Rialto. The chocolate cake, which may have been Austria's legacy to Venice, is greed satisfied. And nobody does a nicer club sandwich.

The deck of the Gritti on the Grand Canal, with its oblique view of the splendors of Santa Maria della Salute (reputed to have been a favorite vantage of Marcel Proust's), offers front-row tables on the most spectacular aquacade on earth. Against the backdrop of the palazzi you get the pageant of water traffic: gondolas, work barges, a funeral cortege, a wedding party, the postal boat, the coast guard, the *vaporetti* (steam launches), and the motor launches. In the lagoon you can see the cruise boats that make Venice a port of call. The food is consistently good and the service is high style, as befits candlelight dining on the Grand Canal.

The Cipriani, five minutes away as the seagulls fly, is Venice as a resort. A shuttle launch operates between the hotel and a landing at San Marco. The Cipriani offers an Olympic-size swimming pool, gardens fronting the lagoon looking toward the Lido, a formal dining room with Fortuny curtains and Murano chandeliers, and a poolside dining room and terrace for lunch. The hors d'oeuvre buffet is so vast and varied that one tends to choose the help-yourself rather than ordering from the menu.

The big three are the summit of *luxe*. To balance the diet, there is the year-round favorite *trattoria* of Venetians. La Colomba, at Piscina di Frezzeria 1665, has a long, awninged sidewalk terrace, walls of paintings encouraged by the Deana family, and in season an eye-stopping construction of eggplants, sweet peppers, zucchini, and onions held together by wooden picks and garlanded perhaps with chili peppers. The waiter remembered after a two-month interval—that I don't like cucumbers in a mixed salad. This recollection welded me to the Colomba.

The Ristorante Al Theatro next door to the Teatro La Fenice is animated at all times, serves drinks, snacks, and full meals, and is a fine place to taste that old Venetian specialty, sardines *in saor* (with sweet-and-sour sauce).

A high proportion of the visiting artists singing at La Fenice stay at the aptly named Hotel La Fenice et des Artistes, a complex of old buildings rearranged into sixty-five rooms with baths. A few of the rooms have rooftop terraces, and the atmosphere is personal enough to tempt one into a long sojourn. Also in the second-category charm group is the Hotel Flora, midway between the Gritti and San Marco, but withdrawn in a little flowered patio. Like the Hotel La Fenice, it offers only breakfast.

An impressive group of personalities from many countries and many fields make it a yearly habit to stay at the first-category Hotel Monaco Grand Canal with twenty-five of its eighty rooms over-looking the Grand Canal. The kitchen is serious, with a talented young chef being actively supported by the management. The Hotel Saturnia, on the smart walkway of Via XXII Marzo, is another first-category hotel. It has a tucked-away patio for meals called the Cortile, plus a highly rated restaurant, La Caravella.

Visitors coming to Venice for long stays are loyal to an old-fashioned *pensione* with personality, the Seguso, located on the broad canal where the big ships come in.

The true Venetian *pazzo* opts for the early autumn season. When the summer hordes have melted away and the prices have sub-sided, the city begins to amuse its natives with opera, theater, con-certs, and exhibitions. In the autumn Venice removes her domino to reveal her seductive charms to the year-round Venetians, who are just plain mad about their city and its outposts up the Brenta.

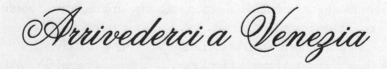

Arrivederci a Venezia

Traveling at Home

BY RENATA ROSSO

~

editor's note

As I mentioned earlier, I prefer not to include excerpts from books in *The Collected Traveler;* nor do I commission articles for this series. But in reviewing my files for this edition, I realized that I did not have enough material on the smaller towns of the Veneto (or what I did have was not sufficient). So when I learned that my friend Renata Rosso, who is from Treviso but lives in New York, was going back home for a month, I asked her if she would write something about her hometown and the area around it. She agreed, because she is incredibly passionate about northeastern Italy. When I listen to Renata talk about the Veneto, her eyes light up, and I am reminded of a quote from the beautiful book *Venice and the Veneto* (text by Sylvie Durastanti; photographs by Sonja Bullaty and Angelo Lomes, Abbeville Press, 1998): "To wander over terra firma is to step straight into the landscapes seen in the paintings of Cima da Conegliano or Giovanni Bellini— the spectacular Dolomites, the rolling hills surrounding Asolo, Mount Berici near Vicenza, the Colli Euganei close to Padua, the grapevines of Soave and Valpolicella, the meadows of Negrar. The Veneto has everything you might long for should you grow weary of the lagoon." So even though this piece is making its appearance here for the first time, I hope you'll agree it was worth the effort.

RENATA ROSSO is the U.S. correspondent for the performing arts magazine *Prima Fila,* based in Rome, and New York correspondent for *World Architecture,* based in London.

I was born and grew up in the Veneto region, in the northeastern part of Italy. Treviso is my hometown. I have been living in New York for the past ten years; therefore I consider myself both a New Yorker and a Venetian. Since living here I have a different relationship with my past. I feel split between the person who lives in

New York and the person who is Venetian. The key to this double nature is reflected in my name: *Renata*, from the Latin *renatus, (a)*, born twice.

But where is my home? Whenever I go back to the Veneto, I feel like a traveler. I look at everything with different eyes. I rediscover old places constantly. The streets, the buildings, the echo of my steps under the porticoes of Treviso remind me of my youth, but with a different dimension. I rediscover the beauty and poetry in little details, the way people gesture, or walk, the modulation of their voices. I notice there is a certain innate elegance in the way people say *buon giorno, prego* (good morning, thank you); the way they smile and the natural grace that most of the women have. I never noticed those things quite so much before. For example, I can hear the solemnity of my *r* and the elegance of the *z* when I say the formal *La ringrazio* (I thank you). I feel so much subtle pleasure in just two simple words.

I get lost in my thoughts when it comes to the sound of words. I start paying attention to it in a detached way as if I were watching and the sound didn't belong to me. This detachment seems to have started when I began going to the Metropolitan Opera in New York City. It never happened before, when I was going to Italian opera houses. In the United States I started being a spectator of my own language. I was able to observe how complex and musical Italian is. This had a lot to do with the fact that I was living in a new country with a new language.

The house where I grew up is located near the sixteenth-century Porta San Tomaso in Treviso. This is one of the three main entrances to the city. In my opinion it is the most beautiful one, with its imposing white facade and the Saint Mark's statue of the lion protecting the access to the historic center. Treviso, like many Italian cities, is surrounded by walls, whose construction started around 1315 and that were later modified and completed in 1532.

The historic part of the city is within these walls, and across the street from my house there is an embankment, topped by horse chestnut trees, that follows their perimeter. People enjoy taking walks *sulle mura* (along the walls). From the top of the embankment, one notices below a series of intersecting channels streaked with little tongues (strips) of land covered by grass, trees, bushes, and flowers, where ducks, swans, and all kind of birds find a perfect ecosystem.

Treviso is a city of water. The important River Sile is emerald green and runs silently through the city along the so-called Riviera Garibaldi. It has always fascinated me for its deep color and clear waters. The river's and channels' intersection is so mesmerizing that Dante Alighieri—the famous Italian poet born in Florence in 1265—identified the city of Treviso in his *Divina Commedia,* by mentioning the Sile River and the intersecting Cagnan channel: *"E dove Sile e Cagnan s'accompagna,"* Paradiso, canto 9, verse 49. He had been a "poet in exile" at the northern Italian courts since 1302 and visited Treviso around 1306, at the court of Gherardo da Camino.

Recently the Riviera Garibaldi area has been restored. The building that once belonged to the "old hospital"—founded between 1261 and 1269—has been transformed into a university. It is like a small citadel: a beautiful new square surrounded by restored palazzi, all built at different times. A narrow channel skirts them. The old small bridges have been given new life by the architect Paolo Portoghesi. This new square has provided a new dimension and horizon to the city. An impressive wooden bridge has been built across the Sile, the Ponte dell'Università. This makes for a pleasant walk even for those who are not students but simply wish to enjoy the combination of the elegant architecture of the palazzi, the winding course of the channels meandering across the Sile River, and the trees marking the water's flow.

One of my favorite spots beside the Riviera Garibaldi on a quiet sunny morning is the Piazzetta (Little Square) del Monte di Pietà, adjacent to the Palazzo dei Trecento, which is behind the main square, Piazza dei Signori. It is easy to find. There are a few places for a good cappuccino, or at noon a *spritz,* which is not the most interesting *aperitivo* but which one identifies with Treviso and Venice. I like its bittersweet taste and the contrast between its red color and the orange slice. I don't know the exact proportions, but it is made with Prosecco, a dry white wine, sparkling mineral water, and a shot of Campari or Aperol (for the light version).

All the cafés in the Piazzetta have outdoor tables, and I carefully choose their location. At the Bottega del Caffè I go for the *scorcio incantevole* (enchanting view). From my table it is as if I were at the theater. The backdrop is the fifteenth-century Palazzo del Monte di Pietà, with its elegant facade and its marble-framed grated windows sided by candles, towered over by the campanile of the Chiesa di San Vito. On the right side of this splendid set is the brick-red back wall of the Palazzo dei Trecento, and opposite stands the rigorous facade of an eighteenth-century building. The cobblestones of the sloping pavement complete the scene.

A few steps away we find ourselves in the heart of the city at the *loggia* of the Palazzo dei Trecento. While sitting at the table of either the Bar Biffi or Beltrame, we can enjoy the amplitude of its arched ceiling and watch the people. These two bars serve the best *panini con porchetta* (roasted yearling pork) that one can ever taste. The *porchetta* has been a tradition in Treviso since 1922, when the Beltrame family started a new recipe by cooking ham for seven hours in a special oven, then slicing it by hand and filling small warm rolls with it.

Whenever I come to Treviso, I stay at my aunt Adelia's. She turned eighty on August 1, 2001, and with my brother Alessandro and sister Antonia and the children, we organized a party for her birthday at a typical restaurant near the Venetian Lagoon, Al Cavallino. We decided to go to a restaurant near the Venetian Lagoon because my aunt is from Venice. (My mother's whole family is originally from Venice; my aunt and my mother moved to Treviso during World War II.) The two cities are very close, twenty minutes by train. (The Venetians dominated Treviso from 1339 to 1381 and then again from 1388 to 1797.)

To get there, we drove on the Treviso-mare highway, beyond Lido di Jésolo (a popular beach), to that charming street that runs along the lagoon, recognizable by its characteristic *barene* (marshes), scattered all over. The restaurant is located in an area that still has the flavor of the past, with faded small-scale buildings surrounding the little square. At its center is a bronze sculpture of a little horse, the Cavallino, from which the restaurant takes its name. A silent calm exudes from the lagoon. The seafood was superb, typical of a cuisine that is not sophisticated but genuine. The fish from the lagoon in general are small (so-called *pesce piccolo della laguna*). I recall all the dishes in Venetian dialect: *schie* (lagoon shrimp), *canestrei* (sort of jurel), *cappe sante* (small scallops cooked in the oven in their own shells), *sarde in saor* (marinated sardines; the fish is fried, then marinated with onions, vinegar, pine nuts, raisins); *canoce* (*cicala di mare,* mantis prawns).

For me it was like revisiting my childhood. We used to go to this restaurant with my parents. The village and the atmosphere haven't changed much since then.

Despite her age my aunt is still a great cook. Typical of Italians, what she cooks depends on the season, encompassing all of the traditional Venetian recipes. (Thank goodness Mother recorded them for us in a beautiful red leather book.) Her almond cake is famous among relatives and friends as well as her *zaletti* (yellow cookies made with wheat flour and cornmeal), and her *tiramisù,* which, by the way, was invented in Treviso. During the Carnival period every-

one is after her unbeatable *fritoe venexiane (frittelle veneziane)*,
Venetian pancakes made with flour, apples, raisins, and pine nuts.
In wintertime I love her homemade ravioli, filled with *radicchio
rosso di Treviso* and ricotta cheese.

The *radicchio di Treviso,* also known as *spadone* because of its
elongated sword shape, is considered king of the winter tables. It is
a true specialty of this area; its unique flavor is due to the combination of the slightly bitter crispy white ribs and the sweet red
leaves. One can appreciate the particular taste of radicchio in a variety of dishes: as a simple salad or grilled, in a risotto, or with tagliatelle, ravioli, and lasagna.

I get lazy when I am in Treviso, and traveling implies an effort.
Sometimes I want nothing more than to stay with my brother and
sister, playing with my wonderful nieces and nephews: Giulia,
Francesca, Nicola, and Lorenzo. Yet I like to travel and discover new
places and rediscover old ones, and visit friends as well: what a
dilemma for me.

On a hot Thursday in August, I took the train to Vicenza to visit
one of my dearest friends, Dina, who wanted me to see her newly
renovated apartment in the Palladian Palazzo Bonin, on Corso
Palladio, which is one of the main streets in Vicenza.

To get there, I took a local train, without air conditioning. In
spite of the heat, I didn't mind it at all. I liked the feeling of summer,
hearing the chirping of the indefatigable cicadas at every train stop,
and feeling the warm wind caressing my face. I felt as if I were on a
journey to the past. I enjoyed it completely, even when the train
stopped in the middle of a cornfield and the sun hit perpendicularly
on the cars. I had become part of that languor: the vivid green of the
trees' leaves, the smell of the newly cut grass. It was so refreshing.

Dina, a dignified lady with big green eyes, picked me up at the
train station and took me to the sixteenth-century Palazzo Bonin,

which has a gigantic wooden main entrance and a beautiful arch that leads to a private courtyard covered with cobblestones.

She renovated the apartment with incredible taste inspired by the famous architect Flavio Albanese. The results are charming and colorful. Red and orange velvet is everywhere. A wonderful collection of Venini blown glass covers the shelves of an entire wall. My room was all white, with a Philip Starck bed. My window offered a view of the top of a medieval tower, the Torre di Porta Castello.

Dina had prepared a wonderful dinner of grilled fresh vegetables from her country house and a *torta salata* (quiche). This was served with a good glass of cold white wine. We dined in the cozy modern yellow-orange kitchen. Her friend Giovanna Dalla Pozza, an art historian, joined us. After dinner we walked around the streets of Vicenza until past midnight. Giovanna gave us the most incredible tour of the city, with detailed explanations about the palazzi. After our tour we stopped at the Caffè Garibaldi, on the Piazza dei Signori. It faces the breathtaking Basilica Palladiana. On the way back to Dina's, I noticed a few people following us, intrigued by the explanations of the *professoressa,* who just happens to be the president of Italia Nostra, an association for the preservation of Italian artistic sites.

I left the following day to join my brother Alessandro for a trip to Asolo. My brother is an interior designer and was going there to meet with Gianfranco Gazzola, a famous craftsman known for his exquisite furniture. While riding in the car, I enjoyed a chat with my brother. Treviso is only 33 kilometers from Asolo. To get there, one has to pass through Montebelluna, a small town that is the world capital of shoes and where one can visit the mountaineering boot museum. When we were little, we used to go with my mother to Montebelluna for shoes at Colognese, a store on Via Mazzini that carries very high-quality shoes. The store is still there. For me it was *un disastro*. I couldn't help it: I bought a pair of every color of their sandals!

Via Forestuzzo, the narrow road that leads up to Asolo, serves as a splendid prologue to the city, with green galleries created by the trees' lush branches. Almost at the top of the hill, elegant houses take the place of nature. Without realizing it, we found ourselves on the Via Browning, with its series of arches and pillars that lead to the main square, Piazza Garibaldi.

The Caffè Centrale is right in the middle of the square, in front of the Fontana (fountain) Maggiore. The Caffè Centrale is the quintessential place for leisure: under its orange tent, protected from the sun, we enjoyed one of the small pleasures that life sometimes reserves for us and immersed ourselves in a sea of tranquillity. It is an international place, where you will usually find at least some British, American, French, or German visitors. On the backs of the yellow cotton chairs is printed the names of famous people who have come to Asolo: the Cypriot queen Caterina Cornaro, the poets Pietro Bembo and Robert Browning, the actress Eleonora Duse, and the composers Igor Stravinsky and Arnold Schoenberg, to mention only a few.

We had a light lunch at the café. One can get fresh salads, quiches, and a variety of tasty sandwiches. The ice cream is excellent and can be topped off with good espresso.

Alessandro helped me with my suitcase to the Hotel Duse, which faces the square and is located on Via Browning. Lorenza, the friendly young manager, was eager to please me. She accommodated my need for "the perfect view" by allowing me to check all the available rooms in the hotel. I chose the one with the beautiful view of the Torre dell'Orologio (clock tower), the roof of the Duomo, the Fontana Maggiore, the Via Cornaro, and the Renaissance-style Palazzo della Loggia, with its remarkable frescoes.

The end of August is off-season in Asolo, hence the best time to be there. My room was very cozy—I felt at peace and happy there. My brief sojourn in Asolo sustained this feeling, with a delightful view at every new hillside and a picturesque corner at every turn. Each morning I got up early and took a brief walk to the Hotel Al Sole, on Via del Collegio. I would go there to have breakfast on its terrace. Gabriella very kindly brought my cappuccino and complimentary cookies outside to my table. From there the view of the main square, and farther down the *campagna veneta* (Veneto countryside) with the profile of the Colli Euganei (Euganean Hills) in the background, was enchanting. "This was the view that the actress Eleonora Duse had from her bedroom, which is located above the terrace," Gabriella told me.

Eleonora Duse (1858–1924) traveled extensively during her career, and Asolo was one of her favorite places to find calm and rest. At that time her rival for the title of world's greatest actress was Sarah Bernhardt. Duse, at her best in tragedy, was the opposite of the flamboyant Bernhardt. She was quiet and withdrawn, an actress of great strength and subtlety, an enigmatic person. Her lover, the Italian poet Gabriele D'Annunzio (1863–1938), who wrote most of his plays for Eleonora, "stayed at this hotel as well," said Gabriella with an understanding smile, "but not in the same room, the one just across the hall." The rooms, though renovated, still bear the names of the two artists.

Each afternoon I took a short nap and did some reading in my room. Then I was ready to please my eyes and soul with another walk and panoramic view.

In the twilight I usually took Via Cornaro toward Via Canova (high heels are not recommended since the worn-out marble sidewalk can be very slippery) to go to Hotel Cipriani for a Bellini. The outdoor garden of the hotel is enclosed but has an open view of the valley. I would pick a table near the parapet, with a view of the hills and the sixteenth-century Villa Armeni, rising on the Colle (Hill)

Messano, with its meadows, cultivated land, vineyards, olive trees, and isolated ancient houses. A pleasant breeze followed the sunset. The view reinforced a forgotten silence. Ernesto always took my order, and after a couple of days he knew what I wanted before I spoke. Besides the impeccable Bellini—with fresh peach juice and Prosecco—he presented me with fresh fried *fiori di zucchine* (zucchini flowers) and olives.

I skipped Cipriani's restaurant for lunch and dinner since I could live without its *risotto all'asolana,* which in his New York restaurant is called *risotto primavera.*

In the mornings I wanted consistency and would repeat the ritual of having cappuccino and cookies. For lunch, however, I liked lingering in different places. One time I went to visit the tomb of Eleonora Duse in the cemetery of Sant'Anna. It was very sunny and hot, and I got quite tired walking in Via Canova. I stopped for some calm and shade in the Church of Santa Caterina. I liked it there. It was almost unadorned except for some fifteenth-century fragments of frescoes with partially faded but delicate pastel colors. The atmosphere was imbued with peace. I continued my walk and arrived on the top of a small hill, at the little Church of Sant'Anna, where Duse used to pray. It was closed, but I read some verses dedicated to the actress that the Italian poetess Ada Negri had written on a memorial stone. I entered the church's cemetery, which has a very well-kept garden with a variety of trees and plants and a profusion of jasmines. The tomb faces Monte Grappa and is famous for its simplicity and austerity. Then I looked for the tomb of one of the greatest Hellenists in history, Manara Valgimigli, who had been the professor of my favorite uncle Teodolfo (*il mio grande maestro,* he used to call him) at the University of Padua. Unfortunately I couldn't find it. Then a thought crossed my mind. In all my days in Italy, I had been to my parents' chapel in Treviso only once. Here I was in a cemetery paying homage to people I didn't know. I felt somehow guilty and rootless. At the same time I realized I was too hard on myself. After all, by visiting a cemetery, any cemetery, one pays homage to all the dead. I never feel my parents in a cemetery.

That visit was a solemn experience for me, one of the rituals in life one needs once in a while. I find it reassuring—I don't know of what. It just happens.

That same night a dark storm came up, as if big gray clouds were fighting one another for the same spot in the sky. The brightness of the gray, white, and yellow of the sky enhanced the colors of the rooftops surrounding the Torre dell'Orologio. Even with the storm, I continued to be happy with the view from my balcony.

Since it was raining, I decided to go out and walk under the porticoes of the Via Browning, to find a place for dinner. Lorenza at the reception desk smiled at me without saying a word. I was probably the only guest going out in that weather.

I had passed by the Enoteca alle Ore several times and remembered it from previous trips to Asolo. Its look of authenticity had always intrigued me. That night I decided to go inside. (It had the added advantage of being the closest place to my hotel.) I was immediately impressed by the tasteful decor. The walls are covered floor to ceiling with wooden shelves generously filled with bottles of wine, all perfectly lined up like soldiers waiting for their orders. The outfits of the hosts—black slacks and shirts with brown leather aprons—seemed very fashionable.

At that moment I didn't realize that this was going to be one of the most memorable evenings of my Italian summer. Besides the allure of the place, the most interesting attraction for me turned out to be the *oste* (host) and oenologist Stefano Gislon, a very charming man from Friuli who could talk about wine as if it were poetry. He told me that his *enoteca* (cellar) had more than a thousand different labels. While giving me its history, he opened all kinds of bottles and brought beautiful glasses of different shapes and sizes: flutes, goblets, Paris goblets, balloons for the red, port glasses, and more. With the savoir-faire of a gentleman, he asked me, "What would you like to drink? *Secco o bollicine?* (Dry or bubbles?)" "*Secco,*" I answered.

With a calm and warm timbre of voice he explained, "My *enoteca* carries only Italian wines. They represent all regions of Italy. I want people to start knowing Italian wines, and to promote natural wine, which means wine produced without using any kind of nontraditional technology." Meanwhile he was pouring me a glass of Terralba, from Castello di Lispida, in the *Piemonte* (Piedmont) region, a natural nonfiltered white wine. "This cellar produces only five thousand bottles a season," he pointed out. "The wine hasn't been filtered; therefore its color is opaque yellow, and the body is the same as red wine, very rich in taste. The *vino naturale* (natural wine) is pressed with bare feet, as in the past. Wine pressed with feet is much softer than that made by a winepress.

"The grapevine is a very sensitive plant," he emphasized. "The best way to cultivate it is by hand." And with even more seriousness, he said, "I can tell immediately when the vineyard is stressed." The conversation was becoming more intriguing with every sip of deliciousness. I had never heard of a "stressed" vine. From living in New York I knew that stress could affect people, dogs, and fish— but wine? Smiling, he asserted, "The grapevine is very sensitive to noise. For example, a tractor creates terrible vibrations in the soil that bother the roots. The roots, which naturally branch out and grow close to the surface, try to avoid these vibrations by going deeper and deeper. Consequently the taste of the grapes gets spoiled, since the minerals, the salts, and the water near the surface are all different from those much deeper in the ground."

The Enoteca alle Ore has been in this sixteenth-century building since 1720. It has always been an *osteria* (a place that serves only wine). The place has been renovated, but it has maintained the same antique shelves, counter, and wall clock.

Hans, a young Brazilian who was helping Stefano Gislon, brought some appetizers to help me appreciate the wine better. The plate was perfectly arranged with some freshly sliced bread, *porchetta, fesa di tacchino* (turkey), *mortadella,* and *lardo di colonnata* (the best-quality lard).

"We accompany the wine with this simple food. This is not a restaurant. One can also have fresh vegetables made to order either raw or grilled, along with a variety of Italian cheeses," said Gislon. "Hans is a specialist at decorating the plates. He worked for years in Berlin."

A group of people from Milan and Florence arrived and greeted him as an old friend. There was a very friendly atmosphere. Gislon, like a conductor in concert, made sure that everyone was drinking the right wine.

Sitting at my table, he continued his fascinating lecture: "Four, five generations ago, wine was considered an aliment [a necessary part of the diet]. Farmers would leave in the morning to till the soil, and they would typically bring with them, for lunch, a piece of bread and two liters of wine. They considered wine food, like pasta. But they were not eating pasta. Now, the younger generation has rediscovered wine. They are curious about it. When they come here, they ask me all kinds of questions."

I wanted to know which wines from the Veneto he would recommend. "A serious cellar is Villa Maser, owned by the Countess Volpi. They produce a good Pinot Nero." The vineyard is located at the famous Palladian Villa Barbaro Volpi, in Maser, ten minutes from Asolo. There one can get an idea of the lifestyle of Venetian society in the second half of the sixteenth century. The architect Andrea Palladio and the painter Veronese worked together on this project, perfectly integrating architectural and pictorial space.

"I would like to mention also the Rosso dell'Abbazia [made of Cabernet Sauvignon and Merlot grapes, so-called *bordolese*] from the cellar Serafin and Vidotto in Nervesa della Battaglia [a little town in the Montello hill]," Gislon continued. "Their 1998 Phigaia, 'after the red,' is a good Cabernet. Among the Prosecco [a dry white local wine], I would recommend one produced by the Consorzio del Montello e dei Colli Asolani, which is a cooperative wine-growers' association. Other good cellars are the Agostinetto and the Primo Franco. From Conegliano I recall Giovanni Grigoletto's Prosecco and his Merlot and Cabernet."

Then he asked me: "Would you like to join Hans and me for dinner? I am going to make some scampi with spaghetti, just for the three of us." Of course I said yes. He went to the kitchen and after a little while came out with an excellent dish. Fresh peeled and diced tomato, organic olive oil, and basil made a sauce that complemented the scampi perfectly. While we dined, he explained to me that for cooking he used a special olive oil—as with the wine, the olives are also harvested by hand—produced in Bassano del Grappa (in the province of Vicenza) by Stefano Zonta, who is also a wineproducer. Zonta's Tocai di Breganze and Malvasia Veneta *"sono vini armonici di grande struttura,"* he said at the end of the evening. He gave me a bottle of the special olive oil before I left.

It was midnight when I made my way back to my room thinking, "This has been one of those great unexpected experiences that makes one appreciate life and human beings more than ever."

I slept deeply, *a stampo,* as I used to say in my teens to my mother. When I woke up, it felt "as if the sleep were a mold removed from my body." The morning was a typical *quiete dopo la tempesta* (calm after the storm). The sky was blue and clear, the air thin and pure.

I set out for Possagno on the *navetta* (shuttle bus), which goes downhill toward Ca' Vescovo, and caught the *corriera* (bus) to the town. I hadn't been there since I was sixteen for an art history class at the *liceo*. I wanted to visit Canova's Temple and the Gallery of Plaster Casts (Gipsoteca Canoviana). My ride to Possagno lasted thirty minutes. I enjoyed passing by the little towns of Monfumo, Paderno del Grappa, and Crespano del Grappa. They are all worth a visit.

The bus driver suggested a visit to *le malghe,* a place where one can see the process of cheese-making and taste all kinds of local cheeses produced there (Montasio, Caciotta del Grappa, Latteria, Casatella). Unfortunately I didn't have time for that, but I would for sure on my next trip.

Off the bus in Possagno, I immediately spotted the house (now a museum) where the neoclassical sculptor Antonio Canova was born in 1757. Then I headed directly for the gallery. The first time I saw this museum, it had a strong impact on me, and I became fond of Canova's work. I wanted to admire again the refined bust of Napoleon, portrayed by Canova in 1804, when he went to Paris as the emperor's official sculptor. At sixteen I thought this face of Napoleon was the most beautiful one I had ever seen.

Plaster casts of many of Canova's famous marble statues are in this unique gallery. It was great to appreciate again the perfection of the *Tre Grazie,* whose original in marble is at the Hermitage in St. Petersburg, and *Amore e Psiche,* which is at the Louvre and the Metropolitan Museum. The whiteness of the place is overwhelming, as well as the beauty of these masterpieces.

Soon after my visit to Possagno, I left Asolo and returned to Treviso by bus with my five-year-old nephew Nicola, who had spent a couple of days in Asolo with me. This was his first time taking a bus—an exciting experience. Upon my return to Treviso, I had only a few days left before leaving for New York.

I decided I must visit a remarkable lady, Ettora Arman, who owns one of the most typical *osterie* (wine shops) in Treviso. I hadn't seen her in years. Located on Via Manzoni, *"entro le mura"* (within the walls), her *osteria* is close to my house and across the street from my grandfather's house, where my sister now lives.

"Arman is an old *osteria*. My family owned it since 1872," Ettora told me with a voice-pitch worthy of a coloratura soprano. "Originally," she continued, "it was a place where you could only have wine. My great-grandfather owned a vineyard in Col di San Martino, in a village called San Vigilio. That was the wine he served in the *osteria* in Treviso. Still today we serve only the wine we produce, a *prosecco frizzante naturale* [sparkling natural Prosecco]." Prosecco is a white wine produced in the province of Treviso, in an area that stretches from the hills of Valdobbiadene to the hills of Conegliano. The road connecting the two towns is called the Strada del Prosecco. Along this road one can find, among others, the sweet slopes of Col San Martino, which is covered with golden grapes.

Arman's interior is very simple, with wooden tables in an ample space. Four generations have been working there, and Ettora renovated the place starting with *la cucina* (kitchen). "It's open all year round from eight in the morning to eleven in the evening. I am seventy years old and have never taken a vacation," she told me. "There is a lot of warmth in this place. Human relationships are most important. Here people come to chat, to play cards, to be with others and drink a glass—or more—of wine." Modulating her voice, she added, "Working is my life. It gives me energy and strength. I manage the place by myself with five women who work for me. During regular days at least four hundred people come here." A customer came over and stated, "She is our queen. What would we do without her?"

With a light smile Ettora continued: "Here there are people of all ages. In the morning and afternoon they are mostly retired. Many are lonely. Here they can find a home. They feel welcome. In the evenings and on the weekends, there are many young people.

They prefer to come here for dinner with their girlfriends instead of going to a disco."

While drinking a glass of wine, one can always find a little snack available at the counter: half an egg with a *cipollina* (pearl onion), a little cube of *mortadella* and a *grissino*, a *panino con sopressa* (sandwich with a local salami), or a *frittatina* (little frittata) with green peas, onions, or zucchini.

After taking care of a customer, Ettora returned to me. "Around seven, seven-thirty, in wintertime—a season more suitable for *osteria*, when we yearn for some warm food—I take a kilo of rice and make a risotto with radicchio or spinach, potatoes, or a *primavera* [mixed vegetables]. When it's ready, I ring the bell my customers gave me a while ago as a present, and announce *"La cena è pronta!"* (Dinner is ready), as if we were a family. They can have a *"piatto di risotto e un bicchiere di vino per cinquemila lire* [risotto and a glass of wine for $2.50]." Smiling, she showed me the bell. "It is the same bell I ring at eleven P.M. when it is time to close. They all know they have to respect my schedule."

When I asked why she didn't cook lunch and dinner regularly, she told me something that made me admire her even more: "I don't want to be in the kitchen all the time, because I wouldn't be able to take care of my customers as I like to. I know all of them by name, and I have a nice word for everyone. I know who is lonely and needs this place for company. For some, this is a place of great comfort. They come here because of me."

While showing me around she mentioned, "Furthermore, here I organize art exhibitions. As you notice, the walls are all covered with paintings. I am booked for exhibitions until the year 2004. I try to help young artists, and this place is well known." Then she brought out some note cards to show me: they were from all over the world, East, West, and even from New York. A couple from the

West Village thanked her and expressed how much they missed her *deliziosi pranzetti* (delicious informal luncheons).

"If you want to have dinner here you have to make a reservation. One can find, according to season, *pasta e fagioli* [pasta and beans], *baccalà* [salt cod], on Friday *polenta e seppie,* and on Tuesday *trippa in brodo e alla parmigiana* [tripe soup and tripe parmigiana]. In addition there are fresh homemade desserts, and my *sbreghette* [biscotti] that I make once a week with flour, dried figs, almonds, and wild fennel seeds."

I was particularly impressed and touched by Ettora Arman. Her eyes shone with calm and serenity. It is not easy to find someone so in love with what she does, so giving and loving of people. The uniqueness of this wonderful woman is that she is always like this—she never gets tired of it.

My stay was coming to an end. I still had to go to Conegliano to visit the headquarters of a world-class company: Permasteelisa. Conegliano, the home of Prosecco, is a delightful town with many artistic sites. This time I didn't go for the fresco-decorated palaces on the Via XX Settembre, or for its castle and the nearby restaurant Al Castello, which has a beautiful terrace from which to enjoy the view as you savor *polenta e funghi chiodini* (polenta with mushrooms). This time I went to visit a company renowned for the most advanced technology in construction.

The first time I had heard of Permasteelisa was at the opening of an exhibition on the architect Frank Gehry at the Guggenheim Museum in New York. Permasteelisa, a company based in Conegliano, was the contractor for the titanium panel cladding for Gehry's Guggenheim Museum in Bilbao. In New York the same titanium paneling had been employed for the Condé Nast Cafeteria, also designed by Gehry. This fact aroused my interest in visiting the company headquarters.

The chief engineer, Marc Zobec, director of research and development, is a friendly young Australian. He explained to me that Massimo Colomban had founded the company in the 1970s. The company's first important commission was the curtain wall for the Sydney Opera House. "This was the first building in the world to use structural silicon and suspended vertical glass on a large scale," he pointed out.

In a relatively short span of time, the company has grown quite fast. At the moment it counts sixteen factories worldwide and is a leader in the external cladding of buildings. "We focus on research and work in connection with major Italian and American universities. [MIT is one of them.] We try to find new heating and ventilating solutions, aiming to lower the costs and to protect the environment." As a matter of fact Colomban's motto is "Architectural building is a challenge against time and against the limitations of technology and common knowledge."

In an outdoor garden at the company headquarters, details of building facades are displayed in real scale. It was quite impressive to see the number and variety of buildings that Permasteelisa has supplied worldwide. I recognized the sample of the interlaced golden steel structure for the great Olympic Fish. This monumental sculpture by Frank Gehry was commissioned for the Olympic City in Barcelona.

I noticed as well the sample of external cladding supplied for the European Parliament building in Brussels, the one for the Galerie Lafayette in Berlin, and the one for the elegant ultramodern Bangkok City Tower in Thailand, designed by the architect Kenzo Tange. Being in that environment was like experiencing the most innovative technology and design in building cladding exteriors. In a way this was a completion of a trip that had started in the past and ended in the most ultimate of modernity. *Il Nordest* (the Northeast) is not only a region of the past. In the last forty years, it has also been home to phenomenal industrial development. Large companies, but above all small and medium-size industries as well, have made the Northeast the area with the highest per capita income in Europe.

My trip was over. It was time for me to go to the Marco Polo Airport in Venice and leave for New York. My brother drove me. It takes only fifteen minutes from Treviso if one rides the highway Venezia–Vittorio Veneto. Now my Italian self had to make room for my New York self, but part of my soul would remain there.

Italy's Beneficent Lake: The Charms of Lago di Garda

BY WILLIAM PETROCELLI

༚

editor's note

Some maps refer to the eastern half of Lake Garda as belonging to the Veneto and the western half to Lombardy. For the purposes of this book, I have considered the lake to be part of the Veneto. In addition to its beauty and setting, this gorgeous lake also offers restorative benefits of a spiritual nature: on the shores of the lake (or not far away) are ten sacred sanctuaries to visit, such as Madonna di Montecastello, San Felice del Benaco, and Peschiera del Garda. The tourist office published a good brochure—"Sacred Places for Meditation"—in time for jubilee year 2000, and it is still widely available at tourist offices here in the United States.

WILLIAM PETROCELLI is co-owner, with his wife, of the outstanding bookstore Book Passage, which has a deserved reputation for its travel book selection. He wrote this piece for the Book Passage newsletter. (See the Bookstores entry in *Informazioni Pratiche* if you'd like to subscribe.)

What makes Lago di Garda so special? It's the mountains and the water, the buildings and the history. But mostly it's the people and the stories.

Signor Bonetti's small building is visible for several blocks in Torri del Benaco, a small, picturesque town on the eastern shore of Lago di Garda. Until 1994 the hand-painted letters NCERE could be seen high on the wall that faces down the main street. Between the window and those letters was a huge smudge mark like a giant erasure.

The letters were painted on the wall in 1944, when Bonetti was a little boy living in the upper stories of the building that now houses his real estate office. That was a bleak wartime year, and Mussolini and his "Italian Social Republic"—a puppet government installed by the Nazis—were headquartered just across Lake Garda in the town of Saló.

According to Bonetti, the fascist Black Shirts liked to race around the lake painting slogans on walls to whip up enthusiasm for the war. One night they propped a ladder against Bonetti's house and painted the word VINCERE (conquer) in big letters. When they left, Bonetti's mother was so angry that she reached out the window to wipe off the offending word. But she could reach only the first two letters. The others remained on the wall for forty years as a sad reminder.

U.S. travel writers don't often write about Lago di Garda, and we hate to disagree with the May 12 *New York Times* ("Idyll by Blue Waters"). But the author got it wrong! He stayed on the western side of the lake. That side is unquestionably beautiful, and that's why those of us on the east like to look at it. Choosing the wrong side of the lake isn't a character flaw, mind you, but rather a rookie mistake—like taking your first California trip to Los Angeles instead of San Francisco.

The eastern and western shores of Lake Garda are decidedly different. The western shore, with larger hotels and a grander lakeside promenade, has a nineteenth-century feel. The eastern shore, with Veronese castles and Venetian buildings, seems older and a little less formal. For years the frontier ran through the lake, separating, first Verona, then the Republic of Venice, and finally the Austro-Hungarian Empire from the rest of Italy, and that accounts for many of the differences. There's no hostility between the people on the two sides anymore, but rather a puzzlement that someone would choose to go to the other side. In fairness to Saló, however, the civic leaders have erased every trace of Mussolini's regime, so people from the eastern shore don't have that grudge to bear.

There's a north-south cultural difference as well. During World War I the frontier with Austria-Hungary crossed Lake Garda near the northern tip, and the fighting near the lake was bloody and furious. Today the area around the charming northern town of Riva del Garda is part of the semiautonomous Trentino–Alto Adige region and marks the beginning of Tyrolean Italy.

Lago di Garda will break your heart. On a clear day it is so breathtakingly beautiful, you can't stop looking at it. But on an overcast day, or a particularly hot day when the *foschia,* or foglike mist, rises off the lake, you'll curse the lake's existence, wondering why you're denied the beauty of its view.

The lake was praised by Catullus, Virgil, Pliny, and other Roman writers, and it was known to them as Lake Benacus, the Beneficent Lake. Although Garda is the largest of the Italian lakes (51.6 kilometers long, ranging 3 to 17.5 kilometers in width), it's not as well known—at least to Americans—as Lago Maggiore or Lago di Como. It's further east than those lakes. If you drew a line from Milan to Venice, Lago di Garda would sit comfortably on the line at its midpoint.

It's not just history that makes the lake so diverse but geography as well. At the south end, where the lake is at its widest and its water the warmest, the rolling hills around the lake are simply an extension of the Po Valley plain. Here the famous Sirmione peninsula juts into the lake on a tiny spit of land so flat and narrow that the thirteenth-century Scaligeri castle is able to straddle both sides. Olive trees and cypress trees abound here, sharing the landscape with vineyards. On the eastern shore are the famous wine communities of Bardolino and Valpolicella. In the west is the Franciacorta region.

But Lake Garda changes dramatically near the midpoint, becoming narrower with the surrounding terrain wildly mountainous. The change comes near Punta di San Vigilio where Winston Churchill holed up after World War II to write his memoirs (and, no doubt, to look across the lake with a slight smile at the last redoubt of the fallen *duce*). The western shore is so steep in the north that at one point the road runs under the overhanging rocks, and mountain towns, like Tremosine, stare down at the lake at close to a 90-degree drop. The eastern shore, separated from the western by only 3 kilometers, is almost as sheer and even higher, rising 2,200 meters above the lake. This entire side of the lake is one mountain— the famous Monte Baldo, whose terrain is wild and diverse enough to support more than 960 species of butterflies, some of which are found nowhere else. Between these two mountain chains the waters of Lago di Garda become colder and the winds wilder, making the northern end of this lake the wind-surfing capital of Europe.

You can drive around the lake, but during the tourist season it is crisscrossed by ferryboats, steamers, and hydrofoils. There's also a car ferry that crosses from Torri del Benaco to Maderno. (During the winter, alas, boat service is severely curtailed.)

Lago di Garda should be seen in its entirety, and if anyone wants to tell you a story, pull up a chair, order an espresso or a grappa, and listen.

Things to See, Places to Eat

Sirmione

Sirmione is perched on the south end of Lago di Garda like a protozoan sitting on its tail. From the castle at the town entrance, take a scenic walk up the east side of the peninsula to the **Grotto di Catullo,** which is a wonderful complex of Roman ruins. On a warm day, eat in the garden of the **Grifone Ristorante** (030.916097; fax: 030.916548) right across the moat from the castle. Just east of Sirmione is a great restaurant, **Vecchia Lungana** (030.919012; fax: 030.9904045), on the road to Peschiera del Garda.

Gardone Riviera

We should probably suggest Gabriele D'Annunzio's famous **Il Vittoriale,** but it's always impressed us as an artistic train wreck or maybe a Fascist wet dream. However, the **Villa Fiordaliso** (0365.20158; fax: 0365.290011), once home to D'Annunzio—and later to Mussolini's mistress Clara Petacci—has been converted into the most quietly elegant restaurant on the lake.

Malcesine

Malcesine's castle, built in the twelfth century by the Scaligeri of Verona, is the best, and it has the best view. There's a wonderful lakeside promenade south of Malcesine. If you lust for the ultimate view, there's a three-stage funicular from Malcesine to the top of Monte Baldo. (Go early to avoid the lines.)

Torri del Benaco

A great small town with a charming harbor. The **Hotel Gardesana** (045.7225411; fax: 045.7225771) was headquarters for the "Captain of the Lake" in Venetian times, and today it's a good place to stay or to dine.

Winston Churchill's villa is now a small hotel and restaurant. **Locanda San Vigilio** (045.7256688; fax: 045.7256551) serves elegant fare overlooking the lake and informal meals on the small pier. There's a walk from there to the town of Garda (if you don't mind wading a few steps near the beginning).

Kings and Emperors Passed This Way

BY PAUL HOFMANN

∼

editor's note

The following two articles are the only ones in this book to focus on the Dolomites and Trentino–Alto Adige. As I outlined in the *Alpi Dolomiti* entry in *Informazioni Pratiche,* most of the publicity that this region of Italy receives focuses on skiing and outdoor adventures, which it rightly deserves; but there's quite a lot of history and culture here too, as this first piece attests. The second article *is* about skiing, because one can't very well omit the slopes from a volume like this entirely.

PAUL HOFMANN, one of my favorite writers on Italy, is the author of *The Sunny Side of the Alps* (1995), *Umbria: Italy's Timeless Heart* (1999), *That Fine Italian Hand* (1990), *Seasons of Rome* (1999), and *Cento Città* (1991), all published by Henry Holt.

Motorists driving on Italy's National Highway 12 near the Austrian border see a big sign on the northern outskirts of Bressanone-Brixen with the outline of an elephant and an arrow. It points the way to the Elefant Hotel, named after one of the town's most famous visitors. In December 1550 an Indian elephant was trudging up to the 4,495-foot-high Brenner Pass, 27 miles to the north. The animal was a gift from King John III, the Fortunate, of Portugal to Emperor Ferdinand I; it had been shipped from Goa, then a Portuguese colony, to Genoa and was being driven through the mountains in the same way Hannibal's African elephants crossed another section of the Alps nearly eighteen hundred years earlier.

In Bressanone-Brixen the pachyderm's handlers let it rest for two weeks in the barn of the High Field Inn, causing a local sensation. The inn's owner, the postmaster, Andrä Posch, at once changed the name of his business to Inn at the Sign of the Elephant and commissioned a local painter, Lenhard Mair, to commemorate the event. The fresco portraying the animal and its escort of turbaned Indians can still be seen on the street facade of the hotel's old wing. (The stoic elephant did make it to the imperial court in Vienna by late 1551 and would live another few years.)

The core of Bressanone, its old town, looks essentially the same today as it did when the elephant passed through. The narrow, arcaded houses with their bow windows and battlements on Grosse Lauben (Via Portici Maggiori), Kleine Lauben (Via Portici Minori), and the side alleys are from the fifteenth and sixteenth centuries. The covered passageways, however, shelter espresso bars, restaurants, fashion boutiques, and other smart stores. Three stout gates of the medieval walls survive.

Bressanone is, in fact, the oldest town in Italy's autonomous province of Alto Adige–Südtirol. The 430,000 inhabitants of that picturesque area south of the main crest of the Central Alps speak three languages—the Tyrolean version of German, Venetian-tinged

Italian, and Ladin, an ancient idiom related to the Romansch of St. Moritz and nearby areas of Switzerland.

Predominantly German-speaking, Alto Adige enjoys a measure of self-government, and with the autonomous province of the Trentino to its south, where only Italian is spoken, it forms a region that has more independence from the central government in Rome than other Italian regions.

Bressanone, which until 1918 belonged to Austria-Hungary, is bilingual. Street signs are in Italian and German, and business is done everywhere in both languages. There are separate Roman Catholic services in German and Italian; churches and chapels abound.

The ecclesiastical complex, only a few steps from the arcaded, pedestrian-only area, has a cathedral, three other churches and chapels, a splendidly frescoed cloister, and an impressive episcopal palace with a wall and moat.

The town has seen plenty of traffic during the thousand years of its recorded history. Sixty-six kings and emperors came through here on their way south to be crowned by the pope, to embark on a Crusade, or to meddle in some Italian power struggle.

Millions of other travelers, following one of Europe's principal north-south routes, also passed through over the centuries, and quite a few stopped here for the night or for a longer stay. Today Bressanone-Brixen is a winter sports center, and its 17,000 permanent residents welcome plenty of Italian and international guests during the summer months as well. They are drawn by the Alpine Renaissance architecture, the chestnut-lined river promenades, and a celebrated spa.

Since the early Middle Ages, Bressanone has been the "Tyrolean Rome"—a religious center in the Alps. Its bishops once headed the Roman Catholic clergy in a vast crescent-shaped mountain area, and between the eleventh century and 1803 they were also political rulers as princes of the Holy Roman Empire of the German Nation.

Many of them came from aristocratic families, and some from the imperial House of Hapsburg. The bishops administered their large territory through hereditary bailiffs—noblemen who had their own castles and henchmen and often did very much as they pleased. Bressanone's Cathedral Square still conveys a sense of clerical power, although the bishops have resided since 1973 in Bolzano-Bozen, the capital of the bilingual province. The square's east side is dominated by the twin-towered Cathedral of the Assumption of the Virgin Mary. Most of the edifice was rebuilt in triumphant Baroque style in the middle of the eighteenth century at the site of a medieval basilica; only the two towers are older than the bulk of the present structure. To the left of the cathedral is the late-Gothic parish church of St. Michael from the end of the fifteenth century, with a tall whitish tower crowned with a needle-shaped roof. An arcaded courtyard between the two buildings contains tombstones with reliefs of imperious- or pious-looking prelates of past centuries as well as the town's war memorials.

The right (south) side of the cathedral is adjoined by the famous cloister with recently restored fourteenth- and fifteenth-century frescoes representing scenes from the Bible and church history. The frescoes are by various local artists (their identities are a matter of conjecture) and date from various times—whenever a prelate or some other patron commissioned a panel. The paintings, therefore, do not constitute a cycle; instead they present random scenes and figures from the Hebrew Bible and the Christian gospels—Adam and Eve, Moses, Job, the Madonna, the Passion of Jesus, the Apostles. The cloister, around a garden with shrubbery, provides access to the former private chapel of the bishops and to a small baptismal church.

The other sides of Cathedral Square are taken up by the town hall, with its crenelated front, old burgher houses, and two cafés with outdoor tables.

Nearby, on the narrow Domgasse (Cathedral Lane), is an old tavern where members of the cathedral chapter, the ecclesiastical body assisting the bishop, once used to relax. It is known as Finsterwirt, or Dark Host, because it seems the clerical patrons could eat and drink here even after the curfew that the prince-bishop had imposed, as long as no candle or torch was lighted. Thoroughly modernized in the interior, the Dark Host is today a restaurant and café with cozy rooms and a pretty courtyard.

The former episcopal residence, the Palace of the Prince-Bishops, a four-hundred-year-old Renaissance palace a short walk to the southwest of Cathedral Square, is now a museum. The ground-floor rooms contain a collection of crèches—statues representing the Nativity—from three centuries, a total of 10,000 figurines. The former state rooms of the prince-bishops and the Diocesan Museum, displaying sculptures, paintings, and liturgical objects, can be visited on two upper floors. The delightful palace gardens are now a lovingly nursed public park with a profusion of flowers.

In season, much greenery and many flowers are in evidence else-where in and around Bressanone; the extended esplanades along the Eisack, or Isarco, River invite strollers and joggers. The town, 1,834 feet above sea level and surrounded by high mountains, has a dry, sunny, and relatively mild climate. (Though it does drop below freezing in winter, it doesn't stay that cold for long, and it's gener-ally sunny.) During the Victorian era Bressanone was a resort where well-heeled Central Europeans with pulmonary ailments would sojourn. Today, instead, the name *Bressanone* conjures to Italians the image of a fashionable place to slim, eat healthy food, get plenty of exercise, and undergo hydrotherapy and other treatments.

An institution that can provide all this is the Sanatorium Dr. von Guggenberg, in a park on the town's southeastern outskirts near the confluence of the Rienza River and the Eisack-Isarco. It's the oldest and among the most prestigious of Italy's many health farms.

The sanatorium was founded in 1890 by the physician Otto von Guggenberg, who had long worked with the Rev. Sebastian Kneipp (1820–97), a Bavarian priest who advocated "natural" lifestyles and the copious use of water to treat a vast range of diseases. The "Kneipp cures" won many followers in Central Europe. Dr. Markus von Guggenberg, the sanatorium's head, is a grandson of its founder; a fourth-generation Guggenberg, his twenty-nine-year-old daughter Johanna, a graduate dietitian who has developed new health-food recipes, is in charge of the kitchen.

Bressanone's "house mountain," the 8,215-foot-high Mount Plose, is nearby. A road and a funicular go up to spots near the summit of this year-round recreation area, and chairlifts take tourists and skiers farther up.

There are several restaurants at the summit, good more for the view than for the food, and the resort area is modern and well developed. The skiing here, while not particularly challenging, is fine for intermediate and even beginning skiers. There are tracks for cross-country skiing at the foot of the mountain near the river.

Wine lovers trek or drive along the east bank of the Eisack upstream for two miles to sample the vintages, mostly white, of the Augustinian canons at Neustift, or Novacella. The canons' monastery, eight hundred years old, is a cluster of buildings from various epochs surrounded by vineyards and gardens. Neustift-Novacella, which includes not only a winery but also a boarding school, is noteworthy for its sumptuous library with a gallery and Rococo stucco work and for its curious Chapel of St. Michael. This circular structure from the fifteenth century looks like a scale model of Castel Sant'Angelo near the Vatican and was indeed planned to resemble that former papal fortress on the Tiber. St. Michael's is locally called the Engelsburg, or Angel's Castle—a fitting landmark of the "Tyrolean Rome."

Visitor's Guide to Bressanone-Brixen

Getting There

Bressanone-Brixen is about four hours by train or car from Milan, Venice, or Munich, two hours from Innsbruck. Driving on super-highways instead of on the more scenic national highways will shorten the trip up to an hour. The area code for Bressanone is 0472.

Where to Stay

The top establishment is the five-hundred-year-old **Elefant** (4 Weisslahnstrasse; 32750; fax 36579), with 44 comfortable rooms in the main building and in an annex in the hotel's park across the street. The Elefant, despite its first-class status, is essentially still a Tyrolean inn.

Dominik (13 Unterdrittelgasse; 30144; fax 36554), looking out on the Rienza River, is small and elegant.

Jarolim (1 Bahnhofplatz; 36230, fax 33155), is opposite the railroad station but quiet, with a swimming pool in its garden and good food.

Schwarzer Adler (2 Kleine Lauben; 36127) is in the Old Town.

All four places have restaurants and offer full-board arrangements including room and all meals, at 60 to 90 percent above the room-and-breakfast rate, as well as half board at 30 to 45 percent above the basic rate.

Health Farm

Kuranstalt Dr. von Guggenberg (17 Unterdrittelgasse; 35525; fax 34014). There is often a waiting list for the institution, which has 56 well-appointed rooms with 68 beds. Full board only. Closed December and January.

Things to See

The cathedral and the other nearby churches as well as the Cloister are open from 7 A.M. to noon and 3 P.M. to nightfall. Admission is free. The Palace of the Prince-Bishops (30505) is open from 10 A.M. to 5 P.M., Monday to Saturday, from March 15 to Oct. 31. Admission.

Eating Out

Local food is an amalgam of Tyrolean and Italian (especially Venetian) cooking: Knödel (large dumplings) in broth or polenta; speck (flue-cured ham) or Venetian-style liver; pasta dishes or Schlutzkrapfen (spinach-filled ravioli in melted butter). Also, game in season and trout.

The leading restaurant is **Fink** (4B Kleine Lauben; 34883), in the Old Town with a café and snack bar on the ground floor and dining rooms upstairs in a 220-year-old arcaded building. A recent lunch for two with fine ravioli, veal schnitzel, and green salad, with a carafe of red house wine and gelato, was about $60.

Elefant, the opulently decorated restaurant of the old hotel, is for serious eaters. Its specialty is the Elefant Platte, a gargantuan composition of mixed grill, sausages, ham and potatoes that serves three to six persons at around $40 a head.

Finsterwirt (3 Domgasse; 32344). A recent dinner featured South Tyrolean wine soup (a heady concoction of bouillon, egg yolks, white wine, and secret ingredients), deer goulash with polenta, and apple strudel. The very substantial meal, with more wine, was around $50 for two.

Downhill in the Dolomites

BY ERIC WEINBERGER

৵

ERIC WEINBERGER has spent several winters working and skiing in the Alps.

The Dolomites of northern Italy are less forgiving than other mountains in the Alps. Here the flesh of the earth has been ripped open, and from this wound jagged peaks and needles protrude, so sharp and scaly that you feel that if you ran your finger lightly over them you would cut yourself.

Yet harsh as these mountains appear, they are softened immeasurably by their color, changing throughout the day: now blushing rosy-pink, as soft as earthen clay; at sundown a flaming red; and then, seemingly within seconds, ashen-gray, like a human face passing straight from life to death.

This is one of the leading ski areas of Europe, and the skiing is around these serrated pinnacles and sheer cliffs, wherever there is room, on steep chutes and angular spaces cut from the rock, and on long, sloping meadows cantering downward to gentle valley streams.

The pearl of the Dolomites—as the tourist literature proclaims—is Cortina d'Ampezzo, host of the 1956 Winter Olympics. And indeed, basking in its long valley, encased by mountains in a rough, irregular shell, it does resemble a pearl not yet pried from its oyster. The town, at about 3,980 feet, is dominated from every point of view by its bell tower, whiter than any snow surrounding it; the fields in summer are a shimmering green.

Cortina is a year-round resort, offering nearly as much in the way of recreation in summer as in winter, and for most of the century has been a mountain hideaway for the rich and fashionable of Rome and Venice. In winter, nonskiers outnumber skiers, the boutiques compete with the best of Rome and Milan, and the bars and pastry shops and cafés fill up long before four, when the lifts close.

This is one part of the Dolomites that has retained its Italianness. Much of the rest of the region has a Germanic feel, and often a German name to go with it—a reminder that in Cortina we are close to the South Tyrol, which until 1919 was part of Austria, not 15 miles away. For those accustomed to skiing in Europe, Cortina is thus something of an anomaly, a place where you will not hear the usual French or German, or even Dutch or English—the other two de facto languages of the Alps—only Italian. During a week's stay chances are you will never see a soul sitting in a café or pasticceria with a copy of *The International Herald Tribune* spread open on the table. The signs at the lift stations giving information about snow and weather conditions, lift closings and alpine dangers are all in Italian and rarely translated.

Cortina's skiing is dispersed among several areas, none close to another, much less connected. Shuttling between them is never convenient, and although there is a free bus service for skiers, this is one resort where it is useful to have a car. If you don't, the best approach is to pick one area for each day and stay there; if you find you have exhausted its possibilities after a few hours, as an experienced skier might, you always have the comfort of a good restaurant handy and, of course, the superlative mountain views. There is even a cable car for sightseers only, the final link of the Freccia nel Cielo tramway, which begins in town near the Olympic skating rink and ascends in three stages toward the summit of Tofana di Mezzo, at 10,500 feet the highest you can go in this area.

Underneath Tofana, at the end of the cable car's second stage, is the small enclosed ski area of Ra Valles, served by two chairlifts and one Poma (a button lift). This is the highest piste (trail) skiing in Cortina, good for third- or fourth-year intermediates who like a fast run on a wide, easy slope. The higher of the two chairs, Bus Tofana, offers a little more variety, including some lips and rolls and a steepish midsection. At the top, good skiers can traverse wide to the left for some bumps or fresh powder in the shadow of a wall hewn from Tofana's rock.

When the snow is good, which it wasn't the week I visited Cortina last January, the adventurous can pursue the celebrated black (difficult) run Forcella Rossa, which drops through the gap at Ra Valles down to a point below Col Drusciè, giving access to the greater part of Tofana's skiing, known generally as Pomedes, and leading to the gentler slopes of the beginner areas, Socrepes and Pocol.

Coming down here from Ra Valles on the lift, and then on skis along a trail through the woods from Col Drusciè, I could see opening before me Cortina's vast winter playground, the best and most varied skiing in the valley, and suitable for families who ski at different levels, beginner through advanced. Directly below Col Drusciè, at a turn in the road called Rumerlo, two chairlifts in succession take the skier over the Olimpia piste, first to the Duca d'Aosta restaurant, named for an Italian aristocrat of the 1930s whose favorite ski field this was, then to Pomedes itself, underneath the great pyramidal wall of the second of Tofana's three peaks, Tofana di Rozes.

The chairlift is a dramatic ride through two tremendous stone pillars hovering over a steep pitch, the Pomedes schuss of the Olympic racecourse, still used each winter when the women's tour comes to Cortina for the World Cup downhill. On each side of Pomedes's pillars are red (intermediate) runs that start high then run low through the trees, breaking off into branches, sometimes blue (easy), often red, back to Rumerlo. They lead on to Socrepes, where all the pistes are blue: safe, groomed runs popular with young families and the ski school, but where there is seemingly enough room for the faster skier to cut loose.

All around here are huts selling snacks and beverages, and some good restaurants too; but for the best views you have to go high, to the refuge huts at Duca d'Aosta or Pomedes, on a shelf well above the road leading up from Cortina to the pass at Falzarego, ten miles distant. Viewed from the terrace of either of these restaurants, the landscape is broad and desolate, but characteristic of the Dolomites, for within the rocky rubble yet another small ski area has been carved, that of Cinque Torri, with two lonely chairlifts, a nearly empty parking lot and, one is told, seldom any skiers.

It would be possible to take one's entire vacation and never budge from Tofana's snowfields, but to do so would mean missing out on a lot more opportunities. When the snow is good—no guarantee on these sunny, south-facing slopes—both beginners and weak intermediates will enjoy the assurance of the Mietres and Pierosá pistes across the valley from Tofana, with a banked meadow running below the lifts that is good for sledding. Stronger skiers should not miss the chance to try Faloria and Cristallo, loosely linked to each other on the other side of Cortina from Tofana.

Access is by a second cable car departing from the archway by the main bus station to a shelf of red runs that in the winter shade are prone to become icy and pebbly, especially in the lower reaches below the treeline. The most important lift here is the speedy Vitelli quad, rising to the ridge at Tondi.

All runs from Tondi lead back to the bottom of Vitelli, but the best and longest run here is hard to see. Although it is marked on the piste map, there are no signposts, and from the chair it looks to be off-piste. It's a sharp left from the top of the chair, and runs well below Vitelli to another chair deep in the woods, Pian de ra Bigontina. Still lower is the connecting trail to Cristallo, involving a lot of laborious poling on the flat to reach the parking lot at Rio Gere. A slow double chair begins here, rising to Son Forca, an area much like Ra Valles, its mirror image across the valley, with the added benefit of a long, fast cruising run widening almost to a highway back to the parking lot.

Looming farther over Son Forca is the second of Cortina's famous black runs, the notorious Forcella Staunies, an extremely tight and narrow couloir, a sliver of snow wedged between Cristallo's teeth.

Cortina is unusual for Alpine resorts in that nearly all ski areas are penetrated by roads, at all altitudes, and so the mountains are open to everyone, not just those on skis. In the restaurants and on lifts, sitting on chairs and sunning themselves, or enjoying mountain walks were nonskiers, content to enjoy time on their own while friends and relatives tore around the pistes.

Cortina is a winter retreat as much as a ski resort, and one of great sophistication. And unlike Kitzbühel or Zermatt, where everyone goes up the mountain at eight or nine in the morning and comes down again at four o'clock, the traditional hour of après-ski before dinner, Cortina begins its après-ski not long after lunch.

Cortina's main thoroughfare, the Corso Italia, lined with hotels and expensive shops, its facades gaily painted in pastels and colorful faded frescoes, is closed to cars and is lively at all times of the day, with shoppers and walkers and aimless passersby, few dressed for skiing but many in extravagant leather and fur coats and carrying mobile phones.

In Cortina style is the thing, and the village is the only ski resort I have visited with a Porsche showroom on its main street. In the window were four shiny new cars and a gaggle of men, accompanied by their wives, waiting patiently for the chance to sit in the driver's seat for a few moments. A sign announces that the vehicles are not for sale; it is an exhibition: the car as a work of art. For more works of art, the town has several galleries and a museum, in the main square, the Piazza Venezia, housing in one building a collection of modern painting and a "paleontological-ethnological" museum.

Despite the town's reputation for stylishness, this is a place for serious skiers. One thing I had hoped to do while in Cortina but couldn't was travel the Sella Ronda, a circuit on skis through four valleys around the nearby Sella massif, one of the great tours of the Dolomites. I had been advised to avoid Cortina both early in the season and late, and this was still early. Thin snow had thwarted me in many respects, closing runs I would have liked to try. The Sella Ronda was closed in both directions. No matter. With nearly a third of Cortina's runs closed, including most of the better ones, I had no choice but to quit early most days and begin my après-ski at two or three o'clock, along with everyone else.

The Tab for Skiing and Sleeping

Getting There

Venice and its airport are two hours away by car. The nearest train stations are at Dobbiaco, to the north, and Calalzo, southeast, both about 19 miles distant. Buses run regularly to Cortina from both towns and cost about $3 one way. In winter there is also a daily bus service to and from Venice. From Milan, one can drive the four and a half hours to Cortina or take a train to Venice and transfer at Padua for a local to Calalzo.

Skiing

High season is the period encompassing Christmas and New Year's, that is December 20 to January 7; and again from February 3 to March 16 and from March 30 to April 14.

In addition to lift passes for one day or several days, another option, and one that all skiers at an intermediate level or above should consider, is the Dolomite Superski Pass, which is only slightly more expensive. The Superski Pass admits you to perhaps the largest ski area in the world under one ticket, covering several dozen towns and villages, 464 lifts, and 735 miles of piste.

Cortina joins the rest of the Superski region at the top of the Lagazuoi cable car at Passo Falzarego, which can be reached by bus from town; but once on skis and descending into the next valley at Armentarola, you will need to arrange your own transport to get back. Taxis are fairly cheap and usually easy to find.

Where to Stay

During high season, the rates per person for all hotels can double. The standard of Cortina's hotels is high. I stayed at the **Hotel Italia** (2 Via Guglielmo Marconi; 436.5846; fax 436.5757), a pleasant hotel in traditional style with a good dining room, situated on the ring road around the Old Town, facing the main bus station.

There are more than forty hotels in Cortina of this standard or higher, culminating in the **Miramonti Majestic** (103 Via Pezzie; 436.4201; fax 436.867.019), which is about a mile from the center of town. A double room in low season (half-board) costs about $300.

For those who prefer to stay in town, there are three fine hotels along the main street, the Corso Italia, each with sumptuous lounge and public rooms: the **Parc Victoria** (436.3246; fax 436.4734), the **Ancora** (436.3261; fax 436.3265), and the **Hotel de la Poste** (436.4271; fax 436.868.435).

Information on hotels and other accommodations, including apartments and beds in private houses, is available from the Tourist Office, 8 Piazzetta S. Francesco, 32043 Cortina d'Ampezzo (BL). The telephone number is 436.3231; fax 436.3235.

Biblioteca

A Guide to the Brenta Riviera: History, Art and Customs, Giovanni Formenton, Medoacus Edizioni, 1988. I found this little pocket-size paperback at a bookstore in Venice, and I think it is the best of its kind. I saw other books, some of which were of the coffee-table variety, but I didn't want a book that heavy or pretty; I wanted one to carry around with enough history and background but with color photos too. To the best of my knowledge, this one isn't available outside of Italy, so if you know you'll be visiting the Brenta, stop into one of Venice's excellent bookshops before you depart.

An Italian Education: The Further Adventures of an Expatriate in Verona, Tim Parks, Grove Press, 1995. *Italian Neighbors, Or, a Lapsed Anglo-Saxon in Verona,* Tim Parks, Grove Weidenfeld, 1992 (hardcover), Fawcett, 1993 (paperback). Tim Parks is an award-winning novelist and has translated the works of Moravia, Calvino, and Calasso, but it is for these two memoirs of life in Verona (where he teaches English) that he is best known. Like reading Peter Mayle when you are in Provence, reading Tim Parks when you're in the Veneto is *essenziale*. The first book focuses on his arrival from England to Italy, and his initiation that followed, while the second is more about his adventures as an ex-pat father in and around Verona. (Personally, I enjoyed the second one better.) Either way, you don't have to read them in sequence, and they're both great companion reading.

Veneto Villas, Valeria Bove, Arsenale Editrice, 1998. This pocket-size paperback—in the same series as *Secret Venice*—is a good little compendium of the architectural details of the villas in the provinces of Belluno, Padua, Rovigo, Treviso, Udine, Venice, Verona, and Vicenza. (A chapter is devoted to the villas in each region, and color photos accompany each of the fifty-seven entries.) Author Bove reveals two important facts: First, the term "Veneto villa" is very specific, and does not indicate any residence in the Veneto area. On the contrary, the site itself has to have specific characteristics (it does not, for example, refer to the Veneto region per se, but to the so-called *Territorio da Terra* dominated by the Serenissima Republic, which covers the entire Triveneto). Second, there are 3,477 officially registered Veneto villas. I, for one, admit that my interest in the villas of the Veneto had been until recently purely architectural. That is, I never really understood how unique the villas were to this part of Italy, or that they could have significance beyond architecture. As Bove notes, it was in the fifteenth century that Venice annexed Vicenza (1404) and Padua and Verona (1405), and from that time the "Venetian villa" was thought of as a distinct architectural category. "Various reasons have been given for Venice's political and economic development: the sudden availability of large tracts of land, the difficulties faced by maritime commerce due to the changes in sea routes following Portugal's discovery of new lands and the Turks' conquest of Constantinople, as well as the increase in agricultural prices in the early 16th century. But above all there was a change in mentality; the idea of the 'merchant' and 'market' acquired different meanings. The traditionally mercantile dominant class in the Veneto seems to have followed a trend set by the nobles of the dominant city. That is, this new class, which was still strictly linked to a feudal past, saw in the re-population and empowering of the countryside a legitimate means of reacting against the Republic's annexing of their cities, which had effectively weakened their real control over the cities themselves." This book features only the more significant villas and is meant to generate on the part of the reader an interest in further discovery; it is not a practical information guide and does not include opening hours, admission prices, or directions. For that more specific information, see Hallenstein's "Splendor in the Grass" and inquire at the local area tourist offices in Italy.

The Villas of Palladio, photographs by Philip Trager, text by Vincent Scully, Bulfinch Press, Little, Brown & Co., 1986 (hardcover); 1992 (paperback). Unlike Formenton's and Bove's pocket-size books, this is a large coffee-table book and all the photos are in black and white—but oh, what gorgeous photos they are! (Readers may be familiar with a more recent photography book by Trager, *Changing Paris: A Tour Along the Seine,* which I very much admire.) Especially impressive in this volume, I think, are the fifteen photos (including the cover shot) of Villa Almerico Capra, better known as La Rotonda, proving that the exterior and grounds of the villa are just as impressive as the interior. (I note this because visitors are admitted inside the villa on an extremely limited schedule. But don't let the limited hours prevent you from at least visiting the outside—even the grounds are "worth a detour.") Other featured villas include Pojana, Godi, Pisani di Bagnolo, Caldogno, Sarego, Barbaro, Badoer, della Malcontenta, Cornaro, Pisani di Montagnana, and Emo, plus nine less-known villas. There is a helpful map at the back, a selected bibliography, and a brief list of the villas with their dates and owners.

pasticceria

MARCHiNi

venezia

A Tavola!—
La Cucina Veneziana
(To the Table!—The Cuisine
of Venice and the Veneto)

*"What sort of food accorded with the contradictory charac-
teristics of the Venetians? They were earners (the men) and
spenders (the women), combining an acute respect for the
value of money with readiness to dissipate it lavishly on luxury. Solidity and extravagance: they managed to marry in
Venetian society and they managed to marry (and happily at
that) in Venetian cooking."*

—Waverly Root, THE FOOD OF ITALY

In Venice, Delectable Tastes
of the Sea

BY MAUREEN B. FANT

editor's note

As readers of my previous editions know, I am reluctant to include articles recommending restaurants, as I feel this is not the province of *The Collected Traveler*. I believe that travelers will be better served by reading about the food and drink unique to the Veneto (and Friuli–Venezia Giulia) and how these are prepared and served. Some specialties of Venice and the Veneto to look for include *risi e bisi* (rice and peas), scampi (shrimp, usually tails only, that are served baked, sautéed, grilled, or boiled), polenta (served both hot and cold), risotto (made only with Italian Arborio rice and served in a nearly infinite variety of ways), *fegato alla veneziana* (liver with onions), *baccalà mantecato* (nearly identical to *brandade de morue* in Provence, made with salted cod, milk, olive oil, and garlic), many varieties of *seppie* and *seppioline* (cuttlefish and smaller, tender ones), *pasticciata* (*pastizzada* in dialect), *alla veneta* (beef marinated in vinegar and stuck with garlic slivers, then lightly floured and browned in butter and onions), *masaro a la valesana* (wild duck), *coniglio bollito al sale aromatico* (rabbit cut into pieces and stewed with herbs and garlic), a very great variety of vegetables but especially peas, artichokes, tomatoes, onions, cabbages, and squash (Waverly Root wrote that "the market gardens of the Veneto coast are famous"), and—my favorite—*sardelle in saor* (sardines—or sole or other small fish—lightly fried and layered in a casserole with onions that have been slow-cooked in vinegar; pine nuts and currants are also often added, and in every type of place where I've eaten this dish—whether a famous Venetian restaurant or an informal trattoria-pizzeria—it is *always* good). When you know about a particular dish, you will know when you come across an authentic version of it, which is a good sign that a kitchen prepares all—or most of—its dishes with care.

Though I remain reluctant to feature many articles about restaurants, I admit that some guidance from respected authorities is very welcome. I do not want to deny anyone the experience of eating at Osteria da Fiore, Osteria al Mascaron, or Harry's Bar, and by checking several sources, you'll begin to see a few of the same names, usually with good reason. But the point is, you should know what kind of food to expect at a restaurant versus an *enoteca* or *trattoria,* and if one place or another has closed its doors or has truly declined, you'll have a good meal somewhere else, or you might discover a favorite of your own. I am happy to include the following three articles reviewing restaurants for two reasons: first because the reviewers— Maureen B. Fant, Gael Greene, and Faith Heller Willinger—write about food and the people who prepare it with great enthusiasm, not simply about the pleasures (or pitfalls) of dining out; secondly, because restaurants in Venice and the Veneto do not open and close, or rise and decline, with the frequency found in other, larger cities; therefore older articles are not to be disregarded. Some items may no longer be found on restaurant menus, and some establishments may have undergone a renovation, but generally the places held in high regard—be they neighborhood wine bars or renowned restaurants—still are.

MAUREEN B. FANT lives in Rome and writes regularly about food for the travel section of *The New York Times.* She is the coauthor, with Howard M. Isaacs, of *Dictionary of Italian Cuisine* (Ecco Press, 1998) and is author of *Trattorias of Rome, Florence & Venice: A Guide to Classic Eating, Drinking, and Snacking* (Ecco Press, 2001).

No tourist destination is more loved and more reviled than Venice, especially when it comes to food. The creatures of the Venetian lagoon in the hands of an expert chef are as memorable as they are rare, but most visitors to *La Serenissima,* trapped in the world of mass tourism or deterred by appalling prices at the top end, come away with the impression that Venetian food is not very good and way overpriced.

On a February weekend, my companion, Franco, and I scouted for the great food we knew Venice could offer.

On the ecclesiastical and social calendar this was the beginning of Carnival; on the gastronomic calendar it was the beginning of soft-shell crabs, slightly ahead of *castraure,* the local small wild artichokes, and still in full radicchio season. In the seven years since our last visit, our two favorite restaurants, not always the household names they are today, had been lauded in the press with considerable hyperbole; intimations that praise had turned their heads had begun to circulate. We wanted to see whether they were still as good as we remembered (they were) and try others we had missed. Our criteria were simple: local ingredients, fair prices, and tranquil surroundings. With one irresistible exception, we steered clear of the expensive hotel restaurants and enjoyed several delicious meals in good restaurants that are admired by the dwindling local population.

Osteria da Fiore

Hyperbole? If we had spent five hours on a train from Rome in the morning and returned the same afternoon, our lunch here would have been worth the trip. This is a small, serious, modern, high-toned restaurant (with a Michelin star); its recently renovated elegant dining room lies behind the facade and front room of an old *osteria*, or wine shop. An enormous staff of pleasant young men in dinner jackets back up Maurizio Martin, the co-owner (his wife, Mara, is the chef), in the dining room. The menu is all seafood from the Venetian Lagoon, and specific provenance is often noted on the menu. The cooking style is traditional Venetian taken to the nth degree of refinement with bursts of artistry.

After a *stuzzichino (amuse-bouche)* of soft white polenta, zucchini, and *schie*—miniature shrimps cooked and eaten whole—came the quintessentially Venetian antipasto, *baccalà mantecato,* three divinely creamy scoops of stockfish (air-dried cod, not salt) flaked and beaten with olive oil until it can be spread, served with toasted polenta slices. Another antipasto was three perfect scallops presented in their shells and sprinkled with fresh thyme; it was like tasting both flavors for the first time.

For the pasta course, I had another exciting interpretation of an old favorite, *bigoli in salsa,* whole wheat spaghetti with onions cooked to a creamy sweetness with sardines that slowly disintegrate into a richly flavored sauce.

Tagliolini with scampi (langoustines) and *radicchio di Chioggia* (which comes in a round head and is less bitter than the more celebrated *radicchio di Treviso*) were baked, which gave a rich texture but none of the heaviness of a *pasta al forno*.

Franco's grilled eel from the island of Burano, skinned after cooking, was lean but unutterably tender. My *involtini di triglie con radicchio di Treviso* could have been a painting, a study in red: fillets of red mullet wrapped around chopped *radicchio di Treviso* leaves (the highly prized bitter long-leafed variety).

Although extensive wine lists are rare in Venice because of the logistical difficulties of storage (or of doing anything underground), the Martins do have a good list, emphasizing regional labels. We drank the excellent house Soave Classico Superiore Pieropan 1998 ($17.50, at 2,000 lire to the dollar).

Our desserts, too, were thrilling interpretations of traditional ones: an exquisite cake called *pinza,* a sort of firm custard studded with raisins for flavor in a crust served with cold zabaglione as a sauce, and *cremini fritti,* delicious deep-fried cubes of custard.

Al Covo

To add to the already cheery atmosphere of this charmer founded fourteen years ago by Cesare and Diane Benelli, some people came to Saturday dinner during Carnival in costume. A foyer with service bar separates the two simple, comfortable dining rooms (one non-smoking), where Mrs. Benelli, who is American, assisted by solicitous waiters describes the menu's offerings, mostly superb local seafood.

There is frequently a nonfish option too. Cesare Benelli, the chef, modestly describes his cooking style as doing as little as possible to the best ingredients.

The antipasto of spider crab salad was shredded crabmeat

replaced in its large red and white shell. It was served at just the right temperature, not too cold, and its predominant flavor was crab-perfection.

Refinement and subtlety defined the pasta we tried—*tagliolini* (very thin noodles) with oysters and *scorfano* (red *rascasse,* a scary-looking fish with tender white flesh), in light, delicate, but paradoxically rich sauce based on the broth of the *scorfano,* all sprinkled with fine parsley. The nonfish *pasta e fagioli* was a velvety, flavorful purée of cranberry beans with fresh fettuccine and a small slice of *musetto (cotechino)* sausage.

A tempura-style *fritto misto,* light as a feather, was enough to share as a main course with a salad of soft, young mixed greens. In addition to a multitude of perfect shrimps and scampi, the *fritto* contained a few vegetables, such as *radicchio di Treviso,* and two of the lagoon's most cherished morsels, namely, a small soft-shell crab, *moleca,* the first of the season, and two ethereal lagoon scallops, *canestrelli.*

How can anything so delicate have so much flavor?

Our wine, Gambellara I Masieri DOC 1998 ($9.50), was a bargain from a good list.

Mrs. Benelli is also the deservedly renowned dessert chef. Her *semi-freddo* (molded ice cream) drenched in grappa and covered with small raisins was accompanied by a brittle made of almonds and pine nuts. The *torta di pere e prugne,* pear and plum pie, was another treasure.

Antica Trattoria Furatola

Known to connoisseurs as a serious fish place, this spruce little restaurant with an unprepossessing facade keeps a low profile. After a cramped anteroom, with one little table and a service bar, comes a single long room with low ceilings and white walls, old photos and copper pots and pans, and an open kitchen. On a

Saturday at lunch, it was practically empty despite crowds thronging the city.

Our excellent seafood antipasto came in two stages, the delicate boiled version, *bolliti,* first and the more strongly flavored marinated version, *marinati,* second. The first included octopus, mantis shrimp *(canocchia),* ordinary shrimp, and the tiny brown shrimp called *schie* locally, as well as subtly flavored white cuttlefish roe, which we had to have identified for us. Despite the inclusion of geographically irrelevant salmon and sun-dried tomatoes, the second half was delicious too: marinated anchovies, called *sardoni* locally, and sardines *(sarde)* in *saor,* fried then marinated, were delicious and very typical.

What I really wanted next was spaghetti with mantis shrimp, but I allowed Franco and the waiter to talk me into spaghetti with *sugo della casa,* dark rich fish sauce with a little tomato and a lot of squid, fish pieces, and *schie* parts. The portion was enormous but came with the reassurance that I needn't feel obliged to eat it all. Franco's fish soup was in the same key, made on a similar base, and we felt that while both were good, we'd have been happier with the mantis shrimp. A very nice grilled *coda di rospo* (monkfish) followed; we were glad we had insisted on sharing it.

The wine list is limited but adequate; we tried Incrocio Manzoni Vitigno 6.0.13 (yes, that is its name, derived from an agricultural experiment) Colli Trevigiani IGT Gregoletto from the Veneto ($11.50), though a crisper wine would have suited the food better.

Large glasses of *sgroppino,* liquid lemon sherbet to cleanse the palate, appeared next. In an assortment of desserts that followed, the best was an excellent *crostata,* or tart, of mixed fruit.

Fiaschetteria Toscana

We tried this highly recommended Venetian classic on a weekday evening with two American friends. We found superb service, excellent ingredients, but somewhat hit-or-miss cooking. The dullness of the apparently unplanned decor of the upstairs main dining room was enlivened by exuberant glass sconces laden with glass fruits.

The antipasti were good: sole *in saor* was the typical sweet and sour treatment applied to tasty fried sole fillets, layered with onions and succulent raisins; the excellence of the crab salad was marred by its chilly temperature; raw small scampi, shelled, were perfect. Risotto with *carletti* (a wild green called silene in English) for two was fine but too subtly flavored to go the distance in such a large portion. Franco's gnocchi with scampi and zucchini were livelier. A nice grilled monkfish was slightly overcooked by any standard, and severely overcooked for our friend from New York, who had begged to have it practically raw—not to Italian taste.

Had the monkfish been pulled off the grill a minute sooner, my *frittura la Serenissima* might have reached me just that much warmer. Nevertheless, it was a lovely superbly deep-fried mess of zucchini strips, artichoke wedges and shrimp, scampi, and *moscardini* (tiny octopus); it also earned me a souvenir plate (given by the restaurant association I Ristoranti del Buon Ricordo to diners who order a specific dish). This was fry for sissies—no heads, no shells.

Franco's *fritto misto,* for true connoisseurs, included no vegetables, no souvenir plate, but plenty of whole small fish—the works—and it was even better than mine.

An unusually lengthy and interesting wine list emphasizes the Veneto and neighboring regions. Since we wanted a light red, which our guests preferred to white, we chose a Zeni novello di Teroldego IGT 99, from Trentino ($13).

Homemade *sfogliatine* (puff pastries), some filled with whipped cream (much loved in Venice), were a delightful conclusion.

Vini da Gigio

In an enticing air of rusticity and informality, this friendly restaurant serves about forty in its two low-ceilinged rooms (one non-smoking). Unusually for Venice restaurants, the wines are a bigger attraction than the food. Our Rosso del Veronese Brolo di Campofiorin Masi 1995 ($25) was a rich and velvety Valpolicella.

The simple but good seafood antipasto consisted of boiled octopus, mantis shrimp, shrimp and cuttlefish eggs, tepid and dressed only with olive oil, as well as *baccalà mantecato* and toasted polenta. Deserting the lagoon, we then shared ravioli filled with purée of winter squash, sauced with a zabaglione of melted *taleggio* cheese; that was tasty, as were our simple main courses. These were the classic *fegato alla veneziana,* small pieces of liver sautéed with onions accompanied by slices of toasted polenta, and half a local roast duck, which was hearty and flavorful.

For dessert a *crostata* of thin pear slices and whipped white *robiola* cheese was exquisite.

Cip's Club

By noon on Sunday, Carnival was under way. A cat can look at a king, and for the price of even a light lunch, the harried visitor can step aboard the Cipriani Hotel's private launch to the luxurious complex on Giudecca, the island facing San Marco.

The hotel's main restaurant, by all accounts superb, was still closed for the winter, like the hotel itself. Only Cip's, which passes for the hotel's informal (sort of cashmere instead of silk) dining room, is open for most of the year. Small, square, and bright, the dining room is cleverly designed to convey an impression of coziness without making you elbow your neighbor. As soon as the weather is warm enough, tables are set on a deck outdoors with a view toward San Marco that is worth at least half the considerable price of the lunch.

The patrons at our Sunday meal included a table of Americans, a French couple, and the rest Italian, some local. Everyone received the same deferential and highly professional service. While not large, the menu is intelligently composed to offer something for everybody without straying very far from local ingredients and dishes, except to the extent of offering a pizza menu too.

An antipasto of just-cooked mantis shrimp draped elegantly over soft mesclun with a little balsamic vinegar was delicious, and a microcosm of the whole show: local basics, international high-level presentation, with a little something expensive and completely superfluous (the *balsamico*), because the customers might not understand leaving well enough alone. Our shared pasta, *tagliatelle* with Gorgonzola and *radicchio di Treviso,* was braver: nothing much added to the two basic ingredients, so the dish was wonderfully rich and assertive but never heavy. *Fegato alla veneziana* again, thin and tender, and a turbot fillet garnished with small vegetables; its rhomboid shape evoked the Italian name of the fish *(rombo)* but was the only element in our lunch that reminded us we were in a hotel.

Dessert was Cippamisù—the definitive *tiramisù,* not substantially different from the norm except in its compact cylindrical shape, just better. Our superb, flavorful white Breganze di Breganze Maculan 1998 from the Veneto was at $28 the least expensive bottle on the brief but choice list.

We left the peace of Giudecca and the exhilaration of San Marco and returned to Rome. Never mind the hats and masks: from now on for us Carnival in Venice will evoke the delicate creatures of the Venetian Lagoon.

Bill of Fare

It is a measure of the importance of foreign tourists to the local economy that many restaurants in Venice do have no-smoking sections. Be aware, however, that if you choose to sit there, you may find yourself dining with a greater proportion of foreigners than Italians.

Prices are for a meal for two with either a house wine or a bottle from the low end of the list. Credit cards are accepted except as noted.

Al Covo, Campiello della Pescaria 3968, Castello; tel. and fax: 39.041.5223812. Closed Wednesday and Thursday. Nonsmoking room available. No charge cards. About $125, at 2,000 lire to the dollar. From San Marco, walk along the Grand Canal toward the Castello; turn left when you reach the Gabrielli Sandwirth hotel. The restaurant will be on your left after a few steps.

Antica Trattoria Furatola, Calle Lunga San Barnaba 2870, Dorsoduro; 39.041.5208594. Closed Monday lunch and Thursday. About $80.

Cip's Club, Hotel Cipriani, Fondamenta de le Zitelle 10, Giudecca; 39.041.2408575; fax: 39.041.5203930. Open daily for lunch and dinner. About $130. Take the hotel's launch from San Marco.

Fiaschetteria Toscana, San Giovanni Crisostomo 5719, Cannaregio; 39.041.5285281; fax: 39.041.5285521. Closed Monday lunch and Tuesday. About $80.

Osteria da Fiore, Calle del Scaleter 2202A, San Polo; 39.041.721308; fax: 39.041.721343. Closed Sunday and Monday. About $150.

Vini da Gigio, Cannaregio 3628/a, Fondamenta San Felice; 39.041.5285140; fax: 39.041.5228597. Nonsmoking room. Closed Monday. $65.

Venice's Answer to the Coffee Break

BY GAEL GREENE

～

GAEL GREENE has been the restaurant critic for *New York* magazine for thirty-three years and travels frequently to Italy. She is also the author of *Blue Skies, No Candy* (William Morrow, 1976, hardcover; Warner Books, 1978, paperback) and was the cofounder, with James Beard, of New York's Citymeals-on-Wheels. For this piece, she embarked on a *cantina* crawl and sampled a mouthwatering variety of *cicchetti*.

Early in my winter-long stay in Venice, an artist friend ends his morning of sketching by leading me to a wine bar, Antico Dolo. We stand at the counter sharing a plate of wonderful boiled tripe and, finally, a melt of Gorgonzola on a polenta square that has taken the kitchen forever to warm up. Definitely worth the wait. On another morning my Venetian landlord introduces me to his banker (who has the best exchange rate for lire) and, with an air of equal generosity, to the ancient wine bar Do Spade (Two Swords), in a vaulted passage just steps from the Rialto. There I fall in love with the *Giapponese Paperino:* chopped fresh tuna and spicy rice on soft crustless white bread. At seven-thirty one evening not long after, we meet new Venetian pals for an aperitif and a meatball on a tooth-pick at Enoteca Mascareta, one of the rare cantinas, or *bacari,* known more for good wine than for snacks—though I can imagine making a late-night supper of their splendid meats and cheese on crusty country bread.

Our friends are initiating us into a Venetian sacrament, not unlike the American coffee break. It's their ritual twice-a-day snack pause: a glass of wine with *cicchetti* (tapaslike snacks) in the local *bacaro.* Here where each *sestiere* (or borough) is like a small village, everyone moves mostly on foot, up and down over endless bridges, constantly bumping into friends, socializing on the street. Each neighborhood has its *bacari*, a word derived (depending on your source) from Bacchus or from an Apulian wine popular in eighteenth-century Venice.

In late morning and again in the evening, these wine bars come alive with people—street sweepers, bankers, shopkeepers, and housewives with strollers, each nibbling (or even lunching) on *cicchetti,* and sipping *un'ombra* (a glass of wine). Legend has it that wine sellers in the Piazza San Marco would move the barrels to keep them cool in the shadow *(ombra)* of the campanile. The workers' convivial "Let's go to the shade" came to mean "Let's get a glass of wine." And in Venice, where, to be cruelly frank, it isn't easy to get a great meal (except in a few very expensive restaurants), *cicchetti* and the homey dishes served in these bars may be the best food you'll eat. Each *bacaro* has its magnum opus. It might be crisp-fried mullet, grilled sardines, stuffed peppers, baby octopus, or simply an array of plump sandwiches.

As a restaurant critic, I have no patience for mediocre food. I resent each greasy croquette as a theft of time and abuser of calories. I am determined to find out where discerning Venetians snack. Michela Scibilia, author of a charming Venice dining guide, *Osterie & Dintorni* (published by Vianello Libri; available in English), is curious to meet another professional foodie. She agrees to lead a *bacari* crawl for me and my companions.

We might easily spend the day savoring luscious snacks all over town, but to avoid running us ragged Michela has targeted a cluster of favorite *bacari* in and around the Rialto. We meet just before noon at Vivaldi, on the busy path between the Rialto and Campo San Polo. We are: Michela in a bright red coat, tall, with a tangle of black hair, and passionate, piercing brown eyes. Her photographer husband, easygoing and agreeable Daniele. Jill, a fine-arts major from St. Louis, with her Venetian *amore,* architect Diego. My mate, photographer Steven Richter, faithfully wiping the grease from his lens. And his six-foot-six son, Nico, who could have eaten all day and remained rail thin. Now I see why it's good to start snacking early. Vivaldi's cheese-stuffed sardines, calamari fritters, and everything else that's deep-fried are still crisp, hot, and delicious. At the better *bacari,* such as this one, they disappear fast. At others, what's left over from lunch may be dragged out for reheating at the aperitif hour and dinner. Guido Giuman, the charismatic ponytailed host of Vivaldi, urges us to try wonderful baby octopus *(folpetti)* and the crumb-battered salt-cod croquettes Venetians like with their first *ombra* of the day.

Our next stop, the dark and venerable Cantina Do Mori with its lineup of wooden kegs and hanging copper kettles, is on tourist agendas now. But the Venetian faithful go anyway, because the traditional *cicchetti* are so good and so cheap. Our group is busy sharing bites. We pass around *crostini* with *salsa al radicchio* and with chopped liver; a fabulous combo of Gorgonzola and *speck* (bacon); and what seems like the best fifty-cent nibble in the world—an itsy pocket of *coppa* (head cheese) with pecorino. Do Mori's sandwiches are celebrated, and choosing from the selection is traumatizing. The larger ones in soft white bread are called *tramezzini;* half a *tramezzino* is a *francobollo* (postage stamp). Though my co-conspirators seem content to sip dollar-a-glass *ombre,* I have my eye on a Gaja Barbaresco, one of several serious bottles sitting on the counter, opened but sealed with a gizmo that supposedly keeps the wine from spoiling. How much for a glass? Alas, any replies to my bold Italian are way beyond my comprehension. Did the guy say 5,000 lire (less than three dollars)? Jill is sure she heard 2,500. "I was thinking how amazing," she confides later. But the bill is even more amazing. My not very thrilling pour of Barbaresco costs 25,000 lire, or about $13.50—my most wanton slurp in Venice.

From a labyrinth of narrow alleys alongside the Rialto, we emerge into what is fittingly called the Campo delle Beccarie, where the Osteria Sora al Ponte is drawing a crowd. Michela wants to check it out, but one bite of a rubbery calamari ring and she turns on her heel. Next she herds us to Vini da Pinto, a pocket-size bar that spills onto the Campo with tables, empty now in the frosty air but sure to draw dozens for lunch on the next warm day. Michela and the mom-and-pop owners seem to be shouting at one another, wagging fingers, chopping the air. "I took him out of my latest roundup because he's become too touristy," she explains. "But," she tosses her head defiantly, "he still does the best *baccalà mantecato* in Venice." Indeed, the rich smear of salt cod beaten with olive oil into a mayonnaiselike paste makes sensational *crostini*. We also order the spot's obligatory *crema*—farm wine in the tiniest glasses, very minor, but pleasant at about 65 cents a glass.

It's almost two, and so much snacking has left us exhausted and—hard as it may be to believe—hungry. Michela ushers a docile brood to a window table at Vecio Fritolìn in the Santa Croce district for one last round of *cicchetti,* followed by lunch. I realize I've passed this place twice a day for weeks and never ventured in. Venice once was full of *fritolìn,* or carry-out fry shops, Michela explains. This one closed a few years ago, to be revived by a feisty little blonde from the northernmost region of Italy who takes our order in an accent even I recognize as foreign. Her *fritto misto* of calamari, whitebait, and a scallop or two is freshly fried and a bargain too.

By now I'm craving something sweet. Our waitress comes up with a couple of S-shaped cookies to dip in *vin santo,* and fabulous cellophane-wrapped almond brittle, a Venetian sweet I've sworn off a dozen times and so far have not resisted. My motto in life: Too much is just barely enough.

Canoce (canocchie)—a shrimplike crustacean

Capelunghe—razor clams

Coda di bue in francobolli—oxtail in tiny sandwiches

Fragolino—strawberry dessert wine, both red and white

Frittata—a room-temperature omelette

Garusoli—sea snails

Musetto—spicy boiled sausage

Panini—small sandwiches

Polpettina—meatball

Nervetti—boiled veal tendons, served with onion, parsley, oil, and vinegar

Prosecco—sparkling white wine

Sarde in saor—fried sardines, marinated with onions, raisins, pine nuts, olive oil, and vinegar

Seppie—cuttlefish

Sfogie—small sole

Tramezzino—a triangular overstuffed sandwich on soft bread

Michela's Favorite *Cicchetti* Stops

Antico Dolo, *778 San Polo, Ruga Vecchia S. Giovanni;* *041.522.6546.* Order the boiled tripe and polenta with *baccalà.*

Da Alberto, *5401 Cannaregio, Calle Giacinto Gallina;* *041.523.8153.* Try the *polpettine, baccalà,* and *sarde in saor.*

Cantina Do Mori, *429 San Polo, Calle dei Do Mori; 041.522.5401.* Oxtail in *francobolli!*

Da Dante, *2877 Castello, Corte Nova; 041.528.5163.* Very Venetian, with a courtyard, billiards, and traditional *cicchetti.*

Do Spade, *860 San Polo, Calle do Spade; 041.521.0574. Tramezzini* and *bruschette* are specialties.

Enoteca Mascareta, *5183 Castello, Calle Lunga Santa Maria Formosa; 041.523.0744.* A wine bar associated with the restaurant Mascaron.

Vecio Fritolìn, *2262 Santa Croce, Calle della Regina; 041.522.2881.* Order the *fritto misto* (mixed fried seafood).

Vini da Pinto, *367 San Polo, Campo de le Becarie; 041.522.4599.* Great *baccalà mantecato* (creamy salt cod spread).

Vivaldi, *1457 San Polo, Calle de la Madoneta; 041.523.8185.* Heavenly fried fish and baby octopus.

Venice: A Food Lover's Guide

BY FAITH HELLER WILLINGER

❧

FAITH HELLER WILLINGER lives in Florence and is a contributing editor of *Gourmet.* She is also the author of *Red, White & Greens: The Italian Way with Vegetables* (HarperCollins, 1996) and *Eating in Italy: A Traveler's Guide to the Hidden Pleasures of Northern Italy* (William Morrow, 1998).

I used to hate Venice. I believed it to be expensive, pandering— with Disney-like gondola rides and carts of kitschy souvenirs— and crowded with tourists feeding the pigeons of San Marco and recording the act for posterity. Then I met Marcella and Victor Hazan, both born-again Venetians.

The Hazans teach in-depth courses on Italian food and wine, limited to six students, at their home in the Canareggio district. In their company I encountered Venetian chefs who took me into their kitchens, went with fishmongers at dawn to the Tronchetto wholesale market, and tramped through the Malamocco vegetable gardens. I dined in unassuming restaurants and wine bars and discovered the sweetness of seafood from the Venetian Lagoon. By the time I started to understand the lilting local dialect (ignore *l* except when it begins a word), I was hooked.

Founded in A.D. 421 by refugees from the mainland fleeing barbarian invaders, Venice looked westward to Europe and eastward to Byzantium, part metropolis and part seraglio. Resting in the heart of two hundred square miles of partially navigable salt marsh, its 118 islands are intersected by more than 150 canals and joined by some four hundred bridges. Theodore of Amasea, traditionally depicted with a crocodile, was the city's patron saint until two enterprising Venetians snatched the body of Saint Mark (whose symbol was a far more impressive winged lion) from Alexandria in 828 and turned the honor over to him. This should serve as fair warning: a city that stole its patron saint will probably have an easy time stealing your heart.

Although the piazza honoring Saint Mark is generally considered the center of the city, travelers interested in Venice's *culinary* center should head for the Rialto market. I usually start with a visit to San Giacomo di Rialto, the oldest church in Venice, followed by a stroll through nearby stands selling domestic and imported produce. Local specialties include *radicchio di Treviso* (white ribs edged with deep red leaves from that nearby commune); vibrantly orange-fleshed *zucca* (squash) sold in wedges; trimmed, lemon-rubbed, chartreuse-colored *carciofi* (artichokes); *castraure* (slightly bitter artichoke sprouts); and when the weather is damp, *chiodini* and *porcini* mushrooms. The spring cornucopia includes *carletti* (wild greens), *bisi* (tender peas), chunky white and slender purply-green asparagus, and the green beans called *tegoline*.

Fruit picked ripe and rushed to the Rialto from islands in the lagoon can be spectacular, with intense flavors only hinted at by most commercially grown produce. White peaches dripping with juice make a wonderful dessert or a refreshing drink when puréed and combined with Prosecco (Treviso's sparkling wine) to create a Bellini. Green or purple-black figs, tiny summer berries, and sweet golden-green or dark purple Fragolino grapes that taste like strawberries are also sold at the Rialto alongside somewhat less exciting fruit from the mainland and beyond.

Venice has some of the world's greatest seafood. Fish from the Adriatic or the lagoon is sweet and delicate, requiring simple cooking and little more than a splash of mild extra-virgin olive oil to achieve perfection (no lemon—it overwhelms such fragile flavors). The best way to become familiar with local bounty is to indulge in a do-it-yourself fish market tour, which should begin with spotting bivalves: *caparozzoli* (carpet shell clams, called *vongole veraci* throughout the rest of Italy); *capelunghe* (razor clams, called *cannolicchi* in Italian); *peoci* (mussels); and the scallops known as *capesante* (*canestrelli*, a smaller, rarer variety, are harder to find). Mollusk mavens will recognize *bovoletti* (small snails) and the spiky twisted shells of *garusoli* (murex snails); *seppie* (cuttlefish) and *seppioline* (baby cuttlefish); *calamari* (squid), *calamaretti* (baby squid), *polipi* (octopuses), and *folpetti* (small octopuses); but they may be puzzled by *latte di seppia*—it's said to be a gland.

The next step should be crustaceans: *gamberi* (shrimp); *gamberetti* (tiny pink shrimp); *schie* (even tinier gray shrimp); *scampi* (Dublin bay prawns, supersweet when fresh); spiky, long-legged *granceole* (spider crabs); and brownish-gray, flat, strange-looking *canocie* (*canocchie*) (mantis shrimp). *Mazanete* are thin-shelled female *moleche* (soft-shelled crabs), "the Rolex of seafood," says one local chef.

In flat fish, *sfogi gentile* are so small—ten inches long at the most—that they barely resemble what passes for sole in the United States. *Branzino* (sea bass, called *spigola* elsewhere) is an elegant fish, silver with a pale belly and dark back. Yellow-and-black *gò* (catfishlike goby) are used in classic risotto preparations. Navy, turquoise, and silver *sarde* (sardines) appear at almost every stand, as do *bisati* (eels), swimming in tubs. Oddly enough, for a town obsessed with fresh fish, Venetians are crazy about what they call *baccalà mantecato,* which is reconstituted cod (actually air-dried, not salt, cod) cooked and then beaten with extra-virgin olive oil, milk, and a hint of garlic.

Venice isn't the best town for carnivores, but they can seek solace in *fegato alla veneziana* (calves' liver and onions) and *carpaccio* (paper-thin sliced raw beef), which was invented at Harry's Bar. And to the delight of waterfowl fans, the practice of cooking birds from the lagoon—*masorini* (mallard), *ciossi* (widgeon), and *sarzegne* (teal)—has been revived.

Such signs of onetime Austrian dominion as *krapfen* (yeasty doughnuts) and strudel abound in pastry shops, along with traditional Venetian *zaletti* (raisin cornmeal), *baicoli* (butter), and *amaretti* (almond) cookies, each meant to be served with a glass of dessert wine. When in the mood for something more substantial, I opt for that regional classic, *tiramisù,* coffee-soaked biscuits layered with *mascarpone* custard. Venice is also wild about *gelato* made with both milk and cream. A visit to Nico on the Zattere for *gianduiotto* (a blocklike chunk of chocolate-hazelnut *gelato* with whipped cream), to the Lido for fantastic custard *gelato* at Tita, or to the Hotel Cipriani's restaurant for a scoop of dark chocolate *gelato* topped with bitter-orange sauce shows why.

Not surprisingly, Venice produces no wine of its own and, being a city with no cellars, has never been very interested in quality wine in the past. Restaurants have, however, awakened to the oenological revolution taking place in the surrounding Veneto and Friuli regions, once sources of simple quaffing wines purchased in bulk. There modern vintners release traditional white wines—straightforward, crisp, and delicately perfumed—or innovative *vini da tavola,* often varietal blends and sometimes aged in wood. (Light and fruity reds are also produced, but Venetian drinkers generally prefer whites.) In the Breganze area, first-rate Torcolato, one of Italy's finest dessert wines, is made by Maculan; Soave, by Anselmi and Pieropan; Bianco di Custoza, by Le Vigne di San Pietro and Zenato; Pinot Bianco and aromatic Alpianae, by Vignalta; Corbulino Bianco, by Scarpa; and the summertime thirst-quencher of choice, sparkling Prosecco di Conegliano, is at its best from Primo Franco, Zardetto, and Gregoletto. Whites from Friuli are usually named for the grape involved: Pinot Bianco or Grigio, Tocai Friulano (not a sweet wine), Ribolla Gialla, Sauvignon, and Chardonnay. Labels to look for are Livio Felluga, Jermann, Ronco del Gnemiz, Rodaro, Abbazia di Rosazzo, Borgo del Tiglio, Gravner, Dorigo, Le Due Terre, and Vie di Romans. Grappas (distilled grape pomace, which can range from mild to throat-burning) are carefully produced and beautifully packaged by Nonino from Ribolla Gialla, Fragolino, and Picolit grapes.

When Venetian locals bump into friends, or when hunger strikes, they head for the nearest *bacaro* (neighborhood wine bar) for an *ombretta* ("little shade," from the custom of cooling off in the shadow of San Marco's bell tower with a swallow of wine), often consumed standing at the bar. And because Italians don't drink without eating, *bacari* serve a wide variety of snacks called *cicchetti* (little tastes). Boiled baby octopuses, whipped salt cod, meatballs, anchovies, hard-boiled eggs, marinated vegetables, *nervetti* (calf's-foot salad), and sandwiches with their fillings piled high in the middle are among the traditional offerings. *Sarde* (sardines) are given the *saor* treatment (pickled lightly with onions, raisins, and pine nuts) and must be boned by the diner.

Shaped like a tunnel with doors at both ends and decorated with copper wine buckets hanging from the ceiling, Do Mori is always crowded, the air alive with Venetian voices. Locals burdened with briefcases and shopping bags elbow to the counter, order, and step back three paces to a shelf, upon which they place their wineglasses and plates full of canapés of whipped cod (with or without garlic), prosciutto wrapped around breadsticks, octopus, *sarde in saor,* and such sandwiches as the best-selling *coppa di toro* (soft whole-wheat bread spread with ham and olive paste). One pays when finished. Owner Roberto Biscontin doesn't stop pouring, slicing, wrapping, adding, and chatting up the regulars until his *bacaro* slows down around one P.M., when everyone has gone home for lunch. It's a perfect stop before or after a morning visit to the Rialto.

Vino Vino, steps from the La Fenice opera house, has a fantastic selection of wines, many available by the glass, and a wide variety of snacks prepared in the kitchen of its sister restaurant, the elegant Antico Martini. Large oval platters of *cicchetti,* displayed behind glass at the bar, include the ever-present *sarde in saor,* marinated vegetables, and octopus. Marble tables fill two tiny dining rooms, one of which overlooks a quiet canal.

L'Aciugheta is a *bacaro-pizzeria,* an uncommon combination that features a well-chosen list of wines, chalked on slates behind the bar, and rolled-anchovy sandwiches and mini-pizzas to snack on at the counter or at any table that's not set. (Close to mealtimes, many tables are reserved for more formal dining.)

Osteria d'Alberto may be hard to find, but the search pays off. The selection of *cicchetti* is enormous: fried stuffed olives, meatballs, sausages, boiled eggs with pickled onions and anchovies, fried *scampi* on skewers, octopus, and more. In the early afternoon a hot first course is served—pasta, gnocchi, or risotto. Customers either stand at the bar or eat at one of the few tables in the back.

My favorite *bacaro* in Venice is Al Mascaron, which has evolved into a restaurant without abandoning the wine-bar tradition or its regular clients. Offering *ombrette* and *cicchetti* at the bar in the morning as well as full meals at wooden tables in two dining rooms, owner Luigi Vianello and chef Giancarlo Seno work hard making octopus and celery salad, boiled shrimp, grilled marinated vegetables, *moleche* (soft-shelled crabs), pastas, risottos, and soups. The ambiance is convivial, although service may suffer at the busiest times. Venetians mix at the bar and play card games of *madrasso, scopa,* and *briscola* at the tables in off-hours. In a country where practically everyone smokes, Al Mascaron's nonsmoking dining room is miraculous.

A more sophisticated incarnation of the *bacaro,* Harry's Bar was created in 1931 by Giuseppe Cipriani as a luxury bar with a clubby atmosphere, a place for local artists and writers, expatriates, and visitors to hang out. Food was almost an afterthought here and, in the beginning, was often cooked by Signora Cipriani herself. Popular demand and a clientele that didn't want to go elsewhere to eat led to expanded service and a menu that ranges from humble *sarde in saor* to caviar and white truffles. Arrigo Cipriani, son of Giuseppe, presides (when he's not overseeing his restaurant in New York City), assisted by the charming Lucio Zanon. Barmen Claudio Ponzio and Valentino Carlon prepare perfect versions of the standard cocktails—Martini drinkers rejoice!—but I always order Harry's Bellini, paired with chicken or shrimp salad sandwiches. Dining here *is* expensive, but enthusiasts insist you haven't been to Venice if you haven't been to Harry's.

Restaurants in Venice have always had two tiers of service and food, and in the past visitors without Venetian accents tended to pay more for lesser fare and attention. But in 1992 a group of chefs and restaurant owners joined forces to form Ristoranti della Buona Accoglienza (Warm Welcome Restaurants), whose member establishments—which include all of the restaurants described below, apart from the Hotel Cipriani's—promise good regional food and wine and cordial service at stable prices.

Chef Cesare Benelli was one of the founders of Ristoranti della Buona Accoglienza, and no visit to Venice is complete for me without at least one meal at his cozy restaurant, Al Covo. Cesare and his Texan wife, Diane Rankin, are obsessed with local ingredients and recently revived the dying art of cooking fowl from the lagoon, usually stewing it in red wine. Such first courses as sugar-sweet mantis shrimp dressed with fine extra-virgin olive oil; already boned *sarde in saor;* and ethereal whipped cod are hard to resist. Of the main-course pastas, I opt for Al Covo's spaghetti, sauced with either carpet shell clams or *datteri* (sea dates), when they're available. Deep-fried soft-shelled crabs, baby cuttlefish, sweet Dublin Bay prawns, and tiny sole are crisp and greaseless. Diane's chocolate cake and favorite Venetian and American cookies work well with dessert wines from the reasonably priced list.

I often get lost on my way to Osteria da Fiore, which is located on a quiet lane near the Frari church and is always packed with discriminating diners. Chef Mara Zanetti and her husband, host Maurizio Martin, present customers with the tiniest, lightest, crunchiest deep-fried baby shrimp and a glass of Prosecco while the difficult decisions regarding the menu are attended to. The mixed seafood starter—on my last visit it included razor clams, spider crab, octopus, mantis shrimp, and scallops, cooked in various ways—is a tribute to the lagoon. The risotto is black with cuttlefish ink or flavored with prawns. Homemade *sorbetti* are a wonderful conclusion, as are the more substantial desserts.

Ai Mercanti is perched on a little bridge around the corner from the Rialto market. The restaurant is small, with a low beamed ceiling. Mushrooms are on chef Bruno Paolato's menu most of the year—raw or cooked, alone or with seafood (as in the warm scallop and wild mushroom salad). Diners tired of fish also will find here lamb, rabbit, or waterfowl. The wine list offers some unusual gems from wineries such as Russolo, Specogna, and Edy Kante.

In spite of its name, the Fiaschetteria Toscana serves classic Venetian cuisine. Owner Albino Busatto welcomes guests to the warm rose-colored, stone-floored restaurant with wooden ceilings, and his son Stefano presides in the kitchen, preparing, among the starters, *tagliolini* with crab and tiny potato gnocchi dressed with prawns and zucchini. (Mariuccia Amato, Albino's wife, is the pastry chef.) Fish are superfresh and cooked simply: sea bream sauced with butter and capers and baked baby monkfish or sea bass. Seasonal vegetables, especially the grilled radicchio, are world-class. Light-as-a-feather *zabaione* (foamy whipped custard) is made with Marsala Stravecchio, a fortified dark dessert wine that has been aged at least ten years. Albino cares about wine, and his list reflects this.

Corte Sconta has had its ups and downs, but it is now better than ever. Two rustic dining rooms and a hidden courtyard (hence the restaurant's name) are always crowded for dinner. Chef-owner Claudio Proietto rules the kitchen, while his wife, Rita, and her sister-in-law Lucia Zambon keep things under control up front. Between meals locals stop in for a glass of wine and *cicchetti* or to play cards at a table in the back. The core of Corte Sconta's generous mixed antipasto platter is grilled razor clams and scallops, tiny shrimp with polenta, whipped cod, and boiled baby octopuses. Spaghetti with inky cuttlefish sauce, *tagliatelle* with basil and scallops, and goby risotto turn up as *primi* (first courses); and main courses of grilled eel, squid stuffed with radicchio, and *fritto misto* (mixed fried sole, sardines, prawns, and squid) are equally inviting. Fruit ices, berries, and cookies are available for those who can still manage dessert.

Ai Gondolieri, around the corner from the Accademia and not far from the Peggy Guggenheim Collection, is another welcome relief for those not enraptured by fish; the emphasis is on meat, local waterfowl, and vegetables. One look at the selection of red wines behind owner Giovanni Trevisan's bar would be enough to convince most wine lovers to try this restaurant, and chef Marisa Oboe's skills will win over at the table: risotto with radicchio, asparagus, wild greens, or mushrooms; squash or potato gnocchi; simple soups; grilled vegetables; truffles in season; and rabbit and other game.

The pleasures of staying at the Hotel Cipriani are legendary, but one need not be in residence to enjoy the excellent cuisine. A private launch waits at the San Marco dock to whisk guests to the hotel and restaurant, on the far side of the Giudecca, where waiters bustle around tables graced with exquisite flower arrangements. The food is as sophisticated as the setting, a mixture of Spartan simplicity and innovative flavor combinations. Squid-ink pasta sauced with fresh tomatoes and scallops, perfectly executed risottos, and grilled sturgeon and monkfish never disappoint. Desserts are at times inspired, like the grappa parfait and the golden *zabaione* made with a Fragolino dessert wine, but one shouldn't forget that chocolate *gelato*—it is in a league of its own.

Obviously, I've fallen for Venice. I've started to enjoy the swirly intricacies of Venetian glass chandeliers. I even like some of those kitschy souvenirs, especially the scarves and fans. And just thinking about *caparozzoli* and *canocie* and *moleche* makes me want to hop on the next train from my home in Florence. But I haven't changed my mind about the pigeons.

For more information on Ristoranti della Buona Accoglienza, write to the organization at Casella Postale 624, 30100 Venice or call the offices in that city at 523.9896. The Hazans, unfortunately, no longer live in Venice and teach only occasionally. They do, however, still write about food and wine.

Wine Bars

L'Aciugheta, Campo SS. Filippo e Giacomo, 4357, Castello (041.522.4292)

Do Mori, Calle do Mori, 429, San Polo (041.522.5401)

Harry's Bar, Calle Vallaresso, 1323, San Marco (041.528.5777)

Al Mascaron, Calle Lunga Santa Maria Formosa, 5225, Castello (041.522.5995)

Osteria d'Alberto, Calle Malvasia, 6015, Castello (041.522.9038)

Vino Vino, Ponte delle Veste, 2007/a, San Marco (041.523.7027)

Restaurants

Corte Sconta, Calle del Pestrin, 3886 (near the Arsenale), Castello (041.522.7024)

Al Covo, Campiello della Pescaria, 3968, Castello (041.522.3812)

Fiaschetteria Toscana, Salizzada San Giovanni Grisostomo, 5719, Canareggio (041.528.5281)

Ai Gondolieri, Fondamenta Ospedaletto, 366, Dorsoduro (041.528.6396)

Ai Mercanti, Campo delle Beccarie, 1588, San Polo (041.524.0282)

Osteria da Fiore, Calle del Scaleter, 2202/a, San Polo (041.721.308)

Ristorante Hotel Cipriani, Giudecca, 10 (041.520.7744)

This article originally appeared in *Gourmet*, September 1994. © Faith Heller Willinger. Reprinted with permission.

Wines of the Veneto

BY BILL MARSANO

❧

editor's note

Here is an excellent piece presenting an overview of the variety of wines from the Veneto, which, according to Joseph Bastianich and David Lynch in *Vino Italiano,* "ranks third in Italy in the quantity of wine produced, trailing only Sicily and Puglia. The difference is that the vast majority of Sicily's and Puglia's wines leave in tanker trucks, not in bottles. And yet the Veneto isn't just bargain-rack wine. Soave can be a rich, aromatic, mouth-filling white. Valpolicella can be a luscious, ageworthy red. Even Prosecco, the wine for carefree nights in Venice, can be a serious sparkler. Amarone, of course, is Amarone: there's nothing quite like it."

BILL MARSANO, introduced in the *Informazioni Pratiche* section, won the 1999 James Beard Award for his writing on wine and spirits in *Hemispheres,* the in-flight magazine of United Airlines.

Veneto is a blessed region—perhaps overblessed or even unfairly blessed. Lovely Veneto has flatlands and rolling hills and mountains; she has a coast on the Adriatic and a fine stretch of lakefront property, if you will, on the eastern shore of Lago di Garda; she has Venice and Verona and Vicenza; has villas Palladian and vistas arcadian. And vines. Vines in superabundance.

Wine has been made here since the Veneti tribe settled the region about 1000 B.C. The Etruscans and Romans carried on, and the vine thrived under a later tribe, the decadent Venetians of *La Serenissima,* the "Most Serene Republic." Today Veneto ranks third in wine production among Italy's twenty regions, behind only Puglia and Sicily. As she also ranks seventh in population, the role of exports is obvious. Her wines are well known internationally and easy to find.

They're equally easy to enjoy. Artisan winemakers provide excellent bottlings from small estates (some only two acres), but even industrial-scale producers have, in recent decades, managed to combine quality with quantity. As a result, Veneto leads in production of DOC *(denominazione di origine controllata)* wines, annually providing more than twenty percent of Italy's total. DOC wines are made according to strict regulations that control the process from vineyard to aging. Overall, the wine-drinker routinely receives good value whether he pays a few dollars for a clean, well-made picnic white or sustains the substantial damage imposed by something like a long-aged Bertani Amarone, a Maculan Bordeaux blend, or an upscale Prosecco from Mionetto.

The vineyard is bewilderingly diverse, with eighty or so grape varieties officially permitted. Even some of the important local vines are little known elsewhere, and many lesser varieties are merely vestigial these days, having fallen from favor or having been uprooted for such foreign favorites as Chardonnay, whose tentacular reach knows no limits.

There are pockets of stubborn resistance. Near Verona, for example, Dott. Sandro Boscaini of Masi and its sister estate Serègo Alighieri will have no truck with outlander grapes. Instead he looks into the past for inspiration, working to get the best out of the Veneto's heritage. He has reintroduced the neglected *ripasso* method (of which more anon) and personally rescued Oseletta from extinction, having searched out perhaps the last half-dozen surviving vines. The grapes go into his latest creation: Osar, a fine red produced in necessarily small quantities.

Veneto's principal white wines are Soave and Prosecco; her chief reds are Valpolicella (actually a close-knit family of wines), Bardolino, and a varied collection of Bordeaux types.

In the postwar years, Soave was one of Italy's wine ambassadors to the United States, elected by acclamation after Americans discovered it while seeking Romeo and Juliet in Verona. Producers of this light, fruity, refreshing wine quickly made sure they could get it at home, none more successfully than Bolla, whose fictional spokesman, "Franco Bolla," pitched it as a wine that "goes with everything." In time, many consumers thought of Soave Bolla as a single word.

Demand rose and quality fell as the vineyard was overextended. The hills had produced the best wine and the new vineyards on the plains merely produced *more* wine. Swelling amounts of undistinguished filler grapes smothered the delicate lemon-almond character of Garganega, Soave's essential variety. Only recently has the wine recovered from this abuse.

The wine writer Victor Hazan said, "I like Soave best when I have to think about it least." He meant no disrespect: it is quintessentially a refreshing, casual wine, and reasonably priced, from such important houses as Bolla, Bertani, and Masi. Leonildo Pieropan and Anselmi are among the star producers, and excellent bottles also come from Cantina del Castello, Coffele, Gini, Pasqua, Monte Tondo, and Suavia.

Identifying Soave can be tricky because of its checkered past. Today some producers prefer to emphasize proprietary names on their premium versions. Bolla, for example, labels its best with the name Tufaie in large type and Soave in small, barely legible type just below. Also look for *classico* on labels; it indicates the wine was grown in those superior hillside vineyards; *superiore* indicates a slightly higher level of alcohol. The sweet dessert version is labeled *recioto*.

Prosecco is little known to Americans, but recently Mionetto, one of the most forward-looking producers, has mounted a full-scale marketing effort in the United States. Sergio Mionetto, head of the house, is convinced Americans will fall for its gentle seduction as Italians have. Indeed, in the Veneto this light, low-alcohol sparkling white is routinely made at home by basement winemakers for family consumption, and it is the only wine that has its own bar—the *Proseccheria*. Venetians in particular are addicted to it. At least once a sweltering summer's day they stop for the glass of Prosecco they call an *umbra* or *umbretta,* which freely translates as "a little bit of shade." "The *umbra* is always Prosecco," Sergio says, noting that Asti would be too sweet and champagne too assertive.

An alternative cooler is the Bellini, which also requires Prosecco. (Champagne would overwhelm the delicate peach nectar.) "The nectar must be from white peaches," Sergio says, adding that the Bellini "was popularized by Harry's Bar on the Grand Canal, but it wasn't invented there. It's what our grandmothers often drank—sometimes with peach nectar, sometimes with strawberries."

The wine is found in two versions. One is *amabile* (slightly sweet) and *frizzante* (lightly bubbly)—and easily identified: its naked cork protrudes from the neck of the bottle and is tied down with string. This, says Sergio, is the traditional Prosecco; the fully bubbly *spumante,* which is dry or just barely sweet, is a more recent development. The hilltowns of Valdobbiadene and Conegliano produce the best; wines from the former are crisper, with more finesse than the softly fruity wines from the latter. Either name may be on the label or, when grapes from the two areas are blended, both.

Prosecco from the subzone of Cartizze, near Valdobbiadene, is a highly regarded wine but a somewhat iffy proposition. If you know the producer, buy; if not—not. Burton Anderson has noted that the amount of Cartizze or Superiore di Cartizze bottled is rather larger than the vines can actually provide.

Mionetto is among the largest producers, but there are plenty of others to seek out, including Adami, Desiderio Bisol, Fratelli Bortolin, Col Vetoraz, Spumanti Dal Din, De Faveri, Conte Collalto, Nino Franco, Masottina, Angelo Ruggeri, Ruggeri & C., and Tanorè.

Pinot Grigio sparked a fad in America some years ago, but in truth the best comes from nearby Trentino–Alto Adige and Friuli–Venezia Giulia, two regions that, with Veneto, make up the "superregion" called *Le Tre Venezie*. Bolla's new Pinot Grigio, Arcale, for example, is from Friuli–Venezia Giulia, not Veneto. Better to look for the less-known but very good Bianco di Custoza, which is reminiscent of Soave, from the likes of Arvedi di Emilei, Corte Gardoni, Lamberti, Giacomo Montresor, Albino Piona, and Santi.

Bardolino, a light, fruity red or *chiaretto* (rosé), was another postwar ambassador, partly because it caught the eye with its straw-wrapped flat or "mandolin" flask. (No doubt many consumers mistook it for Chianti.) Again it's important to look for the *classico*, and for the same reason. Bardolino is best when it comes from the hill vineyards above the pretty lake town for which it is named. Bertani and Masi are again the big names; other notable producers incude Arvedi di Emilei, Corte Gardoni, Lamberti, and Fratelli Zeni. But forget about the mandolin flask: like Chianti's quaint *fiasco,* it has been retired.

Valpolicella is the red that rules here, however, and it is not so much a wine as a family or clan of wines. A blend of the same grape varieties, Corvina, Molinara, and Rondinella, produces the standard Valpolicella, the *ripasso* style, Recioto della Valpolicella, and Amarone della Valpolicella.

Basic Valpolicella, especially the *classico,* is similar to but more complex and longer-lived than cheerful Bardolino; ruby red and fuller bodied, it's for dinner rather than lunch, usually at its best when no more than three years old. A heightened version, called *ripasso,* is made by the old practice, revived by Masi, of giving Valpolicella more character by refermenting it on the pomace of Amarone. (Pomace is the residue of fermentation.) Masi's Campo Fiorin was the first of the *ripasso* revival; Bolla's Le Poiane is the latest. The term may or may not appear on labels or back labels.

Valpolicella from neighboring Valpantena is usually a lighter, lesser wine—but not always. A recent Bertani Valpolicella Valpantena was substantial enough to stand up to a *classico*, even a *ripasso*.

Recioto della Valpolicella is a sweet red *passito* wine, usually still but sometimes sparkling, made from grapes partly air-dried by breezes off the nearby river Adige. It goes well with or instead of dessert. It is also a wine of celebration and a gesture of welcome, offered to guests as Vin Santo, also a *passito* wine, is in central Italy.

Amarone della Valpolicella is a dry, rich, powerful, and distinguished red whose roots are entwined with *recioto*. In making *recioto*, fermentation is arrested to achieve maximum sweetness; for Amarone, fermentation continues until all the sugar is converted to alcohol. It is a seductive wine because its richness gives an impression of sweetness; at fifteen degrees or more of alcohol, it is also decidedly muscular.

Indeed, some old-timers in Veneto call Amarone a "failed" *recioto* or, as Patricia Guy says in her book *Amarone* (published by Morganti), "a *recioto* that got away." (She adds that an old dialect term for it is *recioto scapà*, or "escaped.") Given Amarone's stature, growing internationally over the past decade or so, you can be sure no producer is pleased by the notion that it is the result of a mistake or "forgotten barrels."

Amarone is difficult to match with food; it is what I think of as a "fireplace" wine and what Italians call a *vino di meditazione*. It goes best with a log fire, accompanied by close friends and much talk about past glories, future possibilities and, of course, the wine itself.

Amarones from Bertani, Bolla, and Masi (including Serègo Alighieri) have achieved renown, with Bertani particularly noted for vintages long aged before release to the market. Fine smaller producers include Stefano Accordini, Allegrini, Luigi Brunelli, Fratelli

Tedeschi, Le Sallette, Quintarelli, and Romano dal Forno, and good bottles also come from Lorenzo Begali, Tommaso Bussola, Michele Castellani, Giuseppe Campagnola, Corte Sant'Alda, Giacomo Montresor, Novaia, Angelo Nicolis e Figli, Roberto Mazzi, Raimondi Villa Monteleone, Trabucchi, Massimino Venturini, Viviani, and Fratelli Zeni.

Veneto has more than a hundred thousand producers, and it stands to reason that there is much experimentation and innovation, particularly since Chardonnay is now widely grown and Bordeaux types (Cabernet Sauvignon, Cabernet Franc, Merlot, and Sauvignon Blanc, among others) have grown here so long as to be naturalized citizens.

They are bottled as single varieties (such as Bolla's Colforte and Maculan's Palazotto), blended among themselves (Maculan's Ferrata and Russolo's Doi Raps are examples), or blended with local grapes (as in Bertani's Catullo). Other names to look for are Ca'Lustra, Cavazza, Conte Collalto, Conti A&G da Schio, Dal Maso, Inama, La Cappuccina, Alessandro Piovene, Le Ragose, Tenuta S. Antonio, Vignalta, Vigneti Due Santi, and Villa da Ferro.

For greater detail, a wine-lover will want to consult Burton Anderson's *Wines of Italy,* published by Mitchell Beazley. Travelers may want to seek the familiar names of major producers on returning, but while in the Veneto the venturous spirit should prevail. Seek out wines you *won't* find at home.

Italy's classification levels, top to bottom, are DOCG *(denominazione di origine controllata e garantita),* DOC *(denominazione di origine controllata),* IGT *(indicazione geografica tipica),* and VDT *(vino da tavola).*

DOCG wines are rare because this classification is extremely demanding, but it is easily identified by the DOCG neck label on every bottle. Veneto has one DOCG: Recioto di Soave.

DOCs are more common, but the standards are still rigorous. As of this writing, there are seventeen DOC zones in Veneto; they appear on labels in this form:

Amarone della Valpolicella
Denominazione di Origine Controllata

If a wine from a DOC zone is based on a specific grape variety, the label will look like this:

Cabernet di Breganze
Denominazione di Origine Controllata

IGT, a looser classification, refers to "typical geographic indications": a skilled and knowing taster should be able to sip and say, "Yes—this is from Veneto." You, of course, may simply say, "This is delightful—pour me another."

VDT, lowest and loosest of these disciplines, indicates simple but well-made wines—enjoyable but of no particular distinction or pedigree; they are often the cheapest.

This is not always the case. Innovative producers sometimes experiment with nontraditional grapes and blends; the results, even if superb, are classified VDT solely because they don't meet the requirements of higher classifications. When such wines prove their worth, they may move up to IGT, a level created so that innovation might be rewarded. Nevertheless, all "new" wines begin as VDTs. If you spot a VDT from a renowned producer, pause before passing on: it might be a splendid surprise.

Salute!

This piece was originally intended for a cookbook project, but is appearing, with alterations for travelers, for the first time in this volume. Copyright © 2001 by Bill Marsano. Reprinted with permission of the author.

Sampling the Best of Italy, in Verona

BY FRANK PRIAL

〜〜〜

editor's note

I have been a frequent patron of wine bars in Italy, though none with as happy a name as the Bottega del Vino, in Verona, the subject of this piece.

FRANK PRIAL is the wine columnist for *The New York Times* and writes about wine for a variety of other publications. His work has been featured in the *Central Italy* and *Provence, Côte d'Azur and Monaco* editions of *The Collected Traveler*. He is also the author of *Wine Talk* (Times Books, 1978) and coauthor, with Rosemary George and Michael Edwards, of *The Companion to Wine* (Prentice-Hall, 1992).

The center of this ancient city is reserved for walkers. Not the grim heads-down striders of New York or London, but relaxed strollers, wandering in and out of shops, chatting, laughing, and casually inspecting each other in the time-honored Italian way.

Just off the main pedestrian thoroughfare, the Via Mazzini, is the tiny Via Scudo di Francia. In the middle of the block, a small electric sign announces the Bottega del Vino, one of the best-known gathering places in Italy. Politicians, business people, tradesmen, students, occasional tourists, and people from the wine trade fill the *bottega* nightly.

Each spring, when Verona is host to a big wine trade fair known as Vinitaly, Bottega del Vino runs almost around the clock. On most days, service is supposed to end at one A.M., but no one seems to watch the clock. I wandered in for dinner around eleven one night, and when I left at three-thirty A.M., a handful of die-hards were still eating dinner—or a very early breakfast.

As I left, Severino Barzan, the *bottega*'s owner, said, "You will be back for lunch, yes?" The answer was yes because the lunch had been scheduled in advance; dinner was a last-minute decision. Lunch, a multicourse, multiwine affair with Mr. Barzan presiding in his own basement dining room, lasted from one to five.

Verona has two Michelin-starred restaurants, but the Bottega del Vino isn't one of them. The red guide for Italy awards two stars to Il Desco and one to Tre Marchetti. The *bottega* manages to rate only one crossed fork and spoon, which means "quite comfortable." No matter. One eats well in Mr. Barzan's care. Dishes are traditional, and portions are generous. Pastas are made fresh daily, and everything else comes from local farms and butchers. My favorite dish: *bigoli all'anatra,* a thick local pasta mixed with pieces of roast duck.

But food at the Bottega del Vino is a mere backdrop. As the name implies, this is a serious place for wine.

Forget the eighteen different vintages of Penfolds Grange from Australia that Mr. Barzan stocks; forget the Opus One and reserve cabernets from Robert Mondavi and the fifteen vintages of Château d'Yquem, many of them in double magnums and jeroboams.

Instead, concentrate on the Italian wines, especially the wines of the surrounding region, the Veneto. The glory of the Veneto is Amarone, a rich, powerful red wine. Mr. Barzan is an Amarone fanatic, but he confines his passion mostly to two labels, Bertani and Masi.

He stocks twenty-seven vintages of Bertani's Amarone riserva, beginning with 1959, and thirty-five vintages of various Masi Amarones, starting with 1974 and including *riservas, classicos,* single-vineyard Amarones, and even some made especially for the *bottega.* Also from Masi are Amarones made from the vineyards of the Serègo Alighieri Estate, whose ownership descends in an unbroken family line from the son of the poet Dante.

Mr. Barzan also offers a dazzling display of wines, mostly Barolos and Barbarescos, from the Piedmont region of Italy: twenty-one from Angelo Gaja; eleven from Bruno Ceretto, including a rare 1970 Zonchetta Brunate; twenty-five wines from the Marchesi di Gresy; and eighteen from Prunotto. The list of Tuscan wines has fifty-seven listings from Frescobaldi, including all vintages of Luce, Lucente, and Danzante, the wines from the recent joint venture of Frescobaldi and Mondavi.

As with any restaurant whose owner is devoted to wine, some of the Bottega del Vino's best bottles are not on the list. The only way to unearth them is to challenge Mr. Barzan to bring forth something truly different.

Like any successful restaurateur, Mr. Barzan is omnipresent at the *bottega*. He seems to know half his customers by name. Some *bottega* regulars insist there must be two or three Severinos, because he also owns a hotel and a theme park on Lake Garda, twenty miles west of Verona, and two restaurants and a supermarket in Yalta, the Crimean resort on the Black Sea.

The Yalta ventures came about after Mr. Barzan met the mayor of Yalta when Mikhail Gorbachev visited Italy in the early 1980s. "That was the time of *glasnost*," Mr. Barzan said. "They invited me there and gave me everything I wanted. It was almost too easy."

Everything but what he needed to run restaurants. "At first, we brought in 100 percent of what we needed," he said. "Now it's 30."

Even though he has a variety of thriving businesses, Mr. Barzan's first love is still the *bottega*. "It is a part of Verona," he said. "In fact, it *is* Verona." He then led me into a back room, whose walls are decorated with old newspaper clippings. "During the war," he said, "this was a meeting place for the anti-Fascists, intellectuals, and political people who needed a place to gather, to plan the future, or just to eat and play cards. We keep it just the way it was then. When I was a kid, working in hotels," he added, "I dreamed of owning the Bottega del Vino. Now I do. I'll never change it, and I'll never sell it."

Roman Holiday

BY DOUG PEPPER

~

editor's note

....

Ignore, if you will, the title of this piece. The writer did indeed travel to
Venice as part of a trip throughout Italy, using, of course, Fred Plotkin's
Italy for the Gourmet Traveler as his gastronomic guide. What the writer
doesn't mention in this piece is that when he and his wife-to-be were in
Venice at the Trattoria Anzolo Raffael, recommended in Plotkin's book,
they were astonished to meet another North American couple whose last
name was Plotkin. It turns out that the Plotkin couple were of no relation to
Fred, and they had just landed in Venice and had come straight to this
restaurant, based on the other Plotkin's recommendation. The foursome
were the only North Americans in the entire restaurant, and after dinner
they all walked to Harry's Bar for a drink. This was, as you'll read, where
the writer had decided to propose, but the privacy in which to do it was not
easily granted him by the Plotkin couple. On several occasions, the writer's
significant other suggested they call it a night, but of course the writer
couldn't allow for that and desperately ordered round after round of drinks.
Finally, after untold drink dividends (a *dividend,* by the way, is a term I
learned from my good friend John D., whose father coined the word for
those occasions when your glass, usually filled with martinis, is-not-quite-
empty but is refreshed anyway—dividend!—ensuring you never know how
many glasses you've consumed) and the obligatory photo taken in front of
Harry's, the Plotkin couple departed, leaving the writer to do his deed.

DOUG PEPPER, a Canadian by birth, is a vice president and senior editor at Crown Publishers in New York, where he lives now. He contributed
this piece to *Elm Street,* a magazine for Canadian women.

It started with an egg—as so many things do—fried, to be precise.
I can't remember exactly what age I was, early teens probably, but
it was at the house of my close friend, Howard, and he was the one
making breakfast. He was the product of divorced parents and, as

such, was left to make his own meals a lot. I had many breakfasts with him, but they always consisted of much the same thing: two eggs sunny-side up with a pinch of paprika sprinkled on the yolks, accompanied by a sliced tomato, buttered whole-wheat toast, some smoked bacon, and freshly squeezed orange juice. Not especially glamorous, but it was the first time I had seen someone my age cook anything other than macaroni and cheese. And Howard did it with the kind of care and technique that you would not expect from a teenager. Watching him taught me something about the joy of cooking and turned on a light in me that has shone brighter over the years.

Since then, I've done a lot of cooking; it has, in fact, become my hobby. I have the same reverence for my kitchen as many men do for their toolsheds. I pride myself on its order and setup: everything in its place, copper shining, knives sharp, pantry well stocked. I also like to talk to cooking professionals, attend food conferences, go out to eat, hang out in food stores, read—and publish—cookbooks, watch cooking shows on TV, you name it. But if there is one thing I keep coming back to—a cardinal rule that defines what I think is best about cooking and eating—it is that we should keep things simple and use only the best, freshest ingredients available.

This philosophy became abundantly clear to me on a recent trip to Italy. The vacation was something of a culinary adventure for me and Susan, my then girlfriend, as we scheduled our whole trip around where we wanted to eat. Our destinations were Rome, Venice, Bologna, and the Ligurian Coast—in particular the Cinqueterre (the five towns) region south of Genoa; our food of choice was fish and simple pastas.

We ate fresh clams and other shellfish, enjoyed lunches of steaming fish soup, sampled fresh sardines in olive oil, lemon, and capers, gnocchi so good it made us want to weep, and wonderful, infinitely drinkable wines to wash all the food down. We toured markets, such as the Campo dei Fiori in Rome; food stores, like Tamburini in Bologna; and every type of restaurant, from a charming spot in Portovenere, south of Genoa, that made the world's best pesto, to an *osteria* in Venice that served excellent *polpettini* (meatballs), to an extraordinary, plain little restaurant just off the Piazza Navona in Rome called Ristorante Il Pellicano.

The chef at Il Pellicano, a woman named Maria Romani, had some 450 dishes (including twenty-four soups) in her repertoire, and patrolled her kitchen in a white smock and a pair of beat-up slippers. We ordered a tasting menu—*Faccia pure come vuole* ("Go right ahead and do as you think best")—which featured fresh fish from the Adriatic—mackerel, anchovies, marinated salmon—and a broad range of local ingredients. The Italians must have quite a different idea of what constitutes a tasting menu: it turned out to be a fifteen-course meal, each dish better than the last. At the end of the evening, as we waved our white napkins in surrender, Maria came up to the table and took a well-deserved bow. I was overcome with emotion and told her that she was a genius, although I don't think she understood a word I said. She beamed, took my face in her hands, planted a big kiss on each cheek, and headed back to her *pesce*.

Everywhere we went it was the same, although Maria was the only chef to kiss me. The food was fresh—sometimes still alive—the presentation simple, and the tastes out of this world. The Italians, of course, love food, and it showed. I imagined duels being fought over ravioli, suicides following botched meals, old men and women spending fifty years perfecting a baked risotto timbale.

One Venetian mecca that we visited was Harry's Bar. A place of myth almost, Harry's is, however, a great restaurant. We didn't eat there on this trip, but rather stopped for drinks after a glorious meal at Trattoria Anzolo Raffael. We ordered the only things one should drink there—a martini for me: ice-cold, painfully dry, and lovingly mixed, and Harry's exclusive Bellini, fresh peach juice and Prosecco, for Susan. As a plate of cannelloni and another of fresh pasta with shaved truffles wafted by, the combined culinary sensations from the last week and a half filled my head, and I decided to propose. I'd been thinking about doing it for the entire trip, even came pretty close at Il Pellicano, except that I was too stuffed to get the words out. But there is very little a man can't accomplish with a good martini in hand, in a place like Harry's Bar, on vacation in one of the world's most beautiful cities with the one he loves. So I uttered the fateful words. Luckily, she accepted (after asking me if I was serious), and the couple who had ordered the cannelloni and truffle pasta smiled at us and sipped their wine.

Since I can't stay in Italy for the rest of my life, my solace on returning home was my kitchen and several shelves of cookbooks. The latter combine three of my passions: publishing, reading, and cooking. I spend weekdays publishing cookbooks, weekday evenings reading them, and weekends cooking from them. I own hundreds, well thumbed and splattered, and no category is more comprehensive than that devoted to Italian cuisine. I'm also blessed to live in Toronto's Little Italy, surrounded by wonderful Italian grocery stores. So my first Saturday back I created a meal for my family to officially announce our engagement.

I started with an antipasto plate of juicy black olives, roasted peppers with olive oil and capers, wedges of Asiago cheese, Italian salami, thinly sliced prosciutto, and crusty bread rubbed with garlic. Accompanying this were grilled fresh sardines soaked in olive oil, lemon, and parsley, just as we'd had in the Cinqueterre. I followed with artichokes Roman style—braised in olive oil and stuffed with parsley and mint—a simple, satisfying way to cook a very Italian ingredient. The pasta course was ziti—long, thick macaroni—with pepper sauce, garlic, and basil. As if this wasn't enough I was taking Maria's concept of a tasting menu to heart—I served as the main course a *zuppa di pesce*. This is not for the "rush-hour" cook or someone looking for a quick fix, but it's worth it: fresh fish, vegetables, wine, and saffron providing layers of flavor and a velvety consistency. The soup recipe follows and I urge you to try it. I don't know that anyone had room for the sour-cream coffee cake, but the grappa went over well.

It wasn't Italy, but at least I was cooking. At one point, I closed my eyes, imagined I was in some tiny kitchen somewhere in Rome, could speak fluent Italian, and had 450 recipes in my head. For the time being I'll have to settle for a functional kitchen and a smattering of Italian, with great cookbooks within reach. And as long as I know how to make decent fried eggs, I'll happily and simply survive.

Zuppa di Pesce

Makes 6 to 8 Servings

According to *The Harry's Bar Cookbook* by Harry Cipriani (Bantam, 1991), from which this recipe is adapted, Harry's fish soup "is a combination of the French *bouillabaisse,* with its rich saffron flavour, and the Venetian *brodo di pesce,* a lighter soup using more vegetables and fewer kinds of fish."

2 stalks celery
2 medium onions
1 carrot
⅓ cup olive oil
1 medium tomato, peeled and seeded
½ cup all-purpose flour
1 cup dry white wine
8 cups hot fish or vegetable stock
¼ tsp. saffron threads
1 bay leaf
pinch cayenne

salt and black pepper

½ lb. each 2 kinds of boneless, skinless white fish (such as sea bass, monkfish, or halibut), cut into ½-inch pieces

½ lb. medium shrimp, shelled, deveined, and cut into thirds

¼ cup brandy

1 clove garlic, minced

2 canned anchovy fillets, drained and chopped

3 flat-leafed parsley sprigs, chopped

1 fresh rosemary sprig, leaves removed and chopped (or a pinch of dried)

1 fresh thyme sprig, leaves removed and chopped (or a pinch of dried)

Cut celery, onions, and carrot into julienne strips. Heat 2 tablespoons of the oil in a large saucepan over medium heat. Add celery, onions, and carrot. Cook, stirring often, for 5 minutes or until vegetables are softened but not brown. Cut the tomato into julienne strips, add to saucepan, and cook for 1 minute. Stir in ¼ cup of the flour and cook for about 2 minutes, stirring constantly. Stir in wine and bring to a boil, then simmer, stirring often, for 2 to 3 minutes, until mixture has thickened. Stir in stock, saffron, bay leaf, cayenne, and salt and pepper to taste, then bring to a boil. Reduce heat to medium-low and simmer, partially covered, for 20 minutes.

Meanwhile, combine remaining flour with ¼ teaspoon each salt and pepper in a shallow dish. Add fish and toss to coat well. Heat 2 tablespoons of the oil in a large skillet over medium-high heat. Add fish and shrimp, then cook, stirring, for 2 to 3 minutes, until browned and just cooked. Don't overcook. Add brandy to skillet to warm it, then, standing well back, ignite brandy. (Be careful; the flames may be quite high.) Swirl the skillet at arm's length until flames die down, then add contents of skillet to soup.

Wipe out skillet, and heat remaining oil over medium heat. Add garlic, anchovies, parsley, rosemary, and thyme, then cook for 2 to 3 minutes, stirring constantly, until garlic is pale golden; be careful not to let garlic burn. Strain this flavored oil through a sieve into soup. Stir well, then taste and adjust seasoning, if necessary. Serve at once.

Biblioteca

I believe that one cannot separate Italian food from Italian history. Really good cookbooks—ones that offer tried-and-true, authentic recipes, as well as detailed commentary on the food traditions of the country or region and the history behind the recipes and the ingredients unique to the cuisine—are just as essential to travel as guidebooks. I read these cookbooks the way other people read novels; therefore the authors have to be more than just good cooks, and the books have to be more than just cookbooks. All of the authors and books listed below fit the bill, and because they are *all* my favorites, I feature them alphabetically. I couldn't envision my kitchen without a single one. I do not provide lengthy descriptions of these titles as I think it is enough to state that they are definitive and stand quite apart from the multitude of cookbooks crowding bookstore shelves. All of them are *essenziale,* in one way or another. I have also included a few articles I was unable to feature in this collection, as well as some titles that aren't strictly cookbooks but are equally as interesting and relevant.

Mediterranean Cookbooks and Food

A Book of Mediterranean Food, Elizabeth David, Penguin, 1988.
Cod: A Biography of the Fish That Changed the World, Mark Kurlansky, Walker & Co., 1999. I include this wonderful book here because, as Kurlansky notes in one of the chapters, "from the Middle Ages to the present, the most demanding cod market has always been the Mediterranean." Fresh or dried salt cod is

a Mediterranean staple (except in the Muslim countries), making an appearance in dishes such as *baccalà mantecato* and *baccalà alla vicentina* in the Veneto, *sonhos de bacalhau* in Portugal, *brandade de morue* in France, and *filetti di baccalà all'arancia* in Sicily. The fascinating story of cod crisscrosses the globe from Newfoundland to New England, the Basque coast of Spain, Brazil, West Africa, Scandinavia, and beyond, but the Mediterranean is never very far from the thread.

From Tapas to Meze, Joanna Weir, Crown, 1994.

Invitation to Mediterranean Cooking: 150 Vegetarian and Seafood Recipes, Claudia Roden, Rizzoli, 1997.

Mediterranean: The Beautiful Cookbook, Joyce Goldstein, Collins (produced by Welden Owen), 1994.

Mediterranean Cookery, Claudia Roden, Alfred A. Knopf, 1987.

Mediterranean Cooking, Paula Wolfert, HarperCollins, 1994.

The Mediterranean Diet Cookbook, Nancy Harmon Jenkins, Bantam, 1994.

A Mediterranean Feast: The Story of the Birth of the Celebrated Cuisines of the Mediterranean, From the Merchants of Venice to the Barbary Corsairs, Clifford A. Wright, William Morrow, 1999. An outstanding and exhaustively researched book. If you want to read only one book on Mediterranean cuisine, this is the one. Wright reveals, "I wrote this book in an attempt to extend one man's—Fernand Braudel's—vision, love, and scholarship, and I augmented it with my own research and love of Mediterranean food, in the hope of providing a guide to the Mediterranean that has not been attempted before. The weaving of history and gastronomy in *A Mediterranean Feast* was meant to reveal the culinary structure of the Mediterranean—its rugged contours, oppressive reality and blue delight—through the eyes of geographers, travelers, historians, and cooks, what Braudel means by 'total history.' Braudel's writings were an attempt to seek out the 'constant' of Mediterranean history, the structures and recurrent patterns of everyday life that provide the reference grid. For myself, and this book, the constant is the food of the Mediterranean, its cuisine and recipes."

Mediterranean Light, Martha Rose Shulman, Bantam, 1989.

The Mediterranean Kitchen, Joyce Goldstein, William Morrow & Co., 1989. A unique feature of this wonderful book is that Goldstein indicates how, by changing only an ingredient or two, recipes can go from being Italian, say, to French, Portuguese, or Moroccan, which illustrates the core ingredients each country shares and also allows for more mileage out of nearly every recipe.

The Mediterranean Pantry: Creating and Using Condiments and Seasonings, Aglaia Kremezi, photographs by Martin Brigdale, Artisan, 1994.

Mostly Mediterranean, Paula Wolfert, Penguin, 1988.

The Feast of the Olive, Maggie Blyth Klein, Aris Books (Addison-Wesley), 1983; revised and updated edition, Chronicle Books, 1994.

Olives: The Life and Love of a Noble Fruit, Mort Rosenblum, North Point Press, 1996.

Italian Cookbooks

The Art of Eating Well: Italy's Most Treasured Cookbook, Pellegrino Artusi, translated by Kyle M. Phillips III, Random House, 1996.

La Bella Cucina: How to Cook, Eat, and Live Like an Italian, Viana La Place, Clarkson Potter, 2001. I had to include this book here under Cookbooks—the bulk of the book does, after all, feature more than 125 recipes—but it is *much more* than a cookbook. If you've ever wondered about the supposed "secrets" to the healthful and joyful Italian way of life, you'll find them revealed here. (They're not secrets, by the way, just commonsense ways of living, but these are often antithetical to America's puritanical and competitive ways.) "A Civilized Lunch During the Workday" should be required reading for every American; I'm also especially fond of the *"La Bella Vita,"* "Inside an Italian Kitchen," *"La Natura,"* and "A Blueprint for Eating Like an Italian" essays. The fuss-free recipes celebrate the simplest ingredients and techniques and are an invitation not only to a meal but to a way of life.

Celebrating Italy: The Tastes and Traditions of Italy as Revealed Through its Feasts, Festivals, and Sumptuous Foods, Carol Field, William Morrow, 1990; HarperPerennial, 1997. Featured celebrations from northeastern Italy include the *Festa del Redentore* (Venice), *Sagra dell'Uva* (Merano), *Venerdi Gnoccolar* (Verona), and a great entry for *Carnevale,* all over Italy, not just in Venice. In addition, a forty-three-page traveler's calendar (most thorough and helpful) features nine *feste* in Trentino–Alto Adige, seven in Friuli–Venezia Guilia, and sixteen in the Veneto. Appropriate recipes follow each celebration. All books have to be categorized, and this one rightly belongs in the cooking section; but if I were a bookseller, I would also shelve it in Italian history and travel. As Field notes, every day, somewhere in Italy, people are celebrating something. "Italians are so connected to the deep meaning of their *feste* that they have continued to observe the same rituals and sacraments over many centuries . . . the rhythm of scarcity and abundance, darkness and excess punctuates the Italian year in an endless round, an explosion of beauty and energy that pays tribute to the mysterious forces of life and to the riches that the earth provides." With dozens of engravings and drawings and a serious, eleven-page bibliography.

The Classic Italian Cook Book, Marcella Hazan, Alfred A. Knopf, 1976, and three others by Marcella: *More Classic Italian Cooking* (1978), *Marcella's*

Italian Kitchen (1986), and *Essentials of Classic Italian Cooking* (1992), all also published by Knopf, in hardcover editions; some editions are in paperback.

The Cooking of Italy, Waverly Root and the editors of Time-Life Books, photographed by Fred Lyon, 1968. The collaborative effort to produce this book (one of the volumes in the Foods of the World series) was extraordinary, the likes of which we'll probably never see again. (A separate spiral-bound recipe booklet accompanied each hardbound volume.) Some of the best commentary on Italian food I've ever read is presented by Luigi Barzini, who contributed the foreword: "The apparently simple cooking of the Italians is, in fact, more difficult at times to achieve than the more elaborate and refined French cuisine. Things have to be good in themselves, without aid, to be exposed naked. In other words, a pleasant French dish can sometime be made successfully even with very ordinary ingredients, while the excellence of many Italian dishes depends on the excellence of the things that go into them. The old saying that good cooking begins in the market is truer in Italy than in France." Barzini goes on to point out, "Fruit and vegetables must be picked at the right time, neither one day too early nor too late. They must not travel far, must not be preserved beyond their allotted season by chemicals or refrigeration." One chapter is devoted to the Northeast, and though this book is, obviously, long out of print and hard to find, it does turn up at tag sales and in used bookstores.

Enoteca: Simple, Delicious Recipes in the Italian Wine Bar Tradition, Joyce Goldstein, photography by Angela Wyant, with wine notes by Evan Goldstein, M.S., Chronicle Books, 2001. Though this book isn't devoted to northeastern Italy, I include it here because it's one of the few (perhaps the only) book devoted to that wonderful Italian institution the *enoteca* (plural: *enoteche/enotechi*). Readers of my books on Paris and central Italy know that I am an enormous fan of wine bars and also of Joyce Goldstein. For this book, she has collected a wide variety of recipes for little dishes typically served at *enotechi* throughout Italy. (A handful from northeastern Italy are included.) These are divided into fritters and frittatas; savory pastries and breads; pastas and grains; fish and shellfish; meat and poultry; vegetables; cheeses, condiments, and preserves; and sweets. I have enjoyed a number of the recipes, but I must admit my disappointment with Evan Goldstein's wine recommendations. While I agree with him when he states, "Your happiness at the table is what counts," I firmly believe that food and grapes that grow together, go together. When he asks, "Do sardines *in saor* truly taste better with a Soave from the Veneto than with any other wine?" my answer is a definitive yes. Though he does offer a few Italian wine suggestions first, I think that when he recommends "alternative wines," as he refers to them, he has missed the barstool completely, so to speak. The world of Italian wines is quite large and diverse, and it's a pity that these *vini* are not better known in North America. This book should have been a golden opportunity to allow the Italian wines to shine in the star role they play in *enotechi,* in the same way Evan suggested such appropriate wine choices in *The Mediterranean Kitchen.* (I discovered *so many* new wines in that book!) Additionally, it is also not helpful when he recommends, for example, "Spanish or Portuguese simpler reds" with the recipe for "Griddled Flatbread from Romagna," since most Americans are, sadly, woefully unfamiliar with either Spanish or Portuguese wines in general and would most likely not know how to identify a "simpler" red without enlisting the help of a knowledgeable wine merchant. I recommend this book in the wonderful spirit in which it was written, but I urge you to consult *Vino Italiano* below for selecting wines to match with these authentic recipes.

Giuliano Bugialli's Foods of Italy, photographs by John Dominis, Stewart, Tabori & Chang, 1984. Bugialli's recipe for the Venetian classic *risi e bisi* (risotto with fresh peas) is the best one I've found. It's more time-consuming than most (you have to boil the shelled pea pods) but results in a superior dish, which is how it became famous in the first place.

In Nonna's Kitchen: Recipes and Traditions from Italy's Grandmothers, Carol Field, HarperCollins, 1997.

The Italian Baker, Carol Field, HarperCollins, 1985. Positively the only book to have if you want to tackle making your own Italian baked goods. Field's recipe for *tiramisù* (a Venetian specialty) is the best one I've ever eaten and is the only one worth attempting. (Tip: if you've only eaten *tiramisù* made with ladyfingers, you have eaten only a cheap imitation; true *tiramisù*—the word means "pick-me-up"—can be made only with *pan di spagna.*)

Italian Cooking: An Illustrated Guide to Classic Italian Cooking, Elizabeth David, Smithmark Publishers, 1996. Among the many observations in this book: "'Italian' cooking is a concept of foreigners—to Italians, there is Florentine cooking, Venetian cooking, the cooking of Genoa, Rome, Naples, Sicily, Lombardy and the Adriatic coast. Not only have the provinces retained their own traditions of cookery, but many of their products remain localized."

The Italian Country Table: Home Cooking from Italy's Farmhouse Kitchens, Lynne Rosetto Kasper, Scribner, 1999. Because I have not yet reached the Emilia-Romagna region of Italy, readers do not yet know of my special appreciation for the work of Lynne Rossetto Kasper. (Her book *The Splendid Table: Recipes from Emilia-Romagna, the Heartland of Northern Italian Cuisine* is perhaps the finest cookbook I've ever seen.) In addition to the great recipes here (some are from the Veneto and Trentino–Alto Adige), the noteworthy feature of this book is the "When in Italy" section, in which Kasper shares some of her favorite guest farms (*agriturismo*), country life museums, and restaurants.

Italian Festival Food: Recipes and Traditions from Italy's Regional Country Food Fairs, Anne Bianchi, Macmillan, 1999. Similar to Carol Field's *Celebrating Italy* but not as all-encompassing and with black-and-white photographs.

Italy, The Beautiful Cookbook: Authentic Recipes from the Regions of Italy, recipes by Lorenza De'Medici, text by Patrizia Passigli (1996) and *Italy Today: The Beautiful Cookbook,* recipes by Lorenza De'Medici, text by Fred Plotkin (1997), both published by HarperCollins and produced by Weldon Owen.

Lidia's Italian-American Kitchen, Lidia Matticchio Bastianich, Alfred A. Knopf, 2001. There are a few other Italian-American cookbooks on the shelves, but I think this one is head and shoulders above them all. Lidia truly explores the history and diversity of Italian-American food in more than four hundred pages. In defining this cuisine—"Is it Italian, American, or a piece of Americana with Italian roots?"—Lidia concludes that it is unquestionably some of each. Many of the great recipes you've watched her prepare on her public television shows are here, but what I like even better are the family stories and photos she shares throughout the book, as well as the e-mail letters from fans. Lidia credits the excellent book *La Storia* (see the *La Cronaca Mondana biblioteca*) with providing much essential background information in her quest to learn more about the enormously popular Italian-American cuisine. In her introduction she ponders what foodstuffs her *compatrioti* (countrymen) found in America five hundred years ago. It is doubtful they found the fresh herbs and ripe produce, virgin olive oil, true Parmigiano-Reggiano, or fresh mozzarella that were so essential to their cuisine back home. "They had to cook with the ingredients that were available, led by the memory of the flavors they recalled. And therein lies the beginning of the answer to 'What is Italian-American cuisine?'" Notable about Lidia's approach is that she is less concerned with authenticity in a dish than with flavor and freshness; this is not to say that she doesn't appreciate Italy's culinary specialties, but she does not slavishly follow a recipe for the sake of authenticity alone. If you enjoy these classic dishes, this is a book you'll cook from again and again.

Pasta Classica: The Art of Italian Pasta Cooking, Julia della Croce, Chronicle Books, 1987.

Patricia Wells' Trattoria: Healthy, Simple, Robust Fare Inspired by the Small Family Restaurants of Italy, William Morrow, 1993.

Red, White & Greens: The Italian Way with Vegetables, Faith Heller Willinger, HarperCollins, 1996.

Riso: Undiscovered Rich Dishes of Northern Italy, Gioietta Vitale with Lisa Lawley, Clarkson Potter, 1992. Rice, of course, is the starch of choice in northern Italy, while pasta dominates in the South. In addition to a section devoted to risotto, there are recipes for rice soups, hot and cold salads, *risi in bianchi* (Arborio rice dishes like risotto but less time-consuming), and desserts.

Saveur Cooks Authentic Italian: Savoring the Recipes and Traditions of the World's Favorite Cuisine, by the editors of *Saveur,* Chronicle Books, 2001. The third book in this series—Authentic American and French have been previously published—is also a must-have, even if you subscribe to *Saveur* and have read all these articles and recipes before. I think *Saveur* is an excellent magazine, and its contents are deserving of a home between hard covers (unfortunately for me, perhaps, because the appearance of this Italian cookbook prevented me from including any material in my own book!). The book is divided into chapters on the foods—as opposed to the regions—of Italy; the Veneto and Friuli–Venezia Giulia are abundantly represented, Trentino–Alto Adige less so. The book is profusely illustrated with color photographs on nearly every page, and the recipes—some from restaurants in the United States—are winners. *Essenziale.*

Savoring Italy: A Celebration of the Food, Landscape, and People of Italy, Robert Freson, HarperCollins/Callaway Editions, 1992. The successor to Freson's *The Taste of France,* this is my favorite book on Italian food. Twenty regions of Italy are featured, with essays contributed by noted Italian authorities such as Carol Field, Leslie Forbes, Barbara Grizzuti Harrison, Nadia Stancioff, and Louis Inturrisi. There is a separate chapter on the Northeast. As with the France book, Freson was interested in recording, "while it was still possible, the relationship between regional resources, climate, produce, and people." This wonderful volume is inexplicably out of print but is worth finding.

Verdure: Simple Recipes in the Italian Style, Gioietta Vitale with Robin Vitetta-Miller, Clarkson Potter, 2001. A companion volume of sorts to *Riso* (above), this book is dedicated to vegetables prepared in the style of northern Italy. In addition to the healthful benefits these recipes offer, they are terrific weeknight dishes, with few ingredients (though of high quality) and quick preparations.

Venetian Cookbooks and Food

The Cuisine of Venice & Surrounding Northern Regions, Hedy Giusti-Lanham and Andrea Dodi, Barron's Educational Series, 1978. This out-of-print book is a remarkably thorough compendium of appetizers; soups; pastas, polenta, risotto; egg dishes; fish; poultry; veal; beef; lamb, pork, sausages; vegetables and salads; and desserts of northern Italy, from Geneva and Turin to Trieste and the Austrian border. The majority, however, are from the Veneto. Giusti-Lanham, at the time this book was published, was the U.S. delegate of the Accademia Italiana della Cucina, and she and chef Dodi founded the Scuola Italiana di Cucina in New York. Thirteen of the recipes are exclusively Dodi's, and others are from prominent hostesses throughout the North; all of them are fairly easy to prepare. I have especially enjoyed *sogliole fredde al vino bianco* (cold filets of sole in white wine), *pere in forno al rum* (pears baked with rum), and *cavolfiore con salsa di acciughe* (cauliflower with anchovy sauce).

The Harry's Bar Cookbook, Arrigo Cipriani, photographs by Christopher Baker, introduction by Jan Morris, Bantam Books, 1991. Were it not for this cookbook, I would probably still not know the story of how the bar that came to be known as Harry's came into being. I won't spoil it for you by revealing it here, but it's a great, heartwarming story, one that reinforces the uniqueness of this Venetian landmark. I haven't attempted any of the dessert recipes in this book, but the others I've tried were all very good, almost as good as being in Venice at . . . well, no, they're *not* as good as being at Harry's. I'm sorry to say that no recipe or ambience you create in your home is as good as being at Harry's, but this cookbook is as close as one will ever get.

The Traveling Gourmet: Venice and Its Regions, text by Gilles Plazy, photographs by Mark E. Smith, recipes by Toni Vianello, Flammarion, 2001; originally published as *L'Esprit du Gout: de Venise à Verone,* Plume, 1999. This is the only book I know of that is devoted to both Venice and the Veneto, that marries history and recipes with beautiful photographs. I've cooked from this book only a few times, but I love it all the same and highly recommend it.

Venice & Food, text, illustration and calligraphy by Sally Spector, Arsenale Editrice, 1988. This is a very special volume and is a personal favorite in my collection. When I first saw it, at the Rizzoli Fifty-seventh Street store in New York, I was completely mesmerized by its beautiful clothbound cover, and I felt an immediate affinity with the author, who dedicated the book not only to the memory of her parents (which made me sad) but also to "the past, present and future of the Mediterranean." I have never had the fortune to meet Sally Spector, but I sure would like to, and I hope other Mediterranean destinations inspire her to create more books like this. Mixed in between recipes for *cicheti,* rice dishes, grain and pasta, polenta, fish, vegetables, and sweets are essays on a number of related topics, such as water and wells, farming implements, the history of the fork (the Venetians were the first modern Europeans to eat with one), cheese, olive oil, the *Festa del Redentore, radicchio rosso di Treviso,* spices, and Marco Polo. Many of the recipes appear in other Venetian cookbooks, but what makes this one different is the extra details Spector adds. Just one example is her recipe for *sardelle in saor,* my most favorite Venetian dish. Other versions of this recipe are typically very short; it's true that it's not a complicated or time-consuming dish (although it does have to marinate for at least twenty-four hours), but in my experience it's the simple dishes that need not only superior ingredients but thorough explanation. Spector provides good tips, especially in steps four and six, and the result is that this is the best version of this famous dish I've ever made. With illustrations lovely enough to frame and fascinating digressions aplenty, this book is hard to set aside.

Italian Restaurant and Food Guides

A word about guides that rate eating establishments: Understand that they are all subjective, and that one should not be a slave to them. Ed Behr, in his fall 1999 newsletter *The Art of Eating,* noted that the two most influential food guidebooks in Italy are *Espresso* (which I have not yet seen) and *Gambero Rosso Ristoranti d'Italia,* while the Michelin Guide is most effective at filling tables at establishments awarded the most stars. The Slow Food guides are also used by those looking for more traditional places, but Behr found that the Italian guides are widely seen as corrupt, whereas Michelin is seen as having too obvious a French bias. Wine and food industry friends of Behr told him they rarely or never follow the guidebooks because they don't agree with them; rather, they follow leads from people whose palates they trust. "There's no perfect way," Behr concluded. I couldn't agree more, which is why I emphasize the importance of trusting the author not only of food guides but hotel guides too. I very much respect the authors and the books I recommend here, but readers should know that I typically follow the opinions of rather picky critics with exacting standards—I am not a fan of the popular single-city Zagat survey guides, for example, because they are compiled not by critics but by the general restaurant-going population, the majority of whom do not cook, read cookbooks, or travel and wouldn't know an authentic Venetian dish if it hit them on the head. Behr has written that Zagat "has all the defects of democracy," and William Grimes, restaurant critic of *The New York Times,* has written about "the self-levitating phenomenon that I think of as the Zagat Effect, in which a restaurant, once it has achieved a top rating, continues to do so year after year, regardless of the quality of the food. Diners flock to it, Zagat guide in hand (either literally or metaphorically) and, convinced that they are eating at a top-flight establishment, cannot bring themselves to believe otherwise." Once I have determined that I trust a food or wine writer, I will happily follow his or her leads, knowing that I will eat and drink well if not always fabulously. It's true that places that appear repeatedly in numerous guides can sometimes slip in quality; but if you set out with an optimistic, not-too-beholden attitude, I think you'll agree with these critics' opinions and have some very excellent meals indeed (and hopefully discover some good places on your own that I hope you'll share with me!).

Dictionary of Italian Cuisine, Maureen B. Fant and Howard M. Isaacs, Ecco Press, 1998. This is a brilliant and eminently practical achievement. As Fant and Isaacs inform us, there are many good books on Italian cooking in English that are aimed at *either* cooks or travelers—rarely both—and are still not quite comprehensive enough for those looking at a regional restaurant menu. As they note, "In Italy, all cooking, like politics, is local." Some shapes of pasta are not known in a town only an hour away, and some vegetables are known by two or three different names throughout the country, which is why it's necessary to have this book of six thousand entries. There are words not only for things to eat but also for cooking techniques, utensils, and important place names. For those who are serious about Italian food and drink, this is *essenziale*.

Eating and Drinking in Italy, Andy Herbach and Michael Dillon, second edition, Open Road Publishing, 2001. This is one volume (others include Spain, Paris, and France) in a new series that I love. First of all, each book—paperback, approximately 6½ by 4 inches—fits easily in a pocket, so you won't look like a nerd in a restaurant as you look up a word. More important, it's really thorough: seventy-one pages of English-to-Italian, helpful phrases, and Italian-to-English menu words and *methods and styles of cooking* (which as we all know is what trips people up the most). Some examples are *affumicato* (smoked), *affettato* (sliced), *cannelloni alla Barbaroux* (pasta stuffed with ham, veal, and cheese), and *al guanciale* (cooked with bacon and onions). Plus, these guys are funny: after the entry for *fega* (liver), they write, "Liver in Venice, liver in Milwaukee . . . *no grazie*"; after *testa di vitello* (calf's head), they write "I'll pass"; and after *nervetti* (tendons of calves' feet, a Venetian specialty), "I don't think so." Their mission? "No Menus in English." As they explain, "When we're in Italy, we want it to look Italian. We don't want to see the golden arches near the Leaning Tower and we don't want to see a menu in English. As we see it, a menu in English is the first step in the Americanization of the restaurants of the world, the first domino. And once it's not foreign, what's the point of going?" Herbach and Dillon also provide a list of some of their favorite restaurants around Italy (seventeen in the Northeast), and some of the useful phrases they provide include "I want to reserve a table," "this evening," "tomorrow," "the day after tomorrow," "near the window," "outside," "do you accept credit cards?" "undercooked," "overcooked," "how much does this cost?" and "this is not what I ordered."

Eating in Italy: A Traveler's Guide to the Hidden Gastronomic Pleasures of Northern Italy, Faith Heller Willinger, William Morrow, 1998. Though not as extensive (or as heavy) as Fred Plotkin's *Italy for the Gourmet Traveler,* this is an outstanding, authoritative book that I could not live without.

The Food of Italy, Waverly Root, Atheneum, 1971; Vintage Books, 1992. The best summation of this excellent work comes from Samuel Chamberlain's introduction, in which he says, "This is destined to become a classic work on the subject of Italian food and wine, and a reference book that will retain its value through decades to come." A chapter is devoted to "The Domain of the Veneti" and is accompanied by a good map clearly indicating Venezia Euganea, Venezia Giulia, and Venezia Tridentina and the towns within them that have, in Root's opinion, "great" eating and "good" eating.

Italy for the Gourmet Traveler, Fred Plotkin, Little, Brown & Co., 1996. The wonderful and trusted Plotkin recommends restaurants, *trattorie,* food fairs, festivals, bakeries, coffee bars, wine bars, bookstores, gourmet shops, markets, vineyards, farms, wineries, olive oil producers, and cooking schools throughout every region of Italy (and he even shares a few recipes). To ask if this book is *essenziale* is akin to asking if the pope is Catholic; I can't imagine planning a trip to *anywhere* in Italy without this book. It is, however, more than seven hundred pages long, so it's too heavy to qualify for a bring-along, unless one is planning on traveling extensively. A really great feature of this book—which not only sets it apart from others but proves how well Plotkin knows Italy—is his selection of a "Classic Town" for each region of the country. As he explains, travelers can spend weeks exploring the gastronomic and economic riches of a region without ever setting foot into another, so he decided to select one city in each region that "gathers within its walls much that embodies the character, history, and gastronomic personality of the region." For the Veneto he has selected Treviso, for Friuli–Venezia Giulia he chose Udine, for Trentino he singled out Trento, and for Alto Adige it's Brixen/Bressanone. (Plotkin has created separate chapters for Trentino and Alto Adige, explaining that in the minds of many Italians, these are linked as one region, and they were granted autonomous status by Rome in 1948; "but for readers of this book I felt there are significant differences between the two and that they merit separate chapters, even though these two provinces are legally designated as one."). Plotkin avoided selecting regional capitals as classic towns, with three exceptions: Trento, Bologna, and Rome. One could plot an entire journey through Italy by visiting the classic towns, and it would be one swell trip indeed.

Osterie d'Italia 2001, Slow Food Editore.

Ristoranti d'Italia, Gambero Rosso Editore and Istituto Geografico de Agostini. This annual guide is a hefty paperback (over eight hundred pages) and unfortunately is only available in Italian and in Italy. (Alternatively, you can order it in advance of your trip from *Gambero Rosso,* Speedimpex USA, 35-02 48th Avenue, Long Island City, New York 11101; 800-969-1258; fax: 718-361-0815; e-mail: gambero@gamberosso.it; www.gamberorosso.it). Though I do not read or speak Italian, I do not find the language barrier to be a problem when deciphering descriptions—some of the words will be obvious to anyone who cooks frequently from Italian cookbooks, and the accompanying symbols help fill in the blanks. I think this is a worthwhile book to buy when you arrive in Italy: there are reviews of nearly three thousand *ristoranti, trattorie, pizzerie,* and wine bars, in more than a thousand localities in Italy, and more than two hundred color maps of individual cities and towns. Plus, there is a forty-four-page *atlante* (road atlas), at a scale of 1:750,000 at the back of the book, featuring every part of Italy, including Sardinia and smaller islands off the coast of Sicily. Eating establishments are ranked with *tre forchette* (three forks, meaning a score of 90–100 points), *due forchette* (scoring 80–89 points), and *gli emergenti* (scoring 70–79 points). Of the seventeen establishments receiving *tre forchette* in the 2001 guide, two were from the Northeast: La Siriola de l'Hotel Ciasa Salares in San Cassiano (Bolzano) and Il Desco in Verona.

Trattorias of Rome, Florence, & Venice: A Guide to Classic Eating, Drinking, and Snacking, Maureen B. Fant, Ecco Press (an imprint of HarperCollins), 2001. I have long been a fan of Maureen Fant's food writing in the travel section of *The New York Times.* She lives in Rome, but she writes about other places in Italy too and is the coauthor, with Howard Isaacs, of *Dictionary of Italian Cuisine* (above). I was happy to learn that she had written this great guide, and as it's the only one to focus on *trattorie,* it's a welcome addition to the other restaurant books listed here. While I love to eat at restaurants, when traveling—especially in the middle of the day—I prefer casual, fun-loving places where the food is not fussy and the wine flows freely. This book is so handy and so reliable that I hope a regularly updated edition is planned. Though the title mentions only *trattorie,* wine bars too are included in the listings, as well as more elegant restaurants that "in one way or another have a *trattoria* at heart or in their past" and some *gelaterie* that are "too good not to point out." For my last trip to Venice, I scanned the twenty-three entries and plotted out each day of my trip, ensuring I would make a stop—even if it was for a quick glass of Prosecco—at all the places I wanted to go (which was nearly every one, as it turned out). On this particular trip, I was traveling alone with my daughter for most of it, and every one of the places I stepped into proved to be welcoming and accommodating to children. Besides the listings, Fant provides a glossary (condensed from *Dictionary of Italian Cuisine*), an outline of cooking styles, etiquette, and tips, and most important, a list of places open on Sunday and Monday. (As she explains, Sunday and Monday are the two most difficult days of the week for finding open eating places in Italy.) I think that perhaps Fant's introduction to the Venice section of the book provides the best summation of eating out in this city: "In fact, one of the stupidest notions propagated by travel guides is that the food in Venice is awful and the city's eateries one big tourist trap. Certainly you can pay dearly for food in Venice. Imagine the logistical difficulty of operating a business where everything has to be brought in by boat; imagine the temptation to cut corners and inflate prices when your main customer base is transient. Furthermore, with a declining local population, tourists (many of them day trippers) and university students do most of the eating out in Venice, favoring low-end stodge parlors and high-end hotel dining. You might think that would cut out the interesting middle ground of diligent trattorias catering to average locals and informed visitors, and yet, miraculously, they exist."

Treasures of the Italian Table: Italy's Celebrated Foods and the Artisans Who Make Them, Burton Anderson, William Morrow & Co., 1994. Not a cookbook, but something better: profiles of people—true culinary artisans—who continue to produce food by traditional methods, eschewing the ways of mass production. Anderson has been called "the world's greatest expert on Italian wine," and the Italian foods he has chosen to highlight in this book are *tartufi bianchi d'Alba* (white truffles of Alba), *pane toscano* (Tuscan bread), pasta, *olio extra vergine di oliva* (extra-virgin olive oil), *pizza napoletana* (Neopolitan-style pizza), *Parmigiano-Reggiano* (the one and only Parmesan), *vino* (wine), *culatello* (a pork specialty from a pig's buttocks), risotto, *bistecca alla fiorentina* (beef from the white cattle of Chianina, cut in a certain way by Florentine butchers), *aceto balsamico tradizionale* (true balsamic vinegar from Modena), and *caffè espresso.* Obviously, with the exception of risotto, the majority of these specialties do not have their origins in northeastern Italy, but visitors are likely to find many of them on menus or in food shops. Anderson recommends favorite restaurants and retailers where these delicacies are available.

World Food: Italy, Matthew Evans, Lonely Planet, 2000. When I first learned of Lonely Planet's World Food series (some other editions include Spain, France, and Italy), I imagined that each book would be authored by the food authorities relevant to each country's cuisine. They're not, but it turns out the authors are knowledgeable culinary enthusiasts. (The author of this edition was formerly a chef and is now a restaurant critic, food writer, and recipe columnist in Australia.) Each title in this series is small enough to fit in a large pocket or handbag, and in addition to an Italian culinary dictionary (a pretty good one too, for a book of this size) and glossary, this edition features chapters on the culture of Italian cuisine; staples and specialties; drinks (including wine); home cooking and traditions; celebrating with food; shopping and markets (including a floor plan of the amazing Padua market, which I found quite helpful); where to eat and drink (including some tips for vegetarians and vegans); and regional variations, which includes individual sections for Trentino–Alto Adige, Friuli–Venezia Giulia, and the Veneto. I don't consider this a bring-along, but it's definitely worth reading before you go.

Articles

The November 1999 issue of *Saveur* is entirely devoted to Venice. "Magical City, Irresistible Food" is how the editors described this special edition, and if you missed it, it is very, very much worth ordering a back issue. Perhaps my favorite feature within this compendium is the one entitled "Venetian Classics," which highlights ten recipes—both ancient and modern—that define the food of Venice; these include *fritto misto, risi e bisi, fegato alla veneziana, bigoli in salsa, tagliolini alle vongole veraci, sarde in saor, pasta e fagioli* (somewhat surprising, as we so associate this dish with Tuscany), *baccalà mantecato,* and *tiramisù.* To order, contact *Saveur* at 800-429-0106. Back issues are $5.95 each (three or more issues are $3 each), shipping and handling is $2 per issue (or $1 per issue for three copies or more), and credit card orders are accepted by phone. To send a check, write to DC Reader Services, Back Issues Department, P.O. Box 2898, Lakeland, Florida 33806, and include a note indicating the issue date.

About Wine in General

Great Wines Made Simple: Straight Talk from a Master Sommelier, Andrea Immer, Broadway Books, 2000. One chapter, "A Little Italy," is devoted to the major wines of the country, including Soave, Prosecco, Amarone, Recioto, Tocai, Teroldego, Valpolicella, and Pinot Grigio. In 1997 Immer, one of only nine women in the world to qualify as a master sommelier, was named Best Sommelier in America.

Jancis Robinson's Wine Course, BBC Books, London, 1995.

Making Sense of Wine, Matt Kramer, Quill (William Morrow), 1989.

The Oxford Companion to Wine, edited by Jancis Robinson, Oxford University Press, 1994.

Pairing Wine and Food: A Handbook for All Cuisines, Linda Johnson-Bell, Burford Books, 1999.

Tasting Pleasure: Confessions of a Wine Lover, Jancis Robinson, Viking, 1997. Italy and some Italian wines are mentioned or featured throughout the twenty-four essays. (I guess you can tell I'm a Jancis Robinson fan.)

Vineyard Tales: Reflections on Wine, Gerald Asher, Chronicle Books, 1996. Two of the twenty-nine essays are about Italian wines.

The Wall Street Journal Guide to Wine, Dorothy J. Gaiter and John Brecher, Broadway Books, 1999. One chapter is devoted to Italian whites and one each to Barolo and Dolcetto.

About Italian Wine

Italian Wine, Victor Hazan, Alfred A. Knopf, 1982. Victor is as passionate about Italian wine as his wife, Marcella, is about Italian cuisine. Do not be put off by the fact that this edition is almost twenty years old. The general information about Italian wines and wine appreciation is excellent, and the results are a joy to read. Hazan has organized the book not by region but by red wines (big, medium range, and light), white wines (light and crisp, and full and fruity), and sweet wines. A few wines to try that are unique to northeastern Italy include Amarone wines from the Veneto (the only "big" red wine in the Northeast), Malbec, Pinot Nero, Lagrein Dunkel (from Trentino–Alto Adige), Refosco (Friuli–Venezia Giulia), Schiava, Marzemino, Müller-Thurgau/Sudtiroler and Müller-Thurgau, Soave, Prosecco, Ribolla, Malvasia, Tocai, Bianco del Collio, Moscato, Picolit, Recioto di Gambellara, Verduzzo di Ramandolo, Vin Santo di Gambellara, and Vino Santo Trentino. In case you're wondering (I certainly have been), Hazan will not be updating this seminal work. In an interview with *Town & Country* (July 2001), he admitted that when he finished this book in 1982, he was optimistic that a publisher would ask him to take a second look at Italian wine, and he looked forward to the task. In the early 1990s, he was approached with an offer for a new book, though it was to be devoted only to red wine. (Hazan feels that "no dry white wine can match the pleasure-generating depth of flavor of a comparable red wine.") So he began visiting new producers and retracing his steps to those he had met while working on his first book, but after several years, he found that he had to abandon the project. Hazan explained that in the intervening years, Italy's producers had nearly perfected the art of wine making—that is, they were able to rid wine of many of its defects (thinness, sourness, astringency, oxidation)—and in the process they lost much of their individual character. Many of these wines are, as Hazan noted, "unusually skillfully made and agreeable to drink," but he feels they reflect the people who made them more than the places where they were grown. As a writer, Hazan regrets the loss of a subject very close to his heart, but as a drinker, he said he has no cause to lament: while there are many Italian wines he doesn't care to write about, there are still many he cares to drink.

The Italian Wine Guide: Where to Go and What to See, Drink, and Eat, Touring Club of Italy, 1999. A comprehensive, well-designed companion published by the respected Touring Club Italiano, covering everything to do with wine in twenty chapters. Each chapter is introduced with an outline of the local viti-culture and maps of the DOC zones. Descriptions of wine towns, wineries, and wine stores are included, as well as wine routes and tours suggested by TCI (with maps, of course). The "Round About Wine" sections feature facilities associated with wine, such as museums and libraries. Recommendations for hotels, restaurants, golf courses, antiques fairs, *agriturismo* properties, wine shops, and cultural institutes are featured in the margins within each chapter. There are individual chapters for Trentino–Alto Adige, Veneto, and Friuli–Venezia Giulia, and the "Drinking Well in Venice" section includes good suggestions for *enotechi* and restaurants with superior cellars. There isn't a general description of Italian wine labels (surprising), but there are explana-tions of IGT, DOC, and DOCG terms. This book is so jam-packed with infor-mation, I'd qualify it as a bring-along (in all, 744 wineries offering guided tours and tastings are featured), but it's heavy, and unless one is planning on really using it thoroughly, I'd recommend spending time with it before you go.

Italian Wine for Dummies, Mary Ewing-Mulligan, Ed McCarthy, Hungry Minds, 2001. It would be disingenuous of me to admit that I have not been a fan of the *Dummies* series. As I think is clear from the books I recommend in my annotated bibliographies, I look for authoritative titles in each category, and the *Dummies* titles simply are not the exhaustively thorough volumes I prefer. But then again, they're not supposed to be. So there I was browsing the bookshelves at Italian Wine Merchants in New York (see *La Bella Vita* for more details) when I came upon this new addition to the wine series. (Others feature French wine, red wine, white wine, champagne, and wine buying.) I read the endorsements on the cover by Lidia Bastianich and Piero Antinori and thought I should take a closer look: this is a good book, both for newcomers to Italian wine and to those who know quite a bit. In addition to an introductory chapter covering the grapes of Italy and the Italian wine label, each wine region of the country is addressed separately. The chapter on northeastern Italy covers Trentino–Alto Adige, the Veneto, and Friuli–Venezia Giulia. The authors excel at hitting the highlights, and there is a two-sided cheat sheet at the very front of the book. The book closes with ten commonly asked questions about Italian wines and ten common Italian wine myths exposed: Are Italian wines so much better with food? The authors reply that "Italy's wines come alive with food—it's true. That's because Italians always drink their wines with meals (lunch *and* dinner), and the style of wine that has evolved in Italy is therefore a meal-friendly style. The lack of sweetness, crisp acidity, and fairly subtle flavors of most Italian wines enable them to accommodate and complement food, rather than compete with it." In light of the fact that there aren't many books available and in print on Italian wine, this is a welcome and useful book presenting a very good overview of the wine trade in Italy.

Italian Wines 2002, Gambero Rosso Editore/Slow Food Editore. This annual paperback is the English-language version of *Vini d'Italia,* jointly published by the esteemed magazine *Gambero Rosso* and the Slow Food Association. In its fifteenth year, this guide is for both professionals and enthusiasts, and to my mind there is no better guide to current Italian wines. For the current edition, more than eleven thousand wines were evaluated and ranked in categories ranging from a simple mention to the highest award, *tre bicchiere* (three glasses). What I especially like is that the guide is filled with wines that are not well known, if at all, in North America and that I would otherwise never learn of, and while some of these prove difficult to find outside of restaurants, they end up on my shopping list when I go (or someone I know goes) to Italy. This guide is sold in bookstores throughout the United States and Canada, but if you have difficulty finding it, contact the distributor (Antique Collectors' Club, 91

Market Street Industrial Park, Wappingers Falls, NY 12590; 800-252-5231; e-mail: info@antiquecc.com) or *Gambero Rosso* (Speedimpex USA, 35-02 48th Avenue, Long Island City, NY 11101; 800-969-1258; fax: 718-361-0815).

Touring in Wine Country: Northeast Italy, Maureen Ashley, series editor Hugh Johnson, Mitchell Beazley, 1998. This paperback series is a good addition to wine touring books, though the various editions are not meant to be comprehensive. Each edition is slender and lightweight, good for carrying around, and is profusely illustrated with color photographs. This one covers Trentino–Alto Adige, Friuli–Venezia Giulia, and the Veneto, and it includes detailed vineyard maps and wine routes, recommended wine cellars and producers to visit, hotel and restaurant recommendations, local places of interest, special events, and food specialty shops. The author shares a good suggestion for readers interested in visiting a wine estate: she notes that the vintners' main business is the business at hand, and that almost without exception travelers should call ahead and make an appointment with the vintners, "if only to save them the embarrassment of not being able to offer the level of hospitality they would like, or maybe so they can, for example, get a friend or a neighbor in to act as interpreter." She adds that tourists should always ask for thorough driving directions, as relatively few estates are signposted.

VINO—Italian Wines: The Quality of Life, Burton Anderson, Italian Trade Commission, 1992. This is actually a small paperback booklet (105 pages) that is a very good overall reference guide to the twenty wine regions of Italy. Anderson explains the Italian wine label, and there are maps for DOC white and red wines and a good glossary. Most helpful is a food-and-wine pairing chart at the back. This is what I read first when I started down the path to learning about Italian wine. Inquire about available copies from the Italian Trade Commission (Italian Wine Center, 33 East 67th Street, New York, New York 10021; 212-980-1500; fax: 758-1050; www.italtrade.com).

Vino Italiano: The Regional Wines of Italy, Joseph Bastianich and David Lynch, recipes by Lidia Bastianich and Mario Batali, Clarkson Potter, 2002. As wonderful as Victor Hazan's and Burton Anderson's books are, it was time for an updated book on Italian wines, and here it is. I'm happy to say that this edition is a worthy successor to those two other milestones of publishing. It *is* different, however, and what I would recommend to readers who are seriously interested in learning about Italian wines and how they have changed over the last twenty years is to seek out either the Hazan or Anderson (or both) and then read this one. Joseph Bastianich is perhaps uniquely qualified to write this book: together with chef Mario Batali, he co-owns three of the most popular Italian restaurants in New York (Babbo, Lupa, and Esca), and also with Batali, he co-owns Italian Wine Merchants, an exclusively Italian wine shop near Union Square in Manhattan. Additionally, Joe grew up in a home surrounded by Italian food and wine, as he is the son of Lidia Bastianich, chef, restaurateur, cookbook author, and television host. One of the major reasons I am so fond of this book is that it encourages readers to try the wide variety of Italian wines and *drink them with the food they are meant to accompany*. As Batali notes in his foreword, "The bottom line is, Italian food is best enjoyed with Italian wine. The Italians, sometimes to their disadvantage, have traditionally created wines that are at their best with food. . . . And there's nothing quite like pairing a Roman dish with a Roman wine, or a Friulian dish with a Friulian wine. There's no substitute for that kind of elemental combination." Bastianich and Lynch emphasize this again in the introduction, when they write, "Without Italian food and Italian culture to go along with it, Italian wine has no context . . . in addition to who's who and what's good, this book attempts to describe the *ambiente* of Italian wine. The Italian word *ambiente* literally means 'environment,' or 'habitat,' but it also refers to ambiance, the feel of a place. Applied to wine, *ambiente* is not just the geology, topography, and climate of a vineyard but the culture that surrounds it. The experience of drinking an Italian wine isn't complete without the food products that grow in the same soil, nor without some sense of the culture that created it. Italians truly thrive on personal contact, and they think very carefully about how everything at their table—the wine, the food, the people, the place—fits together." *Vino Italiano* begins with four chapters on the basics of Italian wines (including one entitled "*Il Viaggio del Vino*—How Italian Wines Get to the U.S. and Why They Cost What They Do"—which is one of the most interesting in the entire book and is required reading for anyone who buys wine at retail) and outlines each of the wine-growing regions of Italy. Separate chapters are devoted to Friuli–Venezia Giulia, the Veneto, and Trentino–Alto Adige, and there are appendices featuring a glossary of Italian wine terms, Italian grape varieties, DOC designations, and a producer directory.

The Wine Atlas of Italy, Burton Anderson, Simon & Schuster, 1990. This out-of-print and extremely hard-to-find book is still one of the best ones, in my opinion, on Italian wine. If you are very diligent, a copy may turn up, but it won't be cheap: expect to pay at least $40. Kitchen Arts & Letters in New York (see Bookstores in *Informazioni Pratiche* for details) maintains an ongoing waiting list for this book, which surveys the entire country's vineyards in superb detail.

Of Related Interest

Cheese Primer, Steven Jenkins, Workman Publishing Co., 1996. Though not exclusively about Italian cheese, cheeses from Italy figure large in this excellent cheese bible. Jenkins, the first American to be awarded France's Chevalier du Taste-Fromage, created and/or revitalized the cheese counters at such venerable New York food emporiums as Dean & DeLuca and Fairway. In addition to presenting the cheeses of Italy and twelve other regions of the world, he explains how cheese is made, the basics of butterfat, and the seasons that are best for making and eating cheese. (Yes, most cheeses have a season, which is determined by pasturage—vegetation that cows, goats, and sheep have been eating at the time of milking.) Jenkins also offers great suggestions for buying and serving cheese and creating cheese plates. And for travelers, he provides the names of cheeses—most never exported—to look for in various regions. This is the most comprehensive book on cheese I've ever seen.

The Joy of Coffee: The Essential Guide to Buying, Brewing and Enjoying, Corby Kummer, Chapters Publishing (Houghton Mifflin), 1995, 1999. A comment I hear often from people who visit Italy is that the coffee is so much better there. It's my opinion that it's not the coffee that's better but the quality of the dairy products. Coffee, after all, does not grow in Italy, and roasters and vendors can buy excellent beans as easily as anybody else around the world. (That said, it's also true that a lot of coffee consumed in America is inferior, overroasted or burnt, weak, or—worst of all—artificially flavored. Making coffee is indeed an art, and each step along the way to a perfect cup has to be right. Proper roasting will not cover up inferior beans, outstanding beans can be ruined by improper roasting, the wrong grind will not extract the right flavor, an unsure hand at the espresso machine will result in a lousy cup, and, as I've said, milk that's been pasteurized and homogenized to death will make for a less rich cup all around.) Anyway, if you're a coffee drinker, you can judge for yourself, and I've included this book here for those who want to know more about the elixir they love. I find this to be the best volume on coffee ever published. Kummer, who is a well-known food journalist, is a senior editor of *The Atlantic Monthly* and has also contributed to *Martha Stewart Living, New York, Food & Wine,* and other periodicals. He covers coffee plantations, cupping, roasting, grinding, storing (the best place, if you drink it every day, is not in the freezer, as many people mistakenly believe), and brewing, plus separate chapters on espresso, caffeine versus decaf, and a country-by-country guide. There are also recipes for baked goods that pair well with coffee. (I've made almost all of them and can vouch that they are yummy; the Unbeatable Biscotti are definitely the best ones I've ever made, and I've baked *a lot* of biscotti.)

Miramare

Soprintendenza per i Beni Ambientali, Architettonici, Archeologici, Artistici e Storici del Friuli-Venezia Giulia

CASTELLO DI MIRAMARE - TRIESTE 150

ITALIA

PIAZZA UNITA' D'ITALIA

già
PIAZZA GRANDE

Il Friuli–Venezia Giulia
(The Region of Friuli–Venezia Giulia)

"Friuli–Venezia Giulia is now creating an identity of its own, although at times it seems like putting together pieces from several different jigsaw puzzles. The population in the east speaks Slovenian, while the Carnia and Julian Alps have a sizeable German minority. Trieste has large Jewish, Greek, and Serb minorities, and in the middle, around Udine, you have the Friulians themselves, who, like the Ladins in the Dolomites, speak a language similar to the Swiss Rhaeto-Romansch. It's a melting pot, Italian-style, and one that is becoming spicier all the time: the reopening of Central and Eastern Europe in the 1990s means that Friuli–Venezia Giulia is no longer Italy's dead end, but an important link to its future."

—Dana Facaros and Michael Pauls,
Cadogan Guide: Venetia & the Dolomites

Italy's Secret Garden

BY FRED PLOTKIN

~

editor's note

I was so happy to see this piece when it appeared in the food section of *The New York Times* because before it ran, my files on Friuli–Venezia Giulia were rather thin. After it ran, many more publications began featuring articles on this lovely and fascinating region.

FRED PLOTKIN, who was introduced on page 268, is a walking encyclopedia of all things Italian but especially Friuli–Venezia Giulia. He is the author of a number of excellent books, notably *La Terra Fortunata: The Splendid Food and Wine of Friuli–Venezia Giulia, Italy's Great Undiscovered Region* (Broadway Books, 2001) and *Recipes from Paradise: Life and Food on the Italian Riviera* (Little, Brown & Co., 1997).

There is a place, at the very geographic center of Europe, that is home to one of the most refined food and wine cultures in the world.

Hemingway, Joyce, D'Annunzio, Rilke, and Pasolini all lived in this place, and yet it is nearly unknown in the United States, and even in much of Europe. It has been occupied by Julius Caesar (for whom it was named), the Celts, Attila the Hun, the Ottomans, Napoleon (who brought French grapes), the Hapsburgs, Yugoslavia, and ultimately, by Italy. It suffered some of the heaviest damage in Europe during two world wars. Much of it was leveled in 1976 by earthquakes. Yet, its people rise again and again, roll up their sleeves, plant food and vines, and plan for a better life.

Friuli–Venezia Giulia is the tiny region on the far northeast fringe of Italy where Europe's three principal cultures—Latin, Slavic, and Germanic—converge. It is the home of a subtle cuisine that combines local products with influences that are, literally, all over the map. The land provides an outstanding array of fruit and vegetables that are eaten only in season. And the Alps offer exquisite herbs that women gather to use in soups, pastas, omelets, poultry dishes, and desserts.

The region is also the birthplace of grappa and the source of an astounding variety of wines, despite its diminutive size. The town of San Daniele has produced a sweet, delicious prosciutto for centuries that rivals Parma's.

Friulian rivers are full of trout, the forests full of mushrooms and game, and the plains are planted tall with wheat, rye, hops, barley, and corn for white and yellow polenta.

Underappreciated culinary regions of Europe don't stay that way for long (just think of Provence or Emilia-Romagna), and then come the tour buses. But here, in this utterly distinct and yet diverse place, the people are careful guardians of their land and traditions. It feels as if it will stay that way for a long time.

I first went to Friuli–Venezia Giulia in May 1976 to help clean up after a series of earthquakes and found the people so warm, despite the terrible hardship they had endured, that I vowed to return. I've done so often—I spent much of the last four years there.

Italians tend to see the region as Germanic or Slavic and not really part of their own nation, though much blood was spilled to claim it. Germans, Austrians, Slovenians, Croats, and Serbs see it as some middle ground between themselves and Italy.

I quickly learned that Friuli–Venezia Giulia is deeper, more subtle, and infinitely more interesting than its neighbors.

The area called Friuli (from Forum Julii, or Julius's Forum) makes up about 70 percent of the region, mostly in the south, west, and north. The main city is Udine, a handsome, hard-working city of 200,000, distinctly Venetian in aspect. There are more than one hundred special little towns in Friuli, like Cividale, which has superb art treasures, excellent local cooking, and wonderful wine produced nearby. It is also home to *gubana,* a yeasty cake filled with nuts and spices and soaked with grappa or plum *eau de vie.*

The Friulani are fanatically industrious and have what they call "brick sickness"—an insatiable desire to build. After the 1976 earthquakes, they rebuilt whole cities.

The remaining part of the region is Venezia Giulia (Julian Venice), also named for Julius Caesar. Its citizens, known as Giuliani, resent the fact that most people call the whole region Friuli. When Friuli was a backwater, Venezia Giulia was a jewel of the Austro-Hungarian Empire. Venezia Giulia's largest city, Trieste, ranked just after Vienna and Budapest in importance and was the empire's chief port. Cormons is renowned within the region for fantastic food and wine.

Most people in the region speak Italian, and many speak Furlan (the native tongue that incorporates Latin, Slavic, and Germanic influences), while Trieste has its own singsong dialect.

Trieste is certainly the most cosmopolitan city in Italy. Rome, Florence, Venice, and Naples, for all their charms, are quite provincial. In the end, Milan is trendy and Euroglitzy. In Trieste, people with many religions and languages all live side by side and interact much in the way New Yorkers of every origin do. There is a vibrant café society rivaling Paris's and Vienna's, where literature is read, art displayed, and the issues of the day debated. This has always been a city of ideas and was the first in what is now Italy to embrace Freud and psychoanalysis. In the twelve years Joyce lived in Trieste, he wrote *Dubliners, Portrait of the Artist as a Young Man,* and part of *Ulysses.*

Trieste is the leading coffee-importing and -roasting city in Europe, the home to Illy Caffè and Cremcaffè, among others. It is also a major spice port: cinnamon, nutmeg, poppyseeds, pepper, and other flavors entered local cooking as they were transported to

Vienna and Budapest. Paprika came from Hungary. Phyllo arrived from Greece and Turkey (and also Vienna).

Just south of Trieste is Istria, a large peninsula on the Adriatic that many Giuliani regard as an amputated limb. In 1954 most of Istria was handed over to Yugoslavia. This led to a mass migration of 350,000 Istrians (in a scene that resembled the recent exodus from Kosovo), many of whom settled in Queens and Los Angeles.

One of the most famous of them is Lidia Bastianich, who moved to New York as a child and grew up to become one of the city's leading chefs, restaurateurs, and cooking teachers. The dishes at her restaurant, Felidia, are mostly from Istria and Venezia Giulia, while Friulian food can be found at Frico, which Ms. Bastianich owns with her son, Joseph. (A *frico* is a crisp made of Friulian Montasio cheese and is the calling card of most restaurants around Udine.)

The people of this region, a product of so many foreign influences, are above all a product of their own land—from the high Alps to the gorgeous hills of the wine country, from the incredibly fertile plains to a mostly pristine and fish-rich part of the Adriatic.

It is land that gives these people their identities. Not long ago, I met a seventy-year-old Friulian—a former mayor, a businessman and quite worldly, yet in love with his region. He told me, with misting eyes, "When I go for a walk on the land and then come home, I almost feel guilty when I scrape the soles of my shoes."

For its variety, delicacy, sophistication, and sheer pleasure-giving, the cuisine of Friuli–Venezia Giulia is on the level of the cuisines in Emilia-Romagna and Liguria, Italy's finest food regions.

If one were to construct a seasonal Friulian menu, it would begin with a springtime of fresh herbs—like mint, verbena, valerian, and tarragon—cooked in omelets, with seafood, and pounded as sauces for meat. The star dish is *cjarsòns,* an Alpine filled pasta served as a first course that contains about forty ingredients, including a dozen herbs, cinnamon, nutmeg, chocolate, lemon, and ricotta. In the plains, white asparagus is served with chopped boiled egg that has been softened with wine vinegar. *Orzotto,* or barley risotto, is made with fresh-picked hops. Soft pork sausage is shaped in patties and sautéed in delicate wine vinegar.

Summer means seafood, so fish stew from Grado might be featured, along with *polipo alla dalmata* (octopus with potatoes), *cozze alla triestina* (mussels in a broth made with thyme, onion, garlic, white wine, bread crumbs, and parsley) and sea scallops broiled in their shells with local olive oil and thyme. Omelets will contain zucchini flowers and smoked ricotta. Gnocchi are filled with the fruit of the moment (apricots, then cherries, then plums) and are served with cinnamon, sugar, and melted butter.

In autumn, delicate *prosciutto di San Daniele* will be served with September figs (with grated fresh horseradish at other times). After the harvest, grape skins will be used to make grappa or to ferment beets to make a dish called *brovada.* Vegetable soups are typical first courses, followed by venison cooked with spices or berries.

Although polenta is eaten year-round, it is the central dish of winter. Large copper pots yield slow-moving rivers of this meal, which is poured onto round wooden boards, where it hardens and is cut into sections with thread. Stews, including goulash made of equal parts beef and onion, are supporting players. When polenta cools, it can be grilled, pan-fried, or served to children with cinnamon and sugar. Hearty soups, grilled pork, stewed fruit, and *frico* all come to the table, with warming snifters of grappa.

And then there is the region's wine. With sheltering hills, generous sun, cooling sea breezes, and skilled growers and winemakers, Friuli–Venezia Giulia is one of the world's great zones, although its production is quite small compared with other regions'. The Collio zone (in Venezia Giulia) and the Colli Orientali (in Friuli) are the most outstanding. Native white grapes like Tocai, Ribolla Gialla, Malvasia Istriana, and Verduzzo make wines of distinct character.

Pinot Bianco, Pinot Grigio, Chardonnay, Riesling, Traminer Aromatico, Müller-Thurgau, and especially Sauvignon Blanc have found congenial terrain there. Often winemakers will blend different grapes to produce wines of extraordinary structure, depth, character, and finish, like Collio Bianco, a blend of Tocai, Ribolla Gialla, and Sauvignon Blanc.

Friulian red wine is not as well known, in part because most people associate fine Italian red wine with the Tuscany's Chianti and Brunello or the Piedmontese Barbaresco and Barolo. A native Friulian red grape, Pignolo, is only now being discovered abroad, and at its finest (by Walter Filiputti and Abbazia di Rosazzo, and some older Dorigo vintages) it makes a miraculous wine, with flavors of sun, earth, and fruit.

Lighter native reds like Refosco, Schiopettino, Terrano, and Tazzelenghe are distinctive on their own or in blends. Pinot Nero, Cabernet Sauvignon, Cabernet Franc, and especially Merlot make outstanding wines.

All of these grapes are used to make grappa. In the early 1970s, the Nonino family were the first to realize that each grape had its own properties, and rather than blend them into harsh firewater, they distilled each grape individually for a range of postprandial libations of great delicacy. With its splendid fruit, Friuli also produces some of the finest distillates of plums, peaches, pears, cherries, and apricots.

Friulian winemakers have also invented another blend, fitting for a place so close to the Kosovo war, yet where Catholics, Protestants, Jews, Muslims, and Orthodox followers of the Greek, Serbian, and Russian churches live in harmony. It is called Vino della Pace, Wine of Peace. A blend of international grapes, it is sent to world leaders as a metaphor for coexistence.

As planes return to their hangars in NATO's Aviano air base in Friuli, the people of this region, who have known too much war and have chosen peace, will be making the last Vino della Pace of the century, and will toast to the moment when enjoying the pleasures of the table and companionship will be more important than finding yet another way to cause suffering.

Finding Friuli in New York

The food and wine of Friuli–Venezia Giulia are not easily found outside its borders, but there are places in New York City where it's possible to sample the cuisine. Its leading exponents are the restaurants owned by the Bastianich family: Felidia (243 East 58th Street, 212-758-1479) makes careful preparations of Istrian and Giulian dishes, including herb omelettes and *krafi* (potato-filled pasta with a light citrus sauce), while the calling card at Frico Bar (402 West 43rd Street, 212-564-7272) is, of course, its *frico*.

The wine lists at San Domenico (240 Central Park South, 212-265-5959), I Trulli (122 East 27th Street, 212-481-7372), and Babbo (110 Waverly Place, 212-777-0303) have real depth and quality in wines from the region, especially whites.

There is a private social club in College Point, Queens, called Famee Furlane (20-10 127th Street, 718-445-4163) where regional customs are kept, the Friulian language is spoken, and Friulian food is served. It is often possible to dine there (call first). The Istria Sport Club (28-09 Astoria Boulevard, Astoria, Queens, 718-728-3181), open to the public, serves Istrian specialties.

Cremcaffè (65 Second Avenue, near Third Street, 212-674-5255) is a small bar and restaurant where one can sample Cremcaffè, a coffee that is a local favorite in Trieste. The chef there, Romano Michelus, usually features Triestine dishes as specials. The restaurant has begun to feature wines from Trieste's hinterland, including varieties like Malvasia Istriana and Moscato Istriano.

Cremcaffè also serves *cappuccino triestino,* which you must ask for specifically. (In Trieste it is called *un cappo.*) This is coffee in an espresso cup with a small amount of steamed milk. You are served a dollop of whipped cream on the side, which is then stirred in gradually as you drink from the cup.

New Yorkers should remember, when ordering espresso, to ask that it be *ristretto* (short), so that the proportion of water to coffee is what one would find in Italy. If lemon rind finds its way onto the saucer, throw it away and complain to the person who put it there.

Trieste

By Francine Prose

∽

editor's note

Jan Morris, in her most recent book *Trieste and the Meaning of Nowhere* (see *biblioteca* for details), notes of Friuli–Venezia Giulia's major city, "The elusive flavour that I enjoy here is really only the flavour of true civility, evolved through long trial and error. I have tried to get the hang of many cities, during a lifetime writing about them, and I have reached the conclusion that a peculiar history and a precarious geographical situation have made Trieste as near to a decent city as you can find, at the start of the twenty-first century. Honesty is still the norm here, manners are generally courteous, bigotries are usually held in check, people are generally good to each other, at least on the surface. Joyce said he had never met such kindness as he did in Trieste. Mahler just thought its people 'terribly nice.' So do I." I would echo that sentiment, but I also admit that Trieste takes time to get to know, and I think it either grows on you or it doesn't. My friend Lorraine, who has visited Trieste a dozen times or more, admitted to me last summer that she *still* isn't quite sure what she thinks of the city, and when pressed, she said she downright can't get her head around all the *angst*. Read the following articles and decide for yourself—and let me know!

From across the Caffè San Marco, the most splendid and the-atrically Old World of Trieste's historic coffeehouses, I find myself unable to stop staring at the elderly man who, like certain figures you see when you are traveling, seems conjured up, by magic, to enhance the ambience of a place. Perhaps it's just the setting—the glossy, dark wood paneling, the golden walls, the marble-topped tables, the paintings of masked revelers, the uniquely Triestian mix of Vienna and Venice—but it's easy to imagine that the elegant cof-fee drinker has been at that same table with his newspaper for the century or so since the café was founded.

I keep thinking of the characters of Trieste's greatest novelist, Italo Svevo, gathering in coffeehouses like this one to discuss their romantic and financial affairs: businessmen-artists, cosmopolitan hicks, patriots who love their city yet fear that it has somehow fallen off the edge of the known world, isolated by its position on the bor-der of Italy, Austria, and the Balkans, cut loose by its years as a bar-gaining chip in the forging of treaties and alliances. Colonized by the Romans in the second century B.C., Trieste was taken over by the Venetian Republic in 1202. In 1303 it placed itself under the pro-tection of the Hapsburgs and remained part of the Austro-Hungarian Empire until the end of World War I, when it was returned to Italy, only to be overrun again, first by the Nazis, then by Marshal Tito of Yugoslavia. Not until 1954 did the city again become part of Italy.

This troubled history has left its scars on Trieste's landmarks (the Caffè San Marco, which opened in 1914 and was restored after being damaged in World War I) and on its older residents, many of whom have the haunted, slightly otherworldly look of the elderly man in the café. When at last he rises, folds his paper, and leaves, I half expect to see the filtered late-morning light shining through his ethereal frame.

Trieste is proud of its melancholy ghosts. The tourist office has run out of brochures that direct visitors to the locations frequented by James Joyce during the eleven years he lived here with his family, taught English at Berlitz, finished *Dubliners,* and nearly starved to death. But at the Museo Sveviano—a modest collection of mementos and vintage photographs housed on the second floor of the musty, fabulously old-fashioned public library—you can pick up a map of the places where Svevo lived and wrote the bittersweet novels that themselves function as guides to this moody and beautiful port city on the Adriatic.

In Svevo's fiction, the climate is often inclement, a further torment to his brooding heroes as they wander the rainy, windswept waterfront in search of impossible loves. But during the bright early autumn days I spent in Trieste with my husband, Howie, the Adriatic was tranquil and blue, the hills surrounding the city a sort of silvery California green, and the weather couldn't have been balmier.

Everything in Trieste and in the surrounding province of Friuli–Venezia Giulia reminds you of so many disparate places and historical periods that the result is like nothing else, like nowhere else. Unlikely combinations crop up in every aspect of the life of the region, from its local cuisine to its urban and rural landscapes.

In *trattorie* that resemble Tyrolean chalets, you can order pasta with goulash, prune gnocchi, ravioli sauced with butter and cinnamon, and a delectable sort of potato pancake (called *frico*) filled with melted cheese. The hills of the Collio, north of the city, one of

Italy's major wine-growing areas, look—except for the onion-domed churches—like Tuscan vineyards. In Trieste itself, it's possible to wander along a wide canal (the Canale Grande) past a nineteenth-century version of a Venetian palazzo, then past the blue-domed Serbian Orthodox church of San Spiridone and into a small square lined with brightly painted houses reminiscent of Ljubljana, in Slovenia, or Prague. Alternately, you can wander the Borgo Teresiano, a Hapsburg grid of orderly streets, banks, and office buildings decorated with heroic, aggressively Rococo nude statuary and then, minutes later, enter the mazelike alleys of the medieval city. They wind beside a well-preserved Roman amphitheater and up the hill of San Giusto to a cathedral decorated with twelfth-century mosaics, smaller, plainer versions of those at Ravenna.

The trip up to San Giusto is particularly rewarding (take the city bus or risk keeling over from motor-scooter pollution on the steep hike uphill). The cathedral is very much a work in progress, still under renovation when we visited; successive revisions and additions range from the Roman portrait busts embedded in the facade to mosaics from the 1930s. In the churchyard are the ruined pillars of the Roman basilica and forum, as well as a rugged castle begun in the fourteenth century—only serious medieval armor buffs will want to linger in its museum—surrounded by walkways and turrets offering spectacular views of the sea, the busy harbor, and the limestone hills beyond. You can feel the energy rising up from the city, the hum and buzz of Trieste's reawakening from its postwar torpor, partly thanks to the computer industry, drawn to the area by factors that include the physics center down the coast at Miramare, not far from the castle at Duino where Rilke was inspired to write his elegies.

Even on the sunniest days, Trieste casts deep shadows. A few steps downhill from the cathedral, the Civico Museo di Storia ed

Arte contains a fine collection of antiquities, Egyptian mummies, and treasures from Roman tombs. On the grounds is a chapel housing the remains of the archaeologist J. J. Winckelmann, who was killed while on a trip to Trieste in 1868. According to one story, he made the mistake of showing off some gold coins to an acquaintance and was murdered—presumably for his art treasures—by an eavesdropping waiter. A charmingly and romantically gloomy garden—the Orto Lapidario, or Stone Garden—is decorated with sculpture and features a large structure, a sort of shed, sheltering tombstones, and votive objects exhumed from the graveyards of the ancient and medieval world.

As we walked the trail that winds through the attractively shaggy garden, church bells began to toll, disturbing the dozens of semiferal cats who make their home there. Like a feline version of the elderly coffee drinker at the Caffè San Marco, a black cat appeared and ran just ahead of us, pausing every so often to look back over its shoulder. The whole scene—the funerary monuments, the tomb of the murdered archaeologist, the gauzy greenery, the tolling bells, the cat—had the obvious but effective spookiness of a dream sequence in an early Bergman film.

Yet another attractive aspect of Trieste is that you never feel the guilt-inducing pressure of a long list of art sites you think you should probably visit. Most of the city's museums, in former private houses, still retain their original furnishings and architectural details, which are generally more interesting than the art—the result of the somewhat spotty collecting tastes of the city's princes of commerce and finance. The Museo Revoltella, in particular, is a kind of wonderland of nineteenth-century kitsch, displaying paintings with titles like *Listening to Beethoven* and *After the First Communion*.

Like Marseilles and Miami, Trieste is not a city to which you go to see much of anything in particular but rather just to be there, to experience the pulse and rhythm of the place: dodge its swarming Vespas; browse the antiques shops on the Via dei Rettori; walk the Corso Cavour at dusk when the whole population, it seems, turns out for a leisurely stroll; look out your window in the Duchi d'Aosta (one of the city's excellent hotels) to see the last rays of sunlight strike the golden mosaics on the facade of the Palazzo del Governo, across the grand sweep of the monumental Piazza dell'Unità d'Italia; or eat *fritto misto* at a waterfront restaurant, watching ships come and go and listening to your fellow diners switch effortlessly back and forth between Italian and Slovenian.

There are great art treasures in Friuli. About forty-five miles northwest of Trieste; the prosperous, sleepy, immensely pleasant—and rarely visited—city of Udine calls itself, with good reason, the "City of Tiepolo." The Duomo contains several works by the Venetian master, as does the nearby small Oratoria della Purità, where the ceiling is decorated with Tiepolo's newly restored *Assumption*. On the day we visited, the chapel was being prepared for a wedding; bouquets of white roses and ribbons adorned the pews, and a tenor, a violinist, and an organist were rehearsing the "Ave Maria."

By far the most numerous and magnificent frescoes are in the Gallerie del Tiepolo, a section of the Museo Diocesano in the Palazzo Patriarcale, in which there is also an engaging collection of Friulian religious sculpture from the thirteenth through the eighteenth centuries. Commissioned by the region's archbishop, Dionisio Delfino, the frescoes of the gallery and the ceiling over the staircase were painted between 1726 (when Tiepolo was about thirty) and 1730. Representing his first major commission, they have the assurance and the exuberance of a great artist proving himself and coming into his own. The colors in the Old Testament scenes that cover the gallery—*Sarah and the Angel, Rachel Hides the Idols, Abraham and the Angel, Jacob's Dream*—are splashier and livelier (and the human drama more individual and intense) than in Tiepolo's earlier work.

In the so-called Pink Room, you can almost watch him discovering the fun that can be had with perspective, trompe l'oeil, the viewer's position in relation to the image. In *The Judgment of Solomon,* the baby (whose mother pleads for its life with the cruel soldier who holds her child nearly upside down) seems to dangle, terrifyingly, directly over our heads. These daring experiments with the energies and dizzying possibilities of space seem already perfected in *Banishment of the Rebel Angels,* a portrayal of the guilty and unhappy angels repenting—too late!—as they are sent spinning through space, sprouting bat wings and tails. The painting's placement, over the staircase descending several stories, dramatically increases our sense of the distance that the angels are going to have to fall as they plummet past us down the stairwell.

To see the frescoes in this setting is very different from viewing Tiepolo among the dutiful crowds in Venice. On a Saturday morning, Howie and I spent an hour and a half, mostly in the gallery, and in that entire time, only one other couple came into the museum. The privacy and quiet also made it possible to see *The Rebel Angels* as we did—lying flat on the stairs and looking up at the ceiling.

The pace and the prettiness of Udine make you fantasize about living there, visiting the Tiepolos every now and then, and in the evenings going out to eat (or even to stay) at Scacciapensieri, one of the *agriturismo* farm-inns that dot the Friulian countryside, cooking and serving up extraordinary meals, with many locally grown ingredients. But in case you are eager to see another major wonder of the world of art, less than an hour south, the third corner in the triangle of short drives from Trieste—you can proceed to Aquileia.

Once the fourth-most-important city of the Roman Empire, a regional capital of about 100,000, Aquileia never quite regained its prominence after being sacked by Attila and gradually dwindled into a small provincial town. It has an amazing archaeological museum, and there is a walk you can take along the Via Sacra, once the principal street of Aquileia's important river-port system and now an astonishingly beautiful lane lined with cypresses, lush lawns, a canal, and archaeological fragments. The floors of private Roman houses remain in a field near the Via Sacra and across the main road; these well-preserved mosaics depict animals and geometric forms that give you a sense of the domestic architecture and of the layout of a neighborhood in ancient Rome.

Any of this would be enough to merit a trip to Aquileia, even if it weren't for its real eye-popper: the patriarchal basilica, founded in the fourth century and worked on for almost a millennium, with a floor the size of a soccer field and a fourth-century pavement, more than eight hundred square yards, completely covered with a prodigious mosaic portraying writhing animals, faces, birds, a fight between a rooster and a turtle, and a detailed and animate fishing scene. These images out of some paleo-Christian Looney Tunes assume the additional weight of being early Christian symbols. There are two crypts, one painted with twelfth-century frescoes of the life of Saint Hermagoras, a martyr and an early bishop of Aquileia, and another in which you can see, through a Plexiglas floor, more recent excavations exposing yet more mosaics.

Just outside the basilica, I watched a group of men working in a cordoned-off area, carefully digging and brushing dirt and dust off a mosaic floor. It is possible, given Aquileia's remoteness, that these workers were the direct descendants of the original Romans who lived here, or of the invading Huns, or both. But who knows if they were thinking about any of this on a warm cloudy September morning, as they labored to unearth what has been buried for centuries beneath the layers of history that underlie so much of Friuli, and Trieste?

More ghostly beauty can be found at the palace of Miramare, some five miles up the coast. This huge nineteenth-century castle sits on a promontory by the edge of the sea, a giant white cream puff with terraced gardens that combine formal Italian plantings with the salubrious lawns and woods of a Hapsburg health spa. Though the ocean views from the castle's rooms are stunning, Miramare's decor resembles that of many European palaces from around the same era. How much less poignant and affecting it might seem if you didn't know that the Archduke Francis Ferdinand stayed here en route to Sarajevo, that it functioned as German headquarters during the Nazi occupation in 1943, and that the Archduke Maximilian, who built the palace, lived here for only three years. Sent off to Mexico in 1864 to become emperor, he was executed by troops loyal to Benito Juárez, widowing the Empress Carlotta, who later went mad. How can this knowledge not influence the way in which we view the heartbreakingly cozy bedroom with its low ceilings and paneled walls, designed by Maximilian to carve out—from the vast spaces of the palace—the scaled-down comforts of a stateroom on a ship?

A Tale of Three Cities

Trieste

Antico Caffè San Marco, 18 Via Cesare Battisti (040.363.538), serves pastries and cake along with espresso. Closed Monday and August.

Grand Hotel Duchi D'Aosta, 2 Piazza dell'Unità d'Italia, Trieste (040.7600.011; fax: 040.0366.092; e-mail: reservations@grandhotelduchidaosta.com), right on Trieste's historic main square, is old-fashioned and elegant, with a helpful staff. There are fifty-five rooms, all with bath, and a double room costs about $190, including breakfast. The restaurant is closed for renovation. Open all year.

Al Teatro, 1 Capo di Piazza Bartoli (040.366.220; fax: 040.366.560), is in the center of the city, not far from the waterfront. There are forty-five simple, basic rooms, thirty-four with private bath. A double bedroom with bath costs about $90, including breakfast. No restaurant. Open all year.

Al Fiori, 7 Piazza Hortis (040.300.633), has an inventive chef who serves up northern Italian dishes; there is an excellent tasting menu and a congenial staff. Homemade bread is a specialty, as are seafood dishes; the seafood is kept in a tank on the premises. Dinner for two, with a bottle of local wine, costs about $85. Credit cards accepted. Closed Dec. 25 through Jan. 1 and three weeks in July.

Udine

Astoria Hotel Italia, Piazza XX Settembre 24, Udine (0432.505.091; fax: 0432.509.070; astoria@hotelastoria.udine.it), traditional and well run, is on a pleasant square in the center of town, near the Duomo. There are seventy-four bedrooms, all with bath, and a double room costs about $150, including breakfast. Open all year. Specialties of the hotel restaurant include asparagus soufflé, risotto with fresh herbs, homemade pasta, and roast lamb. Dinner for two, with a bottle of local wine, is about $60.

All Vecchio Stallo, 7 Via Viola (0432.21296), a friendly neighborhood *trattoria,* serves prosciutto with melon, pasta pomodoro, gnocchi, frittata, and *bacalà* (salted cod). Dinner for two, with a bottle of local wine, costs about $35. Closed midday, Sunday, and Dec. 24 through Jan. 5. Cash only.

Scacciapensieri, 29 Via Mopurgo, Buttrio (043.267.4907; fax: 043.268.3924; e-mail: brutmus@tin.it), is a charming agrotourism inn overlooking terraced vineyards, not far from Udine. There are six rooms, all with bath, and a double costs about $75, including breakfast. Closed January. Its wonderful country restaurant serves such local dishes as *frico,* made with potatoes and cheese, and tagliatelle with goose ragout. Dinner for two, with a bottle of wine, costs about $35.

Aquileia

Hotel Patriarchi, 12 Via Giulia Augusta, Aquileia (0431.919.595; tel. and fax: 0431.919.596; e-mail: patriarch@wavenet.it), is a comfortable, no-frills hotel within walking distance of most of the town's attractions. There are twenty-one rooms, all with bath, some offering beautiful views of the basilica. A double room costs about $70, including breakfast. Closed for two weeks in February. The hotel restaurant offers mostly fish specialties, some of them *alla gradese* (with vinegar). Also on the menu are polenta and *panzerotti* (large tortelloni) with fish stuffing. Dinner for two, with a bottle of local wine, is about $40.

Trieste, Filtering Tradition

By Susan Herrmann Loomis

~

editor's note

Just when you think you've got the Italian coffee lingo all figured out, you land in Trieste and it's all different, as the author notes in this piece. It doesn't take very long, though, to master the definitions, and one of the greatest pleasures I've had in life is hanging out in Trieste's famous and beautiful coffeehouses.

SUSAN HERRMANN LOOMIS is a food writer and the author of, among others, *On Rue Tatin* (Broadway, 2001), *The Italian Farmhouse Cookbook* (Workman, 2000), and *The French Farmhouse Cookbook* (Workman, 1996).

By seven A.M. the aroma of coffee and the clink of espresso cups resonates through Trieste, on the northern shore of the Adriatic Sea, the last major city in Italy before Slovenia. Hundreds of cafés shiny with mirrors and polished bars serve the 230,000 residents of Trieste some of the best coffee in Italy.

On my first visit to the city, though the air was cool, the sun shone, and I migrated outside along with the rest of Trieste to sip coffee, enjoy the sea air, and look out over the Gulf of Trieste. The city's famed wind, the *bora*, had blown all the clouds away the night before, and though I couldn't see it, I was told that on an exceptionally clear day the cupola of San Marco in Venice is visible across the Adriatic.

Trieste has been a prized destination for centuries. James Joyce lived there at different times and began writing *Ulysses* there. Rainer Maria Rilke and Sigmund Freud frequented the small city, which also spawned a handful of Italian writers, including Umberto Saba and Italo Svevo.

When I was in Friuli a year ago, everyone I met pointed me in the direction of Trieste, insisting that I couldn't visit the region without experiencing its crown jewel. I didn't make it on that trip, but fortunately it was only a few months before I was able to return for five days in March.

What attracted me was a blend of history, elegance, and coffee. I once spent a week in Budapest, and my image of Trieste was similar, though smaller, and Italian. I wasn't disappointed. I understood immediately its appeal to writers, for while it offers the bustle of an Italian city, it is also gentle, soothing. For those same reasons it is a wonderful spot to simply stop and explore.

Known as Tergeste when it was a Roman colony, Trieste was governed by count-bishops in the Middle Ages and, after many years of struggle with the Venetians, placed itself under the protection of the Hapsburg Leopold III in 1382, eventually settling into the Austrian domain. There it stayed until the end of World War I, when it became part of Italy.

At the start of the eighteenth century, Emperor Charles VI declared Trieste a free port, which immediately sparked trade with the rest of Europe. The enlightened rule of his daughter, Empress Maria Theresa, brought Trieste to its zenith of architectural, commercial, and cultural development. The city became a gateway to eastern Europe, and diverse religions, cultures, and philosophies were encouraged. Education took on a prominent role, a legacy Trieste maintains in its institutions of higher learning, internationally recognized for science and technology.

The free port status attracted the coffee trade in the eighteenth century, signaling the birth of Trieste's coffee culture. The Arabica beans the city imports and its long tradition of roasting them account for the quality of the local brew. As Andrea Illy, part of the family that owns the largest coffee-roasting company in Trieste, puts it, "By the end of the eighteenth century, coffee had become part of the city's genetic code."

There are twenty-odd privately owned coffee roasters in the city, and

30 percent of the Mediterranean region's coffee still passes through the port, where coffee traders, blenders, and decaffeinaters ply their trade.

In the nineteenth century, Trieste solidified its position as a world center of shipping and shipbuilding. Attracted by the international trade, banks and insurance companies established their headquarters, and most of the city's grandest buildings have their names incorporated into the facades. The city was largely built by insurance companies, and their image here is an elegant one.

After World War I Trieste became part of Italy. World War II brought German domination, and Marshal Tito's troops occupied the city in 1945, claiming it for Yugoslavia. In 1947 the region was divided by treaty, with most of Istria, which had been Italian, given to what was then Yugoslavia. Thousands of Istrian Italians fled their land and settled in and around Trieste. The city was occupied by American and British military personnel until 1954, when it came under Italian administration once more.

In 1963 Trieste was named the capital of the newly formed region of Friuli–Venezia Giulia, and in 1975 the border between Italy and what is now Slovenia became official. Today, four of the five districts of the province of Trieste, neighborhoods right outside the city center, have street signs in Italian and Slovenian. Residents communicate in both languages, and over-the-border trade is brisk.

Changing borders, air travel, and fluctuating taxes at other European ports have combined to deflate the economy of Trieste. The city's residents, who once felt discreet nostalgia for its heyday, are now eager for it to thrive again. With politics relatively settled in neighboring Slovenia, Trieste is readying itself to become once more the "gateway to the East."

All of this history is essential background for a visit to Trieste. I already knew, from my time spent in Friuli, that the region is full of surprises, and so is Trieste.

The city vies with Naples for the honor of making the finest coffee in Italy. The local cuisine runs to boiled and smoked pork, with sauerkraut, goulash, strudel, and nut-filled pastries, all more Slovenian and Austrian than Italian. Most of the pastries are studded with bits of wonderful chocolate, which is Italian, and pasta and gnocchi are easy to find, but as culinary accessories rather than mainstays. The architecture is a blend of Baroque and grand neoclassical, which is more Austrian, but the Mediterranean hues of the buildings are clearly Italian.

It is also an energetic city. Even though the economy has faltered, Trieste has managed to maintain its treasures. The Teatro Comunale Giuseppe Verdi, built in 1801 and inspired by La Scala in Milan, is one of the country's thirteen official state opera theaters. After a spring symphonic program, an international opera festival is held here from the end of June to early August. The Museo Revoltella in one of the city's most luxurious palazzi reopened in 1990 after a twenty-year restoration and offers a look into nineteenth-century Trieste life as well as a modern art collection.

Trieste is studded with Roman ruins, many of which are either restored or in the process of restoration, and many of its finest buildings are newly painted. The cafés are always full, and the smaller eating establishments called *buffet* (pronounced boo-FAY), where boiled pork, *krauti,* and tear-inducing fresh horseradish reign, are open—and busy—all day.

Trieste is easy to navigate, particularly on foot. Its nerve center is the Piazza dell'Unità d'Italia looking directly out to sea. Bordered by ornate nineteenth-century buildings, it is awe-inspiring, hard to walk across without breaking into a jubilant run.

By nine A.M. on Sundays a low hum emanates from the piazza, the collective sound of Triestini of all ages there to socialize, sip coffee on the terrace of the Caffè degli Specchi, stroll across the street and the Riva Mandracchio onto the Audache pier, or simply wander the pedestrian streets directly around the piazza.

Each third Sunday of the month the network of old, narrow streets around the nearby the Piazza Vecchia and the Via dei Rettori turns into a flea market, as antique shops and other merchants set up tables outside to display their wares.

Trieste wakes early, and walking along the street that lines the port was my favorite postsunrise activity. Fishermen were just unraveling their lines to dip into the water, and the sun was burnishing the same facades—painted in wonderfully rich ochers, roses, yellows—that passenger ships first saw when they came in numbers earlier in the century. Traffic was already nervy, so crossing the street was an act of faith.

I am always attracted to fish markets, and I walked into the one at the Pescheria Centrale, a lovely building with a small bell tower. Although it no longer bustles, the building is worth a look; high, open, light, it is lovely, and there are enough fresh Adriatic fish to make it interesting. The Aquarium is right next door, with live versions of what one sees at the market.

Going west from the piazza along the Riva Tre Novembre is the Greek Orthodox Church of San Nicòlo dei Greci. Even its faded blue-green door is beautiful, and inside it is a universe of dark painted walls and ceilings, wooden benches that line the open interior, and icons framed in brilliant silver. Near the church is Caffè Tommaseo, which still has vestiges of its nineteenth-century elegance and is a very pleasant spot to sip coffee.

Farther on past the Palazzo Carciotti, now the harbor office, is the Canal Grande, where sailing ships once moored in the heart of the city. Flanked by impressive neoclassical buildings, it is now host to gaily colored fishing and pleasure boats. At the head of the canal is the hulking church of Sant'Antonio Nuovo, topped by statues of six Triestina martyrs. To the right, just in front of the church, a fruit, vegetable, and clothing market unfolds on one side of the Piazza del Ponterosso six days a week (closed on Sunday).

Behind the church, up the Via delle Torre, through the Piazza San Giovanni, and up to the Piazza Goldoni, there is a different Trieste. Traffic hums, people rush, and the energy is high, perhaps fueled by smooth coffee from Cremecaffè, right on the square.

Here is one of Trieste's best-loved meeting places. Jammed no matter the hour, it has one long bar where patrons sip small glasses of coffee touched with milk and often topped with unsweetened whipped cream. On the other side of the café, patrons line up to buy freshly roasted coffee, both beans and ground.

Crowning Trieste are the hilltop Castello and the Cathedral of San Giusto, the Museo di Storia ed Arte, and the remains of a Roman forum, which can be reached by a very long flight of stairs from the Piazza Goldoni, or by strolling up behind the Piazza dell'Unità d'Italia and past the remains of the Roman theater. It's worth walking up the stairs for the view of the city, and the stunning cathedral offers ample reward for the effort.

Two basilicas joined together in the fourteenth century, it is filled with treasures, including a mosaic of the Assumption and a breathtaking collection of jewelry kept behind thick wrought-iron gates. The museum is a jumbled but fascinating collection of finds ranging from the Neolithic era to objects traced with pre-Roman writing.

Trieste's pebbled beaches are another attraction, and once the water warms, the city moves out to them. Some are within walking distance of the center. The two beaches at Grignano, which require an admission fee, can be reached from downtown by bus number 36.

It is hard to decide what is best about Trieste. The city is still a bargain, perhaps one of the last in Italy. Walking its streets is a great pleasure, and its relative lack of tourists means there is lots of room to explore. And it is a study in contrasts, a place to experience several cultures that have all dominated at one time or another and now are comfortably blended.

Coffee Talk

Knowing the vocabulary of coffee in Trieste makes ordering it a pleasure and cuts back on surprises. If you order a *cappuccino* in Trieste, it will come in an espresso cup with a light layer of foamed milk and will often be served with a glass of water.

If you look distinctly foreign, you may get a normal-looking Italian cappuccino, which has a lot of milk in it, so insist on the traditional Trieste version.

On the other hand, if you want a large cappuccino, the kind you get in the rest of Italy, ask for *caffè latte*.

To try cappuccino in a glass, which many Triestini prefer, ask for a *capo in b*, or *cappuccino in bicchiere*, which will come in an oversize shot glass with a bit more milk.

And if you want an espresso, ask for a *nero*.

Coffee prices vary depending on the function of the bar. If it is also a *torrefazione*, or coffee roaster, such as Cremecaffè, prices by the cup are less expensive. In general, a cappuccino costs about 85 cents, an espresso slightly less.

Where to Taste

To the sorrow of Trieste, its grande dame of cafés, the Caffè San Marco, recently closed. It is expected to reopen, though no date has been set.

There are few as lovely as the San Marco, but the city has plenty of other coffee bars. They are generally open from early morning into the evening.

Cremecaffè, 10 Piazza Goldoni (40.636555), is an essential stop. Closed Sunday.

Bar Rex, 1A Galleria Protti (40.367878), is a chic meeting spot at the head of the Corso Italia, with a huge terrace that fills quickly on a sunny day. Closed Sunday in winter.

Bar Urbanis, 15 Piazza Borsa (40.366580), is a friendly neighborhood spot. Closed Wednesday.

Caffè Piazza Grande, 5 Piazza dell'Unità d'Italia (40.369878), is a sophisticated bar that offers books and newspapers to read in a tea salon with a view of the piazza. Closed Sunday.

Caffè degli Specchi, 7 Piazza dell'Unità d'Italia (40.365777), is right on the piazza. Though harshly restored some time ago, it still holds a place dear in the hearts of Triestini.

Pasticceria Bianchi, 3 Via delle Torri (40.638892), is a simple café hidden behind display windows filled with seasonal chocolates and decorations. Inside, the small, shiny bar is a haven, the coffee and pastries very good. Closed Sunday.

Caffè Tommaseo, Rive Tre Novembre 5 (40.366765), is a grand old café with many small rooms, elegant marble-topped tables, excellent coffee, and very decent pastries. The only jarring note is the taped rock music it plays.

Places to Stay

It is most enjoyable to stay right in the center of the city, within walking distance of everything.

The **Duchi d'Aosta,** 2 Piazza dell'Unità d'Italia (40.7600011; fax: 40.366092). A double is about $200 including breakfast. The best rooms look out over the piazza.

The **Hotel Al Teatro,** 1 Via Capo di Piazza Gianni Bartoli (40.366220; fax: 366560). Home to actors performing at the nearby

Teatro Verdi, this small hotel offers pleasant, clean, and affordable if slightly faded lodging in the heart of Trieste. Double rooms, about $91 a night with breakfast.

The **Hotel Greif Maria Theresa,** 109 Viale Miramare (40.410115; fax: 40.413053). A two hundred-year-old hotel with an exterior that looks like an Austrian pastry. About three miles from the center of Trieste, right across the road from the bay. Double rooms, about $206 including breakfast.

Places to Eat

Trieste's border cuisine reflects the city's mix of cultures. While pasta mixed with tomato-based sauces can be found, hearty platters of boiled pork served with *krauti* and freshly grated horseradish, gnocchi with clams, goulash, and other dishes of central European influence are common, as are tiny breaded and fried sardines called *sardoni savor,* stuffed baby squid, a wonderful bean and potato soup called *jota,* and dark bread with caraway seeds.

Beer is almost as common as the hearty red local wine called Terrano, or the lighter, fruitier white Tocai from the hills around nearby Cormons. Desserts run to thick crepes stuffed with marmalade, apple strudel with a hint of chocolate, or sumptuous Linzer torte.

The casual, lively buffet is a signature dining experience here, offering mostly counter with a few tables, paper napkins, and plenty of wonderful boiled pork, fine bread, and homemade *krauti.*

Arguably the best buffet is **Da Pepi Buffet,** 3 Via Cassa di Risparmio (40.366858). A platter of succulent boiled pork parts, from tongue through ribs, costs approximately $9; a boiled meat *panino,* or sandwich, about $2.50; a glass of wine about $1.25. Cash only. The place is jammed at mealtimes.

Trieste is also full of *trattorie,* small family-run restaurants. Among those recommended are these:

Da Giovanni, 14/b Via S. Lazzaro (40.639396), specializes in Istrian cuisine, which includes stuffed cabbage leaves, roast veal shanks, salt cod in tomato sauce with polenta, and a variety of pastas, including dressed with goulash. A full meal with wine is about $20 a person. Cash only. Open for lunch and dinner.

Città di Pisino, 7 Via Boccardi (40.303706), is a simple family-run jewel a few blocks from the Piazza dell'Unità d'Italia. Goulash is subtly flavored; the antipasti of marinated squid, tiny sardines in lemon, and fried sardines with marinated onions is filled with flavor, the apple strudel out of this world. Dinner with wine is about $25 a person. All major credit cards. Open for lunch and dinner.

Trieste Pick, 1 Via Pozzo del Mare (40.307.997), aims to be all things to all people, with drinks and snacks at a bar, take-out food, and a handful of tables seating perhaps thirty people. The food is simple and somewhat sophisticated, ranging from crabmeat dressed with olive oil and pepper, to a succulent pasta of small shrimp and wild greens. Dinner with wine, about $34 a person. All major credit cards. Open for lunch and dinner.

A glimpse of true old Trieste is **La Bomboniera,** a pastry shop at 3 Via XXX Ottobre (40.632752), which glimmers with hand-wrought pastries and chocolates. The confections start at $1 on up.

Nearby Excursions

Aside from Venice, which is about one hundred miles southwest, there is Udine, about forty-five miles north, a pristine and bustling city with plenty of monuments and shops to fill a day. In between is Cormons, the capital of the Friuli wine-growing region.

Closer to the city center is what the Triestini refer to as the Carso, or Karst, a stretch of rocky highland pocked with underground caverns. The area has small neighborhoods, farmland divided by winding stone walls and roads filled on Sundays with city dwellers out for a drive or a bicycle ride.

Of the many small restaurants dotted about, one of the more popular is **Mezzaluna,** 54/a Loc. Malchina, 34019 Duino Aurisina (40.291529), where diners sit at long tables and eat the products of the house—smoked or cooked hams, wild herb frittatas, or cannelloni. A meal, with wine, starts at about $15 a person. Cash only.

There are also many small wine producers called *osmizze* dotting the Carso. They serve young wine by the glass, along with slices of prosciutto, sausage, and perhaps cheese, signaling that they are open (generally in late spring and summer) by displaying a large bouquet of leaves somewhere, either on the roof or by the front gate.

Il Castello di Miramare on Grignano Point (40.224/43) is a palace on the sea that houses the state museum. Built in the mid-nineteenth century by the Archduke Ferdinand Joseph Maximilian of Hapsburg-Lorraine, it is surrounded by a lush fifty-five-acre park. Entry fee to museum; the park is free.

The Castello, visible from Trieste, can be reached by bus Number 36 to Grignano. A good stop for coffee nearby is **La Baia,** at the beach (40.224.193).

La Grotta Gigante (40.327.312), about nine miles from the center of Trieste, is an underground cavern some 375 feet high; visitors can take a guided tour from one end to the other. Open Tuesday through Sunday year-round. Admission about $19.

To get there, take the Trieste-Opicina tram from Piazza Oberdan. At the terminus take bus Number 45 to Borgo Grotta Gigante; it is a ten-minute walk to the Grotta entrance.

This article originally appeared in the travel section of *The New York Times* on May 11, 1997. Copyright © 1997 by Susan Hermann Loomis. Reprinted with permission of the author.

Trieste: Frontier Town

BY ALFREDO ANTONARUS

∾

editor's note

Here is a series of articles about Trieste that appeared in the wonderful magazine *Gambero Rosso* (see Periodicals entry in *Informazioni Pratiche* for more details).

If they still greet outsiders with some reserve around here, it's easy to understand why. Until just a handful of years ago, this city tucked into the northeastern corner of Italy had its back to one of the hottest borders on the whole continent. And Trieste had the job of keeping its shoulder to the Yugoslav door to be sure it stayed firmly shut. All century long the city had been expected to keep vigil over an immobile landscape that had to stay unchanged to protect the interests and equilibrium of the great powers.

But Trieste had never had an easy time with foreigners. Pushed around by the Romans, strangled by the Emperor Augustus, vandalized by the Visigoths, looked after by Attila, destroyed by the Huns, devastated by the Lombards, kicked around by the Byzantines, the city bore up under the insults of the Venetians, the bad manners of the Austrian feudal lords, the weight of the Viennese empire, and the villainies of Napoleon's army. It finally was able to catch its breath under the Hapsburgs. Then a series of hot and cold wars tore through the zone in the names of Risorgimento and Nationalism.

When, at the end of the 1950s, a famous journalist asked the great poet Umberto Saba, then a very old man, to describe his own city, he spoke of a sense of tragedy that hovered over Trieste. Today, if you go to Saba's landmark secondhand bookstore, you find his best friend's son in charge. He talks, as everyone does, about too many old people and too few parking spaces. But a sense of tragedy? "Things that poets say," he answers. But perhaps what's tragic now is this: Trieste is a place that has the potential for grandeur but manages only to be marginal. The Intercity train leaving from Bologna makes at least five stops on the way, and even when it starts out full, it's half empty by the time it reaches Trieste. The city is a beautiful, elegantly dressed and made-up woman who doesn't know what to do with her looks. "Besides San Giusto Cathedral, Piazza Unità, and the Miramare Castle, we don't have great monuments," observes the bookseller. But the whole city is attractive: its setting, its outskirts, its urban layout. Yet it feels as if it's all here just for the pleasure of the *Triestini*.

"It's a place that you can't just pass through on the way to somewhere else. It has to be your destination," says one hotel keeper. In its role as bulwark, as outpost, as border, Trieste has always required the desire, the determination to get there. For decades it was a dead end fated to be on the periphery, to be the gateway to a border that, more than geographic, separated two universes—another language, another political system, market, religion, regime. This provoked a conservative mentality, of being the last bastion before the endless barbarian steppes. But it also encouraged a rigid exploitation of the advantages of such a position, a passive enjoyment of the lack of competition. Today the conflict is not between the left and the right but between the worlds of small city-based businesses and powerful industries that want more contacts with the outside. The war, once again, is taking place down at the harbor where monopolies have taken over without making big investments. The debate is about the waterfront and its future.

The palazzi in the historic center, the old cafés, the promenade along the sea, the antique shops, the parks are all part of this debate. They should rightly be the scene of more vivacious tourism than what you see in Trieste today. Most visitors are still Eastern Europeans more interested in cheap goods, cash-and-carry frontier shopping, than in the artistic pleasures of the city. The money-changers do a big business in Slavic banknotes turned in for a few bills to be hurriedly spent in the megamarkets.

Most of the dozens of wine shops, the *osterie* that once were a feature of the city, have disappeared. At number 8 Via Malcanton, there's one, labeled *vini tipici,* that sells a modest Tocai and a Refosco that goes down like sandpaper. The other museum piece of an *osteria* is at number 12 Via dell'Industria (in the San Giacomo neighborhood, a quarter of hills, steps, and laundry at the window that resembles a working-class Lisbon or an orderly Naples). It's one room, chipped and peeling, with barrels and demijohns piled up behind the counter. Yellowing postcards are stuck into the frame of a mirror that last saw Windex under Franz-Joseph.

The young don't drink wine anymore. The more daring ones order a *spriz.* The others stick to Coke. The average wine-drinker is well over forty. Marino Vocci, an expert in Trieste's cuisine, told us that the city discovered the pleasure of very good wine quite late, especially when compared to other areas of Italy. Wine was most commonly served from a demijohn, and until the mid-1970s bottled wine was offered in only a couple of restaurants. It was a question of tradition, not of ignorance. The *Triestini* went, and many still do, directly to the producers' outlets in the country where they found a fresh, honest, unpretentious wine, but never one they could fall in love with. So the job of improving local wines began very late, and mostly because of Edi Kante from Prepotto. He introduced quality wine to a city where tastes had traditionally favored wines with a deep color and a strong, acid flavor. As you walk around, you'll notice that *spriz*—a barbaric drink half wine, red or white, and half fizzy water—is still popular. Wine in Trieste was always associated with the sweaty, working-class poor. The middle class hung out in the cafés and drank beer. But not even beer is doing well here. Almost all the famous beer halls closed at the end of the 1970s. Forst, after closing for ten years, reopened recently, offering beer and karaoke.

A journalist does his job by being curious and a pain in the neck. So I go into bars, pose questions, ask customers leaning on the counter how life is in Trieste. They look at me a little suspiciously and sometimes answer something like "All in all, life is pretty decent here, thank God." And that "pretty decent," rather than "not too bad" or "passable," means that they live prudently, modestly, with admirable manners and good taste. It means that they live quietly, minding their own business, without having anyone, if possible, bother them while they are drinking a *spriz* with their elbows on the counter. Obviously, every now and then I find a speechmaker, a monologist, who tells me that Trieste is a mess, that you live worse here than in Rome or Milan, that there are too few inhabitants so it isn't considered a metropolis, that salaries are low and the cost of living high.

I hear a lot about the high prices in Trieste's shops. The shoppers that come from the East had gotten merchants used to a constant and spontaneous consumer, one they learned to take advantage of. But here too things are changing. There's no longer a socialist wilderness over the border. The Slavs who still come to Italy to shop have learned that by going half an hour more on the train, or by traveling north and west to Udine or Pordenone, they can buy better merchandise at lower prices. Many stores have closed, and the ones that survived learned that they had to build a clientele, and that demand had to be encouraged. It can't be easy to sell in this city. There are very few young and too many elderly. The city overflows with retired people. If you want to get an idea of the average age in Trieste, go for a cappuccino at Caffè Italia, at number 2 on Piazza Giovan Battista Vico. (You get there by going out of the center toward San Giusto.) There's a crowd of *bocce* players during a championship. They range from sixty to one hundred years old. Geezers who play cards, drink *spriz,* and chat quietly, elegantly.

As far as restaurants go—since I'll have to answer the question "How's the food in Trieste?"—the best description is, again, pretty decent. Even though there isn't a marvelous place to eat, one that offers unforgettable food, there isn't a rash of trashy places that will put anything at all on your plate. The *Triestini* themselves prefer to go out to eat in the country, with the result that fine places in the city have never even tried opening. But in general, restaurants are pleasant. During the winter many, and not only Pepi S'ciavo and Marascutti, can suggest local dishes that, since they are mainly based on pork and served with horseradish and potatoes, are more suited to cold weather. It's easy to find soups and tripe that are part of the venerable Friuli peasant tradition. Above all there's Suban, where they really know how to make the most classical country dishes. From the first sign of warm weather until the end of fall, restaurants favor that other tradition, food from the sea. With no trouble at all you can always find decent spaghetti or soup. The *Triestini* waiters are a pleasure: they learned to say please and thank you in childhood and are unfailingly courteous. The bill is always correct. The table linens are always freshly laundered. As for the rest, it's always just the essential. The *Triestini* dislike excess. The most you'll see is one candle or a bouquet of dried flowers in a glass.

It's above all while dining that you feel how many different cultures have influenced this area. First of all, you feel the legacy of Istria, the peninsula south of the city that is now part of Slovenia. Many *Triestini* are originally from Istria and still go back to restaurants there. Most fresh fish is still brought in from those waters. Austria is still in the boiled beef, the sauerkraut, the *jota* (bean soup). The poppyseed is Slovenian, the sauces Hungarian, the soups from Friuli. But above all Trieste is Mediterranean. Even though it

is the most northern corner of this sea, and in the rain or when buf-
feted by the *bora* it has a dark Nordic mood, it never completely
loses the sunny feel of olive trees, pines, oleander, and cypress. The
nearby town of Duino could have been stolen from the Amalfi coast
and slipped in here. Sandorligo della Valle, the zone for the best
olive oil, is a scrap of Liguria.

I visited Trieste about eight years ago, writing an article similar
to this one, and my impression was of an immobile city, a place tor-
mented by waiting. A place that was impatient, yet didn't even
know what it was waiting for. I found a city that ran its rough past
through its fingers. This time as I questioned shopkeepers, met with
restaurateurs and hotel managers, and talked to people on the
street, I felt that everything had changed. Many circumstances came
together: the crumbling of the Wall, the end of the Eastern regimes,
the political changes in Italy, the election of a new mayor, coffee
entrepreneur Riccardo Illy.

I felt as if the city were joyfully connecting with its hinterlands,
stitching together connections that had torn apart. It used to be a
difficult, complex city. It still is, but it recognizes a new challenge.
The former mayor bragged that he had never set food in Slovenia or
Croatia. Riccardo Illy visits Ljubljana more often than Rome. He
has a new compass, has shifted the city's direction and turned attitudes upside-down. Slovenia was connected to Trieste in the past for
historical reasons, but today it is even more linked to the city for
economic and political ones. Trieste is opening its doors, looking
around. There has been an improvement in the city's quality of life
(it is ranked as one of the most livable in Italy by a recent Census
Bureau survey) and in its attitude toward outsiders. You feel waited
for, welcomed.

Trieste: Cosmopolitan Cooking

BY ROSSANA BETTINI

∾

The Old *Osterie*

A faded sign that suggests you drink Amaro Alpino is all that remains of the Antica Trattoria all'Olmo. Founded in 1860, it was one of the oldest *osterie* in Trieste. After World War II it became the property of my paternal grandfather, Nino Stelco. My mother loves to tell about the long journeys into the country looking for good wine, driving from Prosecco to Conegliano. At Da Nino, besides wine by the glass, everyone drank *mis mas* (half wine and half fizzy water), *mezza lana* (half white and half red), *biancoA* (half white and half orangeade), and beer. There was only one brand, Dreher. The cook was German and made the best hash brown potatoes (*patate in tecia*) I have ever tasted. When I was little they let me eat in the *trattoria* once in a while, and when I did, it always felt like a party. My grandfather was from Istria, but sometimes a kitchen worker from the south who was busy in the pantry gave advice about the correct preparation of spaghetti. That's what the old *osterie* were like. When it wasn't the owner's wives in the kitchen, it was former ships' cooks, foreign wives of retired sailors, or ex-soldiers.

Very few of these authentic *osterie* are left, I mean places that still have their period furniture and dark wooden floors. In Via Pascoli, a little past the gilded Madonna, is one that has survived intact: **Osteria da Mario** (Via Ugo Foscolo, 040.76.06493). **Da Giulio** has changed its address but not its tables (Via F. Venezian, 11/f; tel. 040.30.6800) or its neighborhood, the now-fashionable, once infamous Cavana quarter. **All'Antica Ghiaccieretta** (Via

Fornelli, 2; tel. 040.30.5614) is in the same neighborhood; the cooking, the service, and the smells make it seem as if time has stood still. **Buffet da Pepi** (Via Cassa di Risparmio, 3; tel. 040.36.6858), also known as **Pepi S'ciavo,** is run by three superefficient partners who haven't touched a thing in the bare and unfussy restaurant, unchanged for over a century. The buffet is a custom that the *Triestini* love. For centuries they have been used to the *rebechin,* or *merenda,* which means "mid-morning snack." The common denominator in the buffet is the boiler, a huge stainless-steel container where all the tastiest cuts of pork simmer together at a constant temperature: head, tongue, pancetta, pigs' feet, *cotechino* (large fresh pork sausage), and Vienna or Cragno sausages blend together to emit an unmistakable fragrance. Generally you eat a dish of mixed pork meats with fresh grated horseradish, sauerkraut, and a generous dollop of mustard. You drink beer, red Terrano wine, or white from the Collio zone. Among the buffet specialists: apart from **Pepi S'ciavo** there is the centrally located **Marascutti** (Via Battisti 2/b; tel. 040.76.06064) and **Da Toni,** near the Torre del Lloyd (Viale Campi Elisi, 31; tel. 040.30.78529), where they also serve a tasty fixed-price menu that includes regional dishes like bread gnocchi and changes weekly. But this is not the whole of Trieste gastronomy.

Country *Trattorie*

In the summer, the *Triestini* spend their Sundays at the beach. On their return, they stop to enjoy the cool evening in one of the many open-air restaurants in the countryside known as the Carso, just outside Trieste. Some specialize in fish, such as mixed fried or breaded fish, or grilled scampi, like the **Trattoria Sociale di Prosecco** (Prosecco, 280, tel. 040.22.5039). The indoor dining room is modest, but the garden is shaded by century-old horse chestnut trees. Not far away, in Gabrovizza, is the **Trattoria Sociale di Savina** e **Anna** (Gabrovizza, 24; tel. 040.22.9168). From Friday through Sunday they have excellent venison with polenta. On other days gnocchi, *panzerotti* (stuffed pasta), strudel (salty, not sweet), roast veal with potatoes, breaded vegetables, hash brown potatoes, and for dessert, perfect apple strudel. The red wine is always from Terrano, whether in carafe or bottled, but they do have a few whites. Indoors is rustic and simple, but from April to June you eat in the perfumed shade of the wisteria. During the summer tables are under the grapevine pergola.

In Monrupino, on the slopes of the Zolla hill (peek into the lovely little church) is **Furlan** (Monrupino, 19; tel. 040.32.7125), famous for its traditional Triestino and Carso dishes. According to the season, you can dine on game, wild asparagus with eggs, porcini mushrooms, fried frogs' legs. There's a small choice of local wine to pair with the regional food. The dining room is spacious, but outdoors is cool and shady. **Trattoria Gregori** (Padriciano, 36; tel. 040.22.6112) is near Opicina, going toward Basovizza. Although only about five miles from the center of Trieste, it is rustic and has tables outdoors. Among its specialties are *chifeletti,* which are made from the potato dough for gnocchi rolled, curved, and fried. Bread gnocchi are served with a meat sauce, and *panzerotti,* also made from gnocchi dough, are filled with spinach and meat and seasoned with the juices from roast meats. Another standard is roast pork with potatoes and spinach purée. As usual, the wine is usually from a demijohn rather than sold by the bottle, but this is true even in the center of the city, where places with a decent selection of wine are rare. Even when the food is quite good, the wine cellar is nonexistent.

City Restaurants

One of the rare places where the wine cellar is at the level of the food is at Dario Basso's **Hosteria Bellavista** (Via Bonomea 52; tel. 040.41.1150), a classical, appealing, cared-for place with a flowered terrace where you can eat outdoors starting from the first sunny days of March. The view over the Gulf of Trieste is breathtaking, and the foie gras and prosciutto equally exceptional. The menu includes Dalmatian and Venetian dishes, a rich choice of French cheese, and a fine *bollito* served from a cart from which you can choose the cuts of meat that appeal to you. The high quality of both the wine cellar and the food make **Bellavista** the best restaurant in the city.

The unrivaled stronghold of traditional Triestino cooking is **Antica Trattoria Suban** (Via E. Comici, 2; tel. 040.54.368), in business since 1865. This is the place where locals bring their out-of-town guests to sample the best local dishes: *jota* (bean soup made with sauerkraut), smoked pork ribs with fresh horseradish, and stuffed or sautéed cabbage. The selection of wine is generally not worthy of the excellent food, but with a little patience, you may find a good bottle or two.

Along the waterfront are restaurants that specialize in seafood. Fresh fish, marinated or poached, breaded or fried, is the daily fare at **Al Bagatto** (Via Venezian, 2; tel. 040.30.301771). The wine list is acceptable. If you manage to find a table, owner Gianni Marussi will not let you get away without having the ice cream "drowned" in coffee dessert, the *affogato*. No tables outdoors at Al Bagatto, but good air conditioning.

Bandierette (Riva Nazario Sauro, 2; tel. 040.30.0686) faces the old fish market, right on the waterfront. The atmosphere is pleasant, and the seafood—oysters, lobster, crabs, scallops, and every sort of mollusk or fish—is outstanding. Bandierette is another place with a good choice of wine. Nearby, Arturo Rimini's simple, clean restaurant **Ai Fiori** (Piazza Hortis, 7; tel. 040.30.0633) matches fresh fish to seasonal vegetables and pays special attention to soups. A large purification tank for shellfish is in the middle of the restaurant: it is meant to be reassuring for those who like to eat their oysters and mussels raw. Good wines from all over the world.

The tasty mussels from the Gulf of Trieste are in great demand all over Italy and can be sampled in all the city's fish restaurants. The delicately fragrant, little-known extra-virgin olive oil grown in the area is low in acidity, and the better restaurants offer it on the poached fish or on vegetables. The best producers (Ota, Sancin, Starec, and others) are all members of the Frantoio Sociale in San Dorligo della Valle (tel. 040.382555) where you can find their addresses and phone numbers. Triestino olive oil, Carso wines, and other local products are shown off also at the **Trattoria Risorta** (Riva De Amicis, 1; tel. 040.271219), located about seven miles from the center of the city in Muggia. The restaurant faces the small port and the fourteenth-century Marquando Castle. In the summer, meals are served on the geranium-lined waterfront terrace.

Sweets from Another Era

Economically, socially, and artistically, Trieste is in a brisk new phase, but its culinary ties to the past are firm and deeply rooted. Austrian and Hungarian influences are evident in the city's pastry. Cake names like Dobos, Pischinger, Linzer, and Sacher are everywhere. *Presnitz* (a flaky, filled twist), *putiza* (a yeast cake), and *krapfen* (doughnuts) are common local favorites. After mass on Sunday or a stroll on Corso Italia, the *Triestini* buy little pastries to have after lunch or enjoy in the afternoon with tea if they are planning on eating in a restaurant.

The **Bomboniera** pastry shop (Via XXX Ottobre 3; tel. 040.63.2752) has been turning out Austro-Hungarian sweets since it opened in 1850. Among the tempting choices are Sacher torte, a delicate chocolate cake known as *rigojanksi,* a selection of tiny pastries, pralines, and a sweet known as *lettere d'amore.* **Pirona** is another bakery that has not changed its appearance or quality (Largo Barriera Vecchia, 12; tel. 040.63.6046). Its pretty turn-of-the-century shop windows are full of irresistible pastries. The best Sacher torte in the city is at **Penso** (Via Diaz, 11; tel. 040.30.1530). Also try their fragrant custard and apricot-jam-filled *krapfen*. Among the newer pastry shops, we are impressed by **Saint Honoré** (Via di Prosecco, 2; tel. 040.21.3055) in Opicina, one of the Carso hills reachable on the little white and blue train. Roberto, the phlegmatic owner, turns out vast quantities of bread, cakes, cocktail tidbits, cookies, and chocolates that range in size from minimouthfuls to ten-pound mountains. The workshop next door is much bigger than the shop itself.

Café Life

Trieste is famous throughout Italy for its cafés. The best known is **Caffè Tommaseo** (Riva 3 Novembre, 5; tel. 040.36.6765), established in 1834. It was founded by Tommaso Marcato, who thrust it immediately into the limelight by introducing newly fashionable ice cream and by substituting newfangled gas lamps for the older, more complicated ones that burned oil. Six years ago the *caffè* was completely restored, and despite the difficulties of the project, the results are satisfying. The clientele is of every generation, depending on the time of day. Among the favorite *aperitivo*-hour drinks are Champagne, Spumante, and wine. Two young sommeliers can guide you in your choice. Keep in mind that *cappuccino* in Trieste means a small coffee with only a few spoonfuls of hot milk. The more evenly balanced mixture in a large cup is called *caffè latte*.

Another important *caffè* is **San Marco** (via Battisti, 18; tel. 040.37.1373), opened in 1914 by Marco Lovrinovich and restored about eight years ago. The place has always had a strong political atmosphere and even today the clientele is young, almost all students who nurse a tiny espresso while they study and smoke. The older regulars generally have their own reserved tables. A visit here to see the original decorations and furnishings is a must. Before dinner, the *Triestini* meet "in piazza," which means at the Galleria Tergesteo, in the **Caffè Tergesteo** (Piazza della Borsa 15; tel. 040.36.5812). After a friendly chat, everyone moves on to other bars in the neighborhood. The most handsome and elegant is **Caffè Piazza Grande** (Piazza Unità 5/c, tel. 040.36.5962), recently restored with period furniture and woodwork. Nearby is the **Bar Unità** (Via Pitteri 1; tel. 040.36.5962), which attracts an unconventional crowd. In Piazza Unità is the Hotel Duchi d'Aosta bar and restaurant, **Harry's Grill** (Piazza Unità 2; tel. 040.76.00011). Its eighteenth-century Murano chandelier was admired by Hemingway. But the best-known and best-loved bar in the city is the **Caffè degli Specchi** (Piazza Unità 7; tel. 040.36.5777), about which even nostalgic songs have been written.

Hotels

The neoclassical palazzo of the **Hotel Duchi d'Aosta** (Piazza Unità 2; tel. 040.76.00011) has been sentimentally described as "a precious stone set in the silvery light of Piazza Unità." It is a handsome, well-maintained period building and the outstanding hotel in the city. It has four stars, forty-eight rooms, air conditioning, and a restaurant with a view over the sea. Artists and visiting intellectuals love **Hotel Al Teatro** (Capo di Piazza Bartoli 1; tel. 040.36.6220). The hotel, built in a palazzo from 1780, is right near the Palazzo Comunale, the Palazzo Modello, and the newly reopened Teatro Comunale Giuseppe Verdi. Even though not much has been done to preserve its looks, it's still considered *the* hotel for those who like to explore the oldest corners of the city on foot. It is right by the one-time Ghetto, near all the antique shops and secondhand stores. On the third Sunday of the month, the neighborhood hosts an antique market. Two stars, clean and neat and reasonably priced, the hotel has forty-five spacious rooms, some with a view of the sea and others on the piazza.

Where to Stay in Friuli

La Subida, Cormòns, Gorizia, (0481.60531; fax: 0481.62388)
Country-style one- and two-bedroom apartments and houses for a minimum of three nights. Comfortable accommodations, blissfully serene surroundings. Horseback riding, swimming pool, bicycles. Owned by Josko and Loredana Sirk, also proprietors of the excellent restaurant Al Cacciatore da Sirk.
Apartment with 2 beds: $95 per night. Apartment with 7 beds: $200 per night.

L'Ultimo Mulino, Via Molino, 45, Fiume Veneto, Pordenone (0434.957911)
This romantic little hotel (eight rooms) is also a restaurant. Right by the willow-lined river, its setting is enchanting. The only noise is rushing water and quacking ducks. The building dates from the eighteenth century and has been lovingly restored by the owners, Carlo and Franca Balestieri.
Double: $112. Breakfast: included.

Villa Luppis, via San Martino, 34, Pasiano di Pordenone (0434.626969; fax: 0434.626228)
The entrance to this elegant hotel, once the family home of the noble De Luppis family, still preserves the arches and the paving of a thirteenth-century convent. The glamour of the entranceway is matched by the rooms, each in a different style. Tennis court and swimming pool.
Double: $150. Breakfast: $9. Credit cards: AE, MC, Visa.

Rikhelan Haus, Sauris di Sopra, Udine (tel. & fax 0433.86082)
Mountain lodgings, ideal for skiing in the winter and with a

swimming pool for the summer. Perfectly restored old house with wooden beams, antique furniture, and a balcony outside each room. Delightful little restaurant.

Closed: November. Double: $138. Breakfast: included. All major credit cards.

Astoria Italia, Piazza XX Settembre, 24, Udine (0432.505091; fax: 0432.505070)

Classic, centrally located, elegant, in a restored building. Air-conditioned and sound-proofed rooms furnished with handmade furniture. Spacious bathrooms, all with tubs. Charming little garden with an old well. Well-known restaurant.

Doubles: $112–157. Breakfast: $12. Credit cards: AE, DC, Visa.

Romantik Golf, via Oslavia, 2, San Floriano del Collio, Gorizia

Most of the rooms of this lovely hotel are in two seventeenth-century dwellings near a castle that today houses a restaurant, living room, and three other bedrooms. The whole is surrounded by a pretty park. Swimming pool, tennis courts, and nine-hole golf course.

Double: $175. Breakfast: included. All major credit cards.

Food and Wine Festivals

San Daniele

During the last weekend of August, a colossal food festival called **Aria di Festa** celebrates this town's famous ham. In the course of the four days, more than 2,500 prosciutti are consumed together with rivers of Friuli wine (0432.504743). Stay at the attractive Alla Torre hotel in the middle of town (tel. & fax 0432.954562).

Cormòns

On the second Sunday in September, in the middle of the grape harvest, this town lets loose. The streets are lined with food- and wine-tasting stands. Floats, bands, and dancing celebrate the area's renowned wine, and white wine pours from the special wooden fountain mounted for the occasion (0481.630371).

Grado

This ancient town on the gulf, not far from Trieste, is a tangled web of tiny streets and pretty *piazzette* that resemble those of Venice. During the summer its sandy beaches are popular with families. A white asparagus festival takes place at the end of April and the beginning of May a few miles outside this seaside resort, in the town of Fossalon di Grado. Restaurants offer asparagus-based menus and the prized locally grown vegetable is served in risotto, with eggs, in soup with shrimp, with scallops as antipasto, and in dozens of other ways (0431.8991; fax: 0431.899278).

Valli del Natisone

Several towns near Cividale del Friuli, such as Pulfero, San Pietro al Natisone, and Grimacco have organized a yearly celebration of regional cooking. During most of October and November, eighteen local restaurants offer special very reasonably priced *prix fixe* lunches featuring traditional dishes. For a list of the restaurants and their menus, contact the Cividale tourist bureau (0432.731398).

This piece, composed of five separate articles featuring different aspects of Trieste, originally appeared in issue No. 11, 1997, of *Gambero Rosso*. Copyright © 1997. Reprinted with permission.

Because Friuli–Venezia Giulia is still relatively unknown to North American travelers, I thought I would ask two of the most enthusiastic champions of this region to contribute a list of their favorite things. Here, then, are the *cose favorite* of Lidia Bastianich and Fred Plotkin.

My Friuli Favorites

BY LIDIA BASTIANICH

∾

1. Eating *frico* and *prosciutto* at La Frasca in Lauzacco, with a glass of Bastianich Tocai.
2. Sitting in Piazza Unità in Trieste sipping an espresso.
3. Going to La Risorta in Muggia for some wonderful fish.
4. Chatting away and sipping grappa with Giannola Nonino in Percotto.
5. Early-morning fishing with local fisherman in the lagoons of Grado.
6. Watching La Barcolana.
7. Being part of the lunch-hour rush at Trattoria da Giovanni while eating *trippa*.
8. Spending a warm afternoon looking at the mosaics in Aquilea.
9. Foraging for wild spring asparagus in the Carso area.
10. Quietly praying in the Church of San Giusto.
11. Watching the cats sunbathe in the ruins of the Roman theater in Trieste.
12. Carnival in Muggia.
13. Dancing to folksongs in one of the many *balere*.
14. Visiting the many *osmize* when the new wine comes out.

My Essential
Friuli–Venezia Giulia

∽

Asking me to identify my greatest pleasures in Friuli–Venezia Giulia is akin to asking a helpless romantic to list the highlights of his sentimental journey. As in love, knowledge of this place is an accumulation of memories and experiences that are meaningful in their totality because so many of them were singularly special—and so personal. That said, it *is* possible for another person to build a rich archive of sensations in Friuli–Venezia Giulia, but only if you give yourself over entirely, as one would do in love.

It is not avoiding the question to say that the principal attraction of the place is the 1.2 million citizens of the region. They are unmatched in their warmth and generosity, and are so pleased when someone new comes their way. Nowhere is their sociability more in evidence than in their *osterie,* which are so much more than wine bars. The *osteria* is the place where you check your anonymity at the door, and after one glass of the region's sensational wine (here are some of the world's best whites, and some outstanding reds as well), you have a circle of new friends. No city matches handsome Udine for its selection of *osterie,* and this place also has more great works by Tiepolo than anywhere else. It is no slight to the men of Friuli–Venezia Giulia to observe that the region's women are quite extraordinary. They combine strength, tenacity, and immense patience in the face of adversity, with great beauty and boundless humor.

498   V e n i c e

Friuli–Venezia Giulia is also special for its places, sights, sounds, and smells. Its wine country is prettier than most of Tuscany and Piedmont. My favorite spots are San Floriano del Collio and Capriva. Just as lovely, in a different way, are the endless flat zones (the Bassa Friulana) full of cornstalks that stand tall in fields—carpeted with herbs and vegetables—that surround villas and old farmhouses. It seems absolutely quiet in these areas until you listen very closely and hear the riotous music of nature. A typical spot for these exquisite pleasures is Gradiscutta di Varmo.

I could not go to the region without returning to Aquileia, the greatest center of ancient Roman civilization in northern Italy. Then too there is Cividale del Friuli, the region's most beautiful town, where I would munch on gubana, the best cake found in the region with Italy's top baking. To work off all the marvelous cake, I would go for long peaceful walks in Carnia, the alpine zone that is the repository for ancient Friulian culture. And then to restore my strength I would have a plate of *ciarsons,* the divine forty-ingredient-filled pasta that is wonderful at the Ristorante Salon in the perfect little village of Arta Terme. Before leaving the northern fringe of the region, I would hike in the Fusine Lake District above the important border town of Tarvisio, the place in Europe where the Latin, Slavic, and northern cultures converge.

At some point, and sooner rather than later, I must pause for the wondrous cheese crisp called *frico,* have a couple of silken slices of *prosciutto di San Daniele,* and pair them with a glass of Tocai—this is the holy trinity of Friulian food culture. And if it is springtime, I must have a couple of stalks of white asparagus. My favorite food market is in the city of Gorizia, which has incredibly friendly people. The two best restaurants in a region full of great places to eat are in the beguiling wine town of Cormòns. The entire meal at La Subida will be unforgettable, as will the loving care that is lavished by the Sirk family. But dining is just as wonderful at Il Giardinetto, and if *gnocchi di susine* (gnocchi filled with plums) are in season, I would crawl over broken wineglasses to get to them.

The seascape, with Italy's cleanest beaches and water, is yet another attraction. I love to cycle along the skinny paths that rise just above the waterline in the lagoon between Grado and Lignano.

But no visit to Friuli–Venezia Giulia is complete without immersing oneself into Trieste, Italy's most cosmopolitan city. No place else is like it, with its blend of peoples and religions and marvelous caffès (the San Marco, Tommaseo, and Pirona being the most famous of more than forty), with Italy's best coffee. A *cappuccino triestino* is an intense espresso tamed by a small dollop of fresh whipped cream. The Pirona ranks in the top three for baking, along with La Bomboniera and the Royal. The *Triestini* love their pristine seafood, but the favorite eating institution is the *buffet,* which can only be described as a pork bar. All manner of pork cookery happens here, and it is irresistible. My favorite is Da Pepi, just next to the *borsa* (stock exchange).

Trieste's history is written in its streets, buildings, and monuments. The Roman theater, Miramare Castle, and the Risiera di San Sabba are essential, as is an extended visit to the Piazza Unità d'Italia. I would sit there in the late afternoon, at the Caffè degli Specchi or the restaurant of the Duchi d'Aosta hotel, and read the works of one of the many writers that Trieste has inspired: Joyce, Hemingway, Rilke, Italo Svevo, Claudio Magris, or Jan Morris, and feel grateful that even though Trieste has been radically altered by the dramas of history, the flavor of the city today is still the one those writers knew.

Even if it seems as if I have described every pleasure one can have in Friuli–Venezia Giulia, I know better: this marvelous little region is a custodian of boundless treasures and pleasures. But don't take my word for it—go discover them yourself.

Biblioteca

A Ghost in Trieste, Joseph Cary, line drawings by Nicholas Read, University of Chicago Press, 1993. "The city made of books" is how Cary describes Trieste, home to novelists James Joyce and Italo Svevo and poet Umberto Saba, among others. This volume is part travel diary, part guidebook, and part literary history, and Trieste is featured in wonderful drawings, paintings, and maps. Truthfully, Cary presents Trieste not only as a city of exiles but as an exiled city, and while not always flattering, this one-of-a-kind volume is an important one devoted to the Adriatic city's literary history.

Microcosms, Claudio Magris, Harvill Press, London, 1999. This is the only title by Magris that I have read (most of the others are in Italian, I believe), and I enjoyed it very much. If you are looking to read something that will convey the very soul of Trieste and the essence of Friuli–Venezia Giulia, no other writer comes closer than Magris.

Trieste and the Meaning of Nowhere, Jan Morris, Simon & Schuster, 2001. As most readers probably know, I am an enormous fan of Morris, as both James and Jan, and when I heard from Fred Plotkin that she had written a single volume on Trieste, I knew it was the perfect last book for one of my most favorite travel writers. As Morris relates, her acquaintance with the city spans the whole of her adult life. She writes, "I cannot always see Trieste in my mind's eye. Who can? It is not one of your iconic cities, instantly visible in the memory or the imagination. It offers no unforgettable landmark, no universally familiar melody, no unmistakable cuisine, hardly a single native name that everyone knows. . . . There are moments in my life, nevertheless, when a suggestion of Trieste is summoned so exactly into my consciousness that wherever I am, I feel myself transported there." This lovely and wonderful little book is divided into seventeen short chapters that appear in the table of contents with titles and a quote from the chapter, such as "Trains on the Quays": "Far away from where? Exile is no more than absence." Among the larger and more personal topics Morris raises in this evocative history are nationalism, lust, love, exile, and aging. Morris concludes by noting, "It seems to me that if Trieste were ever impelled to advertise itself on road signs, like towns in France ('*Son Cathedral, Ses Grottes, Ses Langoustines*'), all it need say about itself is '*Sua Triestinità.*' To my mind this is an existentialist sort of place, and its purpose is to be itself." An outstanding and *essenziale* volume.

DEGUSTAZIONE
CREMCAFFE' S.R.L.
P.ZZA GOLDONI 10
TEL. 040-636555
P.IVA 00900670324

OPERATO1   #0003

   1 EURO = 1936,27
        2X   3.300
MINAS GR. 250   6.600
CAFFE' VEN.   6.600
     TOTALE   6.600

FRIULI · DOC

VINI · VIVANDE · VICENDE · VEDUTE

UDINE
ti aspetta

4 - 7
ottobre
2001

A Tavola!— La Cucina Friulana (To the Table!—The Cuisine of Friuli–Venezia Giulia)

"The food of Friuli–Venezia Giulia, like its people, is much more international than that of most of the rest of Italy. Although palpably and unmistakably Italian in terms of the preparation of most dishes, it has stylistic influences from elsewhere. So the more prominent use of spices and many vegetable and fruit flavorings in some dishes draws from surrounding areas but also is particular to this place. The region's cooks make little effort to be international, but rather endeavor to express ideas and flavors that speak of their own fortunate land. It cannot be emphasized too strongly that it is a mistaken assumption that just because the region was long under foreign domination it therefore absorbed the ways of its occupiers. If anything, the people of Friuli–Venezia Giulia wanted to protect and exalt that which was innately theirs."

—Fred Plotkin, LA TERRA FORTUNATA

Friuli: Giving the North Its Due

BY STEFANO POLACCHI

~~

editor's note

....

The cuisine of Friuli–Venezia Giulia is a complex weave of Italian, Austrian, and Slovenian flavors, as you'll comprehend more fully after reading the following pieces. Fred Plotkin, in *La Terra Fortunata,* reminds us that we should not be surprised to learn that this region "always tops the list as the cleanest in Italy, with no polluted beaches and mostly pure lakes and rivers." As he explains, this corner of Italy has seen an inordinate amount of conquest and spilled blood, and therefore the people feel they are real caretakers of their land, treating it as a precious, life-giving commodity. Friuli–Venezia Giulia was apparently the first Italian region to regulate and adopt organic farming, and as Plotkin adds, "grape-growing and wine-making practices are environmentally sound, with few if any added chemicals."

STEFANO POLACCHI writes frequently for the Italian food and wine magazine *Gambero Rosso,* where this piece originally appeared.

You see those hills above Cormòns? That's the olive and grape border. And over there is the imaginary line where our custom of smoking meat disappears. From here, water flows into the Adriatic. On that side, it flows into the Black Sea." Josko Sirk points out the invisible markers that divide the Collio territory. A few miles away is Slovenia, another nation with a Collio territory all its own.

Sirk's restaurant, La Subida, is a major landmark in Friuli, this complex region in the northeastern corner of Italy. Along with Giardinetto, also in Cormòns, and the Torre di Spilimbergo (in the town of the same name), La Subida is a key place to explore the frontier's flavors. Central Europe's fondness for sweet and sour meets the Carnia zone's preoccupation with herbs. Joined to these is what Sirk calls the Mediterranean philosophy of food: "a mix of lightness and irony that leads to modern ways of interpreting ancient traditions."

Although La Subida is locally known for having a "Slovenian kitchen," it's clear that in this area Italian, Slovenian, and Austrian cooking are inextricably meshed. For example, Sirk's *saccottini*, little pasta packages, are stuffed with zucchini and served with elderberry sauce. The combination has the substance and depth of a central European dish but the lightness of a Mediterranean one. The same *saccottino*, made with a transparent layer of strudel pastry and filled with ricotta, is flavored with an aromatic Slovenian version of tarragon, *pektran*, an herb that resembles anise; three national traditions meet in this dessert.

When a German couple eating in his restaurant asks Sirk where they can find shank of veal as tender and juicy as the one they've just enjoyed, he says gently, "In your own home." His point is that good quality meat may be found in every country; it's the cooking method that determines the taste. "Even though we don't have the time to cook the way country women used to, we have to be careful about the compromises we make." Sirk describes how his staff, after years of pressing him, finally convinced him to buy a convection oven. They promised they'd watch the roasts carefully, but after a week they began to use the probe and a rapid cooking method, so the veal came out tasting boiled. "You know what I did? I called the company, they took back the convection oven and I bought a traditional one instead. Now and then a shank will burn if the cook is thinking about his girlfriend, but when something comes out of the oven, it has to taste right."

The passing years have brought yet another border to Friuli's kitchens, Josko Sirk points out. "I eat soup at least five times a week. We are a soup-eating people. But I know perfectly well that my children prefer pasta." Giovanna Modotti, the first woman sommelier in the region and an expert in the history of its food, is particularly interested in Friuli's soups. She traces one in particular, *jota,* as carefully as if it were a royal bloodline or a disappearing language group. "In the thirteenth century, in a convent in Cividale del Friuli, a document describes *jota* as a soup made with fava beans. Then the fava beans disappear, and other beans take their place. In the lowlands, the dish contains *brovada,* turnips fermented in *vinaccia* (the skins left after the grapes have been pressed to make wine), but in Carnia, where there are no grapes, *brovada* is made with turnips preserved in pears. Further south, in Trieste, where the Central European influence is more powerful, instead of *brovada,* we find sauerkraut in the *jota.*" In a single traditional soup, Giovanna has explored the history and geography of Friuli–Venezia Giulia (the full name of the region). She sees the past in every plate. "*Frico* is another interesting dish. It came from the countryside. When the women went out to do their chores, they left the crusts and broken bits of cheese in an iron pan on the hot hearthstone. By the time they returned hours later, the cheese had melted to form a thin crispy cheese pancake. Now it's a chic antipasto in New York restaurants."

One venerable figure in Friuli's culinary life, Gianni Cosetti, dedicates time to sensitizing young chefs to their territory's products. He recently organized a cooking competition in which the contestants could use only locally produced foods, among them more than eight thousand varieties of herbs. Cosetti was the chef at the well-loved hotel, Albergo Roma in Tolmezzo, until it closed recently. He has written many cookbooks, researching the recipes of his region. One of his favorites is *schultar.* "This is boiled shoulder of pork that we ate at Easter with sweet focaccia and vermouth. We brought the meat to church to be blessed before cooking it. I've restyled it, serving it with horseradish. I also prepare a sauce with wild apples and a wild orange berry, *olivello spinoso,* which grows on our riverbanks. The sweet-salty combination is very Austrian, but it's all served with a drizzle of good Mediterranean olive oil."

Gianni also tells us about such old-fashioned foods as *sic*, whey that has been soured by adding a piece of wine-soaked bread. The *sic* is added to browned pancetta or pork fat, and the combination is used to dress warm salads, a central European favorite. *Ont* is clarified butter: "There weren't any refrigerators, so when it was three days old, we melted down the butter. Two handfuls of cornmeal carried all the impurities to the bottom. The clarified butter stayed on top and would last for months stored in the cellar." Another memory brings out a deep sigh. "Polenta . . . do you have any idea the difference between stone-ground cornmeal and the modern kind? Two totally different things. An old mill is still operating here in Tolmezzo. The water from the river turns the grindstones. There's one woman who continues to run it—a real act of love. A few farmers still bring down their corn and have her grind it: five thousand lire (about two dollars) for a thirty-kilo bag. It's like a religious ceremony. She can't make more than fifteen hundred dollars a year. And can you believe it—the tax people gave her a hard time."

Social and culinary history is hidden in the little drawers of the chests that peddlers from the Carnia zone (*kramars*) carried on their backs from valley to valley. Antique examples of the chests can be seen at the ethnographic museum in Tolmezzo. "The women in Carnia often went to Venice to work in the homes of the rich. This was an important factor in natural cultural exchange. They probably managed to pocket a bit of spice, especially valuable cinnamon. Their husbands, the *kramars,* could resell it. When the men came home from their travels, they would shake out the little drawers and use the leftover cinnamon to embellish a holiday dish." Every family in this region has its own treasured ravioli (*cialzons*) recipe, but all have two things in common, the combination of sweet-sour or sweet-salty and the use of cinnamon.

Sale e Pepe, a restaurant in Stregna (above San Pietro al Natisone and Cividale) focuses on traditional dishes, among them *torta gubana* made with pastry rolled around a grappa-drenched filling of dried figs, raisins, and nuts. Every element in this dessert is a subject for local arguments, starting from whether or not the pastry should be leavened. Another Sale e Pepe classic, popular in both Friuli and Slovenia, is *frittelle ripieno di vento,* or "air-filled fritters," first mentioned in a fifteenth-century cookbook by Maestro Martino, a chef from Aquilea. In chef/proprietor Teresa Covaceuszach's version, puffy fried balls of pastry are served with chestnut honey (bitter) and fresh grape sauce (sweet). The honey and grapes contrast with the bland pastry in both taste and texture. Teresa, fascinated by culinary history, tells us about plum gnocchi, another dish popular in the Natisone River valleys and deeply rooted in the central European culinary tradition. "Our valleys were very closed in. It wasn't easy to get away, but once a year, in the three-harvest season (cherries, plums, and grapes), the local women were in great demand and left the valleys to go pick fruit. They were not only deft pickers but also experts in drying and preserving the fruit. It was an opportunity for women to look for husbands outside their own inbred villages, and as an extra benefit, they brought back plums and the recipe for gnocchi." Two other centerpieces of Teresa's traditional Friulano menu are a very soft, runny version of polenta called *toc'in braide* served with horseradish and tart local apples, and *musetto e brovada,* a thick warming soup of pork rind and turnips.

Farther south, in Trieste, on the Adriatic coast, the venerable restaurant Suban is loyal to Friuli–Venezia Giulia's soup culture and offers an excellent *jota* of beans, cornmeal, and sauerkraut, but also updated dishes such as cheese strudel and baked ham wrapped in bread. Young chef Marco Talamini has brought international attention to Stefano Zanier's La Torre in Spilimbergo within less than a year of his arrival, and he too has triumphed with a classic soup: barley with seasonal vegetables. But his other dishes are also interesting. Creamy dried cod purée resembles French *brandade*. Pumpkin is featured on *crostini,* a smaller version of *bruschetta.* Barley cooked with ham bone and fennel resembles a light-hearted risotto. Marco explains, "I like all the flavors in a dish to be clear, not confusing. I've done a lot with barley, with veal cheek (a great meat) and *frico*. But once a week I cut loose and do more creative cooking. I don't want to impose anything on this territory, just explore little by little and then gradually introduce new things."

Back in Cormòns we met Paolo Zoppolatti, young chef/proprietor—with his brother, Giorgio—of Il Giardinetto. An Austrian influence rules the kitchen here, but Paolo explains, "I inherited a passion for cooking from my mother, and I tried to figure out all her tricks. At last I realized you could express your own feelings in a dish. I found it difficult, though, to have a menu that didn't include pasta, since many of our clients are Austrian and they expect spaghetti when they cross the border. It was embarrassing until finally I introduced *blecs,* which is fresh flour-and-water pasta cut into all sorts of shapes and served with a pumpkin and goose sauce. I also make *cialzons,* similar to ravioli. A kind of pasta strudel with potatoes, mushrooms, and mushroom sauce makes everyone happy. But the Austrian tradition has many peculiarities." One example of Paolo's style: a warm salad made with bacon, egg, salad greens, chestnuts, balsamic vinegar, and olive oil. The crispness of the bacon contrasts with the sweet softness of the chestnut, and each flavor plays its part.

∾

Out-of-the-ordinary places places to stay in this wine-rich region.

Capriva del Friuli (Gorizia)
Castello di Spessa, via Spessa, 1 (0481.639.914). A wonderful
estate and restored aristocratic residence. Pinot Bianco, Ribolla,
Sauvignon, and Tocai are the most important grapes in Patrizia
Stekar's vineyards. Five rooms; ten more in the *tavernetta*.

Cormòns (Gorizia)
La Boatina, via Corona, 62 (048.161.445). Sixty hectares on this
estate, twenty planted to vineyard on the Collio hills facing the
Isonzo. Their top wine, a Pinot Bianco. Five double rooms: $70

Dolegna del Collio (Gorizia)
Venica & Venica, Loc. Cero—via Mernico, 42 (048.160.177;
048.161.264). A beautiful *agriturismo* in the winery belonging to
brothers Gianni and Giorgio Venica. They specialize in
Sauvignon. Six rooms and two apartments: $60–70

Pulfero (valli del Natisone)
Casa Romina (0432.731.854 [headquarters for all bed and
breakfasts in Friuli–Venezia Giulia]). A farmhouse set in the
valleys of Monte Spignon. Attractive typical *trattoria*.

Torreano di Cividale (Udine)
Volpe Pasini, via Casali Laurini, 3 (0432.715.151). An important
winery relaunched by Emilio Rotolo, a Calabrian who has become
a major force in Friuli's wine scene. Pinot Bianco, Ribolla, and
Chardonnay are his benchmark wines. Twenty rooms: $80

Cormòns (Gorizia)

Al Cacciatori de la Subida, località Monte, 22 (0481.60531). Closed: Tuesdays, Wednesdays. Open: evenings only except Saturdays and Sundays. Cost per person: About $38 (without wine)

Al Giardinetto, via G. Matteotti, 54 (0481.60257). Closed: Mondays and Tuesdays. Cost per person: About $35 (without wine)

Spilimbergo

La Torre, piazza Castello, (0427.50555). Closed: Sunday evenings, Monday. Cost per person: About $30 (without wine)

Stregna

Sale e Pepe, via Capoluogo, 19 (0432.724118). Closed: Tuesdays, Wednesdays open: evenings only. Cost per person: About $20 (without wine)

Trieste

Suban, via E. Comici, 2 (040.54368). Closed: Monday lunch, Tuesdays. Cost per person: About $30 (without wine)

This article originally appeared in issue No. 27 of *Gambero Rosso*, 2001. Reprinted by permission.

Baking from Northern Italy

BY RICHARD SAX

∾

RICHARD SAX was a prolific food writer, teacher, and cook. Among his many cookbooks are *Get in There & Cook: A Master Class for the Starter Chef* (Clarkson Potter, 1997), *Classic Home Desserts: A Treasury of Heirloom and Contemporary Recipes from Around the World* (Houghton Mifflin, 1996, 2000, 2001), and, with Jo Ann Bass, *Eat at Joe's* (Clarkson Potter, 1993). His books have been honored with James Beard and International Association of Culinary Professionals Awards.

In Trieste and the Friuli region of northeastern Italy, pasta and Italian-style braised dishes are startlingly juxtaposed against others with such seemingly non-Italian ingredients as sauerkraut, goose fat, and smoked pork. If you've eaten at Felidia Ristorante in New York City, which features food from this area as well as from Istria—formerly part of Italy but now in Yugoslavia—you know how delicious the amalgam can be.

The region east of Venice, largely unfamiliar to Americans, borders on both Austria and Yugoslavia; it was part of the Austro-Hungarian Empire until World War I. The styles of cooking, ingredients used, and various specialties overlap and ignore national borders.

Baking is a key element of the region's food, notably yeast-raised, coffee-cake–type breads with rich nut fillings. This is not exactly what comes to mind when one thinks of Italian *pasticceria*. Equally surprising is another regional mainstay, *strucolo,* or strudel, reminiscent of the baked goods of Austria and Hungary.

If you visit this area of Italy—and you should, for its gastronomic pleasures, including *prosciutto di San Daniele,* its lovely wines ("more exquisite than renowned," one writer lamented), and especially its warm welcome—one of the first things you'll see as you drive into Trieste from the Venice airport is the Castello Miramare. This was the summer residence of Emperor Franz Josef and his empress, Elisabeth.

Lidia Bastianich, owner of Felidia and a native Istrian, explains that there is a further reason for this region's unique culinary style: "This is an East-meets-West area, and it has always had a distinct flavor of intrigue and movement—all the way back to the Huns, who brought with them a Germanic element. There's always been a lot of flow back and forth."

Delighted by the regional baked goods on a visit last fall, I sought out authentic versions still made by local bakers. My journey into this world began at a raucous lunch at the Trattoria da Giovanni, tucked away on a side street in Trieste. Run by brothers Bruno and Gianni Vesnaver, this lively, rustic hole-in-the-wall is a lunchtime hangout. Standing at the counter, workers nibble and catch up with local goings-on as they drink the season's new Terlano wine, made from the Terlano grape and drawn by siphon from huge casks called *damigiane* (demijohns).

Sitting at a communal wooden table in the back, a group of us were quickly brought pitchers of the wine, as well as mortadella sliced from a sausage two feet in diameter on the bar and ham baked in a flour-and-water crust to trap its fragrant juices. The slivered ham was showered with freshly grated horseradish and served with a sharp, beer-spiked mustard.

We were most excited, though, about thick slabs of crusty olive bread. This turned out to be the work of a local baker called Simone, and Bruno quickly sent a barboy down the street to fetch him so we could pay our compliments in person. Simone Supanz, an ebullient former boxer (with a broken and reset nose as evidence) runs a *panetteria* (bread bakery) in Via San Gazzaro. He began baking at the age of fourteen, and he still keeps alive many of the traditional regional specialties.

Gubana has traditionally been baked at Easter but is now a typical part of several holidays. "Everyone has heard of panettone," says Carol Field in her fine book The Italian Baker, "but even many Italians are unaware of gubana, the Easter bread of Friuli."

Lore has it that this coiled, nut-filled yeast bread originated either in the village of Gorizia or in the village of Cividale. The name, however, indicates Slavic origins and probably derives from the Slavic guba (roughly, "folded"), which describes its characteristic snail shape. Some people claim that the name is derived from bubane, or "abundance" in the Fruilian dialect. (The Italian term is Cuccagna, which Mary Taylor Simeti eloquently describes in Pomp and Sustenance as a mythic land of plenty, with mountains of macaroni and Parmesan cheese. The same term has survived in English as Cockaigne, which the Rombauer family used to designate their favorite recipes in Joy of Cooking.)

Gubana is a luscious bread, with a rich yeast dough spiraling around a mixture of nuts and raisins moistened with grappa and/or other spirits. The time-honored formula calls for equal weights of dough and filling; one local baker told me he uses even more filling than dough for each loaf. Frequently, slices of gubana are sprinkled with additional grappa or slivovitz (bitter plum brandy) when served.

As is frequently the case with regional and folk recipes, there are several versions of gubana, and it also has two close relatives, putiza and presniz (see recipes below); confusion among them is widespread. In one town gubana may be called putiza. Some bakers make a version of gubana using puff pastry instead of yeast dough; just a few miles away, it may be called presniz.

Some might view this as imprecision. I prefer to see it as a lack of dogmatism, and I consider it one of the joys of Italian cooking.

The filling in the recipe below comes from Andrea Purinan, who, with his father, runs Il Fornaio di Mario Purinan, an outstanding bakery in the lovely town of Udine, capital of the Friuli–Venezia Giulia region. Here *gubana* and *pinza,* another sweet yeast bread, are available year round. When I visited one October, Andrea was starting a flour and water mixture that would ripen for two weeks. This "mother," which raises the dough without yeast, was the first step in making *gubana* for Christmas. Andrea also uses a slow four-rise method for his dough. The following *gubana* recipe is actually a hybrid, using Andrea Purinan's nut filling and Simone Supanz's dough and assembly method.

Gubana (Coiled Yeast Bread with Nut and Raisin Filling)

For the filling

1⅓ cups pine nuts

2 sticks (1 cup) unsalted butter, melted

½ pound almonds with skins (about 2 cups)

¼ pound *biscotti* or butter cookies

½ cup sugar

1 cup raisins

1½ tablespoons cinnamon

2 tablespoons vanilla

½ cup marsala, or to taste

¼ cup plus 2 tablespoons curaçao or other orange-flavored liqueur, or to taste

¼ cup grappa or brandy, or to taste

For the dough
2 packages (about 5 teaspoons) active dry yeast
1½ cups milk
about 6 cups unbleached all-purpose flour
⅔ cup sugar
2 large whole eggs
2 large egg yolks
¼ cup heavy cream or half-and-half
2 teaspoons coarse salt
1 tablespoon freshly grated lemon zest
1½ sticks (¾ cup) unsalted butter, cut into bits and softened

an egg wash made by beating 1 large egg yolk with
    1 teaspoon water
sugar for sprinkling the loaves

Make the filling: In a heavy skillet cook the pine nuts in 1 teaspoon of the butter over moderately low heat, stirring, for 5 to 7
minutes, or until they are pale golden. In a food processor pulse the
pine nuts with the almonds, the *biscotti,* and the sugar until the mixture is chopped coarse, and transfer the mixture to a bowl. Stir in the
remaining butter, the raisins, the cinnamon, the vanilla, the marsala,
the curaçao, and the grappa, stirring until the mixture is combined
well, and let the filling stand, covered, for at least three hours or
overnight.

Make the dough: In a small bowl sprinkle the yeast over ¼ cup of
the milk, heated to lukewarm, stir in 2 tablespoons of the flour and
1 tablespoon of the sugar, and let the mixture stand in a warm place,
covered, for 20 to 30 minutes, or until the sponge is double in bulk.
In the bowl of an electric mixer fitted with the paddle attachment,
beat together the whole eggs, the yolks, and the remaining sugar,
beat in the remaining 1¼ cups milk, the cream, the salt, and the zest,

and beat the mixture until it is combined well. Beat in the butter and the sponge, replace the paddle attachment with the dough hook, and beat in enough of the remaining flour, ½ cup at a time, to form a soft, moist, and slightly sticky dough. Transfer the dough to a lightly floured surface, and knead it, adding enough of the remaining flour to keep the dough from becoming too sticky to handle easily, for 8 minutes, or until it is very smooth and elastic. Transfer the dough to a buttered bowl, turning it to coat it with the butter, and let it rise, covered, in a warm place for 1½ hours, or until it is double in bulk. (Alternatively, let the dough rise, covered and chilled, overnight.)

Punch down the dough, transfer it to a lightly floured surface, and form it into a smooth ball. Let the dough stand, covered, for 15 minutes and divide it in half. Roll one piece of the dough into a 16-by-11-inch rectangle, spread it evenly with half the filling, leaving a 1-inch border on all sides, and beginning with a long side, roll it up carefully jelly-roll fashion, ending with the seam on top. Fold in the ends to enclose the filling, and working very carefully, stretch the pastry lengthwise from the center, forming a narrow filled cylinder, 24 to 26 inches long. Beginning with one end, wrap the pastry into a coil and transfer it, seam side down, with spatulas to a buttered 9- or 10-inch round cake pan or springform pan. (The edge of the coil should come to within 1 inch of the side of the pan but should not touch it; do not tuck under the end of the coil.)

Roll out, fill, and shape another coil in the same manner with the remaining dough and filling, and let the loaves rise, covered with a kitchen towel, in a warm place for 1 hour, or until they are almost double in bulk. Brush the loaves with the egg wash, let them stand for 10 minutes, and sprinkle them lightly with the sugar. Bake the loaves in the middle of a preheated 375°F. oven for 20 minutes, put a sheet of foil, dull side down, over each loaf, and bake the loaves for 20 to 25 minutes more, or until they are golden and sound hollow when tapped. Let the loaves cool in the pans on racks for 5 minutes, remove them from the pans, and let them cool completely on the racks. Makes 2 loaves.

Early on the morning after that raucous lunch, I met Simone Supanz in the labyrinthine work area behind his wood-paneled bakery. The way he stretches the dough for his *putiza* (sometimes spelled *potiza*) is a marvel; once in motion, this sturdy man moves with fluid, athletic grace. Like the *gubana* above, *putiza* is made by spreading a nut filling over a yeast dough, rolling it jelly-roll fashion and stretching it, gently but decisively, before it is coiled into its characteristic snail shape.

Putiza can also be found in cookbooks from Yugoslavia and Czechoslovakia. The etymology of both *putiza* and *gubana* shows the Slavic influences on the Trieste dialect. *Potica* (the Slavic spelling) is thought to be a contraction of *potivica,* from *potive* ("rolled," "wrapped up").

Putiza is excellent with tea; people in this region offer it when visitors stop by for a *caffè* or *grappino*. And Simone also suggests sprinkling the slices with a little more grappa or *slivovitz*.

Putiza (Coiled Yeast Bread with Chocolate Nut Filling)

For the filling
1¾ cups coarsely chopped almonds
1¾ cups coarsely chopped walnuts
¾ cup plus 2 tablespoons golden raisins
⅔ cup pine nuts
¾ cup sugar
½ cup unsweetened cocoa powder
1¾ cups fresh bread crumbs
¾ cup marsala

For the dough
2 teaspoons active dry yeast
½ cup milk plus additional if necessary
2 cups unbleached all-purpose flour plus additional if
  necessary
3 tablespoons sugar
¾ teaspoon coarse salt
1½ teaspoons freshly grated lemon zest
2 large eggs
¾ teaspoon vanilla
½ stick (¼ cup) unsalted butter, cut into bits and softened

an egg wash made by beating 1 large egg yolk with
  1 teaspoon water
sugar for sprinkling the loaf

Make the filling: In a bowl stir together the almonds, the walnuts, the raisins, the pine nuts, the sugar, the cocoa powder, the
bread crumbs, and the marsala until the mixture is combined well,
and let the filling stand, covered, for at least 1 hour or overnight.

Make the dough: In a small bowl sprinkle the yeast over ¼ cup
of the milk, heated to lukewarm, stir in 2 tablespoons of the flour
and 1 tablespoon of the sugar, and let the mixture stand in a warm
place, covered, for 20 to 30 minutes, or until the sponge is double in
bulk. In a food processor pulse the remaining flour a few times with
the remaining 2 tablespoons sugar, the salt, and the zest. Add the
eggs, ¼ cup of the remaining milk, the vanilla, the butter, and the
sponge, and process the dough until it is soft and somewhat sticky.
(If the dough is too dry, pour in additional milk; if it is very sticky,
stir in additional flour, and process the dough for 45 seconds.) On
a lightly floured surface knead the dough, incorporating additional
flour if the dough becomes too sticky to handle easily, for 6 to 8

minutes, or until it is smooth and elastic, transfer it to a buttered bowl, turning it to coat it with the butter, and let it rise, covered, in a warm place for 1¼ hours, or until it is double in bulk. (Alternatively, let the dough rise, covered and chilled, overnight.)

Punch down the dough, on a lightly floured surface form it into a smooth ball, and let it stand, covered, for 15 minutes. Roll the dough into a 16-by-11-inch rectangle, spread it evenly with the filling, leaving a 1-inch border on all sides, and, beginning with a long side, roll it up carefully jelly-roll fashion, ending with the seam on top. Fold in the ends to enclose the filling, and working very carefully, stretch the pastry lengthwise from the center, forming a narrow filled cylinder, 24 to 26 inches long. Beginning with one end, wrap the pastry into a coil and transfer it, seam side down, with spatulas to a buttered 9- or 10-inch cake pan or springform pan. (The edge of the coil should come to within 1 inch of the side of the pan but should not touch it; do not tuck under the end of the coil.) Let the loaf rise, covered with a kitchen towel, in a warm place for 1 hour, or until it is almost double in bulk. Brush the loaf with the egg wash, let it stand for 10 minutes, and sprinkle it lightly with the sugar. Bake the bread in the middle of a preheated 375°F. oven for 40 to 45 minutes, or until it is golden and sounds hollow when tapped, and let it cool in the pan on a rack for 5 minutes. Remove the bread from the pan and let it cool on the rack. Makes 1 loaf.

Presniz is the third and remaining cousin in the *gubana-putiza-presniz* family, and it is frequently confused with the other two. This spectacular version is from Simone Supanz. Unlike its two relatives, a *presniz* is made with puff pastry, and once the dough is filled and wrapped in a loose coil, it is baked on a baking sheet rather than in a cake pan.

Presniz probably evolved from Viennese origins; it is slightly more refined than its relations. The filling, based on a marzipanlike mixture of ground nuts and sugar, is similar to that used for *gubana*, but it is made with hazelnuts, walnuts, and rum. This specialty can be found in Trieste and its surroundings.

If you use an excellent brand of commercial all-butter puff pastry, you can put a fine *presniz* together in minutes. Homemade puff pastry requires considerably more fuss, but some prefer it.

This rich pastry is served on festive occasions, so the amounts are for a large dessert. Leftovers can be reheated in a low oven, in order to crisp the pastry. Serve the *presniz* with coffee or tea, or offer a glass of grappa or brandy alongside.

Presniz (Coiled Puff Pastry with Fruit and Nut Filling)

1¼ cups hazelnuts
¾ cup walnuts
⅓ cup candied citron and/or candied orange peel
¾ cup sugar
½ cup crumbled *biscotti* or butter cookies
¾ cup golden raisins
½ teaspoon cinnamon
1 large egg, beaten
¾ cup rum or a combination of rum and amaretto
¾ pound frozen puff pastry, thawed
1 large egg, beaten

Make the filling: In a food processor pulse the hazelnuts with the walnuts, the candied fruit, the sugar, and the *biscotti* until the mixture is chopped coarse, and transfer the mixture to a bowl. Stir in the raisins, the cinnamon, the egg, and the rum, stirring until the mixture is combined well, and let the filling stand, covered, for 1 hour.

On a lightly floured surface, roll out the dough into a rectangle, 24 to 26 by 6 inches, brush a long edge lightly with cold water, and spread the filling lengthwise down the center of the dough, mounding it into a compact sausage shape. Fold the long edge that has not been dampened carefully over the filling, then fold the dampened edge over it, pressing the dough to seal it, and turn the pastry carefully seam side down. Beginning with one end, wrap the pastry loosely into a coil, leaving about ½ inch between the curves of the coil, and transfer the pastry with spatulas to a buttered baking sheet. Brush the pastry with some of the beaten egg, being careful not to let any drip onto the baking sheet, and chill it for 30 minutes. Brush the pastry with the remaining beaten egg, cut several slits in the top to let the steam escape during cooking, and bake the pastry in the middle of a preheated 375°F. oven for 40 to 45 minutes, or until it is golden. Let the pastry cool on a rack, and serve it warm or at room temperature.

"*Bona pasqua, bone pinze,*" an old saying goes. Serving *pinza,* a golden round of egg-glazed yeast bread marked with a cross or swirl pattern, augurs well for the Easter season. In the old days housewives would start the first of several rises of the dough at four in the morning. Then, on Good Friday, they would bring their *pinza* dough to the village bread baker, covering it with a towel for the last rise. Though the practice has largely disappeared, to this day it is still considered a point of honor to bake a *pinza* at home.

The name *pinza* probably shares its origins with "pizza." *Pinza friulana* or *triestina* is also sometimes called "*focaccia*" or "*focaccia dolce*" and is enjoyed for dessert along with such local sweet white wines as Verduzzo and Picolit, the latter considered comparable to sauternes.

Pinza dough, rich in eggs, butter, and sugar, can also be made with honey. Some versions of this recipe require four rises, with a little of the flour and other ingredients added for each successive rising. Such a method results in more developed flavor and a finer texture; professional American bakers term the method "re-mix." The following recipe calls for only two rises.

Pinza (Sweet Orange Yeast Bread)

4 teaspoons (about 1½ packages) active dry yeast
6 cups unbleached all-purpose flour plus additional if
    necessary
¾ cup sugar
1½ sticks (¾ cup) unsalted butter, melted and cooled to
    lukewarm
¾ cup milk
2 large whole eggs
5 large egg yolks
1½ tablespoons coarse salt
1 tablespoon freshly grated orange zest
an egg wash made by beating 1 large egg yolk with
    1 teaspoon cold water

In a small bowl, sprinkle the yeast over 1/2 cup lukewarm water, stir in 3/4 cup of the flour and 1 tablespoon of the sugar, and let the mixture stand, covered with plastic wrap, in a warm place for 30 minutes, or until the sponge is double in bulk.

In a bowl whisk together 2 cups of the remaining flour and ⅓ cup of the remaining sugar, and in another bowl whisk together half the butter, half the milk, heated to lukewarm, the whole eggs, 3 of the yolks, the salt, and the zest. Transfer the sponge to the bowl of an electric mixer fitted with either the dough hook or the paddle attachment, and beat in the flour mixture alternately with the butter mixture, beginning and ending with the flour mixture and beating the dough after each addition until it is combined well. Beat the mixture for 1 minute more, or until it forms a sticky dough, scrape down the dough from the side of the bowl, and let it rise, covered, in a warm place for 1½ hours, or until it is double in bulk. (Alternatively, let the dough rise, covered and chilled, overnight.)

In a bowl whisk together 2 cups of the remaining flour and the remaining sugar, and in another bowl whisk together the remaining butter, the remaining milk, heated to lukewarm, and the remaining 2 yolks. With the electric mixer fitted with either the dough hook or the paddle attachment, beat the flour mixture into the risen dough alternately with the butter mixture, beating until the dough is combined well. Let the dough rise, covered, for 1½ hours, or until it is double in bulk. (Alternatively, let the dough rise, covered and chilled, overnight.) Divide the dough into three or four pieces, and in the bowl of a food processor process the dough with enough of the remaining 1¼ cups flour to form a soft, slightly sticky dough. Process the dough for 1 minute more, transfer it to a lightly floured surface, and knead it, adding more of the flour as necessary if the dough becomes too sticky to handle, for 5 to 7 minutes, or until it is very smooth and elastic. Divide the dough in half, form each half into a ball, and on a buttered baking sheet let the loaves rise, covered, for 1 hour, or until they are double in bulk. Brush each loaf with some of the egg wash, and with a sharp knife make three curved ½-inch-deep slashes in the top of each loaf, starting each cut from the center of the loaf and forming a Y pattern. Bake the loaves in the middle of a preheated 350°F. oven for 40 to 45 minutes, or until they are golden and sound hollow when tapped. (If the loaves begin to brown too early, put sheets of foil over them, dull sides down, about halfway through the baking time.) Let the loaves cool on a rack, and serve them at room temperature. Makes 2 loaves.

The small crisp almond cookies known as *favette* ("little beans") or *fave triestina* are found in every *pasticceria* window in the region from October through the end of November. They commemorate the All Saints days of November 1, 2, and 3, when souls are released from purgatory. The cookies are colored beige, pink, and tan and are gathered in small cellophane bags and neatly tied with ribbon.

Favette are sometimes called *fave dei morti* ("beans of the dead"), as fava beans figure in the All Saints celebration, as well as in several old superstitions and myths. The Greeks associated favas with funerary rites; Mary Simeti notes that, according to Pythagoras, the hollow stalk of the fava plant provided a pathway to Hades for the spirits of the dead. Over the years, possibly in the eighteenth century, sweet facsimiles, like these little cookies, came to be substituted for the real beans.

Regardless of their macabre connotations, these small macaroons are delicious, easy to make, and successfully stored in an airtight container.

Favette (Little Almond Cookies)

¼ pound sliced blanched almonds (about 1¼ cups)
½ cup sugar plus additional for sprinkling the work surface
    and coating the cookies
1 to 2 tablespoons well-beaten egg
¾ teaspoon maraschino, amaretto, or rum

In a food processor, process the almonds with ½ cup of the sugar until the mixture is a fine powder, add 1 tablespoon of the egg and the maraschino, and process the mixture, adding enough of the remaining egg to just form a thick dough. Turn the dough out onto a work surface, knead it several times or until it is smooth, and divide it into thirds. Sprinkle the work surface lightly with some of the additional sugar, and put some more sugar in a shallow small bowl. Roll each third of the dough into a ¾-inch-thick rope, cut each rope crosswise into 12 pieces, and roll each piece into a ball. Roll the balls in the sugar in the bowl, coating them, and arrange them 1½ inches apart on well-buttered baking sheets. Bake the cookies in the middle of a preheated 300° F. oven for 14 to 16 minutes, or until they are very pale golden, transfer them to a rack, and let them cool. Store the cookies in an airtight container. Makes 36 cookies.

Is there anything more Viennese than strudel? Yet *strucolo,* its name changed but the delicious flaky pastry intact, is one of Trieste's most typical desserts. (One sixteenth-century Italian recipe refers to strudel as *torta alla tedesca,* or "German torte.")

Strucolo di ricotta (ricotta strudel) is one of the best examples of a dish of Jewish origin that has become assimilated into the larger Italian culinary culture. Ernesto Illy, director of the esteemed company Illycaffè, based in Trieste, points out that, as exemplified by this strudel, the Jewish influence in Trieste is difficult to isolate, for Jews have long been thoroughly integrated into the city's cultural life.

Strudel is made in Trieste with either this ricotta filling or with apples (*strucolo di mele*). Many recipes call for lining the dough with dried bread crumbs to absorb the filling's moisture. Strudels are also made with a dough based on mashed potatoes, similar to gnocchi dough. And *strucolo* can also be wrapped in a cloth and steamed or simmered in water, instead of being baked.

This cheese filling is scented with lemon and raisins, a flavor combination typical of the region, and the recipe, simplified by using phyllo instead of hand-stretched strudel dough, specifies ending with a simple sprinkling of confectioners' sugar. Strudels are also, however, frequently served drizzled with a mixture of bread crumbs, sugar, and melted butter; nonsweet versions are topped with melted butter and grated cheese or with meat sauce.

Strucolo di Ricotta (Ricotta Strudel)

For the filling
1½ cups whole-milk ricotta
2 large eggs, separated
½ cup sugar
1 tablespoon freshly grated lemon zest
¼ cup golden raisins
3 tablespoons dark raisins

½ stick (¼ cup) unsalted butter, melted
six 17-by-12-inch sheets of phyllo, stacked between 2 sheets
   of wax paper and covered with a dampened kitchen towel
confectioners' sugar for sprinkling the strudels

Make the filling: Put the ricotta in a cheesecloth-lined sieve set over a bowl, and let it drain for 2 hours. In a bowl stir together well the yolks, ¼ cup of the sugar, and the zest. Add the ricotta, and fold the mixture together until it is just combined. (Be careful not to overcombine the mixture, or the cheese will liquefy.) Fold in the raisins gently. In another bowl with an electric mixer, beat the whites until they are foamy, add the remaining ¼ cup sugar gradually, beating, and beat the mixture until it just forms stiff peaks. Fold the whites into the ricotta mixture gently but thoroughly.

Brush a baking sheet lightly with some of the butter, lay one sheet of the phyllo on the butter, and brush it lightly with some of the remaining butter. Lay another sheet of the phyllo on top, brush it lightly with some of the remaining butter, and lay one more sheet of phyllo on top. Spoon half of the filling along one of the short sides of the layered phyllo, leaving a 1-inch border on that outer edge and a 2-inch border at either end. Fold the short edge of the phyllo gently over the filling, and brush it lightly with some of the butter. Roll the strudel loosely, ending with the seam side down, and press the filling gently toward the center at both ends. Fold each end of the strudel as you would wrap the ends of a gift box by pressing the pastry together, making 2 diagonal folds to form a triangular point, and tucking the ends underneath. Brush the strudel lightly with some of the remaining butter, and pierce it several times on top with the point of a sharp knife.

Form another strudel in the same manner with the remaining phyllo, butter, and filling, and transfer it carefully with spatulas to the baking sheet. Bake the strudels in the middle of a preheated 375°F. oven for 35 to 40 minutes, or until they are browned lightly and crisp. Transfer the baking sheet to a rack, and sift some of the confectioners' sugar over the warm strudels. Serve the strudels warm or at room temperature, sprinkled with additional confectioners' sugar if desired. Makes 2 strudels.

"Of indubitable Austrian origin," says one Trieste source about the various desserts called *coch*. These soufflélike puddings can be made with semolina, rice, almonds, or bread crumbs.

In German the following semolina version of *coch* is called *Griesskoch* and is related to the category of Italian *budino,* or pudding, desserts that include *budino di ricotta*. In his monumental *La Scienza in Cucinae l'Arte di Mangiar Bene,* first published in 1890 (and still in print), Pellegrino Artusi calls this general category of desserts *dolci al cucchiaio* ("sweets with a spoon"), among which are all sorts of creams, zabaglione, and the currently ubiquitous *tiramisù*.

Many of these desserts are served unmolded. This simple, comforting semolina pudding can be inverted and unmolded after baking, but I think its golden surface looks so good that I prefer to serve it right from the baking dish. If you like, add a handful of grappa- or brandy-soaked raisins to the semolina mixture before folding in the beaten egg whites.

Coch (Souffléed Semolina Pudding)

2 cups milk
⅓ cup semolina (available at Italian markets and some
    specialty foods shops)
2 large egg yolks
½ cup sugar plus additional for coating the dish
1 tablespoon freshly grated lemon zest
1½ teaspoons vanilla
3 large egg whites

In a heavy saucepan, bring the milk to a gentle boil, add the semolina in a stream, whisking, and cook the mixture, whisking, for 3 to 5 minutes, or until it is thickened and smooth. Remove the pan from the heat, whisk in the yolks, one at a time, ¼ cup of the sugar, the zest, and the vanilla, and let the mixture cool to lukewarm, whisking occasionally.

Butter a 1½-quart soufflé dish, and coat the bottom and side with the additional sugar, knocking out any excess. In a bowl with an electric mixer, beat the whites with a pinch of salt until they are frothy, add the remaining ¼ cup sugar gradually, beating, and beat the mixture until it just forms stiff peaks. Stir a large spoonful of the beaten whites into the semolina mixture, fold in the remaining whites gently but thoroughly, and pour the mixture into the soufflé dish. Put the soufflé dish in a larger baking pan, and pour enough boiling water into the pan to come about halfway up the side of the dish. Bake the pudding in the middle of a preheated 375°F. oven for 40 to 45 minutes, or until it is golden and just set (the center will shake slightly), and let it cool in the dish on a rack. The pudding may be served warm or at room temperature directly from the soufflé dish or unmolded. (It may crack slightly if unmolded.) Serves 6.

In the Vineyards of Friuli

BY EDWARD BEHR

~

editor's note

I have long been trying to include the writing of Edward Behr in *The Collected Traveler*, without success, until now. Behr is the founder and editor of the outstanding quarterly newsletter *The Art of Eating* (see Periodicals in *Informazioni Pratiche* for more details). He is, not surprisingly, working on some book projects derived from his research and writing in *The Art of Eating*, and he had been concerned that his material would become stale if it appeared in too many places. Happily, when I asked permission to include this piece on the wines of Friuli–Venezia Giulia, he granted it. I like to think he agreed because the piece is very good and deserves a wider audience and that *The Collected Traveler* is an admirable home for it; but it may very well be because he was anxious for me to stop pestering him. Whatever the reason for his consent, this is an excellent overview of the white and red wines of the region, and though it originally appeared in 1993, it has lost none of its accuracy.

ED BEHR has been writing and editing *The Art of Eating* for sixteen years.

Of all the products a contadino *can produce at home, the most delicate is wine,* [which is] *even more delicate than milk. One must be the friend of wine, and love life.*

—Doro Princic

☙

Of the three regions that produce most most of Italy's great wine—Piedmont, Tuscany, and Friuli—the one that excels in white wines is Friuli. It may be capable of producing even finer reds. But few non-Italians can name the wines or place Friuli on a map. The region lies northeast of Venice, bounded by the Adriatic to the south, Slovenia to the east, Austria to the north, and the Italian region of the Veneto to the west. Friuli is not big, only ninety miles from end to end.

Its best-known wine is Tocai Friulano, a dry white that nonetheless suggests sweetness and comes from the grape of the same name. (The typical order in a Friulian bar is a *tajut,* a glass filled to the rim with Tocai.) But even this much knowledge can be confusing. Tocai Friulano is wholly different from the luscious Hungarian wine Tokay and from Tokay d'Alsace (which is made from Pinot Gris).

Friuli has a particularly well-adapted climate for wine grapes, superior soil and sites, and fine indigenous grape varieties. The native grapes counter the all-too-predictable international twins— Chardonnay and Cabernet Sauvignon—though these and other French varieties are also produced in Friuli. The region has a two-thousand-year-old wine tradition, but it is still coming of age, wrestling with style, technique, and geography. It has become an important modern producer only in the last twenty years.

Friuli is where Slavs, Germans, and Latins meet, as one can tell by many winemakers' Slavic or German names—Radikon, Princic, Attems, Gravner, Jermann. I write Friuli, but I mean Friuli–Venezia Giulia, the full name of the region. Friuli is the larger portion, which historically belonged to Venice. Its principal city is Udine, a pleasant walking city of 100,000 people. The reduced territory of Venezia Giulia, which until 1918 was part of the Austro-Hungarian Empire, extends south along the coast. What remains of Venezia Giulia today are the small provinces of Gorizia and Trieste. After World War II, part of the wine-producing area of Collio and most of the peninsula of Istria were ceded to Yugoslavia, in exchange for Trieste.

This year I visited Friuli–Venezia Giulia for the second time, just as the grape harvest was ending. Hardly any Friulian wine-maker speaks a useful amount of English, and my Italian is limited. But I was lucky. Fred Plotkin, a friend with full command of the language, was going to be in Italy at the same time and would be happy to join me. Fred, who wrote *The Authentic Pasta Book* (1985), lived in Italy for five years; he has keen senses and knows an impressive amount about the food and more than a little about the wine.

Friuli is not on the ordinary tourist itinerary. It is little visited by foreigners, scarcely at all by English-speaking ones. The region may not have the profoundly beautiful landscape or artistic riches of some Italian regions, but descending arms of the Alps offer quiet drama behind undulating vine-covered hillsides, marked here and there with small castles. There are impressive Roman ruins at the ancient port of Aquileia, whose magnificent Duomo has an extraordinary, huge fourth-century mosaic floor. The compact town of Cividale has a gracefully arched bridge, the beauty of the tiny eighth-century chapel called the Tempietto, and an exceptional museum of Longobard, or Lombard, decorative art. The people of Friuli are usually sincere and honest. Bicycles, not yet rare as adult transportation, are left unlocked even on the streets of Udine. The initial reserve of the Friulani quickly gives way to warmth and abundant hospitality.

Friulano cooking is symbolized by the *fogolar,* the still-common raised hearth with open sides, capped by a suspended chimney that rises through the roof. The *fogolar* traditionally sits in the center of a room and is circled by high wooden benches where once the family kept warm in winter. This room is the *çjasa,* the home; the rest of the building is the *lûc,* the house. Meat, formerly a luxury, is now common but is usually overcooked, or it appears in long, slow preparations. On my fall trip, I found such game as wild boar and wild duck. The most perfectly cooked meat, tender and with a trace of pink, was a fillet of "small" horse, served by one wine-maker at lunch.

Beautifully fresh Adriatic fish is nowadays available far inland. Prosciutto from San Daniele del Friuli is almost as famous as that from Parma. Aged cow's-milk malga cheese is especially good. Polenta is common and well prepared. And from Sauris, in the mountains of the Carnia to the north, come delicious smoked ricotta and lightly smoked ham. A typical preparation, served as an appetizer, is *frico,* which is either a thin layer of cheese fried crisp as a cracker or else a thicker round of cheese, brown and crisp outside and lusciously flowing within. Other dishes are barley and bean soup, *frittata alle erbe* (omelette with chopped native greens), *gnocchi di zucca* (dumplings made with winter squash), *gnocchi di susine* (dumplings enclosing plums, served as a first course), grilled meats of all kinds from the *fogolar, stinco di maiale* (slowly cooked pork shank) from the *spolert* (the wood-burning kitchen range and oven), *golas* (goulash), and *brovade,* which is turnip preserved in the fermenting pomace left from pressing grapes. The origin of some dishes is clearly middle European. I especially like the simplicity of a mound of polenta, sauced with butter in which raw polenta has been browned, with smoked ricotta grated on top.*

The potent distillate grappa is a fondly regarded Friulian product. It was once a rough drink of the poor. After the tenant-farmers' grapes were pressed by the landowner to make wine, the mash of skins, stems, and seeds was returned to them. They extracted the remaining value by distilling the alcohol from it. Thanks to the successful marketing efforts of the remarkable Nonino family, Giannola and her three daughters, the drink now also exists in many smooth versions.

Friuli's best-known product for the table is wine. The many well-made white wines have a particular harmony, with soothing texture and clean, often-delicate, persistent aromatic flavors—ideal with the delicate Adriatic fish, with *salame,* wild mushrooms, and many things. The many competent red wines fill the role of red wines everywhere; the few top ones have exceptionally concentrated fruit flavors.

Friuli's best vineyards lie in the hills near the Slovenian border,

---

*A visitor to Friuli can find these and more dishes, although many humble restaurants serving truly homelike food have disappeared in recent years. A few survive, and traditional dishes are also preserved in certain fancy restaurants. Among these, Ai Cacciatori della Subida near Cormòns earnestly preserves the past and has well-selected wines. In San Giovanni al Natisone, the restaurant of the Hotel Campiello stresses fish and offers superb traditional *gnocchi di susine, ravioli di zucca con ricotta affumicata,* and *casunziei* (folded pasta filled with beet and sprinkled with poppyseeds); Dario Macorig is a warm host and has a passionate interest in the region's wines. Al Giardinetto in Cormòns offers an admired mixture of old and new styles. Near Dolegna, Aquila d'Oro, which is quite luxurious, uses Friulian materials to make new or revised dishes, which sometimes provoke mixed reactions. My recent meal at Gianni Cosetti's restaurant at the Albergo Roma in Tolmezzo was not special, but he has a reputation for masterful presentations of the food of the Carnia.

Less expensive places with homier food can be as good or better. A favorite cook of many is Leda della Rovere at Da Romea in Manzano (no menu, put and nearly all the best wine producers are no more than a dozen miles apart. They are split into two DOC (*denominazione di origine controllata*) zones, divided by the small Judrio River, which was the old boundary between Italy and Austria. The zone on the Udine ("Italian") side is Colli Orientali, meaning "eastern hills"; the zone on the Gorizia ("Austrian") side is Collio. Italian DOC demarcations aside, Collio extends into Slovenia, where some of the finest vineyard sites lie. Collio and Colli Orientali have confusingly similar names, but that matters little, since the differences are more in history than in the wine. Much of the best soil of the hills is marl, or *ponca,* in dialect. The generous rainfall is unpredictable from year to year; dry periods are often broken by short-lived rushing floods. But the hills need no irrigation, which encourages shallower roots and less-fine grapes. The Alps block cold from the north. More important is that the center of the area is only fifteen miles from the Adriatic. Because of its tempering effect, the northernmost point of olive cultivation in Europe is in Friuli. Winds dry the higher vineyards, keeping the vines healthily free of certain diseases.

yourself in her hands); she knows and cares a great deal about wine. Fred Plotkin led me to the humbler Ai Cacciatori (also called Da Maria) in Cerneglòns, where the unintermediated home-style food includes *frico* (the cheese melting within), barley and bean soup, *frittata alle erbe,* and flavorsome rabbit. Fred's skill also led us to a pleasant Slovenian place called Trattoria Blanch, near Mossa, only five hundred yards from the border.

In the Carnia, one should taste the curious but I think persuasive *cjarsons* (a pasta dish with innumerable ingredients including spinach, sugar, cinnamon, and chocolate) of Ristorante Salon in Arta Terme. (I heard these called the finest *cjarsons* in Friuli.) High in the mountains of the Carnia, one can buy ham and smoked ricotta in the village of upper Sauris, which was haunting when I arrived in the mist at dusk. In Gradisca, have wine, prosciutto, bread, and soup at Osteria Mulin Vecio. I didn't have time for Trattoria Blasut in Lavariano and Da Toso in Leonacco di Pagnacco, recommended for its grilled meats. (I learned of the last two and some of the preceding from Faith Heller Willinger, author of the useful *Eating in Italy.*)

The terraces are called *ronchi,* a word that sometimes shows up in a winery's name. The land is just steep enough that the grapes must be harvested by hand, happily for the wines.

Altogether Friuli–Venezia Giulia has eight DOC zones. A few accomplished producers can be found toward Trieste in the Carso, in the flat Isonzo, and perhaps even in the vast inland plain of the Grave, producer of most of Friuli's wine. Lowlands are of course warmer than hills and generally more fertile, making the grapes ripen sooner with less-interesting aromas. The best lowland vineyard sites have the leanest soil, which is sometimes gravelly, as in the Grave in Friuli. (Like the Graves in Bordeaux, the name refers to the gravel.) Geography, however, means little without the skill and the decision to exploit it.

Languages of Friuli–Venezia Giulia are Friulano, Sloveno, and, near the coast, the Venetian dialect of Italian. Most people also speak conventional Italian, though not always well. Friulano, of which there are half a million speakers, is a dialect not of Italian but of Raeto-Romance, which is a Latin language with elements of German, Gaulish, Italian, Longobardic, and other contributions. (The best-known dialect of it is Romansh in Switzerland.) I asked several Friulani why, with the commercial potential of such a large

---

Rather than wrestle with a list of unfamiliar names on a menu, in Friuli it is safe to explain that you want local dishes and follow the advice of whoever takes your order, sometimes the owner or cook. It hasn't occurred to the Friulani, unlike the Venetians so close by, that the tastes of foreign tourists are any different from their own, so one isn't steered toward nonlocal or insipid dishes. Sometimes one can have small portions of several characteristic dishes.

For tasting wine by itself, find a popular bar, during the hour before noon or later in the day before supper, and order a *tajut.* A wider though not necessarily more discriminating selection of wines by the glass can be found at Enoteca La Serenissima in Gradisca, the *enoteca* of the Collio consortium in Cormòns, and other establishments, such as Enoteca Volpe Passini (where I have not been) in Udine. Few wineries, unfortunately, have provision for offering tastes to visitors.

group, there was no television station in Friulano. "Because we're occupied by the Italians," said a wine-maker. "We don't have a mother country; we are Friulani." In former parts of Austria, there is nostalgia, but no more than that, for the old connection, and however ambivalent a Sloveno may feel toward Italy, I heard none express the wish to join newly independent Slovenia, where I was told the wine is currently neither cheap nor, with rare exceptions, good.

Much fighting has occurred in Friuli because the hills are low enough to permit invasion; the Alps prevent it farther north. The prehistoric Raeti were conquered by the Romans in 15 B.C. (Friuli is a contraction of Forum Julii, the Roman name of what is now the city of Cividale.) After a brief assertion of independence from Rome by the patriarchs of Aquileia, there came the Barbarian invasion by Longobards and later an invasion by Hungarians. Four centuries of independence (1077–1420) ended with a long, mostly quiet struggle over Friuli between Austria and Venice. (A final invasion by Turks came in 1499.) Under the peace of Prague, Friuli joined unified Italy in 1866.

In the vineyards, the Austrians left a legacy of white wine and such varieties as Sylvaner, Traminer, Riesling Renano, and Riesling Italico. Most red wine and all the best native red varieties come from the former Italian side. At the end of the nineteenth century, vine-destroying phylloxera eliminated many minor native varieties; only the few best were replanted on resistant American rootstocks. At the same time, French varieties were introduced.

The vineyards were devastated by each of the world wars, so the vines had to be replanted. During the First World War, in six months of 1915 the Italians lost 280,000 men in battles along the Isonzo River. (The front was described by Hemingway in *A Farewell to Arms*.) The poverty and hunger that followed the Second World War drove many from their farms to jobs in the local chair factories, and to jobs in construction and industry elsewhere in Italy or abroad. Friuli has exported more workers than any other region in Italy. But some people persevered in the countryside.

Three times in this century, the Friulani say, their vineyards were destroyed—twice physically by world wars and once psychologically by the earthquake of May 6, 1976. Aftershocks continued for more than a year. But the Friulani earned a fresh reputation for honesty and hard work by reconstructing without corruption or delay, in bold contrast to the aftermath of earthquakes in Campania and Sicily.

For most Italians (and, in truth, most French), drinking bottled quality wine is at least as new a phenomenon as it is in the United States. Twenty-five years ago, most wine in Friuli was still sold "loose" in wicker-covered demijohns by the farmers who made it, and the wine was consumed locally in the same year as the harvest. In the 1970s, when there began to be a market in Italy for quality wine, Friuli's farmers leaped from sloppily executed, old-fashioned methods to mastery of the latest technology and bottling. The new wines were hugely better than the poor, oxidized postwar wines. The Friulani made the transformation through determination, hard work, independent spirit, and their tradition of wine-making. No unusual link of white grape varieties with the native soil led to the dominance of white wines; the Friulani simply had the foresight to anticipate the demand for white. Friulian grapes came (as they still do) almost entirely from small farmers, who only then began to specialize in grapes and wine. When the new wines succeeded, one wine-maker told me, the Friulani were euphoric.

The flavor of the new wines depended on temperature-controlled stainless-steel tanks (now sometimes linked and controlled by computer) and earlier, scientifically determined harvest dates. Unlike the French or Americans, at first the Friulani avoided all use of oak barrels with their white wines. Stainless steel is neutral and easily sterilized, and it captured particularly clean, aromatic wines—wines that quickly became popular in Italy for their delicacy, youth, and freshness.

Burton Anderson described the wines in his *Wine Atlas of Italy,* published in 1990 but already moving out of date:

> Most exponents still consider their whites too graceful to benefit from the softening effects of malolactic fermentation or even from wood [a number of wine-makers have changed their minds on these points], and instead seek what they define as a natural expression of the grapes. The fine-tuned balance is hard to achieve, because it depends on fruit at the perfect point of ripeness vinified by a creative tactician able to pay minute attention to detail. When it works—and when the vintage is right—few white wines anywhere are as exquisite as those of Friuli. When it doesn't, wines can seem light and anonymous to palates attuned to bolder tastes.

An American palate tends to like bolder flavors, so the least successful of these delicately aromatic German-influenced wines do indeed come across to Americans as dull, diluted, and grossly overpriced. But the better Friulian whites are rich in extract with a pleasing texture and remarkably persistent aromas. They reveal unsuspected aspects of such varieties as Pinot Bianco (Pinot Blanc) and Pinot Grigio (Pinot Gris). It's telling that the Friulani wine-makers don't speak admiringly of the big wines of Bordeaux, but they speak well of Alsace or the Loire and most often of Burgundy.

The ideas initiated in Friuli only fifteen years ago are already losing some of their force. More wine-makers are allowing malolactic fermentation (which is a natural secondary fermentation that converts the hard malic acid of new wine into softer lactic acid, reducing acidity overall). A younger generation, in particular, is making steady experiments with denser planting, lower yields, and sometimes riper grapes. The wines have fuller flavors and richer texture. In the *cantine* (the winery and cellars), they are looking again at low technology and traditional methods. There is a new emphasis on indigenous varieties. Many wine-makers see Friuli as pursuing too many different wines for the market and too many to produce them all well.

Unfortunately, some of the wines, and especially the reds, are not imported or not easily found in U.S. shops. And compared to Italian wines of the past, Friulian wines are expensive though not necessarily overpriced. As Burton Anderson wrote in his *Atlas,* "It was Friulians who introduced the concept that good young white wine could, indeed should, be expensive." Costs of production aside, price is part of the meaning of a wine, determining when, how often, and by whom it will be drunk. Great wine does not make some of the most enjoyable everyday foods taste great. (In America, where the top Friulian wines are $20 and up, it's no comfort to know that a well-made bottle of wine in Friuli is often around $3 and rarely more than $7 or $8 at the *cantina.*)

The wines of Friuli–Venezia Giulia carry varietal rather than place names. A good twenty varietal wines are permitted under DOC regulations, though not all are allowed in any one zone. Still more varieties appear as *vino da tavola.* Nonnative whites include Pinot Bianco, Pinot Grigio, Sauvignon, Chardonnay, Riesling Renano, Riesling Italico, Traminer Aromatico, and Müller-Thurgau; nonnative red varieties are Merlot, Cabernet Sauvignon, Cabernet Franc, and Pinot Nero (Pinot Noir). Native whites are Ribolla Gialla, Tocai Friulano, Malvasia Istriana, Verduzzo, and Picolit. Native reds are Refosco, Pignolo, Schiopettino, and Tazzelenghe. I was especially attracted to the native varieties because they are unusual and more evocative of the place.

There is a "Friulianness" to nearly all the dry white wines that is hard to mistake. The better white wines are concentrated, or "well structured," as the Friulani prefer to say, but it is not a structure that is familiar to American wine drinkers. Acidity is unusually mild. Instead, the Friulian balance depends on soothing texture and taste in the mouth, generous alcohol, and long-lasting but perhaps less assertive aromas than in the wines we are used to. These Friulian whites are wholly dry, but they have an effect of sweetness from relatively low acidity combined with relatively high alcohol (typically 12½ percent) and glycerine—both of which taste somewhat sweet. No trace of sugar is left in Friuli, as it is intentionally so often in American white wines.

Friuli produces a few exceptional red wines, though many Friulian reds are hard to find in the United States. (I tasted a number through the Friulian-like generosity of a Boston sommelier named Jeanne Rogers.) Unlike the soft, friendly red Merlot that used to be sold in demijohns, as some still is, the native red varieties show good natural acidity. But there is no clear Friulian style with red wines. Even the native red varieties have been scarce for too long to set a pattern.

Among Friuli's native varieties,

Ribolla Gialla is sometimes called Friuli's only truly indigenous white grape, since it has by far the longest history. Ribolla may be the same as a grape called Evola in Roman times. The oldest clear record of Ribolla is a sales document of 1299, and the name appears frequently thereafter, often as an honored wine. Ribolla was heavily replanted after phylloxera. Count Attems, president of the consortium of Collio producers, remembers that during the 1930s it was difficult to get the *coloni,* the tenant-farmers, to plant anything else; some landowners were driven to supply their tenants with other varieties and then feign surprise when the grapes turned out not to be Ribolla. Giannola Nonino, the dynamic force behind

Nonino grappa, prefers grappa from Ribolla Gialla over any other variety.

I paid special attention to Ribolla in Friuli, and yet I am unsure of its true character. The familiar Ribolla is a wine of unusual but agreeable acidity, which lacks the perfumes typical of Friuli's white wines. This Ribolla is above all a wine for fish, though it suits *salame* and many other things. The acidity is admired in Friuli for making the wine *vivace,* vivacious, and it is certainly refreshing and palate-cleansing. Victor Hazan, a great expert in Italian wine, has pointed out to me that the appeal is sometimes the textural effect of the tartness on the tongue. But wine-makers are again exploring Ribolla's possibilities. In some higher, cooler vineyards, Ribolla grapes ripen late enough to produce a very different, mellow wine.

Tocai Friulano, the typical grape of the *tajut,* is still Friuli's most widely grown variety. Unlike Ribolla, Tocai's acidity is only mild, and the wine tastes of peachlike fruit with suggestions of flowers and almonds. Tocai's origins are mysterious. There are old tales of connections with Hungary, but it appears unrelated to that country's Tokay. The earliest certain reference to "Tocai" as the modern variety dates from only 1891. Current thought has it that the variety is either a strain of Sauvignon (the strain called Sauvignonasse or Sauvignon Vert in France, not to be confused with the Sauvignon Vert of California, which is actually Muscadelle), or else Tocai is an old variety that somehow changed name. *Tu kaj* in Sloveno, for what it's worth, simply means "ours."

Malvasia Istriana is probably not a native but a cousin of the fine Malvasia grape, originally from Greece, that produces rich sweet wines and often-bland dry ones. Outsiders condemn dry wine from Malvasia Istriana by comparison to great sweet Malvasia. If Malvasia Istriana had a different name, it might fare much better. In its own right as a dry wine, it hints at almond and apricotlike fruit, though it is more reserved than Tocai. One winemaker told me Malvasia Istriana's characteristic is nutmeg. Unfortunately, because it is little known and hard to sell outside Friuli, the variety is probably headed for decline. Tocai, Ribolla, and Malvasia have long been blended to make standard white Friulian wine.

Picolit has the greatest reputation of any Friulian wine; it is a dessert wine, ascending, due to scarcity and cost, almost to myth. Around 1800, Count Fabio Asquini produced 100,000 bottles of Picolit a year and shipped the wine to the courts of France, England, and Russia. But by the 1960s, the tiny amount of Picolit that was still produced never left the families who made it. Picolit at its best is a luscious syrupy wine, made from very ripe grapes that are *passito,* partially dried, to concentrate their sugars before pressing. Not only for this reason is Picolit a costly wine to produce. Unfortunately, the vine suffers from "floral abortion," meaning many of the flowers are not pollinated at all; those grapes that do form are small. That the variety has survived despite this defect indicates the value placed on a good sweet grape.

Italians call a wine like Picolit a *vino da meditazione,* a wine for meditation, served apart from a meal. They sometimes compare Picolit to Sauternes, but the grapes for Sauternes, unlike Picolit, are enhanced by Botrytis (noble rot), which yields a greater range of flavors. Picolit's most fervent admirers agree that it isn't lush with flavor but slightly austere. Some current critics find that Picolit falls far short of expectations, scandalously so given the price. Burton Anderson is not given to rash judgment. But when I asked him over the phone if he had tasted Picolit that justified its reputation, he answered, "Frankly, no."

I believe most of the problem is in the making. Wine that is very high in sugar stops fermenting automatically at around 15 percent alcohol, leaving the wine syrupy and sweet—traditional Picolit. But nearly all commercial Picolit is produced without a *passito,* so it is short in sugar. Fermentation is stopped early to save some of the sugar. Then the wine must be sterile-filtered to remove the yeast that would ferment the rest of the sugar in the bottle. The pallid wines only hint at the potential taste. As well, even most *passito* Picolit is sterile-filtered. I have tasted good Picolit, and I suspect it is a great wine. But I'm hesitant to generalize about the old, true taste.

Verduzzo Friulano makes a lesser, more golden-colored dessert wine. The most famous comes from the town of Ramandolo in the northern tip of Colli Orientali. Like Picolit, rarely does Verduzzo undergo a *passito,* and most of the wines merely tease with suggestions of flavor. But I have tasted fully sweet Verduzzo that was very pleasing at dessert. As one wine-maker pointed out, Verduzzo has some astringency while Picolit has a mouth-filling persistent sweetness. I'm not convinced that either one shows great value without the *passito.*

Pignolo may be the best Friulian red grape; it is capable of producing wine with powerfully satisfying, mouth-filling fruit. But the vine has smallish grapes and limited production.

Refosco produces full-bodied, well-balanced red wine, but its flavors don't suggest specific adjectives. It may never be very "complex." That adjective sounds like jargon, but complex flavors are an essential characteristic of good wine. Greater complexity is inherently more interesting to taste. Yet it's hard to give specific names to many of these flavors, though a few may cry out—cherry, clove, apple, vanilla, tar. More flavors are perceived with practice, but a vague description can be an honest one.

Refosco is called native in Friuli, but Refosco is the same as France's Mondeuse Noire, the best grape of the Savoie, where it probably originated. The better Friulian strain is Refosco dal peduncolo rosso ("with red stems"); a leaner wine comes from Refosco nostrano, or Terrano, grown in the Carso and Istria.

Schiopettino is also called Ribolla nera. *Schiopettino* means "gunshot," perhaps because of the burst of the thin-skinned ripe grape in the mouth or perhaps because the grape matures late and malolactic fermentation made the wine fizzy in spring, when it would seem to explode in the mouth. Somewhat like Pignolo, Schiopettino has berrylike high notes of fruit. One bottle (1990 from La Viarte, perhaps no longer imported) held delicious fruit flavors for three days after I opened it.

Tazzelenghe, or Tacelenghe, means "tongue-cutter." The young wine was so sharp with tannin and acidity that the old *contadini* couldn't sell it in the first year. The few contemporary examples I've met weren't unusually sharp. Tazzelenghe wine may offer less than Pignolo or Schiopettino, but it is good. Before 1978, all three varieties were almost lost. For a crucial time, under particularly benighted EC regulations, it was against the law to grow them.

Among the most charming of Friulian wine-makers is seventy-nine-year-old Livio Felluga of Brazzano di Cormòns. His energies have not faded. Born along the coast of Istria that was lost to Yugoslavia, he comes from an old family of *contadini*. His children, he said, are the fifth generation "to pull bread from wine," to make their living from it. His father dealt in wine, and as early as 1956, Livio began to buy land near Cormòns. Now the family has 135 hectares in vines in Collio and Colli Orientali and produces 600,000 to 650,000 bottles a year.

Livio Felluga speaks patiently the thoughts that have long been familiar to him. "*È una zona con una grande vocazione vinicola.* It is an area with a great calling for making wine. . . . We have great native varieties of grapes. The negative side is that we have planted too many different varieties—and beyond that we are merely following fashionable trends. What has been forgotten is the importance of the native varieties. . . . Each product of the earth must have its suitable soil and microclimate. Our lands in Friuli, I believe, are mostly suited to white wines, principally in the hills." Livio

Felluga's winery (not to be confused with his bother Marco's Russiz Superiore) will reduce its range of wines to two reds, Merlot and Refosco, and four or five whites, mainly native varieties, which "inherently go beyond fashion." Felluga doesn't approve of the use of new oak with white wines: "It is very difficult to do."

"In the trade of wine," he continued, "tasting is very difficult. First, there is your mood. The wine that you find good today, you don't find good tomorrow, because you are not in the right mood. And what if it is the wine of a friend? Then," he shifted specifically to assessments by journalists, "there is the issue of economics. There are many ways to make someone's knees shake when you judge a wine. It is absolutely necessary to be impartial, which occasionally can be an effort."

He is concerned that metaphorical descriptions of wine flavor and technical language only put people off. "I don't want your readers to become afraid of all these big words. The taste buds simplify the issue; if they say it's a good wine, then it's good." He added, "A person who has a good memory for tastes is someone who can understand wine." In time one can acquire the broad knowledge of viticulture, weather, place, property, maker that goes with wine. "Then, when you drink you have a double pleasure." The winery filters but avoids the use of pumps, removing yeast but not the tinier bacteria. Said Felluga, "The less you filter, the more the wine is good." Fred and I, our perceptions perhaps colored by his sympathetic character, admired Livio Felluga's wines.

Short Thoughts About Buying and Tasting

When purchasing wines, it's hard to know which ones are made well by which producer and which are to one's taste. From Friuli, producers to consider are Castello di Spessa, Dorigo, Doro Princic, Gravner (expensive and not an easy expense to appreciate), Livio Felluga, Lis Neris, Puiatti (four lines at different levels of quality).

Wines from many more producers don't happen to have come my way. New York is probably the easiest city in which to find a broad selection of Friulian wines. Both knowledgeable friends and published advice can be helpful in choosing wine. Equally useful, if not more so, is one of the rare wholly honest shops that keep all its wine below 70 degrees F. and out of the sun. Such a store is likely to attract honest staff as well, eager to share knowledge and experience and point to good values.

Side-by-side comparisons, preferably blind tastings where the identity of the wine is concealed, show how wines stand in relation to each other, and they can reveal, for instance, the common links among one maker's wines. But the best way to taste a wine is to share a bottle of it over a meal, along with a few friends who are interested in wine. The wine changes in the course of an hour or more, its flavors expanding or dissipating on exposure to the air. It's best that some wine is left over, so that it can be retasted the next day and even the day after, a test of how much substance it really has. Aromatic and acidic high notes disappear first, quickly making most wines flat. Many reveal raw oak, a sign the oak was never really knitted with the wine or balanced with the other flavors. But the best wines hold up for a surprising time in an opened bottle.

Biblioteca

La Cucina di Lidia: Distinctive Regional Cuisine from the Host of "Lidia's Italian Table," Lidia Bastianich and Jay Jacobs, Doubleday, 1990. Thorough readers of this book will learn that I am an enormous fan of Lidia Bastianich. I first became acquainted with her, as did most Americans, by watching her cooking show on PBS. There was something different about the way she spoke of Italian food, and the way she imparted instructions to viewers. She was extremely knowledgeable and passionate about food, but she was very calm and relaxed in the television kitchen, and her demeanor gave me confidence that other Italian chefs did not. Later I visited two of her restaurants here in New York, Becco and Felidia, two very different places, and I loved (and still do) them both. (The *krafi,* raviolilike dumplings at Felidia, are extraordinary and are like nothing else I've ever had.) It wasn't until I read this cookbook, however, that I realized how truly accomplished and personable Lidia is, to say nothing of how good the recipes are. Lidia was someone I wanted to know, and though I was interested in the recipes, I was just as interested in her life and her family and the history of the Istrian peninsula. Jay Jacobs remembers that after eating at Felidia the first time, he remarked that "for the first time in this country, I'd eaten an Italian meal that actually might have been prepared on Italian soil. But where, precisely? A good-size town on or near the Adriatic in all likelihood, but I wasn't then familiar enough with the east coast of Italy to pinpoint the provenance of a style I found quintessentially Italian, but otherwise geographically uncertain." *La cucina di Lidia* is the distinctive cuisine of her native Istria, about ninety miles from Venice. The Istrian peninsula has been ruled by Venice, Hapsburg Austria, Italy, and Yugoslavia, among others. After World War II, when the peninsula was under Tito's control, the ethnic Italians in Istria were given permission to "return" to Italy, and after spending some time in a refugee camp, Lidia was taken in by an aunt of her mother's in Trieste. The recipes of Lidia's *cucina* also include the extremely diverse cooking traditions of this cosmopolitan city. Jacobs refers to Lidia as "perhaps the most scholarly and analytical of the hundreds of professional chefs I've known." I think you will have success with these recipes; all the ones I've tried are winners. With sepia photographs, family lore, and a few related essays, this is a unique book about an exceptional person from a special corner of the world.

La Terra Fortunata: The Splendid Food and Wine of Friuli–Venezia Giulia, Italy's Great Undiscovered Region, Fred Plotkin, Broadway Books, 2001. Readers already familiar with food writer and cookbook author Fred Plotkin know that he doesn't simply research and write about food but leaves no stone

unturned, teaching us about Italy's history, language, and traditions and about the central role food plays in the daily life of Italians. (All of Plotkin's food books focus on all or part of Italy: *Recipes from Paradise: Life and Food on the Italian Riviera, The Authentic Pasta Book, Italy for the Gourmet Traveler,* and *Italy Today: The Beautiful Cookbook,* written with Lorenza De'Medici.) *La Terra Fortunata* is the only one of its kind and is positively a must-have. Plotkin notes in the bibliography that when he began his research on this book, he found it remarkable how little material there was (in English; those who read Italian can find a bit more) about Friuli–Venezia Giulia. Most of what he found were recollections of wartime exploits, and some bits and pieces in letters written by some of the many artists and writers who have spent time in the region, such as Joyce, Hemingway, Wagner, and Rilke. Publications about food and wine turned up almost nothing, so Plotkin endeavored "to make this volume the book that this marvelous place deserves." He explains that he felt it was important to quash certain stereotypes and assumptions that most people have about Friuli–Venezia Giulia. "The first is that Friuli–Venezia Giulia is a Germanic/Slavic region that is in Italy by an accident of history. As you can see, this is a region formed by many influences, but it is first and foremost the land of the people who lived there through endless misery and glory. The second is to show you that the language, culture, and food and wine traditions were both created and absorbed, but seldom imposed. Through it all, a regional identity was forged (with Trieste always being a distinct entity) that became essential to survival among a people who did not have the luxury of embracing ideology." In addition to recipes for appetizers; sauces and dressings; eggs and cheese; soups; pasta; polenta, rice, and barley; fish and seafood; meat, poultry and game; vegetables; fruit; and other desserts, there are individual chapters on coffee, grappa, and wines, as well as others devoted to sources for ingredients, and travel in Friuli–Venezia Giulia. The first four introductory chapters of the book address the history, politics, land, and culture of the region, and to my mind these represent the best ninety-eight pages ever written on Friuli–Venezia Giulia and serve as an essential introduction for anyone planning to visit the area. Within these chapters is an A–Z list of no less than sixty-one herbs, spices, bulbs, and plants that are common to this delicious cuisine. "Many food experts agree," Plotkin notes, "that Italy has three great food regions (Emilia-Romagna, Friuli–Venezia Giulia, and Liguria, with Sicily a close fourth) and three great wine regions (Friuli–Venezia Giulia, Piedmont, and Tuscany). So this is the only region in Italy where food and wine are at the same high level." Plotkin ends his introduction to the book by saying that "some people, when I told them I was calling a book about Friuli–Venezia Giulia 'the fortunate land,' thought I was being ironic or even uncaring. Yet in nine years of research I came to realize that I was right. This land, which has been the scene of centuries of wars that have spilled untold amounts of blood, this land, which rumbles with earthquakes causing immense devastation, is nonetheless *una terra fortunata*. Friuli–Venezia Giuilia is a fortunate land because of the people who live on it." This work is not only *essenziale* but tops the list of any bibliography on the region.

La Terra Fortunata: The Splendid Food and Wine of Friuli—Venezia Giulia, Italy's Great Undiscovered Region, Fred Plotkin, Broadway Books, 2001. I've listed this book separately again because Plotkin's coverage of wines is so extensive: in addition to the forty-page chapter entitled "The Vineyard of the World: The Fascinating Wines of Friuli—Venezia Giulia," there is "Discovering the Outstanding Wines of Friuli—Venezia Giulia," a twenty-page outline of some of the notable wine producers of the region. For each entry, Plotkin provides an overview of the various wines each vintner produces as well as contact information. (Note that Venica & Venica, in Dolegna del Collio, not only makes great wines—I tried them for the first time at the *Gambero Rosso*/Slow Food Tre Bicchieri tasting in New York last year—but also offers some *agriturismo* accommodations for travelers.) Also in this chapter, Plotkin provides the addresses for wine consortiums and three *enotechi* worth knowing, as well as some of the best words of advice I've ever encountered about wine: "The key revelation as you approach the marriage of food and wine in Friuli—Venezia Giulia (and anywhere else, for that matter) is that you will discover new things when you combine a sip of wine with a small bite of food. Think about it: Most people eat, chew, and swallow their food, then drink wine, then eat, and so on. They are not truly combining the flavors and discovering the mysteries of the interaction between wine and food. By having a more manageable amount of wine in the glass, this can become possible. Opera, which I love as much as food and wine, is the marriage of words and music. Each on its own is important, but when combined they create something incomparable that resembles neither of the individual components. Once you come to love the fusion of food and wine (you decide which is words and which is music) you will understand why the separate elements are wonderful but the combination is outstanding." And finally, "Wine is first and foremost a source of pleasure, and it should be viewed that way. . . . So gather some friends and family, select yourself a nice bottle, and pour the wine into normal glasses. Admire it, swirl it, breathe it, taste it, and let it slide down your throat as your mouth breaks into a smile. This is the secret to knowing and loving the wines of Friuli—Venezia Giulia."

2000 LIRE DUEMILA
PAGABILI A VISTA AL PORTATORE

1000 LIRE MILLE
PAGABILI A VISTA AL PORTATORE

5000 LIRE CINQUEMILA
PAGABILI A VISTA AL PORTATORE

IL GOVERNATORE
Antonio Fazio
IL CASSIERE

BANCA D'ITALIA

35281

RD 794296 P

RD 794296 P

ITALIA 4000

I Personaggi
(Natives, Expatriates, and Passionate Visitors)

"Many foreigners come back the next year. Some come back more and more often. Some stay a little longer, every time, and decide to live in Italy for a spell. A few eventually discover to their dismay they can no longer leave."

—Luigi Barzini, THE ITALIANS

"The Venetian way is the right way, and the Venetian nearly always knows best . . . for the true son of Venice (and even more, the daughter) is convinced that the skills, arts and sciences of the world ripple outwards, in ever-weakening circles, from the Piazza of St. Mark. If you want to write a book, consult a Venetian professor. If you want to tie a knot in a rope, ask a Venetian how. If you want to know how a bridge is built, look at the Rialto. To learn how to make a cup of coffee, frame a picture, stuff a peacock, phrase a treaty, clean your shoes, sew a button on a blouse, consult the appropriate Venetian authority."

—Jan Morris, THE WORLD OF VENICE

Finding Inspiration from Market to Table with the Queen of Italian Cuisine

BY MARK BITTMAN

editor's note

Though Marcella Hazan's many thousands of fans trust her knowledge of Italian food in general, to my mind she is *the* authority on the cuisine of Venice and the Veneto. In addition to her many cookbooks, for many years she taught cooking classes in her Venice apartment as well as at the Hotel Cipriani's cooking school. I regret never following through with my dream of being a student in one of Marcella's classes, but I content myself with her cookbooks in my kitchen, well-used and oft-consulted. My husband and I have never made a Marcella recipe that didn't turn out exactly as she said it would; the thing to remember is that even her seemingly dull recipes are surprisingly full of flavor: I'll never forget the night I wanted to make a risotto because a friend had just brought me a bag of arborio rice from Venice, but I didn't want to run to the store for any additional ingredients. Searching through Marcella's books, I found a recipe for celery risotto, which may not sound very exciting, but was absolutely delicious.

MARK BITTMAN is the creator and author of the popular weekly column "The Minimalist," which appears in the "Dining In/Dining Out" section of *The New York Times*. He is also the author of *How to Cook Everything* (Macmillan, 1998, a four-time award winner, with over 400,000 copies in print), *Jean-Georges: Cooking at Home with a Four-Star Chef* (Broadway, 1998), *Simple to Spectacular* (Broadway, 2001), *The Minimalist Cooks at Home* (Broadway, 2000), *The Minimalist Cooks Dinner* (Broadway, 2001), and *Fish: The Complete Guide to Buying and Cooking* (Macmillan, 1994). He has also been honored with the coveted IACP (International Association of Culinary Professionals) Bert Greene Memorial Award for best food journalism.

It's not easy to pick Marcella Hazan out in the crowd at the centuries-old Rialto market on Venice's Grand Canal. Unlike other well-known food personalities, she is neither flamboyant nor tall nor an octogenarian nor a television star. In fact, as she selects *canocchie*— a type of Adriatic crustacean not unlike shrimp—she appears to be simply a middle-aged Venetian doing her daily shopping in the jam-packed huddle of stalls that serve this city of 70,000 people.

Marcella, a one-name personality to her admirers, stands out only because of her black sneakers. These are a legacy of half a life spent on her feet in kitchens and in the United States, where sneakers are as common as the pumps and low heels worn by just about every other woman at the Rialto.

When she gets to talking, she is immediately distinguished by her knowledge of food. She points out artichokes in several forms: bottoms only, those in acidulated water, those with stems and those with leaves, a good indicator of freshness. She knows the precise use for each. She chooses a small one to slice raw into a salad. There are fresh porcini by the basketful and other wild mushrooms that she knows intimately. She buys an *ovolo*, an egg-shape white mushroom with a yellow core. They are about $60 a pound, so a single one is roughly $2. Later, she will peel it, shave it on a truffle slicer, and eat it with fresh Parmigiano-Reggiano, olive oil, and lemon juice.

There are varieties of radicchio not seen in the United States. Mrs. Hazan names them all. There are dozens of other fruits and vegetables, common and esoteric; the selection may not be that of a month ago, but it is staggering by American standards. Only *zucca,* a pumpkinlike winter squash, cut and packaged and used for filling pasta, looks fit for a supermarket. For two American visitors Mrs. Hazan buys a small package of *giuggiole,* known as jujubes in English, saying, "You need to try these." These small fruits, some-times also called Chinese dates, are brown, sweet, and acidic.

Then there is the seafood. The Adriatic, a sheltered sea, is justifiably famous for its fish, and the Rialto is the place to buy it; fishing boats begin unloading there (as they used to do at the Fulton Fish Market in lower Manhattan) before dawn each day. The selection is amazing, not just because it is so large but also because nearly every fish is local. There are live fish everywhere: eels are swimming, shrimp are jumping, baby flounder are flipping. There are clams, mussels, crabs, never just one or two species but half a dozen or more. "You have these great fish in the States too," Mrs. Hazan said. "But there you never see them, or you're discouraged from buying them."

Marketing with Mrs. Hazan is instructive, particularly when one considers the powerful influence she has had on a generation of American cooks. Twenty years ago, people who knew how to make spaghetti carbonara considered themselves well versed in Italian cooking. Then along came *The Classic Italian Cookbook* (Knopf, 1976), followed so closely by *More Classic Italian Cooking* (Knopf, 1978) that the two are best considered as a set and have been combined into *Essentials of Classic Italian Cooking* (Knopf, 1995). Thanks to Mrs. Hazan, there were suddenly more "new" Italian recipes than any home cook could possibly use.

There were already Italian cookbooks, of course, and good ones. But none before or since presented recipes that were so clear, simple, and delicious. With her insistence on real Italian ingredients ("Do not under any circumstances use ready-grated cheese sold in jars"), she opened a world to millions of Americans and helped change the way we shop, cook, and eat. Would the Italian food craze have happened without Mrs. Hazan? Probably. Would American cooking be as good, our palates as developed, our demand for good ingredients as strong? Probably not.

Back in Mrs. Hazan's splendidly updated apartment in a five-hundred-year-old building on a typically deceptive Venetian street, her husband and unofficial co-author, Victor, awaits her return. As they cook, it becomes clear that their approach is a combination of rigid-ity and flexibility. She has spent a morning searching for just the right ingredients, but once she begins to put them together, the situation is fluid. There are no measuring cups or spoons, and there is seemingly little precision. This belies Mrs. Hazan's reputation as a dogged recipe tester and Mr. Hazan's as a demanding writer and editor.

"This is cooking, not chemistry," Mrs. Hazan said. "I measure when I'm making a recipe for a book, but even then, I use the average of several measurements; things work differently every time. That's why I tell people it often doesn't make any difference whether you use a cup of something or a half a cup; follow my recipe the first time, then make it your own."

This philosophy, so clearly conveyed in her four books, has enabled her followers to cook decent Italian food and also to learn the spirit that lies behind so much Italian cooking: get your hands on the best ingredients, preferably local ones, and combine them in ways that parade rather than hide their flavors.

Susan Friedland, the editor at HarperCollins who is working on Mrs. Hazan's next book, *Marcella Cucina*, maintains that this combination is what one wants in a teacher or author. "On the one hand," Ms. Friedland said, "she is the quintessential home cook; she doesn't try to create restaurant food, just great-tasting food. On the other, her techniques are impeccable. She is the best guide there is."

When Mrs. Hazan has finished cooking, the couple sit down with their guests to a meal of pasta with clams; *canocchie* with olive oil, parsley, garlic, and bread crumbs; two salmon fillets sandwiched around shrimp, mussels, clams, and seasonings; and bread, salad, berries, and wine. It is all wonderful but disappointingly familiar, until their American visitors realize that they have spent several nights a week for the last twenty years cooking in exactly this style, and it is largely thanks to Mrs. Hazan's cookbooks that they have been able to do so.

Being Everywhere

ANDREA LEE

～

editor's note

The Veneto is reputed to be the wealthiest region of Italy, and Luciano Benetton is one of the region's most successful entrepreneurs.

Keep in mind as you read this piece that it appeared in *The New Yorker* sixteen years ago; but aside from a few dated references, this is an interesting look at the inner world of a giant retail clothing company, the significance of the Veneto region, and the work ethic and creativity of Luciano Benetton, *"una storia di self-made man."*

ANDREA LEE is the author of a number of novels and nonfiction books, including *Russian Journal* (1981), *Sarah Phillips* (1984), *Interesting Women: Stories* (2002), all published by Random House, and, with Ian Frazier, *They Went: The Art and Craft of Travel Writing* (Houghton Mifflin, 1991, in both hardcover and paperback).

Early on a September morning in 1985, five people gathered at the small airport outside the city of Treviso, in northern Italy. They were Luciano Benetton, the head of the international sportswear company that bears his family name and is based in Treviso; Riccardo Weiss, the Benetton area manager in charge of Eastern Europe; Davide Paolini, the public-relations director for Benetton; Renata Sponchiado, an administrative assistant at Benetton who also serves as an Italian-German translator; and I, a writer studying the Benetton corporation. After a few minutes of chatting in the tiny waiting room, empty except for us, we passed through a rudimentary passport control, walked across the airfield, and climbed aboard the Benetton company plane, a Cessna Citation II executive jet. Soon we were flying above the green cornfields and red villages of the Veneto countryside outside Treviso, on a route that would take us north, over Austria and Munich and into Czechoslovakia.

In the eight-seat cabin, Luciano Benetton drank coffee, leafed through two Treviso newspapers, and listened with a calm, attentive expression as Paolini read him choice news stories from other Italian papers. He chuckled at a gossip column chronicling the supposed extravagance of Jacqueline Onassis, then settled down to a discussion of racing-car engines and basketball scores. Benetton, whose leonine curling gray-brown hair and horn-rimmed glasses are familiar to millions of Italians from endless photographs in the press, was dressed in his usual assortment of casual clothes: voluminous khaki pants, brown L. L. Bean–style oxfords, a tweed jacket, and a shirt with a button-down collar. He looked absolutely tranquil, although this was one of the occasions that, as he had remarked in an Italian interview not long before, excited him more than anything else in life: the opening of a Benetton store in a "remote, almost unbelievable" part of the world. We were going that morning to attend a Benetton opening in Prague—an event that would mark the début of the first shop for a Western manufacturer in Czechoslovakia since the inauguration of the Communist regime, in 1948.

The Citation II crossed the Alps: wave after wave—at first, green slopes in sunshine, then slanted shelves of bare rock poking through layers of mist. The clouds got thicker as we traveled north, until we were flying in a muffled gray world; there was the through-the-looking-glass feeling that one often has on approaching Eastern Europe. When we landed at the Prague airport, a cold drizzle was falling. Inside the terminal was a welcoming delegation, including the managers of the new store—one of them a beautiful young Czech woman wearing a Benetton outfit of bright wool, which stood out like a beacon in the drab surroundings. We were passed through customs with the relative ease of official visitors. After circumventing a staring blond horde of Czech travelers, we were soon seated in a small, comfortable bus with a discreet Benetton label on the windshield and riding down a highway lined with posters advertising Aeroflot and Czechoslovak Airlines. Wet green hills and muddy potato fields rolled away from us on either side. In the front of the bus, Luciano Benetton chatted through an interpreter with the Czechs, who leaned toward him looking flushed and tense. Among them, with his kindly, rather abstracted look and tweedy clothes, he resembled a professor in a seminar of nervous students. Watching him, I recalled the final directive in an in-house memo that had been addressed to Benetton staff attending the Prague opening: "Since political authorities will be present, it is advisable to avoid any discussion whatsoever of politics."

As if in response to this thought, our line of traffic was stopped at a temporary roadblock for what grew to be an unconscionable amount of time. After a number of apologies from our Czech hosts, they told us that the president of the Czechoslovak Socialist Republic was passing through, in an elaborate motor cortege, which included big, gleaming finned Chaika limousines, like a vision of the 1950s, and a vast motorcycle escort. The procession brought with it, for an instant, a palpable sense of repression, of the weighty political machinery of the past, which seemed almost a calculated contrast with the spirit of the visiting Italian industrialist, whose company advertising reflects a neo-European style of pacifism, and whose own philosophy, as it's revealed through his work, is a set of inspired variations on simple pragmatism. "What a waste of gas!" Luciano Benetton said softly, looking out the window.

The store in Prague is one of the most exotic offspring of the Benetton Group, the fast-growing twenty-year-old Italian corporation whose sudden appearance and resounding success have caused a medium-size sensation in the international clothing industry and have made Benetton the subject of Harvard Business School case studies. The business of the company is creating stylish Italian casual clothing and marketing it through nearly four thousand Benetton outlets in fifty-seven countries worldwide. Since 1979, when Benetton opened its American campaign, over five hundred stores have opened in the United States—and this figure seems likely to double or triple, since the taste for Benetton clothes is apparently developing from a fad into an institution among fashion-conscious young Americans.

Founded in 1965 as a typical small Italian family enterprise, consisting of Luciano Benetton, his sister, Giuliana, and their younger brothers, Gilberto and Carlo, the Benetton Group is now a complex of manufacturing companies. (Benetton controls, among others, Fiorucci, Inc., the Scottish cashmere company Hogg of Hawick, and the Italian shoe company Calzaturificio di Varese.) It is the world's largest manufacturer of knitwear and the world's largest consumer of virgin wool. Its sales last year totaled $437 million, and the growth of the company is such that a new Benetton franchise opens, somewhere, on the average of twice a day. Behind this phenomenal expansion lies an almost universally appealing product: the bright-colored half-classic, half-modish sportswear designed by Giuliana Benetton, who in the mid-1950s produced the first Benetton sweaters on a home knitting machine. But the main impetus for the extraordinary development of the company has been the marketing genius of Luciano Benetton, eldest brother, chief shareholder, company spokesman, and inspirational force. The Italian press, with its love of fairy-tale nicknames, has christened the four Benettons the Brothers of the Rainbow—a reference to their new-found fortune, and to the many colors that are Benetton's specialty. In addition, the press calls Luciano Benetton the Wizard of Treviso.

"I have never asked myself why I decided to go into business,"

Luciano Benetton remarked to an Italian journalist a few years ago. "The one motivation that, in my opinion, is not valid is an economic one. One doesn't go into business simply to make money." The development of Benetton is in fact a classic rags-to-riches entrepreneurial saga or, as another Italian journalist put it, *"una storia di self-made man."* Viewed from outside, the motivation seems fairly obvious. Luciano was born in 1935 and spent his childhood in the climate of deprivation, bombs, and partisan fighting that the Second World War brought to northeastern Italy. When the war ended, his family developed its own personal tragedy—the illness and death from nephritis of the father, Leone Benetton. The elder Benetton had owned a modest car- and bicycle-rental business; with his death, in 1945, his wife and four young children began a genteel struggle for survival which left the two eldest determined to begin working in early adolescence. Luciano left school at the age of fifteen to take a job in a men's clothing store, and Giuliana, who from childhood had knitted striking sweaters for her family and friends, became, at thirteen, a skein winder in one of many small knitting ateliers in Treviso.

In 1955 Luciano, who had just turned twenty, put into operation the first of the simple, daring schemes that were to make his fortune. He told Giuliana he was convinced that he could market the bright-colored original sweaters she had continued to make as a hobby, so why shouldn't they leave their jobs and start a business? "I felt no fear of failure at the beginning," Luciano said later, in interviews. "When you start with nothing, you don't need to fear failure. And, besides, I had been meditating the idea for five or six years—I had a great deal of time for meditation in the shop. Everything was more or less foreseen."

With thirty thousand lire—the proceeds from the sale of Luciano's accordion and Carlo's bicycle—Luciano and Giuliana bought a knitting machine, and soon afterward Giuliana put together a collection of eighteen pieces. Luciano was immediately able to sell them to local stores. Sales increased steadily over the next few years, until Giuliana had a group of young women working for her and Luciano had bought a minibus to carry these employees to and from a small workshop the Benettons had set up near their home. (A local anecdote has it that Luciano Benetton received a loan for this initial workshop from a priest, who said that by putting poor country girls to work, the Benettons were preventing them from becoming prostitutes in Milan.)

In the early 1960s, Luciano Benetton put into practice several innovative but thoroughly practical ideas that helped turn the company from a small enterprise into a giant. Idea No. 1 was to sell only through specialized knitwear stores (as opposed to department stores and boutiques selling a wide range of clothes), whose owners would presumably be more interested in pushing sales of his particular product. This idea, which eventually developed into that of the Benetton retail outlets, was born when Luciano visited Rome for the Olympics of 1960 and there made the acquaintance of a group of closely related Jewish knitwear merchants, the Anticolis and Tagliacozzos. They subsequently began marketing his clothes. Selling wholesale to this group, Luciano made use of another idea unusual at that time and place: to offer retailers a 10 percent discount if they paid in cash on delivery of his product. At that point, Benetton sweaters did not bear the family name—appealing to the contemporary fondness for things foreign, they had labels like "Lady Godiva" and "Très Jolie"—but they already displayed the Benetton trademark of medium-high quality and stylish design at a mesmerizingly low price. This attractive combination grew out of two more new ideas—this time, ideas for lowering production costs. The first was a novel technique for making wool soft, like cashmere; it was based on a method Luciano had observed while visiting factories in Scotland, where rudimentary machines with wooden paddles beat raw wool in water. The other idea was to buy up and adapt outmoded hosiery-knitting machines, at a price of five thousand dollars apiece. The machines did their new job perfectly; they are still in use and are now valued at almost half a million dollars apiece.

In 1965 Benetton was formed, as Maglificio di Ponzano Veneto dei Fratelli Benetton. Gilberto Benetton was placed in charge of financial strategy, and the youngest brother, Carlo, headed the production system. In the same year, the first Benetton factory went up, in the village of Ponzano, a few kilometers outside Treviso. The factory, highly modern for that time and place, with company parking lots, stores, and lunchrooms, was designed by the well-known Italian architects and designers Afra and Tobia Scarpa, who are themselves natives of the Veneto. During this collaboration, the Scarpas joined the ranks of deeply loyal friends and associates that the company seems to attract. In 1967 they designed the prototypical Benetton store, and the company's first independent outlet opened the following year in the mountain village of Belluno. With its appealing merchandise and its spare, intimate interior—Benetton stores are deliberately small—illuminated by floor-to-ceiling shelves of vibrantly colored sportswear, the shop was an immediate success. Now that the boutique style has conquered America, and bright, small, sparsely furnished stores are the rule even in the remotest suburban mall, it is difficult to imagine how radical a departure the Benetton shop was for Italy in 1968. "It was conceived on the idea of the specialized store, the desire for an alternative to the department store," Luciano later told an American journalist. "We wanted to compete with the department store on a specific level—sportswear. From the beginning, we wanted to create an image—the right people to open our stores, the decor, the colors. We needed lots of colors, because there had to be more than what already existed."

Benetton window design, also developed by the Scarpa team, has an international reputation for starting new trends. At present the windows feature two or three colors combined strikingly in complete outfits, which are displayed not on conventional mannequins but on people-shaped metal forms. Displays are set up not by window dressers but by store managers, who are taught by Benetton area representatives how to tie in their look with whatever advertising campaign Benetton is featuring at the moment. The clothes in the window are set closer to the glass than those on display in other stores and are intended, according to Luciano Benetton, to exert a subtle but cumulative attraction. Company public-relations people quote Benetton as saying, "The first time you pass our windows, you might not notice them. The third time, you go in."

By 1975 the distinctive white-and-green Benetton knitting-stitch logo—designed by the graphic artist Franco Giacometti, who is another longtime Benetton friend and associate—had become the symbol of a phenomenon on the Italian commercial scene. Approximately two hundred Benetton shops had opened in Italy; many of them, but not all, bore the Benetton name. Another of Luciano Benetton's ideas was to have, alongside the classic Benetton shops, variously named stores with differing interiors and differing selections of Benetton clothes, geared to various types of clients. The idea grew out of the intention of avoiding mass flops: if one Benetton store was a failure, others in the same area wouldn't bear the stigma. And today the narrow shopping streets of an Italian provincial town may have, besides a classic Benetton store, a shop of a type called Sisley, which carries higher-priced sportswear; an outlet of the Benetton Tomato chain, which, along with the Benetton Jeans West stores (Benetton entered the jeans market during the denim boom of the mid-1970s), is designed to appeal to teenagers; and an example of the more refined-looking Merceria chain, intended to appeal to the parents of Jeans West customers. Far from glutting the market, this clustering of stores selling basically similar products turned out to promote a profitable sense of competition among shopkeepers, and so it is now an established Benetton strategy. (It is used in America, although besides several variations on the classic green-and-white shop, only Sisley and a children's store called 012 exist in the United States; in New York, on Fifth Avenue alone there are eight Benetton stores.)

In the early 1970s came the development of Benetton's perhaps most widely publicized production technique—one that, like most of Luciano Benetton's ideas, seems completely practical and almost obvious. This was the dyeing of assembled garments rather than yarn. A certain percentage of an item of clothing produced in undyed gray—say, a tabard-front wool sweater—is kept on hand in the dyeing rooms of the Ponzano factory until reports from the stores come in. Then small batches of it are dyed the colors most requested that season. (Benetton became among the first Italian manufacturers to computerize operations—a move facilitating this kind of quick turnaround.) The process is slightly more expensive but has the advantage of allowing production to respond quickly to public demand; Benetton spokesmen claim that they can have requested colors in the stores within ten days. It also allows the company to maintain almost no inventory and to produce mainly to order, in a European version of the Japanese *kanban* system. In interviews with the Italian press, Luciano Benetton has said he feels that if there is one secret of his company's success, it is "the assurance of swift re-selection and stocking." "We try to adjust to the market quickly," he told a journalist for Time-Life in 1984. "In fashion, it's true that one normally tries to impose something to make it easier, but I think the customer has to be respected. He's the one who decides, the arbiter of the situation."

What Benetton was offering clearly appealed to a lot of people. In 1978 the company realized $78 million in sales—almost exclusively in Italy, where opportunities for continued high growth were diminishing. Benetton's solution to that problem was to launch a major export campaign to the rest of Europe, and in the early 1980s all the young women in the countries of the Common Market seemed to be buying Benetton sportswear—including media darlings like Princess Caroline of Monaco and Diana, Princess of Wales. The latter unintentionally gave Benetton worldwide publicity when a sales clerk who did not recognize her refused to allow her to return a sweater to a Knightsbridge Benetton shop. By 1982 sales had exploded to $311 million, and a full-fledged international campaign was launched, raising the number of Benetton stores to its current level.

There are Benetton stores throughout Japan, and in Peru, but the big goal for the company remains the conquest of the United States, where Luciano Benetton would eventually like to see four thousand shops. The marketing organization for America is similar to that for Europe: the country is split into regions, each in the care of an agent, who takes orders for the retail outlets, appoints new shopkeepers, and conveys market information to Benetton headquarters. The small green-and-white Benetton shops springing up in cities and suburban malls are not classic franchises. The retailers who set them up make no formal agreement other than to buy exclusively from Benetton and to conform to a strict set of standards, on everything from merchandising to window display. They do not pay royalties; nor does the parent company invest its own money in the stores. A peculiarly Benetton feature of this system is that store operators are not required to have any merchandising experience—only something that Luciano Benetton has described as "the right spirit" to operate one of his shops.

That spirit might be summed up as youthful, progressive, stylish, but not avant-garde—a collection of qualities that allows the most far-flung of the Benetton shops to reproduce the successful and appealing formula devised by the brains back in Treviso. In an interview with the Italian business magazine *Capital*, Luciano Benetton said, "The classic shopkeeper had to be killed, and we killed him." In his place might be a former hairdresser or florist or philosophy student, carefully chosen for his sympathetic style and attitude by a regional agent reporting directly to Luciano Benetton. "The real strength of our company," Benetton added, "is that of a group that has accepted the same politic of production and sales."

Any company that is marketing fashion keeps a tight control over image, but Benetton seems to do better than most in presenting manufacturer and product as a very attractive whole. The four photogenic Benettons (Luciano, Giuliana, Gilberto, and Carlo have a thick-haired, fresh-faced, perennially youthful kind of good looks, not unlike those of the Kennedy family) have become media favorites in Italy. Although, with the justified paranoia of the Italian rich, they keep their family lives extremely private, there are official photographs of them constantly in circulation; they are shown at sporting events (Benetton sponsors a Treviso basketball team and two Formula One racing cars), in the airy spaces of their Scarpa-designed factories, in a frescoed seventeenth-century country villa that houses the company headquarters. In the United States the Benettons have sponsored an exhibition of the Scarpas' designs, donated T-shirts to Harlem preschoolers, and collaborated in the USA for Africa effort. Even Italians seem bowled over by their ubiquity in the press, some cynics regarding them, with their air of wholesome good health, the way similar Americans might eye the Osmond family. "Every time I open a magazine, I see the four Benettons grinning and holding hands," a young Florentine remarked at a dinner party recently. "I'm waiting for Luciano Benetton to make the cover of *International Boy Scout*."

Nothing did more to fix the image of Benetton in the eyes of the world than two stunning advertising campaigns conceived and photographed by Oliviero Toscani, another of Benetton's brilliant associates. The first series, run in 1983–84, showed crowds of children of all races and nationalities wearing Benetton clothes. The slogan was "Benetton—All the Colors in the World." The second ad campaign, with the slogan "United Colors of Benetton," appeared in 1985 and showed the same international, interracial crowds of children wearing Benetton clothes, and the flags of various countries (not necessarily the countries that the looks of the children would indicate). The children are tumbled together in large, embracing groups, or in significant pairs, such as U.S.A. with U.S.S.R. Toscani gained notoriety in Italy some years ago for his controversial Jesus Jeans campaign. (The advertisements showed a curvaceous jeans-clad female rear and bore the biblical-sounding quotation "He who loves me follows me.") With the Benetton ads, he launched a minor fad for casually bunched crowds in fashion advertising. The pictures hover close to sentimentality but never cross the line. They are saved by a neo-European post-punk look, recalling the quirky, half-classic, nongarish fashion one sees now in the most recent European rock-and-roll videos. Like many of these music videos, which feature racially mixed groups and cross-cultural music with lyrics that have turned away from the nihilist frettings of a few years back, the Benetton ads convey an offhand, low-key idealism, sprung almost reluctantly from a young generation whose first impulse is to be cynical.

Luciano Benetton travels a lot, and when he travels he spends a lot of time walking the sidewalks of the cities of the world studying the surges and dips of street fashion and trying to detect the buzz in the air that signals the direction of popular trends. The Benetton specialty—quick feedback—goes beyond orders for sweaters: in advertising, the company image is an up-to-the-minute reflection of mass youth culture. It would not be going too far to say that the Toscani ad campaigns strike the exact note of the young mood in Europe in the mid-1980s, in which a kind of survivalist pragmatism—born of the new conservatism, nuclear worries, and everincreasing unemployment figures—is balanced with a cautious altruism. They reflect as well the eclectic feel of a Europe flooded with non-European races and cultures. The open stress that the company lays on its techniques of mass production—"It's industrial fashion," Luciano Benetton remarks in interview after interview—comes over as a wry, stylish "in" joke to a generation raised with high technology. The sales message—bright, convenient, not exactly classic clothes at a medium price for bright, young, not exactly classic people—has identified and attracted a whole new world of consumers and spawned a host of imitators. On both sides of the globe, sportswear manufacturers like Stefanel (another family business from the Veneto region), New Man, and Esprit (whom Toscani has furnished with a striking series of new-look ads) are tapping the rich Benetton market—selling vivid colors, medium prices, and a vibrant present-tense image to crowds of willing young consumers.

In the summer of 1985, two months before the first Benetton store opened in Prague, I visited the company headquarters, in the village of Ponzano, outside Treviso, to tour some of the factories and to chat with Luciano Benetton. The Villa Minelli, which houses the headquarters, is an important part of the Benetton image and can also be seen as a symbol of the relation of the organization to the part of Italian society from which it grew. Built for the patrician Minelli family in the early seventeenth century, the villa belongs to the white-and-gold ranks of Palladian and pre-Palladian summer residences on the Veneto peninsula, where noble Venetians passed a yearly *villeggiatura* away from the suffocating heat of August and September on the Rialto; the sight of it evokes the centuries that the area spent under the efficient bureaucratic domination of the Most Serene Republic of Venice, whose doges and diplomats came and went on the archipelago only seventeen miles away.

When the first Benetton factory was constructed nearby, in 1965, the villa was in a ruinous state after a hundred years of neglect that had seen it housing an array of inelegant tenants: chickens, silkworms, wartime evacuees from Treviso, British commandos. Five years after designing the Ponzano factory and overseeing its construction, the Scarpas undertook the restoration of the villa next door. This they did with an eye to achieving strict authenticity: they used replacement materials from other ruined villas of the Veneto region and employed seventeenth-century plastering techniques. The villa consists of a main residence, a barn, a small church, and the so-called Feste building, where the Minelli family entertained, and today all four buildings stand handsomely restored: white and airy on the outside and on the inside teeming with lovely frescoes, attributed in part to the seventeenth-century painter Michelangelo Muraro. These frescoes, done largely in mellow ochre-gold and brick-red tints, depict cherubs, floral flourishes, landscapes, and tumbling Titans, and they are crowded so close on walls and ceilings that some rooms have the embroidered look of a Tibetan tent. Entering the main building, which houses the Benetton executive offices, is like walking into a half-Oriental, half-Venetian dream. Below the frescoes, however, computer screens blink, and the rooms, which have Persian rugs on hand-burnished Tavelle-tile floors, hold ultramodern Italian office furniture in sparse groupings that suggest a New York– or Milan-style preference for uncluttered space.

Immediately in front of the villa courtyard is a parking lot with a guardhouse and an electronic gate, and a few hundred yards away is a low, Oz-like metal-towered roofline. This is the roofline of the factory designed by the Scarpas; in the 1980s, it still surprises. On the summer day I visited the villa, the sun shone on roses and a close-trimmed green lawn in the courtyard, and a number of attractive, earnest-looking young people, wearing loose clothing in bright primary colors, were walking back and forth outdoors between offices in the former barn and the Feste building. The entire scene, with its mixture of elegant rusticity and the appurtenances of high technology, was like a concoction worthy of the *Serenissima Repubblica* itself, whose shrewd merchants, in their heyday, knew best of all how to interweave beauty and big business. The Benetton headquarters, in fact, gives the impression not of a garment manufacturer's headquarters but of a sort of utopian university—an impression that seemed to me to connect, in some not altogether reliable way, with the fact that Luciano Benetton looks more like a scholar than an entrepreneur.

People who work at intermediate levels of the Benetton organization tend to use the words "new," "fresh," and "clear" in describing the company or the man behind it. For example, a young French area representative who was also visiting the headquarters that day said to me, in explaining why she had left her previous job, in public relations at a French department store, "I was bored where I was. It seemed old, and what Benetton was doing seemed fresh."

Earlier that day Tobia Scarpa had said when I called him to ask his impressions of the man who has been his friend and associate for nearly twenty years, "Luciano Benetton is one of the few men I know who are able to suspend sentimentality—and we Italians are very sentimental—and achieve absolute clarity of mind."

Talking to Benetton in his office, I saw that clarity immediately. Low-voiced, with the scrupulous politeness of a born introvert who has become a public figure, he answered every question not with the rote precision one might expect from a man who has been interviewed so many times but in a manner that conveyed a quick, almost inspired feeling of real concentration on the subject. Physically, Benetton is a combination of opposite qualities. Over six feet tall, with the bursting mass of thick hair that seems to be a family trait, and the look of superabundant vitality that marks a natural athlete, he has a longilinear face whose slightly ascetic features suggest a tremendous cerebral energy. Behind the horn-rimmed glasses that have become his trademark, his blue eyes seem remote but not cold. When he talks, he seems to be constantly in the process of returning from some interior vision that is ampler and more satisfying than the world around him. Some journalists have said he looks like Gustav Mahler. One gets the feeling that this comparison would embarrass Benetton, whose every social impulse seems to be one of self-effacement. In a 1982 interview in the Italian press, he described himself as "one who prefers to listen and to meditate rather than to talk." Yet when Benetton does talk, he asks questions and speaks of sweeping business moves with a matter-of-fact aggressiveness and a dynamic grasp of practical detail that make it clear that his talent is not simply for theory—that his is one of the personalities with the curious knack of bringing big ideas to life.

In Luciano Benetton's office—typically, he has chosen a small, rather plain upstairs room in the villa—there is little decoration: just a few red-and-ochre putti in a fresco, a photograph of his four handsome children (Benetton and his wife are separated), and two maps of the world. With us when we talked were his eldest son, Mauro, a shy, affable young man with the family look of exuberant good health, and Sally Fischer, a bilingual Benetton press officer, there to smooth out any language difficulties.

I began by asking about the international expansion of the company, which has many people predicting that it will be another McDonald's. Was that in fact what he wanted? For a minute, he looked amused, and then he spoke with his characteristic intense seriousness: "Not McDonald's for the same level of goods, the same consumer, but, yes, for the distribution all over the world. I would like us to be everywhere. Another company we might compare ourselves to might be Coca-Cola or Pepsi-Cola, since we aim our product at young people. The idea behind Benetton—which is basically that of mass-produced, medium-priced fashion that moves with the trends yet maintains something classic—has not changed since our clothing started to become not just a strictly European product but a product for the whole world. In America, in Australia, in Japan— where we envision having two hundred shops—it has been consistently accepted. In all these countries, the prototype client remains the same—young and female. Naturally, there are regional differences. In America, for example, we reach a public a little different from that in Europe—a more sophisticated public, which travels, and might have seen the product first in Europe."

We began to talk about the Benetton plans for expansion into America, and Luciano said that the organization, which recently raised an international syndicated loan with Citibank for $30 million, expects to be listed on the New York Stock Exchange within two years (since June of 1986, it has been an active player on the Milan Borsa). Another Benetton strategy for the United States, he said, included the setting up of a Benetton factory on American soil—a step designed to help circumvent high import taxes that make Benetton more than medium-priced in the New World. (The factory, in North Carolina, was completed earlier this year.) Another move designed uniquely for American shopping customs, Benetton said, was the creation of a series of mail-order catalogues, with photographs by Toscani.

Talk about the catalogue led to talk about the two famous Oliviero Toscani ad campaigns. Benetton smiled. "Several years ago Oliviero came up with the same image for a photographic feature in the Italian *Vogue*," he said. "All the colors in the world, the children. Later, it naturally fitted with Benetton. We are definitely interested in peace and a kind of universalism. Our clothes are appealing in very different countries, and people who consume the same product have one more way of understanding each other. We wanted to make it possible for young people who don't have much money to have the most fashion for the most democratic price, to be able to change styles two or three times a year at low cost. This isn't just dreaming. It is a practical way to arrange things."

When Benetton talked about matters like the company image and world peace, he used a calm, grave, interested voice, and he used the same voice when, a bit later, he began talking about his personal role in the company. For him, as for many entrepreneurs, the line between business and personal life is a blurred one. He spends hours in consultation with one or another of his siblings, and the four work so constantly together that they prefer not to see each other much outside the office. Half his time he is in Treviso, where he spends twelve-hour days at the office; the other half is spent traveling around the world, selecting future store sites, attending openings of the new stores, and checking the progress of existing stores.

The life seems to suit him. When I asked how he would describe himself, he laughed, looked down, and finally said, "Everyone thinks he is unique, very different from everybody else. But I think of myself as a normal person, with a character that is fairly easy to understand. And the reason is, really, that I am a happy person, a satisfied person, because I have done and continue to do work that I like. Because of that, I don't have any problems. I like people who are stimulating, who have some of my own characteristics—who always look a little bit ahead, who try to see things in perspective, to get a sense of how things happen."

"Was there anyone in your family, or among your friends, who helped inspire you to do what you've done?" I asked.

Benetton put his square hands flat on the table and leaned toward me.

"In our family, there was no one previously who did this kind of work, but in character, yes, there was someone who inspired me. It would have been our father. He was very creative. Only, he died before achieving what he might have. His story was one that might have been very similar to mine. He was a person rich in capacity, perhaps in fantasy, and in his *volontà*, his willingness and desire. It was at a moment during the war, however, when it was hard to do things, when life was precarious. In business there has been for us no one real mentor, but it's certainly true that, thanks to relationships we've had, we've been enriched, enhanced—that, sure. We've had very special acquaintances, encounters, in which we've had faith, and they have inspired us, because this type of work, simplified to the minimum level, implies a rapport. It is not a traditional rapport, not one made of written documents, of concessions, of lawyers, and so on. It is really a rapport made of handshakes, of understanding and knowledge on a human level, and also of extreme faith, total faith. Of that kind of person we've found many. Let's say that we work only with people whom we like on a human level. This has never been said before, but we're not interested in being represented in a city, in being represented at all, if the partner isn't to our liking. We're interested only if we find a person who has our philosophy. If not . . ." He waved a hand.

"And Treviso?" I asked. "How would you say that growing up here might have influenced you?"

For a minute, Benetton, for the first time, seemed at a loss for words. "Treviso is . . . a city of ninety thousand people," he said.

"Everybody knows everybody else; one lives here peacefully, without many problems. We came from a family that was unusual, that did have problems—because we had very little money. This fact probably shows up in our work, and in its results. With us, the work somehow took the place of the myth of America—it is a myth, no?—for the young Italian. Well, there is not always a need to emigrate; America can also be here, in this small provincial city, or in Japan, or Australia—America can be anywhere, if only one is willing to evoke it on one's own."

We were going to have lunch together in a small country restaurant where Benetton eats every day, but first I went for a tour of some of the Benetton factories. At the Ponzano plant, next to the Villa Minelli, I watched workers at computer screens draw colored patterns, which were then transferred to thunderous knitting machines with bright cones of yarn on top. In the dye rooms, reeking of damp wool, mountains of grayish sweaters lay waiting to assume colors on store demand. At a factory in a nearby village called Villorba, a young man wearing horn-rims and collegiate clothes, like Luciano Benetton, showed me how he made changes in computerized designs with an electronic pen to produce a pattern that is eventually used for cutting two hundred layers of fabric at once. Two computer disks can hold the models of, say, all T-shirts produced in the last four years, so that they can be summoned for updating or change. And in the village of Castrette, at the new, $25 million Benetton warehouse—the pride of the company, and said to be one of the most advanced warehouses in the world—I watched computerized robot arms piling boxes on twenty-meter-tall moving storage shelves, colored bright yellow, green, and red, like huge Tinkertoys. Each of the factories had the pleasant, livable modern design that seems to be a Scarpa specialty, and each fitted comfortably into the countryside near Venice, a landscape that is still largely small-town and rural. Through an open door in the vast, smoothly churning complex at Castrette, I could see part of a green cornfield, one of the brick-red farmhouses of the Veneto, and a road where an old woman in black, wearing a straw hat, was bicycling slowly by.

The heart of this landscape, and of the Benetton phenomenon, is the small city of Treviso. It is hardly possible to take a walk through Treviso and not be aware, at least on a subliminal level, of Benetton. There are nine shops tucked under the arcades of the winding medieval streets or among the apartment houses outside the ancient city walls, and Trevisans speak of the company with an almost familial assumption of intimacy. Treviso (the name comes from the Latin Tarvisium) is a beautiful old provincial town of Veneto, not overwhelming in its good looks, like Verona or Padua, but with a pleasant, tranquil sense of solidity joining its pastiche of medieval, *settecento,* and modern architecture, and its jumbled history, which leads from misty Aryan-Illyrian beginnings, through long stints under the hand of the Roman Empire and then the hand of the Most Serene Republic of Venice, to bombardment during two world wars.

If one scans a history of the Venetian Empire, one finds Treviso playing the role of an always-rather-unlucky handmaiden to the opulent neighboring city on the lagoon: various middle European barbarians sweep down on Treviso; plots to unseat doges are hatched there; foreign dukes and princes test their military strength against its much-battered walls, since Venice itself is unassailable. If Venice was founded by men fleeing the Dark Age perils of the mainland, Treviso was built, in part, by those who stayed behind: men with the commercial genius and maritime talents of the Venetians, but sturdier, and rooted, too, in agricultural life; able to stand being washed about a bit in the currents of history. The city lies at the juncture of the Sile and the Botteniga Rivers, on the flat, well-watered plain, covered with vines and cornfields (this is polenta territory), that runs from the archipelago of Venice to the foothills of the Dolomites. Dante mentions Treviso in *The Divine Comedy,* and his son and Petrarch's daughter are buried there. If one walks through the Piazza dei Signori, with its faintly Oriental diapered-stone palace, and along the several streams and canals lined with frescoed houses and brick walls inset with the lion of Saint Mark, one has the impression of calm daily life informed always by richness of design.

The beauty of Treviso, like that of Venice, has always been wedded to an intense practicality. Over the centuries, as part of the efficient bureaucracy of the *Serenissima,* the town grew to be a secondary commercial center for the mainland, and its fields served as the breadbasket for Venice. Nowadays, Treviso and its outlying villages are home to a number of enterprises—Benetton is one of the largest—that have helped to make the modern province of Veneto a vital part of the Third Italy, the newly developed northeastern and central industrial zone that since the Second World War has shown the fastest rate of economic growth in the country.

The development of Benetton is, in fact, only a rather flamboyant example of an interesting process of industrial expansion that has been going on in the villages and towns of previously agricultural regions near Ancona, Florence, Bologna, and Venice. Economists have named this changing area the Third Italy to distinguish it from the older triangle of industry defined by Milan, Turin, and Genoa—the Second Italy. (The First is the agrarian center and the south.) For Italians and foreigners alike, mere mention of the Second Italy conjures up visions of smoky skies and names like Agnelli, Pirelli, and Olivetti. Although Italian economic reporting can be slow and imprecise—annual reports for IRI, the huge state company that controls everything from highways to telephones, are sometimes published eighteen months late—it is still possible to see from available information that the industrial emergence of the Third Italy is a major national trend.

The most recent comprehensive overview of Italian industry, a 1981 census of companies compiled by the Istituto Centrale di Statistica—and, typically, published only in July 1985—makes the point. In the decade 1971–81, Italy, in spite of wobbly governments and rampant inflation, saw a rate of growth faster than that of any of its partners in the Common Market—growth, particularly, in entrepreneurial activity, which led to the foundation of nearly 900,000 new businesses in the period. Most of this phenomenal growth took place in the Third Italy, which in 1981 held a total of a million firms, as opposed to two and a half million for the entire rest of the country.

The industrial expansion in the region is more than fast. It is a different kind of growth, fascinating to both Italian and foreign economists. The enterprises springing up cover the spectrum of contemporary industry, with products ranging from shoes and clothing to automotive parts. They are not clumped together in clearly defined "gray zones" but spread out among villages and small towns, not displacing the native agriculture but coexisting with it. (The image that Italian journalists constantly use to describe the layout is that of a network, or net.) This is possible because most of the new firms are medium-size or very small—many with fewer than ten employees. Yet they are not the artisans' workshops of the past (although many of them are family-run) but technologically advanced collections of workers and equipment, with some of the highest rates of production and earnings in the country.

In a recent study of small businesses in Italy, the economist Michael J. Piore and the political scientist Charles F. Sabel, both of

MIT, write that this new economic model grew up mainly as an answer to the tough conditions imposed on Italian firms by powerful labor unions in the late 1960s and early 1970s; another factor was the high social-welfare taxes—recently as high as 49 percent of wages—that the Italian government forces employers to pay for each worker employed. Moreover, peculiarities of collective bargaining in Italy made it essentially impossible to lay off workers if market demand should require a decline in production. The only way for a company to raise production temporarily without running the risk of increasing its permanent labor force was to make greater use of nonunion alternatives. In response, big businesses began to rely increasingly on the unofficial work that Italians call *lavoro nero:* subcontracting jobs out to firms employing under fifteen people—the legal limit for the size of a company subject to union and state control. Many of the small units were simply sweatshops, or workshops that provided a flexible labor force for the parent firm, but gradually a collection of independent small companies developed, with their own specialized markets, first at home and then abroad. Unhampered by government or unions—the trade unions first showed a sagacious restraint and then, in true Italian fashion, worked out an unofficial modus vivendi with the newcomers—the young firms boasted a high rate of production, based on increasingly efficient (sometimes miniaturized, sometimes computerized) manufacturing techniques. Today, their working conditions and pay scales usually meet union standards; in fact, as in every other sector of Italian life, an orderly solution to a problem has been found by circumventing the established order. According to Sabel and Piore, the new-style companies are able to respond closely to market trends, manufacturing almost entirely on demand; their profitability as a group reveals itself in their success in foreign markets, and, at home, in rising wage levels, technological development, and investments. Highly adaptable, most of them were able to ride out the Italian economic downturn of 1982–83 and move forward with renewed energy into the mid-1980s.

What all this has to do with Benetton comes into focus when one realizes that the company delegates a large percentage of its work to a network of contractors and subcontractors. The company tours don't include small nonunion workshops clustered around the Benetton plants, but according to a Harvard Business School study of Benetton, by 1983 payments for contract work equaled nearly six times the labor expense for work performed in the factories. That year subcontractors performed about 40 percent of the knitting of wool, 60 percent of the garment assembly, and 20 percent of the finishing operations. The use of a flexible freelance labor force puts Benetton in the company of other large firms in the Third Italy that channel their work away from union and government restrictions and enjoy the advantages of a production staff that moves with market demand. And with its family management, artisan roots, emphasis on front-line technology, and smooth fit into the surrounding countryside, Benetton is an example on a grand scale of the new kind of industry growing up among the fields and small towns of northern Italy.

Some proud Venetians claim that their province led the way in what the Italian press calls the miracle of the Third Italy. They say that the new-style economic model was anticipated by *il modello Veneto*. Whatever the case, the postwar growth—intensified during the 1970s, as in other parts of central and northeastern Italy—that increased industrial employment in the Veneto by 235 percent between 1951 and 1981 was unquestionably rooted in certain enduring traits of the Venetian character and landscape. When, before visiting the Benetton headquarters, I spoke with an Italian banker who specializes in relations with banks in the Veneto region (he prefers that I not mention his name), he emphasized the peasant, agricultural background of the new Venetian businesses. "With the exception of Venice and the port of Marghera, the Veneto was primarily an agricultural area until the Second World War," he said. "It had no industrial tradition, no experience of syndicalism, little real trade-union strength compared with other areas in Italy. When it made the jump into the modern industrial age, the businesses that sprang up had a peasant, agricultural structure—usually a paterfamilias and a family work force. Then there is the incredible creativity of the Venetians. Every little locality specializes in one product or another. A Venetian peasant might find a broken-down refrigerator and, from a starting point as small as that, build up a huge volume of business selling cheap appliances that he has rebuilt."

In a report on Veneto in the Italian business daily *Il Sole–24 Ore,* the journalist Dante Ferrari writes that the industrial explosion in the region was encouraged by a strong artisan tradition, by an abundance of labor left from a shrinking agriculture, by hydraulic energy provided by the many rivers and springs, and by a long history of polycentrism—Veneto is evenly dotted with solid, medium-size towns like Treviso—which helped construct the diffused network of industrial units characteristic of the Third Italy. Ferrari also discusses the Venetian character, which he and other Italians describe in terms that Americans might use for New Englanders, or the British might use for Scots: close-lipped, religious, clannish, hardworking, politically conservative, but with odd flashes of radical idealism. Added to these traits are an instinctive distrust of pomp, chatter, and servility, a talent for driving a hard bargain, and an ingrained veneration for thrift. "The towns of the Veneto have this peculiarity," Ferrari writes. "Savings-and-loan banks in the countryside, as with small regional banks, exert . . . moral influence and guidance under the shadow of the church towers. The idea of saving is not only a goal of many people but also a sign of distinction and of nobility, an aspiration felt by everyone, both rich and poor."

Ferrari could have expanded the discussion by mentioning the psychological legacy of the Most Serene Republic of Venice, the nation that perhaps more than any other, before or since, identified itself with commerce, and whose inhabitants seemed to carry in their bloodstream a curiously commingled fascination with profit and with travel. Although it would be romantic rather than illuminating to portray present-day businessmen of the Veneto mainland as heirs to Marco Polo or as modern variations on Shakespeare's Antonio, it is still useful to be aware of the weight of a tradition that gave rise to literature and legend. The phenomenal receptiveness of these small-town businesses to sophisticated marketing and manufacturing techniques and their ability to envision themselves in terms of international markets become more comprehensible if one invokes the memory of past governors for whom, even through the medieval hurly-burly of war and intrigue, world trade was as essential as military action. "One of the secrets of Venice's rise to power lay in the fact that she never saw the twin necessities of defense and commerce as altogether separate," John Julius Norwich writes in *A History of Venice*. "Her war captains . . . were never averse to trading on the side. . . . In feudal Europe, where the fighting nobility remained haughtily aloof from trade, such a system would have been unthinkable, but in Venice there was no separate military caste; the nobles were merchants, the merchants noble, and the interests of both were identical."

Once one begins to look at the region around Benetton, the structure and growth of the firm seem logical, inevitable, making up a fabric as authentically Venetian, as Third Italian, as a Benetton sweater. (Appropriately, many economic descriptions of the area make use of the homely metaphor of knitting.) What has made Benetton bigger and faster than the others is, at least in part, that the imagination of Luciano Benetton has been bigger and worked faster; and this very identification of a company with a personality is part of the classic design. It is also at the base of one pressing question facing Benetton and similar young Italian giants: that of growth and succession. Dante Ferrari puts it very well. "In Veneto," he writes, "the person who gives the orders is the owner, and not simply the manager . . . and the problem that presents itself now is that of the passage between generations. The proprietors of today's big firms were, twenty years ago, employees, or artisans, or, more likely, small-scale producers or dealers . . . people, in short, who were used to being completely in charge of management, with simple but solid rules. Today the members of this generation are beginning to have gray hair and govern in general small- or medium-size businesses with great productivity—but they give orders in the name of a credibility more closely linked to an individual person than to the firm itself. Who will take over the leadership of these companies?" Ferrari's answer is a sentimental invocation of the strength of tradition and family ties for the Venetian: "No region of Italy has succeeded in keeping father and son united as has the Veneto."

For the future of a company like Benetton, the real answer probably involves a strong continued family direction combined with a public offering of shares. A Milanese banker whom I telephoned after my trip to Treviso told me that he expects to see a shift toward greater regionalization of Benetton management and production as the company grows bigger; perhaps, given the strength of the Benetton information systems, it will be possible to have an international firm with the feeling of a small business. When, during our drive to lunch, I asked Luciano Benetton whether the family members expected their children to go into the business, he said that he was exerting no pressure in that direction. "In the second generation, there are fifteen," he said. "I think it's better that each one express his own personality. Later, there might be a possibility of some of them entering the firm, and if so, we'll be fortunate." Some younger Benettons are already intimately involved with the business, as might be expected: Luciano's son Mauro, whom I had just met, is a production manager for Benetton's Sisley division; and two of Giuliana's daughters attended the summer program at the Fashion Institute of Technology this year.

The car in which Luciano Benetton drove me to lunch was an unobtrusive Alfa Romeo sedan, but it was armored and moved along like a tank. He has been the subject of a kidnapping attempt, and three years ago he was held hostage at gunpoint in his house—an experience that forced him to move from the country into a small, easily guarded house in the very center of Treviso. It struck me as incongruous to be thinking of brigands and bulletproof glass while driving between flat Veneto cornfields that suggest nothing so much as North Carolina, but the sight of smallish modern factories at every crossroads reminded me of the tremendous concentration of new wealth in the area. Lunch was at Da Sergio, a tiny restaurant that forms yet another Benetton-family-style circle: it is owned and staffed, Luciano told me, by a husband and wife and their two sons, and at lunchtime, when it is nearly all filled with Benetton staff, it has the clubby, intimate feel of a neighborhood hangout.

As we entered the simply furnished, low-ceilinged room, there occurred among the people eating lunch not exactly a hush—as a boss, Luciano Benetton seems so resolutely democratic that one feels he would be unhappy if a hush were to fall—but a transformation in the set of eyes, of shoulders, which implied that the most crucial person had entered. *"Buon giorno, Signor Luciano,"* said the adolescent waiter, coming up to us with a quick deferential smile. Like all of Benetton's employees and many of his local acquaintances, the waiter addressed him with the "Signor" plus first name—a style that in Italian suggests a formalized and respectful intimacy, often with someone of higher rank. It is a legitimate way of addressing an especially accessible *padrone* and carries strong patriarchal overtones. Benetton sat down at a side table and ordered a frugal lunch of *pomodoro con riso* and a plate of zucchini and green beans. We began to talk about the Treviso basketball team that Benetton sponsors—on the flat Venetian plain, as in the American Midwest, basketball is a big sport. All three of the Benetton brothers play, and Luciano, as he often tells reporters, was never the best player but was always the captain of the team. Then Benetton talked about the company plans for Eastern Europe. "It's taken a lot of time and planning," he said. "But now we have stores in Belgrade and Budapest. Success for us would obviously not be to fill the Eastern bloc with stores on a Western scale. It would be to have perhaps twenty stores, in the major cities—yes, even in Moscow. The Yugoslavian and Hungarian openings have broken the ice: they were both successes, and they created perhaps not a potential market but at least a rapport. Moscow has already made the initial overtures. The rapport with them can be a bit strange, though, because the people in charge of fashion sometimes turn out to be engineers."

Benetton was interested to learn that I had spent time in Russia, which is one of the few countries he has never visited, and as he ate his lunch and drank a single glass of wine, he questioned me closely about life there. The questions he asked were practical and to the point. What was a typical Russian evening with friends? What did they eat? What did they wear? Was it true, as he had been told, that there were no displays in store windows—that most clothing stores were on the second floor, and not at street level? His face as he accepted or rejected each piece of information as useful was animated, even illuminated, by an almost sportive intellectual enjoyment—the kind a bright young student might unwittingly display, revelling in his power to grasp new facts. It was clear that this gathering of information for meditation and eventual use was a great pleasure to him and was linked to a bigger vision, which gave him a tremendous sense of excitement and well-being. He forgot about me for a minute and went off into his own thoughts, and as I watched him, I felt closer than at any time previously to the wide range of imagination, the clarity of thought that people who know him well always mention, at one point or another, in descriptions of him. He touched his glasses, pushed back his plate of beans and zucchini, and stared down at his hands, which he cupped on the table—it was as though all Russia, all Eastern Europe, were a problematical small contraption that he was holding. He said slowly, still looking down, "It would be fascinating to open up that closed box."

The first Benetton store to open in Czechoslovakia was not in the main shopping area of Prague but on Rezniká Street, a side street in a rather quiet neighborhood that held a few innovative shops. (An Italian-style *gelateria* was one of them.) As I flew in with the Benetton delegation from Italy—Luciano Benetton, Riccardo Weiss, Davide Paolini, and Renata Sponchiado—I learned that the Czech government had initially not wanted the store within the city limits at all. It had first planned to allot space only in a suburb; had then, after more negotiation, agreed to open the shop in an outlying area of the city; and finally, had located the outlet in this central but not heavily commercial area. Our bus ride from the airport that morning took us across the Vltava and into the lovely tangle of spires and peaked roofs that is the old city. Riding through the rainy streets filled with traffic and fair-haired pedestrians, I experienced the sense of otherworldliness I always feel in Eastern Europe.

It was strange, in those urban surroundings where advertising and commercial display are restricted to an almost nineteenth-century sobriety, to catch sight of the familiar green-and-white exterior of a Benetton store. Above the front door hung a small sign that read "TUZEX," the word that denotes hard-currency stores in

Czechoslovakia. (As in certain types of *Beriozka* stores in the Soviet Union, where scarce goods are available only for foreign money, customers who shop in Tuzex stores in Czechoslovakia must pay with coupons that show they have received and exchanged a certain amount of Western currency. This generally limits the customers to those Czechs who have permission to travel in the West or are in some way connected with companies outside the Soviet bloc. There are a number of Tuzex stores in Prague, selling clothing, shoes, housewares, and other items. They are not hidden from the general public, like some hard-currency stores in the Soviet Union, but seem to be regarded in the same light as any snobbish high-priced store in the West.)

As our bus came to a halt near the new shop, I saw that a knot of curious observers had gathered by the door, even though the public opening was not to take place until later that afternoon. Inside was a typical colorful, intimate interior, in the prefabricated Scarpa design that the company calls Benetton; inconspicuously placed along the shelves holding variegated stacks of clothing were several very small, almost postcard-size reproductions of Benetton's "United Colors" ads. All in all, it was a standard Benetton shop— the kind that, both in America and in Italy, is generally filled with seventeen-year-old girls chattering back and forth between dressing booths. It was curious, therefore, to see—as we did when we entered—surroundings geared to such an insouciant, well-heeled young clientele filled instead with a generally sombre, generally elderly mass of ministers and other officials of the Czech government. They had the indestructible dark suits and passive bland faces of powerful men in any Eastern European country, and they looked slightly suspicious and confused as they contemplated this capitalist-style paradise for female youth. With them was an entourage of even blander-looking young men, whose impressive physiques suggested a career in preventing security mishaps.

Present there, I found out from reading a program, was J. Kapek, general secretary of the Prague Committee of the Czechoslovakian Communist Party. As Luciano Benetton came through the shop door, cameras flashed, and there was applause. Toasts were drunk in sweet champagne, and an array of pretty, nervous-looking Czech girls wearing Benetton T-shirts, tight pants, and high heels offered hors d'oeuvres made of half a grape and a tiny piece of cheese. An official gave a short welcoming speech in Czech, and more pictures were taken, including one of Luciano Benetton surrounded by the blushing salesgirls—a pose he managed without looking the least bit ridiculous. Meanwhile, the twenty or thirty people crowded inside the shop jostled one another and chatted in Czech, Italian, and German.

"Oh, this will be a big success, very big," said a stylishly dressed black-haired woman, a photographer, who said she worked for Czech news services. "Only, I wonder why the store is so small. I thought an Italian store would be larger, more elegant."

"What they really need to be selling is shoes," said a pale young man, an East German journalist with an almost unbearably cynical smile. "The Czechs already dress like Westerners; the only thing that gives them away is their bad shoes."

I talked with a young Yugoslavian man who heads one of two Benetton shops in Belgrade. He explained to me a complicated hard-currency system for purchases made in the Yugoslavian Benetton; for example, a young woman with Western currency who wants to buy a sweater selects the sweater, fills out a pro-forma voucher for the exact cost, takes the voucher to the bank, where she exchanges it for hard currency from her account, and finally brings the currency back to the store to exchange for her sweater. "In this part of the world, shopping is a real adventure," he added unnecessarily.

When it was time for the Benetton delegation to move on to a luncheon at the Intercontinental Hotel, Luciano Benetton, who had maintained his kind, abstracted smile through the whole festivity, made one of his swift, immediately acted-on decisions: to go from the store to the hotel on foot rather than in the bus, so as to get a good look at the life of the city. With his guide, he at once set off at a purposeful pace, leaving his companions to straggle along behind, confused and a little irritated. "Signor Luciano walks *very* fast," one of the Benetton executives remarked darkly. An enterprising Czech news reporter took out a movie camera and scuttled along crab-fashion, filming Benetton's walk; Luciano maintained an Olympian calm.

We passed through staring noonday crowds and entered the Old Town Square, with its lovely Baroque churches and Copernican clock. The entire way, Benetton peered into shop windows, studied what people were wearing, and asked his typical barrage of questions, listening carefully to the answers. How old was this church? What did Czechs eat, not just for a fancy official lunch but for an average meal? What do Czechs do on weekends? For vacations? If they traveled to East Germany or Hungary, how did they do it— what was the most economical way? As I hurried behind him, I again had the impression, as I had had at lunch a month earlier, of an energetic visionary whose whole basis for planning and action comes, in a typically Venetian style, from a concentrated diet of practical information. "Do you think Czech women are individualistic about clothes?" I heard him ask his guide. "For instance, would you buy a dress if you knew that one of your friends had one like it?"

At the Intercontinental Hotel, in one of the luxurious, slightly oppressive banqueting rooms one finds in modern Eastern European hotels, Luciano Benetton gave a simultaneously translated speech to the group of officials and journalists who had been at the store reception. In his pleasant, uningratiating voice, he said that this was a day filled with emotion for him, that the opening of the store was also the debut of a new type of dialogue between East and West, that the company hoped to open a second Czech store in the following year, and that he wished them all *felicità*. At the elaborate lunch following, I ate excellent Czech ham and drank pilsner beer at a small table with the Italian ambassador to Czechoslovakia, his young attaché, and the Italian trade representative. It was not the head table, where Luciano Benetton sat chatting with Czech officials, and I had the impression that the representatives of the Italian government were feeling a bit left out. It was an impression that I later connected with the knowledge that many young Italian firms like Benetton owe some of their vitality to an ability to circumvent the official bureaucracy. The courtly old Roman ambassador seemed suavely dismissive of the energetic northern businessman, and when I asked the trade representative whether he had worked on the Benetton project, he said, "They didn't ask us. They have their own contacts."

After lunch and a brief tour of the city (chief impressions: Luciano Benetton peering into bookstores, into subway entrances, absorbing the answers to a mile-long string of questions as he strode cheerfully through the drizzle between the black Baroque statues on the bridge of Charles IV), our bus took us back to the shop for its official opening to the public. As the bus turned the corner, we saw a long line of customers waiting patiently to enter—the salesgirls were letting in eight at a time. Success! A smile ran across Luciano's face, and the rest of us broke into applause. It really was impressive, I reflected, if one considered the fact that except for an inconspicuous Benetton sign set amid other low-key foreign advertising in the Slavia Stadium, there had been absolutely no publicity for the store in Prague. Earlier that afternoon I had chatted with the head of the Tuzex organization, a small, sprightly man, and he had told me that if the store was a success (and success in Czechoslovakia means the same thing it means anywhere: lots of sales), then there would be another Prague store. If things continued at this rate, the second store looked like a sure thing.

Inside the shop, the salesgirls were rushing around displaying and refolding sweaters for a clientele that wouldn't have looked out of place in a midwestern American suburb: mostly blond, prosperous-looking young women in their late teens or early twenties, already dressed in Western clothing. Their expressions, excited or self-consciously deadpan, gave away the fact that this was not just another Thursday afternoon—that what they were buying was something special and hitherto unavailable. Some of them bought five or six items at once and walked out into the drizzly gray street laden with shopping bags, and beaming. Luciano Benetton stood by with an intensely involved, slightly searching expression on his face, like a chemist watching the emerging results of an experiment he has set up. He took the store managers aside and, in his calm, painstaking way, reminded them to make the window displays more eye-catching as winter approached, and to turn in sales figures the following Monday. Then he scanned the shelves of colorful clothing, picked up a sweater that was folded wrong, refolded it, and replaced it.

The return flight to Treviso took us out of the mist and rain of Eastern Europe into a sunny late afternoon over the Alps and northern Italy. A relaxed atmosphere prevailed on the Citation II, with Benetton, Paolini, and Weiss discussing soccer and teasing the copilot about some Czech dolls he had bought for his children. I talked to Renata Sponchiado, the pretty administrative assistant, who had done much of the translation work all day. "Oh, Signor Luciano is very pleased with this new store," she said in a joyful voice. "And I am happy. It took two years of long, hard work. We had tremendous difficulty with the bureaucracy at first, and in the end things worked out mainly because of one of our German associates. He had a friend who was a Hungarian minister, and that friend knew a Czech minister—it was all through connections and friends."

When we landed at the Treviso airport, I said good-bye to the others and took the armored Alfa back into town with Luciano Benetton. He was on his way home, and I was to go on in the car with a driver to catch a flight to Rome from Marco Polo Airport, in Venice. It was about six-thirty in the evening, and the sunny streets around and inside the small city were filled with people walking, bicycling, or driving home. It seemed dimensions away from the melancholy gray beauty of Prague and the controlled frenzy of our race from official function to function.

Although Luciano Benetton never looks weary or frazzled—an inexhaustible vitality and an unflappable serenity seem to be two of the secrets of running a worldwide business—in some way, perhaps through a sort of broadening and relaxing of all his molecules, I could sense his absolute comfort in returning to his own small town, which seemed to fit him like one of his well-worn tweed jackets. He told me he was happy with the Prague shop, although the location was not ideal. "The response was good—it was a miracle, when you come to think of it, how many people came. It was on a side street, there was no advertising, everything took place through word of mouth." He adjusted his glasses and thought for a minute as we passed through one of the gates in the ancient city wall of Treviso. "That location might, strangely, turn out to be an advantage," he went on. "It might become chic to go to a place a bit out of the way, where not everyone goes."

He talked earnestly, reflectively, about Czechoslovakia, setting forth, with his usual relish for new facts, some of the information he had gleaned from his indefatigable questioning. I asked him which country he was going to visit next, and he told me that the next day he was leaving for one of his frequent visits to America.

He would stop in New York and in Madison, Wisconsin. "And Oshkosh," he added, with a delighted laugh suggesting that he looked forward to enlarging his knowledge of the world by one more exotic corner. "I've never been to Oshkosh. I like that name."

After the driver let him out at the corner of a cobblestoned street, he said good-bye and, with his swift, direct stride, walked away. Near that corner was a bar I had visited—one of the small, oddly festive bars of Treviso, where pink-cheeked barmen who know everyone serve an excellent Bellini or grappa or beer. Before we drove away, I saw a man come out of the bar and heard him say as he passed Luciano Benetton, *"Buona sera, Signor Luciano."*

As the Benetton driver took me down a two-lane road that led through the green cornfields and vineyards and a scattering of small factories toward Venice and the airport, he asked me if I wanted to listen to some taped music. Looking through the glove compartment, I found a number of cassettes, holding music from all over the world: a few samba tapes, some jazz, Peruvian panpipe music, a few low-key rock vocalists from the United States.

"Whose are these?" I asked.

"They belong to Signor Luciano," the driver said.

It seemed logical: they were all music appropriate for a solitary dreamer—one who, without abandoning a base fixed firmly in the small world of his family and region, seeks out many styles and cultures. I put on a panpipe tape, and as the thin music filled the car with the remote harmonies of the Andes we rode down the highway through the cornfields to Venice.

An Heiress Who Threw Open Gates for Modern Art

By Yorick Blumenfeld

～

editor's note

A great number of articles and interviews about Peggy Guggenheim have appeared over the years, but I have long been fondest of this piece, which originally appeared in *Smithsonian*.

YORICK BLUMENFELD is the author of *The Naked and the Veiled: The Photographic Nudes of Erwin Blumenfeld* (1999), *2099: A Eutopia (Prospects for Tomorrow)* (2000), and *Scanning the Future* (1999), all published by Thames & Hudson.

Many of us dream of leaving an artistic legacy. Few of us have the means or the determination to do so. Peggy Guggenheim, who was regarded during most of her eighty-one years as the enfant terrible of her famous family, always lived on the edge of the surreal, both in art and in her daily life. Her extraordinary passion is now immortalized. She is the only American to have her name emblazoned in large bronze letters along Venice's historic Grand Canal.

Peggy's former home, the Palazzo Venier dei Leoni, has been converted into a museum for her splendid collection of twentieth-century paintings and sculpture, for which she paid less than $500,000 and which now has an estimated value of around $50 million. The range of works, from Picassos to Pollocks, makes it Italy's most important collection of modern art.

The popular image of Peggy as *l'ultima dogaressa* clutching a pair of Lhasa apso terriers while being ferried along the Grand

Canal in her own private gondola was one that she deliberately cultivated. Without doubt, Peggy liked a touch of class, and the elaborately carved golden lions of her craft added the required touch of the fantastic.

In truth, however, Peggy spent a lifetime overcoming basic insecurity about her looks, her wealth, and her position. She always regarded herself as one of the "poor" Guggenheims, and so she was, when compared with her uncles who had founded American Smelting and Refining. What she lacked in capital, Peggy made up with two other Guggenheim traits: a superb sense of timing (knowing exactly when to buy) and an almost unnerving ability to seek out the best advisers.

"Peggy's paradox is that so much good came out of so much doubt and trial and error," says Thomas M. Messer, the director of the Solomon R. Guggenheim Foundation, which runs the Venice collection and the New York museum. Messer, who first met Peggy in 1956, adds, "Everything Peggy did had a touch of elegance. Even if sharp-tongued and proverbially outspoken, she was quite shy and extremely feminine."

Messer says that Peggy had three strong collecting areas: the pioneers of twentieth-century art, such as Picasso, Braque, Léger, Gris, and Duchamp: the Surrealists, including Max Ernst, Dali, Tanguy, Magritte, Delvaux: and the New York School, particularly as represented by Jackson Pollock. "The charm of these works, taken as a whole, is that they speak of a particular moment in collecting history," says Messer, who singled out a few of his own favorites.

"There are three sensational Picassos," he explained, including *The Poet* (1911), which is one of the most fabulous of the Analytical Cubist Picassos and which Peggy acquired in 1941. Messer considers *The Red Tower* (1913) by Giorgio de Chirico as another masterpiece. It is regarded as one of the greatest paintings of de

Chirico's metaphysical period, and it is the first work he ever sold. Among the sculptures in the collection, Messer most highly esteems *Maiastra* by Brancusi and Giacometti's *Standing Woman.*

In her 1946 autobiography, *Out of This Century* (which the more conservative branch of her family referred to some years ago as *Out of My Mind*), Peggy wrote, "I comfort myself by thinking how terribly lucky I was to have been able to buy all my wonderful collection at a time when prices were normal, before the whole picture world turned into an investment market." Peggy was one of the original "trust fund babies." Contrary to general belief, she inherited relatively little from her father, whose private business failed to prosper after he left the family partnership. Tragically, he went down on the *Titanic* in 1912. Nevertheless, because of trust funds set up by her uncles and her mother, she received the income from her first inheritance of $450,000 at the age of twenty-one. She used the proceeds to lead what could justly be described as a life of lusty bohemianism in Europe.

In the roaring Paris of the 1920s, she was often seen in the company of the likes of Marcel Duchamp and Isadora Duncan. Impetuously, she married the writer Laurence Vail in 1922, and their stormy relationship produced two children before ending in a breakup in 1928. Whatever Laurence Vail's shortcomings, he must be credited with introducing Peggy to Venice. Laurence had lived there as a child, and as she wrote in her autobiography, he knew "every stone, every church, every painting." Peggy was captivated by the city's floating unreality. She wanted to buy a palazzo there and then, but her money was locked up in trust funds.

Peggy drifted though several relationships in the 1930s and was at a loss as to how to give meaning to her life. Then in 1938, at the age of forty, she decided to enter the art world. The young writer Samuel Beckett, with whom she was in love during this time, urged her to become interested in contemporary art because it was "a living thing." Another friend and mentor, Marcel Duchamp, proceeded to educate her about values in the art market. "I don't know what I would have done without him," she wrote. "To begin with, he taught me the difference between Abstract and Surrealist art." Equally important, Duchamp introduced her to a galaxy of modern artists.

Peggy rented the second floor of a building on London's fashionable Cork Street early in 1938, and her secretary named the gallery Guggenheim Jeune. Peggy had wanted to give Brancusi the opening show, but when this did not materialize, she decided to exhibit Jean Cocteau. The gallery was a critical success.

Peggy's second show was of the Russian-born painter Vasily Kandinsky, who arrayed a range of his paintings from 1910 to 1937. As she admitted later, she bought only one of his canvases, from 1936, and missed out on "the marvelous early ones." Although she had not yet turned collector, she often bought one painting or sculpture from each show. "Thus, without knowing it, I started my collection," she noted in her memoirs.

Peggy's first sculpture show in April 1938 was to make her famous. She had planned an exhibit to include Brancusi, Arp, Laurens, Duchamp-Villon, Pevsner, and Calder, as well as the then-unrecognized representative from England, Henry Moore. British customs officials, however, refused to admit the works of this stellar constellation as "art." The director of the Tate Gallery was called in to decide whether these sculptures were simply metal, wood, and stone or *whether* truly works of art. His refusal to declare them "art" caused such a storm that the case was brought up in the House of Commons. Peggy won the debate.

Guggenheim Jeune in London was not popular with her rich uncle Solomon Guggenheim in New York. He was being advised by a dogmatic German baroness, Hilla Rebay, to establish a museum of nonobjective art. Hilla thought Peggy was cheapening the

Guggenheim name to make a profit. When Peggy tried to sell a Kandinsky to her uncle, Rebay replied: "It is extremely distasteful at this moment, when the name of Guggenheim stands for an ideal in art, to see it used for commerce so as to give the wrong impression."

Peggy was also having second thoughts. Her London gallery appeared to be a successful venture but was in fact unprofitable. "I felt that if I was losing money, I might as well lose a lot more and do something worthwhile." So she approached a leading English authority on modern art, the writer, poet, and critic Herbert Read, and gave him a five-year contract to direct a new London museum of modern art. Peggy was apparently oblivious to the threatening clouds of war, as she hoped to open her London MOMA in the fall of 1939.

In August of that year, she blithely went to Paris to borrow works from various friends for the opening of her museum. While there it soon became apparent that war would be declared. With regret, she abandoned the museum. Instead, she decided that with the $40,000 that she had planned to spend on it she would start buying an art collection. She put herself on a regime to "buy a picture a day." It was both a timing of genius and an incredible stroke of luck.

Peggy Guggenheim was always known in the art world as someone looking for a bargain. And in Paris in 1939–40 there were bargains all around. It was the perfect "Guggenheim market": all sellers and no buyers. With Marcel Duchamp and the dealer Howard Putzel to advise her, she acquired works like Brancusi's *Maiastra* for only $1,000. The day Hitler conquered Norway she walked into Léger's studio and bought *Men in the City* for another $1,000. The next day she bought a splendid Man Ray. The approaching fall of France did not stop her. In the few months preceding June 1940, she acquired about fifty works.

Finally she had to flee Paris, just three days before the Germans entered the city. But this was not before she had bought *Voice of Space* by René Magritte. Peggy's recollection of the transaction was that she was visiting an art shipper when Magritte appeared with a picture under his arm. He offered to sell her the painting on the spot, and she accepted, paying cash.

As an American, Peggy did not have much trouble ultimately taking her family and her art collection out of France and to the United States. She arrived in New York in 1941 in the company of the Surrealist painter Max Ernst, whose work she had been collecting and whom she would shortly marry. Peggy, it must be acknowledged, often appreciated an artist before she appreciated his work.

Her ambitious program of acquisition continued in New York. She decided to launch a museum on Fifty-seventh Street, which she called Art of This Century. She finally decided it also would be a gallery where she could sell paintings for Max Ernst and for young unknown American artists. At the opening, Peggy wore one earring by Yves Tanguy, the Surrealist, and another by Alexander Calder. She explained to her guests that this showed her neutrality in the conflict between the often hostile schools of Abstractionism and Surrealism. Ernst, who was shortly to divorce her, told Peggy: "You are a lost girl." In terms of espousing any one artistic current, this was probably a correct appraisal, as Peggy embraced all of art.

Soon after opening her gallery, she appointed a jury consisting of Marcel Duchamp, Piet Mondrian, Howard Putzel, plus the top three experts at the Museum of Modern Art and herself, to select forty paintings from among the younger generation of American artists. The selection of the jury showed Peggy's shrewdness. The stars who emerged from that first show were Jackson Pollock, Robert Motherwell, and William Baziotes. Later she was to give first one-man shows to those three, Clyfford Still, Mark Rothko, and others.

Art of This Century soon became a focus for the new Abstract Expressionist movement. Lee Krasner, Jackson Pollock's wife and a notable painter herself, wrote that "Peggy's achievement should not be underestimated. . . . There was nowhere else in New York where one could expect an open-minded reaction." Peggy signed up Pollock to a contract of $150 per month in 1943. If less than $2,700 worth of his paintings were sold, Peggy was to select works to make up the difference. In 1945, she signed him up for a further two-year contract with a stipend of $300 a month. In return, his entire output had to move through her gallery.

The details of this contract and other aspects of Peggy's more idiosyncratic acquisitions have been painstakingly researched by the art historian Angelica Zander Rudenstine in her exhaustive 844-page catalog of the Peggy Guggenheim Collection published last year. This is truly an "essential reference work for all those interested in the field of 20th-century art."

A Bargain Palace on the Grand Canal

By the end of World War II, Peggy was eager to return to Europe. She decided to make Venice, with its floating sense of time and its free spirit, her future home. "I had always loved it more than any place on earth and felt I would be happy alone there. I set about trying to find a palace that would house my collection and provide a garden for my dogs," she wrote.

In the spring of 1949, as the cold war offered another splendid opportunity for panic buying, she acquired an unfinished palace on the Grand Canal for a bargain $80,000. Because of its incomplete condition (one story only), it had the advantage of not being regarded as a national monument. Moreover, it had a large garden with linden trees, plantains, and pines in back and in front a terrace on the Grand Canal. The Palazzo Venier dei Leoni, she realized, would make a superb showcase for her art collection. The palace had been started in 1749 by architect Lorenzo Boschetti. The last male of the famous Venier family died before it was finished.

Peggy enjoyed the idea of living like a duchess in an ivy-clad palace-museum on the Grand Canal. It was near the Palazzo Barbaro, where Isabella Stewart Gardner had lived and where Peggy's favorite author, Henry James, had stayed to write *The Great Condition*.

Many of the Venetian aristocracy were not thrilled by Peggy's plans to fill the palace with "modern art." For these bluebloods, real art had stopped with Guardi and Canaletto in the eighteenth century. Giuseppe Santomaso, a painter and neighbor, explained that to Venetians Peggy represented everything in the contemporary world of art that they rejected.

A Shock for the Aristocracy

The fact that she had exhibited her collection at the XXIVth Biennale in 1948 did not change the aristocracy's reaction to her. Peggy, however, was excited to see the name Guggenheim appear on the maps in the Public Gardens next to those of Great Britain, France, Holland, and other national pavilions.

While she was remodeling her palazzo between 1949 and 1951, her collection was shown at the Stedelijk Museum in Amsterdam, the Palais des Beaux-Arts in Brussels, and in the Zurich Kunsthaus. Then in the spring of 1951, she opened the collection to the public for three afternoons a week. She maintained this practice during the Venice "season," often selling catalogues herself, until the time of her death.

If she outraged the Venetian aristocracy by her free and somewhat surrealist spirit, the ordinary people appreciated her eccentricity. Besides turning her maids into "curators," she also taught her two gondoliers to be picture hangers. She liked to chat with workers of the district, and she dressed with artistic extravagance.

"The more exaggerated one's clothes, the more suitable they appear in this city," she wrote.

Most shocking to the traditionalists, perhaps, was the sculpture by Marino Marini named *The Angel of the City,* placed in front of her doorsteps on the Grand Canal. It is a statue of a horse and rider, whose arms are spread open in ecstasy and whose phallus is in full metallic erection. Marini had the bronze phallus cast separately, so that it could be removed at the owner's discretion. Santomaso, who was by then a professor at the Accademia, recounts that after one party the phallus was missing. It never turned up, so Peggy asked Marini to make her another. At first Marini refused, saying, "I no longer have the model." Eventually he replaced it.

As the years passed, Peggy's collection continued to grow. She transformed her laundry in the basement into a gallery. One by one many of the other rooms followed suit. When all the spatial possibilities of the palazzo were exhausted, she decided to build a pavilion in her garden.

Gradually, in the 1960s, she began to consider what would happen to the collection after her lifetime. There were three main contenders, the city of Venice, London's Tate Gallery, and the Guggenheim Museum in New York, all three of which in earlier days disparaged her taste and art.

In their efforts to secure the collection and the palace, the Venetians made her an honorary citizen in 1962. Then in 1967 she was made a *commendatore* of the Italian Republic. Santomaso advised her: "You will be immortal if you leave this collection to Venice." However, the city lost its chance when, under Italian law, the authorities insisted that she had to pay a tax as the donor. Peggy was outraged at the idea and later, on her eightieth birthday, publicly declared that the Venetians had been very "stupid" about this.

London's Tate Gallery lost out, the apocryphal tale has it, because her pet terriers were not allowed into the country when she was to sign the draft documents. British quarantine laws prohibited their entry. But Santomaso claims he convinced Peggy to keep the collection in Venice.

Messer, on the other hand, diplomatically and persistently pursued her. With strategic insight, he invited her to show her collection at her uncle's museum in New York in 1969. It was on that occasion that she resolved to donate her palace and its contents to the Guggenheim Foundation. "In the end," recalls Messer, "it was a family matter." Harry Guggenheim, her cousin and chairman of the board of the foundation, was particularly pleased about the reconciliation and the amalgamation of these two important collections.

Under the terms of the agreement, worked out by Messer and Peter Lawson-Johnston, president of the foundation, the works of art were to remain with Peggy until she died. After her death the Solomon Guggenheim Foundation would assume effective control of and responsibility for the palazzo and its contents. The collection would be kept in Venice and would remain on view for six months of the year. In her own hand Peggy wrote a postscript: "If Venice sinks, the Collection should be preserved somewhere in the vicinity of Venice."

When Messer took over the estate in December 1979, his most immediate task was to physically safeguard the collection. The changes over the next few years were massive: air conditioning was introduced throughout, a proper security system was installed, and a reinforced concrete storage area was built in which Peggy's collection could safely be stored when not exhibited. In sum, a private palace was converted into a modern museum with quality lighting and humidity-control systems.

The formerly wild garden, which measures about fifteen hundred square yards, was also transformed. The new sculpture garden has flagstones laid out according to an eighteenth-century geomet-

ric pattern. One of the least disturbed areas of the garden is the red-brick wall to the rear where, surrounded by daisies, rest Peggy's ashes. Next to her plaque is another engraved with the names of "my beloved babies," the pet terriers that had lived with her in Venice.

In his basement-level office in the palazzo-museum, collection administrator Philip Rylands commented that the Italians were filled with admiration for the professional basis on which the museum was being run. For example, interns, who stay up to three months each, are guarding the rooms, selling tickets, catalogues, and postcards as well as doing other minor curatorial jobs. Because it is privately owned, the museum can stay open for longer hours than any other museum in Italy, and there are no strikes and no closures. There are now more than 180,000 visitors a year.

Messer feels that Peggy Guggenheim's great accomplishment as a collector "was to gather, with much intuitive perception and freedom from dogmatic assumptions, works that reveal the wide range and ultimate unity of modern art." Messer thought of Peggy as "a lion woman," proud and imperious. Her collection in Venice is now a living monument, a testimonial to her acumen and sensibility.

Just Wild About Harry's

BY RAFFAELLA PRANDI

～

editor's note

....

As I have mentioned elsewhere in this book, and as you'll read so often in guidebooks, Harry's Bar is, for good reason, one of the world's most memorable watering holes (it's a quite excellent restaurant, too). At least part of the legendary success of Harry's is due to the founder's son, Arrigo Cipriani, the subject of this interview.

RAFFAELLA PRANDI is a frequent contributor to *Gambero Rosso*, where this piece originally appeared.

Few Italian restaurants have achieved the international fame of Harry's Bar in Venice. The restaurant's trademark Venetian style, elegance, and reputation have survived the opening of branches in the Americas, and the satellite versions appeal to the same cosmopolitan clientele as the glamorous original. The mystique of Harry's Bar, its famous creations (the Bellini cocktail and *carpaccio* are the best known), and its even more famous habitués (Hemingway, Orson Welles, and Aristotle Onassis, for example) have earned the restaurant a place in Italy's culinary and social history. Well-traveled food enthusiasts from every corner of the world, united by affection for Italian flavors and atmosphere, make their way to Harry's on both sides of the Atlantic and are not surprised to find themselves elbow to elbow with Barbara Bush or Woody Allen or the king of Spain.

Giuseppe Cipriani opened Harry's Bar in 1931 in partnership with a well-to-do American friend, Harry Pickering, who provided the money. It was a tiny space, an ex–rope shop, at the end of a narrow Venetian alleyway. Today the restaurant seats eighty, serving approximately 250 meals a day.

Cipriani later opened a six-room inn on the island of Torcello, in the Venice Lagoon, placing his aunt Gabriella in charge. She ran the Locanda Cipriani until her death in 1980, a few days after Giuseppe himself. The family also owned the Hotel Cipriani on the Giudecca. Both places have been sold and are no longer connected in any way with Harry's Bar.

Somehow Arrigo Cipriani, Giuseppe's son, seems to be everywhere at once, no matter what the city, moving around the rooms of his restaurant with the same casual ease. You can see him in New York scolding a waiter for a creased tablecloth, in Venice rushing into the kitchen to check on a delayed risotto, or in Buenos Aires smiling cordially at departing Japanese guests. We caught up with him at a table in Venice. Although concentrated on our conversation, he relentlessly watched his restaurant's activity out of the corner of his eye, as a mother never loses sight of her child while chatting with a friend.

Today your family runs two restaurants in Venice, two in New York, two in Buenos Aires . . .
There's also a coffee bar in Palazzo Grassi in Venice and the hotel we're opening in New York, a truly extraordinary venture. We've already inaugurated a banquet hall in the old wheat exchange on Wall Street—18,000 square feet, ninety-foot ceiling, space for a thousand people in a nineteenth-century building. Our five-story hotel on the upper floors will be ready in the fall of 1998. We're also building two restaurants in Grand Central Terminal.

Why a hotel in the United States and not in Italy?
Because it's easier to raise money in the United States. We've always found backers among our own clients.

And why a restaurant in Grand Central Terminal?

Because we can appeal to tens of thousands of commuters. I'm always looking for places where I can create a clientele. For example, in Buenos Aires we opened a pastry shop in a mall.

How do you manage to keep track of all this activity?
I have a wonderful son in New York who knows everything that I know and that his grandfather Giuseppe knew.

Do you think of your restaurants as a chain, like Bice, for example?
No, because we run them all ourselves. We are physically there in New York, and everyone who works for us feels like part of a single team.

In your book you describe your experience with Lord Charles Forte, who asked you to organize and run a restaurant on the ground floor of the Hotel Sherry Netherland in New York.
The restaurant, Harry Cipriani, was an enormous success, but after two years, in 1987, the Forte organization suddenly decided they could do without us. The new management introduced nouvelle cuisine, the restaurant failed, and after all the proprietors asked us to come back. In 1991 we returned, and so did all our old clients, from the very first day. We're still going strong today.

Is it difficult to be a restaurateur in New York?
No, because it is a realistic city. That's why nouvelle cuisine never prospered there. You at *Gambero Rosso* are always interested in price/quality ratio, value for money. In New York that's very important, no matter how rich the clients. If they don't get high quality at the right price, the restaurant won't work.

How does Venice come into the equation?
I think Harry's Bar really reflects Venice's spirit. Venice is an elegant city on a human scale, a marriage between people and architecture. It is not a city meant for cars or even bicycles. All this has to be part of the restaurant.

How do you do that?
By treating people as human beings, by having simple, authentic relationships with our clients, offering real service. There's nothing complicated about it. To serve is above all to love.

Your cooking has been faithful to the most classical Venetian traditions, never been tempted by trends . . .
Of course new things have come in, but the basic dishes, the risotto, the pasta, are the same. Have you noticed that very few restaurants make risotto anymore? Because for good risotto you have to have good broth, good rice, and then you have to put them together in exactly the right way. Risotto consists of various components; people and ingredients have to be synchronized. The moment of *mantecazione,* that is, the final blending of butter and cheese, is fundamental. It's then that you make a good, mediocre, or extraordinary risotto. If in those last minutes the cook is not concentrating, he doesn't send out a perfect risotto.

Why are you so opposed to restaurant guides?
We don't need restaurant guides. For example, the books say that we are expensive. But I have 23 waiters here, and 60 people working in 630 square feet, with seating for 80. And in the last year, not one single person has come in carrying a restaurant guide, not *Gambero Rosso,* not Michelin. So I ask myself, who buys the guidebooks? The answer is easy. Restaurateurs. We have our clientele, we created it ourselves, and we know exactly what they want. And they want the opposite of what the guides want.

What do your clients want?
Simplicity and truth, in people and in food.

And what do restaurant guides want?
Guidebooks want snobbishness, stiff service, dishes created by painters and sculptors and not by cooks: appearance and not real-

ity. Instead, we create a restaurant for our customers to enjoy every day. The guidebooks praise places where you might go twice a year.

What do you mean by snobbishness?
Admiring the superfluous, even ridiculous food pairings. Giving a lot of importance to things rather than people, to decor above comfort. Real quality is the opposite. It is the search for the best and therefore, the rarest—the quality you can find not so much in things as in what people can do.

How has the concept of service changed in the last forty years?
In the 1960s, luxury hotels led the way in service and in cuisine. That's not true anymore. Hotel chefs were meticulous teachers and flag bearers of the traditions that were the foundation of the best Italian cooking during the first half of the twentieth century. That all changed with the arrival of the accountants, the multinational hotel companies that looked at the bottom line before thinking about quality. Service became a question of following rules. The client of a luxury hotel became an anonymous customer.

Can you give me an example?
Minibars. Thirty years ago they didn't exist. Now they are in every hotel room. Although it passes for an improvement, it's not. And guidebooks reward this kind of thing. Instead, a client should be able to phone twenty-four hours a day for room service in a hotel where he or she is paying $650 a night. There won't be minibars in the hotel I'm opening in New York.

Are you still training your own personnel?
The two directors we have in New York learned on the job with us. Six years ago they were cleaning ashtrays. Today they are in charge. We always try to promote from inside rather than hire new personnel. It's hard for an outsider to understand our methods.

How are your methods different from anyone else's?
A few minutes ago you heard me get angry with one of the waiters for telling a client that it takes eighteen minutes to make risotto. He must learn that you absolutely should never say something like that. It's in our Cipriani DNA, knowing it's simply not done. It's like saying to the customer that you don't want to make the risotto. You can't set limits like that for a client. Ever.

And how do you manage to reproduce Harry's around the world maintaining the standards you require?
With research, the science of food. I'll give you an example: salt cod. We order it six months ahead in a place in Norway that we know is very, very good. We can be sure it will be perfect. Through research we can reproduce quality.

But what about the atmosphere, the feeling your clients get?
That's the hardest part. We have to research not only what goes into each dish but our service. In New York, for example, 80 percent of our clients come three times a week. That means they are getting just what they want. And what they want is a *trattoria* atmosphere.

So the kind of restaurant you like and have exported around the world has a friendly trattoria *atmosphere and serves home-style cooking?*
Right. For example, we make our own pasta, and we try to make it very well.

New restaurants in New York and London are aiming at the spectacular, big numbers, high quality, big business. What do you think?
I think they'll disappear in no time.

What about star chefs?
Our chefs have to do what we want, not what the chef wants. The same goes for our architects. We can't have people doing their own thing.

But architects are bringing fame and fortune to many restaurants.
More pure snobbishness. Those grandiose restaurants are aimed at impressing the naïve, the provincial.

Does that mean the ordinary person doesn't understand good food?
Everybody understands what's really good. I think Italian taste is universal. For example, the whole world loves our bean soup.

What will your New York hotel be like?
When my father was running it, the Hotel Cipriani on the Giudecca was one of the best hotels in the world. It had its own laundries, which we'll also have in New York, linen sheets, which we'll also have in New York—they give a sense of crispness. My father used to say that when you go to bed at night and close your eyes, you don't see anything. You just feel. It's all in the details.

Whose cooking do you admire in Italy?
Near Harry's Bar in Venice there are two *trattories* I like. I adore Clemi at Castelletto—she's a born restaurateur—and there's Ombre Rosse that opened recently. It's a wine bar. The owner is in the dining room and his wife in kitchen.

What makes a "born restaurateur"?
The welcome—a relaxed, casual welcome that isn't affected. The ability to be oneself. Since Clemi has a terrific personality, even though she can be a little brusque, you feel the human contact. I can't stand the menu-reciters or, for example, the waiter who came here and said, "What are you having?"—a total mistake.

I noticed you were angry, but I wasn't sure what had annoyed you.
You have to educate the staff through fear sometimes and never let anything just pass. They are boys from the provinces; a Venetian

would never have said it like that. I can't let one person ruin everything. Next year at our other restaurant in Venice, Harry's Dolci, I want to run a school, teach the young how to talk to customers.

And how do you feel when important, famous people come into the restaurant?
It's a perfectly normal thing for us. And the famous come because they are treated like normal human beings. Nobody pays special attention to them; they sit where they like, just like everybody else. But I did notice one thing. When the king of Spain came and lit his cigar at the end of the meal, eight tables lit up as well. They felt liberated.

Biblioteca

Casanova

Casanova: A Study in Self-Portraiture, Stefan Zweig, Pushkin Press, London, 1998.

Peggy Guggenheim

Peggy Guggenheim: A Collector's Album, Laurence Tacou-Rumney, Flammarion, 1996. "A Collector's Album" is an apt part of the title, as this is not a biography; nor does it pretend to be. The book is a hardcover filled with color and black-and-white photographs, some of which are arranged like snapshots in a family album, which it really is, since author Tacou-Rumney is married to Sandro Rumney, Peggy Guggenheim's grandson. In some ways I prefer this book to the other, more serious biographies; Peggy's legacy is one of extravagance and controversy, and people have so many opinions about her that it's refreshing simply to let photographs tell the (abbreviated) story of her life. This is really the best book of all for looking at and reading about the artworks and the artists.

Claudio Monteverdi

Claudio Monteverdi (1567–1643) was a pioneer both of Venetian opera—he wrote seven of his operas in Venice—and of the Baroque genre of music. The two works for which he is perhaps best known are the operas *Orfeo* and *L'incoronazione di Poppea.* In 1613 Monteverdi was appointed choirmaster at St. Mark's Basilica and master of music for the republic, a post he held until his death in 1643. Some consider Monteverdi to be the first great composer; certainly his contributions to the world of music, especially opera, are invaluable.
Monteverdi in Venice, Denis Stevens, Fairleigh Dickinson University Press, 2001. This book tells the story of Monteverdi's thirty years in Venice, from the time of his arrival to his death. Stevens, a musicologist and musician in his own right, exposes the modern interpretations of Monteverdi's work (and makes important distinctions between them) as well as Monteverdi's original intentions and musical tendencies. This book will be of interest to readers who seek a little more extensive investigation into Monteverdi's works. There are substantial sources about Monteverdi that are far more general and rudimentary, but Stevens's book allows "the composer to shine through layers of pseudo-musicological varnish that has obscured a large part of his message."

Marco Polo

The Travels of Marco Polo, edited and revised from William Marsden's translation, by Manuel Komroff, introduction by Jason Goodwin, Modern Library Classics, 2001. Not a biography in the way we know biographies today, but as close to one as we'll ever have on the great Venetian traveler. Polo's account was one of the earliest European travel narratives, and it remains the most important. As noted in the brief biography that opens the book, "For generations of Europe, his copious, vivid, and factual account of Eastern ways was the discovery of Asia. . . . Never before or since has a single book brought so much authentic new information, or widened the vistas for a continent."

John and Effie Ruskin

Effie in Venice: Mrs. John Ruskin's Letters Home, 1849–52, edited by Mary Lutyens, Pallas Editions, London, 1999; first published by John Murray, London, 1965.

Giuseppe Verdi

Encounters with Verdi, edited by Marcello Conati, translated by Richard Stokes, with a foreword by Julian Budden, Cornell University Press, 1984. This is a wonderfully researched and well-organized collection of chapters written by cultured and insightful individuals who had the good fortune to have met Verdi. The writings of each of these authors are invaluable contributions to our understanding of the composer's artistic genius as well as to his highly individual perceptions of the world of music.

Verdi, Julian Budden, edited by Stanley Sadie, Schirmer Books, 1996. Budden is the former producer of opera on BBC, a member of the British Academy, and one of the foremost authorities on Verdi today. This book, part of the *Master Musicians* series, is one of the best, if not *the best,* introductions to Verdi. Originally published by Vintage in 1985, Budden explores the life of the great composer and offers insightful commentary about his works, including *La Traviata, Rigoletto,* and *Simon Boccanegra,* each of which premiered at Teatro la Fenice in Venice. Included are a glossary of terms, a "who's who" section, and a list of recommended recordings.

Verdi with a Vengeance: An Energetic Guide to the Life and Complete Works of the King of Opera, William Berger, Vintage Books, 2000. Berger, a librettist and frequent commentator at National Public Radio's *At the Opera,* provides descriptions of Verdi's compositions and the contemporaneous social conditions. Berger offers both plot descriptions of various scenes within Verdi's operas and critical commentary that is also quite humorous. This book caters both to the novice and to the highly literate connoisseur of music and includes a glossary of terms and a list of recommended recordings and films.

Verdi: A Biography, Mary Jane Phillips-Matz, with a foreword by Andrew Porter, Oxford University Press, 1996. This detailed description of the life and works of one of *the* towering musical figures of the nineteenth century deserves a place in any music library. Phillips-Matz is a rather conservative author who perhaps does not capture the dynamism of the man and his music and in so doing attributes to Verdi an almost enigmatic existence. She does, however, make up for her lack of color with her careful attention to detail, which certainly demonstrates her great knowledge of music. Her sweeping commentary may at times evoke dubious reactions from the most knowledgeable readers (to whom this book really caters), but she is to be respected as one of the foremost authorities of Verdi and opera.

Antonio Vivaldi

Vivaldi, John Booth, Music Sales, 1992. This 143-page biography—in the *Illustrated Lives of the Great Composers* series—is more vivid than the average academic biography. Antonio Vivaldi's life remains a great mystery to many of us; most of his operas are entirely lost. But Booth relates Vivaldi's story (at least what is known) in a very appealing way for both the novice and the baroque or classical music enthusiast. Beautiful illustrations add atmosphere to Vivaldi's life and times. This is an enjoyable and comprehensive biography.

Antonio Vivaldi: The Red Priest of Venice, Karl Heller, translated by David Marinelli, Amadeus Press, 1997. An appropriately titled book for the Venetian composer who fell between the baroque and classical periods and who was ordained at the age of twenty-five. Heller's work paints a picture of the political and cultural environment around Vivaldi, which contributed to his difficult life as a composer. This work is most suited for readers who already have a background in Vivaldi and who are serious about understanding his influence on other baroque and classical composers and his great contribution to the Italian concerto.

Vivaldi, Michael Talbot, edited by Stanley Sadie, Oxford University Press, 2001. This book, published in the *Master Musicians* series (the *Verdi* biography noted earlier by Julian Budden is in the same series, though printed by a different publisher), is a true academic resource but does not read like an academic text and is among the most insightful of the Vivaldi biographies. Talbot is an authority on the life and works of Vivaldi, and among his discoveries is an unknown set of Vivaldi violin sonatas. Again, this book is appropriate both for the Vivaldi connoisseur and for the novice.

MUSEI CIVICI VENEZIANI
D'ARTE E DI STORIA

RISORGIMENTO - MUSEI VETRARI DI MURANO
INTERNAZIONALE D'ARTE MODERNA DI CA' PESARO

ITALIA POSTA PRIORITARIA
VENEZIA MARCO POLO
6.12.00

MUSEO QUERINI STAMPALIA · VENEZ

Una antica casa veneziana con arredi e opere di:

Giovanni Bellini, Lorenzo Di Credi,
Jacopo Palma il Vecchio, Jacopo Palma il Giovane,
Bernardo Strozzi, Sebastiano Ricci, Marco Ricci,
Giambattista Tiepolo,
Pietro Longhi, Gabriel Bella, Orazio Marinali,
Giuseppe Jappelli, Antonio Canova

INGRESSO INTERO L. 12.000

SERIE C   N° 45297

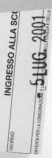

SCUOLA GRANDE S. ROCCO

L. 10.000 € 5.1

N° 30292

INGRESSO ALLA SCU

5.LUG. 2001

GIORNO   OFFERTA PER LA CONSERVAZIONE E IL RESTAURO DELLE OPERE E DELLA

Musei e Monumenti
(Museums and Monuments of Note)

"We have seen famous pictures until our eyes are weary with looking at them and refuse to find interest in them any longer. And what wonder, when there are twelve hundred pictures by Palma the Younger in Venice and fifteen hundred by Tintoretto? And behold, there are Titians and the works of other artists in proportion. We have seen Titian's celebrated Cain and Abel, his David and Goliah, his Abraham's Sacrifice. We have seen Tintoretto's monster picture, which is seventy-four feet long and I do not know how many feet high, and thought it a very commodious picture. We have seen pictures of martyrs enough, and saints enough, to regenerate the world."

—Mark Twain, THE INNOCENTS ABROAD

Venice's Trove of Ties to the Sea

By Susan Allen Toth

～

editor's note

Though I am fond of so many museums and *scuole* in Venice, I can actually name my two favorite museums: the Correr and the Museo Storico Navale. I find nearly everything fascinating in the museum, but I especially like the pennants of Lepanto. Truthfully, they are not as impressive to me as the one in the museum in Toledo, Spain, but they are still awfully amazing.

SUSAN ALLEN TOTH is the author of *England As You Like It: An Independent Traveler's Companion* (Ballantine, in hardcover and paperback, 1995, 1996), *England for All Seasons* (Ballantine, in hardcover and paperback, 1997, 1998), and *Reading Rooms: America's Foremost Writers Celebrate Our Public Libraries with Stories, Memoirs, Essays and Poems* (Doubleday, 1991), among others. She has been an inspiration to me while working on my own series, and I wish she wrote more often on Mediterranean destinations.

Everyone who comes to Venice knows immediately that this city is indeed wedded to the sea: its foundations sunk deep into a lagoon, its myriad canals serving as streets and back alleys, and its faded palaces recalling a past as a great naval power.

But not everyone knows that Venice's long relationship with the sea is recorded in a vast and easily accessible museum.

Although the Museo Storico Navale, or Museum of Naval History, is only a few minutes' walk from the busy Piazza of St. Mark's, it is easy to miss.

Two large anchors stand before its doors on the Riva San Biagio, but its sign is modest and quite small. Any tourist could mistake it for just another part of the off-limits Arsenale, whose water-bus stop is outside the museum entrance.

Few tourists seem to find their way here. On an early October day, when the usual crowds were lining up before St. Mark's, jostling each other in the Doges' Palace, and jamming the doors at the Accademia, the rooms of the naval museum were almost empty.

Except for one party of giggling schoolchildren, who were quickly herded through, my husband, James, and I spent an entire morning virtually alone.

Passing through heavy glass doors, we paid a modest 2,000 lire each (at about $1.40, one of Venice's rare bargains) to tour four floors and what seemed like infinite connecting rooms.

Unlike most public buildings in Venice, the naval museum is light, airy, spacious, and freshly painted, with white walls, gleaming terrazzo floors, handsome wood and glass cases, and—best of all—informative signs everywhere in Italian and English. (Part of the bargain, worth noting to anyone who has experienced the few overused public toilets in Venice, are the museum's large, clean, tiled, and ventilated restrooms.)

The sea almost literally sweeps into the museum. Tall windows line the lagoon side, so, looking up from an exhibit, we would catch a glimpse of a cruise ship, tug, ferry, sight-seeing boat, private motorboat, or *vaporetto* floating by. It was as if the museum wanted to remind us that Venice's life on the sea, however diminished, still rose and fell with the tides.

Just inside the doors, a small room displayed a two-man submersible boat from World War II, used for attaching torpedoes to enemy ships. Naval power in Venice has always been intimately involved with war. A placard told a brief story of a British captain who had captured two Italian commandos. Even when the captain put one of them in the hold near the presumed bomb, the Italian refused to reveal its precise location. The bomb exploded without loss of life. Later this Italian commando served with the Allies, and in a turnabout of fortune, the same British officer awarded him a decoration.

Stories like that, succinct in plot and character, appeared everywhere in the museum, miniature sagas of courage, foolhardiness, pride, and chauvinism.

The flag room, filled with cases of dramatic uniforms and draped with banners from different eras, hinted at many of those qualities. On one pennant, faded crimson edged with gold, a lion holding the coat of arms of the Giustinian family boasted of the historical importance of the city's aristocracy. Another flag, the Imperial Standard of Emperor Napoleon III from 1865, signaled the sad end of Venetian independence.

Attached to the wall of the next room, huge gold letters spelled out VITTORIO VENETO, insignia taken from the stern of a battleship destroyed in 1945. Their polished glamour cast an eerie aura over a roomful of models of World War II battleships, frigates, and submarines.

The life span of most of those ships—and of many of the men in them—was cut short. Reading the placards was like reading epitaphs: sunk in 1943, destroyed in 1944, burned in 1942. (Another room even displayed some spent torpedoes, now bent and crumpled. One, stood on end, looked like a macabre piece of modern sculpture.)

Although the deceptive glitter and inevitable pall of war hung over this section of exhibits, I found myself drawn to the intricate ships' models, constructed in several different scales. In room after room, skilled artisans brought their various ships wonderfully to life. One large, almost dizzyingly detailed model of an eighteenth-century combat vessel, forty-eight oars on twenty-four benches, even had realistic-looking wooden men carved to scale. I thought how their backs must have been breaking.

Other carved figures sat in an eighteen-oar scouting vessel, a twenty-eight-oar brigantine, a fifteen-bench raider. A Venetian xebec, a raider galeotta, a sixteenth-century trireme (modeled in 1801) were all there before me, complete in every detail, sometimes cut into cross-sections or longitudinal sections for further clarity. An actual piece of a stern, faded blue with incredibly ornate gilded carvings, columns, scrolls, and acanthus leaves, from a Venetian vessel of the eighteenth century, evoked the spirit of that luxurious and decadent era.

Bits of ships, mementos of the shipbuilders' arts, hung on the walls or in cases. Some were straightforwardly utilitarian, like a carpenter's plane, a huge old wood docking windlass, or the bow section of a lugger. Others were fragments that looked like flotsam that had mysteriously floated into the museum: ships' bells, part of an anchor chain, figureheads, a mast section, elaborately carved porthole doors.

One eye-catching item, at first looking like a wooden Medusa's wig, turned out to be a sculpture of a sheepskin, a bow ornament that involved an ancient Mediterranean tradition. When launching a ship, the placard told us, sailors sacrificed a sheep and its skin was nailed on the bow as a propitiatory emblem. This ornament would serve the same purpose.

In case a visitor might forget what sailors had to confront on their dangerous voyages, several walls of dark, small oil paintings reminded us. Those primitive Italian paintings, plain and very moving, were hung by grateful crew members in churches as offerings of thanks.

They mostly showed scenes of shipwrecks—sailors swimming in black waters or scrambling onto drifting spars—while Mary and her Son, and sometimes God the Father, looked benignly on, willing everyone to safety.

Not all the naval museum is devoted to war or disaster. Many rooms commemorate the ships and smaller vessels that have always been a part of everyday Venetian life. Meticulously crafted models, often in burnished teak, showed work boats, like the barges used in the Venetian lagoon; light personnel carriers, looking like slender gondolas; medium and small material carriers; and passenger vessels.

The *Shrimp Tail,* a full-size stern boat from the nineteenth century, featured two black leather upholstered chairs, edged with rich black fringe, and a fringed canopy of herringbone linen with cream braid.

But for elegance of line and fitting, the gondolas were hard to surpass. One, labeled Shadow Cool Type (*"o gondola da fresca"*), evoked a vintage British car. A prized exhibit, donated in 1979, was Peggy Guggenheim's personal gondola, from the House Venier dei Leoni, which she made into the Guggenheim Museum of Modern Art in Venice. Gleaming black and adorned with carved lions, this lavish gondola had a magnificent heart-shaped cushioned seat, facing two carved armchairs. The seat was flanked by two gold lions, each holding a trident, with their tails curled aloft. Riding in this gondola down the Grand Canal would, I thought, be as bravura a gesture as one could make in Venice.

But that was before I saw the *Bucintoro.* In a small nearby room, a glass case enclosed a huge model of this entirely gilded, ornamented, and dazzling ship.

The original *Bucintoro* was Venice's ship of state, in which the doge made his ritual appearances, surrounded by select members of the aristocracy. It was destroyed by the French in 1798, but workers in the Arsenale re-created its splendors in this model of 1837.

Next to it was a full-size gilded throne, thought to be part of that last *Bucintoro.* No one could sit in that throne on that boat and remain humble for more than one sweep of the oarsmen below.

Other displays continued to surprise and delight us, making us linger far past our usual museum time. One room was filled with rare models of Chinese junks, another with portraits of champions of Venice's annual regatta, yet another with models of modern ocean liners.

The *Michelangelo*, operated from 1965 to 1975, the last large liner built in Italy, dominated the room at a scale of 1:50 and managed to suggest the size and majesty of those departed ships.

Finally beginning to tire, we did not give the attention it deserved to the Swedish Room, reached by an unlikely staircase from one upper exhibit hall. That room highlighted naval collaboration between Italy and Sweden, two seafaring countries who both sail on landlocked waters, the Mediterranean, and the Baltic.

Yet another door led from the Swedish Room into a hall that was an entire museum in itself. New and shining, the elegant room, donated in 1989, was filled with birch and glass cabinets containing a vast seashell collection. A catalog (in Italian only) lay on a handy table for identification and consultation.

After leaving the main museum, we had one more stop to make. Our ticket also admitted us to a pavilion a short distance down the Fondamenta dell'Arsenale. The pavilion, actually an unadorned warehouse with cement floors and stained wooden rafters, held real—not model—boats. They were cracked, worn-looking, and not at all gussied up.

Although I had thought I couldn't look at any more boats, I wandered among those mute relics with a renewed landlubber's respect for those who brave the sea.

Some were sporting types, like the captain of a bright-red racing motorboat that set several world records in 1935, and some were fishermen, like those who once steered a rush-grass Sardinian fishing boat.

We saw more sleek gondolas, inspected the tiny cabin where the captain's family lived at the rear of a freight-carrying barge, climbed a ladder to the deck of a torpedo boat that displaced sixty-five tons, and examined a life-cutter built in 1887.

Each of those boats had a story, I was sure, though I could only guess at a few of them. A black hearse, with gold ornaments and an angel at the stern, built in 1870, carried former Arsenale workers from the Church of San Biagio, a naval chapel, to the cemetery island of San Michele. I could envision the four rowers pulling their heavy freight, the imposing black boat sliding silently over the quiet water. When we walked out in the gray yet luminous day, with the lagoon glinting before us, I began to count and mentally describe all the different kinds of boats and ships that passed us.

Police boat, ambulance boat, the private taxi from the Cipriani, the glass factory's speedboat to Murano, *vaporetti*—I soon lost track.

But our visit to the naval museum had opened my eyes to other ships as well. Now, I could also imagine on the lagoon a ghostly flotilla—a magnificent *Bucintoro,* a forty-eight-oar combat vessel, an eighteenth-century pale-blue boat with gilded carvings, a working barge, Peggy Guggenheim's gondola of lions, a proud regatta winner standing in the prow of his boat, a red speedboat. The centuries floated by and disappeared. Thanks to my morning among those ships, I had sailed far into Venice's past and returned, perhaps a bit breathless, but in plenty of time to catch a Number 5 water bus home.

This piece originally appeared in the travel section of *The New York Times* on November 7, 1993. Copyright © 1993 by Susan Allen Toth. Reprinted with permission of the author.

All Play and No Work Makes for Great Art

By Elisabetta Povoledo

∿

editor's note

The Ca'Rezzonico, long a favorite museum of mine in Venice, was restored—some say a bit too much—and reopened to the public in the summer of 2001. The restoration will, happily, bring the beautiful building and its collection to the attention of visitors who I think have otherwise ignored the Rezzonico, or else put it on their secondary list of things to see. The collection of small paintings by Pietro Longhi, depicting scenes of daily life of Venetians in the 18th century, is invaluable and worth a visit just to see them. And as the museum is on the Grand Canal, there is at least one balcony where one can stand and pretend the *palazzo* is yours (I never miss an opportunity to pretend I live on the Grand Canal).

ELISABETTA POVOLEDO writes for *Italy Daily,* where this article first appeared.

The Carnival of 1796, held just one year before Venice meekly caved in to Napoleon's troops marking the end of the Most Serene Republic, was one the most lavish in its history.

Oblivious to the inglorious destiny awaiting them, the city's aristocracy gave in to the good life with particular gusto.

Venice's economy may have been in tatters, and its once sizeable political and military clout dwindled away to almost nothing, but the ruling class played on, festooning their gondolas, vying for the most elaborate mask, attending balls and theater performances, gambling, gossiping, flirting, eating, drinking, and dancing the nights away, poised on the edge of an abyss they didn't see coming.

The lavish Ca'Rezzonico, on the Grand Canal, which reopened in 2001 after a lengthy restoration, is a fitting receptacle for a museum dedicated to the pleasure-seeking eighteenth century. The palazzo's first proprietors headed for financial ruin while the second lasted barely sixty years, until the family died out.

Although not cursed like another Venetian palace, the Ca'Dario—whose owners have had a tendency to meet bad ends, most recently Ferruzzi chairman Raul Gardini, who shot himself in 1992—the sheer scale of the Ca'Rezzonico, its opulent halls and expensive furniture, are an indication of how any family could fall into ruin in its pursuit of the good life.

Pursue it the Venetian nobility did, for nearly a century, living off of the wealth accrued by their ancestors through commerce and trade, producing nearly nothing.

Still, to the European aristocracy of the eighteenth century, there was no better place to have a good time than the lagoon city. Venice then was what New York was in the 1980s, the ideal pleasure capital. More than 30,000 foreigners lived in the city, and thousands more came as tourists, drawn by the ephemeral pleasures of its legendary Carnivals and festivities. The celebration of the Sensa, an annual ritual commemorating the city's marriage to the sea, could draw 100,000 revelers.

"It was an evasive time, and the obsession with revelry meant to avoid the economic and political realities of the time," explained Michael Broderick, whose Veniscapes tour company offers specialized tours of the city; one on the age of decadence is coming soon. "The masks were part of society's masquerade, to portray itself as a happy carefree city."

If the aristocracy's over-the-top generosity, the feasts, and the lavish lifestyle—described in some detail by Giacomo Casanova, the era's most appealing cad—were little more than a mere front, a masquerade for that era's decadence, they were still effective, as is appreciated in the Ca' Rezzonico, which recreates a typical palazzo of the time.

The contradictions of eighteenth-century Venice are perhaps nowhere better reflected than in its art.

If the republic was plunging inexorably toward a politically ignoble end, culturally Venice thrived. It quickly became an artistic point of reference for all of Europe. Its musicians, among them Vivaldi, were admired, its painters wooed by the royal courts. Gianantonio Pellegrini and Giambattista Tiepolo spread their unaffected style to the rest of the continent, the golden luminosity and warm colors of the Venetian tradition finding favor among the monarchs north of the Alps.

The palace's gems are the four original ceiling frescoes by Giambattista Tiepolo, one a nuptial allegory to celebrate the marriage of Ludovico Rezzonico and Faustina Savorgnan, the others allegories of more abstract notions such as merit, nobility, and virtue.

Dozens of paintings depict Venetian life. For a society that today would be called "out of touch with its own feelings," blind as it was to the unsustainability of its lifestyle, the eighteenth century was also one of keen self-observation, albeit *sans* self-criticism. The notoriety of many great Venetian artists of the era came from their unique ability to acutely observe the society in which they lived.

The museum is teeming with examples. An entire wing is dedicated to Tiepolo's son, Giandomenico, the painter of society's pleasures, fashions, and foibles, represented here with a series of frescoes from his villa in Zianigo, in the countryside west of Venice.

There are works by the portraitist Rosalba Carriera, who keenly captured the essence of her sitters, as well as an entire room devoted to Pietro Longhi, who specialized in domestic views, and left a precious pictorial testament allowing the modern viewer a momentary peek into history.

Longhi tells us that a rhinoceros was in Venice in 1751; there's even a curious "I was there" inscription. He paints the nobility but also opens doors to the humbler classes that served the rich, portraying fortune-tellers and seamstresses and hairdressers.

He also enlightens us to one of the great fads of the era, chocolate, the ultimate decadent drink. Coffee, imported to Venice the century before, had enjoyed some notoriety with the wealthy, who were wont to dress up in Turkish robes and attempt to outdo each other's porcelain and silver tea sets. But some nobles felt coffee to be too, well, Protestant, because it gave the drinker a burst of energy. Chocolate, on the other hand, was deemed to be more Catholic, more in line with a slower-paced life.

There are rooms with works by the *vedutisti,* the view-painters, foremost among them Antonio Canal, known as Canaletto, who offers snapshots of his native city with freshness and humor. There is also the darker vision interpreted by Francesco Guardi.

The rich collection of paintings was gathered when the museum first opened in 1936 from various municipal collections or else bought on the antique market. Many furnishings come from the Palazzo Calbo Crotta, next to the train station, currently undergoing its own, very expensive restoration.

Begun by Baldassare Longhena in 1649 for the noble Bon family, construction on the Ca' Rezzonico halted in 1682 when the architect died and the family's finances faltered. The palace remained incomplete.

Enter the upstart Rezzonico family, Lombard merchants who had moved to Venice some years earlier and muscled their way to a noble title.

Giambattista Rezzonico bought the building in 1751 and hired the architect Giorgio Massari to finish Longhena's work. It was completed by 1758, when it hosted a series of extravagant balls after

Giambattista's brother, Carlo Rezzonico, bishop of Padua, became Pope Clement XIII.

Fame was short lived, and the Rezzonico family died out in 1810. The palace passed from hand to hand, at one time belonging to the painter Robert Barrett Browning, whose father Robert Browning, the poet, died within its walls. In 1935 it was donated to the city, and a year later the museum of the Venetian *settecento* was opened to the public.

Restoration of the museum was begun in 1978, but money ran out almost immediately, and it remained in a sorry state until 1994. Since then the city has spent more than 23 billion lire scrubbing it back into shape.

The Ca' Rezzonico, like many galleries in Italy, is both museum and historical monument, which made the restoration slow going. "Some laws to update the palazzo are a curse," complained Filippo Pedrocco, the museum's director. "They make no distinction between a historical building and a warehouse in Rho."

Opening only sporadically for the past five years to host temporary exhibits, it finally opened its doors in July 2001.

In October, the third and fourth floors—the latter includes the reconstruction of an apocathery shop—will house the recent donation of 350 paintings given to the museum by Egidio Martini, a Venetian artist, restorer, and collector.

"The eighteenth-century marvels exhibited in the museum make one think of that century as one lived by those who did not know they were going to die," said Venice historian Gino Benzoni.

This piece originally appeared in the August 29, 2001 issue of *Italy Daily*. Copyright © 2001 by Elisabetta Povoledo. Reprinted with permission of the author.

Restoration of a Renaissance Jewel Box: Santa Maria dei Miracoli

BY RANDOLPH H. GUTHRIE

~ᴖ~

editor's note

....

While working on this edition, I became extremely interested in the works that Save Venice has cleaned and restored over the years, and especially in exactly how a work is saved from certain destruction. I thought other readers would be equally as curious, so I asked the chairman of Save Venice, Randolph Guthrie, if there were any summaries of particular projects I could include in this anthology; he suggested this piece, which he wrote as the introduction to an upcoming book about the restoration of the stunning church of Santa Maria dei Miracoli. (The book, by the way, will be published in Italian, though the first five pages will be in English, and will have photographs by Ralph Liebermann, the finest photographer of architecture today; the book will be available through Save Venice.)

RANDOLPH H. GUTHRIE, introduced earlier in this book (page 172), is a surgeon by profession whose passion for Venice knows no bounds.

The restoration of the Church of Santa Maria dei Miracoli began with a dream—that Save Venice could be transformed from a tiny organization of three hundred supporters raising $25,000 a year into a powerhouse that would comprise thousands of supporters and raise a million dollars a year. It was an ambitious dream, perhaps even presumptuous, since we were taking responsibility for a project that would cost us almost $4 million at a time when we had almost nothing but faith. In the end, after ten years, all was accomplished. Save Venice and its many friends had risen to meet the challenge.

Santa Maria dei Miracoli is an extraordinarily beautiful church. It is unique in its unadorned, jeweled marble surfaces; in its harmonious sarcophagus form; in its painted, coffered ceiling; in its incredible stone carvings by the Lombardo family; in its elevated apse; and in its feeling of intimacy. It is no wonder that it is the favorite wedding church of Venice. There are few buildings in the world of this stature. It was a joy to restore.

Two years of studies preceded the restoration. A detailed, minute, visual inspection was made. Almost life-size drawings were created using laser beams. Every inch of the walls was tapped with an electronic hammer connected to a computer to turn up defects by measuring the speed of sound waves. Numerous small holes were drilled, into which humidity and temperature sensors were inserted and attached to a computer. These and other studies turned up a number of discoveries; I would like to relate some of those most interesting to us laypeople.

For a starter, it was feared that the structural brick had been so weakened by salt invasion that the walls were in danger of simply turning to powder and collapsing, just as had happened to the bell tower in San Marco in 1904. To the contrary, the brick walls were found to be in reasonably good condition, probably because the German private committee had, in the early 1970s, put a barrier layer in between two lower courses of the walls to block rising lagoon water. Further, we found that the water in the walls was mostly fresh and indeed was rain water leaking into them through defects around the windows. Having water in the walls is not normally a good thing, but in this case it had been diluting and driving out the salt in the bricks ever since the Germans had created their barrier.

The marble slabs and carvings in the left front corner of the nave were in much worse condition than anywhere else in the church. People speculated that this was due to the nearness of the adjacent canal, but the whole left wall lay alongside the canal, and only the front was affected. The computer-controlled temperature and humidity sensors placed throughout the church showed that, from time to time in this corner, suddenly, the temperature would drop and the relative humidity rise. Sometimes it would happen two or three times a day. Other times several days would pass without anything happening. The computer printouts were clear in their information, but no one could interpret it.

Finally, in our frustration, we assigned a person to sit next to the computer and observe exactly what was happening in the church at the time of the atmospheric changes. In the end, the answer was simple. The left front corner wall contained a door going down steps to the sacristy, which, being in the bowels of the church, was cold and wet. Opening the door allowed a burst of wet cold air to escape, which naturally led to condensation of water on the nearby walls. This door is now permanently sealed, and the door at the right front of the nave is used instead (with some changes inside to alleviate the phenomenon).

Another intriguing question arose from the studies: what was the original surface of the walls above the cornice? The cornice runs around the inside of the church about ten feet off the floor. Both below and above it, the walls are surfaced with marble slabs. The slabs below the cornice seem to be part of the original design. But the slabs above are peculiar in that, where they abut the window frames, the frames do not stick out into the room beyond the slabs. In fact, they fail to stick out even half the thickness of the slabs. Now normally the frame of a door or window sticks out further than the thickness of the wall surface, allowing the frame to hide any imperfections in the edge of the wall. This is true of the exterior sides of the window frames of the Miracoli but not of the interior. Why?

No one can be sure, but it is likely that the original wall surface above the cornice was of one-quarter-inch-thick marmorino. If so, during the Austrian restoration in the 1870s, the marmorino, for reasons unknown, was replaced with marble slabs. These, being an inch and more thick, stick out farther into the room than the window frames, whose depth had been designed for the thinner marmorino. For a while there was debate about removing the slabs and resurfacing with marmorino. In the end it was decided not to make so great an alteration. We hope that this was not a mistake. If the architects intended the walls to carry marmorino, they are now carrying a great deal of unintended weight. The architects of older times knew exactly what they were doing. How else can one explain the survival of the great cathedrals floating on no more than tiny finger columns—just wisps of stone? We can only trust that the architect, Pietro Lombardo, put in a little extra strength for good measure and future meddlers.

The slabs on the lower walls were taken down for salt removal. They were placed in specially built, large steel tubs containing circulating distilled water and left there until testing showed that their salt content was minimal. Some of these slabs were found to be reused tombstones with elaborate carvings on their back sides. Some were original from 1489. Some had been replaced over many years. All were returned to the walls. Of great interest was the method of connection of the slabs to the walls. The old Venetians, cleverer by far than any of us, knew all about high water rising in the brick, bringing with it its corroding salt. They protected the valuable marbles by hanging them on bronze hooks with a space between the brick and the marble that the water could not cross. The eighteenth-century restorers must have believed that the old Venetians didn't know any other way to attach the marbles, so they took away all the hooks and plastered the marbles back with cement. The cement was doubly evil. It made a connection that allowed the salt water to cross into the marble, and it added the even more corrosive calcium salts to the water. We removed all the cement and restored the hooks. The latter had to be hand made.

The intricate wood and metal webbing of the rose window was totally rotted and had to be remade from scratch. Marvelous craftsmen were found who created a new window exactly like the old, and it is extraordinarily beautiful. The same goes for the wood of the doors, altar frames, benches, and especially the ceiling.

We had decided not to touch the ceiling. It is entirely of wood, containing fifty carved wooden coffers draped over the curve of the barrel vault, each holding a painted prophet. The paintings were restored in the 1960s, but the wood had not been touched. Before we started the work, all looked reasonably bright, but after the marbles had been restored and the church was gleaming, the ceiling woodwork looked dirty and drab. Fortunately, an angel was found to share the cost, and the ceiling was also restored to its former splendor.

It is difficult to believe that we could have found our way through without architect Mario Piana. As the chief official of the Superintendency of Monuments assigned to the project, he shepherded it from beginning to end. He watched over all of the work that was done on site as well as supervising the selection and work of subcontractors. He kept close guard on all expenses, which, with so many different suppliers and craftsmen, was not easy to do. He ensured that the highest standards of restoration were observed. The Lombardi could not have had a more worthy guardian. Mario has our heartfelt gratitude.

Where can we find enough words of praise for Ottorino Nonfarmale, the man whose company performed all the restoration and who was on site every day, year in and year out? He oversaw everything. When chemicals were tested on the stones, he made sure that they were the right strength. When the woodwork of the ceiling was being stripped, he did the first part himself to be sure how far to go. When others did the rose window, he instructed them exactly what to do. For Ottorino, this work was not for profit but for love. And it shows. We are truly grateful.

Of the literally thousands of generous donors who gave through Save Venice to this restoration, three deserve special mention. The first and most touching is Carmela Gennaro, a lifelong schoolteacher in New York City. Born in New York of Sicilian-American parents, she traveled to Europe in 1950 and fell in love with Venice. Though she never was able to return, she treasured her memory of the beautiful fabled city, and when she died, she left a quarter million dollars, half her estate, to benefit its restoration. The second is Save Venice's much-esteemed board member Paul Wallace, who was our "angel" for the ceiling and gave a matching grant of a quarter million dollars. Lastly, the Getty Grant Program contributed another quarter million dollars. Getty grants are so prestigious that receiving this award was a great stimulus and morale-builder for all of us.

Nothing would have been possible without the extraordinary performance through the years of the staff of Save Venice—our executive director, Beatrice Guthrie; our New York director, Karen Marshall; and our Venice director, Melissa Conn. Starting in 1987, they revitalized the organization. Membership exploded. Money was raised in ever increasing amounts. Systems, especially computerization, were developed that became the envy of other similar organizations. The five-day Regatta Week Gala in Venice and its journal were created. The newsletter became an annual publication. The brochure documenting all the restorations in our history was assembled. We originated our fund-raising trips and cruises. We began the lecture series in New York, featuring eminent experts on various aspects of Venice. The organization was roused from a deep sleep and made alive. It was an exciting time, and it allowed us to restore Santa Maria dei Miracoli, as well as taking on a host of other projects.

After ten years the work was finished in 1997. It is the only church in the world to be totally refurbished from top to bottom, inside and out. When it was done, the old sacristan, who had shuffled about during the years of work, doing his best to accommodate everyone, stood in the back of the building and cried. The people in the fully packed church showed no less emotion during its official reopening, presided over by the patriarch and the mayor of Venice. It was a great day.

I said that day from the podium, "We would like to recognize all those who have helped bring about this new miracle—those of you who are here and those many who are not here—who have contributed to the restoration of this church, Saint Mary of the Miracles. Without you, we could have done little. Our thanks and gratitude go out to all of you. We are finished. We can go in peace."

Jewish Tombs on a Venice Sandspit

BY PETER HELLMAN

editor's note

After nearly two centuries of neglect, the Jewish cemetery on the Lido has been restored and reopened to the public. It's one of the oldest in Europe (established in 1386), and visiting the cemetery was a highlight of my last trip to Venice. It's just a short walk there from where the boat from Piazza San Marco docks.

PETER HELLMAN contributes frequently to *The New York Times* and is the author of *When Courage Was Stronger Than Fear: Remarkable Stories of Christians Who Saved Jews From the Holocaust* (Marlowe & Company/Balliett & Fitzgerald, distributed by Publishers Group West,

1999), *The American Wine Handbook* (Ballantine, 1987), and *The Auschwitz Album* (Random House, 1981), among others.

"Now I feel my trip to Venice is complete," said a Jewish tourist from Texas as she and her husband entered the sixteenth-century square of the city's former ghetto, the first of its kind in Europe. Yes, there's much to see here, including five synagogues, a museum, and a grim Holocaust memorial. But few visitors who tour this quarter realize that the place that most sweepingly evokes six tumultuous centuries of Venetian Jewish memory is neither in the ghetto nor even on the main islands of Venice.

That site is the ancient Jewish cemetery, hidden away behind high brick walls on the northern end of the Lido, the chic sandspit across the lagoon that shields Venice from the open Adriatic Sea. The cemetery's euphemistic Hebrew name is Beit Chaim—House of the Living. The oldest legible tombstone to have been found here is that of "Samuel, son of Samson," dated 1389. Of all the ancient Jewish cemeteries in Europe, only the one in Worms, Germany, can claim any existing monument more venerable.

After the opening of a new Jewish cemetery around the corner in 1774, the old one long lay abandoned and battered. Yet with its tombstones chiseled in Hebrew, half hidden and askew amid wild-flowers, vines, and scrubby trees, the cemetery appealed greatly to the sentiments of such romantic luminaries as Byron and Shelley, who rode horseback on the unspoiled Lido in the nineteenth century. More recently, the rare tourist who was curious about the cemetery had a hard time gaining access to it. The best one could do was to peer in through the bars of the padlocked iron gate.

Now the situation is at last on the verge of change. Following a yearlong restoration, just completed, the House of the Living is ready for a close-up look: tours of the cemetery started in February 2000.

The oldest tombstones in the cemetery, following the German tradition of the founding Jews of Venice, bear simply carved Hebrew epitaphs. But the Sephardic Jews who arrived in Venice after the expulsion from Spain in 1492 and from Portugal in 1497 brought with them a taste for surprising, even exuberant tombstone images. Look no further, for example, than the pair of rectangular stone sarcophagi from the early eighteenth century, belonging to Vidal and Esther Amar, that flank the entrance gates a few steps into the cemetery. Glaring out from their corners, between side panels carved with garlands and fruit, are the heads of unsavory, thuglike creatures. The top panels are adorned with large, elaborately carved lion's heads, each inset with a fruit, perhaps a pomegranate. In all, this vigorously carved decoration seems as if it belongs on a Renaissance palazzo on the Grand Canal rather than in a graveyard. Just beyond these sarcophagi is a tombstone with an inescapably Old Testament decoration: two naked men carrying a hanging bough of giant grapes, which they have just brought back to the Israelite encampment from Canaan.

No one can pinpoint the year in which Jews first appeared in Venice. The first notice is negative—a tenth-century regulation banning Venetian ships from carrying Jewish merchants, perhaps lobbied for by their competitors. Then, in the late fourteenth century, the republic, reeling from a costly war with Genoa, sought to revive its liquidity by inviting Jewish moneylenders, mainly from the mainland city of Mestre, who were required to provide below-market interest rates.

The Jews were later expelled, then reinvited. Finally, in 1516, the community was formally installed in a poor quarter that was a foundry site (*getto* in Italian). The population in 1552 is estimated to have been around 900, out of a total of 160,000 residents in the city. At night the three ghetto gates were locked and guarded by Christians whose salaries were paid by the Jews within. The key difference between this mother of all ghettos and its vile Hitlerian successors is that the doges never laid a finger on the Jews of Venice.

The burial ground granted to the community in 1386 was "the most out-of-the-way place the authorities could imagine," says Aldo Izzo, a retired sea captain who lives on the Lido and is president of the local Jewish burial society. An adjoining Benedictine cloister, which had previously controlled the cemetery land, failed in a legal proceeding to have the land returned. Next the Jews protested against vandalism in the cemetery and even the unearthing of the dead. In 1391 the republic directed that a wooden fence be built around the cemetery. That seems to have brought peace between the monks and the Jewish dead.

Rather than leave some of the oldest tombstones unguarded in the old cemetery, Mr. Izzo removed them, a few years ago, to the new cemetery. Among them is that of Samuel, son of Samson. More than twelve hundred monuments remain in the old cemetery, though not necessarily in their original locations. Hundreds have been set along the perimeter walls.

Walking the grounds with Mr. Izzo, I was puzzled to see that many tombstones bear an image of upraised hands. Mr. Izzo explained that these were graves of *kohanim*, who are regarded as descendants of temple priests in biblical times. The upraised hands symbolize the priestly benediction. Another frequent image is that of water being poured into a bowl—a symbol of the Levites, who were charged with washing the hands of the priests. The winged angel on a tomb of the Malach family, Mr. Izzo explained, is there because in Hebrew the name means "angel."

A rarity in this or any Jewish cemetery is the scorpion carved on the tombstone of Sara Copio Sullam. It's an allusion to the maiden name of the deceased, which is derived from *scorpio*. Copio Sullam, who was known for her blond-tressed beauty and for her lively literary salon in the ghetto, died in 1641. Many Marranos (Jews who were forced to become Christians under the Spanish Inquisition but practiced Judaism secretly) converted back to Judaism upon reaching Venice but held on to their combative heraldics—prancing Castilian lions, castles, and suits of armor being prominent on their coats of arms.

One of the simpler tombstones in the cemetery belongs to Venice's most renowned Jewish figure, Leone Modena, an extrordinary man-about-town, revered in circles both Jewish and Christian, religious and secular. Modena, who died in 1648, wrote numerous books, including *The History of Jewish Rituals* and an autobiography of life in seventeenth-century Venice, in which he listed his pursuit of twenty-six professions ranging from composer of Italian sonnets to marriage broker. Modena needed plenty of work since, as an admitted compulsive gambler, he was constantly in debt. In his will, he directed that the elegist at his funeral point out that "he was not a hypocrite, that his heart was the same inside as out, and that he feared God and fled evil more in secret than in the open."

Beginning in the 1670s, the dead no longer rested in peace in the old cemetery, as the republic took over its northern portion and built fortifications against the threat of a Turkish attack. The tombstones that got in the way were simply piled in the rear of the remaining cemetery grounds. The community then opened its new cemetery, farther inland, in 1774. Napoleon, to whom the republic succumbed without a blow being struck in 1796, liberated the ghetto but heaped further indignity on the old cemetery, according to Mr. Izzo, by using tombstones as cannon platforms. Later, the northern portion became a shooting range, which is active to this day. The coup de grâce came in the 1920s, when a new coastal road was cut through the front of the old cemetery. By then its original five acres had been whittled down to just under one acre. There were no protests. "Nobody cared about this place," explains Mr. Izzo, "not even the Jews."

Indeed, Venetian-born Jews I queried were short on memories of the old cemetery. But one, Mino Vianello, had a chilling memory of a burial in the new one. In September 1943, with Italy under Nazi occupation, the police had demanded a list of local Jews from Giuseppe Jona, head of the community. Rather than comply, Mr. Jona committed suicide. By night Mr. Vianello's father and three other men brought the body by boat to the cemetery on the Lido for burial. "They were frightened," remembers Mr. Vianello, who was then a boy, "but there was no choice." Of two hundred Venetian Jews deported by the Nazis, only seven survived.

In the 1970s, the small Venetian Jewish community, numbering well under a thousand, began the restoration of the ghetto. "We had no energy left over to work on the old cemetery," explains Cesare Vivante, head of the committee on Jewish monuments. Finally, in 1996, local and regional government agencies, heeding Mr. Vivante's prodding, provided funds to begin the restoration, including clearing, regrading, landscaping, and draining a salt marsh that had formed at the rear of the cemetery, as well as cleaning and repairing tombstones. That work came up to speed with grants from the New York–based Steven H. and Alida Brill Scheuer Foundation. Other donors included Save Venice, Venice in Peril, and the World Monuments Fund.

The rear of the cemetery is rather sterile-looking because of the swamp draining, resembling a well-groomed suburban cemetery. The front, which was not under water, has more mature trees and foliage. One surprise that emerged from the muck during the draining: fourteen tomb markers in the form of Doric columns bearing tablets carved with epitaphs of the Cividal family and their seal showing Samson fighting a lion.

After the uniquely intense splendor of Venice, an excursion to the Lido for a look at the old cemetery provides a fascinating change of pace. It's a fifteen-minute ride on the *vaporetto* from San Marco to the lively Piazza Santa Maria Elisabetta—not a Gothic or Renaissance structure in sight!—on the Lido. On a fine day last fall, my thirteen-year-old daughter, Kate, and I rented bicycles on the square. We headed across the Lido, a mere quarter mile wide, to the sea beach, and came upon the vast, elegant, yet vaguely melancholic Hotel Des Bains, where Visconti filmed Thomas Mann's *Death in Venice*. Farther along we licked *gelato* cones as we gazed at the grand fantasy of the Hotel Excelsior, half-expecting men in tights wielding crossbows to appear in the tower crenelations. I got my biggest kick, however, from a hotel that isn't even on the beach. It's the Art Nouveau Hungaria Palace Hotel, at mid-island on the Gran Viale. Every inch of its facade is clad in pastel-tinted majolica tile, themed to a grape harvest carried out by smiling maidens. It's a ten-minute ride north from the Hungaria Palace to the gate of the old cemetery.

As we returned to Venice, the late afternoon sky was precisely the uncanny turquoise blue of Venetian landscapes by Canaletto—a tint I'd always suspected was one part painter's license. But the painter wasn't wrong. Across the lagoon, the muted sun was backing behind the dome of Santa Maria della Salute. The Venetian waterfront, dominated by the Piazza San Marco, positively glowed. At that moment I felt that my daughter and I owned our own perfect Canaletto.

Tour Basics

Guided tours of the Jewish cemetery are offered every Sunday starting February 6, leaving from the main cemetery door. The February 6 tour will be at 10 A.M.; thereafter, tours will be at 2:30 P.M.

There will also be cemetery tours by reservation on Wednesdays and Fridays if a minimum of twenty people is reached.

For reservations and information, call the Jewish Museum of Venice (041.715359). The cemetery tour costs $6.40, at 1,875 lire to the dollar; a combination ticket that includes a museum tour is $11.75.

The Number 1 *vaporetto* and the Number 14 *motonave* (a larger boat) leave from San Zaccaria, near San Marco, to go to the Lido, as do several lines from San Marco. Allow ten to fifteen minutes to walk to the cemetery. The A bus also goes there.

Bicycles may be rented on the Piazza Santa Maria Elisabetta.

Palmanova: An Ideal Fortress

BY SILVANO BERTOSSI

~

editor's note

Palmanova is simply that rare example of a perfect city in the utopian Renaissance style. It has been referred to as the "brightest star in the constellation of Venice's defenses," and to me it is the most fascinating site in all of Friuli–Venezia Giulia. The impeccable star-shaped plan of the city can really only be appreciated by a bird's eye view—contact the tourist offices in either Trieste or Udine, or Pro Loco Palma (0432.929106) for more information. But even if the view from a small airplane is not part of your itinerary, do not miss visiting the town, its streets, and the Duomo.

SILVANO BERTOSSI contributes frequently to *Italy Italy*, where this piece first appeared.

Born as a citadel, the little city of Palmanova is actually a romantic fortress that has laid down its arms and looks like something out of a storybook. Nevertheless, it testifies to the ingenuity of man. Palmanova is a living monument, challenging the passage of time and offering a tantalizing glimpse into the past.

At the dawn of the fifteenth century, the Republic of Venice conquered Friuli, the region in northeastern Italy that for many years had been ruled by the patriarchs, the prince-bishops of Aquileia. Venice's rival in conquest was the Austrian Empire. Eager to strengthen its overseas commercial network, Austria had long had its eye on the ports of the northern Adriatic Sea. Venice also had to defend itself from the Turkish Empire, encroaching on its eastern border. The Turks had already conquered Bosnia. They were also staging incursions into Croatia, Slovenia, and Carinthia and had then begun to press westward toward Friuli.

The first of the invasions feared by the new Venetian occupiers of Friuli came in 1472, when the Turks threatened Rocca di Montefalcone. Venice was also obliged to defend its territories from invasion by sea. In the momentous Battle of Lepanto in 1571, the Venetian navy was pitted against the Turks in what military historians say was the largest battle of the modern era involving ships powered by oarsmen. The Venetian ships had 1,815 cannons and 74,000 men. Their fleet was composed mainly of galleys, a flat and narrow type of ship widely used from the Middle Ages until the nineteenth century. There were also six galeasses (ships larger than galleys) and thirty smaller ships.

One hundred and five Venetian galleys were commanded by Sebastiano Venier. His fleet was flanked by seventy-nine Spanish galleys under the command of Andrea Doria of Genoa, and a dozen papal galleys under Marcantonio Colonna of Rome. Three more galleys were sent by the duke of Savoy, three by the Order of Malta. The Turkish fleet was composed of 222 galleys and sixty galiots (smaller and swifter than galleys), with 750 cannon and 88,000 men. The outcome was disastrous for the Turks. Fifty of their ships were destroyed and 117 were captured; 8,000 Turks died and 10,000 were taken prisoner. The Venetians lost a mere fifteen galleys, though 7,500 men in all were killed in the fierce combat.

Despite the victory at Lepanto, the war between the Turks and the Venetians was not over. The Ottomans never again reached Friuli, but life in the Venetian Republic was anything but quiet. There were conflicts with the Austrians and with pirates from the Balkan territories who, with their fast launches, disrupted Venice's sea trade and staged quick but damaging incursions by land. Precisely for these reasons, the Venetians decided to build a fortress to defend their eastern border.

At that time fortresses were one of the few means of defending a territory. With the introduction of gunpowder, it became necessary to redesign fortresses so they could resist cannon fire. Bastions, the mighty structures that jut out from defensive walls at regular intervals, had to be strengthened. The length of the walls between the bastions was increased to adapt to the longer range of the new weapons. The walls had to provide shelter within them for troops, and they had to defend the entrances of the fortress and offer secure positions for cannons.

All of this required a new way of conceiving the design of fortresses, in which military needs took priority over civil ones. Whereas Renaissance architects imagined ideal cities that had regular geometric shapes and urban plans offering a minimum of comfort to their inhabitants, military architects preferred radial plans, with streets leading directly to the bastions and city walls, for maximum efficiency in emergencies. Civil architects, by contrast, proposed grid-shaped plans with streets leading to the city gates. Early in 1593, three architects presented projects for the proposed fortress. The Senate of Venice chose the project drawn up by Giulio Savorgnan, with some later changes. The plan of the city itself was influenced by the ideas of Bonaiuto Lorini and Vincenzo Scamozzi, a pupil of the great architect Palladio. Scamozzi held that the piazzas should have closed corners. (According to previous tenets of urban planning, the streets leading to the city gates should initiate at the corners of the main piazza.)

A number of military and civil engineers took part in the construction of the fortress. It was Savorgnan, however, who played the most important role, even though the fortress he had built at Nicosia had been taken easily in an assault. Savorgnan attributed this failure to the weakness of the garrison; to the winding roads of the old town, which slowed down the troops; and to the fortress's vulnerable position at the foot of hills from which the enemy could easily fire inside the walls.

Palmanova has nine lanceolate bastions that give it a starlike plan. The interior was laid out on a geometric plan based on the number three and its multiples. Three streets (called *borghi*) lead from the large central piazza directly to the three monumental city gates, beyond which were three rural estates. The interior has six neighborhood districts, each with a smaller piazza at its center.

Because of its size, Palmanova is one of the most ambitious projects carried out in the Renaissance. It was a unique "military machine," a model for other star-shaped cities built in Europe up to the mid-eighteenth century. Construction began with the measuring of the land on October 9, 1593, when the positions of the bastions were defined. The earth dug up to create the moat was used to raise the bastions and the defensive walls. The tools employed were very simple, and great numbers of them were required. They included pickaxes, shovels, wheelbarrows, carts, and *zarletti* (containers for transporting earth that were strapped to the backs of the laborers).

Special mechanisms were used for digging and hoisting weights. The earth piled up for the defensive walls was packed and shored up with stone and brick. This laborious work proceeded slowly. Several times it stopped altogether. But by 1599 the main structures were in place. Building the rest took another thirty years and the toil of 7,000 men. It was not easy, at the time, to construct a fortified enclosure almost 4.5 miles long, with underground passages almost

3.5 miles long, in addition to the rest of the structures. The construction of the outer fortifications of the walls alone required moving 40,500 cartloads of material.

Palmanova has three rings of fortifications. These were built at different times and give the city the appearance of a star, or a snowflake. The first and the second rings were built by the Venetians. The second consists of the outer fortifications that protect the three city gates. The third and outermost ring was initiated in 1806 by Napoleon. A system of covered galleries and exterior passages that offered cover from enemy fire provided a safe and direct link between the city's innermost fortifications and the outermost defensive positions. Thanks to this new defensive concept, the fort was able to withstand Austrian sieges in 1809 and 1813.

Today Palmanova remains just as it was originally planned by those sixteenth-century architects. The city offers a tangible, fully accessible example of how a fortress could be built to defend a border, a territory, or an entire civilization. With its star-shaped plan, its three monumental city gates, and its defensive walls framed by a deep moat, Palmanova has an important place in the history of architecture.

The city-fortress is also beautiful. The clean lines of its nine-point stellar plan rest lightly on the vast plain, as if it had blown in on the wind and had set itself down there to be admired. Presently, Palmanova is a small city with a population of 3,500. It is a friendly place, where people know one another and value human relations. Fortunately, it was never destroyed by war. However, it would have been razed were it not for a timely intervention that prevented the destruction of this great example of sixteenth-century military architecture. The "military machine" withstood the attacks and the assaults of war. It would have been a real shame if all that work, the mental and physical labor of thousands, had been lost forever.

Palmanova's strategic location, chosen by the sixteenth-century Venetians for military purposes, also suits today's travelers. It is simple to include a visit to Palmanova in a tour of some of the other intriguing destinations in the area, all within easy reach. The cities of Udine and Trieste are an ideal base; they are well connected by bus, train and highway with the other places of interest in the region. The airport of Ronchi dei Legionari is about halfway between the two. Udine's Piazza della Libertà is one of Italy's most beautiful, and Trieste's vast Piazza dell'Unità d'Italia is another. Both cities have a medieval core, and each can boast some fine old churches and an impressive castle that now serves as a museum as well as a vantage point with fine vistas. Castles and massive medieval cathedrals are some of the more imposing attractions of the many cities and towns in the region of Friuli–Venezia Giulia in northeast Italy, along with a beautiful seashore and thickly wooded mountains. The smaller towns in the region harbor some artistic treasures as well. In Aquileia, an extraordinary sixth-century mosaic pavement stretches from one end to the other of a thousand-year-old basilica set among the ruins of an ancient Roman city. The charming town of Cividale has preserved its medieval appearance and a gem of a chapel built by the Lombards in the eighth century. Northward, toward the Austrian border, the town of Gemona del Friuli has a magnificent medieval cathedral. On the coast are the romantic castle of Miramare, Grado's picturesque port, and Trieste's splendid seafront promenade.

Biblioteca

Angels A to Z: A Who's Who of the Heavenly Host, Matthew Bunson, Crown Trade Paperbacks, 1996. This is *not* just another angel book—It's a fascinating and useful reference you'll be glad to have. From *abaddon* to *zutu'el* and with numerous black-and-white reproductions of major and minor artworks, this is really a great resource for looking at art. In his foreword, Bunson gives several reasons for the popularity of angels and states, "Finally, and perhaps most important, throughout history one thought has proven powerfully constant and nearly universally accepted by Jewish writers, Christian saints, Muslim scholars, and followers of the New Age: The angel is one of the most beautiful expressions of the concern of God for all of his creations, an idea beautifully expressed by Tobias Palmer in *An Angel in My House:* 'The very presence of an angel is a communication. Even when an angel crosses our path in silence, God has said to us, "I am here. I am present in your life." ' "

From Abacus to Zeus: A Handbook of Art History, James Smith Pierce, Prentice-Hall, 1977. Pierce has keyed the A–Z entries in this useful guide to the second edition of H. W. Janson's *History of Art,* which I mention only to illustrate that this is an extremely thorough and indispensable reference. Entries are presented A–Z within five chapters: "Art Terms, Processes, and Principles"; "Gods, Heroes, and Monsters"; "Christian Subjects"; "Saints and Their Attributes"; and "Christian Signs and Symbols."

History of Art, H. W. Janson, Anthony F. Janson, 6th rev. ed., Harry N. Abrams, 2001. Still enormous (and now slipcased), still a classic, and still a fixture on college and university campuses.

The Illustrated Age of Fable: The Classic Retelling of Greek and Roman Myths Accompanied by the World's Greatest Paintings, Thomas Bulfinch, with a new foreword by Erika Langmuir O.B.E., Stewart, Tabori & Chang, 1998. Someone was really thinking when he or she came up with this brilliant idea for a book. Though not a single painting featured is in a northeastern Italian museum (the closest we get is the Palazzo Ducale in Mantua), I include it here because the very great *Bacchus and Ariadne* by Titian graces the cover (this gorgeous canvas is in the collection of the National Gallery, London) and because it contains paintings by Correggio, Titian, Tiepolo, Carpaccio, and Tintoretto. Additionally, this is an essential book to have. As Bulfinch noted in his original book, first published in 1855, "our book is not for the learned, nor for the theologian, nor for the philosopher, but for the reader of English literature, of either sex, who wishes to comprehend the allusions so frequently made by public speakers, lecturers, essayists, and poets, and those which occur in polite conversation." Bulfinch was aware, as Langmuir notes in her foreword, that many less privileged men and women felt excluded from what he called "cultivated society." Langmuir adds, "His book was designed as much to remove a social barrier as to inform and delight."

The Oxford Companion to Christian Art and Architecture, Peter and Linda Murray, Oxford University Press, 1998. A thorough reference guide with color plates; general background to the Old and New Testaments and Christian beliefs; a glossary of architectural terms; and a detailed bibliography.

The Story of Art, E. H. Gombrich, 16th ed., Phaidon Press, London, 1995. Although Sir Ernst Gombrich has authored numerous volumes on art, this is the one that established his reputation. To quote from the jacket, "*The Story of Art* is one of the most famous and popular books on art ever published. For 45 years it has remained unrivalled as an introduction to the whole subject."

Who's Who in the Bible, Peter Calvocoressi, Penguin Books, 1987, 1999. Though similar to the books listed above, this volume features more artworks—more than 130 both in black and white and in color—and is devoted exclusively to the people in the Bible. With biographies of more than 450 characters (some famous, others less so, others just ordinarily famous "whose names are familiar even when what they did is ill remembered," and the rest completely unfamous) from the Old and New Testaments and the Apocrypha, curious readers can find out the defining qualities of people from the Bible and learn how they have inspired artists, musicians, and writers through the ages. With six genealogical charts, six maps, and a glossary, this is an indispensable monastic companion. (It's paperback too, if you want to pack it.)

In a Category by Itself

Places: A Travel Guide for Music and Art Lovers, Robert Craft, Thames and Hudson, 2000. This most unusual book is indeed hard to categorize, but then Craft is hard to pin down too. He is probably best known for his nearly lifelong friendship with Igor and Vera Stravinsky (interested readers should turn to his *Chronicle of a Friendship* for more on that), but he is as well an inveterate traveler, acclaimed conductor (just a few of his credited works are six recordings of Stravinsky—including *The Rite of Spring* and *Firebird Suite*—and six of Schoenberg), a critic of contemporary ballet, and a scholar of twentieth-century and Renaissance music. Craft is a travel writer in the mold of Norman Douglas and Bruce Chatwin, conveying an enormous wealth of knowledge and an equally enormous vocabulary. (I admit I have been sent to the dictionary on more than one occasion while reading this book.) I was drawn to him because it's obvious he is a *Collected Traveler* type: he enjoys reading up on his chosen locale before he arrives, and his luggage apparently always holds a mini library of books. It has been said of Craft that "his gift is for identifying and absorbing the quintessence of the place and communicating his discoveries with the infectious enthusiasm of a detective solving a puzzle or a prospector finding gold." The chapters in *Places* feature destinations in Europe, Africa, the United States, and Asia and an entire one for Italy. ("La Serenissima" is one essay.) It is worth quoting from a review by Michael Dirda, for *The Washington Post Book World,* so that readers know exactly what they're getting into when they pick up Craft: "He alludes to authors by last name only, drops in phrases from Latin, Italian or French, expects you to be interested, as well you should, in Carthage, Roman ruins in North Africa, gamelan music, church architecture, art restoration, the painters Klimt and Schiele, Hindu mythology, Christian iconography, Kafka, landscape design, Moorish Spain, Chinese archaeological digs, Canova, exhibitions at the Met and odd facts." Now you're forewarned, but don't misunderstand: this is great stuff, if perhaps not for those without an exhaustively quizzical mind.

Italian Art and Architecture

The Architecture of the Italian Renaissance, Peter Murray, Schocken Books, 1963, 1986. Related chapters include one on palace design in Venice and elsewhere; Sanmicheli and Sansovino (Sanmicheli's work in Verona, Sansovino's works in Venice); and two different ones on the works of Palladio.

The Art of the Italian Renaissance: Architecture, Sculpture, Painting, Drawing, edited by Rolf Toman, Konemann, 1995. This book includes a thorough glossary and lineage charts for the Sforza, Este, and Gonzaga families, the popes, and the doges of Venice.

The Arts of the Italian Renaissance: Painting, Sculpture, Architecture, Walter Paatz, Prentice-Hall and Harry N. Abrams, 1974. This is still among my favorite books on the *quattrocentro*. It is long out of print, but I think it's the best single volume one can find. With 301 illustrations, including 61 in color, it is a very comprehensive edition, with an excellent bibliography.

The Italian Painters of the Renaissance, Bernard Berenson, Phaidon, 1952. To my mind, this is without a doubt the single best book on Italian Renaissance painters. There are, of course, dozens of other worthy titles, and this one is out of print; but I urge you to check in your library or used bookstores for this fine edition. (It's a 488-page hardcover.) The first chapter opens with the line, "Among the Italian schools of painting the Venetian has, for the majority of art-loving people, the strongest and most enduring attraction." Following the final chapter—"The Decline of Art"—there are more than 200 pages of black-and-white reproductions. (Color tip-ons appear throughout individual chapters.) One of the reasons I and many others are so fond of Berenson is perhaps best explained by this excerpt from the preface: "Yet too much time should not be wasted in reading about pictures instead of looking at them. Reading will help little towards the enjoyment and appreciation and understanding of the work of art. It is enough to know when and where an artist was born and what older artist shaped and inspired him, rarely, as it happens, the master or teacher who first put pen pencil and brush into his hands. Least profit is to be got from the writings of the metaphysical and psychoanalytical kind. If read one must, let it be the literature and history of the time and place to which the paintings belong." *Essenziale.*

Lives of the Painters, Sculptors and Architects, in two volumes, Giorgio Vasari, translated by Gaston du C. de Vere (translation first published in 1912), with an introduction and notes by David Ekserdjian, Everyman's Library. The opening line of the introduction is the only recommendation one need ever read or hear on this masterpiece, originally published in 1550: "Giorgio Vasari's *Lives of the Painters, Sculptors and Architects* is the Bible of Italian Renaissance—if not all—art history." *Essenziale.* A wonderful companion volume is *The Great Masters* (Beaux Arts Editions, Hugh Lauter Levin Associates, 1986), which pairs Vasari's biographies on Giotto, Botticelli, da Vinci, Raphael, Michelangelo, and Titian with related paintings, sculptures, drawings, and architecture in 120 color plates and 127 black-and-white illustrations. There are also twenty gatefolds of selected works.

Looking at Pictures with Bernard Berenson, selected and with an introduction by Hanna Kiel, with a personal reminiscence by J. Carter Brown, Abrams, 1974. Kiel, who translated several of Berenson's works into German and prepared the bibliography at the end of this book, here combines text from Berenson's books, diaries, and letters with 150 great Italian paintings from museums and private collections in Europe and America. Only three of the works reproduced here are actually to be seen in the Veneto (*Flight into Egypt* by Tintoretto in the Scuola di San Rocco, Venice; *Noblewoman with Old Maid and Lapdog* and *Landscape* both by Veronese and both in the Palladian Villa Barbaro at Maser), so I wouldn't qualify this as *essenziale* unless, like me, you really enjoy Berenson; but there are lots of works by Venetian masters in other museums.

The Panorama of the Renaissance, Margaret Aston, Thames and Hudson and Harry Abrams, 1996. I was late in learning about this book, having only discovered it by chance while combing the shelves at Hacker Art Books in New York (see Bookstores entry in *Informazioni Pratiche* for contact information). But better late than never. Aston has had the ingenious idea of presenting the entire epoch of the Renaissance with more than a thousand illustrations spanning the whole of Europe. Thus we see what is happening in Belgium, for example, at the same time as in Italy and Spain, and in all areas: art, science, exploration, war, personalities, religion, daily life, fashion, architecture, eroticism, royalty, music, women, great cities, banking and business, and philosophy. The reference section at the back of the book includes a biographical dictionary, timelines of Renaissance history and culture, a map, a glossary, and a gazetteer of museums and galleries with collections of Renaissance art; this sixty-three-page section alone is worth the price of the book. *Essenziale.*

Venetian Art and Architecture

Another Venice, Jacopo Fasolo, Arsenale Editrice, 2000. This little pocket-size paperback is a gem of a book. Fasolo brings to our attention sixty-one lesser-known *monumenti,* complemented by beautiful watercolors and small color photographs of each entry. Fasolo describes Venice as a "large 'shared house' where the *campi* are the rooms and the *calli* the corridors," and he notes that the city's place-names reflect the differences between the *sestieri* and represent an account of the birth and growth of the city. "Thus we cannot but see Venice's architecture, whether it be humble or monumental, as forming a single unit that pulsates with the ideas of profound necessity and fully-fledged culture—each and every architectural manifestation therefore demands and deserves the visitor's close attention. And this is a sign of the attention paid to 'another' Venice, a Venice which is not exclusively monumental. In terms of the 'readability' of its details and the smaller size of its building, this 'other' Venice is perhaps much more accessible to us, much more intimate as well as fascinating and surprising in its more variegated solutions." Fasolo recommends that the best way to see the buildings of the "other" Venice is to be in a boat, gliding through small canals; but a great number of these monuments are to be found on regular walking routes, or else a short distance from them. One could plan an entire itinerary around these; on my last trip, I selected ten I wanted to see and easily worked them into my daily plans. Fasolo shares a surprising amount of history and information on each building, and with a map of each *sestiere,* this is quite a substantial and fascinating volume.

The Basilica of St. Mark in Venice, edited by Ettore Vio, Scala/Riverside, SCALA GROUP, Antella (Florence), 1999. Scala is known for publishing affordable books of high quality, and this (very affordable, about $19.99) paperback is the best I've seen of its kind. It's profusely illustrated in color with diagrams and cross-sections, and the quality of the reproductions is excellent.

Decorative Floors of Venice, Tudy Sammartini, foreword by John Julius Norwich, photographs by Gabriele Crozzoli, Merrell, 2000. "Venice is, par excellence, a city of detail," as John Julius Norwich notes in his foreword. I couldn't agree more, and just one example in Venice where this is particularly true is inside the St. Mark's Basilica. The first time I walked through, with my husband, I was so dazzled that I had to walk through again. It's true that I was awed by everything inside, but I couldn't keep my eyes off the floor. This is a sumptuous book in every way, with 240 color photos illustrating one of the least-documented aspects of the arts of Venice.

Painters of Venice: The Story of the Venetian "Veduta," Bernard Aikema, Boudewijn Bakker. This book was published on the occasion of an exhibit of the same name at the Rijskmuseum in Amsterdam (December 15, 1990— March 10, 1991). Artists featured include Canaletto, Caspar van Wittel Israel Silvestre, Johan Richter, Michele Marieschi, and Francesco Guardi.

Venetian Art from Bellini to Titian, Johannes Wilde, Oxford Studies in the History of Art and Architecture series, first published 1974; reprinted 1995.

Venice: Art & Architecture, Marion Kaminski, Konemann, 2000. Readers have a choice between one small, square, chunky volume or two large, heavy volumes for this title in Konemann's Art & Architecture series. (Others include Andalusia, Egypt, Paris, Tuscany, the Uffizi Gallery in Florence, and the Musée d'Orsay.) I like both sizes, and since neither one is lightweight enough to qualify as a bring-along, the larger may be the better value. But the one I have in my home is the smaller book, and I do not think it is lacking, except perhaps in the fine details of particular artworks. I don't think there is a page in the book without an illustration, color photograph, or floor plan (all of high quality), and the text is excellent. Chapters are devoted to a historical overview, the streets of Venice, the Grand Canal, individual *sestieri,* and the islands, with a great appendix featuring a glossary, biographies of artists, and—my favorite—a fold-out chronological timeline from 1150 to 1800. *Essenziale.*

Series

Masters of Italian Art, Konemann. The list is long of the artists featured in this series: Botticelli, Brunelleschi, Canaletto, Caravaggio, Donatello, Duccio, Fra Angelico, Ghirlandaio, Giotto, Gozzoli, Leonardo da Vinci, Mantegna, Michelangelo, Piero della Francesca, Pontormo, Raphael, Tiepolo, and Titian.

The Scrovegni Chapel: Padua, Bruce Cole, George Braziller, 1993. This lovely volume in the Great Fresco Cycles of the Renaissance series is meant to highlight the frescoes painted in chapels and town halls across Italy. Each volume in the series is written by a leading scholar in the field who sets the frescoes in their artistic and historical context.

Single Artist Books and Museum Catalogs

The following are definitive volumes (or catalogs that accompanied museum exhibitions) and are worth a special effort to track down. Some are *catalogues raisonnés,* or they represent an artist's work in Venice or northeastern Italy.

Giovanni Bellini

Giovanni Bellini, Anchise Tempestini, edited by Abigail Asher, translated by Alexandra Bonfante-Warren and Jay Hyams, Abbeville Press, 1999. When Giovanni Bellini was in his seventies, German master Albrecht Dürer described the artist as "very old, but still the best painter of all." This authoritative source explores twenty-five of Bellini's most important works.

Giovanni Bellini, Roger Fry, Ursus Press, 1995. Fry, a painter himself, belonged to an elite group of critics and connoisseurs who, in the latter part of the 19th century, embarked on a large artistic revisionist project with the task of clarifying Italian Renaissance art. In the first edition of Fry's book (dated 1901), he provided a succinct but definitive view of Bellini's career. He not only examined Bellini from a scientific perspective, for which he was clearly an authority, but also observed Bellini's innovative use of semitransparent oil glazes, his psychological motivation, and his affinity and great respect for nature. Fry is truly an authority on the Italian Renaissance, and his highly individual and knowledgeable assessments remain decisive.

Antonio Canale (Canaletto)

Canaletto, J. G. Links, Phaidon Press, 1982. Michael Kimmelman, writing in *The New York Times* at the time of the 2001 Biennale, noted that as a young painter trying to make his mark, Canaletto was much more experimental and less predictable than he was to become, "churning out nearly interchangeable panoramas for complacent collectors who wanted picturesque spectacles that effectively embalmed Venice." Canaletto may indeed have become rather clichéd, but it's impossible to consider the history of painting in Venice without him. J. G. Links, who sadly passed away in 1997, was acknowledged as the leading living authority on Canaletto. (He was also the author of my most favorite book on Venice, *Venice for Pleasure*—see the Guidebooks entry in *Informazioni Pratiche*.) In addition to this authoritative work, Links was the author of *Townscape Paintings* and *Canaletto and His Patrons* (neither of which I've seen), and he was partly responsible for the largest-ever exhibition of Canaletto's work at the Metropolitan Museum of Art in New York (1989–90).

Vittore Carpaccio

Carpaccio: The Major Pictorial Cycles, Stefania Mason Rinaldi, translated by Andrew Ellis, Skira, 2000. Carpaccio's (c. 1450–1522) glorious narrative works are a montage of fifteenth-century Venice. For many, two of his pictorial cycles (*Life of Saint Ursula* in the Accademia and the *Episodes from the Lives of Saints George and Jerome* in the Scuola di San Giorgio) are a major highlight of a trip to Venice. This edition displays these cycles, and others, wonderfully, accompanied by Mason's enlightening explication. This may be the finest source—after standing in front of the original works—for understanding and comprehending Carpaccio's use of imagery, so important to the Venetian school.

Pietro Longhi

Pietro Longhi: Paintings and Drawings, Terisio Pignatti, translated from the Italian by Pamela Waley, Phaidon, first published 1969. This is an excellent work, with mostly black-and-white reproductions, a few in color.

Giambattista Tiepolo

The Religious Paintings of Giambattista Tiepolo, William Barcham, Clarendon Studies in the History of Art, Clarendon Press, Oxford, 1989.

Giambattista Tiepolo: 1696–1770, edited by Keith Christiansen, Metropolitan Museum of Art, distributed by Harry Abrams. This book was issued in conjunction with the exhibition of the same name, presented on the three hundredth anniversary of the artist's birth. Organized by the Soprintendenza ai Beni Artistici e Storia di Venezia, the Assessorato alla Cultura del Comune di Venezia, and the Metropolitan Museum of Art, it was held at the Museo del Settecento Veneziano, Ca'Rezzonico, Venice, (September 5–December 9, 1996) and at the Metropolitan Museum of Art, New York (January 24–April 27, 1997).

Tiepolo, William Barcham, Harry Abrams, 1992. This edition, like others in the very good Masters of Art series, contains about a hundred illustrations, including forty color plates. It is an excellent introductory volume at a good price.

Tintoretto

Tintoretto: La Scuola Grande di San Rocco, under the direction of and with commentary by Giandomenico Romanelli, translations from Italian to French by Françoise Liffran, Gallimard/Electa, Paris, 1995.

Tiziano Vecellio (Titian)

Le Siècle de Titien: L'âge d'or de la peinture à Venise, foreword by Micheal Laclotte and Giovanna Nepi Scirè, curators, Éditions de la Réunion de musées nationaux, Paris, 1999. This book was published in conjunction with the exhibition of the same name at the Grand Palais, Paris (March 9–June 14, 1993).

Titian and Rubens: Power, Politics, and Style, with critical commentary by Hillard T. Goldfarb, David Freeberg, Manuela B. Mena Marqués, Isabella Stewart Gardner Museum, 1998. This book was published to accompany the exhibit of the same name (January 23–April 26, 1998).

Titian the Magnificent and the Venice of His Day, Arthur Stanley Riggs (Officer of the Royal Order of the Crown of Italy), Bobbs-Merrill, 1946. This rather rare volume is one of my favorites, if not exactly authoritative or entirely accurate. It's just an unabashed love song to "the greatest painter in most respects that Italian art ever produced."

Titian: Prince of Painters, edited by Susanna Biadene, Prestel USA, 1990. This book was published on the occasion of the exhibition of the same name, Palazzo Ducale (June 2–October 7, 1990) and the National Gallery of Art, Washington, D.C. (October 28, 1990–January 27, 1991).

Titian's Women, Rona Goffen, Yale University Press, 1997. Renaissance scholar Goffen offers an interpretation of Titian's fascination with and exploitation of women, placing them in the context of sixteenth-century Venetian life.

Gardens

The Garden Lover's Guide to Italy, Penelope Hobhouse, Princeton Architectural Press, 1998; first published in Great Britain in 1998 by Mitchell Beazley, London. Hobhouse is a world-renowned gardener and writer, and she has a special affection for Italian gardens. This edition is divided into five regional chapters. Addresses, fax and telephone numbers, hours and brief directions are provided, as well as color photos, maps, a glossary of Italian gardening terms, and a good selection of related biographies.

Italian Gardens of the Renaissance, J. C. Shepherd and G. A. Jellicoe, Princeton Architectural Press, 1993; originally published in 1925 by E. Benn, London. This work is a classic. Shepherd and Jellicoe were fifth-year students of London's Architectural Association when they set off on a grand tour of Europe. While in Italy, they studied in great detail selected gardens dating from the fifteenth to seventeenth centuries, and they produced this masterful project. As Reuben Rainey notes in the foreword, the gardens appear in a general chronological order, but readers are not told the criteria for the gardens chosen for inclusion. No matter—serious garden and Renaissance lovers will rejoice at this collection. With black-and-white watercolors, line drawings, and photographs of twenty-six major Italian villas.

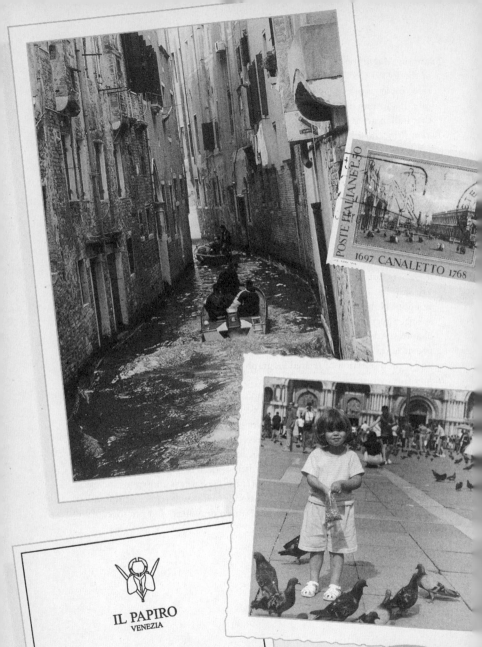

IL PAPIRO
VENEZIA

La Bella Vita
(Good Things, Favorite Places)

"Historians have pointed out the many innovations devised by the Serenissima over the centuries, among them capitalism, the income tax, public debt and financing, and organized tourism. In addition, Venice was first to perfect an intelligence service, complete with secret agents and informers. However, historians fail to point out that Venice—cynical, commercial, violent, scheming, all-powerful, imperialist, ultra-wealthy, and the medieval capital of the world—also invented the art of living."

—Frédéric Vitoux, LIVING IN VENICE

An American in Venice: Jackson Pollock Beads from a Former Banker

BY JOHN BRUNTON

❧

editor's note

....

I first learned of the unique work of Leslie Genninger in 1990, when I was wandering aimlessly around the streets of the Rialto and suddenly spied some beautiful jewelry in a window. Stopping to take a closer look, I stepped inside and met Leslie, who was then creating her own designs in the studio of Lucio Bubacco. In the years since then, she has branched out on her own, and now has two outposts in Venice: Genninger Studio (2793/A Dorsoduro, calle del Traghetto, next door to the Ca'Rezzonico museum) and a small shop within walking distance of Piazza San Marco. I have continued to buy her stunning creations since the day I stumbled upon them twelve years ago, and I have been happy to see that I was, in a way, a trendsetter in this regard: Genninger's work has since been recommended by writers for *Travel + Leisure* and the Fodor's *Venice* guide. The best way I can describe her work is to say that after you've seen miles and miles of Murano glass, all of it nearly identical, Genninger's designs truly stand apart. Both her studio and shop offer a full line of bracelets, necklaces, hat pins, earrings, wineglasses, lamps, pins, etc. Interested readers may find out more by viewing the website (www.genningerstudio.com), calling the studio in Venice (041.522.5565), phoning or sending a fax in the U.S. (513-784-7989), or sending an e-mail (leslieg@tin.it).

JOHN BRUNTON lives in Paris and writes for *The International Herald Tribune,* where this article originally appeared.

To walk through the narrow streets encircling Venice's Rialto market is to explore the ancient commercial heart of the city. But the tiny shops that centuries ago stocked spices and silks from the Orient have by and large been replaced by souvenir sellers, catering to demands for Taiwanese plastic gondolas and made-in-Hong Kong masks.

Many of these boutiques specialize in Murano glass, one of the symbols of Venice ever since the art of making crystal glass was rediscovered here back in the tenth century. But it's hard these days to find anything original among the mass of kitsch.

One shop stands out—an Aladdin's cave that displays contemporary glass sculptures of the Venetian artist Lucio Bubacco and the fun, colorful jewelry of Leslie Genninger, a young designer from Cincinnati, Ohio.

Genninger abandoned a profitable career as an investment banker in the United States to travel around Europe and look for a different direction. Her wanderings brought her to Venice in the summer of 1988, where she fell in love with Murano glass.

"I was both fascinated and, at the same time, appalled by what was being done with glass here in Venice. The opportunities for creating new designs and colors are incredible, but sadly most producers insist on the safe policy of endlessly reproducing the same old designs."

Six years later she is still here and has successfully set up her own line of jewelry, Murano Class Act, which sells as quickly as she can make it.

Fashion designers in Milan and the United States have used her work in their shows, stores stock pieces in Tokyo and New York, and she is just about to embark on a selling trip around Europe's capitals.

"I started off by representing Lucio Bubacco's work in America," she said. "He was the one artist in Venice who I thought was really doing new things with glass. I used to spend a lot of time hanging out in his workshop, where I discovered a huge pile of old glass beads and ancient necklaces.

"I'd rip them apart, mix them up, then make my own earrings, brooches, and bracelets. They all sold as soon as I put them in the shop window."

With the money she made from these designs, Genninger bought 220 pounds of 1940s and 1950s beads from Murano—about four thousand pieces in all—and again everything sold out once she'd turned them into her brand of contemporary jewelry.

Still, she felt that she could go only so far using old beads, and the next logical step would have to be producing her own beads, creating designs that were different from anything else being shown in Venice.

How did the closed, male world of the Murano master bead makers react to a brash young American woman who could hardly speak a word of Italian—let alone the local dialect—and who dared to suggest they change the tried-and-true colors and shapes of their beads?

"From the very first meeting, the reaction of these maestros of bead making has been fantastic," she said, perhaps diplomatically. "The master craftsmen, who have been creating beads for twenty or thirty years, have given me incredible support and encouragement, and I think that being a woman and a foreigner has actually been an advantage."

What Genninger discovered was that the "maestros" were for the most part bored—leading a profitable, easy life, but caught in a rut of reproducing the same old designs for the big companies.

"I asked them to show me their fantasy beads and they leaped at the chance, because they all have a burning passion for beads and were just waiting for the spark to relight the fire. I'd show them a picture of a Jackson Pollock painting and say 'Hey, make me a Jackson Pollock bead!'

"It's a perfect partnership, because they have the technique and skill that I lack and can understand perfectly what I want to do. Each day we're going further with new colors.

"Take our latest idea, where we've just created a wonderful opaque salmon-pink bead, with twenty-four-karat gold-leaf peeking in and through the design, then covered with clear crystal glass, which captures the colors within."

Last year, Genninger created eight hundred bead designs, collaborating with three maestros who flame-work solid glass beads and a dozen artisans working on glass-blown ones. They produced a total of 100,000 beads, which she then transformed into necklaces and bracelets, earrings and cufflinks, brooches, buttons, and stickpins that can adorn a hat, a scarf, or a lapel.

Typical of the way she has taken on the Murano glass establishment is the success of her delightful glass pins. These are tiny molten drops of glass that are cut away and discarded when a large object is being blown.

"For centuries these *scarti di vetro* were just thrown away," she said. "But I found there was a little bit of beauty within each one, especially if you painted on a dab of gold or silver leaf.

"At first, the glass factories just laughed in disbelief and gave me them for nothing—until they saw how fast people bought them! Now every showroom in Venice is selling them."

With her jewelry business firmly established, Genninger has decided that her next challenge will be to design chandeliers, off-beat glass mobiles à la Calder, and sculptures. If that works out, she may well find herself as the first lady maestro of Venetian glass, a long, long way from the world of power breakfasts and investment bankers.

This piece originally appeared in the January 24, 1994, edition of *The International Herald Tribune*. Copyright © 1994 by John Brunton. Reprinted with permission of the author.

La Bella Vita

Granted, it's quite personal, but this is my list—in no particular order and subject to change on any day of the week—of some favorite things to see, do, and buy. I am happy to share some of these with you here in the hope that you will also enjoy them, and that you will, in turn, not hesitate to share your discoveries with me.

A word about shopping: I am not much into acquiring things, so as a general rule shopping is not one of my favorite pastimes; but I do enjoy buying gifts for other people, especially when I'm traveling. To borrow a quote from a great little book called *The Fearless Shopper: How to Get the Best Deals on the Planet* (Kathy Borrus, Travelers Tales, 2000), shopping is "about exploring culture and preserving memory—the sights, sounds, smells, tastes, tempo, and touch of a place." Most of what I purchase, therefore—even for myself—falls into the food and drink category, because for me, food and drink are inextricably linked to a place. Venice, however, is a place that is quite different with regard to *ricordi* (souvenirs). I am not sure I can name a single other Mediterranean destination with as many appealing craft traditions as Venice. Frédéric Vitoux, in *Living in Venice*, writes, "The artisans of Venice—glassmakers, porcelain manufacturers, weavers, goldsmiths, lace makers, gondola builders—continue traditions passed down over centuries. Whether a length of sumptuous hand-finished velvet or a magical glass from Murano, each object created is a splinter, a piece of Venice, fashioned to ensure that visitors never stop dreaming of the city."

Food and drink can be extended, of course, to pottery (for which I have a particular weakness), glassware, and a full array of items for the table. To quote again from Kathy Burrus, "I am surrounded—not by things but history and culture and memory." I have found that even the *supermercati* of Italy sell beautifully packaged items of yummy stuff that in the United States are either hard to find or expensive or both.

A word about stores: I have a particular knack for "discovering" shops that a year or so later end up in books and periodicals; therefore, as it would be redundant to list some of my favorite retailers that are also featured in the books under Shopping/*I Ricordi* in the *biblioteca* that follows, I have mentioned them only if I had something extra to say about their wares or service. And you might want to adopt my motto of "when in doubt, buy it now." I learned years ago that the likelihood of being able to retrace my steps to a particular merchant *when the shop was open* was slim. If you spy a *Carnevale* mask or some Murano glassware in a window, or smell something delicious from one of the little *alimentari,* go and get it, for Giovanni's sake. One has regrets only for the roads not taken, or the object not purchased! Remember, most stores honor the afternoon siesta, and many are closed on Sunday and Monday morning.

~*Baicoli* (singular: *baicolo*), a traditional Venetian cookie. Visitors will see packages and tins of *baicoli* throughout Venice, and I encourage you to take some home. They are not among the most delicious cookies you'll ever eat, but they are, to my mind, incredibly addicting. *Baicoli* are made of the most basic ingredients—flour, yeast, sugar, butter (I don't think in great quantity), and water—but according to Sally Spector in *Venice & Food,* they are very deceiving since, "while it is not technically difficult to make them, it requires three days and a lot of kneading: prepared in stages, the dough is left to rise twice; once baked, it is left to sit for two days, then thinly sliced and the slices are all laid flat on cookie sheets and rebaked." She adds that there are no variations in *baicoli.* Only one company, Colussi, makes them, and even accomplished cooks agree that there is no reason to make them at home since the commercial product is so consistently good. Plain cookies like these cry out to be dipped into something, and indeed Venetians often dip them into hot chocolate, coffee, tea, zabaglione, or dessert wine (in much the same way that Tuscans dip their *biscotti* into *vin santo*). *Baicoli,* as Spector goes on to say, are sometimes described as being *pan biscoti,* special biscuits the Venetian Republic made for its navy; but it's more likely that *baicoli* are merely inspired by these other biscuits, which were more like a cracker "with the amazing quality of being completely immune to worms and insect larvae and, in addition, were extremely nutritious and tasty." The Venetian government started making *pan biscoti* in 1335, and they could only be made in the ovens of the Arsenale, the official state shipyard. Apparently, the recipe has never been found, so we'll never know what the secret was to their remarkable preservation; but Spector notes, "Proof of their extraordinary resistance was established in 1821, although already well-known, when some *pan biscoti* were found, in perfect condition, on Crete, called Candia by the Venetians. The Republic had ceded this island to the Turks in 1669 so it is presumed that the *biscoti* had been there for at least 152 years."

~*Piazza* by Alberto Giacometti, in the Peggy Guggenheim Collection (Palazzo Venier dei Leoni, Dorsoduro), Venice. And— the rest of Peggy's outstanding collection of twentieth-century art notwithstanding—spending time on the outdoor patio, which overlooks the Canal Grande, is *grande* indeed.

~Well-heads (*vere da pozzo*) in Venice. As Sally Spector outlines in *Venice & Food,* the Venetians developed an ingenious system of underground cisterns—*pozzi*—that collected, purified, and stored rain water. I love coming across these while walking around Venice, and I especially like those decorated with amphora, terracotta vessels that were used to transport olives, olive oil, wine, and other Mediterranean staples around the sea in antiquity.

~Hotel ai Due Fanali (Campo San Simeon Grande, Santa Croce; 041.7184.90; fax: 041.71.83.44; e-mail: request@aiduefanali.com; www.aiduefanali.com), Venice. This wonderful family-run hotel is a real find. It has the advantage of being about two hundred yards from the Grand Canal but is on its own *campo*, meaning that it is crowd free and blissfully quiet at night. (The name, by the way, refers to the two large lamps flanking the entrance to the front patio.) The Due Fanali is about a five- to seven-minute walk from the Ferrovia *vaporetto* stop (though on the opposite side of the canal) and is also a short walk from the Riva di Biasio stop on the Number 1 line. In addition to its off-the-beaten-track location, the hotel itself is also quite lovely and tastefully decorated, with a welcoming staff (who are also very accommodating to children). The pretty lobby is also a sitting room with a little library of books about Venice, and there are good views from the third-floor breakfast room. (Breakfast is rather substantial too, with fresh-squeezed juices, cereals, a variety of breakfast breads, cheese, hard-boiled eggs, jams, and fruit.) Rooms are not large but are carpeted and quite comfortable with good storage space for luggage and items to be hung or put in drawers. The owners recently acquired the Ca' Nigra, once the school of the Church of San Simeon Grande, on the opposite side of the *campo*. They are restoring this thirteenth-century palazzo, and when complete—sometime late in 2002 or early 2003—it will be an extension of the hotel. It wasn't easy to obtain approval to renovate the palazzo; it was once owned by a famous patrician, Nigra, who even had a covered slip for his private gondola—in other words, a separate "room" was built into the side of the palazzo, enabling him to dock the gondola and, two steps out of it, enter a ground-floor entrance room. (This is exceptional in Venice; most private gondolas were docked outdoors.) On a tour I was shown room after beautiful room, each with unique architectural features, some with huge windows looking out onto the Canal. This annex is truly going to be a very special hotel in Venice, but until it's complete, guests will be warmly received at the original Due Fanali. Note that visitors who arrive by water taxi will have no need of a porter: the boat docks alongside the *campo,* and the hotel is literally straight ahead, entrance on the left.

~Artigian Carta (Frezzeria 1797, San Marco; 041.522.5606; www.artigiancarta.com), Venice. This beautiful and wonderful little shop is one of several in Venice specializing in marbled handmade paper and leather bookbinding. The small store is jammed with a great number of enticing items—bound journals, stationery, fountain pens, inks, picture frames, bookmarks, photo albums, and more. Just a short five-minute walk from Piazza San Marco, this is a great place to find unique gifts, each carefully wrapped in brown paper featuring old images of the Venetian skyline. On my last visit, I took the plunge and bought some ink and a glass fountain pen. I love using the pen so much I may get rid of my entire collection of floaty pens. (Well, no, I love my floaty pens too, but I think it's definitely time to say good-bye to all those other inferior pens.)

~Paintings by Venetian masters, lots of them. In the article by Thomas Hoving that I mentioned in the introduction, he shared his list of must-see masterpieces, not all of which are paintings: the series of pictures by Vittore Carpaccio in the School of Saint George; Giovanni Bellini's altarpiece in the Church of Saints Giovanni and Paolo; Andrea del Verrocchio's bronze equestrian statue of Bartolomeo Colleoni in the *campo* outside the Giovanni and Paolo church; *The Tempest* by Giorgione and *Christ in the House of Levi* by Veronese in the Accademia; "the gloomy, moody, frightening, dark and admirably sinister cooking of St. Lawrence on a monstrous griddle" in the Church of the Gesuiti; the Tintoretto paintings in the Scuola Grande di San Rocco; Tiepolo's nine canvases portraying Saint Simon Stock in the Grand School of the Carmine; the Palazzo Dario on the Grand Canal; the Marciana Library; the Palazzo Ducale; the *Last Judgment* mosaic in Santa Maria Assunta on the island of Torcello; and Piazza San Marco. Some of Hoving's favorites are among my own (with a special nod to the *Last Judgment* mosaic on Torcello). Here are two others: *Battaglia di Lepanto,* by Veronese, in the Gallerie dell'Accademia, Venice; and *Nettuno che offre a venezia i doni del mare* by Tiepolo, in the Palazzo Ducale.

~The Rialto Bridge, Venice. Not only do I love the shape and design of the bridge, but I love the way the *vaporetto* conductors pronounce it—ree-*AHL*-to—as the boat approaches the stop. Incidentally, there is a painting by Guardi, in the fine collection of the Calouste Gulbenkian Museum in Lisbon, entitled *The Rialto Bridge After the Design by Palladio.* The painting dates from 1770 and shows a three-arched bridge topped by a very Palladian-like temple. I admit I actually like this design too, but it could not be more different than the shape of the Rialto today.

~La Zucca: Osteria Con Cucina (Calle del Megio, Santa Croce 1762; 041.5241570), Venice. This small restaurant is one of those neighborhood places you always read about and hope to find but rarely do. It had been held in some regard, at least by the Venetian expatriate community, for quite a while, and Venetian friends took me here to see if it was still as good as it once was. I'm pleased to report that they felt it had indeed held up, and as a first-timer, I thought it was outstanding. The kitchen specializes in vegetables, and as its name implies, it also has a way with different types of squash (*zucca* means "pumpkin" or "squash"). I can remember each dish we ordered distinctly, but perhaps the pièce de résistance was the pumpkin soufflé, which my friend Johnny H. said he thought might more properly be called pumpkin pie it was so rich; it was so addictively delicious I could not stop eating it. I can't wait to come back here, and I think you would like it too for a light meal a bit off the beaten path. La Zucca is a five-minute walk from the San Stae *vaporetto* stop and close to San Giacomo dell'Orio.

~The Hotel Cipriani (Island of Giudecca), Venice. Okay, even if this is the first book in my series you've picked up, you know by now that I do not approve of gratuitous expense on a hotel. Hotels that are just expensive, with less than stellar service and bored staff, should not be allowed to remain in business until they either drop their prices substantially (to match their mediocre quality) or demonstrate they have learned the true definitions of *customer service* and *distinction*. The Cipriani has remained at the top of Venice's best-hotels list because it delivers what it promises, which is due to the rigorous standards of Natale Rusconi, its hotelier par excellence. So back to the beginning: I have never spent a night at the Cipriani, but I have spent time on its spectacularly lovely grounds—in view of its swimming pool, the only outdoor pool in all of Venice—and eaten at Cip's Club. Most important, I was meant to feel welcome as I walked around wherever I wished, peeking into here and there. (I have not yet seen the suites in the fifteenth-century Palazzo Vendramin, though my friend Naomi B. gave me a beautiful etching of one by Sally Spector, author/illustrator of *Venice & Food*.) Yes, it's extremely expensive (as I write this, "bargain" rates are being offered at $378 for a double room), but the Cipriani is one place I believe I can wholeheartedly tell you is worth every penny. Everyone I know who has stayed there not only raves about it but compares it to other, equally well-known and expensive Venetian hotels, and well, the differences are bluntly made. (If you are inclined not to trust the opinions of people I know but you don't, see "As Good as It Gets (Trust Us)" in *Travel + Leisure*, September 2000, by Christopher Petkanas, someone who stays in a *lot* of hotels.) Ask around and you will hear the same accolades, and if the price is a bit too much for your wallet, do yourself the favor of at least taking a meal at Cip's Club—from its tables, you will have perhaps the best view of Venice in the entire lagoon.

~Museo Civico Correr (Piazza San Marco, in the Procuratie Nuove), Venice. There never seem to be crowds here, but this wonderful collection presents the history of Venice, and from some of the windows you have outstanding views of the piazza—you can even lean out and take some great photos. I love nearly everything in here, but I especially like the fresco *Le Stagioni* by Giovanni Carlo Bevilacqua, the Armory Room, and the "Venice and the Sea" room, in which there is the Edict of Egnazio, written by Giovanni Battista Cipelli (1478–1556) and also known as *Venezia Forma Urbis:* "The city of Venetians, through the will of the Divine Providence founded on water, surrounded by water, is protected by water instead of walls: whosoever therefore should cause damage in any way to the public waters will be condemned as an enemy to the country and will be punished no less severely than he who has violated the sacred walls of the country. May the law of this Edict be immutable and perpetual." Carpaccio's famous *Two Venetian Ladies* is also here and is much better than the reproductions in books. There is a small café where one can find sustenance in the form of *panini* (sandwiches), cold drinks, coffee, and pastries.

~An *enoteca* anywhere. It would be impossible for me to name a single favorite, as I have not "discovered" a single one on my own—I simply follow the noses of other reviewers, like Maureen B. Fant, Fred Plotkin, and Faith Heller Willinger, and I've never been disappointed. However, there are a few that come to mind: Enoteca Mascareta (Calle Lunga Santa Maria Formosa, 5183; 041.523.0744, Venice) and Enoteca Regionale del Friuli–Venezia Giulia "La Serenissima" (Via Battisti, Gradisca d'Isonzo; 0481.99528).

~Piazza San Marco, Venice. I read somewhere that a ridiculously high percentage of visitors to Venice never leave Piazza San Marco. This is a great pity, of course, but I'm not ashamed to admit that I love it all the same. A piazza is a great thing, wholly unlike anything we have in the States, and I am especially fond of Piazza della Signora in Florence and Piazza del Popolo in Todi. But perhaps none compare to San Marco, the only piazza in Venice.

~Basilica di San Marco. Even more predictable than the piazza

is the basilica, especially the long lines to get into it. But the basilica may be that perfect example of a tourist site that became famous
for a reason: it is truly something to see. The first time I went
through it, I was so stunned with the opulence of it all that I think
my mouth may have been hanging open. I had to go through a second time to understand what I was seeing. The only way to see the
basilica, of course, is to *get there early*, unless it is the off-season,
though you'll still have to wait even then. I think a planned visit to
the basilica is a perfect excuse to have (another) morning coffee at
Florian's; then you can saunter over when you're ready to get in line.
(The line really isn't bad first thing in the morning, and it moves
quicker than it appears.) The exterior of the basilica is almost as
impressive as the interior. I am especially fond of the four horses
that grace the central doorway, and though it is told often that they
were taken from Constantinople, then to Paris, then back to Venice
again, I rarely come across references of the horses' origins.
According to H. V. Morton in *A Traveller in Italy,* "They are almost
certainly the horses which Theodosius II took from Chios to deco-
rate the imperial box, the Kathisma, in the Hippodrome of
Constantinople. They stood upon the roof of what was a large
building where the Emperor and the Empress and their court assembled to watch the chariot races. . . . All this was complete when the
Christians of the Fourth Crusade sacked Christian Constantinople.
The four horses escaped by some miracle. Their beauty and their
splendour, as they stood proudly above the circus, penetrated even
minds debased by greed and hatred, and instead of being hacked to
pieces or melted into coin, they were carefully loaded in the galley
of Morosini and consigned to Venice."

~Rigattieri (San Marco, 3535/36, between Campo Sant'Angelo
and Campo Santo Stefano; 041.2771223; fax: 041.5227623), Venice.
This famous shop—you'll read of it in many books—has specialized in beautiful ceramics and other tabletop items, much of it from

Bassano del Grappa in the Veneto, since 1948. If you are walking down the narrow street where it's located, you cannot help but notice its artfully decorated windows, which are so enticing to people (like me) who have a weakness for ceramics; once inside, you will have a difficult time leaving empty-handed. On my last visit, I acquired some off-white plates from Bassano with a cut-out design along the rim, as well as a stunning ceramic "string" of hanging pomegranates. The staff—consisting of Signora Rigattieri and an assistant or two—is wonderfully helpful, though their English is limited, and they will gladly convert prices for you on their calculator if your head is spinning because you're afraid you might be spending too much money. (You probably are, but for the most part, this stuff isn't available in North America.) Best of all, the staff will happily ship your purchases home. (A note about this, however: about two weeks after I arrived home, I received a notice from UPS that a driver had tried to deliver my big box from Rigattieri but that first I needed to leave a check for $30, addressed to Rigattieri; when I called UPS to confirm if the $30 was for a customs charge, the representative could not say, and I have not yet been able to determine what the charge was for, and I don't exactly understand why it was not simply added to the total on my credit card. I explain all this just so interested readers will not be surprised if they receive the same charge; whatever it was for, it has not taken anything away from my enjoyment of the plates.) Rigattieri is actually two shops side by side, but no internal hallway connects them, so you have to go from one to the other by walking back out onto the street. The shelves are packed; decisions are difficult; but if you're looking for something for yourself or for a gift, this is one of the best shops in Italy for ceramics. (Needless to say, I've been to a lot.)

~A gondola, Venice. I refer both to the craft itself, which is sleek, beautiful, and unique in all the world, and to a ride in one. I used to think that *nothing* in Venice was as touristy as a ride in a gondola—who would spend that kind of money when one could ride the *vaporetto?*—until I understood that if one wanted to see anything off the Grand Canal, there is only one way to do it: by gondola. If you long for some tranquil waterways where tourists rarely set foot and do not have an opportunity to take a seat in someone else's boat, a gondola ride will ensure that you see the "other" Venice, one you may remember better than your ride along the Grand Canal. Remember to arrange the price and duration of your journey before you climb aboard, and decline the singing unless you are truly a romantic—after all, it's tranquillity you're after, not a bad version of "O Sole Mio."

Writer Nicholson Baker, in an article in the June 15, 1998 issue of *The New Yorker,* proposed an excellent idea to both give the gondola renewed appreciation and help solve the problem of waves in Venice: "Shouldn't it be possible to institute an *ora-remi*—an hour or two in the middle of the afternoon (when business slows down anyway), during which only human-powered vehicles would be allowed on all the canals? . . . Imagine the history-sheltering silence. Gondolas would pour from their moorings to celebrate, wedding bells would swing in their leaving towers, women would kiss their husbands or their gondoliers, and everyone would weep and spend lots of money."

~A Bellini at Harry's Bar (Calle Vallaressa 1323, San Marco; 041.528.5777), Venice. A Bellini is a most luscious concoction, of the most beautiful color, made with Prosecco and white peach juice. Years ago Williams-Sonoma stores used to carry small jars of white peach juice from Italy, but not many months later, when I could no longer find it, an employee told me that efforts to keep it in stock had become a nightmare. No matter; yummy as my blended versions were, they *never* tasted as good as they did at Harry's, possibly the most famous bar in the world. Even if you decline tasting a

Bellini (which would be a mistake, but there are other things to drink), you can't leave Venice without setting foot in Harry's.

~A nighttime ride up or down the Grand Canal, Venice.

~The *sestiere* of Cannaregio, Venice, and the Campo Ghetto Nuovo. A plaque in the far corner of the *campo* reads, "The city of Venice remembers the Venetian Jews who were deported to the Nazi concentration camps on December 5, 1943 and August 17, 1944."

~Hostaria e Masaniello (Campo Santo Stefano, 2801; 041.52.09.003), Venice. Normally, I prefer to eat local cuisine when I travel, but Venetian friends wanted to try this place, which specializes in cuisine from the Amalfi coast. At the time we visited, the restaurant had been open only a short time, but word on the *strada* was that it was quite good. With tables set up outside on the *campo*, just a stone's throw away from the Palazzo Barbaro and right next to a beautiful well-head, eating here would be memorable even if the food were mediocre. As it happens, the food is memorably delicious—especially the *bruschetta* and *spaghetti alle vongole*—and is served on the most beautiful made-on-the-Amalfi-coast platters. After dinner one in our party asked the waiter for a special, off-the-menu *digestivo* that is among the most delicious concoctions I've ever tasted: a mixture of creamy chocolate and a potent liqueur, possibly grappa. I never did learn the name, or if it is something unique to the Hostaria. If you do eat here, ask for this—neither the hostess nor the waiters appear to speak English, so do your best. You will not believe how good it is! (And then, if you wouldn't mind, please ask someone to write the name down and then write and tell me what is called so I can figure out how to get some!)

~Piazza San Marco, Venice, when the Campanile strikes midnight.

~Fraschetteria Toscana (Cannaregio 5719; 041.5285281; fax: 041.5285521), Venice. This casual, well-regarded restaurant can be a bit confusing to find because it's close to the Rialto Bridge but is technically in the *sestiere* of Cannaregio. (A good landmark to look for is the Coin—pronounced co-EEN—department store.) As noted previously, Sunday night is not the best night to eat out in Venice, and my friend and I felt the service was a little rushed the particular night we were there. (She had been there eight months previously and had had a more leisurely meal.) Nonetheless, our waiter was really very helpful, and we had an excellent meal of sole *in saor* with grilled polenta, John Dory with zucchini and bits of tuna, *tagliarini con gambero,* and delicious raspberry gelato. Everything was prepared with care, and I would gladly return.

~Caffè Florian (Piazza San Marco), Venice. Say what you will about Florian's popularity or its prices—if the orchestra is playing, an additional sum of about three dollars is added to the tab. I *love* Florian, especially sitting inside in the beautiful, period rooms, and I *love* the orchestra, and I love the classy way in which my order is served. I am aware that the Quadri, on the opposite side, is the other grande dame on the piazza, but the Florian is somehow more elegant and friendlier, and it's also one of the oldest *caffè* in Italy. The Florian also has its own line of signature products, including espresso cups and saucers, creamer, coffee and coffee tin, chocolate, and best of all, two compact disks: *Concerto al Caffè* and *Un Caffè in Musica 2000*—brand marketing at its finest, and it sure sucked me in hook, line, and sinker. (But truthfully, the stuff is well made, beautiful, and practical, and what a great gift for someone who loves Venice!) And when you're back home and wishing you were sitting at Florian, you can visit its website: www.caffeflorian.com.

~Scuola Grande di San Rocco (Campo San Rocco, San Polo 3054), Venice. The Archbrotherhood of Saint Roch (born in Montpellier, France, in 1295) was the wealthiest of the six *scuole grandi,* which were unique to Venice in that they were both repositories of art treasures and social institutions and obeyed the state rather than the Church. The history is interesting on its own, but the real reason to come is to see the magnificent paintings of Tintoretto, which literally cover the ceilings and walls of the ground floor hall and great upper hall. A very thoughtful touch is the mirrors found in the corners of each room, allowing one to see the paintings on the ceiling without having to crane your neck or lie on the floor.

~Venetia Studium, campo dei Frari, San Polo 3006; 041.713.393, Venice. This is not the premier Venetia Studium shop in Venice (the other more famous one is in the Mercerie), but I like that it is less known and small. I had no idea it was here until I found myself peering into the beautifully decorated windows. I had thought the silk Fortuny scarves were another of those Venice *ricordi* whose charms were exaggerated; but I was wrong, wrong, wrong. A Fortuny scarf—or handbag, lampshade, pillowcase, whatever—is a true thing of beauty. It will set one back about $80, but it will last forever and simply does not look like any other scarf in the world.

~Museo Querini Stampalia (Santa Maria Formosa 5252), Venice. The only example of the preservation of an entire estate of an ancient family of the Venetian aristocracy, the Querini Stampalia is one of the lesser-known museums in Venice. It deserves to be better known, especially for its more than one hundred paintings of scenes of daily life in Venice. The painting collection includes works by Bellini, Jacopo Palma il Vecchio, Tiepolo, Longhi, and Gabriel Bella, and in addition to the paintings, the museum/house contains eighteenth- and nineteenth-century furniture, a china collection, sculpture, and globes that give a complete picture of art in the Venetian Republic from the sixteenth to the eighteenth century. You can also visit the area restored by architect Carlo Scarpa, which is one of Scarpa's finest and most fascinating works.

~Strada del Vino, Trentino–Alto Adige. This designated wine road runs in a fairly straight line from Bolzano to Cortina all'Adige, but what a beautiful straight line it is! There are vineyards on either side as you motor along, passing hardly a single other vehicle, and the route takes you through the little towns of Caldaro, Termeno, Cortaccia, Magre, and Rovere, each of which has something to do with wine. There is a wine museum in Caldaro, although I've not visited it. At the end of the route drivers can connect with the *autostrada*—at the Mezzo-Lombardo entrance—or avoid the highway altogether and remain on the lesser roads.

~Villa Luppis (Via San Martino 34, 33080 Rivarotta di Pasiano, Pordenone; 0434.626969; fax: 0434.626228; www.villaluppis.it), Friuli–Venezia Giulia. The beautiful Villa Luppis is one of the loveliest and most relaxing places I've ever been in my life, and I would tell anyone planning to visit this region of Italy to make sure to secure a reservation here. I read about the villa in the Abitare la Storia brochure (see the Accommodations entry in *Informazioni Pratiche* for details), and in fact Villa Luppis is the only Abitare property in Friuli–Venezia Giulia—but it's not far from Venice (only fifty kilometers) and offers a free shuttle service to and from Piazzale Roma. The grounds of the villa are particularly inviting, with stone statuary, a large pool, and flowering plants. In warm weather lunch and dinner are taken outside on the main patio, and breakfast (which may consist of such yummy things as cereals, yogurt, prune *crostata,* salami, cheese, fresh-squeezed juices, cappuccino, and almond torte) is offered under umbrellas on the terrace overlooking the pool. There is a gym near the pool, where among the thoughtful amenities are water toys and swimming wings for children. There are also tennis courts, and the villa offers a discounted ski pass (for the nearby slopes of Piancavallo), special greens fee pass at a nearby golf course, a shopping card that allows special purchases from name-brand manufacturer outlets, and a cooking school and wine-tasting course for individual and small groups. Rooms at the villa are fairly large, nicely appointed, and air-conditioned in summer. The main hall is a large, comfortable room with individual seating areas and a bar, where drinks are served every evening. This is a room I could spend many hours in. The staff is unobtrusive and efficient; especially helpful is a handsome young gentleman named Davide, who can usually be found at reception. The restaurant at Villa Luppis is rather renowned, but more impressive to me than our dinner one night was the impromptu lunch the kitchen staff prepared for us when we arrived at three-thirty in the afternoon. They apologized for the "meager" little lunch, but it was one of more satisfying, perfectly prepared pastas I've ever had, with a fresh, perfectly ripe salad, delicious bread, and crisp white wine. The indoor restaurant and chapel are the oldest parts of the vast central building, and though the chapel is generally closed, if the staff isn't too busy they might show it to you. It's one of the most charming and unusual sanctuaries in the world and is the only example of this art in Europe, inspired by the ceiling of the Castle of Cracovia. There is a beautiful painting of Saint Francis on one wall, and the rest is done up in a folk art style. The ceiling is segmented into squares with faces of family ancestors in each square as well as a moon, star, sun, and a hand in bright shades of blue, red, green, and gold. Some plaques on the wall attest that some of the men in the family apparently died fighting for their country, both in 1913 and 1942. In every way the Villa Luppis is a very special place, and I look forward to my next visit with my family—for more than one night!

~Maria Sello, *bottega artigiana* (Via Portanuova, 15), Udine. A little shop with beautiful, hand-made items ranging from scarves, objets d'art, clothing, and jewelry. Great for unusual gifts.

~Al Vecchio Stallo (Via Viola, 7), Udine. This *osteria* (formerly a stable for mail carriage horses, as you'll see from all the horse paraphernalia hanging around) was recommended in two books, so I really wanted to try it. When my friend Lorraine and I arrived in Udine, we had allowed for plenty of time for lunch, but after a delay in the parking lot (the machine ate our credit card, which we were able to retrieve by calling the posted phone number), we were dangerously close to missing our opportunity entirely. We started to climb up the hill, determined to get there before two o'clock, but at a certain point we were a little confused about exactly which way to turn. We decided perhaps we would have to find a different place for lunch, since the clock was ticking, so we asked a young woman who was walking by for a recommendation of a place with good local food that was close by. She replied that there really was only one good place, Al Vecchio Stallo, and when we said we were actually trying to get there but were worried about being too late, she offered to take us there herself! Quickening our pace, she kindly led us right to the door, and after thanking her profusely we stepped inside to find not a single table free—except for one on the patio that was not yet cleared. We indicated to the hostess that we were willing to wait for that table, and although the day's specials were gone, we enjoyed a few dishes from the regular menu. Al Vecchio Stallo is a place the locals love—we were the only tourists there—and it is very much worth the hike up the hill.

~Caffè degli Specchi (Piazza Unità d'Italia), Trieste. There are other cafés on Trieste's grand piazza, but I like this one best. Seated at one of the piazza-side tables, one has a more central view of things, like the lovely Duchi d'Aosta hotel on the opposite side.

~Sunbathers young and old along the waterfront of Trieste on a sunny, summer day. The stretch of coastline from Miramare to downtown Trieste is rocky, with little coves but no sandy beaches. This does not deter the inhabitants from seeking the sun: they simply lay their towels chock-a-block along the cement "boardwalk," which is filled with little bars and restaurants, and carry on.

~Duomo di San Giusto, Trieste. Not only is this Roman cathedral beautiful, but the view from up there is spectacular.

~Cremcaffè (Piazza Goldoni, 10), Trieste. Though I am immensely fond of the Caffè San Marco in Trieste, the Cremcaffè is a much different place, all hustle and bustle with no table service and everyone standing at the counter talking excitedly or in line to buy bags of coffee. Cremcaffè is positively not the place to go if you want to sit quietly, reflect, or read a book. (For that, the San Marco is unbeatable.) But it is definitely the place to go if you want to see local *Triestini* enjoy their morning *copa* and catch up on the gossip. The protocol at Cremcaffè is to first pay the cashier, who sits in the center of the *caffè* near the entrance, and then take your *scontrino* to the counter, which is along the right side and stretches all the way to the back of the *caffè*. You give the *scontrino* to one of the very busy people behind the counter, and he or she will fetch your order. After your order is brought to you, the *scontrino* is stamped "*annullato*," indicating that you have paid and received. This all makes perfect sense, except that unless you are a regular, you don't know what is being offered (besides the coffee) since you can't see any of the pastries or rolls from the cashier's counter. I simply marched on back and took a look, then returned to the cashier. On the opposite side of the *caffè*, Cremcaffè coffee—whole bean or ground—is available in vacuum-packed bags good for traveling (and great for gifts). A word of warning about the selection: be sure to ask if what you're buying is regular coffee or Turkish-style. It's impossible to read the type on the bags from the other side of the counter, and I did not know until I returned home that I had bought three bags of beans that were "good for Turkish coffee." I tried grinding the beans coarsely and making coffee in my French press and ended up with a weak brew. (Later, I ground the beans fine and made Turkish coffee in a brass *ibrik* I bought in Egypt, and it was delicious.) At any rate, the Cremcaffè is an experience, and the coffee is outstanding.

~The Corso Italia thoroughfare in Trieste.

~Hostaria Bandierette (Riva Nazario Sauro, 2; 040.300.686; fax: 040.306.894), Trieste. This almost water-side restaurant specializing in *cucina di pesce* was recommended in *Gambero Rosso,* and I can report that its seafood risotto is outstanding. The Bandierette has a sister restaurant, Città di Cherso on via Cadorna, but I haven't tried it. (It too specializes in *cucina di pesce*.)

~Except for once or twice a year, or by appointment, most wineries in this part of Italy do not accept visitors. In addition to the amazing wines by the glass I've had at *enotechi* and restaurants, a few moderately priced bottles I've particularly enjoyed include Agno Costo, Colli Euganei Pinot Bianco, Vignalta 1999, and Bianchese di Villa, which is the house wine at the lovely Villa Luppis and comes simply as *vino da tavola* white and red. This last is really the kind of wine I wish I had cases and cases of for everyday drinking, and it's made from grapes grown throughout Friuli–Venezia Giulia. (Villa Luppis does not have its own vineyard.) Guests may buy a few bottles from the villa, but otherwise it can't be had.

~Every inch of the historic section of downtown Vicenza, designated a UNESCO World Heritage Site.

~Basilica Palladiana (Piazza dei Signori), Vicenza. Though this monumental building is impressive from any angle, it's almost more interesting when one hasn't yet seen it but catches a glimpse of it down a side street from the Corso Palladio. Once you see it, you cannot help but find your way to it, and then you stand in awe of it.

~*Teatro Olimpico* (Piazza Matteotti, 11), Vicenza. It is, I think, utterly impossible to describe this *teatro* to someone who has never seen it. Even when you read about it, you will never truly comprehend its magnificence, its trompe l'oeil perspective, or its uniqueness. But when you are finally seated inside the theater, you will understand why people come from all over the world to see Europe's oldest surviving indoor theater. (By the way, it's made entirely of wood and plaster and painted to look like marble.)

~Museo della Grappa and the Ponte Vecchio, Bassano del Grappa. The Palladian bridge, with the Dolomites in the background, is what people come to see, but don't miss the little museum at the end of the bridge. It traces the history of distillation back to Egyptian times, and shows how grappa and Italian *acquavite* are made from the distillation of *vinaccia,* the remains of skins, pits, and stems left after the grapes have been smushed.

~Italian Wine Merchants (108 East 16th Street, New York, NY 10003; (212) 473-2323/fax: -1952; www.italianwinemerchant.com). Yes, you're reading this correctly: this shop is in New York City, not geographically anywhere near northeastern Italy. But I have included this wonderful shop in these listings because readers who enjoy Italian wine, or want to learn about Italian wine, should know about it. To say Italian Wine Merchants is unique is to state the obvious: it is one of only two stores exclusively devoted to Italian wine in North America (the other is in Portland, Oregon). From the moment you walk inside the store, you know it's not like any other wine emporium you've ever seen: there are huge circular chandeliers—reminiscent of those in Turkish mosques—beautiful wooden tables, and antique corkscrews and wine accessories. Only one bottle of each wine is on display, and when you select one, it is delivered via an old dumbwaiter from the cellar—which is temperature and humidity controlled—below (temperature variance is the most common cause of a wine's deterioration). Red and white wines are displayed separately, and are arranged from least expensive to most expensive, a system I particularly like. If this were all there was to Italian Wine Merchants, I probably wouldn't mention it here; but wine is not just *sold* in this establishment, it's *celebrated.* Behind the selling room is the Studio del Gusto, a "taste salon" with a serious kitchen, where wine tastings are held with gastronomic authorities and wine experts. The kitchen is also home to a *salumeria,* where artisan salami, cured meats and olives are made, reinforcing the oft-forgotten truth in North America that wine is meant to be drunk with food. All of this is brought to us courtesy of Italian wine and food authorities Joe Bastianich, Mario Batali, and

Sergio Esposito. Most readers know Joseph and Mario through their successful forays in the Italian restaurant world and the Food Network; Sergio is not a television personality, but he absolutely runs the show at the shop. His may not be a name you recognize, but Sergio grew up in Italy, studied and traveled throughout the great vineyards of Europe and the United States, and has worked as a sommelier, consultant, and general manager for top restaurants. With the partners' extensive knowledge and direct links to wine producers in Italy (their combined visits to Italy average thirty times annually), they hand select the best wines per price point. This is worth noting, because, as Sergio explained to me, the wines they select represent good value: whether a bottle is $10 or $100, it is a good value within its field. (There are a good many bottles priced at $20 and under, by the way.) Sergio also noted that though the shop offers wine from every region of Italy, he is not beholden to stock wines from each region equally: if a region does not produce a great quantity of good value wines, it is reflected in the stock, and therefore there might be only one bottle from that particular region. Yet another reason I feel compelled to share Italian Wine Merchants with you is that 98% of the store's business is over the telephone, meaning that out-of-state mail orders are welcome and shipped regularly (except, of course, to those no-no states that have quaint customs about alcohol). Additionally, Sergio himself excels at wine portfolio management, and a number of clients rely on him and the staff to guide their purchases. Again, because of such frequent travels to Italy, the IWM team have positioned themselves as the eyes and ears of the Italian wine industry. A full schedule of events in the Studio del Gusto is offered throughout the year, though reservations are required (out-of-towners are welcome, but you need to reserve in advance). Like Viana La Place invites us to do in her book *La Bella Cucina: How to Cook, Eat, and Live Like an Italian*, the Italian Wine Merchants propose an education in the Italian lifestyle.

Biblioteca

Classics

The Merchant of Venice, William Shakespeare, many editions.

Romeo and Juliet, William Shakespeare, many editions, including a Modern Library hardcover (2001) slender enough to bring along.

The Taming of the Shrew, William Shakespeare, many editions.

The Wings of the Dove, Henry James, several editions, including a clothbound Everyman's Library volume, 1997; first published 1902.

Fiction, Short Stories, and Mysteries

Dead Lagoon, Michael Dibdin, Pantheon, 1994.

Italian Fever, Valerie Martin, Alfred A. Knopf, 1999.

Italian Folktales, selected and retold by Italo Calvino, Pantheon, 1992; originally published by Giulio Einaudi editore, S.p.A., 1956; English translation by Harcourt Brace Jovanovich, 1980.

The Nature of Blood, Caryl Phillips, Alfred A. Knopf, 1997.

Partisan Wedding, Renata Vigano, University of Missouri, 1999. Though this story collection is fiction, it is based on the true efforts of women who were members of the Italian Resistance in World War II, the author included.

Partita in Venice, Curt Leviant, Livingston Press, 1999, 2000.

The Secret Book of Grazia dei Rossi, Jacqueline Park, Simon & Schuster, 1997.

The Things We Used to Say, Natalia Ginzburg, translated from the Italian and introduced by Judith Woolf, originally published in Italian under the title *Lessico Famigliare* by Giulio Einaudi S.p.A., 1963; Arcade Publishing, 1999. Ginzburg asked that this be read as a novel, but it is actually autobiographical, and she makes the single best short observation about World War II in Italy that I've ever read: "We thought that the war would immediately turn everyone's lives upside down. Instead, for years many people remained undisturbed in their own homes and went on doing the things they had always done. Then just when everyone thought that in fact they had got off lightly and that there would not be any devastations after all, nor houses destroyed nor flights nor persecutions, then all of a sudden bombs and shells exploded everywhere and houses collapsed and the streets were full of rubble and soldiers and refugees. And there was no longer a single person who could pretend that nothing was happening and close their eyes and stop their ears and bury their head under the pillow, not one. That is what the war was like in Italy."

Zeno's Conscience, Italo Svevo, Everyman's Library Contemporary Classics, 2001.

Bringing Italy Home: Creating the Feeling of Italy in Your Home Room by Room,
Cheryl MacLachlan, photographs by Bardo Fabiani, Clarkson Potter, 1995.

Italia: The Art of Living Italian Style, Edmund Howard, photographs by Oliver
Benn, first published in Great Britain, 1996; published in the United States by
St. Martin's Press, 1997. Although encompassing all of Italia, there is enough
material in this beautiful book on Venice and the Veneto to make it worth consulting even if you never travel to other parts of Italy. Chapters are organized
by theme, such as "Interiors," "Gardens," and "Details," and there is a visitor's
guide at the back of the book, plus a bibliography.

Italian Country, Clarkson Potter, 1988.

Living in Venice, Frederic Vitoux, photographs by Jerôme Darblay, Flammarion,
2000; originally published as *L'art de vivre à Venise,* Flammarion, 1990. I am
immensely fond of Flammarion's "Living in . . ." series (other editions include
Rome, Paris, Portugal, and Istanbul), and this edition on Venice is especially
appealing. There are individual chapters on the lagoon, decor, interiors, traditions, and rendezvous, and the final is a Venetian notebook, a district-by-
district guide to hotels, restaurants, wine bars, shops, museums, private tours,
antiques, markets, and so forth, and a Venetian calendar of annual events. "An
art to living in Venice!" writes Maria Teresa Rubin de Cervin in the preface.
"What a strange and obvious title. No other city has raised to such a degree of
perfection this art—of happiness and of loving, of dying and of living."

Shopping/*I Ricordi*

When I'm looking for singular gifts other than culinary items, I've enjoyed consulting *Made in Italy: A Shopper's Guide to Florence, Milan, Rome & Venice*
(Annie Brody and Patricia Schultz, Workman, 1988). I know this book is over
a dozen years old, but I still recommend it if you are at all interested in discovering some unique shops, bargains, workshops, and manufacturers' outlets.
Many of the establishments listed are not only still in business but thriving, and
this book is much more than a shopping guide: it includes a very good—and
still applicable—"Shopping with Know-How" section, covering things such as
money matters, size chart, symbols for reading labels, shipping services, and a
glossary of words for shops, food stores, store signs, and so on. Short essays
are provided for local specialties, such as Ferragamo, factory outlets, Gucci,
the *erboristeria,* international antiques fair, and extra-virgin olive oil.

~Another good book, and certainly more up to date, is *Frommer's Born to
Shop—Italy: The Ultimate Guide for Travelers Who Love to Shop* (Suzy
Gershman, updated annually). One of the best things about this paperback is
its size, which is so slender it will fit in any bag or large pocket. There is a sep-

arate chapter on Venice. ~Remember that customer service as we know it in the States is an unknown concept in Italy. Customers are almost never right, and you should not expect to return anything you've purchased, for any reason. ~If you're buying packaged foods, look for the expiration date (*data di scadenza*). Dried mushrooms in particular, of any variety, can and do go bad and shouldn't be stored over hot summer months. Pasta, rice, and polenta can be purchased vacuum-packed, and even though these packages are rather lumpy to pack in your bag, they're better for traveling. ~Useful vocabulary: *prezzi fissi* (fixed prices).

Travel Anthologies and Other Good Things

Italy in Mind, edited and with an introduction by Alice Leccese Powers, Vintage Departures, 1997. Book excerpts from works by Homer Bigart, Harold Brodkey, Elizabeth Barrett Browning, Lord Byron, Eleanor Clark, Lawrence Durrell, Mary Morris, William Murray, Tim Parks, John Ruskin, Bernard Malamud, Susan Sontag, R. W. B. Lewis, Mark Twain, and others.

Desiring Italy: Women Writers Celebrate the Passions of a Country and Culture, edited by Susan Cahill, Fawcett Columbine, 1997. A very fine anthology of book excerpts by women writers, including Barbara Grizzuti Harrison, Edith Wharton, Mary McCarthy, Shirley Hazzard, Rose Macaulay, Mary Taylor Simeti, Kate Simon, Iris Origo, Jan Morris, Muriel Spark, and Francine Prose, among others.

Edith Wharton Abroad: Selected Travel Writings, 1888–1920, edited by Sarah Bird Wright with a preface by Shari Benstock, St. Martin's Press, 1995, 1996. Included in this selection of seven of Wharton's travel pieces are two essays on Italy: "Italian Villas and Their Gardens" and "Italian Backgrounds." Wharton traveled widely in the years before World War I. The other essays in this collection are on Algiers, Tunis, Greece, Turkey, France, and Morocco. With twenty black-and-white photos and illustrations and a glossary of foreign words and phrases used throughout the text.

Just Visiting, George Grant and Karen Grant, Cumberland House, Nashville, Tennessee, 1999. An unusual collection, which brings together quotations, poems, remarks, and even recipes that emphasize the effect that some of the world's greatest cities—in this case, London, Edinburgh, Paris, Venice, Florence, Vienna, New York, Washington, Jerusalem, and Rome—have had on some of the best writers, observers, and leaders throughout history. More important, the Grants share a view of travel that is so akin to my own that I include it here enthusiastically and highly recommend this edition. Travel, they write in the introduction, "has always been a component part of a well-rounded education. The banal prejudice and narrow presumption that inevitably accompany all unexposed, inexperienced, and undiscerning existence can often be ameliorated only by the disclosure of the habits, lifestyles, rituals, celebrations, and aspirations of the peoples beyond the confines of our limited parochialism. The great Dutch patriot Groen van Prinsterer aptly commented to his students, 'See the world and you'll see it altogether differently.'" Very much worth reading.

Murano, poem by Mark Doty, glass from the collection of the J. Paul Getty Museum, Getty Publications, 2000. A gorgeous book and a creative idea. A good gift too, if you could ever part with it.

The Riddles of Venice: A Book of Six Treasure Hunts in Venice, Douglas M. Sardo, with an introduction by John Julius Norwich, edited by Beatrice H. Guthrie, Save Venice, 1989. This most wonderful book is difficult to describe because the title may give one the impression it's only a book for children. It positively is not, though with adult supervision it is the very best form of Venetian entertainment for children that I've ever seen. (Older kids could definitely make a go of it without the pesky adults.) The book contains six walking tours of Venice, one for each *sestiere,* and each walk is designed as a treasure hunt. Each hunt begins with a map of the *sestieri,* showing the route to be taken to complete the unfinished paragraph as indicated. (The paragraph reveals a quotation about Venice.) No historical knowledge is necessary to solve the riddles, and all walks are accessible by *vaporetto.* If you are ambitious enough to complete all six hunts, you then search for the color-coded letters throughout the book and copy them in sequence into boxes on the final page. Only at this point will you have solved the final riddle of Venice, and if you accomplish this, telephone the Save Venice office (041.52.85.247) and inquire if you may collect a small treasure. Norwich notes in his introduction that the treasure hunts are unique in three important respects: "There is not one treasure, but a thousand; these treasures are not hidden, but are constantly exposed to view; and they do not lie at the end of the trail, but everywhere along it." Except for very young children, under the age of two, kids of all ages will find lots to like about these hunts. With this book as a companion, one can easily fill an entire morning, afternoon, or day in hunting through one or two *sestieri,* or an entire week if one wanted to tackle all six. Norwich reminds readers to imagine for a minute how difficult—if not impossible—it would be to do these walks in any other great Western city. He also suggests that we might, as we walk along, discover Venice's most important secret: "that however spectacular the buildings you pass on your way, however splendid the palaces or opulent the churches, the whole city remains somehow greater than the sum of its parts. The greatest miracle of all, in other words, is Venice herself: more glorious and at the same time more mysterious than all of her thousand treasures, to which some of us devote a whole happy lifetime of hunting, and yet never entirely find." I for one am never going to Venice again without this book, and I think you—and friends, family, and children—will really love it too. It's not available in any store, only through Save Venice (see the Save Venice entry in *Informazioni Pratiche* for contact information).

~Scarf of Venice or Italy, or France, Madrid, Seville, New York, Barcelona, and others. A company called Silksoie has created a nifty line of scarves—in two sizes, 11 by 11 inches and 17 by 17 inches—that reproduce maps of capital cities and countries around the world. According to Silksoie, maps reproduced on silk were originally used by the Allies during World War II. They were easy to hide, lightweight, and water resistant, all qualities that are equally good for travelers. A store in New York's SoHo neighborhood, Cité (100 Wooster Street, between Prince and Spring; 212-431-7272), sells the full array of silk scarves, which I think are irresistible. Or, readers may contact Silksoie directly in Montreal (514-272-9516; www.microsoie.com).

"For more than a thousand years Venice was something unique among the nations, half eastern, half western, half land, half sea, poised between Rome and Byzantium, between Christianity and Islam, one foot in Europe, the other paddling in the pearls of Asia. She called herself the Serenissima, she decked herself in cloth of gold, and she even had her own calendar, in which the years began on 1st March, and the days began in the evening. This lonely hauteur, exerted from the fastness of the lagoon, gave to the old Venetians a queer sense of isolation. As their Republic grew in grandeur and prosperity, and their political parties hardened, and a flow of dazzling booty enriched their palaces and churches, so Venice became entrammelled in mystery and wonder. She stood, in the imagination of the world, somewhere between a freak and a fairy tale."

—Jan Morris, *The World of Venice*

W. Kent Inv.ᵗ   I. Ware Sculp.ᵗ

F I N I S.

Additional Credits

Page x: Henry James, *On Italy*, Wiedenfeld & Nicolson, 1988.

Informazioni Pratiche: J. G. Links, *Venice for Pleasure*, Pallas Athene, seventh revised edition, 2001.

La Cronaca Mondana: Denis Judd, from the Preface to *A Traveller's History of Italy*, Interlink Publishing Group, 2000. Luigi Barzini, *The Italians: A Full-Length Portrait Featuring Their Manners and Morals*, Atheneum, 1996; originally published in hardcover by Atheneum, 1964.

Venezia—*"La Serenissima"*: Mary McCarthy, *Venice Observed*, Harvest Books, 1963; originally published in hardcover by Heinemann, London, 1956.

Il Veneto: Gilles Plazy, *The Traveling Gourmet: Venice and Its Regions*, Flammarion, 2001. Photographs on page 312 courtesy of the Italian Government Tourist Board.

A Tavola!—*La Cucina Veneziana*: Waverly Root, *The Food of Italy*, Vintage Books, 1992; originally published in hardcover by Antheneum, 1971. Photograph on page 386, bottom left, courtesy of the Italian Government Tourist Board.

Il Friuli–Venezia Giulia: Dana Facaros and Michael Pauls, *Cadogan Guide: Venetia & The Dolomites*, Cadogan Guides, London; distributed in North America by Globe Pequot Press, 2001. Photograph on page 450, top right, courtesy of the Italian Government Tourist Board; photograph on left courtesy of Hotel Villa Luppis, Rivarotta di Pasiano, Friuli–Venezia Giulia.

A Tavola!—*La Cucina Friulana*: Fred Plotkin, *La Terra Fortunata: The Splendid Food and Wine of Friuli–Venezia Giulia, Italy's Great Undiscovered Region*, Broadway Books, 2001. Photograph on page 502, bottom right, courtesy of Hotel Villa Luppis, Rivarotta di Pasiano, Friuli–Venezia Giulia.

I Personaggi: Jan Morris, *The World of Venice*, Harvest Books, 1995; originally published in hardcover by Pantheon, 1960.

Musei e Monumenti: Mark Twain, *The Innocents Abroad*, originally published in 1869 by American Publishing Company.

La Bella Vita: Frédéric Vitoux, *Living in Venice*, Flammarion, 2000.

Page 691: Photograph courtesy of the Italian Government Tourist Board.

Photographs not credited were kindly contributed by Lothar Tschanun, Gottfried and Romi Brandel, and Mark McCauslin, as well as the author. Special thanks to Lothar, Gottfried, Romi, and Mark for sharing them with readers of this book!

The journey has just begun! Don't miss the other books in **Barrie Kerper's Collected Traveler** series—each one a rich source of literary delight and practical travel advice.

Paris: The Collected Traveler
0-609-80444-8. $16.00 paper
(Canada: $24.00)

Morocco: The Collected Traveler
0-609-80859-1. $16.00 paper
(Canada: $24.00)

Provence: The Collected Traveler
0-609-80678-5. $16.00 paper
(Canada: $24.00)

Central Italy: The Collected Traveler
0-609-80443-X. $16.00 paper
(Canada: $24.00)